MAKING THE CASE
An Argument Reader

MAKING THE CASE
An Argument Reader

Laurence Behrens

University of California, Santa Barbara

Prentice
Hall

Upper Saddle River, New Jersey 07458

Library of Congress Cataloging-in-Publication Data

Behrens, Laurence.
  Making the case : an argument reader / Laurence Behrens.
    p. cm.
  Includes index.
  ISBN 0-13-015400-8 (pbk.)
    1. Legal composition—Problems, exercises, etc. 2. Legal opinions—United
States—Problems, exercises, etc.   I. Title.

KF250 .B44 2001
808'.06634—dc21
                                                                    00-062373

AVP/Editor in Chief: *Leah Jewell*
Acquisitions Editor: *Corey Good*
Editorial Assistant: *Jennifer Collins*
AVP/Director of Production and Manufacturing: *Barbara Kittle*
Director of Marketing: *Beth Gillett Mejia*
Marketing Manager: *Brandy Dawson*
Managing Editor: *Mary Rottino*
Project Manager: *Alison Gnerre*
Prepress and Manufacturing Manager: *Nick Sklitsis*
Prepress and Manufacturing Buyer: *Mary Ann Gloriande*
Line Art Manager: *Guy Ruggiero*
Interior Design: *Circa 86, Inc.*
Cover Design: *Kiwi Design*
Electronic Illustrations: *Maria Piper*

Acknowledgments for copyrighted material may be found beginning
on p. 555, which constitutes an extension of this copyright page.

This book was set in 9.5/12 ITC Century Book by DM Cradle Associates
and was printed and bound by Courier/Westford.
The cover was printed by Coral.

© 2001 by Prentice-Hall, Inc.
Upper Saddle River, New Jersey 07458

Printed in the United States of America
10 9 8 7 6 5 4 3 2 1

ISBN 0-13-015400-8

Prentice-Hall International (UK) Limited, London
Prentice-Hall of Australia Pty. Limited, Sydney
Prentice-Hall Canada, Inc. Toronto
Prentice-Hall HispanoAmericana, S.A., Mexico
Prentice-Hall of India Private Limited, New Delhi
Prentice-Hall of Japan, Inc. Tokyo
Pearson Education Asia Pte. Ltd., Singapore
Editora Prentice-Hall do Brasil, Ltda., Rio de Janeiro

To the memory of my parents,
Cyril and Freda Behrens

Brief Contents

Contents

Chapter 1: Law and Society   1

Chapter 2: Arguing Effectively   57

Stories and Exercises I   81
Norman Brand and John O. White

- Three Quick Writes
- Charlie and Jack
- Red and Sue
- Roman Round
- George and Mabel
- Jones and Green
- Baker and Abba
- Mrs. Trueblue
- Eel O'Brien
- Abner and Judy
- Sample Answer: Abner and Judy
- Chris the Cocktail Waitress

Stories and Exercises II   91
Leonard Tourney

- A Short Guide to Writing Effective Issue Statements
- Incident at the Airport
- Sample Student Response: Incident at the Airport
- Once in a Blue Moon
- Jail Bird

Models for the Opening Statement and the Closing Argument   96
Sheldon J. Stark, B. Henry Allgood

Chapter 3: Emotional Distress   107

Group 1 Readings: Introductory   109

Take $2,000 and Call Me in the Morning   110
Howie Carr

The Case of the Tardy Rabbi 112
David Margolick

The Spelling Bee   113
McDonald v. Scripps Newspaper

Photojournalism, Ethics, and the Law   115
Mike Sherer

The Cat in the Casket   116
Corso v. Crawford Dog and Cat Hospital

Shunned by Jehovah's Witnesses   117
Paul v. Watchtower Bible and Tract Society of New York

Chapter 4: Homicide   172

Chapter 6: Freedom of Speech   353

Chapter 7: Search and Seizure   419

Preface

Making the Case is a composition reader focused on legal issues. It aims to help you develop your skills in written argument by stimulating you to think and write about compelling cases that have actually appeared before the courts.

You may have an image of the law as impossibly complex, musty, and boring, and—let's face it—much of it is, even to lawyers. But if you peer beneath the sometimes intimidating language—here reduced to a bare minimum—you can often discern the outlines of intense human drama. Viewed in one way, legal cases are stories. They are morality tales. *A* has done something wrong to *B*. *B* claims injury. *A* denies the charge. *A* may be a person or a company. *B* may be a person, or a company, or the government—speaking for "the people." *A* and *B* hire champions to argue their cases. An impartial judge and jury hear the opposing arguments. They take account of the facts. They take account of the law that applies to these facts. And they make a decision. Using the material in this book, you will be called on to make these decisions—and to explain why you decided as you did.

Legal cases are rooted in conflicts, and most conflicts are inherently dramatic and interesting. These conflicts often raise questions about our duties and responsibilities to other people and to society at large. Writing about legal disputes is an ideal approach to developing your skills at logical thought and argument. Role-playing as jury members, as prosecutors, or as defense attorneys, you make *claims* (that is, arrive at verdicts) based on *support* (the facts and evidence of the case itself), and apply *standards* (the relevant laws). Writing about cases tends to be purposeful—in terms of arguing for a particular verdict—even as it implies larger ethical questions. And, usually, writing essays about particular cases is more enjoyable than writing about more general or theoretical issues.

Each chapter in this book focuses on a particular issue and comprises groups of related readings. While the main chapters focus on broad issues such as homicide, freedom of speech, and sexual harassment, a series of brief segments at the end of the book focuses on narrower issues: high school athletic injuries, hot coffee spills, parental responsibility for the destructive acts of their children. Each group of readings and cases focuses on a particular aspect of the issue in question. By reading and discussing such related cases, you may see how judgments on aspects of an issue (for instance, harsh and insulting language in emotional distress cases or the particular conditions of a claimed hostile work environment) are affected by the specific circumstances of the case, and you can compare and contrast such cases—in effect, using your judgments about one case as precedent for your judgments on another.

More general reading selections in each major chapter provide social, psychological, or historical contexts for the issue in question. For example, a chapter dealing with sexual harassment includes not only cases of sexual harassment that have been taken up by courts, and sections from the relevant statutes and the judge's instructions to the jury, but also passages from books or articles on the matter. Beginning with Chapter 3, each group of reading selections is preceded by an introductory headnote and is followed by a set of discussion and writing assignments: "For Deliberation and Argument."

Making the Case therefore allows you to practice the essential college-level and professional skills of *analysis* (applying one or more general principles or rules to one or more specific cases), *comparison-contrast* (examining key similarities and differences), *summary* (summarizing the relevant case or cases and the legal principles that apply), *narration* (relating the key events), *definition* (defining key legal concepts, such as *negligence* or *malice*), and *evaluation* (examining the evidence and determining how well it supports the conclusion being argued).

The texts of cases treated in *Making the Case* are drawn largely from primary sources on the law. The facts of each case derive from the narrative—and generally highly readable and interesting—sections of court decisions. These narratives are followed by extracts of the law that apply to that case, drawn from relevant codes and statutes and from the judge's instructions to the jury—instructions designed to explain key terms and concepts to people untrained in the law.

To encourage you to compose logical, well-supported, and well-written essays, *Making the Case* will introduce you to the IRAC (Issue, Rule, Application, Conclusion) approach to composing arguments. A typical writing assignment asks you to render a verdict on the case, explaining your reasoning in IRAC format. Often you will be asked to role-play—sometimes as a member of a jury, sometimes as a prosecutor or defense attorney faced with the task of writing a memo to your superiors or a closing argument to a jury. Other assignments are less structured, allowing you to explore the moral or personal dimensions of the case.

The opening chapter on law and society sets the law into the context of larger social concerns; selections explain how the American court system operates and how a variety of people view the world of law and lawyers. The second chapter focuses on composing arguments and provides a number of practical strategies for organizing your ideas and making your points effectively. A glossary of legal terms concludes the book.

In their readability and inherent interest, the cases presented in this book are *not* representative of those typically found in legal casebooks. But that is intentional. Someone once defined drama as life without the boring parts. You are about to plunge into the world of law—without the boring parts.

◼ A Note on the Appeals Process and the Case Descriptions in this Book

Most of the cases that appear in this book are culled from appellate court decisions—also called *opinions*—published in legal volumes called *reporters*.

Civil and criminal trials are conducted in lower courts, such as municipal courts, small claims courts, family courts, district courts, or superior courts. The party that sues is called the *plaintiff*; the party being sued is called the *defendant*.

In some cases a trial court judge will, upon petition by the defendant, dismiss the case without trying it or hearing testimony. This *summary judgment* is handed down if the judge agrees with the defendant that the plaintiff does not have a *cause of action*—that is, cannot offer facts that, assuming they are true, show that the defendant has breached a legal duty. (For a fuller description of the American legal process, see Hricik, pp. 2–11).

A defendant who loses in a *civil* case is found *liable* and is subject to payment of monetary *damages* to the plaintiff. Examples of civil offences include assault, battery, infliction of emotional distress, trespass, negligence, invasion of privacy, defamation, violation of civil rights, fraud, breach of contract, and wrongful death. A defendant who loses in a *criminal* case is found *guilty* and is subject (depending on the seriousness of the offense) to payment of a fine, imprisonment, or in extreme cases, death. Examples of criminal offenses include burglary, robbery, extortion, rape, arson, kidnapping, and homicide.

Generally, the proceedings of lower court trials are not published, although transcripts are available from the court clerk. The losing party in the trial—either the plaintiff or the defendant—may appeal the verdict, or a summary judgment, to the next higher level court, the *appellate* court. (The first name in a case—as in *Smith v. Jones*—is the name of either the original plaintiff, or, in some jurisdictions, if the case has been appealed, the petitioner for appeal. Thus, if Smith sues Jones, and Jones then loses and subsequently appeals, the appellate case may be called *Jones v. Smith*. If the appeals court reverses the trial court and finds for Jones, and then Smith appeals to a still higher court, the case once again may become *Smith v. Jones*.) If the court accepts the appeal—and it may not—the panel of judges constituting the appellate court will review the record of the case, as conducted in the trial court, along with the associated evidence, and will render a *decision* (representing the judgment of a majority of its members), either *affirming* the verdict of the trial court or *reversing* it. Appellate judges do not hear additional testimony from witnesses or gather additional evidence. The appeals court has none of the traditional "courtroom drama" of the trial court. The judges on the court render their judgment on the basis of briefs and oral arguments by the attorneys for the plaintiff(s) and the defendant(s), as well as *amicus curiae* briefs (those submitted by interested parties) and of course the transcript of the trial itself. They base their legal analysis on both *statutory law* (passed by legislatures) and *case law* (legal opinions by judges that serve as *precedent* for future cases).

An appellate court may reverse a verdict if it believes that the trial judge has erred in interpreting or applying the law, or if it decides that there is a compelling reason to overturn precedent established by lower courts. If the trial court verdict is partially or entirely reversed, the appeals court may *remand* the case back to the lower court for retrial. In such a case, the trial court judge is bound to follow the rulings of the appellate court. This may result in a different verdict, though of course the jury is free to render whatever verdict it thinks right.

Appellate court rulings are generally published in legal journals called *reporters* (such as the *Federal Reporter*, the *Pacific Reporter*, or the *North-*

western Reporter), which are available at any law library. (When you see rows and rows of uniform-looking legal volumes behind a judge or attorney on TV or in the movies, you're generally looking at bound collections of reporters.) Judgments of intermediate appeals courts may be appealed to the state supreme court or (if the case has been tried in federal courts) to the U.S. Supreme Court. At any point in the trial or appeal process, the parties in a civil case may decide by mutual agreement to reach a *settlement*. Settlements avoid the time and expense of further court action. The fact that so many cases are either remanded back to trial court or settled out of court (in which case the results are not readily available) sometimes makes it difficult to determine the ultimate outcome of a case.

The case descriptions in this book are excerpted from those sections of the opinions, generally near the beginning, in which the judge or judges hearing the appeal summarize the facts of the case before beginning their legal analyses. In these legal analyses, the judges apply the law to the facts of the case—generally in modified IRAC format (see Charrow, Erhardt, and Charrow, pp. 59–72) before arriving at their conclusions and their decisions. These analyses have been omitted from the case descriptions in the text, although sections of them show up in the case law accompanying a set of readings in a group.

■ Case Outcomes

Also omitted from the case descriptions are accounts of how the cases turned out—or at least (since, as noted earlier, ultimate case outcomes are sometimes difficult to determine) how the appellate courts ruled. This is an intentional omission made to avoid biasing your responses to the facts of a given case. If you know in advance what the appellate court decided, there is a strong possibility that you might adopt that conclusion as your own and tailor your reasoning to support the court's decision. If, on the other hand, you don't know how the court ruled, then the question of whether the plaintiff or the defendant has a stronger case becomes a much more open one. For the purpose of this text, it's much less important that you come to the "right" decision or predict the winner than that you undertake to argue logically—to systematically apply general principles to specific facts in order to arrive at logical conclusions.

If, at the end of this process, your curiosity about a given case simply *must* be satisfied, ask your instructor, who can then consult the *Instructor's Manual* and tell you how the appellate court ruled.

■ Note to Instructors

The *Instructor's Manual* may also be accessed through the Prentice Hall Web site: *www.prenhall.com/english*. For a passcode to the Instructor's section, contact your Prentice Hall representative.

■ Citing Sources

In writing about the cases in this book, credit your sources as follows:

Give the full citation only once, the first time you mention the case. (On subsequent mention, you can give an abbreviated reference, such as *People v. Markham* or simply *Markham* and the appropriate page number.) After the case name (in italics or underlined) insert the legal volume citation and the date of the case, which is provided in this book at the bottom of the first page on which the case is reprinted. Example: *Lawrence v. Stanford*, 655 S.W.2d 927 (1983) or Commonwealth v. Carroll, 194 A.2d 911 (1963). The first citation means that the case appears in volume 655 of the *Southwestern Reporter*, Second Series, beginning on page 927, and was decided by the court in 1983. The court that wrote the opinion is indicated in the case heading; so in your discussion you can refer to the fact that the case is being heard by a particular mid-level appellate court or supreme court (state or federal). (See Hricik, p. 3, for more on citing legal sources.)

Full legal citation requires reference to both the "official" and "unofficial" printings, as well as the appellate court that wrote the opinion; for example 2d Cir. (the U.S. Court of Appeals for the Second Circuit), or Ariz. (the Arizona Supreme Court). But because your essays are being written to develop your skills in argument, rather than to stand up in court, you can dispense with such full citations here.

For sources other than cases, cite by providing their titles in the text of your discussion ("According to the 'Jury Instructions on Homicide' . . ." or "The *Restatement of Torts, 2d* specifies that . . ." or "We were guided in our deliberations by the judge's instructions on emotional distress . . .") and give the page number in parentheses. Because you probably won't have access to the document as originally reprinted, give page references for this book. If you don't mention the source in the body of your own text, cite it in parenthesis. Examples: (*Restatement (Second) of Torts, 2d*, 116 (1965)) or ("Jury Instructions on Emotional Distress" 23).

Your instructor may prefer citations to appear in footnotes. If you have a word-processing program that can handle footnotes (such as Microsoft Word), pull down the "Insert" menu at the point you want to insert a footnote. Select "footnote" from the menu. The screen will split, a footnote number will automatically appear in both the upper screen (the text section) and the lower screen (the footnote section, which will appear at the bottom of the page). Type your footnote in the lower screen. The program will automatically number footnotes consecutively and keep them on the same page as their numbered references in the text. (Note: in MS Word, you must be in "Page Layout" or "Print Layout" view to see footnotes.)

■ Acknowledgments

To the many people who have encouraged and assisted me throughout the development of this project I extend my grateful thanks. Those who reviewed the early and later stages of the manuscript and offered numerous insightful suggestions include Beverly Braud, Southwest Texas State University; John C. Briggs, University of California, Riverside; Kim Donehower, University of Maryland; George Gadda, UCLA; Richard Grande, Pennsylvania State University; John F. Jebb, University of Delaware; Susan L. Hoffman, Indiana State University; Catherine Metcalf, California State University, Fullerton; Joan Latchaw, University of Nebraska at Omaha; Troy Nordman, Butler County Community College; Elizabeth Roeger, Shawnee Community College; Daniel Scripture, University of California, Santa Cruz; and Paul J. Voss, Georgia State University. My thanks also to the staff of the Ventura County Law Library, in Ventura, California, where most of the research for *Making the Case* was conducted.

Amy Atchison, law librarian at the University of Southern California and currently at the Rand Corporation in Santa Monica, California, directed me to numerous legal reference materials and was always cheerfully available to assist me in locating obscure and yet-unpublished cases and to suggest additional sources. She also reviewed the draft manuscript. Thanks also to my friend and colleague in the University of California, Santa Barbara, Writing Program, Leonard Tourney, who allowed me to sit in on his legal writing course in preparation for teaching the course myself, who provided me with numerous ideas for this project at various stages in its preparation, who reviewed the entire manuscript, and who created and generously provided some of the essay topics that appear in Chapter 2. My students Alyssa Mellott and Mark Tseselsky worked exceptionally hard and diligently under tight deadlines to compose and revise the model student papers that appear in Chapters 3 through 7. These papers clearly illustrate how to do many of the typical writing assignments accompanying the cases in this book. Their commentary upon their own processes of writing and rewriting is a particular highlight of their work.

My gratitude to my editors at Prentice Hall, Leah Jewell and Corey Good, who enthusiastically supported this project and offered expert editorial guidance and suggestions, and to project manager Alison Gnerre and editorial assistant Jennifer Collins at Prentice Hall. Finally, my thanks to my wife, Bonnie, who suggested the psychological material in Chapter 3, who helped me make some tough decisions about which cases to keep and which to drop, and who endured numerous phone calls assuring her that I'd be home from the library as soon as I checked out "one last batch" of cases.

Laurence Behrens
University of California, Santa Barbara

Law and Society

WILLIAM ROPER: So now you'd give the Devil benefit of law!

THOMAS MORE: Yes. What would you do? Cut a great road through the law to get after the Devil?

ROPER: I'd cut down every law in England to do that!

MORE: Oh? And when the last law was down, and the Devil turned round on you—where would you hide, Roper, the laws all being flat? This country's planted thick with laws from coast to coast—man's laws, not God's—and if you cut them down—and you're just the man to do it—d'you really think you could stand upright in the winds that would blow then? *[Quietly.]* Yes, I'd give the Devil benefit of law, for my own safety's sake.

—Robert Bolt, *A Man for All Seasons*

In Sir Thomas More's view, the law's role in society is to protect it from anarchy—from the "winds that would blow" in a lawless civilization. Indeed, civilization is barely conceivable without some form of law, some system of rules that govern the mutual rights and duties that human beings have to one another. For all of our distrust of "money-grubbing lawyers," our scorn at the flood of litigation that clogs our courtrooms, and our dismay at unjust verdicts, without the law to protect our rights, daily life would truly be a matter of the "survival of the fittest." From the Bill of Rights to the laws guaranteeing a minimum wage to the legal prohibitions against theft and murder, we depend on the law to safeguard our freedoms and our prerogatives. That is, at least, the ideal. The reality (which includes the ideal) is that the law is administered by human beings; that its administration is often maddeningly cumbersome, slow, and unjust; and that there are huge areas of life that the law cannot reach, remedy, or improve.

The readings in this chapter offer several perspectives on the way that law and lawyers work in society. David Hricik's "The American Legal System" provides an overview of the purpose and operations of American law and will serve as an essential foundation for your understanding of the cases that comprise most of this book. In "A Crumbling Hive of Humanity Fit for Dickens," David Ferrell offers a vivid portrait of the Los Angeles County Courthouse, a place of high ideals, broken dreams, and bursting water pipes. In "Gulliver on Lawyers" satirist Jonathan Swift delivers (in 1726) a savage indictment of the legal profession. A defense of this profession, "About Real Lawyers," is offered by Judge Victor A. Fleming. Novelist Scott Turow then presents an account of his first contract law class at Harvard—taught by the renowned and feared Professor Perini. In "The

Memo" Cameron Stracher recounts a chastening experience preparing a legal memorandum as a first-year associate at a New York corporate law firm. Next, William R. Keates explains why many young corporate lawyers are deciding that the six-figure incomes they earn just aren't worth it. In "The Imperfection of Law and the Death of Lilly," Chinese-American attorney Ji-Zhou Zhou tells how a profoundly moving experience with one of her clients revealed for her the limitations of the law. On a more upbeat note, in "To Work for Social Change," African-American criminal defense attorney Robert C. Johnson, Jr., describes his rewarding experiences working in a succession of public-interest jobs. The chapter concludes with an amusing story by Czeck writer Karel Capek about a parrot, a suit for defamation of character, and a defendant who refused to accept a "not guilty" verdict.

The American Legal System

David Hricik

What is the difference between a plaintiff and a defendant? What exactly is a legal case? How does the loser in a case appeal an adverse verdict? Why do we need both state and federal courts? These and other questions about the law are addressed by David Hricik in the following selection, excerpted from Law School Basics: A Preview of Law School and Legal Reasoning *(1996). Although his book is intended as an introduction to law school for prospective law students, Hricik's explanations of the law and the legal system will be fundamental to your understanding of the cases that you will read and write about in the rest of* Making the Case.

David Hricik, a graduate of the Northwestern University School of Law, is a practicing attorney at the Houston law firm of Slusser and Frost. In addition to teaching legal writing at the University of Houston Law School Center, he helped create the America Online "Law School Basics" course. He has published articles and given lectures on such topics as judicial reform, patent litigation, and legal ethics.

Here are some basic questions: What is the "law"? Where does "law" come from? What is the purpose of law?

1

The last question first: What is the purpose of law?

2

What Is the Purpose of Law?

For our purposes, it is easier to begin by saying what the purpose of law is not, rather than what it is. Laws are not the same as personal or individual morality. This is easy to prove: some things are legal, yet are considered immoral by some

3

"The American Legal System." *Law School Basics: A Preview of Law School and Legal Reasoning.* Copyright © 1996, 1997 by David Hricik. Published by Nova Press.

people. *See, e.g., Roe v. Wade*, 410 U.S. 113, 119 (1973) (abortion is protected by the United States Constitution). . . .[1]

Some things which are moral to some people are nonetheless always illegal. *See, e.g., Reynolds v. United States*, 98 U.S. 145, 167 (1878) (polygamy is illegal). Some laws even require people to do things which they find utterly immoral. For example, Christian Scientists may be forced to accept blood transfusions, even though they believe it damns them to eternal hell. Laws are not morals—at least not an individual's or a particular group's morals. That much is clear.

There are many theories about why we have laws, about what purpose is served by our explicit, institutionalized and complex legal system. Some view law as merely a tool to oppress people; others argue that laws express reason and order. Many view law as a system of rules which, when applied to facts by judges and juries, should result in rational and reasonable results to particular cases—to particular facts. We will not decide who is right. As with most things, the truth no doubt lies somewhere in between.

For our purpose, we do not care too much about what the purpose of law is, at least not on this fundamental level. For lawyers and law students, the law is a set of "rules" which create "duties," the breaking of which may result in "liability," usually in the form of money damages. Put at its simplest, "the law" is an expression of the social policy that people have a duty to follow the rules, and those who don't will incur liability for any harm they cause.

The "rule" is very often something so vague as having a duty to "act reasonably under the circumstances." Or, the rule can be very specific: having to stop at a stop sign, having to drive no more than 30 miles per hour, having to do what you have agreed in a contract to do.

"Liability" for breaking a rule often comes in the form of a "judgment" for money damages, which is a court's order for one person to pay money to another person. It can also take the form of an "injunction," which is a court order prohibiting someone from doing something. For example, a court could enjoin a party from selling dangerous products. (In criminal cases, "liability" can take the form of a jail or prison sentence or a fine—which is a court's order that a person pay money to the government.)

So the "purpose" of law is to have rules which create duties which, when broken, result in some sort of liability to the injured party. Obviously that is an

---

[1] You have just seen a case cited . . . as a lawyer would do in a brief or memorandum. A few words about case *citations* is in order here. Look at the cite for *Roe*. The words "*See, e.g.,*" mean "See for example." "*Roe v. Wade*" means that someone named Roe is involved in a suit with someone named Wade. (You can't tell who sued whom, though, not just from the *style* of the case.) "410 U.S. 113, 119" means that the Roe versus Wade case is "reported" (*i.e.,* printed) at volume 410 of the United States Reporters, beginning at page 113, and that the specific words from the case to which I'm referring are on page 119 of that Reporter. The fact that it is in the United States Reporters means it was decided by the United States Supreme Court, as that particular reporter publishes only its decisions. The date in the parentheses is when the case was decided. The parenthetical explanation of "abortion is protected by the United States Constitution" is what *I* say that the court said. It is one way to let the reader know what a case says.

oversimplification: for example, some of the law comprises those rules that define *how much* someone who breaks a "rule" must pay the injured party. But, as a general concept, law is meant to define the duties which people owe one another.

Where Does "Law" Come From?

As to where this "law" comes from, it is again probably easiest to first say what   10
the law is *not*. The western world's legal systems are of two primary kinds: common law and civil law. For our purposes, the "common law" system which we have in the United States can be described by contrasting it to civil law systems. By illuminating the differences, we can better see the common law methods. Understanding how the common law system works will help you understand why you spend so much of law school reading cases.

Civil law jurisdictions[2] place their primary emphasis on legislation—statutes   11
or codes enacted by a parliament or similar legislative body. The governing legislatures of civil law countries try to enact comprehensive codes on every subject. These statutes or codes provide the main source of the legal rules. In theory, everything necessary for the legal operation of society is covered in a code or statute. Consequently, in civil law countries, decisions by courts are not as important as those codes. The courts play a role, to be sure, but it is comparatively less than in common law countries.

In contrast, under the common law system, like we have in the United States,   12
the society places less overall emphasis on statutes and codes. The "common" law plays a much greater role because there are *no* statutes or codes governing *most* legal issues. Instead, most of the "rules" are in the form of previously-decided judicial opinions, not statutes or codes. Unlike civil law systems, in common law countries, *judicially*-developed "rules"—that have never been approved by any voters or elected legislative body, such as a Congress, a state legislature, or even a city council—provide much of the governing legal framework.

The common law method means building up the law by court opinions, case-   13
by-case, as opposed to creating the law by legislative enactment. The facts surrounding origins of the English system are illuminating:

> England had laws just as Continental countries did, even though these laws were not 'written' in the Romanist sense of being declared in authoritative texts. The rules established by general custom were declared not by a single judge alone but by the whole court of the king, which represented the magnates of the kingdom; *but there was no authorized version of these rules.*[3]

Under our common law system, most law comes in the form of these judicial   14
opinions: there is no big encyclopedia of "rules" setting out what can, must, or should be done under any set of facts or circumstances. You will seldom go to a

---

[2]An example of a civil law jurisdiction is France.
[3]2 *Dictionary of the History of Ideas* 694 (emphasis added).

"rule book" to find an "outline" of legal rules on the issue you are researching. As will become more clear later, the common law is really a series of *cases*—not rules—which can be applied to later fact patterns.

The point is so important that it bears repeating: most "law" in common law systems is case law, decided by judges and memorialized only in written "opinions"—not statutes, codes, or other "rule books." For instance, the "elements" which must be alleged to effectively claim that a party was negligent in injuring another person were essentially created by the courts of England in the sixteenth century, and were adopted by America's state courts throughout the nineteenth century. Likewise, most contract law is primarily found only in cases decided over hundreds of years by judges. Similarly, the rules governing real property come from cases which were written by judges in England long, long ago involving fee tails, fee simples, and other legal concepts whose importance has left us, but whose labels have not.

Of course, there are specialized statutes in common law jurisdictions such as the United States. Statutes provide a very comprehensive set of legal rules for some issues. For instance, significant federal legislation, called ERISA, governs employee benefit plans. ERISA is a complex statute, and the government has promulgated hundreds of pages of rules and regulations which further clarify and add to the statute. The patent statutes are comprehensive, as are some of the federal environmental statutes. Similarly, many state legislatures have enacted very detailed state statutes on various subjects. For example, the Texas Deceptive Trade Practices Act (often called the "DTPA"), provides a fairly complex codification of law designed to protect consumers. There are also a *lot* of federal and state regulations which are relatively comprehensive.

Nonetheless, with certain exceptions, statutes play a comparatively insignificant role in the common law system. For example, even though the DTPA is probably one of the longer Texas statutes, the legislature left many issues for the courts to decide by applying the statute to various facts. Those judicial interpretations are as important—if not more so—than the words of the DTPA statute itself.

The main supposed benefit of the common law system is its flexibility: a judge can decide that the facts before him or her are different enough under the rules so that a different *result* from an earlier case should be reached. Courts can also create a different, new rule when needed to apply to new problems or social changes. The common law has an additional benefit: judges decide cases based on actual, concrete disputes, not hypotheticals. A statute cannot be written which will govern every possible fact pattern, but a court can decide what rule should apply to specific facts, and a jury can decide what result is just under all kinds of different and unforeseeable fact patterns. The common law system allows for a lot of discretion in order to achieve justice in each dispute.

Most people are surprised to learn that many, if not most, of the laws that lawyers rely on in their day-to-day practice were never passed by a legislature or by Congress, but instead evolved over hundreds of years as courts developed and applied judge-made rules to the facts presented in each new dispute brought before them. That arguably makes judges very powerful. That power, in turn, means that *your* ability to effectively argue the law can shape the outcome of your client's cases. Knowing how to find the law and how to write about it will make you a more effective, and therefore a more powerful, lawyer.

To sum up, the "purpose" of law is to create duties which, if broken, mean that   20
the wrong-doer must compensate the injured party. This "set of rules," however, exists only in the form of case law; there is no "rule book," as there is in civil law countries.

Why Do We Have "Cases" Anyway?

Lawyers use the word "case" to refer to many very different things. "Case" means   21
a dispute: your client has been sued by IBM. That is a case. "Case" also refers to the published opinions which judges have written when they decided earlier disputes. Thus, if IBM's case against your client went to trial and the judge wrote an opinion explaining the case, that opinion is also a "case." I will refer to the latter kinds of "cases" as "opinions" whenever I think the context is confusing.

How are opinions created? As next shown, a court may, when it decides a   22
case, write an opinion that will be published in a reporter. Those published opinions then become *precedent*—the law—for other courts to use when deciding later cases. To understand why opinions get written, you need to understand how lawsuits are resolved. To illustrate, I will give you something you will not get in law school: a brief and over-simplified synopsis of a lawsuit.

The *plaintiff* is the party which sues. The plaintiff files a "complaint." The   23
complaint lays out the allegations which, plaintiff claims, show why the defendant (the party being sued) owes the plaintiff money. Put in terms of the "purpose" of law: the plaintiff alleges facts which show that the defendant owed a duty to the plaintiff, breached that duty, and injured the plaintiff. For example, in a case you will read as a 1-L,[4] the plaintiff claims that the defendant had agreed to deliver a load of coal to the plaintiff's lumber mill; because the defendant failed to deliver the coal on time and as promised, the mill had to shut down, causing the plaintiff to lose business; because he had no coal, he could not run the mill, and so could not cut wood to sell to his customers.

After being served with the plaintiff's complaint, a defendant must file an   24
"answer." The defendant will "deny" those allegations in the plaintiff's complaint which, the defendant contends, are not true, and will assert any "affirmative defenses" he might have. Again, for example, the defendant will deny that there was a contract to deliver coal; if there was a contract, it is legally unenforceable because it was not in writing; even if there were an enforceable contract, the damages were caused or at least exacerbated by plaintiff's failure to order coal from some other supplier.

The judge will then issue a "scheduling order." Scheduling orders typically set   25
the case for trial in a year or so, and establish certain deadlines along the way, the

---

[4]1-L—the first year of law school.

most important of which is a "discovery cut-off" deadline. The parties will have up to that date to take "discovery" of each other. Discovery consists of asking each other written questions (called "interrogatories"); asking each other to produce documents which are relevant to the suit (called "requests for production"); and taking each other's sworn answers to oral questions (called "depositions"). . . .

Typically, at some point near the end of the discovery period, one side or the other will file a "motion for summary judgment." This motion says that the moving party is entitled to "win as a matter of law": the *movant* will argue that given the undisputed facts and under the controlling case law, it is entitled to have the court enter judgment in its favor. For example, the defendant coal supplier could file a motion for summary judgment contending that there had been no enforceable written contract, and so a judgment should be entered in the defendant's favor ordering that the plaintiff "take nothing" for the lawsuit. The other side will oppose this motion by filing a response in which it argues either that a jury must be allowed to decide the case because there are disputed facts, or, for various legal reasons, that the controlling opinions do not mean that the movant should win as a matter of law. So, the plaintiff in our coal case might contend that there really was a written contract and that a jury needs to decide whether to believe the plaintiff's story that his dog had eaten it.

When the trial court judge grants or denies the motion for summary judgment, she may write an opinion which explains the facts of the case and the controlling legal principles, and then *applies* those legal principles to the facts of that particular lawsuit to explain why the court reached the result it did. Judges write opinions so that the parties understand why she ruled as she did; so that the appellate court can review whether her decision was correct (if there is a later appeal); and, in a larger sense, so that in the future other parties can conduct themselves in accordance with the law. This is one way the published opinions are created: district court judges sometimes write and publish opinions when deciding cases.

If the trial judge determines that the movant is entitled to win the case as a matter of law, the losing side can appeal after he writes the opinion. If the judge denies the motion, then there must be a jury trial, after which the losing side can still appeal. Judges sometimes write an opinion even after a jury trial, when denying the losing party's motion for new trial or motion for judgment as a matter of law. This is another way published opinions are created: by district judges when explaining why the result reached after a trial by jury was correct and fair.

Any appeal will be decided by an intermediate appellate court (the exact name of which depends on whether the suit is in state or federal court). The party that *lost* in the lower court will appeal, and will be called the "appellant." The party that won will be called the "appellee." The parties will file their *briefs* in the appellate court. After reading the briefs and perhaps allowing a short oral argument, the appellate court will write an opinion that either *affirms* the trial court's judgment as correct, or *reverses* the trial court because it committed some reversible error. Any appellate court opinion which is published becomes part of the common law that can be applied by later courts. This is another way the published opinions are created.

The loser in the court of appeals can then try to appeal to the highest appel-   30
late court (usually called a supreme court). As with appellate court decisions, the
published opinions of the supreme court join the common law decision.

Thus, we have opinions because of the way by which we resolve lawsuits in   31
the common law system. The parties need to know *why* one side won. The
reviewing appellate court needs to be able to check whether the lower court got
it right. Society needs to know what the legal rules are so that in the future,
people can avoid breaking the rules. That's why we have all these opinions.

The State and Federal Court Systems

The next piece of the puzzle which no one will ever *explain* to you in law school   32
is how the courts are structured. You are just supposed to already know it, or you
are supposed to figure it out from reading opinions for class.

There are at least two reasons why you need to understand the court systems.   33
(System*s*, not system.) First, it will help you understand cases better when you
are preparing for class. When you read the case, and it says that the plaintiff lost
in the trial court, but won a reversal in the appellate court, you will know that the
plaintiff will be the appellee in the decision in the supreme court. Second, the fundamental principle of legal reasoning is the doctrine of precedent. You have to
know which earlier cases are *controlling* precedent over the particular court your
case is in. In order to know which cases are *binding* on your court, you have to
understand how the state and federal judicial systems in the United States are
structured. (You'll see why in a moment.) The doctrine of precedent is crucial in
the practice of law and in the United States legal systems.

The fact that the United States has the federal judiciary, along with fifty inde-   34
pendent state court systems, as well as countless administrative and quasi-
judicial bodies, makes it probably the most complex judicial system in the world.
Welcome to it!

The Structure of the Federal Court System

The federal court system has a pyramid structure. The federal district courts, of   35
which there are about ninety, are at the base. Twelve federal appellate (or
"circuit") courts make up the middle. At the top of the judicial pyramid sits the
United States Supreme Court.

We'll study the federal judicial pyramid from the bottom up.   36

UNITED STATES DISTRICT COURTS As mentioned, there are about ninety federal dis-   37
trict courts. Each state has at least one, and most states are divided into several
districts.

Lawsuits must originally be filed in district courts. All federal trials take place   38
in the district courts. Witnesses testify, evidence is received, and juries reach their
decisions *only* in these district courts. District courts are the only courts which
find facts; appellate courts cannot do so, but instead merely apply the law to the

facts as found by the district court, or determine whether there is evidence to support the district court's fact-findings. Appellate courts merely review the written "record" of testimony and exhibits taken in by the trial court and apply the law to double-check whether the trial court was correct. . . .

UNITED STATES COURTS OF APPEAL—THE CIRCUIT COURTS Appeals from district courts, with few exceptions, are heard by federal appellate courts, called "circuit courts." The United States is divided into twelve regional circuits—the first through eleventh, plus the Court of Appeals for the District of Columbia. (There is also the "Federal Circuit," which takes appeals from all over the country, but only on certain issues, like patent cases.) 39

An appeal from a district court must go to the circuit court for that particular region. For example, Texas is within the Fifth Circuit. California is within the Ninth. New York is in the Second. Illinois is in the Seventh. The District of Columbia has its own circuit. If you look in the front of any volume of the "F.2d's" (the Federal Second) Reporters, you'll see a map of which states are in each circuit. So, if you lose a case in a federal district court in Texas, you file your appeal with the Fifth Circuit. If you lose one in a California federal district court, you appeal to the Ninth Circuit. 40

Whoever lost in the district court may appeal. The loser—called in the appellate court the "appellant"—will file an opening brief in the circuit court which explains why the district court's decision was wrong. Typically, the circuit courts limit appellants' briefs to fifty pages. Whoever won below will file an appellee's brief, which is also typically fifty pages. The appellant then usually gets a 25-page reply brief. 41

The appeal will be assigned to a "panel" from among the judges in that particular circuit. A panel usually has three judges. These three judges then read the briefs and sometimes permit a 30-minute (15 minute per side) oral argument. (Oral argument is becoming rare, which—you guessed it—is [one] reason why legal writing is so important.) Some time after oral argument, the court will issue a written opinion explaining why the district court was right or wrong, and so whether it is affirming or reversing the decision of the district court. 42

Lawsuits may not originally be filed in the appellate courts—each appellate court only *reviews* the decisions of the district courts in its circuit. As Justice Thurgood Marshall was quoted by *The Wall Street Journal*, "such appeals should await the outcome of the trial." It is hard to argue with that. 43

THE UNITED STATES SUPREME COURT If the loser in the court of appeals wants to try, it can ask the United States Supreme Court to review the case. Again, the United States Supreme Court sits alone at the top of the federal judicial pyramid. 44

The principal way by which cases reach the Supreme Court is through the writ of *certiorari*. Whoever lost in the appellate court will write a "petition for a writ of *certiorari*," which argues why the Court should issue an order (a "writ of *certiorari*") directing the lower court to send up records of the case so that the Supreme Court can consider the issues which it is interested in, to see if the result 45 reached in the case was correct. The loser is called a "petitioner" in the Supreme Court because that's what it's doing: it is petitioning the Court for a writ of *certiorari*. The winner in the circuit court will write a brief opposing *cert* (pronounced like the candy), arguing that either the circuit court decided the issues correctly, or that essentially the issues are just not important enough to warrant the Supreme Court's time, or both. The winner below is called a "respondent" in the Supreme Court because that is what it is doing: it is responding to a petition for a writ.

Nine justices (not, mind you, "judges") sit on the United States Supreme   46
Court. Like all federal judges, they are appointed by the President, subject to approval by the Senate, and serve for life unless impeached. One of the nine is appointed Chief Justice, also subject to Senate approval. He (there has never been a female Chief Justice) presides over the Court's sessions and determines which justice will write each opinion.

If the Court grants *cert*, then the parties write briefs, much as they did in the   47
circuit court. The Supreme Court then holds an oral argument and will later issue an opinion deciding the case. . . .

The Supreme Court is the ultimate judicial tribunal: if you lose there, it's   48
"game over."

The Structures of the State Court Systems

The vast majority of cases are handled by state courts. Why? There are far more   49
state courts than federal district courts, there are far more disputes which can be heard only in state court, there are more state laws than federal laws, and there is virtually no federal common law—only federal statutory law. Federal courts are courts of *limited jurisdiction*. Only suits which are expressly recognized by federal law may be filed in federal court. Everything else must go to state court.[5] There is very, very little federal law governing divorce, car wrecks, breach of contract, products liability, and most common disputes. Thus, most cases must go where most of the governing law subsists: in state court.

The structure of each state court system varies by state. Each state has   50
between two and four levels of courts. Generally, most states have lower courts of limited jurisdiction. Examples of this kind of court include county courts, family courts, municipal courts, JP (justice of the peace) courts, or small claims courts. The next higher level are the district or superior courts, which also act as appellate courts for cases decided by the courts of limited jurisdiction. Next up are the "true" appellate courts often thought of as intermediate appellate courts. Finally, at the top, sits a court of last resort, usually, but not always, called the state's "supreme court."

---

[5]There is something called ``diversity jurisdiction," which allows people to file a lawsuit in federal court only because the defendant resides in a different state than the state in which suit is brought. Even in such suits, however, state law is applied to the merits of the dispute.

COURTS OF LIMITED JURISDICTION At the bottom of each state court "pyramid" are   51
its courts of limited jurisdiction. These can include municipal courts, JP courts,
small claims courts, family courts, and the like. These courts have limited jurisdiction. This means that they have jurisdiction to handle cases involving only
smaller amounts of money, or only certain kinds of cases (for example, landlord-
tenant disputes).

Generally, these courts are informal. Parties often file suits without a lawyer;   52
the rules of evidence may not apply; and the judges probably never write opinions
that will be published in the reporters. These courts are critically important to
solving the problems that confront people every day, but they generally do not
add much to the common law, because they do not write opinions that are published in the reporters.

DISTRICT OR SUPERIOR COURTS Just above the courts of limited jurisdiction are   53
the district courts. In some states, they are called superior courts. District
courts handle the bulk of the state court caseload. They also handle appeals
from the courts of limited jurisdiction: the loser in a lawsuit filed in a court of
limited jurisdiction can "appeal" up to the district or superior court, although
usually the "appeal" takes the form of a completely new trial—"*de novo*
review"—rather than the review only by written briefs which takes place in the
typical appeal.

Practice before a state district court is, in broad view, much the same as in a   54
federal district court (discussed above). The procedural rules can be quite different, however, and so the actual daily practice may be very different. For our
purposes, however, they are quite similar: the written practice consists of pleadings and motions supported by briefs. . . .

INTERMEDIATE APPELLATE COURTS Intermediate appellate courts exist in many   55
states, and are much like the federal circuit courts. In most states, as a matter of
right the loser in a district court can appeal and have a state court of appeals
review the district court's decision for error.

The briefing practice in state appellate courts is much as it is in the federal   56
circuit courts: main brief, response; reply, followed (perhaps) by oral argument. . . .

COURTS OF LAST RESORT: STATE SUPREME COURTS At the top of state court systems   57
is a court of ultimate review. In a deliberate scheme to confuse you, New York
calls its supreme court the "court of appeals," and Texas has *two* supreme
courts—one for criminal matters and the other for civil suits. Most states, thank-
fully, have only one highest court, and they call it the supreme court.

Most state supreme courts act like the United States Supreme Court, taking   58
only those cases in which they are interested and ignoring the others. They will
decide whether to take your case based only on the written briefs. This means
that only your *writing* can persuade the court to review your case. (Which, you
guessed it, is yet another reason writing is so important.)

• • • •

Discussion and Writing Topics

1. How does Hricik's description of law—dealing with rules, duties, and liabilities—tally with your own view of law before reading this selection? To what extent did Hricik's explanations add to, deepen, or change your prior understanding of how the law and the legal system work? Give examples.

2. Have you or someone you know had experience with the legal system in this country? If so, describe what happened. Was it a civil or a criminal case? Was it in state or federal court? Based on these experiences, what advantages and disadvantages do you find with the system of justice and legal procedure that were encountered? What recommendations do you have for legal reform in this area?

3. If your college or university library has a set of legal reporters such as Hricik describes (for example, the *Supreme Court Reporter*, *United States Reports*, the *Federal Reporter*, or a regional reporter, such as the *Pacific Reporter*), browse through them and write an account of what you find. How are cases presented? How are individual legal opinions organized? What seems to be the logic behind the organization? What sections do you understand? What sections don't you understand, and why?

Note: You can also find legal opinions on the Web. The most important legal sites are Westlaw and Lexis-Nexis, but these are accessible only to subscribers. (Your college or university may subscribe; check with a librarian.) For a good free site, go to Findlaw at http://www.findlaw.com and follow the links to federal or state cases. You can find the full text of U.S. Supreme Court opinions through Findlaw, as well as certain other recent appellate cases (searchability varies from state to state). Other important law sites are maintained by the Cornell University Law School (<http://www.lawschool.cornell.edu/library/>) and the Emory University Law Library (<http://www.law.emory.edu/LAW/refdesk/toc.html>). The Indiana University Law School maintains a law section for the World Wide Web Virtual Library at <http://www.law.indiana.edu/v-lib/>. See also WashLaw Web, the Washburn University School of Law site, at <http://www/washlaw.edu/>.

A Crumbling Hive of Humanity
Fit for Dickens

■——■

David Ferrell

David Ferrell's article provides a vivid description of the activities and the conditions inside a big-city courthouse—in this case, the Los Angeles County Courthouse. It is meant to be impressionistic rather than systematic. Unlike

————
Los Angles Times, 10 Apr. 1999: 1+.

Hricik, who, in "The American Legal System," attempts to provide his readers with a broad overview of the law, legal cases, and the state and federal court systems, Ferrell focuses on some of the details of life at one particular location. Hricik provides a series of longshots; Ferrell offers a series of close-ups.

This article originally appeared as a front-page feature in the Los Angeles Times *on 10 April 1999.*

Los Angeles' main house of justice is a Rube Goldberg apparatus, a vast, shuddering contraption where lofty ideals gnash against harsh realities like broken-tooth gears.

It juts from the flanks of Bunker Hill with the spartan lines of an electrical transformer. Constructed 40 years ago out of marble, bronze and fluorescent tubes, the L.A. County Courthouse has been left to slip into disrepair pretty much ever since. The building has rats, asbestos, broken acoustical tiles, bad pipes and chronically overflowing toilets that send water trickling down through light fixtures below.

The varnish is gone from the oak-paneled courtrooms and from everything else, leaving an ambience of crass functionality, a place bleak and institutional and packed nine stories high with quirks. Some of the third-floor ceilings leak; they're beneath the hillside and a cracked outdoor walkway. The marble clock on the fifth floor has no hands. Underground tunnels branch off in mysterious directions. There are lawyers who have spent years trudging through that dank realm to pull old case files with no idea what lies down intersecting pathways— shadowy nether regions filled with industrial noises and jets of steam.

In contrast to courts devoted to criminal matters, this is the bench of the people, a detangling mechanism for everyday entrapments: apartment fires and fuel-tank explosions, car wrecks, broken contracts, paternity disputes, divorces and custody issues, landlord-tenant fights, probate battles. If you're ever going to go to court in L.A. County, chances are it will be here, or a smaller version of it.

Nearly 2 million people a year push through the glass doors at 17 entrances on four different levels. Yet that only hints at the complexity of the place, for the building is more than a single civil courthouse; it is two of them, fused together like the halves of an engine block.

Step inside at 111 N. Hill St. and you are in the main building of the nation's largest Superior Court system. But go up the hill and walk in on the fourth floor, at 110 N. Grand Ave., and you will find separate filing windows, separate clerks and a separate roster of judges. You are now in the flagship of the nation's biggest Municipal Court.

Into these dual conduits flow tragedies and grudges at the staggering rate of about 13,000 new cases a month. The anxiety and pain seem to hang like a fog, filtering down luminous hallways, leaving black soot marks where it recirculates through the ceiling vents.

These windowless halls are the conveyor belts of strife, people moving against their will. You can feel the torque of lives bending, the tremor of things not right. There is something unfeeling in the way the light hits the white marble walls and poorly matched beige terrazzo floors. Hard surfaces here and hard edges, the inhospitable backdrop to hard times. No one smiles. No one would be here if they could be anywhere else.

Wood benches are scarred with graffiti, cigarette burns, the petrified rings   9
from long-ago soft drink cans. Legal combatants stare from them like zombies, or grab a minute for tense dialogue with their lawyers.

Conversations tend toward a singular tone, the singsong dirge of lives in   10
crisis: *"If you decide to do it, you'll have to make some sacrifices. . . . That's what the code says; just follow the code. . . . Do whatever you can, OK? It's all in your hands. . . . It's not going to settle; you know it's not going to settle. . . . The way she operates. . . . Anything we can get done in the hall, when the meter's running, is smart, as opposed to. . . . Do you want me to get off the case?"*

Winners emerge smiling, even jubilant. Some are granted multimillion-dollar   11
judgments, others extract themselves from poisonous marriages, turning points that will alter their lives. But they hurriedly take their happiness and go, leaving the building to those still burdened by their troubles.

A Murder Within

Wall signs are in English and Spanish, but that fact is a poor barometer of the   12
social diversity. Testimony has been rendered in more than 100 languages and dialects, from Afghani to Zambal. You can run into supermodels and window washers, stooped old men in plaid shirts and Armenian women pushing strollers.

This remains one of the only courthouses in Los Angeles with no metal detec-   13
tors. Three years ago, a combatant in a divorce case named Harry Zelig horrified bystanders, including his own young daughter, by pulling out a handgun and murdering his wife near the second-floor escalator. Not many have forgotten it, least of all the judges who pass down life-altering rulings and the bailiffs responsible for maintaining order.

Two or three times a day someone, often a judge, presses a hidden button   14
wired to an ancient panel of alarm lights in an upper-floor office. Bailiffs rush to break up a fight, defuse a threat or usher some angry litigant out to the street or to jail. Metal detectors are due to be installed this summer.

Of all the traumatic experiences in Los Angeles, few are more wrenching than   15
arriving here for the first time to face legal warfare. Navigate the downtown traffic and you find yourself with lines to stand in, procedures to worry about. Your life is wobbling out of control, and you are forced to put your trust in mirthless strangers: a judge, sitting like God on high, and lawyers, some billing small fortunes every hour.

Gila Yashari, a Beverly Hills real estate agent, is crying outside the courtroom   16
before a hearing in her divorce case. "I'll tell you, it's scary," she says. "You have no idea what's going on, and there's no book about it. You wait in the halls for hours. . . . It's like they dip you in hot water about 50 times a day, and you wake up in the morning and you know you're going to get dipped again."

Dungeon of Tension

Walk through any chambers of the Family Law courts, scattered on floors 2   17
through 6, and you enter a dungeon of tension, anger and frustration. Cases
involving custody disputes have been known to drag on for 18 years—from the
moment a child is born until legal adulthood.

Rich husbands steal away assets in the Cayman Islands. Wives take their chil-   18
dren and diamonds and flee to France. A woman named Molly Yuen files for divorce
from her rich husband, Henry, fully expecting a share of his millions. To her apparent
shock, she discovers that Henry has already divorced her a dozen years earlier—
without her knowledge, she says—well before building his financial empire.

Fascinating battles sing across the gossip wire, discussed and second-guessed   19
in the third-floor judges' lounge where bagel breakfasts are held Friday mornings,
at the fast-food eateries where clerks grab lunch and in bars where lawyers drop
their briefcases at sundown.

The tension comes out in laughter, jokes about it all, but there is always an   20
underlying awareness that the theater is real. Good people get crushed. Children
are kidnapped, manipulated for selfish ends. Neighbors butt heads in tiffs that
will leave both sides bleeding.

Some of the most riveting struggles occur in Probate, where wills are   21
reviewed, estates divided and unclaimed possessions sold at auction. Here, grief
over the death of a loved one is sometimes overshadowed by angry jousting over
who will inherit what. Desire for money, sports cars and wine collections pits
brother against brother, sister against sister.

Slip into Department 5, Commissioner Ronald H. Hauptman's courtroom, and   22
you can stare into the life of Shirley Hollingsworth, a proud former USC history
professor, now 77 and struggling fiercely to maintain her independence.

Her vitality has ebbed: arthritis, thyroid disease, a peptic ulcer, osteoporosis,   23
chronic obstructive pulmonary disease, hypertension. Hollingsworth is now thin
to the point of anorexia and moves about with a walker or a wheelchair. Her son
John filed the petition to put her finances and personal care in the hands of a con-
servator, citing the massive disarray at her home in Pacific Palisades. Photographs show floors strewn with trash—plastic bags, pill bottles, pots,
glassware, jars, rolls of toilet paper, rat feces.

A psychologist sent out to administer a battery of 15 tests—abstract rea-   24
soning, problem-solving and the like—found a woman of exceptional intelligence
with signs of dementia. "She . . . is believed to drive with no license and no insurance," the examiner reported, "and drives dangerously, according to neighbors.
She eats one meal a day. Her home is run-down with no heat, a broken stove and
electrical problems."

Even weighing all that, the issues are delicate and reach deep into us all.   25

"You're asking the court to make Solomonic decisions," her lawyer, Gary Rut-   26
tenberg, tells a reporter outside court. "She is cognizant of everything around her.
She says she's capable of handling her own things and should be left alone to do
what she wants to do."

Each human drama is but a grain of sand on a mountainous beachhead of lit-   27
igation. The sad chronicle of Shirley Hollingsworth's later years is detailed in file
No. BP 054 172, a color-coded folder that looks much like any other in Room 112,
the Records room, a cavern of high metal shelves containing some 450,000 other
files. Many, like Hollingsworth's, are but a single thin volume. Others grow to
massive dimensions. A case against Paradise Memorial Park, a cemetery where
graves were dug up and plots resold, now fills 13 boxes, a load that can only be
moved on dollies. That file is housed alongside other humongous cases in an
adjoining room with a hand-printed sign over the door: "Odd Files."

Mountains of Paper

The paperwork is the mainspring that drives the whole building. The files in 112,   28
and in the Muni Court stacks three floors up, are in ceaseless motion: Dozens at
a time are trundled on metal carts to trials and hearings. Clerks are forever
moving old cases down to Archives, a onetime bomb cellar accessible through
underground tunnels. Each motion, each judgment means still more paperwork
to be sorted and moved.

Glitches are inevitable. Every lawyer has some horror story about papers—or   29
whole cases—that disappeared. About 10 files a day go missing. There are ways
to track them—bar codes and computer programs that key on transposed
numbers—but a search can sometimes take days. Occasionally a trial must be
postponed while harried clerks search the proverbial haystack. Frustrated
lawyers are always on the phone: "Where's the file? What's going on?" Bearing the
responsibility for victory or defeat in the courtroom, they often exhibit thinly
veiled disdain for the ever-changing cast of clerks.

"They're county employees," complains one attorney, "so if there's one person   30
in line or 10 people in line, they're going to move at the same speed."

The clerks answer with sarcastic humor. A paper sign behind the information   31
desk in Records advertises, "Answers: $1. Answers which require thought: $2."

You can wait in line and find out the file is not in the stacks because it has just   32
been returned—i.e., dumped down a short metal chute and hidden in a pile of
other returns. Or your file may not be in Records at all. It may be in one of the
courtrooms. Or it may be in Archives, the dim, cave-like repository of about 1
million older case records stored in folders and on microfilm.

So, for example, should you wish to explore the reasons that Sylvester Stallone   33
sued a woman named Barbara Guggenheim the day after Christmas in 1989—a
case that involved millions of dollars in artwork—Archives is your destination.

Getting there is a journey into Wonderland. First you hunt your rabbit hole, a   34
rusted, free-standing elevator on a grassy mall across Hill Street. There is no
building around it, just the elevator in a badly eroded kiosk. Or you can take the
more adventurous route—the long, square tunnel that begins in the courthouse's
canted underground garage.

Dark, slanting passageways, braided with overhead pipes, branch off to   35
Archives, the Criminal Courts Building, the Hall of Records and to one unnamed

place, barricaded with chain-link. The tunnel takes you to an escalator that goes down one more level to a high-ceilinged bunker crowded with tables, a long counter and shelves that rise like skyscrapers. Buttressed between two of them, thin boards support a trash can to catch incoming rain.

This dour cellar, like other warrens, has its own strange constituency, an ebb and flow of stoic men in ball caps, women in baggy sweats, motivated by circumstance to track down old divorce papers, Social Security files or records of criminal proceedings. One young woman recently came in to scour files on train and streetcar accidents going back to 1880. A man from the Genealogical Society of Utah was after divorce files dating to the same period. 36

Back at street level, jurors stream into the courthouse at the rate of about 200 a day, compelled here from a 20-mile radius. Before being assigned out to various chambers, they crowd into a second-floor assembly room and drift next door to Elias' Snack Shoppe, run by a nearly blind, rheumy-eyed Egyptian named Elias Thomas. Along with coffee, hot dogs and slices of pizza, Thomas hawks $5 tapes of himself playing Middle Eastern tunes on the lute. He squints to make change and dreams that someone will discover him here and make him a star. 37

Court employees and county messengers bag up mounds of mail and whisk it down the hall, and through the tunnels, on orange motorized carts. Out front is a shoeshine man, Peter Wiggins, who kicked a heroin habit and escaped a past that included prison time for armed robbery. Now, smiling and dapper in a tie and fedora, he brags of the lawyers and judges who give him $6 for a $4 shine. 38

In the filing rooms you will find a species of litigant known as the *pro per*, the hard-bitten individual who dares to handle his own lawsuits. These men and women, independent-minded and often dressed accordingly, are an exasperation to the judges, because almost invariably they bungle their cases and lose. The very worst— the most prolific—are eventually branded "vexatious litigants," at which point they are forbidden to file further legal actions without the consent of the presiding judge. 39

This blackball list in Los Angeles County runs to more than 130 names. Some are notorious, among them a guy named Harold, a dogged but exceptionally unlucky man who was moved to launch a dozen ill-fated lawsuits over a span of years. One suit targeted a neighbor who was alleged to have committed a long list of transgressions: slashing Harold's car tire, blowing cigarette smoke in his face, pounding on his door, subjecting him to long, threatening stares, and making an enormous number of hostile phone calls. 40

"[He] has already punched me unconscious with permanent brain damage, continues to intimidate and harass me, and may attack again," Harold charged in his hand-written appeal for a restraining order. 41

There are times, when the dockets overflow at other courts, that criminal trials are transferred here from the Criminal Courts Building on Temple Street, even though the building is poorly equipped to handle dangerous inmates. Two dim lockups occupy the seventh floor, but there are no secure avenues for moving suspects to various courtrooms, so violent gang members and third-strikers are transported up and down a freight elevator and marched through public halls in handcuffs, only a few feet from passing women and children. 42

If nothing else, the building is solid—a concrete monstrosity that was viewed   43
as something of a Taj Mahal when it opened in 1959. Its cost was $24 million, well
over budget, making it, at the time, the nation's most expensive trial court. There
were touches of splendor then: All 101 courtrooms were paneled in eastern white
oak. Entry doors were framed in bronze.

Backdrop of Decay

The four designers, including Paul R. Williams, the city's first prominent black   44
architect, were looking more for understated elegance than outright pizazz. They
eschewed the intricate facades of earlier, now-razed courthouses and opted for a
look that was later described by one architectural critic as " '50s modern
attempting to be classical and public."

Today's critics more often call it bland. Inside, the finery has become less and   45
less salient against the intruding backdrop of decay. A broad section of marble
has come down in the eighth-floor hallway. A room on the third floor contains
hundreds of acoustical ceiling tiles, rubble from the Northridge earthquake.
Doors are broken, ditto for courtroom chairs.

Janitors who prowl the dark hours complain about rats, roaches, fleas and   46
water beetles. The building has more than 215 restrooms, but not one has a floor
drain, a design oversight that has brought decades of exasperation. When toilet
valves stick, or some vandalizing litigant jams paper towels or cafeteria fruit
down the commode, the water spills out with nowhere to go. Problems that begin
after hours often turn into floods before they are noticed, with the water dripping
down into copy machines and computers on the next floor.

Pipes burst so often that some custodians think every last one should be   47
yanked out and replaced. Floods of mysterious origin seep under the north wall
of the evidence room, a gray hovel, enclosed in chain-link, where thousands of
documents, maps and other exhibits are stored, including a dummy head used to
argue some long-ago police brutality case that no one remembers.

In spite of its abundant flaws, the courthouse has been the scene of countless   48
historic cases, some of which have shaped the evolution of civil law. Famous litigants began with Charlie Chaplin and Errol Flynn and continue even now with the
likes of Kim Basinger, Pamela Anderson, Bette Midler and Carroll O'Connor.

In the old days, cases were doled out from huge master calendars. On   49
Mondays, hundreds of attorneys would gather in a few massive courtrooms to
hear where their trials would begin. Hucksters sold tip sheets about judges and
prospective jurors. Lawyers billed their clients untold thousands of hours for time
spent sitting around waiting.

That problem was solved with beepers. Lawyers were paged when trial was   50
about to start. Now cases are assigned to judges the moment they are filed, a
system that has eliminated years of backlog but not the anxiety. Attorneys still
fret over the assignment of judges. The notion that they are all interchangeable
parts—rational, objective arbiters of truth—is seen as naive foolishness. The fact
is, a judge's personality strongly influences the machinations of justice.

Victor E. Chavez, the presiding judge of the Superior Court, rode down the   51
aisle at his wedding on horseback. Judge Alan Buckner lives on a yacht. Lawrence
Crispo sings opera. Some are diplomats; others are reputed to be tough as
rawhide.

Ronald Sohegian is one of the latter, a judge who inspires fear in more than a   52
few lawyers. "If you deserve a head-cracking," one attorney says, "he'll crack your
head."

Judge Robert O'Brien, up on the eighth floor, handles injunctions and tempo-   53
rary restraining orders. Known as a stickler for punctuality who frequently arrives
at the building before dawn, O'Brien likes to see motions filed no later than 8:45
a.m. If you have to pull a case in Records, or track down a file elsewhere, you may
risk a day's delay, a failure that might be critical in a TRO [temporary restraining
order] case that requires freezing assets or blocking a business deal.

Lawyers are loath to criticize the bench, fearful of paying the price in some   54
future ruling, but privately they admit to having favorites—and others that sour
their stomachs.

"Sometimes you just feel like a guy doesn't like you," one attorney says.   55
"Something about your tie, about your hair."

Few victories come easy here in this grand old hall of jurisprudence, but for   56
dedicated attorneys there is the chance to leave a mark, one way or another.
Some do it through insightful briefs or brilliant oratory. Down in Department 2,
the lawyers of the master-calendar era did it another way.

In those days, when attorneys were allowed to sit in the jury box as they   57
waited for their assignments, lawyers in the last row would tilt back against the
white-oak paneling.

You can still see the line of amoeba-shaped oil spots, the stains of old Vitalis.   58

● ● ● ●

Discussion and Writing Topics

1. The title of Ferrell's article refers to the novelist Charles Dickens, whose vivid
   descriptions of the places and often appalling social conditions of Victorian
   England remain compelling to readers today. (See, for example, *Our Mutual
   Friend*, *Great Expectations*, and *Bleak House*, the story of a legal dispute that
   spanned generations.) What aspects of Ferrell's article make it novelistic in
   feeling? What techniques does he use to help his reader not only understand but
   also almost *feel* what it is like to be inside the Los Angeles County Courthouse?
2. Imitating Ferrell's style, describe a place you know well in a way that you hope
   makes it come alive for readers.
3. Describe an experience that you or someone you have known has had with the
   legal system, providing the kind of detailed description that characterizes "A
   Crumbling Hive of Humanity." Was it in criminal, civil, or traffic court? Did a
   judge or a jury decide the verdict? Was the case settled?
4. Compare Ferrell's view of a real courthouse with the courthouses shown in
   popular TV programs and movies.

5. How would you feel, as a plaintiff or defendant, if you were a litigant in the surroundings that Ferrell describes? Consider the scenarios presented in the article: the physical surroundings, the litigants, the court employees.

Gulliver on Lawyers

Jonathan Swift

The following selection is from Jonathan Swift's memorable satire of human folly, Gulliver's Travels, *first published in 1726. Assuming the form of a travel book, a popular type of narrative in England during the eighteenth century,* Gulliver's Travels *purports to be the true account of Lemuel Gulliver, a sailor who endures a series of shipwrecks and ends up in a number of strange lands. In describing the customs and attitudes of the inhabitants of these lands,* Gulliver/Swift *is actually satirizing the customs and attitudes of his contemporaries in England.*

Gulliver first lands in Lilliput, where he is a giant among tiny people; next he finds himself in Brobdingnag, where he is a midget among giants. His third voyage, to Laputa, affords Swift the opportunity to ridicule the science of his time. But his most savage and broad-ranging satire is reserved for the fourth voyage. Here Gulliver finds himself among the Houyhnhnms, a race of intelligent horses. When the hapless hero attempts to explain the customs and practices of his native England to his superrational hosts, they simply cannot comprehend the various idiocies and barbarities of "civilized" Europeans. In this selection, Gulliver attempts to explain law and lawyers to his Houyhnhnm master.

[My Master] added, That he had heard too much upon the Subject of War, both in this, and some former Discourses. There was another Point which a little perplexed him at present. I had said, that some of our Crew left their Country on Account of being ruined by *Law*: That I had already explained the Meaning of the Word; but he was at a Loss how it should come to pass, that the *Law* which was intended for *every* Man's Preservation, should be any Man's Ruin. Therefore he desired to be farther satisfied what I meant by *Law*, and the Dispensers thereof, according to the present Practice in my own Country: Because he thought, Nature and Reason were sufficient Guides for a reasonable Animal, as we pretended to be, in shewing us what we ought to do, and what to avoid.   1

I assured his Honour, that *Law* was a Science wherein I had not much conversed, further than by employing Advocates, in vain, upon some Injustices that had been done me. However, I would give him all the Satisfaction I was able.   2

I said there was a Society of Men among us, bred up from their Youth in the Art of proving by Words multiplied for the Purpose, that *White* is *Black*, and *Black*   3

Text of "Gulliver on Lawyers" is from Vol. III of the collected works of Swift, published in Dublin in 1735.

is *White*, according as they are paid. To this Society all the rest of the People are Slaves.

For Example. If my Neighbour hath a mind to my *Cow*, he hires a Lawyer to prove that he ought to have my *Cow* from me. I must then hire another to defend my Right; it being against all Rules of *Law* that any Man should be allowed to speak for himself. Now in this Case, I who am the true Owner lie under two great Disadvantages. First, my Lawyer being practiced almost from his Cradle in defending Falshood; is quite out of his Element when he would be an Advocate for Justice, which as an Office unnatural, he always attempts with great Awkwardness, if not with Ill-will. The second Disadvantage is, that my Lawyer must proceed with great Caution: Or else he will be reprimanded by the Judges, and abhorred by his Brethren, as one who would lessen the Practice of the Law. And therefore I have but two Methods to preserve my *Cow*. The first is, to gain over my Adversary's Lawyer with a double Fee; who will then betray his Client, by insinuating that he hath Justice on his Side. The second Way is for my Lawyer to make my Cause appear as unjust as he can; by allowing the *Cow* to belong to my Adversary; and this if it be skilfully done, will certainly bespeak the Favour of the Bench.

Now, your Honour is to know, that these Judges are Persons appointed to decide all Controversies of Property, as well as for the Tryal of Criminals; and picked out from the most dextrous Lawyers who are grown old or lazy: And having been byassed all their Lives against Truth and Equity, lie under such a fatal Necessity of favouring Fraud, Perjury and Oppression; that I have known some of them to have refused a large Bribe from the Side where Justice lay, rather than injure the *Faculty*,[1] by doing any thing unbecoming their Nature or their Office.

It is a Maxim among these Lawyers, that whatever hath been done before, may legally be done again: And therefore they take special Care to record all the Decisions formerly made against common Justice and the general Reason of Mankind. These, under the Name of *Precedents*, they produce as Authorities to justify the most iniquitous Opinions; and the Judges never fail of directing accordingly.

In pleading, they studiously avoid entering into the *Merits* of the Cause; but are loud, violent and tedious in dwelling upon all *Circumstances* which are not to the Purpose. For Instance, in the Case already mentioned: They never desire to know what Claim or Title my Adversary hath to my *Cow*; but whether the said *Cow* were Red or Black; her Horns long or short; whether the Field I graze her in be round or square; whether she were milked at home or abroad; what Diseases she is subject to, and the like. After which they consult *Precedents*, adjourn the Cause, from Time to Time, and in Ten, Twenty, or Thirty Years come to an Issue.

It is likewise to be observed, that this Society hath a peculiar Cant and Jargon of their own, that no other Mortal can understand, and wherein all their Laws are written, which they take special Care to multiply; whereby they have wholly confounded the very Essence of Truth and Falshood, of Right and Wrong; so that it will take Thirty Years to decide whether the Field, left me by my Ancestors for six Generations, belong to me, or to a Stranger three Hundred Miles off.

---

[1] The profession.

In the Tryal of Persons accused for Crimes against the State, the Method is much more short and commendable: The Judge first sends to sound the Disposition of those in Power; after which he can easily hang or save the Criminal, strictly preserving all the Forms of Law.

Here my Master interposing, said it was a Pity, that Creatures endowed with such prodigious Abilities of Mind as these Lawyers, by the Description I gave of them must certainly be, were not rather encouraged to be Instructors of others in Wisdom and Knowledge. In Answer to which, I assured his Honour, that in all Points out of their own Trade, they were usually the most ignorant and stupid Generation among us, the most despicable in common Conversation, avowed Enemies to all Knowledge and Learning; and equally disposed to pervert the general Reason of Mankind, in every other Subject of Discourse as in that of their own Profession.

● ● ● ●

Discussion and Writing Topics

1. What do you think Gulliver's Houyhnhnm master means when he says that "Nature and Reason were sufficient Guides for a reasonable animal"? To what extent do you share this assumption?
2. Respond to this portrait of law and lawyers expressed by Gulliver. Clearly, the portrait is a caricature, but to what extent, based on your own knowledge and experience, is this caricature based on reality? On which aspects of the law and lawyers does Gulliver focus? How valid are his criticisms? Be as specific as possible in your discussion.
3. In the spirit of Swift, write a satirical account of some other professional group—for example, dentists, teachers, police officers, football coaches, rock singers, talk radio hosts. You might try your hand at imitating Swift's style.

About Real Lawyers

Victor A. Fleming

In this article, which originally appeared in Trial *magazine (September 1993), Victor A. Fleming argues that lawyers and the legal profession have been the victims of bad press and misperceptions by the public—starting with misinterpretations of a famous antilawyer line in one of Shakespeare's plays. Fleming, the author of* Real Lawyers Do Change Their Briefs *(1989), is a judge in Little Rock, Arkansa and writes a weekly column, "I Swear."*

I grew up in the fifties and sixties. It seemed a simpler time as I passed my childhood years in a small Mississippi Delta town. Among my favorite quotes is the line from Tom T. Hall's "Old Dogs and Children and Watermelon Wine": "I tried it all when I was young and in my natural prime." I tried it all, too—or most of it

Trial, Sept. 1993: 84–85.

anyhow: athletics, drama, journalism, literature, politics, religion. Some of it stuck with me, some of it didn't. I was good at some of it, bad at some. But I had an ability to sympathize and empathize that would later be helpful in the practice of law.

For four years I called Davidson College home and almost grew roots in Meck-   2
lenberg County, North Carolina. By age 23, I had earned money in a dozen or more different jobs—service station attendant, janitor, cook, deejay, waiter, bartender, fork-lift driver, journalist, salesman (cars, clothes, advertising), soldier, truck driver, and more. Most of these were temporary day jobs (for a paycheck) while I struggled to write the Great American Something during the evenings.

When I realized I was never going to make any money as a writer of great lit-   3
erature, some prophetic words of my mother came back to me. Even now, I remember the dialogue:

Mother: You could be a great lawyer, son, because you love to argue so much.   4

Me: I do *not* argue, and I don't love to argue, and that's the last I want to hear   5
about this arguing business.

So I applied for and was accepted into law school.   6

I did not realize, however, that my chosen profession would become the con-   7
stant object of cruel epithets and tacky jokes. What really hurt was that so many of the remarks I endured weren't justified.

I recall once trying to persuade someone to stop repeating malicious gossip   8
about a mutual acquaintance. "It's *hearsay*, right?" came the sarcastic response. "You lawyers are all the same!"

Another time, among friends, I suggested an easier way to keep score in our   9
golf matches. Someone immediately quipped, "Leave it to a lawyer to try to complicate things."

Someone in my golf group (by accident, I believe) once tried to close the trunk   10
of a car while I was leaning in. After being restrained by one of the others, this fellow exclaimed, "Can you imagine anything worse than slamming a trunk lid on a lawyer?"

Someone piped up, "It might not be so bad. You might kill him."   11

Another voice chimed in, "That would have pleased Shakespeare."   12

At that remark I saw red. Folks who invoke Shakespeare around me are   13
meddlin', since I was an English major and a Shakespeare buff. Few things rankle me quite as much as the allusion to Shakespeare when the notion of killing a lawyer comes up.

I doubt most of the people who insist on quoting the line could correctly name   14
the speaker (it was not Henry VI), let alone describe the context of the passage. They are content to let it stand alone, suggesting that all lawyers are rapscallions. In *The Second Part of King Henry the Sixth* (or *Henry VI, Part II*, for the nonpurist), a basic part of the plot was a planned revolution headed by the Duke of York. York enlisted one Jack Cade as a general. That Cade was a lowlife rebel is emphasized particularly in one scene, in which a messenger describes Cade and company: "His army is a ragged multitude of hinds and peasants, rude and merciless." (Act IV, scene iv.) Plotting secretly to become king himself, Cade says, amid a group of his cronies,

There shall be in England seven half-penny loaves sold for a penny: the three-hooped pots shall have ten hoops; and I will make it felony to drink small beer: all the realm shall be in common, and in Cheapside shall my palfrey go to grass. And when I am king—as king I will be . . . there shall be no money; all shall eat and drink on my score; and I will apparel them all in one livery, that they may agree like brothers and worship me their lord.

Whereupon the semi-comical (but definitely ignorant) Dick speaks the infamous line: "The first thing we do, let's kill all the lawyers." (Act IV, scene ii.) And, indeed, with the idea of bringing down the kingdom, Cade and his followers set out to kill all "scholars, lawyers, courtiers, [and] gentlemen." (Act IV, scene iv.) Gives you a bit of insight into the character of the man journalists are so fond of quoting.   15

Denouncing lawyers has been a popular pastime historically. The story is told that once at the offices of Sir William Jones, a British barrister of significant repute, a large spider dropped to the floor in the presence of Jones and a philanthropist friend, Mr. Day. Jones shouted, "Kill that spider, Day!"   16

Refusing to carry out the order, Mr. Day is said to have responded coolly, "I will not kill that spider, Jones; I do not know that I have a right to kill that spider! Suppose when you are going to Westminster Hall, a superior being who, perhaps, may have as much power over you as you have over this spider, should say to his companion, 'Kill that lawyer, kill that lawyer!' How should you like that, Jones? And I am sure to most people a lawyer is a more obnoxious animal than a spider." (10 Modern Eloquence—Library of After Dinner Speeches, Lectures & Occasional Addresses 52 (Thomas B. Reed ed., 1900.)   17

Although an early example of a tacky lawyer joke, Day's poking fun at Jones lacks the universally demeaning aspect that typifies current lawyer jokes. Clearly, in the last quarter-century things have gotten out of hand.   18

Given the image painted by the U.S. media and foisted on a sensation-starved public by Hollywood, it is no wonder that "Americans love to hate their lawyers." I'll attribute that quote to F. Lee Bailey,* although I doubt he said it first. In Bailey's opinion, however, "a lawyer's stock in trade is to attack people." People thought of as attackers are not generally well liked by others.   19

Few nonlawyers realize it, and the F. Lee Baileys of the world notwithstanding, the vast majority of Real Lawyers do not consider themselves professional attackers. And they certainly don't aspire to evoke hatred in people. They spend most of their time analyzing and solving the problems of others.   20

It is important that nonlawyers realize that lawyers are human beings. They had childhoods. Many were kind to their mothers. Some had other aspirations before choosing law as a career. In many instances character traits unfairly attributed to legal training were ingrained in the lawyers long before practicing law entered their minds.   21

---

*A prominant criminal defense attorney whose clients included Patricia Hearst and O. J. Simpson.

This country needs a concerted movement to depict accurately the ethics and activities of the average Real Lawyer. There is a need for the media to inform the public that most Real Lawyers engage in mundane activities that their counterparts on the screen never get around to because of the excessive glamour in their fictional lives. 22

Television has emerged as this century's most pervasive influence on public opinion, and the TV image of the law leaves much to be desired. Homicide cases are routinely resolved by courtroom confessions, often at preliminary hearings ("Perry Mason"). A public defender routinely represents defendants arrested by her husband ("Hill Street Blues"). Defense lawyers play tricks on witnesses and, in effect, wind up offering their closing arguments as testimony ("Matlock"). 23

Then there is "L.A. Law," where judges mercilessly lecture the lawyers once a week. Lawyers who try to be ethical get thrown in jail. Seasoned litigators appear in each other's offices without appointments to read case law. Every deposition results in a shouting match. And there's the inter-, intra-, and extra-firm sleeping around that gets in the way of folks' ability to cope with the pressures of law practice. 24

These shows are, at best, caricatures of the Real Thing. This county needs some legal realism from its TV heroes. 25

A popular soap opera should feature an attorney who refuses to take a case because of a conflict of interest. A prime-time drama should air an episode in which some rich tycoon is told by his lawyer that he should settle a case rather than go to trial because there is no guarantee of victory for him. How about a sitcom in which a lawyer handles a case for free for an indigent child? 26

This happens daily in the lives of Real Lawyers. Month-long murder trials, million-dollar jury verdicts, lawyer-judge yelling matches, and homicides solved by courtroom confessions are rare occurrences indeed. The Real Lawyer experiences these once in a blue moon. 27

Art Buchwald wrote, "It isn't the bad lawyers who are screwing up the justice system in this country—it's the good lawyers." But when he decided to take off after Eddie Murphy for a share of movie profits, you can bet he hired the best legal eagle he could find. 28

It's the dishonest attorneys—from those who challenged the ministry of Jesus (*see Luke* 11–14) to those who participated in Watergate—who have caused the erosion of public confidence in lawyers and have stripped away the honor that law deserves. If we could somehow restore the proper image of attorneys, then we could perhaps recapture the glories of an age when law was—as Gilbert and Sullivan's *Iolanthe* puts it—"the true embodiment of everything that's excellent." 29

● ● ● ●

Discussion and Writing Topics

1. Victor A. Fleming argues that most people's perceptions of lawyers are based on a false image created by the media, especially television. To what extent do you think he is right? How are your own perceptions of lawyers and the legal professional, favorable or unfavorable, based on what you have seen on TV

and in movies? To what extent does your personal knowledge of real lawyers (what Fleming calls "The Real Thing") influence your perceptions? Or to what extent does this knowledge of real lawyers contradict the image offered by the media?

2. Watch one or more episodes of legal dramas on TV (for instance, *Ally McBeal*, *The Practice*, *Law and Order*, *Judging Amy*, or *Family Law*). Suppose that your entire knowledge of lawyers and the legal profession were based on what you saw on these shows. Write an essay discussing the two or three most important conclusions you would draw from these shows, supporting your conclusions with specific references to what happens during these episodes.

■ The Great Perini ■

Scott Turow

Scott Turow is most well-known as the author of popular legal thrillers such as Presumed Innocent *(1987),* Burden of Proof *(1990),* The Laws of Our Fathers *(1996), and* Personal Injuries *(1999). Before writing these novels, however, Turow, himself a lawyer, penned an account of his first year at Harvard Law School,* One L *(1977). (The title refers to the label for first-year law students.) The experiences described by Turow are typical of those that have been endured in law school by many of America's attorneys.*

Although legal education is slowly undergoing change (there is now a greater emphasis on legal ethics and on the social context of the law than in the past), the basic format of instruction in law school remains the Socratic method—named after the fifth-century B.C. Athenian philosopher Socrates, who drew insights and truths from his students by asking a series of questions. Students read cases in their casebooks, and then in class are questioned (or grilled, as the case may be) on the facts and legal significance of these cases. In this selection, Turow describes the opening session of a contracts law course, taught by a famous legal scholar, Rudolph Perini.

(For another view of first year at Harvard Law School, see James Bridges's 1973 film The Paper Chase. *In that film the Perini-like figure is the fearsome Professor Kingsfield.)*

I should say a word or two about law books, since they are plainly the focus of so   1
much of a law student's attention. There are three general categories. The first are the casebooks, the thousand-page volumes out of which class assignments are regularly made. The cases in the book are usually edited and have been selected for their importance in the development in given areas of the law. In the second

One L. New York: Penguin Books, 1977: 42–50.

category, a kind of academic purgatory, are the "hornbooks," brief treatises produced by well-known legal scholars which summarize leading cases and which provide general descriptions of the doctrines in the field. Professors discourage hornbook reading by beginning students. They fear that hornbook consultation will limit a 1L's [first-year law student] ability to deduce the law himself from the cases and also that it will decrease a student's interest in class, since the hornbooks often analyze the daily material in much the same way that the professors do themselves. In the final category, the nether world well beneath academic respectability, are the myriad study aids, commercially prepared casebook and course and subject-matter outlines, and other kinds of digests. The best-known series is the Gilbert Law Summaries. Although law students have gotten by for generations with the aid of these and other prepared outlines, there are members of the faculty who claim to have never heard the word "Gilbert's" from a student's lips. Before I started, I myself was somewhat incredulous that students would buy a course guide rather than prepare it themselves. It seemed to border on plagiarism.

Whatever category, two generalizations about law books usually hold true. 2 They are quite large—I'd already had to invest in a big orange knapsack to haul all of them around. And they are expensive. The casebooks are especially dear, $16 to $25 when bought new [editor's note: now between $60 and $70], the prices probably inflated because the publishers recognize that casebooks are required reading and have to be purchased. Faculty agitation for lower prices would probably do little good and in any event is unlikely, since the professors are most often the editors or authors of the books they assign. In all but one of my first-year classes, the required casebook had been produced by either that professor or another member of the HLS faculty. Used-book exchanges like the Lawbook Thrift Shop are the only means students have to lessen costs.

Terry emerged with a heavy green book which he showed me at once. "Got 3 that yet?"

I examined the title page. It was a Contracts hornbook, written, as was our 4 casebook, by Gregory Baldridge and Rudolph Perini.

"Two buddies of mine say that the dude's whole course is in there," Terry told 5 me.

"He wrote a hornbook, huh?" I asked, still fingering the cover. 6

" 'Wrote a hornbook?' Hey, man, this guy *is* Contracts—he is *the* authority. 7 That is *the* hornbook." .

"I thought profs say don't read hornbooks for a while." 8

"That's what they say, man—that's not what people do. At least, that's what I 9 hear."

I shrugged and handed him the book back. But I worried. How did I know 10 what was right? I felt my faith should be in the professors, but I didn't want to fall behind my classmates, either.

"I'll wait," I said. 11

"Your choice," Terry answered. 12

"I want to see how bad Perini really is, first." 13

He nodded and we went off together toward the classroom in Austin where   14
we would both find out.

Most law-school classrooms are arranged in roughly the same way. Broken   15
usually by two aisles, concentric semicircles of seats and desks issue back from
the podium, resulting in a kind of amphitheater. In Pound [Hall], where we had
met [Professor] Mann, the newly constructed classrooms had been built with
remarkable compactness. But in Austin the rooms were ancient and enormous.
The seats and desks were in rows of yellowed oak, tiered steeply toward the rear.
At its highest, the classroom was nearly forty feet, with long, heavy curtains on
the windows and dark portraits of English judges, dressed in their wigs and robes,
hanging in gilt frames high on the wall. It was an awesome setting, especially
when its effect was combined with the stories we had all heard about Perini.
There was a tone of tense humor in the conversations around me, most voices
somewhat hushed. As I headed for my seat, I overheard a number of people say,
"I don't want it to be me," referring to whom Perini would call on.

I introduced myself to the men sitting on either side of me. One was a former   16
marine from Ohio, the other a kid named Don, just out of the University of Texas.
The three of us gossiped about Perini, exchanging what little information we
knew. Don said that Perini was a Texan. He had graduated from the University of
Texas Law School, but he had been a professor at HLS for twenty years. Only in
the late '60s had he interrupted his teaching, when he had briefly been some kind
of counsellor to Nixon.

It was already a few minutes after ten, the hour when we were supposed to   17
start. The class was assembled and almost everyone was in his seat. Don asked
me what Perini looked like.

"I don't know," I answered. "No idea."   18

Greg, the ex-marine on the other side, said, "Just take a look."   19

Perini moved slowly down the tiers toward the lectern. He held his head up   20
and he was without expression. My first thought was that he looked softer than
I'd expected. He was around six feet, but pudgy and a little awkward. Although
the day was warm, he wore a black three-piece suit. He held the book and the
seating chart under his arm.

The room was totally silent by the time he reached the lectern. He slapped the   21
book down on the desk beneath. He still had not smiled.

"This is Contracts," he said, "Section Two, in case any of you are a little uncer-   22
tain about where you are." He smiled then, stiffly. "I have a few introductory comments and then we'll be going on to the cases I asked you to look at for today.
First, however, I want to lay out the ground rules on which this class will run, so
that there will be *no* confusion in the future."

He spoke with elaborate slowness, emphasis on each word. His accent was   23
distinctly southern.

Perini picked up the casebook in one hand.   24

"The text for this class is *Selected Cases in the Law of Contracts*. The editors   25
are Baldridge and"—Perini lifted a hand to weight the silence—"et cetera." He

smiled again, without parting his lips. Around the room a few people snickered. Then he said, "Needless to mention, I hope you bought it new," and got his first outright laugh.

"We will proceed through the book case by case," Perini told us. "Now and then we may skip a case or two. In that event, I'll inform you in advance, or you will find a notice on the bulletin boards. You should stay three cases ahead, each day." 26

Between the desk on which the lectern sat and the students in the front row, there was a narrow area, a kind of small proscenium. Perini began to pace there slowly, his hands behind his back. I watched him as he came toward our side of the room, staring up harshly at the faces around him. He looked past fifty, coarse-skinned and dark. He was half-bald, but his black hair was styled carefully. There was a grim set to his mouth and eyes. 27

"This class will deal with the law of obligations, of bargains, commercial dealings, the law of promises," Perini said. "It is the hardest course you will take all year. Contracts has traditionally been the field of law of the most renowned intellectual complexity. Most of the greatest legal commentators of the past century have been Contracts scholars: Williston, Corbin, Fuller, Llewellyn, Baldridge—" He lifted his hand as he had done before. "Et cetera," he said again and smiled broadly for the first time. Most people laughed. One or two applauded. Perini waited before he began pacing again. 28

"Some of your classmates may find the Property course in the spring the hardest course *they* take. But you will not feel that way, because you will be taking Contracts with me. I am not"—he looked up—"an easy person." 29

"I expect you to be here *every* day. And I expect you to sit where the registrar has assigned you. On the so-called back benches, I should see only those persons who are visiting us seeking a momentary glimpse of something morbid." Laughter again from a few places. 30

"I expect you to be very well prepared, *every* day. I want to be absolutely clear on that. I have *never* heard the word 'pass.' I do not *know* what 'unprepared' means. Now and then, of course, there are personal problems—we all have them at times— which make full preparation impossible. If that is the case, then I want a written note to be handed to my secretary at least *two* hours before class. You can find her on the second floor of the Faculty Office Building in room two eighty-one." 31

I wrote it all down in my notebook: "No absence. No pass. No unprepared. Note to sec'ty 2 hrs. b-4 class, FOB 281." 32

Holy Christ, I thought. 33

As expected, Perini told us to read nothing aside from class assignments for the first few months—not even "a certain hornbook" we might have heard of. For the present, he assured us, we would have our hands full. Then he described the course in some detail. In that discussion too, Perini maintained that tone of barely veiled menace. We may have been Phi Beta Kappas and valedictorians, but this was Harvard Law School now—things would not be easy. 34

There were moments when I was certain that Perini was only half serious. There was such obvious showmanship in all of this, the deliberateness of the gestures, the 35 archness of his smile. It was almost a parody of the legendary tough professor, of the Perini of rumor. But if it was an act, it was one which he was determined would be compelling. He revealed no more than a trace of irony and there were often moments, as when he had looked up at us, that he seemed full of steel.

As he went on describing the subjects with which we would soon be dealing—   36
offer, acceptance, interpretation; the list was extensive—I began to think that, like Mann, he would let the hour slip away. No one would be called and we'd all be safe for one more day. But at six or seven minutes to twelve he returned to the lectern and looked down at the seating chart.

"Let's see if we can cover a *little* ground today." Perini took a pencil from his   37
pocket and pointed it at the chart. It might as well have been a pistol. Please, no, I thought.

"Mr. Karlin!" Perini cried sharply.   38

Nearby, I heard a tremendous thud. Five or six seats from me a man was   39
scrambling to grab hold of the books that had been piled before him, two or three of which had now hit the floor. That, I was sure, was Karlin who had jolted when he heard his name called. He was a heavyset man, pale, with black eyeglasses. He was wearing a yarmulke [skullcap worn by Jewish men and boys, particularly during religious services]. His eyes, as he struggled with his books, were quick with fright, and at once I felt terribly sorry for him and guilty at my own relief.

"Mr. Karlin," Perini said, ambling toward my side of the room, "why don't you   40
tell us about the case of *Hurley* v. *Eddingfield*?"

Karlin already had his notebook open. His voice was quavering.   41

"Plaintiff's intestate," he began. He got no further.   42

"What does *that* mean?" Perini cried from across the room. He began   43
marching fiercely up the aisle toward Karlin. "In-*tes*-tate," he said, "in-*tes*-tate. What is that? Something to do with the *stomach*? Is this an anatomy class, Mr. Karlin?" Perini's voice had become shrill with a note of open mockery and at the last word people burst out laughing, louder than at anything Perini had said before.

He was only five or six feet from Karlin now. Karlin stared up at him and   44
blinked and finally said, "No."

"No, I didn't think so," Perini said. "What if the word was 'testate'? What would   45
that be? Would we have moved from the stomach"—Perini waved a hand and there was more loud laughter when he leeringly asked his question—"*else*where?"

"I think," Karlin said weakly, "that if the word was 'testate' it would mean he   46
had a will."

"And 'intestate' that he didn't have a will. I see." Perini wagged his head. "And   47
who is this 'he,' Mr. Karlin?"

Karlin was silent. He shifted in his seat as Perini stared at him. Hands had shot   48
up across the room. Perini called rapidly on two or three people who gave various names—Hurley, Eddingfield, the plaintiff. Finally someone said that the case didn't say.

"The case doesn't *say*!" Perini cried, marching down the aisle. "The case does   49
not say. Read the case. *Read* the case! *Care*fully!" He bent with each word, pointing

a finger at the class. He stared fiercely into the crowd of students in the center of the room, then looked back at Karlin. "Do we really care who 'he' is, Mr. Karlin?"

"Care?"

"Does it make any *difference* to the outcome of the case?"

"I don't think so."

"Why not?"

"Because he's dead."

"He's *dead!*" Perini shouted. "Well, that's a load off of our minds. But there's one problem then, Mr. Karlin. If he's dead, how did he file a *law*suit?"

Karlin's face was still tight with fear, but he seemed to be gathering himself.

"I thought it was the administrator who brought the suit."

"Ah!" said Perini, "the ad*min*istrator. And what's an administrator? One of those types over in the Faculty Building?"

It went on that way for a few more minutes, Perini striding through the room, shouting and pointing as he battered Karlin with questions, Karlin doing his best to provide answers. A little after noon Perini suddenly announced that we would continue tomorrow. Then he strode from the classroom with the seating chart beneath his arm. In his wake the class exploded into chatter.

I sat stunned. Men and women crowded around Karlin to congratulate him. He had done well—better, it seemed, than even Perini had expected. At one point the professor had asked where Karlin was getting all the definitions he was methodically reciting. I knew Karlin had done far better than I could have, a realization which upset me, given all the work I had done preparing for the class. I hadn't asked myself who was suing. I knew what "intestate" meant, but not "testate," and was hardly confident I could have made the jump while under that kind of pressure. I didn't even want to think about the time it would be my turn to face Perini.

And as much as all of that, I was bothered by the mood which had taken hold of the room. The exorbitance of Perini's manner had seemed to release a sort of twisted energy. Why had people laughed like that? I wondered. It wasn't all good-natured. It wasn't really laughter *with* Karlin. I had felt it too, a sort of giddiness, when Perini made his mocking inquiries. And why had people raised their hands so eagerly, stretching out of their seats as they sought to be called on? When Socratic instruction had been described for me, I had been somewhat incredulous that students would dash in so boldly to correct each other's errors. But if I hadn't been quite as scared I might have raised my hand myself. What the hell went on here? I was thoroughly confused, the more so because despite my reservations the truth was that I had been gripped, even thrilled, by the class. Perini, for all the melodrama and intimidation, had been magnificent, electric, in full possession of himself and the students. The points he'd made had had a wonderful clarity and directness. He was, as claimed, an exceptional teacher.

As I headed out, Karlin, still surrounded by well-wishers, was also on his way from the classroom. I reached him to pat him on the back, but I had no chance to speak with him as he went off in the swirl of admiring classmates. A man, and a woman I'd met, a tall blonde who had gone to Radcliffe, Karen Sondergard, had stayed behind. I asked them about Karlin.

"He's a rabbi," Karen said, "or else he trained for it. He was at Yeshiva in New York." 63

"He did quite a job," I said. 64

"He should have," the man told me. "He said he read Perini's hornbook over the summer." 65

I stared for an instant, then told the guy that he was kidding. 66

"That's what he said," the man insisted. "I heard him say so." Karen confirmed that. 67

Nazzario came up then and I had the man tell Terry what he had said about Karlin. 68

"Over the *summer*," I repeated. 69

Terry glanced at me, probably suppressing "I told you so," then shook his head. 70

"Folks around here sure don't fool around," he said. 71

We all laughed and the four of us went off together for lunch. Afterward, I went back to the Lawbook Thrift Shop. I wasn't sure if it made me feel better or worse when I bought Perini's hornbook. 72

● ● ● ●

Discussion and Writing Topics

1. Discuss your reactions to the class session, and to Perini's instructional tactics, as described by Turow. How does the class session differ from that of a typical undergraduate course? To what extent do you think that Perini's tactics are appropriate for the training of future attorneys? To what extent might your reaction, had you been a student in this course, been the same as Turow's?

2. Describe, in a degree of detail similar to Turow's, the opening session of a course you have taken that was particularly memorable. It does not need to be a session that provoked fear or dread in you (although it may well be)—just one, as a result of the instructor's distinctive style of teaching, that has stayed with you, and perhaps changed the way you approach learning.

The Memo

Cameron Stracher

A reviewer of Cameron Stracher's Double Billing *believes that it "promises to become for the hordes of junior associates in large corporate law firms what [Turow's]* One L *is for law students—a classic must-read."* Double Billing: A Young Lawyer's Tale of Greed, Sex, Lies, and the Pursuit of a Swivel Chair *is*

Double Billing. New York: Wm. Morrow, 1998: 94–101.

based on Stracher's own experience as a junior associate in a large New York City law firm, with the fictional name of Crowley and Cavanaugh. The book demonstrates why, although the top law school students eagerly hope to land jobs at big city corporate law firms where they can earn six-figure incomes within a couple of years, the human price they will pay in meeting their quota of "billable hours" is considerable—and often, unpayable. (Stracher himself quit the corporate law life after two years.)

In this early excerpt from the book, Stracher has a One L–like moment (see Turow, pp. 26–32) when he realizes how unprepared he is to do his part on the case he has recently been assigned. The case involves a class-action lawsuit charging a securities firm, TriCom, with fraud after some of its stock suffered a precipitous decline and clients experienced huge financial losses. Stracher's law firm represents the defendants.

Stracher is a graduate of Harvard Law School and author of a novel, The Laws of Return. Double Billing *was published in 1998.*

Dinner plates circle the conference room like wagons savaged by Indians. It's late. 1
Sane people are sleeping. I tiptoe past Daniel's [another associate, also assigned to the case] office as if I'm afraid I might wake him.

"Going home?" he says, looking up. 2

I shrug casually. "I'm coming in early tomorrow," I say. "I thought I'd get some 3
sleep." My eyes ache from a week of reading thousands of footnotes in law review articles.

"Good idea," he says, as if approving a theory. On his planet sleep, like gravity, 4
is hardly necessary.

"Good night." 5

"See you tomorrow." 6

Tomorrow, for him, may be later today. I don't ask. 7

A black Lincoln Town Car waits on the street as I revolve through the doors. 8
The driver is asleep, a newspaper folded over his face. He startles awake when I open the back door, reaches for something inside his jacket—a gun?—then relaxes. Car service is a luxury that even in this tightwad decade lawyers won't surrender. No sensible person should have to hail a Yellow Cab.

The driver offers me his paper, and I sift through the stories I missed that 9
morning. Subway crashes, murderous children, diabolical cops. The shortwave radio cackles in a babble of tongues. Russian? Armenian? Hungarian? The driver carries on a conversation with the dispatcher, or he's ordering terrorist strikes. I flip the page.

The car cruises up Central Park West, then turns onto my street. I help the 10
driver read the numbers from the front of the buildings. At 257, I tell him to stop. He stops at 323, the next block. I don't argue with him; he doesn't look happy. We're both working late, but he's driving me home. I sign the voucher and skip out onto the street.

It's warm, too warm for March. Two kids sit on a stoop smoking dope. A home- 11
less man pushes a shopping cart toward the river.

I walk back toward the intersection. Another cab slows, honks; I wave him on. 12
Farther down the street, on Broadway, a black man tries to hail him. The cab
cruises right by. The man steps into the street, nearly straddling the fire lane.
Empty cabs sail past as if he were invisible.

At the corner grocery, a Korean man sits on a wooden crate snapping the 13
brown ends off green beans.

There are worse things than earning $93,000 a year, being driven home in a 14
Lincoln Town Car, ordering meals from any restaurant you choose, commanding
the respect of strangers.

Far worse things. 15

Seven-thirty A.M., sweaty, tattered, my ears chilled with dew, I stagger to the 16
food court in the basement of our building for my morning bagel. Renaldo, behind
the counter, asks about my run, clucks when I tell him the mileage. "You should
be asleep," he says. "It is not healthy."

I thank him for his concern, and wonder which of us, three-hundred-pound 17
Renaldo or sleep-deprived me, will survive the millennium.

As I walk out, I see Daniel sitting at a nearby table drinking from a Coke 18
bottle. I duck my head, but in that instant he catches my eye and I quickly re-
adjust my face to feign surprise.

"You ran?" he says incredulously. 19

"Just a little," I say apologetically. 20

"That's insane." 21

So is working all night, but I don't tell him. 22

He asks where I will shower and change, and I tell him about the partners' bath- 23
room, explain my system. He seems impressed, if a little stupefied, at my routine.

"Why breathe more air than you have to in this city?" he asks. 24

I consider his question seriously. "It's something I've always done," I say after 25
a moment. "I didn't want to give it up."

My answer leaves us both quiet, as if remembering what we have relinquished. 26
Once, we all listened to new music, drank cheap beer, danced with lovers, stayed
out until dawn. When we awoke, we hadn't been dreaming of practicing law.

Daniel drains his Coke, slaps both hands on the table. "I left you a memo," he says. 27

"A memo?" 28

"It's just a draft. Some cases I found." 29

The walls close around me. Memo? He wrote a memo? We were supposed to 30
be working together. No one said anything about writing a memo.

"You don't have to read it," he says, as if he thinks I am panicking about time. 31

I try to play cool, ask him calmly how long it is. If I have a few free minutes 32
maybe I could read it.

He shrugs. He's never been good with numbers. "Thirty pages?" he guesses. 33

"Thirty pages!" 34

"Thirty-five pages?" 35

I have barely begun to collect cases, to read the heavily footnoted law review 36
articles describing the economic analysis underlying the fraud-on-the-market theory.
I am weeks away from putting anything in writing. Months from comprehension.

"It's not final," he repeats. "We need more case support, and I left your sections blank." [37]

My sections? Did I have a section? [38]

"The theoretical stuff," he says when I don't respond. [39]

"Yes," I say, swelling with pride at my theoretical expertise, a chance to redeem myself, to stake my contribution to the argument. If I only I could understand what I've been reading. [40]

He looks around at the motley assortment of homeless men who have staked out tables in the public space as soon as the building opened. "Do you always get here so early?" he asks. [41]

"Yes," I lie. [42]

"That's insane," he repeats. [43]

So is working all night, but I don't tell him. [44]

We work through the weekend, Daniel and I, expanding the case law and economic analysis in the memorandum, transforming it from an examination into an argument. Daniel's first draft was heavy on precedent, but undiscriminating; he threw all the cases he could find into the mix without regard to jurisdiction or the strength of their similarity to the TriCom case. Now we hone our support to the cases we think are strongest. Daniel refers to it as "our" memorandum, and I don't disagree. I have nothing to show for my efforts but a stack of highlighted law review articles and the memorandum. If he cut me loose and exposed my fraud, I would sail into shark-infested waters without precedent. Surprisingly, he seems to believe I have contributed equally to the memorandum, which means I will share equally in the Fall. [45]

I'm still not certain that I like Daniel, or that I trust him, but as the weekend grinds on, I come to admire him. In part, it's because he seems to like me, and to believe that I work hard. It helps that I've arrived earlier than he on both Saturday and Sunday, and that I look overburdened with a small mountain of law review articles. When we eat lunch and dinner together he floats his legal arguments for my analysis. I try to say intelligent-sounding things, or to keep silent when I know I will betray my ignorance. He listens to my sounds, and seems to regard them favorably. At some point I realize that though he has written most of the memorandum, and done most of the research, I have made enough of a contribution that to claim the memo for his own would be a truly heinous act, an act of which I don't believe he's capable. It's then that I relax. [46]

"We're going to lose," I say. [47]

"I never thought we could win," he says. [48]

"Then why are we doing this?" [49]

Daniel shrugs. His down jacket squeaks like a deflated balloon. He's been wearing it all weekend, protection against an overzealous air-conditioning system. It's odd to see Daniel in his civilian clothes: khakis, white T-shirt, down jacket, hiking boots. He looks surprisingly collegiate, as if he had just ventured out from a fraternity, his eyes squinty and dark, face unshaven, hair like red yarn. He's a deliberate study in contradictions: a lawyer who dresses like a preppy logger, a competitive workaholic who shares credit selflessly, an avowed misan- [50]

thrope who socializes with his co-workers. Which half is to be trusted? Which half is the real half?

"You've got to make the argument," he says. 51

For whose sake? I wonder. If TriCom knew the probability of success, would 52 it want to spend $100,000 on the motion? [The attorneys are preparing a motion asking the judge to dismiss the suit against TriCom.] Would the insurance company? Do they know where their money goes? Perhaps they do and they don't care. With millions at stake, what's a hundred thousand? It's all part of the game.

"The cases suck," I say. 53

Daniel grimaces. I realize I have inadvertently insulted him. It's not the cases 54 that suck, I quickly explain, it's the case law. He's done a great job with bad law. While there are plenty of opinions in which courts have said the market absorbs new information instantly, no courts have ever dismissed a case at the beginning of a lawsuit because the market did not react to negative information. In fact, we've actually found several cases where courts have held that negative information can, over time, affect the stock price even if it has no effect at first. Those cases are distinguishable, Daniel has written, because the negative information did not concern the allegedly fraudulent representations. Still, on a motion to dismiss, before any factual issues have been investigated, courts are reluctant to dispose of cases unless the issues are clear-cut.

"You've read the theory," Daniel pleads. "It's a good argument." 55

A good argument, an interesting argument, a theoretically challenging argu- 56 ment, a losing argument. Charlie told us we had to "educate" the judge, as if she were credulous and green instead of a federal district court judge with a sterling reputation and years of experience as a securities litigator. *It took six months before the stock price fell.* Is it worth $100,000 to tell her? She won't dismiss the case, not now. Will the mountain of paper we're about to dump on her desk alert her to problems with the lawsuit, or will she just be annoyed at the futility of our argument?

Despite his misanthropic attitude, Daniel thinks I'm too cynical. A lawyer has 57 an ethical obligation to advance any argument that could help his client; we can't decide the odds are too slim. In fact, it would be unethical not to make an argument that has a chance of succeeding, no matter how small. In a war, you use every weapon. You never know whom you might kill.

I've heard the argument from Julia, and before her from my professors, and 58 from other associates quoting partners, mentors, colleagues. It infuses the very air we breathe.

"You said we would lose," I remind him. 59

"I always say that," he says. 60

"Our argument doesn't make sense." 61

"It doesn't have to," he says. "It's the law." 62

We labored for two more weeks and one weekend on the memo. During that 63 time, we worked on nothing else. Though Daniel had several copyright issues he promised Jensen he would investigate, and I had another reinsurance liability issue that Barry Katz asked me to research, we put all callers on hold while we read through the remaining stack of cases and law review articles. Then we copied and collated, cut and pasted, revised and revamped, until the memo sparkled with brilliance. In the end, I spent seventeen straight days, twelve to eighteen hours a day, most of it billable, on the memorandum. Total cost: $32,000. Daniel's time was about the same.

When we finished, Jackie printed the memo and placed it in an envelope, which a messenger delivered to Charlie's [a senior member of the firm who assigned the case to Daniel and the author] office, five flights above ours. A week later, Charlie chewed up our forty-two pages, digested it, and spat out an entirely new thirty-five-page Memorandum in Support of TriCom Inc.'s Motion to Dismiss Plaintiffs' Complaint or, in the Alternative, for Summary Judgment. It wasn't so much that he revised our memo; he simply wrote a new memo. As I reviewed his draft, circulated for our "comments," I didn't recognize a single sentence from our original version. He used most of the same authorities, and even some of the same quotations, but he arrayed them differently and structured the argument to follow his new order.

His memo was better.

I hated to admit it. My second impulse, after Denial, when I saw that Charlie had rewritten every word, was Anger. He was just stroking his ego, I thought. He couldn't bear to let two first-year associates do his work, and do it well. But after the anger passed, and I read the memo in a more dispassionate moment, I felt Grief that I had disappointed Charlie. I could have done a better job, I thought, if only I had more time, if only I understood the cases better, if only I hadn't let Daniel dictate the argument. Charlie's memo truly was an improvement: cleaner, more persuasive, more closely reasoned. He distilled the important facts from the cases we cited and analogized them succinctly with our facts. He never let the court forget that there was an actual controversy before it: our case.

In retrospect, my confidence was laughable. I had never written a memorandum to be submitted to a court before. My only legal writing experience was in Moot Court and the small research projects of the last year and the previous summer. Charlie was a skilled practitioner who had been writing briefs and memoranda for six years. Clients paid $280 an hour for his time. He should know what he was doing.

Barry Katz had praised Charlie as the best writer at the firm. When he heard I was working with Charlie, he told me how much I would learn. He was right, in part. I learned that Charlie was very bright and I learned that Charlie was a good writer. But I did not learn How to Write like Charlie in Five Easy Steps. My secretary placed a memo in an envelope, had it delivered to Charlie's In box, and, presto, a new memo emerged from his Out box. He left no fingerprints.

Daniel shrugged when I complained about the lack of feedback. "It's not law school," he said. Daniel had more reasons to care than I—about thirty-five more pages of reasons—but he seemed not to. Perhaps it was part of his act: a studied indifference toward what he cared about deeply. I assumed he was still dating Abby, if only from her reticence to discuss it, yet at work I rarely saw them together and when I did they acted like strangers. Was it indifference, or was his nonchalance a shield behind which he guarded his heart from romantic paralegals and supercilious senior associates? I didn't ask, and he wasn't telling.

The night before we filed the memorandum with the court, we did not sleep. 70 Last-minute changes were made, cases checked and rechecked, typos caught, copies velobound, supporting documents attached in an appendix. Sometime around two in the morning the chicken salad sandwich I had ordered for dinner at midnight began to churn in my stomach. Food poisoning, I thought. I scurried to the bathroom, just in time to vomit into a urinal. I lay on the tile floor, stomach heaving, eyes watering. If I didn't feel so awful, I could have appreciated the metaphor. The physical manifestation of my emotional state. As it was, I just felt sick. Finally, as I prepared to drag myself out of there, Charlie appeared.

"What are you doing?" he asked, as if I had a choice.   71

I explained my predicament.   72

"Do you want to go home?" His tone clearly conveyed that he couldn't imagine 73 anything less appropriate, that whatever malady I suffered was the product of my own indolence and imagination.

So I stayed, and vomited two more times before dawn. Daniel told me I looked 74 green, and Charlie wondered why I had ordered chicken salad. By morning I had a fever of 102, and remained in bed for the rest of the day.

● ● ● ●

Discussion and Writing Topics

1. Based on this brief account, what can you infer about the daily life of a junior associate at a corporate law firm? How does Stracher illustrate the advantages and disadvantages of such a life? To what extent does the subject matter of this selection relate to the subject matter of the earlier selections by David Hricik ("The American Legal System"), on the one hand, and Scott Turow ("The Great Perini"), on the other?

2. Write an account of a work experience in which you felt unprepared for the demands of the job. Alternatively, narrate and explain how you handled the challenging demands you faced.

A Young Corporate Lawyer Burns Out

William R. Keates

Like Cameron Stracher, William R. Keates has chronicled his experiences as a first-year associate in a big-city law firm. Like Stracher, Keates eventually decided that corporate law was not for him. In this excerpt from Proceed with

Proceed with Caution. Chicago and Washington: Harcourt Brace Legal Pubs., 1997: 116–20.

Caution: A Diary of the First Year at One of America's Largest, Most Prestigious Law Firms *(1997), Keates sums up his disillusionment and the reasons he decided to quit and practice a different kind of law. In this selection, the first four paragraphs represent an extract from the diary that Keates kept during his first year. The following section is his later commentary on the diary entry.*

It's Sunday night and I'm bitter. I spent the whole damn weekend working in the office on the Allegheny Industries case. Last night, I was there until 10:00 p.m.   1

Actually, I'm not bitter because I had to work the whole weekend. I don't mind working hard. In fact, I prefer to work hard as long as I believe that I'm accomplishing or producing something valuable and important. The problem is, I rarely feel that way at work. I've done little or no "sophisticated" legal work, and hardly any work that I've actually been interested in.   2

I've always got a ton of work to do, but it's so damn boring. I was bored out of my skull on Friday, when I forced myself to become a glassy-eyed drone and churn out some billable hours. Sometimes I get so bored that I wonder how I'm going to make it through the afternoon, let alone the week, the year, the decade. I can't believe I could conceivably spend the rest of my life practicing law.   3

I've been thinking a lot lately about whether I can do something else for a living. I don't even need to make the kind of money I'm earning. I'd rather have my life back. I just want a good salary that will let me live my life without worrying about money everyday. It's not like I don't want to be successful. I do. I just want to be successful at something I actually like doing—or at least that I don't dislike doing. Why is that such a problem?   4

As my diary shows, by the time I approached the end of my first year at the firm, I was seriously questioning my career choice. I wasn't alone in second-guessing myself; job dissatisfaction is a serious problem plaguing the legal profession. More and more, lawyers are questioning whether the rewards of their jobs outweigh—or even justify—the stress, personal sacrifices, and unwavering dedication that accompany those rewards. The increasingly common answer to that is "no," as lawyers change careers in record numbers.   5

I know that from the outside looking in, it's tough to feel sorry for people in their mid-twenties with prestigious jobs, earning upwards of a $100,000 a year— no matter *how* many sacrifices they make and how many hours they work. After all, investment bankers, accountants, doctors, and other professionals also "live to work," routinely putting in 60 to 100-hour workweeks, including weekends. It's possible for *any* professional to lead a full and happy life if they enjoy their work and find it fulfilling. Conversely, you can be happy even if you don't find your work fulfilling; many blue-collar workers don't enjoy their work, but because they work shorter workweeks, they have enough leisure time to enjoy their personal and social lives, which compensates them for what they *don't* get from their jobs.   6

But many large-firm lawyers have the worst of both worlds, as I did: I lived to work and I didn't find that work fulfilling. As a lawyer you've got to do what your clients need done, but it will rarely involve anything you find genuinely inter-   7 esting. A colleague of mine at another firm, who did corporate work, said to me, "I wouldn't find a prospectus interesting under the *best* of circumstances. At 3 o'clock in the morning, when I'm at some printer waiting for the damn thing to be printed, it's the last thing I want to read."

Some professionals can rationalize the sacrifices they have to make now by looking down the road, at the long-term benefits they can reap from their labors. But I found, as many junior associates do, that that doesn't work too well in a large firm. It takes 8 to 10 years to make partner in a big firm, but due to tough competition and few partnership openings, there's no guarantee that if you put in the time, you'll become partner. That makes it difficult to relate your daily activities to the ultimate goal of partnership. Even if you *can*, partnership may be no panacea. A 1990 study by the American Bar Association showed that almost a quarter of male partners at law firms are dissatisfied with their jobs, and almost half of female partners feel the same way. Hating what you do now, and unable to see any long-term payoff for it, you're likely to find resentment creeping into your inevitable neglect of personal relationships, hobbies, and interests.

You might be asking yourself why I didn't foresee that my work would be unfulfilling. After all, I spent 3 years in law school, and then I spent 3 months in my firm's summer associate program before coming in as a permanent associate. Shouldn't I have been wise to what I was in for? Unfortunately, I wasn't, and I don't think many people *are*. Most people in law school—and even those contemplating going to law school—are high-minded, envisioning themselves as using the legal system to right social wrongs, further just causes, and otherwise contribute to society. Law school encourages these lofty ideals by encouraging you to provide *pro bono* (free) legal services and represent the poor and needy. In law school, your work and your idealistic pursuits become indistinguishable.

When you enter the real world of big-firm practice, however, you find those goals difficult, if not impossible, to achieve. Most large firms claim that they'll give you opportunities to do *pro bono* work, but in fact their attention to the bottom line means those opportunities are limited or nonexistent. Let's face it— those $100,000 salaries have to be paid by *someone*, and it's not indigents. As a result, your clients are often huge corporate institutions rather than oppressed people trying to stand up for their right. In fact, you're more likely to represent the *oppressors* than the oppressed since they're the ones with the money to pay the huge legal fees large firms demand. You will be fighting to make rich clients richer. Your work will be boring and your hours will be long. In short, you'll find that the practice of law isn't what you envisioned at all.

Before I practiced law, I also had a vision many law students share, of being able to perform free legal work for friends, family, and community organizations after work and on weekends. Unfortunately, this wasn't the case, even if there was the time to do it. That's because associates at most firms, particularly large firms, agree to perform legal work only for their firms' clients. If you want to do *pro bono* legal work for people or organizations who aren't clients, you need to get permission from your firm's management committee. This policy is based on the necessity of avoiding conflicts of interest, as well as the law firms' belief that any legal work performed by their salaried associates should be on behalf of one of their clients. In short, they bought your legal services and you can't give them away—even to your family.

Maybe you think you can put up with all of these pitfalls because you've got your eye on the immediate prize—the huge salary junior associates get. That reminds me of a famous quote from Orson Welles in the movie *Citizen Kane,* where, as [a character says], "It's not difficult to make a lot of money if what you want to do is make a lot of money." But if you're honest with yourself, you realize it's *not* all you want. I soon discovered that no amount of income, prestige, or professional pride can adequately compensate you if you believe your legal career is damaging your personal relationships and ruining your life. The high salary, large expense accounts, and chauffeured sedans waiting to whisk you to airports and meetings sound glamorous, but they quickly become meaningless, and, worse, you begin to resent them as representing the very things you feel are wrong with your life.

12

● ● ● ●

Discussion and Writing Topics

1. What are the main reasons that Keates decided to quit his job? To what extent do you sympathize with him and share his values?
2. Consider your own career goals. Where do you see yourself five to ten years from now? What kind of expectations do you have for the rewards of your chosen (or *a* chosen) career? What drawbacks and problems do you anticipate? What steps do you think you might be able to take, what research might you be able to do, to help avoid the kind of disillusionment and burnout that Keates eventually felt—a disillusionment that has been experienced by numerous other young professionals for whom the reality of their jobs turned out to be very different from their expectations?
3. Talk to a practitioner in the career field in which you are interested. Ask about working hours versus private hours, salary versus less tangible rewards, the professional's own expectations versus the reality. How well does the reality presented to you match or compare to *your* expectations for a career in your field of study?

The Imperfection of Law
and the Death of Lilly

■ ━━━━━━━━━━━━━━━━━━━━━━━━━━━━━━━━━━━━━━ ■

Ji-Zhou Zhou

Born in China, Ji-Zhou Zhou graduated from Brigham Young University's School of Law in Provo, Utah. She is a writer and legal consultant for the city of Phoenix, Arizona, on international projects. This selection first appeared

My First Year as a Lawyer, ed. Mark Simenhoff. New York: Signet, 1994: 69–77.

in an anthology, My First Year as a Lawyer: Real-World Stories from America's Lawyers *(1994).*

"Autopsy?" inquired the dead woman's father, in Chinese. Peering at me, he   1
seemed uncertain about whether to render his thought as a full-blown question.
"Should we conduct an autopsy on my daughter?" I discerned a sense of guilt and
hesitation in the way he pronounced the word *autopsy* in reference to Lilly.

Next to me, silently suffering, sat the husband the dead woman, Lilly, had   2
left behind. He was a skinny man, and he trembled throughout the meeting,
which had been called to discuss how to address the messy legal legacy of her
death. With me was my more experienced co-counsel, Greg, a respected personal injury lawyer. Although I was there in my capacity as a lawyer, nonlegal
thoughts kept intruding while I concentrated on doing my job. My mind strayed
to the broken-hearted husband and the young daughter he would have to raise
alone.

"Autopsy?" the father asked again.   3

I turned to Greg and translated the question into English. "Do you think we   4
should have an autopsy done?"

Greg leaned back in his armchair and emitted a deep sigh. "You are asking a   5
very personal question." He paused. "It is so personal that I cannot even answer
it. But if it were my wife, I wouldn't do it, for sure. No."

"From the perspective of an attorney, will you suggest one way or the other?"   6
the father prodded Greg, probably fearing a yes. I made the translation, and this
time Greg spoke as a lawyer.

"What an autopsy does, usually, is to identify the cause of death. In this case,   7
the cause is clear. An autopsy may or may not discover evidence of medical malpractice. But if we find out for sure there was no malpractice, your case is over.
Plus, do you know what they do to the body? They don't even try to put it back
together again after the autopsy is complete."

I didn't translate the portion of the conversation about cutting up the body   8
into pieces. It would be too painful for the family. Though neither the woman's
father nor husband spoke English, I sensed they intuitively understood the
painful delicacy of the conversation taking place. The issue of an autopsy was
dropped. A period of silence ensued while Lilly's grieving husband buried his
face in his hands. Her father stared at the floor, motionless. I felt hearts were
bleeding.

Just days earlier, Lilly had been killed riding her bicycle to the university,   9
where she taught and studied. Witnesses said the accident appeared to be the
driver's fault, not Lilly's. She was an outstanding student who had struggled
against the odds in her Communist homeland and to get an advanced degree in
the United States. Lilly recently had been offered a job as a professor in Hong
Kong, and the family was to leave in two weeks.

"Forty thousand dollars in annual income. Forty thousand dollars. That was   10
what she was going to be paid," her father would tell me later. He had continued,
"She said to me, 'Dad, we don't need to settle for the cheapest of things anymore.

We don't need to check around to see which grocery store offers the cheapest food. With my income we can go to a restaurant once in a while, too.'" His voice and face dropped. I saw his lips trembling. He could hardly pronounce the last few words.

After the accident, we discovered that the driver of the van was a part-time   11
hairdresser, earning minimum wage and having few assets. The driver did maintain a minimum $15,000 insurance policy as required by law. The bereaved family refused to accept that amount to settle the case: They wanted to file a complaint and get a judgment against the van driver, even though I had made them aware of the possibility that she would certainly file for bankruptcy and thus be spared having to pay any damages. America's legal system and business interests toyed with the family's fate. The Chinese consulate was reluctant to help, arguing that Lilly was a Chinese student privately sponsored in the United States at the time of her death, even though she was an employee for the Foreign Affairs Department before coming to pursue her doctorate.

I had been referred to Lilly's family by a relative, who told me that the family   12
feared the hospital where Lilly's saga had abruptly ended would try to garnish its bank account for the $40,000 in medical bills. This family needed legal help and they needed it quickly.

As the family's lawyer and language conduit, my job was to inform them of   13
their legal rights and advise them on a strategy for recovering any money they were entitled to for their daughter's unexpected death. I felt a singular sense of responsibility and commitment in this case. Not only was this family having to contend with the loss of a loved one in foreign surroundings but also Lilly had been the primary breadwinner. The family was faced with paying the medical bills as well as trying to figure out a way to get money to live on in the future.

When I first spoke with them, they clearly were barely able to deal with their   14
loss let alone confront the daunting possibility of a protracted legal case. Though most nonlawyers know little of the nuances of what the law entitles them to, they have at least a vague sense of what a lawyer can do for them. It was my job to determine strategy: to find out whether there was a claim warranted in this situation. I had to figure out if we should file against the van driver for negligence, the ambulance driver, or even the attending physicians.

At the meeting, I asked Lilly's father if he would consider petitioning for polit-   15
ical asylum in the United States based on his fear of persecution for providing service to the American army during World War II and having contacted old friends after coming to the United States. He said he would think about it, but he hadn't given me an answer. I think, somehow, it wasn't easy for him to cut off all ties to the place where he was born, grew up, and suffered—at least not without a sense of loss for the land he certainly still loved.

As a lawyer in this case, I not only had the duty of explaining to the family its   16
legal options but I also functioned as a cultural bridge between Greg and the family, on the one hand, and the family and the U.S. legal system on the other.

For instance, I was called upon to tell the family why the county attorney's   17
office, after investigating the accident, declined to bring murder charges against

the van driver. It was necessary to have a basic discussion of the concept and meaning of murder. I explained that Western legal traditions, and specifically in the United States, generally require intent or extraordinary disregard for another's life for an act of killing to be considered a murder.

After the conference, I drove the father and husband home, and they insisted on my going into their apartment to have a cup of tea.   18

A cute little girl of about six opened the door for us. As soon as Lilly's father sat down, she jumped into his lap.   19

"Grandpa, what did the lawyer say about my mommy? Can Mommy come back to dance with me? Why can't she come back?" she asked, either not clearly understanding that her mother had died or perhaps not yet comprehending the finality of death. The grandfather stroked her shining jet black hair gently, incapable of speaking. He had seemed to handle things better in the office. Once home, it was as if something in him collapsed.   20

"You are back! Oh! You are back." A voice came from the hallway leading to the bedrooms. Then I saw a gray-haired old lady, her failing vision fixed on me.   21

Lilly's mother began speaking to me, and it soon became clear that she was confusing me with someone else—Lilly's best friend, as it turned out. "How do you know so quickly? You must have taken a plane here. But I still don't understand how that could happen to her." She grabbed my hands and started to weep.   22

Her husband answered. "No. This lady is not our daughter's friend. She is the lawyer." He gave me an apologetic smile. "She is the lawyer," he emphasized, "who is helping us in the case."   23

He turned to me. "Lilly's mother has suffered from heart disease for years, and last year we found out her brain shrank a quarter. With my daughter gone so suddenly, I am afraid she may not survive either."   24

I didn't know whether Lilly's mother was following the conversation, and I felt uncomfortable talking about her problems in her presence. She moved slowly to the couch and settled herself there.   25

The little girl hopped off her grandfather's lap and bounded up onto her grandmother's. "Grandma, don't cry. Please don't cry." She wiped off her grandmother's tears. "Mommy must be hiding underneath the bed," she said. Tears dropped from the little girl's beautiful brown eyes.   26

I picked her up and held her tightly in my arms, fighting back a choking in my throat, and brushed away my own tears.   27

Then the husband emerged from his bedroom with Lilly's diploma and a couple of picture albums that contained photos they both took in different countries when she worked as a United Nations interpreter before studying in the United States. I took the red-covered diploma from the table. The diploma was identical to the one I received more than ten years ago in China when I had graduated from the university, just after the upheaval of China's cultural revolution. Holding the diploma in hand, I suddenly realized the long way she had come in pursuing advanced studies. I understood every single thing in life she had to sacrifice for her career, every single step at the expense of life's enjoyments. All of a   28 sudden she seemed so familiar that I felt as though I knew Lilly. I knew this woman.

My desire to remain professional and detached finally failed me, and I stood still in the center of the living room and let the tears roll down my face in streams.   29

Later, as I prepared to depart, Lilly's father accompanied me to the door.   30

"We were just a very regular family in China. We didn't have other opportunities except for this daughter. She is the reason we are all here today. Whatever compensation the law allows is not going to compensate me for losing my dear daughter." His face was shining with grief. "My little granddaughter will certainly grow up, even without her mother. My son-in-law can remarry. We will get old and die," he said quietly, sadly. And then, more rhetorically: "But what is to vindicate my daughter's death?"   31

I fled to my car and sat in its comforting darkness. My hands were shaking so much that at first I couldn't find the ignition hole. Three years of law school equipped me with legal principles, logic, and analytical skills. But no amount of law school and training, with or without the rigorous Socratic method, could have prepared me for this. The supremacy of law seemed to lose its omnipotence and seemed somehow deficient and perhaps a little useless. There was so little solace the law could provide to a family that had lost its only hope in life—a daughter who would have provided a lifetime support for her parents, a wife who would have filled the void in the life of her husband, and a mother whose love for her little girl could never be replaced.   32

My thoughts brought to mind a discussion I had eight years ago with one of my best friends, a respected Chinese lawyer, before coming to the United States. He said that sometimes he felt helpless witnessing his clients' dilemmas, and all he could do was to be sensitive and sympathetic as a friend, even though that accomplished little.   33

On this occasion, I looked out the windshield and saw the father still standing under the citrus tree where I had left him. His white hair was fluffy in the evening breeze of late November. The street lights shone down on his shoulders, forming a shadow—a prolonged silhouette of infirmity on the parking lot. Then I abruptly drove away and turned down a quiet street, where I parked and pondered about Lilly for a long time.   34

• • • •

Discussion and Writing Topics

1. How does Zhou contrast the legal and the nonlegal aspects of the situation she is faced with? What does she mean when she says that "America's legal system and business interests toyed with the family's fate"?
2. Discuss the significance of the title: "The Imperfection of Law and the Death of Lilly." In what ways, in the situation Zhou describes, is the law "imperfect"? In what ways, in your own experience or observation, have you found the law to be imperfect?

To Work for Social Change

Robert C. Johnson, Jr., and Richard W. Moll

The following selection, an account of the background and experiences of an African-American criminal lawyer, originally appeared in The Lure of the Law: Why People Become Lawyers and What the Profession Does to Them *(1990). This book is the product of a series of interviews by Richard W. Moll, a former dean of admissions at several colleges and author of articles for such periodicals as* Harper's, *the* Saturday Review, *the* New York Times, *and the* Washington Post.

This law office doesn't have the big plants and the mauve carpets. It is on the 1 tenth floor of a nondescript building in a historic, atmospheric, crowded section of downtown Boston. There are tired murals of the Boston Tea Party on the waiting room walls and the chairs are stark and stiff. The receptionist/secretary, an attractive black woman, is wearing a trendy man's undershirt. She informs me that Mr. Johnson is still in court in Roxbury and will be a bit late for our appointment. I return from coffee in half an hour to find him in, but a little rushed. ". . . I'm spending the weekend in the country. Can't wait . . ." He is gracious and accommodating, nonetheless, and gets right to his story.

As we begin, I notice African prints on the wall of his small office, papers piled 2 in cardboard boxes on the floor with labels such as "Personal Injury," and pictures of Robert Johnson with famous politicos: Johnson with Governor Dukakis, Johnson with Senator Ted Kennedy, Johnson with Shirley Chisholm.

"The early days are, in many ways, the most vivid. I was born in what could 3 be called 'Black Appalachia,' a poor rural area outside Chattanooga, Tennessee. Dad died when I was four, so Mom moved to Boston, leaving my two sisters and me with my grandparents until I was twelve. My grandparents made a tremendous impact on me. Granddad was a preacher and a carpenter, a role model to everyone in the area. And Grandma lived what he preached. I remember this bum showing up almost regularly on our front porch. He would just sit there patiently until Grandma spotted him and quietly came out of the house, whispered a few words of assurance, then fetched him a little food. He would leave as quietly as he came, only to reappear the next day."

Johnson looks rather formal in a dark suit with purple tie. But it took no time 4 at all for his shoes to come off. His stocking feet are on top of the desk now as he talks at a fast pace, recounting early days with ease. His eyes are wonderfully expressive, as are his gestures.

"Mom remarried in Boston, and we kids were called up north. But her new 5 husband died, and we inherited a stepsister. I'll never forget the Dwight School, near where we lived on the fifth floor in the South End. There was no discipline problem there, to speak of, because the principal and teachers ran such a tight ship. We had to *square corners* as we walked in the hallways. If we didn't, we got

---

The Lure of the Law. New York: Penguin, 1990: 70–77.

two strokes on the palms with the teacher's batten—about one yard of solid oak, and *nasty* if soaked in vinegar. My biggest honor was to wash the blackboard—I'd sit up front, and the teacher always rewarded the most alert students by letting them wash the board. I washed the board a *lot* . . ."

Johnson has a great smile. It registers often as he talks on, looking out the   6
window at Boston. Now his feet are on his chair, and he is squatting there (a difficult feat, it would seem).

"By junior high school, I guess they all knew I was a little different—I was   7
interested in school. They'd pick on me, and I was always in fights. In the sixth grade, I was stomped by one big guy, the height of shame. After it happened once, it never happened again. I learned to say with some authority (God knows where I picked it up), 'Come on, come on—I'll kick your ass.' I was holding my own and they laid off.

"At Boston English, my high school, sixty to seventy percent of the teachers   8
taught and the rest didn't do a damn thing. My French teacher would always go next door during class and drink with one of the gym teachers. When he left the room, all the bullies would take over—it was pathetic. Then the guy wouldn't give any tests at all, but would automatically dish out A's to the Chinese students, B's to the whites, and C's or D's to the blacks (about half the kids in the school were black). I didn't learn a word of French until college. Then the biology teacher would tell us all the questions he was going to ask on his tests—our good grades made it look as though he was really teaching us something. Christ!

"Going to college, by the way, just never entered my mind. No one in my family   9
had ever gone to college and it was a foregone conclusion, I guess, that I wouldn't either. And Boston English wasn't exactly college prep. But by the second year of high school I caught on to taking the good teachers. I was in the top five percent of my class, and started going with a lot of the other smart kids to the South End House, a community center, where I got to know Mel King, one of the most respected black politicians in the city. One day he just said, 'How'd you like to go to college?' And my nod and smile in return changed my life, I guess."

Johnson wheels around on his chair and lets out a big breath of relief as   10
though the story has been on edge to this point. He continues, high speed.

"Mel King told me about A Better Chance, a program to get bright disadvan-   11
taged and minority kids to private schools to prep them earnestly for college. Before I knew it, I was heading over to the Commonwealth School in Boston, a progressive day school full of Waspy and Jewish kids from professional families who wouldn't have dreamed of *not* going to college, and wanted highly selective ones at that. The headmaster there, who had founded the school (he's from a wealthy, prominent family), was a taskmaster and one of the really great men I've met. In short, I worked my butt off. Still, though, I was at the bottom of the class early on.

"A couple of formative things were happening just about then. Mom moved us   12
into a pretty rough housing project called Orchard Park. All I remember from the first days there was a huge guy grabbing me by the collar and saying, 'Hey, man, are you messing with my Phyllis? I'll crack your ass with my bare hands.' It scared the hell out of me. The project was like a prison—everyone was vulnerable. But

it prompted sort of a bond with some of my Commonwealth School friends—I'd bring them to visit the project, and they started taking me home to see how they lived. Interesting . . .

"Then too, I got involved with a teenage action group that encouraged play-   13
wrighting. I seemed to have a natural knack at this and my first play, *Coffee and Sour Cream*, was produced to really decent reviews in *The Boston Globe* and the *Christian Science Monitor*. Hey, man—at this point I was off and running!

"How would my secondary school friends have described me? Well, probably   14
as responsible and militant. I wasn't as militant as the Black Panthers, but almost. Outside of school, I helped Mel King run for this and that public office. I was walking a fine line between my old community and my new school. But I was hanging in there academically. What started as C's became B's at graduation. Princeton rejected me but Bowdoin admitted me and I was off to—of all places— *Maine* for college."

At this point, I gaze about the room, stretching a bit. As I spot a color photo   15
on the windowsill of two handsome teenagers, Bob Johnson says: "You're looking at the best part of my first year of college. That big guy on the right was conceived in my freshman dorm at Bowdoin."

A huge, proud smile.   16

"I exchanged a year to Tufts in Boston to be with my girlfriend when she had   17
the baby. Then back to Bowdoin. All kinds of new horizons opened up. I tried astronomy—I had always used the stars as a kid to get away. I'd look at the stars and find some kind of peace, stability. The stars always seemed to be constant in a universe that wasn't. Well, I tried astronomy during a summer at MIT. I had always liked math and science, you see, but my headmaster at Commonwealth quietly told me that he thought I'd do well in the humanities—history and English. He proved to be right. I tried biology at Bowdoin but I was really more taken by a history course about Africa and some of the other humanities.

"But suddenly I found myself a race leader at Bowdoin. Actually, there were   18
quite a few blacks in my class but I pushed right into leadership. We had a Mahalia Jackson* concert to get an Afro-Am House off the ground. During all this, I must say, I was very aware of a Bowdoin black upperclassman, Virgil Logan, who always seemed to provide a bridge between the black students and the white. I noticed how effective his style was, and found myself trying to copy him. I learned a lot from the guy. . . .

"Anyway, I knew all along that this education was going to be put to work for   19
social change. Anything that got in the way I scoffed at impatiently or abandoned. I was in a fraternity my first year, for example, and then bailed out—it just didn't feel right. But I became sort of a team player, although still pretty radical. I played soccer, was on the judicial board, student council, and some of the other mainstream stuff. I was involved and creative—helped to start the Brotherhood Internship Program, for example, through which Bowdoin students went to Boston for

---

*An African-American singer, often called the "Queen of Gospel songs" (1911–72).

a semester to help in the community centers, to teach math and English and lead all kinds of social projects."

Then Johnson turns toward me and puffs out a little. 20

"Two big things happened that meant a lot to me. At the end of my junior year, 21
Bowdoin gave me the Franklin Delano Roosevelt Cup for '. . . that student whose humanity, vision and courage contributed most to making Bowdoin a better college.' And then, at graduation, I won one of those fabulous Thomas Watson Fellowships that allowed me to travel anywhere for one year—I went to East Africa and Kenya to study black migration from our continent to theirs.

"All the way along, of course, I wondered what I would eventually do for a 22
living. Going to divinity or law school had appeal, although at some point I thought I would return to Africa for a period. But after I got caught up in things at graduate school, that just never happened. But not everyone knows, you see, that a lot of black Americans return to Africa, the homeland, just like Jews return to Israel. That story really has to get out more."

There is a quiet moment—there aren't many in this conversation—as though 23
Johnson is reminding himself of this old goal and making a new resolve.

"Anyway, law seemed a powerful tool. It struck me—in the little I had seen— 24
that a lawyer could do anything. Also, I knew I was best when I was in a combative situation—*that* fit law. And I was deeply concerned about protecting people's rights. It just seemed to me that law might be the closest training to fit the bill for what I thought I could do and wanted to do, although I wasn't certain. I decided to try for the best, and put in applications at Yale (rejected), Harvard (wait-listed), and Cornell (admitted). Once again, I was off to some remote place for more education.

"But Cornell didn't prove to be remote at all, at least for social activity. I got 25
involved in bringing in lecturers to address the Attica defense trials issues, and started a prison project twenty miles away at Auburn where, coincidentally, H. Rap Brown[†] was incarcerated. Although Cornell Law itself was very conservative, there were around fifteen blacks in my class of 125. I did a lot of stuff with the Black Law School Association. Maybe too much! My first year was really rough academically, and I, of course, was questioning the relevance of the law school training for what I wanted my future to be. I decided to study concurrently for a masters of professional studies at Cornell in Afro-American Studies. That brought some meaning and totality to the law pursuits. The whole package made sense, although it was tough to manage. But by the third year of law school, I was really in the swing of things academically—even pulled a few surprises like an A in my trusts and estates course! With my J.D. and M.P.S. in hand, I was ready to take on the world—but *how?*

"I had no interest in the private world of corporate law firms, unlike most of 26
the others in my class. Since summers had been spent teaching Upward Bound kids at Brandeis and Boston College, I thought public agency work might be interesting. And that's what happened: I got a job as director of affirmative action for

---

[†]An African-American activist and "black power advocate" (b. 1963).

the Massachusetts Board of Regional Community Colleges—fifteen of them, in total. And right away I knew that my law training was a big bonus—it had given me the power to analyze, to write clearly, to act in an authoritarian manner, and to read statistics and legal gibberish with understanding. We hired two new female presidents, two new black presidents, and I felt good about the social progress that could be made at this level of authority.

"I moved up to director of affirmative action at the University of Massachusetts–Boston, and taught intro courses in law around greater Boston in different colleges. At this point, I had become convinced that involvement in law could indeed bring about significant social change. At U Mass–Boston, for example, we achieved the distinction of having more black faculty than any other college in America. But that wasn't enough—I started challenging the chancellor on affirmative action issues, and ultimately sued U Mass over a tenure dispute." 27

Bob Johnson is rolling now, and moving up and down slowly as though in aerobics class, crouched above feet *on* the desk chair. 28

"I decided to run for office, for state representative. I picked up about one-third the votes, and some fair coverage from the *Globe*. But along the way, I really was saying to myself, 'This fucking system ain't worth shit.' And just about this time, my wife, who has held good jobs in the academic community of Boston, is saying that the once sensitive and caring man she originally knew during college days had changed, beginning with law school, to someone cold and calculating. We split after having two children. But everyone is on good terms now, and I'm seeing the separated daughter of my old headmaster—life takes odd turns, eh?" 29

The head nods to and fro, up and down. 30

"And here I am trying to start up a private firm with one other black lawyer. I'm doing criminal work, discrimination law, and my clients are usually, but not always, black. I'm dealing with little businesses that get into trouble. [Johnson gave me a newspaper article featuring one of his clients, a woman who ran a snack shack at a bus terminal in a desperately poor area and couldn't pay her rent to the bus agency because her stand was robbed so frequently.] Am I making as much of a mark on society as I did in government-related law? I don't know, but I do know that I have to make a living. 31

"I also know that I'm a damn good lawyer. I can make a witness fall apart on the stand. In fact, much of the law school training proved relevant to what I'm doing. On the other hand, law school didn't do enough to make us look at the whole of society in preparation for applying our trade. We weren't trained well in negotiating, for example—and in the big world, that's the way problems should be settled and often are settled. Instead, most lawyers just have the win instinct, want to achieve that at any cost, and take it personally if it doesn't happen. The client too often gets overlooked in the rush to victory. 32

"What will I look like ten years from now? God, I don't know, but I want to write more and spend time in the country—I like to walk through the woods like anybody else, but haven't spent much time in doing it. I have no hope of being a big legal giant—in fact, my living comes largely from my commercial real estate investments. I support the good guys—give money to [former Massachusetts governor Michael] Dukakis and Kennedy campaigns, and serve on boards of places I 33 believe in, like my old day school. And Dukakis appointed me to one of the state college boards of trustees. If he should end up being president some day, I might get a minor post in Justice or Education, and I'd like that.

"But, for the moment, criminal law keeps me in touch with all the people—I'm   34
dealing daily with rape and murder and kidnapping, just making sure everyone gets a fair hearing. The drug dealers I represent are the only ones that put me in a real moral dilemma—do they *deserve* their 'rights'?"

There is a new pensive posture, feet on the floor.   35

"You know, I do have to say that I don't have a very high regard for lawyers. I   36
can't think of a one I've met who I thought I could really trust. And yet I'm glad I'm in law—as an advocate of people's rights. Sure, there are problems with the system—it takes so long for some resolutions. Although there are some great judges, some others are a fucking joke. At times this really does seem like a 'white man's system'—but, on the whole, I can't imagine a better system and I just go in there and do my best, take it less personally than I used to, and think that even though I lose a case, hopefully there is better law in place because my case was well designed and well fought. I guess Grandpa's preaching and being stomped by a bully in sixth grade all remain with me. I'm still trying to put it all together in law, and that's the right place to be. For me."

Discussion and Writing Topics

1. Johnson is clearly a lot happier about his job as a lawyer than Cameron Stracher or William R. Keates were with theirs. How do you account for the difference? What are the advantages and disadvantages of his job, as opposed to theirs? Do you see any similarities?
2. What can you conclude from this piece about Johnson's personal and professional goals in life? How did his goals emerge from his background and his personal experiences? What other professions, besides law, do you think might have enabled him to achieve these goals?

Mr. Havlena's Verdict

Karel Capek

Here is an unusual legal story, one that focuses less on the drama and suspense of the trial than on the motivations and the strange behavior of the defendant—one who instigates a legal action against himself. Its author, Karel Capek (1890–1938), born in Bohemia, Austria (now the Czech Republic), was a journalist, dramatist, novelist, and short story writer. Like his contemporary and fellow Czech Franz Kafka (author of The Trial *[1925], the classic*

Translated by Paul Selver. Reprinted in *The World of Law*, v. 1, ed. Ephraim London. Originally appeared in *Tales from Two Pockets*, by Karel Capek, London: Faber and Faber, 1932.

nightmare account of a man trapped in an unfathomable legal system),
Capek's imaginative works tend to be philosophical rather than dramatic.
Capek is best known as the author of R.U.R. *(1920), a drama about the mecha-*
nization of humanity that anticipated Aldous Huxley's Brave New World
(1932) and that introduced the word "robot" to the language. His other works
include The Absolute at Large *(1922) and* The War with the Newts *(1936).*

"Talking about newspaper," said Mr. Beran, "what I think is this: Most people turn 1
first of all to the police reports. It's hard to say whether they're so keen on reading
them because of a suppressed desire to commit crime, or for their moral satisfaction
and to increase their knowledge of law. What is certain is that they just gloat over
them. That's why the papers have to publish police reports every day. But now
suppose, for example, the court vacations are on; the courts aren't sitting, but there's
got to be a column of reports about them just the same. Or often enough there are
no sensational cases on at any of the courts and the police-news reporter has got to
have a sensational case, by hook or by crook. When things are like that, the reporters
simply have to hatch out a sensational case for themselves. There's a regular market
for these sham cases and they're bought, lent or exchanged at the rate of twenty
cigarettes or so per item. I know all about it, because I used to share diggings with a
police-news reporter; he was fond of booze and he was a slacker, but apart from that
he was a fellow who had all his wits about him and who had a miserable screw.

"Now one day a queer sort of chap, down-at-heels, dirty and bloated, turned up 2
in the café where the police-news reporters used to meet; his name was Havlena,
he'd studied law but never finished it and he had altogether gone to the dogs:
nobody knew exactly how he made a living—in fact, he didn't quite know himself.
Well, this fellow Havlena, this loafer was quite well up in criminal or legal matters;
when this pressman I knew gave him a cigar and some beer, he would close his
eyes, take a few puffs and begin to give the details of the finest and strangest criminal cases you could imagine; then he'd mention the chief points in the defense and
quote the public prosecutor's speech in reply, after which he'd pass sentence in the
name of the Republic. Then he'd open his eyes, as if he had just woken up, and
growl: 'Lend me five crowns.' Once they put him through a test: At one sitting he
invented twenty-one criminal cases, each one better than the one before it; but
when he got to the twenty-second he stopped short and said: 'Wait a bit, this isn't a
case for the petty sessions or even a bench of magistrates; it'd have to go before a
jury; and I don't do juries.' You see he was against juries on principle. But to be fair
to him, I must say that the sentences he passed, though a bit severe, were models
of their kind from a legal point of view; he particularly prided himself on that.

"When the reporters discovered Havlena and saw that the cases he supplied 3
them with were not so hackneyed and dull as those which actually came up
before the courts, they formed a sort of trust. For every case which he thought
out, Havlena got what they called a court fee, consisting of ten crowns and a cigar,
and besides that, two crowns for every month's imprisonment which he imposed;
you see, the heavier the sentence, the more difficult the case. The newspaper
readers had never before got such a kick out of the police news as when Havlena

was supplying his sham criminal cases. No, sir, and now the papers aren't nearly as good as they were in his time; now it's nothing but politics and lawsuits—Heaven alone knows who reads the stuff.

"Now one day Havlena thought out a case, which wasn't by far one of his best, and though up till then none of them had ever caused any trouble, this time the gaff was blown. Reduced to its lowest terms, the case was like this: An old bachelor had a row with a respectable widow who lived opposite him; so he got a parrot and trained it up, so that whenever the lady appeared on her balcony, it screeched out at the top of its voice: 'You slut!' The widow brought an action against him for defamation of character. The district court decided that the defendant, through the agency of his parrot, had made a public laughingstock of the prosecutrix [plaintiff], and in the name of the Republic, sentenced him to fourteen days' imprisonment with costs. 'Eleven crowns and a cigar, please,' said Havlena as a conclusion to the proceeding. 4

"This particular case appeared in about six newspapers, although it was written up in various ways. In one paper the heading was; 'Far From The Madding Crowd.'* In another: 'Landlord and Poor Widow.' A third paper called it: 'Accusation against Parrot.' And so on. But suddenly all these papers received a communication from the Ministry of Justice asking for particulars of the district court before which the charge of defamation of character, reported in number so-and-so of your esteemed journal, had been tried; the verdict and sentence should be appealed against, since the incriminating words had been uttered, not by the defendant, but by the parrot; that it could not be regarded as proven that the words uttered by the said parrot indubitably referred to the prosecutrix; that hence the words in question could not be regarded as defamation of character, but at the very utmost as disorderly conduct or a breach of the peace, which could have been dealt with by binding the defendant over, by duly imposing a fine, or by issuing a court order for the removal of the bird in question. The Ministry of Justice accordingly desired to know which district court had dealt with the case, in order that it might institute appropriate inquiries and so forth; in fact it was a regular official rumpus. 5

" 'Good Lord, Havlena, you haven't half landed us in a mess,' the reporters protested to their retailer. 'Look here, that sentence you passed in the parrot case is illegal.' 6

"Havlena went as white as a sheet. 'What,' he shouted, 'the sentence *I* passed is illegal. Holy Moses, the Ministry of Justice has got the cheek to tell me that? Me, Havelena?' The reporters said they'd never seen a man so offended and angry. 'I'll give them what for,' shouted Havlena, flying into a temper. 'I'll show them whether my verdict's illegal or not! I'm not going to take this lying down.'—In his vexation and excitement he got terribly drunk; then he took a sheet of paper and for the benefit of the Ministry of Justice drew up a detailed legal statement to vindicate the verdict; in it he said by teaching his parrot to insult the lady the defendant had manifested his deliberate intention to insult and disparage her; that hence this was 7

Far from the Maddening Crowd is a novel written by Thomas Hardy in 1874.

a clear case of unlawful intent; that the parrot was not the perpetrator of, but only the instrument for, the offense in question; and so forth. As a matter of fact, it was the most subtle and brilliant piece of legal reasoning which those reporters had ever seen. Whereupon he signed it with his full name, Václav Havlena, and sent it to the Ministry of Justice. 'That's that.' he said, 'and until the matter's dealt with, I'm not going to give any more judgments, I must get satisfaction first.'

"As you can imagine, the Ministry of Justice took no notice whatever of 8 Havlena's communication; meanwhile Havlena went about looking disgruntled and down in the mouth; he looked seedier than ever and got very thin. When he saw that he had no chance of getting any answer from the Ministry, he quite lost heart; he would spit silently or talk treason, and at last he declared: 'Just you wait, I'll show 'em yet who's in the right.'

"For two months they saw nothing of him; then he turned up again, beaming 9 and smirking, and announced: 'Well, I've been served with a writ at last! Whew, damn that old woman, I had the deuce of a job before I could persuade her to do it. You wouldn't believe that an old girl like that could be so inoffensive; she made me sign a paper that whatever happened I'd foot the bill for her. Anyhow, boys, now it's going to be settled in court.'

" 'What is?' the reporters asked. 10

" 'Why, that affair with the parrot,' said Havlena. 'I told you I wouldn't let it 11 slide. You see, I bought a parrot and taught it to say: "You slut! You wicked old geezer!" And a deuce of a job it was too, I tell you. For six weeks I didn't set foot outside the house and never uttered a word but: "You slut!" Anyway, now the parrot says it very nicely; the only thing is that the damned stupid bird keeps on shouting it the whole blessed day; it just wouldn't get into the way of only shouting at the woman who lives on the other side of the yard. She's an old girl who gives music lessons; she's seen better days, quite a good sort; but as there aren't any other females in the house, I had to pick on her for the defamation of character. I tell you, it's easy enough to think out an offense like that, but, holy Moses, when it comes to committing it, that's a very different thing. I just couldn't teach that brute of a parrot to call only her names. It calls everyone names. If you ask me, it does that out of sheer cussedness.'

"Then Havlena had a long drink and went on: 'So I tried a different wheeze; 12 whenever the old lady showed her face at the window or in the yard I opened the window in double-quick time so as the parrot could shout at her: "You slut! You wicked old geezer!" And I'm blowed if the old girl didn't start laughing and called over to me: "Well I never, Mr. Havlena, what a nice little bird you've got!" 'Damn the old woman,' growled Mr. Havlena. 'I had to keep pegging away at her for a fortnight, before she'd bring an action against me; but I've got witnesses from all over the house. Aha, and now it's going to be settled in court, and Havlena rubbed his hands. "I'll eat my hat if I'm not convicted for defamation of character. Those jacks-in-office won't get much change out of me!'

"Until the day when the case came on, Mr. Havlena drank like a fish; he was 13 nervy and restless. In court he was quite the little gentleman; he made a biting speech against himself, referring to the evidence of all the people in the house that the insult was a disgraceful and flagrant one, and demanded the most exemplary penalty. The magistrate, quite a decent old fellow, stroked his beard and said that he would like to hear the parrot. So he adjourned the proceedings and instructed the defendant at the next hearing to bring the bird with him as an exhibit or, should the need arise, as a witness.

"Mr. Havlena appeared at the next hearing with the parrot in a cage. The parrot goggled its eyes at the frightened lady clerk and began to shriek with all its might: 'You slut! You wicked old geezer!' 14

"That's enough,' said the magistrate. 'The evidence of the parrot Lora makes it plain that the expression it used did not refer directly and unequivocally to the prosecutrix." 15

"The parrot looked at him and yelled: 'You slut!'—'But it is obvious,' continued his worship, 'that it makes use of the expression in question toward all persons, irrespective of their sex. Accordingly there is an absence of contumelious intent, Mr. Havlena.' 16

"Havlena darted up as if he had been stung. 'Your worship,' he protested excitedly, 'the unlawful intent to cause annoyance is shown by the fact that I was in the habit of opening the window which gave access to the prosecutrix for the purpose of causing the parrot to bring her into contempt.' 17

" 'That's a moot point,' said his worship. 'The opening of the window possibly indicates some degree of unlawful intent, but in itself it is not a contumelious action. I cannot convict you for opening the window from time to time. You cannot prove that your parrot had the prosecutrix in mind, Mr. Havlena.' 18

" 'But *I* had her in mind,' urged Havlena in self-defense. 19

" 'We have no evidence as to that,' demurred the magistrate. 'Nobody heard you utter the incriminating expression. It's no use, Mr. Havlena, I shall have to acquit you.' Whereupon he pronounced judgment accordingly. 20

" 'And I beg to give notice of appeal against the acquittal,' Havlena burst forth, snatched up the cage containing the bird and rushed out of court, nearly weeping with rage. 21

"After that they used to come across him here and there, fuddled and devil-may-care. 'Do you call that justice?' he would scream. 'Is there any chance for a man to get his rights anywhere at all? But I won't let matters rest there. I'll have it brought up before the high court. I've got to get my own back for the way I've been made a fool of, even if I have to spend the rest of my life bringing actions. I'm not fighting for my cause, but for justice.' 22

"I don't exactly know what happened in the appeal court; all I know is that Mr. Havlena's appeal against his acquittal was dismissed. Then Havlena vanished into thin air; there were people who said they'd seen him loitering about the streets like a lost soul and muttering something to himself; I have also heard that to this very day the Ministry of Justice still receives several times a year, a long and furious petition headed: *Defamation of character committed by a parrot.* But Mr. Havlena has, once and for all, stopped supplying police-news reporters with cases; most likely because his faith in law and order has been rudely shaken." 23

• • • •

Discussion and Writing Topics

1. Several inversions of expected behavior occur in this story. What are they? How do they account for the story's humor?

2. One of the challenges—and delights—of fiction is that we are sometimes hard put to say what, exactly, a story "means" or "is about." How is this enigmatic quality of literature apparent in "Mr. Havlena's Verdict"? What do you think the story says, both about the law and about certain aspects of human nature?

3. Mr. Beran, whom the narrator cites as the source of the story, says that people are eager to read about crime for two reasons: "Because of a suppressed desire to commit crime, or for their moral satisfaction and to increase their knowledge of law." One might argue with Beran's explanations, but his observation seems accurate: We are fascinated with crime, especially of the sensational variety. Why?

2

Arguing Effectively

No one can be a truly competent lawyer unless he is a cultivated person. If I were you, I would forget all about any technical preparation for the law. The best way to prepare for the law is to come to the study of the law as a well-read person. Thus alone can one acquire the capacity to use the English language on paper and in speech and with the habits of clear thinking which only a truly liberal education can give. No less important for a lawyer is the cultivation of the imaginative faculties by reading poetry, seeing great paintings, in the original or in easily available reproductions, and listening to great music. Stock your mind with the deposit of much good reading, and widen and deepen your feelings by experiencing vicariously as much as possible the wonderful mysteries of the universe, and forget all about your future career.

—Supreme Court Justice Felix Frankfurter in a letter to a 12-year
old boy requesting advice on preparing for law school

Ask people to recall memorable legal arguments, and they'll probably think of courtroom dramas in the movies or on TV. Older Americans may remember Gregory Peck as defense attorney Atticus Finch in *To Kill a Mockingbird* (1962), trying to persuade an all-white jury to acquit an African American wrongfully charged with rape. Others will think of Paul Newman as Frank Galvin, an on-the-skids personal injury lawyer, arguing in *The Verdict* (1982) that an eminent doctor is liable for medical malpractice. Or they'll think of John Travolta as attorney Jan Schlichtman, desperately trying to make the case in *A Civil Action* (1998) that two companies in Massachusetts dumped toxic waste into the groundwater. People may also think of closing statements in any of numerous TV legal series, from *Perry Mason* and *L.A. Law* to *Ally McBeal* and *The Practice*.

Dramas like this do indeed contain many memorable arguments, and such arguments are often crucial to winning cases. But an argument doesn't have to be memorable to prevail, and it is not the aim of this book to show you how to write memorable arguments, filled with soaring oratory. Rather, the aim is to help you to write solid arguments—arguments that are based on demonstrable facts, that are clearly articulated and developed, and that yield valid conclusions.

In some ways, good arguments about legal cases share the same essential qualities as arguments in other professions and disciplines: philosophical argu-

57

ments, historical arguments, sociological arguments, literary arguments. All demand systematic thought and adherence to accepted logical methods in that discipline. Perhaps the main distinction of legal argument is that it almost always arises out of particular cases. A political argument, for example, can begin with a general proposition: "The Democratic party is better able than the Republican party to deal with the global economy of the twenty-first century." But legal arguments are based on particular circumstances: "Is the defendant, who told the plaintiff on three occasions that she should be 'nice to him' if she wanted to be promoted, liable for sexual harassment?"

Similarly specific questions may stimulate argument in other fields, however. *Literature*: "Did the narrator in "Bartleby, the Scrivener" do all that he reasonably could have done to aid Bartleby?" *History*: "Did President Truman take into account all available options before deciding to drop the atomic bomb on Hiroshima?" *Business*: "Did America Online make a sound decision in agreeing to merge with Time Warner?" *Environmental Science*: "Has offshore drilling near Santa Barbara harmed the local marine ecology?"

To effectively respond to such questions, it helps to have a method, a pattern, a template for constructing arguments. In arguing legal cases, the most commonly used template goes by the acronymn IRAC: *Issue, Rule, Analysis (or Application), Conclusion.* More specifically: (1) first state the *Issue*, the main question on which the case turns; (2) next, state the *Rule*, or legal principle(s) that apply to cases such as this one; (3) next, *Analyze* the case by Applying the rules, and individual elements of the rules, to the facts of the case; (4) finally, draw a *Conclusion* that represents the answer to the question articulated in the Issue.

This chapter will help you to organize your arguments on particular cases and to present them effectively. It begins with one of the most important selections in this book—Veda R. Charrow, Myra K. Erhardt, and Robert P. Charrow's "IRAC: How to Argue Your Case Systematically and Logically." The principles of organization explained in this selection underlie many of the assignments to come. Next Richard Wydick's "Use Plain English" explains what's wrong with a good deal of legal writing. Wydick's piece is followed by some sound storytelling advice: "10 Ways to Know If Your Story Is Ready to Tell in Court" by professional storyteller Joel ben Izzy, who also serves as a consultant to attorneys. The chapter continues with two sets of "Stories and Exercises" designed to help you practice the skills you will need to successfully complete these subsequent assignments. And because quite a few of the assignments in this book ask you to compose statements to the jury, as if you were a plaintiff's or defense attorney, the chapter concludes with two such compositions: "Models for the Opening Statement and the Closing Argument."

IRAC: How to Argue Your Case Systematically and Logically

Veda R. Charrow, Myra K. Erhardt, and Robert P. Charrow

The following selection is one of the most important you will read in this book. It explains a relatively simple yet highly effective method of organization by which generations of attorneys have been taught to present their arguments. It is useful not just for legal purposes: The IRAC format of Issue, Rule, Application, and Conclusion can be employed effectively in almost any kind of argument in which you are applying rules or principles to a set of facts in order to draw a conclusion about a particular question (the issue). Your success in completing many of the assignments in this book will depend to a considerable degree on your understanding and your application of the principles of effective organization as described in this section.

This passage is excerpted from a widely used textbook, Clear and Effective Legal Writing, *by Veda R. Charrow, Myra K. Erhardt, and Robert P. Charrow. In addition to explaining the IRAC method of writing arguments, the authors also discuss creating arguments based on syllogisms and using analogies to compare and contrast similar cases.*

Note: In "IRAC: How to Argue Your Case Systematically and Logically" the authors indicate that the A in IRAC stands for Application. *To others, A stands for* Analysis. *For our purpose, the two terms mean the same thing: applying the rule(s) to the facts of the case.* Analysis, *broadly speaking, means applying one or more related principles to each element of a subject or study or, alternatively, viewing a subject through a particular perspective or principle in the interest of greater understanding.*

IRAC: Organizing a Complex Legal Document

You must always impose order on your writing. Legal documents, in particular,   1
demand a tight, logical structure. In other documents poor organization may
interfere with readers' comprehension, but in legal documents poor organization
can cause even greater problems. In an adversarial document, for example, your
opponents will be looking for any weak spots they can find. A gap in your logic
caused by poor organization can give your opponents an opening for attack. In a
nonadversarial document, poor organization can make the reader believe that
either your knowledge and research are not thorough or that your thinking is not
logical. . . .

Excerpted from "Getting Organized," Chapter 9 of *Clear and Effective Legal Writing*, 2d ed. Boston: Little, Brown, 1995. Used by permission of the publisher.

Thus, the outline for a complex legal document might look like this: 2

1. Introduction providing a context
2. First claim
   a. What is the *claim* you are making? How are you proposing to resolve the issue or subissue? This can be further subdivided into
      i. A statement of the particular *issue* or subissue you have identified. At this point you may also wish to state how you believe the issue should be resolved.[1]
      ii. The *rule* of law that is most pertinent to the situation.
      iii. Why and how the rule should be *applied* to the facts of your case.
      iv. A *conclusion* based upon your analysis and the application of the law to the facts.
      (IRAC is the mnemonic for this method of organizing a claim.)
   b. What are the *objections* and counterarguments to your claim?
   c. What is your *response* to the objections and counterarguments?
   d. What is your *conclusion*? This section summarizes your reasoning and restates your claim.
3. Second claim
4. Conclusion

This model works well for any level of analysis, from the general analysis of a   3
whole problem down to the analysis of specific subissues. When you have used this model to analyze all of the issues or subissues, you will then be able to come to a conclusion.

1. Identifying and Presenting Issues[2]

Your first step in setting up the structure of a complex legal document is to iden-   4
tify the important issues that you will be discussing in your document. Here is an example of a fact situation and the issues that should be analyzed in a brief.

Jones worked as a salesman for the Southern Corporation. His job required him to provide his own car and deliver perishable supplies to customers on his route. Jones had been told a number of times by his supervisor at Southern that it was extremely important that he stay on a strict time schedule with his deliveries.

On March 10, Jones made a delivery during normal working hours. He returned to the parking lot in which he had left his car and found that Warner's car was blocking his car. After waiting ten minutes for Warner to return, Jones finally decided that he had to leave. Jones tried to move his car, but put a large dent in Warner's bumper and broke one of Warner's headlights in the process.

---

[1]This is especially important in persuasive writing, where you want to make a forceful opening statement.
[2]See also Tourney, "A Short Guide to Writing Effective Issue Statements," p. 91.

Warner returned just as Jones broke the headlight. Warner demanded payment for the damage to his car and refused to move his car so that Jones could leave. Jones angrily got out of his car and moved towards Warner, yelling that he was already late for his deliveries and that it was Warner's fault. Warner angrily shook his fist at Jones and again demanded payment for the damage to his car. Jones, in anger, hit Warner, knocking him to the ground. Warner had Jones arrested.

After Jones's arrest, Southern Corporation learned from the local police that Jones had been convicted of aggravated assault three years before Southern had hired him. When Southern hired Jones, the corporation did not inquire into his background. Warner is suing Southern for the personal injuries he suffered as a result of Jones's attack.

Issue 1: Did the defendant commit an intentional tort [wrongful act] when he knocked the plaintiff to the ground, or was the action privileged?

Issue 2: Is an employer liable for injuries that its employee intentionally inflicted upon the plaintiff while the employee was trying to make deliveries on behalf of the employer?

Issue 3: Can the defendant employer be held liable for negligence in hiring and retaining an employee who has a criminal record for assault if the employer did not investigate the employee's background and does not know of the record?

Once you have identified the main issues, you may find that you can deal with them more easily by breaking them down into smaller, more manageable subissues (or sub-subissues). For example, you might see the following subissues under Issue 1.

1. Did the act of the plaintiff in shaking his fist at the defendant place the defendant in imminent threat of physical injury?
   a. If the plaintiff's act placed the defendant in imminent threat of physical injury, did he have a duty to retreat?
   b. If the defendant did not have a duty to retreat, did he use excessive force in repelling the imminent threat?
2. Did the act of the plaintiff in refusing to move his vehicle constitute the tort of false imprisonment?
3. Did the act of the plaintiff in refusing to move his vehicle constitute the tort of trespass to chattel?

2. Presenting the Rule

The rule of law that you use in your analysis can come from case law or enacted laws. Once you have established the applicable rule in a particular case, you should present it in a way that will make it easy to apply the law to the facts. For example, if you are discussing a particular tort or crime, or the definition of a particular legal concept, describe it by breaking it up into its elements. Thus, if the issue is whether a defendant has committed a battery, a good way to present the rule would be to take the definition from section 13 of the Restatement (Second) of Torts.

> [Section] 13 *Battery: Harmful Contact*
> An actor is subject to liability for battery if
> a) he *acts intending* to cause harmful or offensive contact with the person of the other or a third person, or an imminent apprehension of such a contact, and
> b) a harmful contact with the person of the other directly or indirectly *results* (emphasis added).

If you have to synthesize the rule from case law, this will probably take more   7
time and space. This is because you will often need to go through the steps that you took and the sources that you used in your distillation of the rule.

3. Application: Analyzing Facts and Law

The next step is to examine the facts and decide whether a rule is satisfied or the   8
elements of an offense or tort are present. You should organize this section so that it follows the order of the *elements* of the rule. For example, you could discuss the facts in the Jones case by applying them to the elements of battery.

> First, the defendant, Jones, *acted* when he attempted to strike the plaintiff in the parking lot. Second, the defendant *intended* to harm the plaintiff, since he spoke angrily to the plaintiff, shook his fist at the plaintiff, and then struck him. Third, the defendant struck the plaintiff and knocked the plaintiff to the ground. Thus, the defendant's act *resulted in* the harmful contact to the plaintiff.

The application section of your document is the most crucial, for it is here that   9
you have to convince your audience that your analysis is sound and that your conclusions follow logically. We have presented only the most basic application of facts to law in the example above. . . .

4. Anticipating Counterarguments

One of the best ways to ensure that you have treated an issue thoroughly is to try   10
to anticipate all possible counterarguments and defenses. Put yourself in your opponent's position: List all of the ways that you can attack or weaken your own argument. Be ruthless. After you compile the list, develop responses or rebuttals for each area of attack.

There are a number of counterarguments that the defendant might raise in the   11
battery case. The defendant might attack the way in which you applied the law to the facts; or the defendant might raise the defense that he was using reasonable force to prevent the plaintiff from committing a tort against his property (the plaintiff refused to let the defendant remove his car from the lot) or against his person (the plaintiff prevented the defendant from leaving by holding something of great value to the defendant).

5. Providing a Conclusion

The contents of your conclusion will depend upon the length and complexity of   12
the information that you have presented in the other portions of your analysis.
For example, if your application section is long and intricate, then you might want
to refresh your reader's memory by briefly recounting the steps in your reasoning.
If the application section is short, however, you would probably not want to reit-
erate your reasoning. In either case, you would finish with a statement of your
position or your interpretation of the facts and the law. Here is an example of a
simple way to conclude the battery issue:

> Because all three elements of battery are present in the defendant's conduct,
> the defendant is liable for the tort of battery.

6. Organizing a Complex Legal Document: An Example

Now that we have presented and explained the different parts of the model on   13
page 60, look at the following fully developed issue analysis. This analysis follows
the standard IRAC—issue, rule, application, conclusion—outline.

Issue[3]	The issue presented in this case is whether one spouse can sue the other for injuries caused by the negligence of the other spouse.
Rule	In *Sink v. Sink*, 239 P.2d 933 (1952), this court held that neither spouse may maintain an action in tort for damages against the other. Although a number of states have recently enacted legislation which allows these suits, Kansas has not joined them. This can be seen in the fact that the Kansas legislature has just enacted, in 1981, a law which authorizes any insurer to exclude coverage for any bodily injury to "any insured or any family member of an insured" in its insurance policies. Even though this law does not go into effect until January 1, 1982, it is clear that Kansas's position on interspousal tort immunity has not changed.
Application	In the present case, the plaintiff, who is the defendant's wife, was injured when the car the defendant was driving crashed into a telephone pole. The plaintiff was sitting in the passenger seat at the time of the accident. She sustained a broken leg and cuts and bruises. Although the defendant may have been negligent, the accident obviously involved injuries inflicted by one spouse upon another.

---

[3]See "A Short Guide to Writing Effective Issue Statements," p. 91.

Conclusion	Therefore, this case clearly falls within the mandate of *Sink,* and the plaintiff's case should be dismissed on the basis of Kansas's very viable interspousal immunity.
Counterargument	The plaintiff has claimed that a decision upholding interspousal immunity violates logic and basic principles of justice. She notes that the new law has not yet gone into effect, so that it does not apply to the present case. She also contends that the foremost justification for immunity laws is illogical, since it is based on the premise that personal tort actions between husband and wife would disrupt the peace and harmony of the home. She cites the Restatement of the Law of Torts, which criticizes this justification by stating that it is based upon the faulty assumption that an uncompensated tort makes for peace in the family.
Response	However, it is no more logical to contend that family harmony will be better served if a husband and wife can drag each other into court and meet each other as legal adversaries. In addition, the plaintiff has overlooked a far more persuasive argument for interspousal tort immunity: under Kansas law, any recovery that the plaintiff-wife would obtain if this action were allowed to proceed would inure to the benefit of the defendant-husband. All property acquired by either spouse during the marriage is "marital property" in which each spouse has a common ownership interest. If the injured spouse (plaintiff) should die, the surviving spouse could maintain an action for wrongful death, and could share in any recovery of losses. This result would allow a negligent party to profit by his own actions. This is a result which would be truly offensive to anyone's sense of justice.
Conclusion	The doctrine of interspousal immunity is as viable today as it was when initially enunciated by this court. It not only fosters family harmony, but also prevents a spouse from profiting from his or her own negligence.

For some types of documents, you will want to abbreviate or rearrange the scheme presented above. For example, if you are answering an opponent's brief, you could begin by stating the opponent's objections and then follow with your own claims and conclusions. With this order, a separate "response" section may no longer be necessary, since the response may become part of your main argument. For example:

Issue	The issue presented in this case is whether one spouse can sue the other for injuries caused by the negligence of the other spouse.

Subissue   Does Kansas law presently require interspousal tort immunity?

The plaintiff in this case has claimed that a decision upholding interspousal immunity violates basic principles of justice and current Kansas law. She acknowledges that Kansas has enacted a law which authorizes any insurer to exclude coverage for any bodily injury to "any insured or any family member of an insured" in its insurance policies. However, she points out that this law does not establish blanket interspousal tort immunity. Also, because the law has not yet even gone into effect, it does not apply to the present case.

Rule   The plaintiff's reliance on the nature and effective date of the legislation is misplaced. The law to which the plaintiff alludes is one that the Kansas legislature has just enacted, in 1981. Even though this law does not go into effect until January 1, 1982, Kansas' position on interspousal tort immunity was established long ago and has not changed. In *Sink v. Sink*, 239 P.2d 933 (1952), this court held that neither spouse may maintain an action for tort for damages against the other. Although a number of States have recently enacted legislation which explicitly allows these suits, Kansas has not joined them. In fact, the legislation mentioned by the plaintiff makes it clear that Kansas is not attempting to establish a new policy on interspousal immunity, but is merely incorporating its current policy into the laws which govern insurers.

Application   As the plaintiff has pointed out in her brief, she was injured when the car her husband was driving crashed into a telephone pole. Whether or not the defendant was negligent, the accident involved injuries inflicted by one spouse upon another. As such, Kansas' policy on interspousal tort immunity would apply.

Subissue   Is the rationale behind interspousal immunity illogical?

The plaintiff further contends that the foremost justification for immunity laws is illogical, since it is based on the premise that personal tort actions between husband and wife would disrupt family harmony. She cites the Restatement of Torts, which criticizes this justification by stating that it is based upon the faulty assumption that an uncompensated tort makes for peace in the family.

Rule   The plaintiff and the Restatement have overlooked the even greater illogic behind a premise that family harmony can be better served if a husband and wife can drag each other into court and meet as legal adversaries. In addition, the plaintiff has overlooked a far more persuasive argument for interspousal immunity: under Kansas law, any recovery that the plaintiff-wife would obtain if this action were allowed to proceed would inure to the benefit of the defendant husband.

Application   In the present case, the husband and wife could be forced to endure years as legal adversaries, waiting for an interspousal lawsuit to slowly wend its way through a complex legal system. In addition, the defendant could stand to profit by any recovery his wife receives from the couple's insurance.

Conclusion   The doctrine of interspousal immunity is as viable today as it was when initially enunciated by this court. It not only fosters family harmony, but also prevents a spouse from profiting from his or her own negligence.

SOME CAVEATS There are several caveats to consider when you use IRAC or any   15
similar outline to analyze the issues in a law school problem. Students sometimes get the impression that they have done a complete, well-rounded analysis of a question once they have taken the obvious issues through the IRAC outline. IRAC can give you a false sense of security if you mistake the thorough analysis of an issue for the thorough analysis of a whole problem or question. Once you have completed analyzing the obvious issues, make sure that you reread the problem to search for subissues or elements of issues that you might have overlooked. These are important and can influence the outcome of your problem.

IRAC is merely a framework within which to build your analysis: It should not   16
appear to your readers that you have merely plugged information into a rigid formula. Edit your writing to eliminate the mechanical effects of a series of statements that the issue is W, the rule is X, the analysis is Y, and that, therefore, the conclusion is Z. . . .

Developing a Logical Argument

In order to create a logical structure, think about what you are trying to accom-   17
plish when you deal with a problem in law. You will often find that you are trying to establish that a specific set of facts fits within a well-settled rule of law. One way to do this logically and systematically is to use the principles of deductive reasoning to set up the skeleton of your legal analysis.

1. Deductive Reasoning in Law

You are probably familiar with the basic categorical syllogism. For example: 18

Major premise:	All men are mortal.
Minor premise:	Socrates is a man.
Conclusion:	Socrates is mortal.

Deductive reasoning is the thought process that occurs whenever you set out   19
to show that a minor premise (a specific situation, event, person, or object) fits
within the class covered by a major premise (an established rule, principle, or
truth) and to prove that, consequently, what applies to the class covered by the
major premise must necessarily apply to the specific situation. In short, deductive
reasoning allows you to prove that your particular case is covered by an established rule.

Deductive reasoning is a cornerstone of legal thought. Lawyers are often   20
called upon to decide how a rule of law applies to a given case. Since the rule is
usually stated in general terms and a client's problem is generally very specific,
deductive reasoning can be used to bridge the gap between the general and the
specific. For example:

Rule of Law (major premise): Courts have held that any agreement made in
jest by one party and reasonably understood to be in jest by the other party
will not be enforced as a contract.
Facts of our case (minor premise): Robert agreed to paint Lee's entire house,
but both Robert and Lee understood that Robert was only joking.
Conclusion: Robert's agreement is not an enforceable contract.

These basic steps of deductive reasoning form the skeleton of a legal argument.   21
In fact, the rule, application, conclusion sequence of IRAC forms a simple syllogism: The rule contains the major premise, the application contains the particular
facts of the minor premise, and the conclusion sums up the information. . . .

2. Expanding the Syllogism into a Legal Argument

The syllogism serves as the skeleton of a legal argument. Once you have created   22
the skeleton, you must flesh it out. For example, once you have the major premise
in a particular case, you must present evidence that your specific fact situation
does indeed fit within the class covered by the major premise. In the example
about painting Lee's house, you would have to show that there was a promise but
that both parties knew that it was made in jest, as "jest" has been interpreted by
the courts.

In the rest of this section, we discuss techniques for expanding the different   23
parts of a syllogism. We present the parts in the order of the standard syllogism,
even though you may not always work in this order when you construct your
argument.

A. THE MAJOR PREMISE In most cases, your major premise will either be a given   24
(you are told what the rule of law is and you must apply it to a set of facts), or you
must extract the rule from legal authorities such as constitutions, statutes, regulations, and reported cases. You must then draw the appropriate information from
these authorities and present the information so that your rule is well substantiated. In addition, you must define the abstract terms in the rule in order to clarify
the rule and make it easier to apply the rule to the facts in your case. . . .

B. THE MINOR PREMISE The most important techniques for expanding your major   25
premise are citing authority and defining terms. The most important technique for
expanding your minor premise is analogy, either to the facts of other cases or to
the policies underlying other decisions.

Arguing by Analogy: Similarity of Facts

When you argue by analogy, you reason that if two or more situations are the   26
same in some significant respect, they are likely to be the same in other significant respects as well, so they ought to be classified together. (If you want to *distinguish* your case from others, you show that it is *not* analogous.)

You could link the major and the minor premises of the general welfare case   27
by using the following analogy: Funding should be provided for X Auto Company
because the case is similar to cases in which the Court has approved Congress's
funding in the past. Here is a way you might express this.

The facts in the X Auto Company case are very similar to the facts in cases   28
that have already established the scope of "general welfare." In all of these cases,
the courts agreed that

1. Private individuals or entities may receive funds from the federal government.
2. Individuals and entities may receive money that they did not personally
   contribute to the government.
3. Individuals and entities may receive money from the government when it
   helps them continue to earn money and spend money.

Arguing by Analogy: Similarity of Policy Considerations

Another way to link the major and minor premises is to show that the facts of   29
your case are covered by a particular rule because your case furthers the same
social goals as other cases already covered by the rule. For example, in the X Auto
Company case, you might argue that your case and the previously decided cases
all fulfill the following goals, regardless of the similarities or differences in their
facts.

1. They keep individuals from turning to the state for support.
2. They keep the economy balanced and functioning.
3. They show people that the government will intervene if a segment of the
   population is about to experience an economic crisis.

The first step in making a policy arguments is to identify what the authors of   30
a rule intended when they created the rule. If you are investigating legislation, try
looking at and analyzing legislative history or policy statements in the legislation
itself. If you are investigating an opinion, try comparing your case with other
cases that have been decided under the rule and showing that your case will help

to further the same goals. You can look at any language in these opinions that sheds light on the objectives of the ruling.

Once you have established the purpose of the rule, i.e., what it was intended   31
to accomplish, you can alter your major premise to include this purpose and emphasize the specific facts in your minor premise that suit the major premise. You would then argue that the authors of the rule intended that the rule cover cases like yours and that the principles behind the rule will be dangerously eroded if the court excludes your case.

If you were arguing that by analogy to the *Steward Machine* case X Auto   32
Company should get federal funds, you might use this analogy on policy considerations:

> The courts have found that federal payments to particular groups or individuals such as the unemployed or the elderly can serve the general welfare because, in the long run, these payments benefit the entire nation. This idea is reflected in the words of Justice Cardozo in *Steward Machine* 301 U.S. 548, 586–587 (1937):
>
> > During the years 1929 to 1936, when the country was passing through a cyclical depression, the number of the unemployed mounted to unprecedented heights. . . . The fact developed quickly that the states were unable to give the requisite relief. The problem had become national in area and dimensions. There was need of help from the nation if the people were not to starve. It is too late today for the argument to be heard with tolerance that in a crisis so extreme the use of the moneys of the nation to relieve the unemployed and their dependents is a use for any purpose narrower than the promotion of the general welfare.
>
> X Auto Company employs hundreds of thousands of employees. In addition, there are thousands of other employees who work in industries that depend on X Auto Company. Even though the problems of X Auto Company are not on the scale of the problems of the Great Depression, the loss of part of a major U.S. industry would have devastating effects on the U.S. economy as a whole. If federal funds can help X Auto Company continue to employ its workers, then thousands of private individuals will continue to earn and spend money. This will help protect the health of the nation's economy.

On the other hand, you could counter an argument based on similarity of   33
policy considerations by showing that giving X Auto Company federal funds would widen the scope of the rule beyond the limits intended by those who derived the rule. This widening would have all kinds of adverse effects or troublesome consequences, such as opening the courts to a flood of frivolous litigation.

Setting up an analogy. To set up an analogy between two cases, using both   34
the facts and the policy issues, begin by making a list of similarities and differences. Here is how you might expand the general welfare example to show that one case that has already been decided involving the old-age benefit provisions of the Social Security Act is or is not analogous to the X Auto Company case.

SIMILARITIES	DIFFERENCES
In both situations the recipients may receive money that they only directly paid into the system. For example, Social Security recipients may receive funds in excess of the amount they actually put into the fund. The X Auto Company will receive funds that it indirectly paid in the form of taxes, etc.	The recipients of old-age benefits have paid into an insurance fund over the years, while the X Auto Company would be receiving money from a nonspecific tax fund that it has not contributed to. Taxes and insurance are not the same thing.
Many individuals who need support will benefit from the federal funds; employees in the case of X Auto Company, and older members of the population in the case of old-age benefits.	It is quite a different thing for the federal government to provide funds to a private corporation than to provide them to individuals. The government is set up to benefit members of the general population. It is not the government's purpose to benefit a large private corporation.
The X Auto Company funds will help keep the economy healthy because it will keep a major industry alive and will keep X's employees (and employees of other companies that depend on X) off of welfare and other forms of state subsidy. Similarly, the old-age benefits of Social Security assure citizens that they will have an opportunity to put money into a fund that they can draw on in their old age, provided they have worked the requisite amount of time to qualify. This keeps older people from having to turn to the state for support.	Giving funds to a private business may actually unbalance the economy, disturbing the free market and fair competition.

C. THE CONCLUSION After you have established and developed your major and minor premises, you are ready to reach a conclusion that follows logically from them. You may need to use a cause-and-effect argument to show *how* you came to the conclusion.

    In law you will often be required to show that there is a cause-and-effect relationship between certain events or actions. . . .

    Here is an example of how a cause-and-effect relationship can be established within a deductive argument. First, set up the skeleton of your argument.

35

36

37

General rule (major premise): Under the law of State X, the operator of a
motor vehicle is liable for his or her wrongful act, neglect, or default if it
causes death or injury to another person.

Specific facts (minor premise): The plaintiff was riding in her car on the
freeway when the defendant's car hit her from behind. Two days later, the
plaintiff suffered severe back pains and headaches.

Conclusion: Therefore, the defendant should be liable for the damages the
plaintiff has suffered.

If you terminated your argument at this point, it would appear that you had
based your conclusion on a faulty premise or assumption: "All pain that occurs
within two days of an accident is necessarily caused by that accident." Or your
conclusion may appear to result from a *post hoc* fallacy, in which you assert that
because event B follows event A in time, event A has therefore caused event B.
To avoid the appearance that your conclusion does not follow logically from the
premises, you must articulate the causal link between events. You could do so by
beginning your conclusion with the following information.

There is a good deal of evidence that the plaintiff's injury was caused by the
defendant's act of hitting the plaintiff from behind. First of all, the plaintiff's
medical records show that the plaintiff did not have a history of back problems or headaches, so there is no possibility that her injuries are part of a
recurrent or chronic problem. Also, she has not engaged in any activity or suffered any other injury within the last few years that might have led to back
pain or headaches. In addition, Dr. Jones, the plaintiff's physician, has examined the plaintiff and will testify that the pain the plaintiff is experiencing is
the kind that the plaintiff would be likely to feel several days after a rear-end
collision in an automobile.

You would finish your argument by qualifying your conclusion to reflect the
evidence you have presented:

Because the evidence from medical records and from an expert demonstrates
that, in all probability, the plaintiff's injuries were caused by the defendant's
conduct, the defendant is liable for the damage the plaintiff has suffered as a
result of that conduct.

When you are constructing a cause-and-effect argument, keep the subject
matter in mind. If you are working with causation in a complex statistical argument, you must comply with the generally accepted principles of statistical analysis. For example, you may have to adhere to a scientific definition of causation.
However, if you are writing about more common types of problems, try to appeal
to your readers' sense of how the world works: Present a cause-and-effect relationship that your readers will recognize from their own experience. You can
appeal to your readers' common sense and to the "common wisdom of the community." Remember that judges and other attorneys are part of the community

and that they will share this sense of what probably did or did not happen in a given situation.

● ● ● ●

Discussion and Writing Topics

1. How does IRAC resemble or differ from other approaches to organizing essays that you have been taught?
2. Choose a situation involving a conflict in which you or someone you know has been involved. Alternatively, select a situation experienced by a character in a novel, short story, play, or film, one that also involves a conflict. Discuss this situation in IRAC format, as if it were the basis of a legal case. Before writing your draft, identify the main elements you intend to discuss. What is the main *issue*, the central question on which the conflict turns? What *rules* or principles most properly apply to situations such as this one? How can you *apply* these rules or principles to the particular set of facts that comprise the incident? Finally, how does a *conclusion* emerge from the application of rules to facts—a conclusion that resolves the issue one way or the other?

■ Use Plain English ■

Richard C. Wydick

Although lawyers have an often richly deserved reputation for writing unreadable prose (or to use the more legal term, committing homicide upon the English language), there is no reason why writing about legal cases has to be bad writing. Attorneys often defend the kind of interminable sentences that appear in contracts or insurance policies by claiming that they have to get every possible contingency into one sentence. Otherwise, potential adversaries would be able to quote out of context ("Well, this sentence doesn't say anything about . . .") and their clients may be left legally vulnerable. (Lay people often suspect—and rightly so—that the real reason for "legalistic" jargon is to intimidate and hold at bay possible adversaries, in the same way that sorcerers use portentous mumbo-jumbo to ward off evil spirits.) But such arguments are increasingly being met with skepticism both by the general public and by attorneys and judges themselves. Not only in law, but in business, government, and other professions, plain English has been slowly but steadily gaining ground.

Plain English for Lawyers. Durham, NC: Carolina Academic Press, 1994: 1–17, 23–32.
Footnote 6 and 7 omitted, following footnotes renumbered.

The following selection by Richard C. Wydick, Professor of Law at the University of California, Davis, should be a worthwhile cautionary note about how not *to write in responding to the kind of assignments you'll find in this book. And it should be helpful for courses other than writing. Turgid, lifeless writing is just as likely to turn up in sociology, literature, and environmental studies papers as it is in business and law assignments. The remedies Wydick suggests are as effective in one discipline as another.*

This selection is excerpted from Wydick's book Plain English for Lawyers *(3rd ed. 1994) and was based on an article that originally appeared in* 66 California Law Review 727 *(1978).*

Why Plain English?

We lawyers do not write plain English. We use eight words to say what could be   1
said in two. We use arcane phrases to express commonplace ideas. Seeking to be precise, we become redundant. Seeking to be cautious, we become verbose. Our sentences twist on, phrase within clause within clause, glazing the eyes and numbing the minds of our readers. The result is a writing style that has, according to one critic, four outstanding characteristics. It is "(1) wordy, (2) unclear, (3) pompous, and (4) dull."[1]

Criticism of legal writing is nothing new. In 1596, an English chancellor   2
decided to make an example of a particularly prolix document filed in his court. The chancellor first ordered a hole cut through the center of the document, all 120 pages of it. Then he ordered that the person who wrote it should have his head stuffed through the hole, and the unfortunate fellow was led around to be exhibited to all those attending court at Westminster Hall.[2]

When the common law was transplanted to America, the writing style of the   3
old English lawyers came with it. In 1817 Thomas Jefferson lamented that in drafting statutes his fellow lawyers were accustomed to "making every other word a 'said' or 'aforesaid' and saying everything over two or three times, so that nobody but we of the craft can untwist the diction and find out what it means. . . . "[3]

Starting in the 1970s, criticism of legal writing took on a new intensity. The   4
popular press castigated lawyers for the frustration and outrage that people feel when trying to puzzle through an insurance policy, an installment loan agreement,

---

[1]David Mellinkoff, *The Language of the Law* 23 (1963).

[2]*Mylward v. Welden* (Ch. 1596), reprinted in C. Monro, *Acta Cancellariae* 692 (1847). Joseph Kimble has pointed out that the person who wrote, and subsequently wore, the offending document may have been the plaintiff's son, a non-lawyer. Professor Kimble dryly notes that the son was probably following a lawyer's form. Joseph Kimble, *Plain English: A Charter for Clear Writing,* 9 *Cooley L. Rev. 1,* n. 2 (1992), relying on Michele M. Asprey, *Plain Language for Lawyers* 31 (1991).

[3]Letter to Joseph C. Cabell (Sept. 9, 1817), reprinted in 17 *Writings of Thomas Jefferson* 417-18 (A. Bergh ed. 1907).

or an income tax instruction booklet. Even lawyers became critics. One lawyer charged that in writing as we do, we "unnecessarily mystify our work, baffle our clients, and alienate the public."[4]

The 1980s and 1990s brought progress toward reform. More than a dozen 5 good books are now available for use in law school writing courses, and most law schools now stress the need for simplicity and clarity in legal writing. Some jurisdictions have passed statutes that require clear writing in governmental regulations, consumer contracts, voter materials, insurance policies, and the like.[5] New collections of jury instructions enable judges to convey the law more clearly to jurors. Bar associations and other groups of lawyers and judges in the United States, Great Britain, Australia, New Zealand, and Canada have passed resolutions, created commissions, appointed task forces, and published tracts, all in the effort to improve legal writing.

Progress, yes, but victory is not yet near. Too many law students report back 6 from their first jobs that the clear, simple style they were urged to use in school is not acceptable to the older lawyers for whom they work. Too many jurors give up hope of comprehending the judge's instructions and rely instead on instinctive justice. Too many estate planning clients leave their lawyer's office with will and trust agreement in hand, but without fully understanding what they say. Too many people merely skim, or even ignore, the dense paragraphs of purchase agreements, apartment leases, employment contracts, stock prospectuses, and promissory notes, preferring to rely on the integrity or mercy of the author rather than to struggle with the author's legal prose.

The premise of this book is that good legal writing should not differ, without 7 good reason, from ordinary well-written English.[6] As a well-known New York lawyer told the young associates in his firm, "Good legal writing does not sound as though it had been written by a lawyer."

In short, good legal writing is plain English. Here is an example of plain 8 English, the statement of facts from the majority opinion in *Palsgraf v. Long Island Railroad Co.*,[7] written by Benjamin Cardozo:

> Plaintiff was standing on a platform of defendant's railroad after buying a ticket to go to Rockaway Beach. A train stopped at the station, bound for

---

[4]Ronald Goldfarb, *Lawyer Language, Litigation,* Summer 1977 at 3; see also Ronald Goldfarb and James Raymond, *Clear Understandings* (1982).

[5]For a list of plain English statutes in the United States, see Joseph Kimble, "Plain English: A Charter for Clear Writing," 9 *Cooley L. Rev.* 1, 31–37 (1992).

[6]This premise is taken from David Mellinkoff, *The Language of the Law* vii (1963); see also David Mellinkoff, *Dictionary of American Legal Usage* vii (1992).

[7]248 N.Y. 339, 162 N.E. 99 (1928). I have used Palsgraf as an example because it is familiar to all who have studied law. In general, however, Justice Cardozo's writing style is too ornate for modern tastes. For good examples of modern plain English style, examine the opinions of retired United States Supreme Court Justice Lewis F. Powell or United States Circuit Judge Richard Posner.

another place. Two men ran forward to catch it. One of the men reached the platform of the car without mishap, though the train was already moving. The other man, carrying a package, jumped aboard the car, but seemed unsteady as if about to fall. A guard on the car, who had held the door open, reached forward to help him in, and another guard on the platform pushed him from behind. In this act, the package was dislodged and fell upon the rails. It was a package of small size, about fifteen inches long, and was covered by newspaper. In fact it contained fireworks, but there was nothing in its appearance to give notice of its contents. The fireworks when they fell exploded. The shock of the explosion threw down some scales at the other end of the platform many feet away. The scales struck the plaintiff, causing injuries for which she sues.

What distinguishes the writing style in this passage from that found in most   9
legal writing? Notice Justice Cardozo's economy of words. He does not say "despite the fact that the train was already moving." He says "though the train was already moving."

Notice his choice of words. He uses no archaic phrases, no misty abstractions,   10
no hereinbefore's.

Notice his care in arranging words. There are no wide gaps between the sub-   11
jects and their verbs, nor between the verbs and their objects. There are no ambiguities to leave us wondering who did what to whom.

Notice his use of verbs. Most of them are in the simple form, and all but two   12
are in the active voice.

Notice the length and construction of his sentences. Most of them contain   13
only one main thought, and they vary in length: the shortest is six words, and the longest is twenty-seven words.

These and other elements of plain English style are discussed in this book.   14
But you cannot learn to write plain English by reading a book. You must put your own pencil to paper.

● ● ● ●

Discussion and Writing Topics

1. It's safe to assume that most readers don't like to read wordy, pompous, convoluted prose. And yet many of these same readers, in their professional capacities, will write the kind of sentences they profess to hated reading. How do you account for this apparent contradiction? Why (to quote Wydick) do people "use eight words to say what could be said in two"?

2. Find a legal document—perhaps a contract (like a lease), a tax instruction, or a disclaimer of some kind—that is "wordy . . . unclear . . . pompous" or "dull." Rewrite a section of this document in plain English, guided by the principles Wydick specifies in the last few paragraphs of this article.

10 Ways to Know If Your Story Is Ready to Tell in Court

■_____■

Joel ben Izzy

*In this piece, Joel ben Izzy, a professional storyteller, offers advice to attor-
neys on how to to present the stories of their cases to juries in the most effective possible way—that is, in a way that persuades juries to bring in verdicts
favorable to their clients. Ben Izzy is a partner in Anecdotal Evidence, a consultation service for attorneys based in Berkeley, California.*

As a trial lawyer, you are one of America's most highly paid storytellers. This may   1
not be how you introduce yourself at cocktail parties, and it is certainly not a title
you would ever want to pronounce in front of a jury. Yet, it does describe what
you do.

For what is your job if not to convey your client's side of a story again and again   2
—first in writing, then in settlement talks, and, finally, before a judge or a jury?

Of course, you don't have the same advantages as most storytellers who work   3
in nonlegal settings. For example, courtrooms don't generally have fireplaces for
the jury to gather around and listen to a good old tale. Also lacking in modern
courtrooms are those accoutrements that often set the mood for storytelling—a
feast, music, and a bottle of wine. And while a storyteller can assume that the
audience shares a love of stories, a trial lawyer can only assume that the audience
members all received jury summonses.

Unlike, say, writer and storyteller Garrison Keillor, you face strict limitations   4
on the story you tell. The one you tell is supposed to be true. To make it tougher
still, the rules of the courtroom can make for a very constrained telling. Even in
an ideal setting, it takes some doing for a storyteller to win over an audience. It is
much harder still when there are those in the audience trying to shoot down
everything you say and waiting to shout "Objection!"

All the above, however, do not make you any less of a storyteller—they just   5
make your job more difficult. If anything, you need better storytelling skills than
Grandpa Joe does while sitting in the barber shop. For after the evidence has
been admitted, the experts have been paraded in, and those who were examined
have been crossed, the jury takes to deliberations two stories— yours and that of
opposing counsel.

The obvious opportunities to tell your client's story come in opening and   6
closing. Less obvious, but equally important, are opportunities that arise in every
other part of the trial, from your first motions to voir dire to cross-examination.
A strong story gives shape and form to every element of a case.

_____

Trial (July 1998): 91–93.

With this in mind, it may be worth stepping back from that big case you're   7
working on to ask yourself if your story is ready to tell in court. The following 10
questions will help you decide.

1. Do you know the simple, one-sentence version of the story?

Almost any case you're arguing, no matter how complicated, can be boiled   8
down to one simple sentence. We're not talking Faulkner here. We're talking
about one sentence that states your case in a clear, compelling way.

In that sense, a trial is a lot like a movie. Samuel Goldwyn of Metro Goldwyn   9
Mayer said, "If you can't write your movie idea on the back of a business card, you
ain't got a movie." Just as the vast majority of screenplays never get made into
movies, so, too, the vast majority of cases never get to court. You need one simple
sentence for your case to go where you want it to, and you need to have that sentence just as soon as possible.

Don't think that because it's just one sentence it's easy to write. Anyone can   10
churn out pages and pages of drivel. Creating something simple takes months and
months of work.

Picasso was fond of saying, "It took me 50 years to learn to draw like a child."   11
That simplicity is what you must find if you want to build a solid foundation for
the story you are telling.

2. Do you know your audience?

"Know your audience" is one of the two most basic rules in storytelling; the   12
other is "know your story." A successful story builds a bridge from teller to audience. Once that bridge is built, the two can meet in the middle.

In a courtroom, the most obvious chance to get to know your audience is   13
during voir dire [see glossary]. Behind the questioning of each potential juror—to
the extent the court will allow—are the real questions: How can I reach this
person? What's his or her story, and how will it resonate with the story I am here
to tell? What does a juror need to know in order to reach a just verdict in this
case?

Recent years have seen growth in the business of jury consulting, which relies   14
heavily on statistical methods and questionnaires. These methods work—one
need look no further than southern California and the O.J. Simpson and Rodney
King trials to see their efficacy. But they do not stand alone, for voir dire is much
more than a chance for you to get to know the jurors—it is their chance to get to
know you, human to human.

Any storyteller needs to know what the audience members have in common.   15
While the answer at first may be as little as "they registered to vote," jurors begin
building a base of common experience the instant they show up for jury duty. The
better you can understand and integrate this information into your story, the
better your chance of reaching them.

3. Have you chosen your organizational structure?

When it comes to organizing a story for trial, most attorneys fall back on the   16
default form of storytelling—chronological order. The contract was signed on

March 15. On March 17, there was a meeting, and here is what happened. On March 20, the plaintiff telephoned, and so on.

While chronological order may be a fine choice for conveying your client's story, it is only one possibility. The choice you make needs to be a careful one.   17

Once again, we can learn from movies. Perhaps your story would be better structured as a flashback. You might see it as "before and after" a particular incident. Or a mystery to be solved. Should your one-sentence version of the case have a question mark at the end?   18

You can also choose how tight you want your focus to be. Do you want to start with a wide-angle lens and zoom in to focus on one detail? Or do you want to start with a tight focus and zoom out to show a larger picture?   19

4. Do you know your characters, including the villain?

People often try to convey a character through description. "My client is good, honest, nice, and smart." When used in a story, these adjectives become hollow.   20

A storyteller knows intuitively that characters are defined by their actions. While the trial purports to judge only the actions of your characters within the scope of the events in question, the jury judges them on a broader scale. What incidents shed light on who they really are? How can you get these stories into trial?   21

As for villains, they give shape to a story. While it is possible to build a story without one, you should know that your jury will be looking for one. Deep inside every grown-up is a four-year-old who is fascinated with the battle of good and evil—and much more intrigued by evil than good. Look again at the movies—does anyone care who wears the Batman costume? Hardly. They come to see Mr. Freeze and Poison Ivy.   22

You must be prepared to answer the question, "Who's the villain?" And if your reply is simply, "Not my client," that won't satisfy the jury.   23

5. Have you found the part of the story that makes people ask, "And then what happened?"

Every good story revolves around a pause. Somewhere in your tale is a point where you can stop, take a breath, and feel your audience's interest mount. It is a moment of silence that you can actually hear, when listeners ask themselves, "And then what happened?"   24

These are the moments that connect a storyteller to a listener. They are also the moments that draw your audience out of its usual passive state, ready to listen with the open eyes, ears, and heart of a seven-year-old.   25

To tell your client's story well, you must know when that moment comes in your story. If you can isolate it and take advantage of it, you can reach your audience.   26

6. Do you see the compelling images in your mind's eye?

The images that stand out most in your mind will be the ones that you are best able to convey to a judge or jury. Every case needs strong, visceral imagery. Without it, the words you utter are merely words.   27

Know just which images float your boat. The more compelling the images are 28 to the teller, the easier it is to tell the story. This is particularly true in cases that seem dry, such as contract disputes. Likewise, very complex cases desperately need accessible, compelling imagery—particularly complex medical negligence cases.

All these cases have images running beneath their surfaces. Often they run so 29 deeply that you must dowse them out with metaphors. But when you find the right images, they surface like water in a desert, offering your audience an oasis.

7. Have you found the weak points in your metaphors?

The further you go out on a limb, the greater the risk of that limb breaking off. 30 This is true of metaphors in trials. Finding the right one is like striking gold. Finding a bad one is like striking fool's gold—you think you've got something until you run to show everyone in the saloon and they laugh in your face.

The best way to generate metaphors is through brainstorming. To do this 31 effectively, open your mind to every possible idea. Write down everything, with no critical examination, until you have a long list. Once you've got your list, turn on your critical faculty and sift through the list, seeing what nuggets, if any, lie in the bottom of the pan.

The next step is crucial, for you must test those nuggets to see if they're real 32 gold or fool's gold. The process for testing is reverse brainstorming. Do everything you can to destroy that metaphor, for that is what opposing counsel will do. Invite others to help you tear it to pieces. If your metaphor is real gold, it will pass the test. If not, get out the pan and start again.

A bad metaphor is worse than none at all and can undermine a case. 33 Remember Bob Dole's* plans for "building a bridge to the past"? He probably wishes he never thought of it. Think about the prosecution in the first O.J. trial talking about a "mountain of evidence." It was a useless metaphor that went nowhere until, finally, the mountain became too high and difficult to climb. In frustration, the jury threw down its pitons and ropes and simply disregarded it.

8. Do you really believe in what you are saying?

This can be a tough question for a trial lawyer. As a storyteller, I know that I 34 cannot do a good job telling a story unless I believe in it. While some may say this is the luxury of being a storyteller rather than a lawyer, I say belief is an essential element in a well-told story.

Belief can work on several different levels. One way to understand this is to 35 look at people's belief in the Bible—appropriately enough, the traditional swearing-in book for a witness. Many people believe in the Bible. For some, this means the literal truth in every word. For others, the Bible is a collection of stories that, while not strictly true, have great truths embedded in them.

To tell your client's story well, you must believe in the truth of the case. You 36 can look from many angles to find that truth, but you owe it to yourself and your

---

*Long-term senator from Kansas; Senate Majority Leader; and 1996 presidential candidate against incumbent Bill Clinton, winning only 159 of 538 electoral votes.

client to find a truth that is rock solid. Otherwise, you are not just fighting the other side, but your conscience as well.

9. Does your story answer the most basic question for jurors: "Why should I care?"

It is amazing how often this question is overlooked, especially in large trials. Lawyers often assume that just because a proposed merger of two large corporations may or may not have been interrupted by the alleged involvement of a third corporation in violation of a contract, which may or may not have been enforceable under particular provisions or federal and state law, the jury should care about it. Why?   37

It is your job to make the jurors care. There are many possible reasons why they should. Maybe the story invokes their innate hunger for justice. Or perhaps they act out of self-interest—they feel that on some level the outcome will affect them. Maybe they feel the outcome will affect their children, or their community. Maybe they empathize with your client.   38

Whatever the case, jurors need to care about it. Every story that works does so because it makes us care about something or, more often, someone. People care about people. If you haven't reached their hearts, you haven't reached your audience.   39

10. Have you told your story to someone who is not an attorney?

While this may sound obvious, it is a point where many cases break down. Many an attorney will build a case that is legally brilliant yet utterly incomprehensible to laypeople. And quite likely, these folks will be the ones on the jury.   40

The problem is that by the time you've become a lawyer, you may have lost your ability to think like a nonlawyer. Luckily, there are still many nonlawyers around. Find someone who will sit down and hear your case, not as a set of arguments, but as a story.   41

As you tell it to that person, the weak points will be obvious. You'll see the parts that are confusing, dull, or unbelievable. Once you know these, you can rework your tale, strengthening it until it becomes what it needs to be—the heart and soul of your case.   42

● ● ● ●

Discussion and Writing Topics

1. Browse through the cases that make up the major portion of this book. Select one, role-play as one of the attorneys in this case, and compose an opening or a closing statement to the jury, one that takes account of as many as possible of ben Izzy's ten questions. For example, make sure that at some early point in your statement you sum up the story in a single sentence. Develop an organizational structure that will allow you to tell the story in the most effective way. Present the villain of the case—but be careful not to overstate, or you may lose credibility in the eyes of the jury. Devise compelling images. Try out your story by reading it aloud to a friend or a classmate.

2. Choose a novel, a short story, or a film that you find particularly fascinating. Imagine you are an attorney representing one of the characters in the story, either in a civil or a criminal case, and compose an opening or a closing statement, using ben Izzy's guidelines.

Stories and Exercises I

Norman Brand and John O. White

The following exercises are intended as practice for the kind of writing assignments you will find in later chapters of this book. In each case, you will be presented with a particular story or situation, followed by the legal rules and principles that apply to this situation. Using IRAC format, write an analysis of one or more of these situations, as your instructor assigns.

Note: The exercises generally proceed from short to long. The first three are "quick writes." You should be able to respond to these in a paragraph or so. The next group should be somewhat longer. The most complete response is demanded from the final exercise, "Chris the Cocktail Waitress." A sample response to the previous exercise, "Abner and Judy," will provide you with a model for responding to this final assignment.

These exercises originally appeared in Norman Brand and John O. White's Legal Writing: The Strategy of Persuasion *(1994).*

Quick Writes

These first three exercises are short legal problems. Using the facts and law   1
given, write an answer that demonstrates your analysis of the problem and the soundness of your conclusion.

Quick Write 1

A and B robbed a liquor store. A's gun went off accidentally, and the clerk was   2
shot and killed. The robbery was a felony. A state statute holds that when a victim is killed in the commission of a felony, all defendants shall be charged with murder in the first degree.

Discuss the charge of first-degree murder against B.   3

Quick Write 2

Rodney and Billy were playing war in front of Billy's house. In the course of one   4
battle, Billy threw a rock (hand grenade) at Rodney. Unfortunately, it hit Charles

---

Legal Writing: The Strategy of Persuasion, 3d. New York: St. Martin's, 1994.
Exercises 3, 7, 10, 11, 14 omitted from original; Exercises after 2 renumbered.

who was passing by on the sidewalk. Charles sustained a serious eye injury and wants to sue Billy for the injury.

Discuss Charles's action against Billy.   5

Assume the following to be a valid legal principle: 6

A *battery* is a harmful or offensive touching of another that is intentional, and without consent or legal privilege. *Transfer of intent* exists when one intends a battery against one person and unintentionally causes another person to be harmfully or offensively touched. In that case, the actor is liable to that other person.

Quick Write 3

Huge Hugo, the neighborhood bully, encounters Ronald in an alley. Without   7
moving a muscle, Hugo tells Ronald he is going to jump on Ronald's head. With that Hugo smiles, but not in a friendly way. Ronald leaves immediately and becomes sick from fear. Later he wants to bring an action for assault against Hugo.

Discuss Ronald's action for assault.   8

Assume the following to be a valid legal principle: 9

Assault is an intentional, unprivileged, unconsented act that causes reasonable apprehension of an immediate battery. Words alone do not constitute an assault. A threatening gesture must accompany the words.

Legal Writing Questions

The following [eight] writing exercises present facts, law, and legal issues. Use 10
them to practice writing thoughtful, complete, and clear analytical answers. You may use the rules of law provided, or you may rely on your own knowledge of law.

Writing Exercise 1: Charlie and Jack

Charlie was a local weight lifter and bully who liked to start fights. Although quite 11
strong, he was extremely slow moving, and he limited himself to brawling with people who were considerably smaller than he.

Jack was a small, unathletic man who confined his exercise to daily jogging   12
and attempts to stuff himself with enough food to boost his weight over 115 pounds. Unfortunately, he frequented the same bar as Charlie (a place called the Dew Drop Inn). One day while Jack was drinking a high-calorie banana daiquiri, Charlie lumbered over wearing a malicious grin. "You're next, Jackie-boy," he said. "Next time I see you it's going to be all over."

Jack left immediately and thereafter began carrying a gun every time he left   13
his house. Three nights later, while taking a short-cut through an alley, he saw a huge figure about thirty yards away lumbering slowly toward him. Because the figure was about the same size as Charlie, Jack became frightened, drew his gun, and fired. Then he ran home.

Jack's shot grazed Fred, a construction worker who was cutting through the   14
alley on his way home. He now sues Jack for battery. What result?

Assume the following to be valid legal principles: 15

A *battery* is the harmful or offensive touching of another that is intentional,
unconsented, and unprivileged. However, a person may touch another in self-
defense as long as he or she does not use any more force than is necessary to
prevent an assailant from harming him or her. Furthermore, one has a right
(privilege) to defend oneself even if one makes a *reasonable* mistake as to the
necessity of self-defense.

Writing Exercise 2: Red and Sue

Red, a Los Angeles resident, and his girlfriend, Sue, also a Los Angeles resident,   16
decide to drive to Las Vegas for the weekend in Red's new Cadillac. They stop in
Barstow, California, pick up a bottle of Old Tennis Shoe Rye Whiskey, and
proceed to drink and drive on their way. As they travel at high speed in their
erratic trip across the Nevada desert, Sue, a little drunk, decides her skill at
steering the car is better than Red's and playfully grabs the steering wheel. The
car swerves sharply, the left front wheel comes off, and the Cadillac crashes into
a cactus, injuring both Red and Sue.

Discuss the possible law suits resulting from this accident.   17

Assume the following to be valid legal principles: 18

- According to Nevada and California law, suits resulting from this accident
  may be brought in either state.
- Both California and Nevada hold drinking while driving to be negligent.
  Negligence implies liability.
- If one does not exercise due care and causes another's injury, that person
  is deemed negligent and is liable for the other's injury.
- If one does not exercise due care and contributes to one's own injury, that
  person is deemed contributorily negligent. Contributory negligence is a
  defense to an action in negligence. Recovery is diminished according to
  the amount of fault in causing the injury.
- Both states stipulate that a manufacturer is responsible for any damages
  resulting from defective parts.

Writing Exercise 3: Roman Round

Roman Round, a travelling salesman with districts in the states of Glacier and   19
Forest, married his childhood sweetheart, Susan, in a civil ceremony in Glacier in
1955. In 1962 twin daughters, Annie and Fannie, were born to them. Roman,
however, had a girlfriend named Alice who also lived in Glacier. Alice had a son,
Homer, by Roman in 1962. Susan died in 1963, at which time Roman moved in with
Alice. They lived together as husband and wife, and in 1973 had another child,
Rupert. In addition, they adopted a seventeen-year-old girl named Ruby in 1974. In

1971 Roman had met and married Nora in Forest. He lived with her when in Forest and with Alice when in Glacier. Roman and Nora had a child, Fred, in 1972.

Roman attended a sales convention in Atlantic City in 1994, at which time, while swimming with Rita, a cocktail waitress, he was devoured by a shark. Rita was not injured. Roman left no will, but did leave an estate of $100,000.

Discuss the inheritance rights of all the parties.

Assume the rules in this jurisdiction are as follows:

- When there is no will, both the states of Glacier and Forest divide property equally among the decedent's living legal wife and legitimate children.
- Marriage at common law in both states is valid after seven years of cohabitation.
- Legitimate children are children born of any valid marriages.
- An adopted child is also a legitimate child.
- Bigamy, entering into a marriage while already married, is illegal, and all marriages subsequent to the valid one are void.

Writing Exercise 4: George and Mabel

George and Mabel, on a visit to the city of Saint Frank, buy a ticket for a ride on the city-owned streetcar. They then relax and enjoy the ride as C. Jones, the operator, runs the streetcar and points out the sights. Meanwhile, Ms. Fox, out shopping, had parked her Audi on the tracks, assuming them to be abandoned because no sign was posted indicating they were in service. C. Jones, coming around a curve, saw Ms. Fox's automobile and was barely able to bring the streetcar to a jolting halt before it could strike the car. Mabel and George were both thrown from the streetcar and injured. Mr. Smith, a fellow passenger, jumped from the streetcar to aid George and Mabel, and broke his leg.

Discuss the law suits that may result from this accident.

Assume the following to be valid legal principles:

- The owner of a vehicle parked within five feet of streetcar tracks currently in service is liable for all injuries resulting therefrom.
- One is not required to come to the aid of another, but if he or she does, he or she does so at his or her own risk; that is, he or she cannot recover from the person he or she aided for any injuries he or she may sustain.
- The city is responsible for any injuries resulting from careless or hazardous operation of its streetcar line.

Writing Exercise 5: Jones and Green

Jones orally promised to will his home and property to Green if Green took care of Jones's sister, who lived in Sacramento. Green then moved from San Francisco to Sacramento (a distance of eighty miles), where he acted as a domestic servant, attended to Jones's sister's personal needs, and acted as her nurse until her death five years later. When Green informed Jones of his sister's death, Jones suffered a fatal heart attack, leaving a perfectly valid will that gives all of his property to Thompson.

Green comes to you for legal advice. He tells you that he forsook most of his friends and personal pleasures and gave up other lucrative employment opportunities for this job. He wants to know if he is entitled to the home and property. 27

Assume the rules in this jurisdiction are as follows: 28

- A will may be revoked at any time before the person who made it dies.
- When a person gives up something of value in reliance upon the promise of another, that person can recover the fair value of what was given up.
- The estate of a deceased person is liable for all of the legitimate debts of that deceased person.
- Any contract to make a will must be in writing or it will not be enforced.

Writing Exercise 6: Baker and Abba

Jim Baker, a seventeen-year-old, five-foot-nine-inch, 139-pound boy, was hitch-hiking one afternoon in July. Tom Abba, a heavyset, thirty-five-year-old man, stopped to give him a lift. While driving together, Tom learned that Jim was carrying five thousand dollars to make a drug purchase. Tom stopped the car and suggested that Jim get out, so they both could go for a swim. Both men left the car. Tom pulled a knife and said, "Jim, give me the money." After Jim had handed him the money, Tom said, "I guess I can't leave a witness," and proceeded toward Jim. Jim drew a pistol from under his shirt and fatally shot Tom. Jim has been charged with murder. 29

Discuss whether Jim is guilty of murder under these facts. 30

Assume the rules in this jurisdiction are as follows: 31

- If a person is threatened with deadly force, that person has a duty to retreat before employing self-defense.
- There is no duty to retreat where one cannot do so in safety.
- If a person kills another in self-defense, that person is not guilty of murder.

Writing Exercise 7: Mrs. Trueblue

Mrs. A. Trueblue and her six-year-old daughter went to dinner at the Blue Wolf Restaurant. The waiter, a surly fellow, asked Mrs. Trueblue, "Well, whaddaya want?" Taken aback at his insolence, Mrs. Trueblue nevertheless ordered two rare steaks. The order came shortly thereafter, burned to a crisp. When Mrs. Trueblue protested, the waiter shouted, "You old witch, what do you expect when you come to a place like this?" He ranted at Mrs. Trueblue and her daughter for another few minutes and then left. Mrs. Trueblue, angered but not flustered, indignantly started to leave. The manager, thinking she hadn't paid her bill (which she 32 hadn't, because the waiter had taken the dinners back), blocked her way, demanding payment. When she attempted to leave, he grabbed her purse, breaking the strap. Being unwilling to leave her purse, Mrs. Trueblue remained in the restaurant for four hours arguing with the manager. Finally the manager let her go. Mrs. Trueblue's young daughter subsequently became quite ill and was unable to sleep well for several weeks because of the waiter's accusation.

Who is liable to whom, and for what?   33

Assume the following to be valid legal principles: 34

- *False imprisonment* is the intentional physical or psychological confinement of the plaintiff by the defendant, without consent and without legal privilege. Psychological confinement exists when the plaintiff is placed under no physical restraint but submits to a threat of force or asserted legal authority.
- A *battery* is a harmful or offensive touching of another that is intentional, and without consent or legal privilege.
- *Intentional infliction of mental distress* requires outrageous conduct on the part of the defendant that is calculated to cause and does cause the plaintiff severe mental or emotional distress.

Writing Exercise 8: Eel O'Brien

Although financially down on his luck, Eel O'Brien remained undaunted in his   35
devotion to *Plastic Man* comic books. Unable to afford the slight coinage necessary for procuring the monthly issues, Eel had taken to perusing them at the racks of some of the local drug and grocery stores. Soon, however, having worn out his welcome at these establishments, he ventured onto new territory, Gargantua's Groceries, a dump if ever there was one, with not a soul in sight. Eel enjoyed as best he could the latest exploits of his hero. He then replaced the comic book in the rack and quickly proceeded to the exit, where he encountered Gargantua himself, who, in height, girth, and musculature, seemed a more or less human equivalent of King Kong. Gargantua's body was pressed against the door, removing the exit from sight.

"Gimme it," Gargantua demanded.   36

"G-g-give you what?" queried Eel, uneasily.   37

"Unless you take that comic book from under your coat, you're not walking   38
out of here."

Eel, now nearly hysterical with fright, thought he heard an emphasis on   39
"walking" and assumed it meant that his legs were in danger of being broken. Quickly glancing around the store, he saw a back door and sped to it. Gargantua lumbered after, hurling a gallon jug of cranberry juice that missed Eel but struck a Campbell soup display, a can of which rolled under Eel's feet, nearly causing him to trip as he made his way to the rear of the store and out.

Eel has just stormed into your office, wildly recounting these details and   40
shrieking, "Do something, do something!" What, legally, can you do for him?

Assume the following to be valid legal principles: 41

- *Assault* is an intentional, unprivileged, unconsented act that causes reasonable apprehension of an immediate battery. Words alone do not constitute an assault. A threatening gesture must accompany the words.
- *Intentional infliction of mental distress* requires outrageous conduct on the part of the defendant that is calculated to cause and does cause the plaintiff severe mental or emotional distress.

Problem 1: Abner and Judy

Abner and his cousin Judy left the Midwest to take the trip to Metropolis they had   42
planned for so long. Despite their excitement at visiting the big city, they were
greatly concerned by the stories of muggings and robberies that were often related
to them by friends who had visited there. Consequently, Abner and Judy were more
than usually upset when they discovered that their hotel had no record of their reservations and that they had to walk six dark blocks to a neighboring hotel that could
accommodate them. After walking only one block, they noticed two men walking
behind them and rapidly overtaking them. As Abner looked back nervously, the two
men looked away and appeared to have no interest in them. Still, Abner, who was
very protective of cousin Judy, became more and more apprehensive.

As the two men overtook Abner and Judy, Abner stopped and pulled Judy out   43
of the way. At that the two men also stopped and turned to face the couple. One
said "Hey Buddy . . . ," at which moment Abner, with his souvenir collapsible
Metropolitan umbrella, struck the man sharply on the head, knocking him out.

The other man, Frank, a chef who was carrying his favorite boning knife home   44
to sharpen it properly, pulled it from a bag he was carrying and gracefully thrust
it into Abner's right shoulder, seriously wounding him.

Judy then brandished her own umbrella, slapping it sharply against her hand   45
for emphasis. The man with the knife turned, broke into a creditable sprint, and
disappeared around the corner.

Meanwhile, it began to rain. Concerned about Abner, Judy opened her own   46
umbrella to protect him from the weather until help came. As she opened the
umbrella, however, one of the wires supporting the fabric sprang out and struck
and injured her right eye.

After the police arrived, they discovered that the man who had been knocked   47
unconscious was Mr. Naybor, a well-known businessman and owner of a nearby
restaurant, who claimed he had only been trying to warn the couple to be careful
on such dark streets. The other man, Frank, was his head chef. Abner admitted
he had made a mistake.

Discuss the following issues: 48

1. The businessman, Mr. Naybor, wants to sue Abner for battery to recover his medical expenses.
2. Abner wants to sue Frank for battery to recover his medical expenses.

3. Judy, to recover her medical expenses, wants to sue the umbrella manufacturer for manufacturing a defective umbrella.

Assume the following to be valid legal principles: 49

Battery. A battery is a harmful or offensive touching of another that is intentional, unconsented, and unprivileged. However, a person has a privilege to touch another in self-defense as long as he or she does not use any more force than is necessary to prevent an assailant from harming him or her. Furthermore, one has a right to defend oneself even if one makes a reasonable mistake as to the necessity of self defense.

Product Liability. A manufacturer is absolutely liable for any defects in a product that are caused by the manufacturer and not by abuse of the product.

Sample Answer: Abner and Judy

As a result of a misunderstanding and altercation on a dark street in Metropolis,   50
two actions in battery are in question. A possible action in product liability is also indicated.

NAYBOR V. ABNER (BATTERY). Mr. Naybor, a local businessman, may want to bring   51
an action in battery against Abner, a visitor to the city. Abner, thinking he was about to become the victim of a mugging, struck Mr. Naybor over the head with an umbrella. The question is whether that action constituted a battery.

Battery requires an intentional and harmful or offensive touching. When   52
Abner delivered the blow to Mr. Naybor's head with the umbrella, it was an intentional act that caused harm and was offensive to him. However, a battery must also be unconsented and unprivileged. Although Mr. Naybor did not consent to the blow, Abner may have privilege if he acted in self-defense or even if he made a reasonable mistake as to the necessity of acting in self-defense.

Because Abner was mistaken, the issue is whether the mistake was reason-   53
able. The street was dark, and Abner may have had reason to be nervous about muggers. Naybor himself said he stopped to warn the couple. Still, it is problematic whether Mr. Naybor gave Abner cause to strike him. Mr. Naybor only said "Hey Buddy," a form of address that does not necessarily carry with it a threat, although it isn't particularly cordial. Also, although Naybor and Frank were overtaking Abner and Judy, and they did stop and turn to Abner, Naybor made no other gesture that could be construed as threatening. However, the form of address, the surroundings, and the nature of approach might very well be enough for a reasonable person to think he was about to be mugged.

The next question, however, is whether that reasonable apprehension would   54
be enough to cause a reasonable person to use the amount of force Abner used. Abner may have believed he had to act at that instant or become a victim. However, because he could have spoken to the stranger, and because there was a

high probability of error in his assessment of the situation, Abner probably used more force than he had privilege to use. Therefore, because he did not have privilege to strike Mr. Naybor as he did, he should be liable to him for battery.

ABNER V. FRANK (BATTERY). After Abner had struck Naybor with the umbrella and   55
knocked him out, Frank stabbed Abner with the boning knife he was carrying in a bag. As a result, Abner wishes to bring an action in battery against Frank, the chef.

It is clear that Frank touched Abner intentionally and harmed him. The ques-   56
tion is whether he had any privilege to do so. He may have had privilege if he were acting in self-defense, because one may touch another in self-defense if he or she uses no more force than is necessary.

In this case, the question is whether Frank, by stabbing Abner with a knife,   57
used more force than he had privilege to use. On the one hand, Abner only had an umbrella—a souvenir one at that. Still, it proved effective, as it was sufficient to knock out Mr. Naybor. Also, since it was dark there may be some question as to whether Frank knew what kind of weapon Abner used.

But were there any other options for Frank rather than proceeding directly to   58
potentially deadly force? He could have run away, as he did later, but he would have had to abandon his employer, who was unconscious. He did run away later, but by then the situation had changed, and Abner had been wounded. Frank could also have spoken to Abner to try to see what the situation actually was. But there is no indication that he spoke to Abner. He did react instantly, but was the reaction reasonable?

Because there were other options open to Frank, and because there is no indi-   59
cation that it was necessary at that moment for Frank to use potentially deadly force, it appears that he used more force than he had privilege to use. Therefore, he will be liable to Abner for battery.

JUDY V. UMBRELLA MANUFACTURER (PRODUCT LIABILITY). Following the stabbing,   60
Judy slapped her own umbrella against her hand as she brandished it. The chef turned and ran. Then she opened her umbrella only to have a wire spring out and injure her eye. As a result, she wishes to bring action against the manufacturer of the umbrella because a manufacturer is absolutely liable for any defects in a product that are caused by the manufacturer and not by abuse of the product.

The first issue is whether Judy abused the umbrella. It is true that she slapped   61
it against her hand for emphasis. We do not know the amount of force she used. It may be argued that because an umbrella is not made to be slapped against the hand or used as a weapon, Judy abused it. However, it is also true that an umbrella should be made to withstand normal wear and tear. A manufacturer should foresee that an umbrella may be tossed into a closet or the trunk of a car, or that it may be tapped on the ground to shake off water. It is hard to tell how hard Judy slapped the umbrella against her hand, but that act in and of itself does not necessarily indicate abuse.

The law requires not only that there be no abuse of the product, but that the defect be caused by the manufacturer. Here is a problem. Not much is known about the umbrella. It is not clear if this too is a souvenir—as is Abner's umbrella. Judy's umbrella's age, condition, or prior use is unknown. There is no indication of a defect specifically caused by the manufacturer. 62

Because no abuse of the product can be substantiated, and because no specific defect caused by the manufacturer can be ascertained, there can be no finding of liability in this issue without more facts. Based on the facts presented, the manufacturer cannot be found liable. 63

Problem 2: Chris the Cocktail Waitress

Chris Connors, a cocktail waitress at Earl's Lounge and Restaurant, was walking through the crowded lounge intending to serve a round of drinks when she was touched indelicately by Wilson Smith, one of the customers. She was so startled by the touch that she dropped her tray on the table of a party of four, slightly injuring one member of the party, a law student named Marvin Bailey, and spilling liquor over all of them. Marvin suffered a cut nose. 64

Marvin, very upset at being injured and also at being forced to hurry home to change his clothes before his evening torts class, went immediately to his car and backed directly into a car driven by Dean Gruff. Both automobiles were damaged. 65

Meanwhile, Chris retrieved the dropped tray, cleaned up around the table, brought new drinks, and, on her way back to the bar, took the tray and delivered a convincing blow to the top of Wilson Smith's head. Smith was surprised and offended, because, given the nature of Chris's job and her brief uniform, he assumed she could handle the overt behavior he considered to be appropriate to bar atmosphere. 66

Discuss the following issues: 67

1. Chris Connors wants to sue Wilson Smith for battery.
2. Marvin Bailey wants to sue Wilson Smith for Bailey's injury, his cleaning bill, and for repair to his own and Dean Gruff's car, all as a result of battery.
3. Wilson Smith wants to sue Chris Connors for battery.

Assume the following to be valid legal principles: 68

A battery is a harmful or offensive touching of another that is intentional, unconsented, and unprivileged. However, one may have a privilege to touch another in self-defense as long as he or she does not use any more force than is necessary to prevent an assailant from harming him or her. Furthermore, one has a right to defend oneself, even if one makes a reasonable mistake as to the necessity of self defense.

(Further clarification of intent: If a defendant intends to touch one person, and in the process causes another to be touched, the wrongful intent is transferred to the unintended victim. The defendant will then be liable for resulting damages as long as those results should be foreseeable and as long as there is no intervening cause for those results.)

Stories and Exercises II

Leonard Tourney

This selection begins with a useful guide to writing effective issue statements. The exercises following will provide you with additional practice opportunities for the writing assignments in the later chapters of this book. "Incident at the Airport" is followed by four sample responses—ranging from good to bad. The "good" response will provide a model for the following two exercises, "Once in a Blue Moon" and "Jail Bird."

Leonard Tourney teaches legal writing at the University of California, Santa Barbara. He has authored several novels, including The Players' Boy Is Dead *(1980),* The Bartholomew Fair Murders *(1986), and* Old Saxon Blood *(1988).*

A Short Guide to Writing Effective Issue Statements

An issue statement is a single sentence defining exactly and correctly the legal 1
question to be addressed. To be effective, it must define the point on which the
case turns. Here are some basic rules for formulating such a sentence.

1. Do *not* use personal names in issue statements; instead, refer to parties in
   the case by legal or by relevant occupational categories. An issue statement, while originating in specific factual situation, is a hypothetical
   extrapolation. The names of the individuals involved are immaterial.
2. The issue statement *must* name the specific cause of legal action (i.e., the
   grounds of the suit or prosecution). *Vague* references to defendant's
   wrongdoing, liability, or criminal conduct aren't enough.
3. The issue statement *should* provide specific details of the case, especially
   those relevant to the key subordinate issue.
4. The issue statement *should* be grammatically correct. This means that the
   sentence must be grammatically complete, verbs should agree with their subjects, and relative clauses must be correctly linked to the words they modify.
5. An effective issue statement is concise: it doesn't use unnecessary words
   to achieve maximum communication. Good sentences are fat free.
6. Spell and punctuate your issue statement correctly. Avoid unnecessary
   commas.
7. Use legal terminology accurately.
8. Revise your issue statement carefully. A good issue statement reflects the
   quality of your thinking about the case and increases the likelihood that the
   discussion that follows will have the same qualities.

Exercise 1: Incident at the Airport

Lisa St. John arrived at LAX [Los Angeles International Airport] late in the after- 2
noon after a grueling flight from London via New York and Chicago. She was
exhausted and irritable, ready to chuck her job as a computer consultant for international corporations. Her mood did not improve when she found that Frank

Mason, her fiancé, was not waiting to pick her up as he had promised. She had long suspected Frank of being a closet flake just waiting to reveal himself to her after he and Lisa were married and only an expensive divorce would undo the damage. The upside of his failure to show was that it gave Lisa cause to break things off. While she waited, she steamed and rehearsed just how she would tell him to marry someone else.

The plane had arrived at 4. Frank didn't appear until nearly 7. Lisa had avoided eating so that her blood sugar level would drop. She wanted to feel awful, look awful. Frank deserved what he got: a whining, inconsolable hag. Then she saw him, and her cup of wrath overflowed. Frank was smiling, carrying a dozen roses, and a box that looked very much like Lisa's favorite chocolates. He threw his arms open wide to greet her and in so doing hit Eben Sommers a 90 year old man waiting to get a plane to Detroit. The blow broke Mr. Sommers' glasses and his nose.   3

"You moron, why don't you watch what you're doing," Lisa cried, as Frank struggled with the roses, candy, and Mr. Sommers, whom he was trying to help up off the floor. The old man had reminded her of her grandfather who had died a month earlier. Enraged, Lisa kicked at Frank, but missed, hitting Mr. Sommers in the leg, breaking his tibia. Mr. Sommers cried out in agony. His cries brought Albert Fenstermocker, a German tourist, to his aid. Fenstermocker, thinking Lisa and Frank were assaulting the old man, began to beat Frank over the head with his cane. Seeing her fiancé assaulted by a perfect stranger, Lisa's feelings changed. She threw herself at Fenstermocker, knocking him to the ground.   4

Write an analysis of the case above focusing your attention on Lisa St. John's liability for battery to Frank Mason, Eben Sommers, and Albert Fenstermocker. Use the following rules.   5

1. **Battery.** Battery is a harmful or offensive touching of another that is intentional, unconsented, and unprivileged.
2. **Transfer of Intent.** In tort law, if A, intending to strike B, misses B and hits C instead, the intent to strike B is transferred and supplies the necessary intent for the tort against C.
3. **Self-Defense Privilege.** The right to protect oneself or another from unlawful attack, the law of self-defense justifies an act done in reasonable belief of immediate danger, with use of reasonable force in the absence of more peaceful alternatives.

SAMPLE STUDENT RESPONSES: INCIDENT AT THE AIRPORT _____

Which is the best response? Why? What problems do you find with the other responses?

(Note: Rules are in **boldface** to highlight position only.)

Response A. Does defendant who inadvertently kicked plaintiff while intending to kick a third party who had accidentally struck the plaintiff commit a battery?

Battery is a harmful or offensive touching of another that is intentional, unconsented, and unprivileged.

At LAX, Lisa St. John, defendant, kicked Eben Sommers, plaintiff, breaking his tibia. This constitutes harmful and, surely, offensive touching to which Sommers, a total stranger, did not consent. Sommers was not Ms. St. John's intended victim, however. She was aiming at a third party, her fiancé, Frank Mason, who had accidentally struck Sommers moments before, breaking his nose and glasses. Nonetheless, according to the rule of transfer to intent, **in tort law, if A, intending to strike B, misses B and hits C instead, the intent to strike B is transferred and supplies the necessary intent for the tort against C.** Therefore, Ms. St. John's intent to kick Mason is transferred to the actual victim, Sommers.

But can Ms. St. John invoke the self-defense privilege to shield her from liability? **The right to protect oneself or another from unlawful attack, the law of self-defense justifies an act done in reasonable belief of immediate danger, with use of reasonable force in the absence of more peaceful alternatives.**

Ms. St. John might argue she kicked Mason to protect Sommers from further harm. But since her statement to Mason asking him to "watch what he was doing" suggests she knew Mason's striking of Sommers was accidental and therefore not likely to be repeated since he was immediately aware of what he had done, she cannot be said to have acted to protect Sommers from further immediate danger as the law requires. Nor was the force she exerted reasonable. If she really believed Mason intended another blow against Sommers she could have seized Mason's arms or flung herself at him, as she did later when she threw herself at a German tourist assaulting Mason. The kick was excessive force, reckless given the proximity of bystanders, and more likely motivated by anger against Mason for his tardiness than a desire to protect Sommers.

Given the evidence, it seems likely Lisa St. John will be liable to Sommers for battery.

Response B. Here the issue in this case is whether Lisa St. John is liable for battery against Eben Sommers, a 90 year old man, injured at LAX when Lisa returned from a business trip. **Battery is the harmful or offensive touching of another that is intentional, unconsented, and unprivileged.** Lisa St. John is definitely liable for battery. While she meant to kick her fiancé, she kicked Mr. Sommers instead, causing him harm and offense. Furthermore, he didn't consent to being kicked. The big problem here is transfer of intent. **According to that rule, if A intending to strike B, misses B and hits C instead, the intent to strike B is transferred and supplies the necessary intent for the tort against C.** This means that her intent to strike Frank is transferred to Mr. Sommers. Thus, she committed a battery against Eben Sommers.

Response C. Lisa St. John arrived at LAX late, in the afternoon. She was mad at her fiancé for being late, so when he greeted her she kicked at him, missing and hitting Eben Sommers, who was this old guy. She broke his tibia in doing so, which was a harmful or offensive touching. It was also unconsented and unprivileged. But was it intended? According to the transfer of intent rule it was.

The facts speak for themselves. Lisa is guilty of battery.

Response D. Sometimes we aim at one thing and do another, hurting another person in the process. That's basically what happened in this case, the issue of which is if Lisa St. John committed a crime or tort against Eben Sommers.

Lisa St. John committed a battery. She kicked Eben Sommers even though she did not mean to do it, because the transfer of intent rule applies. Thus she meets all the elements of the following two rules. . . .

Exercise 2: Once in a Blue Moon

Jason Robertson was a student at UCSB majoring in Political Science and hoping for a career in law. Tall and muscular, he worked out six times a week at Gold's Gym and had a job at the Blue Moon Café, a trendy nightspot on lower State Street. His official job description was "security officer," but he was really a bouncer who made sure that none of the café's patrons got out of hand. Generally his intimidating height and bulk ensured orderliness in the patrons with whom he had to deal.   6

On December 10, 1994, Jason was working when he saw Lisa Anderson come in the door with his best friend Randy. Lisa had dumped Jason about a month earlier, but he was still in love with her, and when he saw her with another man, he experienced a renewal of all those emotions which had burned within him during their relationship. Jason also felt betrayed by Randy, in whom he had confided his deepest thoughts about Lisa and who now appeared to have taken advantage of that knowledge to worm his way into her affections.   7

For an hour Jason watched the couple with ever increasing rage. They sat in the corner of the crowded café, their heads close to each other whispering, occasionally glancing at him and, Jason thought, smirking. Finally, Jason could stand it no longer. He approached the couple and a quarrel ensued between Jason and Randy. Just as Mr. Gordon, the café owner, came over to see what occasioned the raised voices, Randy pushed Jason aside, declared his intention to leave, and called Jason an s.o.b. The Jason told Randy he would kill him next time he saw him with Lisa, took a serious swing at Randy, missed, and struck Ludwig Jones, a local accountant, who was sitting at the next table and had been in the process of hurrying himself and his date away from the scene. The blow broke Ludwig's glasses and his nose, causing him to bleed profusely over his shirt and trousers.   8

Later, Jason apologized to Ludwig and Randy apologized to Jason for shoving him and calling him a name. Jason lost his job over the incident, but has managed to patch things up with Lisa and with Randy. Ludwig, however, after relating the incident to his law-student brother-in-law in Detroit, decided to sue Jason for his broken glasses, his medical and cleaning bills, and damage to his car occurring when, upset at the incident, he had accidentally backed into Mr. Gordon's BMW on his way out of the parking lot. Police investigation of the accident revealed that Ludwig's blood alcohol was above the legal limit and he was cited for driving while intoxicated.   9

Write an analysis of Ludwig's claims, discussing which, if any, of the injuries to person or property Jason may be liable for because of the incident. Use the following rules: 10

1. **Battery.** The harmful or offensive touching of another that is intentional, unprivileged, and unconsented.
2. **Transfer of Intent.** If a person intentionally directs force against one person wrongfully but, instead, hits another, his intent is transferred from one to the other and he is liable to the other though he did intend the injuries sustained.
3. **Self-Defense Privilege.** A person is justified in the use of force against an aggressor when and to the extent he reasonably believes that such conduct is necessary to defend himself or another against such aggressor's imminent use of unlawful force. The force exerted must be comensurate with the threat posed and the defendant is allowed to make a reasonable mistake as to the necessity of self-defense.

Exercise 3: Jail Bird

Alfred Peck was released from prison in 1996 after serving eleven years for a crime he did not commit. He had been tried and convicted for bank robbery after Miss Nell Greer had picked him out of a line-up and, with the concurrence of another bank teller, had sworn he was the man who had worn a chicken outfit and held up her bank branch. Nell wasn't fooled. She knew Alfred to be a regular bank customer. He had a distinctive bird-like face, a chirping voice, a round, plump body. Besides, chicken feathers were found in his small apartment along with a wad of marked twenties. Alfred's own mother had testified against him, denying him the alibi that might have proved him innocent.

Then in 1995, Alfred's mother went to the district attorney, confessed that she had committed the crime herself, and even produced the chicken outfit she had worn and the remainder of the money. "I never did spend any of it. I just wanted to find a way to get that kid outta the house. Jeez, he was thirty, didn't have no job, no girlfriend. He was just a couch potato loser. At least in the prison yard they got social opportunities."

The D.A. was, of course, skeptical of her story—until she donned the chicken costume, flapped her wings, and terrified his office staff with a .38 pistol identical to that used in the robbery eleven years earlier. He had to admit the family resemblance was uncanny.

So Alfred was released and Mrs. Peck was sent to the state mental hospital for observation after she claimed a dozen colored Easter eggs she left behind in the D.A.'s office were laid by her.

Alfred was disappointed to learn that he had no legal recourse against those who had falsely identified him, nor against the system that had done him wrong, but in prison he had learned a trade: he had become not a bad cook. Thinking it might be good public relations, the bank gave him a no-interest loan to get his life back on track. Within six months, Alfred had opened up a fried chicken restaurant. The restaurant, called "The Jail Bird," became a popular hangout and quickly threatened to ruin the KFC franchise across the street.

The franchise manager, Dicky Purlane, grew alarmed at his rival's success, and told his employees that Alfred, being an ex-con, must be attracting the criminal element to the restaurant. "He may not be the chicken bandito, but he's still an ex-con," Dicky reasoned. "Why, it's only logical. Those guys might have any kind of criminal background and they do stick together. God only knows what he learned in prison." Lucy Miller, 16, one of his employees, told her father that her boss said the employees at The Jail Bird were escaped convicts, and Mr. Miller, a retired police officer, prepared a petition, accusing Alfred of hiring ex-convicts and subjecting both his customers and the community to the danger of perverts, sex fiends, and murderers. He secured over three thousand signatures demanding that the city council take action to close "The Jail Bird" down as a public nuisance. Alfred's business fell off dramatically, even though subsequent investigation found that only one of Alfred's employees had a criminal record, and that was his accountant, who had been arrested in 1964 for indecent exposure at the YMCA.

Discuss the possible liabilities of Dicky Purlane, Lucy Miller, and Mr. Miller   17
using the rules and precedents below. In writing your discussion you need
quote rules in their entirety only once.

1. **Defamation.** Unprivileged written or oral statements made to third parties tending to harm the reputation of plaintiff or hold him up to contempt or ridicule.
2. ***Craig v. Wright.*** Truth of defamation is a complete defense—even if the communication was made out of pure spite and even if defendant did not believe the statement was true at the time he or she made it.
3. **Conditional Privilege Doctrine.** Defendant may be privileged to defame another if he had a correct or reasonable belief that some important interest in person or property is threatened.
4. **Constitutional Privilege.** The First Amendment protects statements concerning "public officials" and "public figures" and severely circumscribes the occasions when such a plaintiff may recover for defamation.
5. ***Gertz v. Welch.*** A person may be deemed a public figure when (a) he has achieved such pervasive notoriety that he becomes a public figure for all purposes and contexts (e.g., celebrity sports figure) or more commonly, (b) where he voluntarily injects himself or is drawn into a particular public controversy and thereby becomes a public figure for that limited range of issues.
6. ***Magnusson v. Record.*** A person who repeats defamatory statements is as liable to the injured party as one who originates the defamation.

Models for the Opening Statement
and the Closing Argument

Some of the writing assignments in this text ask you to imagine that you are either the plaintiff's attorney (if arguing a civil case), the state's attorney (if arguing a criminal case), or the defendant's attorney. Although you have doubtless heard numerous opening and closing statements on TV and in movies (one trial lawyer noted that the prosecutor's opening statement in the Joe Pesci film My Cousin Vinnie *was "absolutely classical"), you may be unsure about what kinds of things should be covered in such statements. We offer the following two statements as models.*

Although in both opening and closing statements, the attorney reviews the facts of the case at hand, the closing statement is more properly called a closing argument. *In the opening statement, the attorney is not supposed to make arguments, since no evidence has yet been introduced. Essentially, in the opening statement, the plaintiff's attorney or the prosecutor recounts the events that led to the trial (paying particular attention to the "hooks," or attention-getting opening sentences), summarizes the key evidence against the defendant(s), describes the witnesses who will be called to testify, explains the main legal principles of the case, and in general tries to create a favorable impression to the judge and jury for her or his side of the case. The defendant's attorney will, of course, go over some of the same elements of the case, but will emphasize those aspects of the facts and the law that refute the assertions of the opposing side and that place the defendant in the most favorable light.*[1]

The closing argument is made after all witnesses have been called to testify and all evidence has been introduced. Normally, the plaintiff's attorney speaks first, the defendant's attorney gives his argument, and the plaintiff's attorney finishes with a rebuttal to the defendant's argument. Both sides make arguments that review the key facts of the case—including the exact sequence of the activities in question—and show how the evidence supports or fails to support the defendant's liability (in a civil trial) or guilt (in a criminal trial). The attorneys may then argue about the kind of inferences that the judge or jury can reasonably draw from the evidence. They will also explain how the law applies or does not apply to the defendant's actions. Both sides may refer to claims made in their or their opponent's opening statements, showing how the evidence introduced at trial supports or does not support the claims made in those statements. The judge will limit the plaintiff's attorney's arguments if he or she believes that he is arguing inferences based on facts that have not been placed into evidence. The prosecutor also may not tell the jury his or her personal opinion about the merits of the case, unless that opinion is based on evidence introduced at trial.[2]

One commentator has summed up the role of the closing argument in this way:

> *Closing argument is your opportunity to wrap a ribbon around the trial package you have crafted. You should capture the attention of the jurors by eloquently restating the themes of your case, reminding them of the framework on which your argument rests. Your argument should be persuasive*

---

[1]James J. Brosnahan, *Trial Handbook for California Lawyers.* San Francisco: Brancroft-Whitney, 1974: 120.
[2]Brosnahan, 399–400.

but not dogmatic. The jurors should feel that you know the decision is
theirs, not yours—and that you trust them to make the right choice.[3]

The sample opening statement in this selection first appeared in "Opening
Statements: Lasting Impressions," which appeared in Trial, *June 1999. The*
closing argument appeared in a treatise *on "Sexual Harassment" by B. Henry*
Allgood in 62 American Jurisprudence Trials *235 (1977). For brevity's sake, the*
statement has been edited to remove the discussion of "hostile work environment."

Opening Statement*

Sheldon J. Stark *of Royal Oak, Michigan, developed this opening statement for*   1
a case brought under the Michigan Handicapper's Civil Rights Act, now the
Michigan Persons with Disabilities Civil Rights Act. The case involved a 63-
year-old Wayne County, Michigan, employee, Ty Griffin, who had suffered two
heart attacks. Although Griffin's physician approved his return to work
without restrictions, the county's independent medical examiner (IME)
declared him "the most disabled man" he had ever seen, and Griffin was fired.

Stark used a day-in-the-life video of Griffin after his recuperation to refute   2
the IME's assertion. The video showed Griffin carrying a ladder, painting,
using a sledge hammer, building a deck, and climbing the roof of a home he was
restoring.

The jury found in Griffin's favor and awarded a large sum in damages. The   3
judge ordered his reinstatement. The case settled on appeal. (Griffin v. County
of Wayne, No. 92-216404-NZ (Mich., Wayne County Cir. Ct. June 26, 1995).)

There are people in this world who live to work and people in this world who   4
work to live. Tyler Griffin is one of the people in this world who lives to work.

Tyler Griffin loved his job. His job was his passion, his job was his life, his job   5
was his joy.

This case is about Tyler Griffin's effort to recover his job. Tyler Griffin, known   6
as Ty to his friends, was the claims manager for Wayne County, Michigan, in the
risk management department. He supervised the processing of workers' compensation and injury claims against the county. In essence, it was a desk job.

In August 1990, Mr. Griffin had a heart attack. In December, while he was   7
recuperating, one of the grafts from the triple-bypass surgery closed, and Mr.
Griffin had another heart attack. Mr. Griffin took medical leave from Wayne
County. He was placed on long-term disability.

Even though he had been very ill, the following summer Mr. Griffin completed   8
a rigorous cardiac rehabilitation program supervised by his physician and was
ready to return to work. The County of Wayne refused to let him come back

---

[3]Bob Gibbons, "Closing Argument: Consolidating Your Theme." *Trial* (Jan. 1990): 83.
*"Opening Statements: Lasting Impressions," *Trial* (June 1999): 64–66.

despite the fact that both of Mr. Griffin's doctors authorized him to return without restrictions.

The county refused to let him return to work despite the fact that he said, "I'm 9 ready to return to work. I want to return to work." It refused him despite the fact that Mr. Griffin was physically fit. The county wouldn't let Mr. Griffin return despite the fact that his heart condition was unrelated to his ability to do his job.

By refusing to let him work, the county violated a Michigan law that prohibits 10 discrimination against those with a handicap or disability or the history of a handicap or disability when the condition does not interfere with and is unrelated to the employee's ability to do the job.

We're going to ask you, members of the jury, to determine whether Mr. Griffin 11 was ready and able to return to work without restrictions in the summer of 1991 and whether Wayne County's refusal to take him back was unlawful discrimination because of his handicap.

In pretrial proceedings, the county claimed it didn't know Ty Griffin was ready 12 to return to work. We intend to put in evidence to show you that's a pretext, that it just isn't so.

We'll prove that Ty Griffin was one of those employees who, even when out on 13 medical leave, go to the office to say hello, talk to folks. Mr. Griffin was there often—maybe half a dozen times, maybe more. He told people every step of the way, "My cardiac rehab is going good. I'm feeling good. I'm getting stronger every day."

He also called regularly, and to the county's credit, Mr. Griffin's supervisors 14 liked him. They called him regularly and asked, "How are you doing, Ty?" And he would tell them he was ready to return to work.

The county claimed it didn't have an updated report from Mr. Griffin's doctor 15 authorizing his return to work. That's a pretext, too. Mr. Griffin asked on several occasions, "Do you need any medical reports? Do you need anything in writing from my doctor? I've got time on my hands. I could get it for you."

As his wife, Audrey, will tell you Mr. Griffin had fixed everything in the house 16 and was begging her to break something so he could fix it.

Wayne County now acknowledges that Mr. Griffin's doctor had released him 17 to return to work. Joel Mowrey, the Deputy Director of the risk management department, put a note in Mr. Griffin's long-term disability file. The note reads, "Ty got a return to work. He is at our disposal." The county knew Mr. Griffin was ready to return to work. The county didn't ask him for anything from his doctor.

The county scheduled a medical appointment for Mr. Griffin with an indepen- 18 dent medical examiner, Dr. Shapiro. In August 1991, Mr. Griffin went to the county office before he went to Dr. Shapiro's office. He said, "Gang, I am going to be back Monday. Really, Monday."

He knew there would be some paperwork to complete, but he fully expected 19 to pass that medical exam with flying colors because he was feeling good.

There was no mystery about Mr. Griffin's ability to return to work in the 20 summer of 1991. The county knew it.

The principle defense you will hear in this case is that Dr. Shapiro was a 21 respectable doctor who found Mr. Griffin to be totally and permanently disabled on the basis of ischemic heart disease. With this disease, the arteries start to close from deposits. When the arteries close completely, a person has a heart attack.

The county claims it had full confidence in this doctor. We've taken Dr. 22 Shapiro's testimony by videotape, and you will see him testify. We think that when you see his video, you will have some questions. Dr. Shapiro is not board certified in cardiology. That means the American Board of Cardiology has never certified him as an expert in cardiology.

Both of Mr. Griffin's treating doctors are board-certified internists, and his 23 cardiac doctor is board certified in cardiology.

Dr. Shapiro saw Mr. Griffin only once. At most, he spent an hour and a half to 24 two hours with Mr. Griffin. Dr. Shapiro ran a treadmill test and took Mr. Griffin off the treadmill test before he was exhausted.

The electrocardiogram showed no significant changes in the functioning of 25 his heart. The EKG only showed that this was a man who had had heart attacks. Despite the EKG, Dr. Shapiro tried to talk Mr. Griffin into wanting to retire.

I took Dr. Shapiro's testimony on videotape after I had seen a videotape of Mr. 26 Griffin working on a house in Pinehurst, North Carolina. I asked the doctor during his deposition, "Can Mr. Griffin climb up and down ladders?"

"No." 27

"Can he break up pieces of concrete with a five-pound hammer?" 28

"I wouldn't expect that." 29

I asked Dr. Shapiro if he would expect Mr. Griffin to do any of these things. 30 Again his words were, "Not only would I not expect it, I doubt he ever did it."

Well, you will see it. You will see it. 31

Now, on the basis of that report—ignoring the evidence of Mr. Griffin's own 32 doctors who had actually treated him and been responsible for him—Mr. Griffin was fired.

Needless to say, Mr. Griffin was shocked and upset. He expected to return to 33 work. He was more fit than he had been in years. He had gone through a cardiac rehab program; had developed healthier habits than he had had in a long time; never stopped walking 2 miles a day, riding a bike 3 times a week, 10 to 15 miles an hour, 5 miles a shot. And he was fired.

Had Mr. Griffin's doctor, Dr. Miller, missed something? 34

Mr. Griffin went to Dr. Miller, and Dr. Miller ran a sophisticated stress test 35 called MUGA, which measures muscles and the heart's pumping action. Mr. Griffin passed. There was no problem.

Dr. Miller obtained the strips from the stress test Dr. Shapiro ran. Dr. Miller 36 examined the strips, and he said that they did not show a problem, that Mr. Griffin was fine, that he was ready and able to return to work.

The law forbids discrimination on the basis of a handicap. Wayne County fired 37 Mr. Griffin either because he had heart disease or a history of heart disease.

To complain that you have been a victim of handicap discrimination, you must 38 be able to be defined as a "handicapper." And to bring a handicap discrimination case, you have to prove that the condition is unrelated to your ability to work.

Here's the law. A handicap is a determinable physical characteristic of an individual that may result from disease. Ischemic heart disease is a determinable physical characteristic. 39

Mr. Griffin's ischemic heart disease was unrelated to his ability to do the job. His doctors said so. Wayne County's doctor said Mr. Griffin wasn't able to work, and that's why the county fired him. 40

If the heart disease was related to Mr. Griffin's ability to do the work, and you so find, then you find for the county. If you find that the heart disease was unrelated to his ability to do the work, we'll ask that you find for Mr. Griffin. 41

If you do find that Mr. Griffin was discriminated against—that his heart condition was unrelated to his ability to do the work—we are going to ask you to fashion a remedy to compensate him for what he has lost and for what he has gone through as a result of what happened. 42

Now, we can't ask you to reinstate Mr. Griffin, but we are going to ask the judge to do so at the end of this trial. We're not asking you for future damages because Mr. Griffin wants to return to work at Wayne County. 43

We will ask you for full and fair compensation for what Mr. Griffin has gone through, and that includes noneconomic as well as economic damages. 44

Work Ethic

Ty Griffin is a man who was raised at a time when the essence of being a man was working for a living and bringing home the bacon. Wayne County took that away from Mr. Griffin. That humiliated him. Mr. Griffin had told everybody at the office, "I'm coming back." To have to tell people, "They fired me because they say I'm disabled" knocked the pillars out from under him. 45

Mr. Griffin's job was handling county workers' compensation and injury claims. He didn't have a claim. but the county forced him to be disabled. He didn't want to be. He wanted to return to work. His dignity came from being a productive member of society. That's who Mr. Griffin was, and he doesn't have that now. 46

Identity Threatened

You will learn about his sleeplessness. You will learn about his inability to have a meal because he just didn't feel like eating for a period. Not being allowed to work threatened the very identity of the man. For four years, Mr. Griffin has not been allowed to do the work that made him want to get up every morning and get to the office. 47

It's like telling a great chef to stay out of the kitchen; like telling a cowboy, "You can't roam"; like telling a race driver, "You can no longer be in the driver's seat." 48

Evaluate the injury, that blow, that pain. Translate it into a jury verdict to remedy this wrong. 49

We're confident that you will listen to the evidence and that you will evaluate the credibility of the doctors and all the witnesses. And we're confident that at the end of this case you will do the right thing. 50

Closing Argument*

Ladies and gentlemen of the jury, on behalf of my client and myself I would like   51
to thank you for your patience and your attention over the past several days. As
you know, both sides have now completed the presentation of evidence and you
will shortly be asked to deliberate and to render a verdict based upon the evidence that you have heard and seen over the course of the trial. Before you do I
would like to take a few moments to discuss some of the evidence and testimony
that I believe will be most important to your deliberations.

You may remember that, at the start of this trial, in my opening statement, I   52
explained that my client has asserted claims for two forms of actionable work
place sexual harassment: quid pro quo and hostile work environment. What I
would like to do now is to discuss the evidence that we have presented to prove
that [the plaintiff] was subjected to both of these forms of sexual harassment and,
then, to discuss what we believe would be an appropriate damage award given
the evidence presented.

We have first alleged a case of quid pro quo sexual harassment, and, in a few   53
moments, the judge will charge you on the specific elements of this cause of
action. In essence, I expect that you will learn from the judge's instructions that
quid pro quo sexual harassment occurs where a supervisor penalizes an employee
for refusing to provide sexual favors upon request.

In this case, we have established a classic case of quid pro quo sexual harass-   54
ment. In fact, I expect that as you listen to the judge's instructions on this issue
you will somewhat unavoidably think of [individual defendant] and his actions in
dealing with my client.

You probably know the evidence to which I am referring in labeling this a   55
classic quid pro quo case. You have heard, for instance, that [individual defendant],
on [plaintiff's] very first day of work informed her that she would do very well with
the restaurant as long as she used her body in the right way. You have also heard
from my client how [individual defendant] on numerous occasions, and in a pro-
gressively more graphic fashion, asked for sexual favors. He started out politely
enough by merely asking [plaintiff] for drinks. She was not interested in a social
relationship and therefore exercised her prerogative to decline the offer. That
should have been all that was needed to end the matter, but, as you know, it wasn't.

Instead, [individual defendant] grew more persistent, and more graphic, in his   56
efforts, and as [plaintiff] continued to reject his demands, he came more to the
point by expressly warning her that negative repercussions would follow from
future rejections. Consistent with his approach, he also indicated that she would
enjoy increased employment benefits if she relented to his demands, and you of
course know of his self-assigned nickname of "Sugar Daddy." You also know that
the pay reduction and unfavorable schedule change occurred immediately after
[individual defendant's] last demand and ultimatum was rejected. Finally, you
have heard how [individual defendant] was, when asked by [plaintiff], unable to

---

*"Illustrative Closing Argument." "Quid Pro Quo" in 62 *American Jurisprudence Trials:* 235,
377–80, 384–86 (1997).

justify these adverse employment actions, but instead continued the harassment by essentially telling my client that her prior pay level could be reacquired only if she finally capitulated to his sexual demands.

The defense in this case is apparently attempting to suggest, and will likely argue   57
in its closing argument, that [plaintiff's] sudden pay reduction and schedule change resulted from some unspecified "bad attitude" and had nothing to do with her immediate supervisor's sex ultimatum. In the defendants' view this express ultimatum, which was communicated the last night [plaintiff] worked, was simply a coincidence in timing. I am confident, however, that you will find from the evidence that nothing could be further from the truth. You have heard how [assistant manager] demanded sexual favors from my client on a regular basis. You have heard that on my client's last night of work before the pay reduction and schedule change was announced [assistant manager] directly warned my client that she would pay if she did not capitulate that night. This, I submit, is not the stuff of mere coincidence.

And I want to emphasize that we are not relying solely upon [plaintiff's] testi-   58
mony to disprove this defense. In fact, we are relying heavily upon the defendants' own records and actions to establish that [plaintiff] was performing exceptionally and was literally the last employee in need of disciplinary action. For example, when you consider this concocted argument that my client exemplified a bad work attitude, I would like for you to consider her last performance review, which took place a mere six weeks before the schedule change and pay reduction went into effect.

What happened in that review? For one thing, [assistant manager] completed   59
a written performance review, which you will see during your deliberations, and which I urge you to closely study. You will see how the assistant manager, in his own handwriting, noted that my client was performing exceptionally in every measured performance category, including that of attitude. Ask yourselves if such a document would be generated for an employee whose attitude was poor, much less for one on the brink of disciplinary action. What else happened in that six month performance review? In addition to receiving a stellar written performance evaluation, [plaintiff] very consistently received an exceptional pay raise. In fact, the evidence has established that [plaintiff] received an unprecedented merit based pay increase. I ask you, why on earth would the company issue an unprecedented ten percent merit pay increase to an employee whose attitude was so unacceptable that she was on the verge of a pay reduction?

You also will need to consider the testimony of the various customers of this   60
restaurant who have come here to testify as to their experience with and perception of my client. After all, who could be in a better position to evaluate the work attitude of a restaurant waitress than the customers whom she serves? And as you consider this testimony please bear in mind that all of these individuals are independent witnesses with no interest in the outcome of the case. These customers, many of whom were served by [plaintiff] within days of her pay reduction and schedule change, have all quite consistently verified that [plaintiff] reflected nothing but a pleasant and professional attitude at all times. And remember too that the defense has been unable to counter this testimony with a single independent witness. The reason they have failed to do so is simply because they cannot.

This entire bad attitude defense is nothing but a pretext, an excuse manufactured after the fact in an effort to justify the illegal conduct of [assistant manager].

The evidence, when viewed objectively and in its entirety, can support only   61 one conclusion: that [plaintiff] was punished for refusing to sleep with her supervisor. By doing this, the defendants subjected my client to unlawful quid pro quo sexual harassment, and she should be compensated for this.

There is just one more point that I would like to address before leaving the issue   62 of the quid pro quo claim. I will return to this point a few minutes later when I discuss the damages we are seeking, and it is the point of the employer's response. You will learn from the judge's instructions that an employer cannot defend a claim of quid pro quo sexual harassment by contending that it was unaware that the harassment was taking place. But it is important in this case to remember that upper level management was specifically apprised of [assistant manager's] conduct as it was occurring. Remember, [plaintiff] approached the general manager to report her supervisor's conduct and to ask for it to be addressed. And how did [general manager] respond? He told her "if you're really worried about it, just give him a piece and be done with it." I urge you to consider this response as you determine the appropriate amount of damages to be awarded. . . .

As a result of the sexual harassment that we have proven took place, we are   63 asking you to award two types of damages. The first is known as compensatory damages, which, as the name suggests, are intended to compensate the plaintiff for damages suffered. I imagine that you may have some difficulty determining an amount of damages that could possibly compensate a woman for being humiliated at work on a daily basis, and I urge you to consider this important issue carefully. In particular, I ask you to consider exactly what the defendant did in this case.

Consider, for example, the humiliation [plaintiff] must have felt when her   64 immediate supervisor asked her to perform [sexual acts]. . . . Consider the level of stress that [plaintiff] experienced as she went to work each day knowing she would be subjected to obscene comments and gestures from co-workers and from her superiors. Think of the frustration she experienced as her civil rights were disregarded by an employer who actually laughed at her for expecting anything different. And consider too the apprehension caused by her immediate supervisor's threats and ultimatums.

In addition to compensatory damages, we are asking you to award an amount   65 of punitive damages, which are damages intended to deter the defendant from acting similarly in the future. Here, too, I expect that you will need to give some amount of thought to the proper amount and you will again need to look closely at everything the defendants did and, perhaps more importantly, what they did not do. I would like to take those in reverse order.

As for what they did not do, the employer did not bother to follow its own set   66 procedures established to prevent exactly what happened in this case. For example, you heard from [general manager] that the company routinely checks applicant references in order to determine if the prospective employee may present a risk of harm to customers or to other employees. They did not, however, feel the need to check the references listed by [individual defendant].

We know that if they had, they would have learned of his history of sexual harassment.

The company also failed to follow its own procedures with respect to the complaint of sexual harassment that [plaintiff] made. Again, the general manager informed us of what the company was supposed to do in response. The management was supposed to investigate the matter, they were supposed to admonish the offenders, and they were supposed to document the incident. They were also supposed to have the principal offenders sign statements cautioning against inappropriate behavior. For some reason, however, the company did none of these things, and they did nothing because they did not care about the problem and, frankly, they did not want to be bothered by it.   67

Instead of taking actions to correct this serious work problem, the management laughed, literally, at the report. The general manager advised [plaintiff] to just take the foul language and the offensive touching, somehow, as a compliment. He also told her that she should expect things like this to happen. And what was his response to my client's report that her immediate supervisor was demanding sexual favors and was threatening adverse employment action as a penalty for not capitulating? His response was that she should "just give him a piece and be done with it."   68

All of this was clearly inappropriate. More than that, the company's response shows a clear recklessness and unconcern over what was happening. Instead of fulfilling their duty to rid the work environment of sexual harassment, they laughed at it. Ultimately, they in fact exacerbated the problem by causing the conduct to continue in such a fashion that employees laughed at the notion of it being reported again.   69

As I stated earlier, the purpose of punitive damages is to deter a defendant from conducting itself similarly in the future. In this case, a punitive damages award is badly needed so that the defendant will not allow such behavior to run rampant through its work place, so that it will follow reasonable procedures to prevent sexual harassment, and so that it will take seriously the next report of harassment. In short, some amount of punitive damages is necessary to impress upon this company the need for it to abide by its duties and to respect its employees rights. Again, it is for you to determine the appropriate amount of punitive damages, and I ask only that you consider carefully all of the evidence in doing so.   70

● ● ● ●

Discussion and Writing Topics

1. Analyze either the opening statement or the closing argument. How is it organized? What is the sequence of topics? Discuss the probable logic behind this sequence. Consider also the statement's *tone*—that is, the author's emotional response toward the subject matter—and *language* (legalistic? conversational?). How do you think that the statement's content, the tone, and language are intended to work upon the jury? That is, what does the statement's author appear to believe about the psychology of the jury members concerning the events under consideration and their presentation in court?

2. Select either the opening statement or the closing argument and discuss how it incorporates some of Joel ben Izzy's "10 Ways to Know If your Story is Ready to Tell in Court" (pp. 76–80).
3. Select one of the cases in this text and compose either an opening statement or a closing argument based on the facts of that case. Model your response on the kind of material and the style of argument provided in the statements in this selection. In your statement, attempt to anticipate the arguments that will be made by opposing counsel.
4. Select a dispute with which you are familiar. It may be a real dispute—and not necessarily one that has ended up in court—or it may be a fictional dispute. For example, suppose that Lady Macbeth were brought up on charges of being an accessory to murder. Or suppose the man who built the *Titanic* was indicted for gross negligence. Then again, suppose one of your English teachers repeatedly refused to acknowledge the actual quality of your work, or suppose that you bring charges against your cat for vandalizing your sofa and other acts of destructive behavior. Compose an opening statement or a closing argument for your case, modeled on the ones provided in this selection. In your statement, attempt to anticipate the arguments that will be made by opposing counsel.

3

Emotional Distress

> Against a large part of the frictions and irritations and clashing of tempera-
> ments incident to participation in a community life, a certain toughening of the
> mental hide is a better protection than the law could be. . . . No pressing social
> need requires that every abusive outburst be converted into a tort; upon the
> contrary, it would be unfortunate if the law closed all the safety valves through
> which irascible tempers might legally blow off steam.
> —Calvert Magruder, "Mental and Emotional Disturbance in
> the Law of Torts," 49 *Harvard Law Review* 1033 (1936)

In 1990, a Bakersfield, California, couple sued their nineteen-year-old neighbor
for shooting hoops in his back yard at night. The pair charged the pro basketball
hopeful with infliction of emotional distress. That same year two passengers witnessed a fatal accident in a Palm Springs tramway ride. They themselves were not
physically injured, and they did not know the woman who was killed, but they
sued the tram company for emotional distress. In 1997 actor Brad Pitt filed an
emotional distress suit against *Playgirl* magazine for publishing nude shots of
him and his girlfriend Gwyneth Paltrow taken while the couple were vacationing
in the French West Indies.

Such cases seem to confirm the public's suspicions that all emotional distress
cases are trivial or ridiculous and are filed primarily by greedy clients and their
greedy lawyers for the sole purpose of making easy money. But while it's true that
numerous emotional distress claims are bogus, it's also true that many people
who suffer genuine and severe emotional distress as a direct result of the malice
or the negligence of others often have no other recourse than the law if they hope
for restitution.

Even the silly claims are often filed by people who have suffered genuine emotional distress. The question is whether anyone who inflicts emotional distress on
another should be hauled into court. If we sued everyone who inflicted emotional
distress on us, we'd sue our parents for not letting us have our own cell phone,
our bratty siblings on general principles, our girlfriends or boyfriends for
breaking up with us, our teachers for not giving us A's, our employers for not
paying us what we're really worth, and on and on. To be human is to be (at least
some of the time) emotionally distressed. So where do we draw the line between
legitimate and illegitimate claims?

One important distinction, of course, is between minor and severe emotional distress (sometimes termed "mental anguish"). Another is between distress that has

been intentionally inflicted and distress that has been unintentionally or negligently inflicted. For example, a collection agency that threatens a debtor with bodily harm unless he pays up might be liable for intentional infliction of emotional distress, even though the debtor suffers no physical harm. Another person might be liable for unintentional infliction of emotional distress to a parent if his negligence causes an automobile accident in which the parent's child is killed.

Suits for emotional distress are a relatively recent development in the law (although scholars often cite a fourteenth-century case in which a tavern keeper's wife charged emotional distress against an irate customer who had thrown a hatchet at her). And generally, courts have been more inclined to allow lawsuits for intentional than for unintentional infliction of emotional distress. They have argued that emotional distress caused by an act of negligence is usually a side effect of the physical damage (or, to use the legal term, the "impact") caused by that act, and so the defendant should be properly be sued for causing this physical damage. According to this line of reasoning, it is more appropriate to sue the defendant for negligently causing death or injury than to sue for the emotional distress occasioned by this death or injury. If a negligent act has caused emotional distress alone, without physical injury, then (the courts have reasoned) its seriousness is difficult to gauge, and, in any case, the negligent defendant can be held only indirectly responsible. By its very nature, emotional distress is more intangible and subjective than physical damage; it is harder to assess and to verify, easier to fake. Many judges are wary of opening the doors to emotional distress claims wider than they already are, for fear of being deluged with cases of "social rudeness" and garden-variety embarrassment, and with the kind of cases cited at the start of this introduction.

In recent years, however, more judges have been willing to allow claims for mental distress unaccompanied by physical damage. Definitions and illustrations of "severe emotional distress" have been incorporated into the law and provided to juries hearing such cases. Distinctions have been drawn between petty annoyances and outrageous behavior, between the trivial and the serious, between the fraudulent and the genuine, between the transitory and the enduring.

In this chapter, we explore some of the varieties of emotional distress. We begin with a group of readings—commentary and cases—that places the issue of emotional distress in a social context and suggests something of the range of disputes in this area. A second group of readings narrows the focus to insults and harassment by creditors. It includes both cases and statements on the law, as it applies to emotional distress. (This is typical of the composition of selections in reading groups throughout the chapters in this book.) The third group of readings focuses on emotional distress caused by sexual predators. It includes a description of a common legal construct—the "reasonable person"—who is often posited as the ideal standard of behavior and response to a given situation. (A reasonable person would do this. She or he would *not* do that. Compare the behavior of this reasonable person to the defendant's behavior.) The fourth group focuses on emotional distress occasioned in people who have witnessed accidents that have resulted in the death or serious injury of their loved ones.

This chapter also includes the first of a series of *model student essays* in this book. A student responds to a typical assignment, writes a first and a final draft, and comments on the process of planning, organizing, composing, and revising the essay. Such drafts and commentaries should be helpful as you compose your own responses to many of the assignments in this book.

As with the other chapters in *Making the Case*, the readings and the suggestions "For Deliberation and Argument" that follow each group provide opportunities to practice your analytic and rhetorical skills. Playing the role of jury member, attorney for the plaintiff, attorney for the defendant, or just average citizen, you'll hone your ability to argue with logic and cogency, and perhaps even with flourish and flair.

■ Group 1 Readings: *Introductory*

It's no secret that the public has a pretty low opinion of lawyers as a professional class. Many people are convinced that lawyers will sue over anything if they think there's money to be got out of it. This is especially true in cases involving the often intangible and imprecise subject of emotional distress. A physical injury is something definite, perceivable, and difficult to fake—not so (in many cases) an emotional injury. Even the courts have been reluctant and slow to recognize emotional distress as a legitimate basis for legal claims, particularly in those cases where emotional distress results from negligence rather than malice.

Courts have generally shown little sympathy for plaintiffs who have been the victims of disappointment rather than truly outrageous conduct at the hands of others. Of course, not all cases of emotional distress are so groundless. Some people have indeed been victimized by thoughtlessness, negligence, or maliciousness, and in such cases the legal system can sometimes provide recourse. The problem is to devise and then apply a set of standards by which the trivial claim can be distinguished from the legitimate one.

We begin this group of readings with two articles that treat the subject of emotional distress from a social, rather than a legal, perspective. That is, they approach the subject as the public, rather than lawyers, would perceive it (even though one of the authors is in fact an attorney). Howie Carr's "Take $2000 and Call Me in the Morning" is an abridgement of a column that originally appeared in the Boston Globe. *"The Case of the Tardy Rabbi" by David Margolick, was first printed in the* New York Times. *"The Spelling Bee," McDonald v. Scripps Newspaper, was heard in the California Court of Appeal in May 1989.*[1]

In "Photojournalism, Ethics, and the Law," Mike Sherer, who teaches photojournalism and media law at the University of Nebraska at Omaha, describes another case of a plaintiff claiming infliction of emotional distress.

---

[1]As with all the cases presented in this book, the text is taken from the decision written by one or more of the judges on the majority side of the verdict. (A legal decision is generally preceded by an account of the facts of the case.) Judges on the minority side may, if they choose, write dissenting opinions, but these dissents, while often rhetorically powerful and persuasive, have no legal force, either for the present or for future cases.

"The Cat in the Casket" was heard in the Civil Court of the City of New York, Queens County, in 1979. "Shunned by Jehovah's Witnesses" was heard in the U.S. Court of Appeals, Ninth Circuit, in 1987.

Next, we present a composite of "Judge's Instructions to the Jury on the Intentional Infliction of Emotional Distress." At the conclusion of a trial, the judge will instruct the jury on the law or laws that they must apply to the case that they have heard. These instructions summarize in plain and relatively simple terms the often complex language of the actual law. Many of the cases in this book will be accompanied by the standard California jury instructions.[2]

As also with the other cases presented in this book, we purposely omit the part of the decision that reveals whether the court decided for the plaintiff or the defendant. This is not to intentionally inflict emotional distress upon you (although it may do so), but rather to encourage full discussion and debate on the issues presented by the case and to prevent your being unduly influenced by its actual outcome. When your instructor judges the time right, she or he will consult the Instructor's Manual *and inform you of the actual verdict and the court's reasoning.*

In any case, the point is not to guess the "right" verdict but rather to argue logically and persuasively, applying the rules to the facts of the case— or, more broadly, to apply general principles to specific facts, so that you can draw well-reasoned conclusions. The actual outcome of a case may not be readily knowable, as the parties may eventually have settled out of court (such settlements generally being confidential) or the case may have been remanded back to the lower court for retrial.

Take $2,000 and Call Me in the Morning

Howie Carr

A new disease is stalking my home state. It's called Emotional Distress. I learned about ED while perusing the 1994 report of the Massachusetts Commission Against Discrimination (MCAD). Almost everything causes ED. But thank goodness this new malady is treatable—with massive doses of legal tender.   1

Boston Herald, 9 Mar. 1995.

[2] While laws on any given subject vary from state to state, many of the civil—as opposed to criminal—laws in the United States are based on the *Restatements* (see Group 2 Readings), legal references that attempt to standardize the law, and that are accepted by courts in most jurisdictions as the equivalent of statutory law—that is, law passed by legislatures.

Here are some of the people recently cured of Emotional Distress through the   2
dollars prescribed by MCAD:

- A woman, seven months pregnant, applied for a job as a bartender and
  was turned down. MCAD found her ED-positive.
  Prescription: 15,000 greenbacks.
- A guy who's completely deaf in one ear wanted to be a policeman, but his
  city would not hire him because he wasn't "capable of performing the
  essential functions of the job without risk of injury to himself or others."
  Prescription: $25,000 and a job as a cop.
- A female cop in a town north of Boston was told to remain at the police
  station while her colleagues—"men of imposing size"—went on a drug
  raid. A commissioner/physician from MCAD diagnosed this as "the kind of
  stereotypic thinking which the anti-discrimination laws forbid."
  Prescription for this full-blown case of ED: $25,000.

Here's my favorite: A paraplegic has a "legal aid dog," which I guess is like a   3
Seeing Eye dog. Trouble is, this hound apparently tends to confuse restaurants
with fire hydrants. When the owner of one establishment recognized the canine
as the same one that had recently defiled his floor, he told the paraplegic "to leave
the dog outside."

Now, that's ED. Ruled the MCAD hearing officer: "The exclusion of the legal   4
aid dog based on one incident was discriminatory."

Prescription: 5000 pictures of George Washington.   5

You read MCAD's annual report and you don't know whether to laugh or cry.   6
Is *everybody* walking around with a chip on his shoulder? Is *everybody* entitled to
everything?

People file because they have chronic-fatigue syndrome, a sleeping disorder,   7
dyslexia or even "an emotional condition which manifests itself in an extreme
need for personal safety." (She got $97,500.) They file because they're black and
because they're white. They file because they're from Cape Verde, Haiti or
Bombay. Now they've all moved here to Victim Nation, and they've all been struck
down by ED.

A teen-age mother with a 2-year-old kid got her father to file a grievance   8
against a landlord who didn't want to rent to her. No answer as to why her father
wasn't able to find room for his daughter and grandchild to live with him, but he
was available to grab some ED cash—all $3000 of it.

And there's the guy who is legally blind without glasses and had no driver's   9
license, yet went after a company that wouldn't hire him as an auto mechanic. ED
cure: $20,000.

I could go on—and on and on— but I'm sick. You guessed it. After reading this   10
report, I've come down with a full-blown case of ED. Who do *I* sue?

The Case of the Tardy Rabbi

David Margolick

The story could be called "Saturday the Rabbi Arrived Late," though just how late   1
remains in dispute. Or, if you prefer something more musical, it could be "Get Me
to the Synagogue on Time." It's also listed as *Adler v. Frank* in the Broward
County Circuit.

The most recent entry into the bizarre litigation sweepstakes comes from Fort   2
Lauderdale, Fla., where Rabbi Loring J. Frank had united two young lawyers,
Russell B. and Christine Adler, in holy matrimony in April 1989. But the rabbi did
so behind schedule, and that has led to a lawsuit.

Mr. Adler, who's a sole practitioner, and Mrs. Adler, a public defender, say   3
Rabbi Frank showed up for the ceremony an hour and a half late. That, they say,
led to a chain reaction of calamities: an inflated liquor bill, as bored guests took
to drink; vicious gossip that the marriage might be off; for the bride, a long wait
in a stifling room; and for the groom, the re-emergence of an old back injury.

In May, Mr. and Mrs. Adler sued Rabbi Frank for $130,000 in damages—more   4
than seven times the cost of the wedding—for pain and suffering and inconve-
nience. Their lawyer, Kenneth B. Whitman of Fort Lauderdale, said settlement
talks failed after Rabbi Frank offered the aggrieved couple only an inscribed
plaque in his synagogue.

Now they are about to amend their complaint to assert that Rabbi Frank isn't   5
a rabbi at all. As a result, they say, they will have to marry all over again, and plan
to tack on those costs to their damages. Rabbi Frank insists that he is a rabbi, and
that he was only 10 minutes late "at the most." His lawyers call the case a perfect
example of the warping effect of law school and a legal system run amok, in
which people rush off to court for the slightest slight.

"A responsible, seasoned lawyer would never in his wildest dreams either (a)   6
be a plaintiff in this lawsuit or (b) file it for anybody else," said Robert A. Kasky
of Hollywood, Fla., who, along with Eliot Lupkin of Fort Lauderdale, is representing the rabbi. "It shows the depths that some people in our practice will sink.

"The case boils down to a couple of ill-guided children, both of whom have   7
law degrees, trying to squeeze blood out of a rock," he added. "It's just tasteless.
When I first read the complaint, I thought it was a script for 'L.A. Law.' "

The case has already migrated from the pages of *Broward Review*, a local legal   8
weekly ("Newlyweds Sing Wedding-Bell Blues") to *The National Law Journal*
("Day of Bliss Turns into a Bomb") to *The National Enquirer* ("An angry bride and
groom told a tardy rabbi that being late for their wedding wasn't kosher.").

But Mr. Whitman says there's nothing frivolous about the lawsuit. "The only   9
way that people can seek redress for wrongs is to go to court," he said.

The Adler nuptials were held on April 8, 1989, at the Sheraton Bona-Venture   10
Resort and Spa in Fort Lauderdale. Rabbi Frank, who heads the All People's Syn-

"At the Bar." *New York Times*, 27 July 1990: B5.

agogue in South Miami, was paid $300 for his services, and the couple say he was supposed to arrive at 7:30.

Because all of the activities—picture-taking, food and drinks—had been 11 scheduled for after the ceremony, the whole affair was thrown off kilter when the rabbi was 90 minutes late, the couple says. The bride and groom couldn't mill with guests or eat their meal in peace. Worse, the soon-to-be Mrs. Adler was forced to languish in a room with no air-conditioning as she awaited her "grand entrance," resulting in "mental, emotional and physical discomfort and causing a rift between the plaintiffs."

Rabbi Frank does not dispute that he was late; he had been officiating at a bas 12 mitzvah and encountered construction delays on Interstate 595. But he said he arrived with robes on and was "ready to go down the aisle," only to find himself waiting for the the the bride and groom.

He hypothesized that as new lawyers, the Adlers were looking for a high- 13 publicity case to cut their teeth on. He also speculated that they had been pushed into pressing their case by more traditional rabbis who dislike him because he performs inter-faith marriages.

Still, he said, he had received a great outpouring of support, including a letter 14 from a lawyer's wife. "We hope this case receives a hasty dismissal and its plaintiffs a fiery roasting," the woman wrote. Her husband, the woman went on, "views this action with particular disgust because he is a trial lawyer and is all too familiar with hollow causes, dilatory tactics and an increasingly burdened justice system."

How *Adler v. Frank* will be decided is at this point anyone's guess. But it does 15 seem to be in the right courtroom: the judge hearing the case, Stephen Booher, is a former minister, who, he has confessed, once slept through a wedding.

The Spelling Bee

Gavin L. McDONALD, a Minor, etc.,
Plaintiff and Appellant,
v.
JOHN P. SCRIPPS NEWSPAPER, etc.,
et al., Defendants and Respondents.

Civ. B032591.

Court of Appeal, Second District, Division 6.
April 12, 1989.

Gavin was a contestant in the 1987 Scripps Howard National Spelling Bee, spon- 1 sored in Ventura County by the newspaper, the *Ventura County Star–Free Press*. The contest is open to all students through the eighth grade who are under the

---

age of sixteen. Gavin won competitions at the classroom and school-wide levels. This earned him the chance to compete against other skilled spellers in the county-wide spelling bee. The best speller in the county wins a trip to Washington, D.C. and a place in the national finals. The winner of the national finals is declared the national champion speller.

Gavin came in second in the county spelling bee. Being adjudged the second best orthographer in Ventura County is an impressive accomplishment, but pique overcame self-esteem. The spelling contest became a legal contest.   2

We search in vain through the complaint to find a legal theory to support this metamorphosis. Gavin alleges that two other boys, Stephen Chen and Victor Wang, both of whom attended a different school, also competed in the spelling contest. Stephen had originally lost his school-wide competition to Victor. Stephen was asked to spell the word "horsy." He spelled it "h-o-r-s-e-y." The spelling was ruled incorrect. Victor spelled the same word "h-o-r-s-y." He then spelled another word correctly, and was declared the winner.   3

Contest officials, who we trust were not copy editors for the newspaper sponsoring the contest, later discovered that there are two proper spellings of the word "horsy," and that Stephen's spelling was correct after all.   4

Contest officials asked Stephen and Victor to again compete between themselves in order to declare one winner. Victor, having everything to lose by agreeing to this plan, refused. Contest officials decided to allow both Victor and Stephen to advance to the county-wide spelling bee, where Gavin lost to Stephen.   5

Taking Vince Lombardi's aphorism to heart, "Winning isn't everything, it's the only thing," Gavin filed suit against the *Ventura County Star–Free Press* and the Scripps Howard National Spelling Bee alleging breach of contract, breach of implied covenant of good faith and fair dealing, and intentional and negligent infliction of emotional distress.   6

In his complaint, Gavin asserts that contest officials violated spelling bee rules by allowing Stephen Chen to compete at the county level. He suggests that had Stephen not progressed to the county-wide competition, he, Gavin, would have won. For this leap of faith he seeks compensatory and punitive damages. . . .   7

The third cause of action, paragraph 29, states that plaintiff has suffered humiliation, indignity, mortification, worry, grief, anxiety, fright, mental anguish, and emotional distress, not to mention loss of respect and standing in the community. These terms more appropriately express how attorneys who draft complaints like this should feel.   8

A judge whose prescience is exceeded only by his eloquence said that ". . . Courts of Justice do not pretend to furnish cures for all the miseries of human life. They redress or punish gross violations of duty, but they go no farther; they cannot make men virtuous: and, as the happiness of the world depends upon its virtue, there may be much unhappiness in it which human laws cannot undertake to remove." (*Evans v. Evans* (1790) Consistory Court of London.) Unfortunately, as evidenced by this lawsuit, this cogent insight, although as relevant today as it was nearly 200 years ago, does not always make an impression on today's practitioner.   9

Photojournalism, Ethics, and the Law

Mike Sherer

Every photojournalist knows that images of death and destruction carry powerful 1
emotional messages. Run an image of ultimate grief and make way for cries of
outrage from one's audience. Occasionally the emotional impact of ultimate grief
images has led to litigation. People have argued that news photos and/or news
video have hurt them emotionally and physically.

These claims have been made in intentional infliction of emotional distress 2
suits filed against photojournalists and their news organizations.

The key in an intentional infliction of emotional distress suit is the manner in 3
which newsworthy images were gathered and used. The person making this claim
must show that a photojournalist and/or news organization engaged in extremely
outrageous conduct that was either intentional or reckless.

Most of the intentional infliction of emotional distress cases filed against pho- 4
tojournalists and their news organizations have not been successful. Only those
few instances where the behavior was so extreme and outrageous that it went
beyond what is tolerated by a civilized community have resulted in negative
rulings from the courts. Or as one court noted, "There is no occasion for law to
intervene in every case where someone's feelings are hurt."

Unfortunately, there are those rare examples in which a news organization 5
loses sight of how much an image can hurt. Consider, for example, this story:

A reporter and a television news photographer were at a police station gath- 6
ering information about an old murder case. The reporter had learned that the
police had discovered the skull of a six-year-old child who was murdered two
years earlier.

When she arrived, the police chief showed her the skull. After viewing it, the 7
reporter asked the police chief to put the skull back in a box. Then she asked the
chief to remove the skull again and tilt it forward so the photojournalist could
take a close-up shot of the skull.

After the tape was shot, she called her station to tell them what she had. A 8
meeting was held in which some objected to using the video. The news director
overruled objections with the statement, "Fuck it! We're going to run it."

No one reviewed the tape before it was broadcast. It was seen by the staff for 9
the first time when it was broadcast on the 6 p.m. news. No one had called the
victim's family to tell them about the upcoming tape.

The story that evening opened with an emotional piece on a memorial service 10
for the six-year-old victim along with photographs of the child and footage of the
family. This was immediately followed by a close-up shot of animal remains originally thought to be [the] victim's.

News Photographer 52.3 (Mar. 1997): 12.

Then the tape cut to the shot of the police chief taking the skull from the box, [11] zooming in for a frontal close-up of the tilted skull facing directly at the camera while a voice-over identified the skull as belonging to the victim.

The victim's family was watching as the story unfolded. The victim's 12-year- [12] old sister ran out of the room screaming, "That cannot be my sister." As a court later noted, "The emotional impact was devastating."

Someone from the station later called the family and apologized for the story. The [13] news staff later admitted that the family should have been contacted. They also said that the close-up of the skull was not newsworthy and should not have been aired.

A court, in its decision against the station, noted that the shot of the skull was [14] "gruesome and macabre" and was "intentionally included to create sensationalism for the report."

Fortunately, stories such as this are the exception rather than the norm. [15] Unfortunately, stories such as this have been the center piece of law suits which have argued that a photojournalist's news gathering efforts hurt those photographed.

Whether it is a question of intentional infliction of emotional distress or an [16] issue of invasion of privacy . . . images of individuals in tragic moments often raise more questions of ethics rather than laws. In most circumstances, the courts have given wide discretion to those pursuing newsworthy images. As long as one stays within reasonable bounds in pursuing and presenting information, few legal consequences will follow.

However, just because an image falls within legal limits does not necessarily [17] mean that it also falls within acceptable ethical standards. Legal standards address what one can do. Ethical standards address what one should do. . . .

Finally, if the reader will permit a personal observation, the many photojour- [18] nalists that this author has worked with over the past two decades have all adhered to the highest sense of ethical and legal standards. No one that this author has known could ever be on the losing end of an intentional infliction of emotional distress suit. You do it right and you do it well. Your behaviors and beliefs serve as a model for the entire profession.

The Cat in the Casket

Kay CORSO, Plaintiff,
v.
CRAWFORD DOG AND CAT HOSPITAL, INC., Defendant.

Civil Court of the City of New York, Queens County.
March 22, 1979.

On or about January 28, 1978, the plaintiff brought her 15 year old poodle into the [1] defendant's premises for treatment. After examining the dog, the defendant rec-

---

Corso v. Crawford Dog and Cat Hospital, 415 N.Y.S. 2d 182 (1979).

ommended euthanasia and shortly thereafter the dog was put to death. The plaintiff and the defendant agreed that the dog's body would be turned over to Bide-A-Wee, an organization that would arrange a funeral for the dog. The plaintiff alleged that the defendant wrongfully disposed of her dog, failed to turn over the remains of the dog to the plaintiff for the funeral. The plaintiff had arranged for an elaborate funeral for the dog including a head stone, an epitaph, and attendance by plaintiff's two sisters and a friend. A casket was delivered to the funeral which, upon opening the casket, instead of the dog's body, the plaintiff found the body of a dead cat. The plaintiff described during the non-jury trial, her mental distress and anguish, in detail, and indicated that she still feels distress and anguish. The plaintiff sustained no special damages.

The question before the court now is two-fold. 1) Is it an actionable tort that   2
was committed? 2) If there is an actionable tort is the plaintiff entitled to damages beyond the market value of the dog?

Shunned by Jehovah's Witnesses

Janice PAUL, a/k/a/ Janice Perez,
Plaintiff-Appellant,

v.

WATCHTOWER BIBLE AND TRACT
SOCIETY OF NEW YORK, INC.,
Defendants-Appellee.

No. 85-4012.

United States Court of Appeals, Ninth Circuit.
Argued and Submitted March 7, 1986. Decided June 10, 1987.

Janice Paul was raised as a Jehovah's Witness. Her mother was very active in the   1
Church and, from the age of four, Paul attended church meetings. In 1962, when Paul was 11 years old, her mother married the overseer of the Ephrata, Washington congregation of Jehovah's Witnesses. In 1967, Paul officially joined the Witnesses and was baptized.

According to Paul, she was an active member of the congregation, devoting an   2
average of 40 hours per month in door-to-door distribution of the Witnesses' publications. In addition to engaging in evening home bible study, she attended church with her family approximately 20 hours per month. She eventually married another member of the Jehovah's Witnesses.

In 1975, Paul's parents were "disfellowshiped" from the Church. According to   3
Paul, her parents' expulsion resulted from internal discord within their congregation. The Elders of the Lower Valley Congregation told Paul that she and her husband should not discuss with other members their feeling that her parents had

Paul v. Watchtower Bible and Tract Society, 819 F.2d 895 (1987).

been unjustly disfellowshiped. That advice was underscored by the potential sanction of her own disfellowship were she to challenge the decision.

Sometime after the Elders' warning, Paul decided that she no longer wished   4
to belong to the congregation, or to remain affiliated with the Jehovah's Witnesses. In November 1975, Paul wrote a letter to the congregation withdrawing from the Church.

The Witnesses are a very close community and have developed an elaborate   5
set of rules governing membership. The Church has four basic categories of membership, non-membership or former membership status; they are: members, non-members, disfellowshiped persons, and disassociated persons. "Disfellowshiped persons" are former members who have been excommunicated from the Church. One consequence of disfellowship is "shunning," a form of ostracism. Members of the Jehovah's Witness community are prohibited—under threat of their own disfellowship—from having any contact with disfellowshiped persons and may not even greet them. Family members who do not live in the same house may conduct necessary family business with disfellowshiped relatives but may not communicate with them on any other subject. Shunning purportedly has its roots in early Christianity and various religious groups in our country engage in the practice including the Amish, the Mennonites, and, of course, the Jehovah's Witnesses.

"Disassociated persons" are former members who have voluntarily left the   6
Jehovah's Witness faith. At the time Paul disassociated, there was no express sanction for withdrawing from membership. In fact, because of the close nature of many Jehovah's Witness communities, disassociated persons were still consulted in secular matters, e.g. legal or business advice, although they were no longer members of the Church. In Paul's case, for example, after having moved from the area, she returned for a visit in 1980, saw Church members and was warmly greeted.

In September 1981, the Governing Body of Jehovah's Witnesses, acting   7
through the defendants—Watchtower Bible and Tract Society of Pennsylvania, Inc., and the Watchtower Bible and Tract Society of New York, Inc.—issued a new interpretation of the rules governing disassociated persons. The distinction between disfellowshiped and disassociated persons was, for all practical purposes, abolished and disassociated persons were to be treated in the same manner as the disfellowshiped. The September 15, 1981 issue of *The Watchtower*, an official publication of the Church, contained an article entitled "Disfellowshiping—how to view it." The article included the following discussion:

THOSE WHO DISASSOCIATE THEMSELVES
. . . Persons who make themselves 'not of our sort' by deliberately rejecting the faith and beliefs of Jehovah's Witnesses should appropriately be viewed and treated as are those who have been disfellowshiped for wrongdoing.

The Watchtower article based its announcement on a reading of various passages of the Bible, including 1 John 2:19 and Revelations 19:17–21. The article noted further that "[a]s distinct from some personal 'enemy' or worldly man in authority who opposed Christians, a . . . disassociated person who is trying to promote or justify his apostate thinking or is continuing in his ungodly conduct is certainly not one to whom to wish 'Peace' [understood as a greeting]. (1 Tim. 2:1, 2)." Finally, the article stated that if "a Christian were to throw in his lot with a wrong-doer who . . . has disassociated himself, . . . the Elders . . . would admonish him and, if necessary, 'reprove him with severity.' " (citing, *inter alia*, Matt. 18:18, Gal. 6:1, Titus 1:13).

Three years after this announcement in *The Watchtower*, Paul visited her parents, who at that time lived in Soap Lake, Washington. There, she approached a Witness who had been a close childhood friend and was told by this person: "I can't speak to you. You are disfellowshiped." Similarly, in August 1984, Paul returned to the area of her former congregation. She tried to call on some of her friends. These people told Paul that she was to be treated as if she had been dis-fellowshiped and that they could not speak with her. At one point, she attempted to attend a Tupperware party at the home of a Witness. Paul was informed by the Church members present that the Elders had instructed them not to speak with her.

Upset by her shunning by her former friends and co-religionists, Paul, a resident of Alaska, brought suit in Washington State Superior Court alleging common law torts of defamation, invasion of privacy, fraud, and outrageous conduct.

Judge's Instructions to the Jury

INTENTIONAL INFLICTION OF EMOTIONAL DISTRESS

Ladies and Gentlemen of the Jury:

It is now my duty to instruct you on the law that applies to this case. It is your duty to follow the law.

As jurors it is your duty to determine the effect and value of the evidence and to decide all questions of fact.

You must not be influenced by sympathy, prejudice or passion.

The plaintiff _____ seeks to recover damages based upon a claim of intentional infliction of emotional distress.

The essential elements of such a claim are:

1. The defendant engaged in outrageous, [unprivileged] conduct;
2. [a. The] defendant intended to cause plaintiff to suffer emotional distress; or

California Jury Instructions, Civil: Book of Approved Jury Instructions 8th ed. Prepared by the Committee on Standard Jury Instruction Civil, of the Superior Court of Los Angeles County, California. Hon. Stephen M. Lachs, Judge of the Superior Court, Chairman. Compiled and Edited by Paul G. Breckenridge, Jr. St. Paul, MN: West Publishing, 1994.

[b.] [(1) The defendant engaged in the conduct with reckless disregard of the probability of causing plaintiff to suffer emotional distress;

(2) The plaintiff was present at the time the outrageous conduct occurred; and

(3) The defendant knew that the plaintiff was present;]

3. The plaintiff suffered severe emotional distress; and

4. Such outrageous . . . conduct of the defendant was a cause of the emotional distress suffered by the plaintiff.

The term "emotional distress" means mental distress, mental suffering or mental anguish. It includes all highly unpleasant mental reactions, such as fright, nervousness, grief, anxiety, worry, mortification, shock, humiliation and indignity, as well as physical pain.

The word "severe," in the phrase "severe emotional distress," means substantial or enduring as distinguished from trivial or transitory. Severe emotional distress is emotional distress of such substantial quantity or enduring quality that no reasonable person in a civilized society should be expected to endure it.

In determining the severity of emotional distress you should consider its intensity and duration.

Extreme and outrageous conduct is conduct which goes beyond all possible bounds of decency so as to be regarded as atrocious and utterly intolerable in a civilized community.

Extreme and outrageous conduct is not mere insults, indignities, threats, annoyances, petty oppressions or other trivialities. All persons must necessarily be expected and required to be hardened to a certain amount of rough language and to occasional acts that are definitely inconsiderate and unkind.

Extreme and outrageous conduct, however, is conduct which would cause an average member of the community to immediately react in outrage.

The extreme and outrageous character of a defendant's conduct may arise from defendant's knowledge that a plaintiff is peculiarly susceptible to emotional distress by reason of some physical or mental condition or peculiarity. Conduct may become extreme and outrageous when a defendant proceeds in the face of such knowledge, where it would not be so if defendant did not know.

If you find that plaintiff is entitled to a verdict against defendant, you must then award plaintiff damages in an amount that will reasonably compensate plaintiff for all loss or harm, provided that you find it was [or will be] suffered by plaintiff and was caused by the defendant's conduct. The amount of such award shall include:

Reasonable compensation for any fears, anxiety and other emotional distress suffered by the plaintiff.

. . . In making an award for emotional distress you shall exercise your authority with calm and reasonable judgment and the damages you fix shall be just and reasonable in the light of the evidence. ■

• • • •

For Deliberation and Argument

1. How would you define emotional distress? Suppose someone did something—either intentionally or unintentionally—that caused you considerable
emotional distress. How serious would this distress have to be for you to consider suing that person? Provide examples to clarify your responses.

2. How does Carr communicate his attitudes toward the kind of "ED" cases that
he describes? To what extent do you share his attitudes? Do you think that he
is being insensitive toward the people he describes? Have you encountered—
in your reading or your own experience—other examples of the "disease" he
is discussing?

3. Comment on the lawsuit described by David Margolick. To what extent does
Adler v. Frank fit the pattern described by Howie Carr in "Take $2000 and
Call Me in the Morning"? Consider couching your response as an editorial in
a newspaper or a legal magazine. Alternatively, you might consider drafting
your response as a brief to the court filed *either* by the Adlers' attorney *or* by
Rabbi Frank's.

4. Lawsuit aside, how legitimate a gripe does Gavin (*McDonald* case) have
against Spelling Bee officials? Should Stephen have been allowed to compete
at the county level? What flaw, if any, do you find in Gavin's argument? To
what extent did the newspaper's spelling officials inflict emotional distress on
Gavin? How do the judges of the Court of Appeal convey their attitude toward
this lawsuit?

5. Render a decision on the spelling bee case (*McDonald*) as if you were one of
the judges. Explain your reasoning in light of the facts presented to the court.

6. What rules and regulations (if any) do you believe should apply to photojournalists to prevent causing severe emotional distress to their readers or
viewers, such as occurred in the case described by Sherer? In suggesting such
rules, take into account the constitutional right of freedom of the press.
(While the First Amendment does not protect writers or news organizations
from being sued for libel—that is, for knowingly writing or broadcasting false
and defamatory statements—courts have been reluctant to place undue
restrictions on freedom of the press.)

7. Consider the three cases (*McDonald, Corso,* and *Paul*) treated in this group
from an ethical, as opposed to a legal, standpoint. In which case is the action
at the heart of the lawsuit most reprehensible? Least reprehensible? Why? To
what extent might there be plausible justifications (as opposed to reasons)
for these actions?

8. Compare the legal definition of emotional distress contained in the "Judge's
Instructions to the Jury" to the definition you provided in response to the first
question of the Group 1 Readings. To what extent do the definitions essentially cover the same ground? To what extent are they significantly different?
If you were empowered to draw up a legal description of emotional distress—

one that could be applied in lawsuits—how would you modify the "Judge's Instructions": add, remove, or otherwise change existing language?

9. Compare and contrast the *McDonald*, *Corso*, and *Paul* cases. Do you think that all three cases have equal merit (or lack of merit), or do you find significant differences between them? Explain, citing examples and referring to appropriate sections of the "Judge's Instructions to the Jury."

10. Imagine that you are Janet Paul, about to embark upon a lawsuit against the Jehovah's Witnesses. Write a letter to one of your friends or relatives, explaining your decision.

11. To what extent do you believe that religious freedom is an adequate defense for the Watchtower Bible and Tract Society in the "shunning" case? Should religious organizations have more or less complete freedom to regulate their affairs and their congregations, as long as they don't violate criminal laws?

12. Select one of these three cases. If you were a member of the jury, would you find for the plaintiff or the defendant? Draw on the definitions and discussions in the "Judge's Instructions to the Jury" in supporting and explaining your decision.

13. Select one of these three cases. Imagine yourself as attorney for the plaintiff or attorney for the defendant. Write a paper in IRAC format to make your case. Define the *issue* in question format. State or summarize the *rules* about intentional infliction of emotional distress. *Apply* the rules, as explained in the "Judge's Instructions to the Jury," to the facts of the case you have selected. Draw a *conclusion* from the application of these rules.

14. Select one of the cases treated in this group. Imagine that you are representing either the plaintiff or the defendant. Compose either an opening statement or a closing argument for this case. Remember that your audience is the jury. Draw on the facts of the case in a way that is likely to have the greatest impact on the jury. Keep in mind, however, that jury members may turn against you—and your client—if they think that you are overly manipulating the facts, being deceptive, making exaggerated claims, or attempting too crudely to play upon their emotions. For guidance on developing your statement, see the "Models for the Opening Statement and the Closing Argument" at the end of Chapter 2 (pp. 96–105). See also Larry S. Stewart's "Arguing Pain and Suffering Damages in Summation: How to Inspire Jurors" at the end of the Group 3 Readings in this chapter (pp. 149–55).

15. Drawing on your own experience or the experience of someone you know, provide an account of the "facts of the case," as if these facts were being provided as part of a legal opinion in an emotional distress case. You may want to extend your account by actually rendering a decision and explaining your decision in terms of the definitions of emotional distress in the "Judge's Instructions to the Jury."

16. As a variation of the previous assignment, make the plaintiff a character from a novel or a play you have read or a film or play you have seen.

■ Group 2 Readings: *Insults and Financial Harassment*

This group of readings focuses on emotional distress caused by verbal harassment—personal insults or abusive statements by creditors.

"Sticks and stones may break my bones, but words can never harm me" goes the old children's rhyme. But of course that isn't true. Words can be deeply hurtful and frequently result in the kind of severe emotional distress described in the "Judge's Instructions to the Jury" in the previous group of readings. This is particularly true of people who are highly sensitive to verbal abuse because of their age or their psychological or emotional vulnerability.

Of course, it's one thing to morally censure someone who is guilty of verbal abuse; it's another to haul that person into court. Because insults are a fact of life, the law has to draw some distinction between the trivial and the outrageous. As the "Judge's Instructions" note, "All persons must necessarily be expected and required to be hardened to a certain amount of rough language and to occasional acts that are definitely inconsiderate and unkind." If this were not the case, then the majority of the population would be spending most of their lives in court, either as plaintiffs or defendants—or both.

While most personal insults are inflicted by individuals, financial harassment is generally perpetrated by businesses engaged in what they believe is a legitimate enterprise: collecting what is owed them. Almost everyone has been late in paying bills. Sometimes it's because we forget or because we're not very well organized; sometimes it's because we're short of funds that month. Usually, the first notices from creditors are friendly enough, thanking us for our business and gently reminding us to send money. The next few notices are successively less cordial; the reminders become more insistent, gradually evolving into threats to turn the matter over to a collection agency.

For most people, this is more than sufficient to cause emotional distress. But is it the kind of emotional distress that is legally actionable—in other words, the kind that provides grounds for bringing suit against the creditor in a court of law?

The case that leads off this group, Lawrence v. Stanford, *concerning a family that sues an animal hospital for emotional distress caused by financial harassment, is the subject of our first* model student paper, *by Mark Tseselsky. Following a statement of the law that applies to this case, we present (1) a writing assignment typical of those you will find throughout* Making the Case *and (2) a model response to this assignment. Student Mark Tseselsky writes a rough and a final draft of his paper and also provides an account of the process by which he approached the assignment both in initial draft and revision.*

Following Tseselsky's essay is a case of verbal insult, "The Abusive Motorman" (Knoxville Traction v. Lane), *heard in the Supreme Court of Tennessee in 1899. It is followed by the relevant law on "Liability of*

Public Utility for Insults by Employees." The final case in this group, also dealing with financial harassment, "A Department Store Nightmare" (Moorhead v. J. C. Penney), *was heard in the Supreme Court of Tennessee in 1977.*

Model Student Paper:
Pay Up or We'll Kill Your Dog
∎ ∎

**Gwendlyn Daphane LAWRENCE, A Minor,
and Mario Edward Lawrence, A Minor, both by next
friend and Mother, M. Annette Powell and M. Annette Powell,
Individually, Plaintiffs-Appellants,**

v.

**J. L. STANFORD and Ashland Terrace Animal Hospital, PC,
Defendants-Appellees,**

and

William Leech, Attorney General, Intervenor.

Supreme Court of Tennessee, at Knoxville.
Aug. 15, 1983.

The plaintiffs, Annette Powell, and her two minor children, Mario Edward   1
Lawrence and Gwendlyn Daphane Lawrence, brought this action against the defendants, J. L. Stanford, a veterinarian, and Ashland Terrace Animal Hospital, PC, for damages and other relief. The plaintiffs allege that the defendants willfully inflicted emotional injuries upon the plaintiffs by their outrageous and extreme conduct in threatening that they "would do away with" the plaintiffs' little dog as the doctor saw fit unless the plaintiffs paid "in cash and in full" charges made by the defendants for treating the dog for injuries suffered when struck by an automobile, although the plaintiffs had made known to the defendants that they were unable to pay the complete bill in full at the time demand was made and had sought an agreement from the defendants to allow payment over a period of time which request was denied. It was alleged in the complaint that the defendants threatened to "do away with the dog" unless the bill was paid in full by Friday, January 11, 1980. Being unable to raise the money sufficient to pay the bill by the deadline thus set, plaintiffs brought this action on January 11, 1980, to enjoin the defendants from disposing of the dog and asking for damages for the "outrageous conduct" of the defendants.

The defendants answered, admitting that the plaintiffs were told that they   2
could not have possession of their dog until the defendants' bill was paid in full and in cash but denied stating that Dr. Stanford would "do away with the dog as

---

Lawrence v. Stanford, 655 S.W.2d 927 (1983).

he sees fit." The defendants further allege that on February 5, 1980, after the initial restraining order against them had been dissolved, the defendants proceeded to dispose of the dog pursuant to the provisions of T.C.A., § 63–12–134,[1] by notifying plaintiffs that unless the bill was paid within 10 days the dog would be turned over to the humane society for disposal. The defendants filed a counter-complaint against the plaintiffs in which they sought a judgment for $155.00 representing the charges made by the clinic and veterinarian. . . .

Two points should be noted at this point: (1) the defendants did not give the   3 plaintiffs notice of defendants' intention to invoke the provisions of T.C.A., § 63-1234, until January 15, 1980, which was *after* plaintiffs' suit was filed on January 11, 1980, (2) plaintiffs did not challenge the constitutionality of T.C.A., § 63–1234, at any point in the proceedings in the trial court. . . .

We quote from plaintiffs' complaint as follows: 4

VII

That on Thursday, January 10, 1980, plaintiff received several calls from defendants' agent and employee, again threatening plaintiff to pay or defendants would 'do away with the dog.'

VIII

That plaintiffs would aver and show that they own the dog and are entitled to immediate possession of their dog and that defendants' holding of the dog, refusing to return, and threats to do away with said dog are outrageous and so extreme in degree as to go beyond all bounds of decency and are atrocious and utterly intolerable in a civilized society.

IX

That as a result of defendants' outrageous conduct plaintiffs, and each of them, have suffered severe emotional distress. The minor plaintiffs, in particular, have shown severe distress and spent their Christmas holidays extremely upset, having numerous bouts of crying and obvious distress.

These allegations are supported in the record by the affidavit of Annette   5 Powell, one of the plaintiffs and the mother of the two minor plaintiffs. On the other hand, the defendants deny that the threat to "do away with the dog" was made. . . .

Tennessee Code Annotated (T.C.A.)

63–12–134. *Abandonment of animals.*–(a) The term abandonment as used in this   6 chapter shall mean to forsake entirely, or to neglect, or to refuse to provide for, or to perform the legal or contractual obligation for care and support of an animal by its owner or his agent, and such abandonment shall constitute a relinquish-

---

[1]Tennessee Code Annotated [the laws of Tennessee] (T.C.A.) 63-12-134.

ment of all rights and claims of the owner to such animal after notice is given as hereinafter provided.

(b) Any animal placed in the custody of a licensed veterinarian for treatment, boarding or other care, shall be considered to be abandoned by its owner or its agent following ten (10) days' written notice by registered mail being given by the licensed veterinarian to the owner or his agent at the last known address of such owner or agent, and the failure of the owner or the agent to fulfill his contractual obligation within the above mentioned ten (10) days with the licensed veterinarian, and after such abandonment, may be turned over by the licensed veterinarian to the custody of the nearest humane society or dog pound in the area for disposal as the custodian of such humane society or dog pound may deem proper. Nothing contained herein shall be construed as relieving the owner of such animal or his agent from any liability which the owner or his agent may have incurred as a result of the furnishing of such treatment, boarding, or other care by the licensed veterinarian for the entire period the animal has been in the custody of said licensed veterinarian.

(c) The giving of notice as provided herein to the owner, or the agent of the owner, of such animal by the licensed veterinarian as provided in subsection (b) shall relieve the veterinarian and any custodian, to whom such animal may be given, of any further liability for the care or treatment of said animal. The veterinarian or custodian of a humane society or dog pound shall not be liable for disposal of said animal. Such procedure by the veterinarian shall not constitute grounds for disciplinary proceedings under this chapter.

● ● ● ●

Paper Topic: "Pay Up or We'll Kill Your Dog" (Lawrence v. Stanford)

If you were a member of the jury, how would you decide in the case of *Lawrence v. Stanford*: for the plaintiff or for the defendant? Consider the evidence presented in light of the "Judge's Instructions to the Jury: Intentional Infliction of Emotional Distress" (pp. 119–20) and the discussion of emotional distress from "The Law on Intentional Infliction of Mental Distress" (pp. 132–34).

During the course of your discussion, review the Tennessee statute on Abandonment of Animals (T.C.A. 63-12-134) provided at the end of *Lawrence v. Stanford*. In your view, does this statute give the animal hospital the legal right to take the steps that it did against the plaintiff? Why or why not?

MODEL STUDENT PAPER

COMMENTARY BY MARK TSESELSKY

After first reading the case I wasn't sure which way to argue. Should the defendants be liable for willful infliction of emotional distress or not? First, I tried listing all of the issues that I thought were involved, but then realized that writing out the facts of the case would be a better way to start. I also found that trying to figure out in advance which way to argue the case was a waste of time. When I write an essay like this again, I'll try a different approach: simply lay out the facts of the case, then the relevant rules, and then consider how to apply the rules to the facts before drawing a conclusion.

After reading the documents a second time, I decided to argue that the defendants should not be liable for infliction of emotional distress and proceeded to write the introduction, which included an account of the basic facts of the case and the legal issue that I, as a juror, would have to decide in this case. Once I began writing the argument itself, my basic strategy was to start with the rules. Provide a definition of emotional distress. Connect this general principal with the law defining the specific situation of abandoning animals and with the particular behavior of the defendants toward the plaintiffs. Once the rules were presented, my strategy was to write what I was going to concede to the opposite side (the plaintiff's side), in order of importance. The most important aspect of the plaintiff's argument is that the defendants did not have the legal right to withhold the animal. Thus, I intended to concede to the opposite side as much as possible. I was going to compare their strongest argument and my weakest, and show that even having conceded this much, my argument (for the defendant) was still the closest to the spirit of the rules.

Another important aspect of the opposite case is the sheer nastiness of what the defendants did to the plaintiff. So I conceded their lack of compassion, but once again referred the specific situation (defining the dog as "abandoned" and threatening to dispose of it) back to the general principal (intentional infliction of emotional distress) to show that in this case the principle does not apply. Throughout the analysis I referred back to the rules to make sure that I had covered every relevant aspect of the rules I discussed.

Rough Draft

In *Lawrence v Stanford*, 655 S.W.2d 927 (1983), the plaintiffs, Annette Powell, and her two minor children, Mario Edward Lawrence and Gwendlyn Daphane Lawrence claimed that the defendants J. L. Stanford, a veterinarian, and Ashland Terrace Animal Hospital inflicted severe emotional distress on the plaintiffs by threatening to "do away with" their dog unless the plaintiffs immediately paid in full for the treatment of the plaintiffs' animal. The defendants admitted they refused to give back the animal until the bill was paid in full, but they denied the allegation that defendant Stanford or an agent of the hospital ever threatened to "do away with" the dog. Also, the defendants did not notify the plaintiffs of their intention to invoke the Tennessee Abandonment of Animals statute[1] until after the plaintiffs filed their case. In deciding the case, we the jury, considered whether defendants' conduct as described above was so outrageous and extreme, and mental anguish from this conduct so intense and prolonged, as to justify the plaintiffs' claim to have suffered severe emotional distress as a result of defendants' actions.

"One who by extreme and outrageous conduct intentionally or recklessly causes severe emotional distress to another is subject to liability for such emo-

---

[1] *Tennessee Code Annotated (T.C.A.)* 63-12-134.

tional distress."[2] "The term "emotional distress" means mental distress, mental suffering or mental anguish. It includes all highly unpleasant mental reactions, such as fright, nervousness, grief, anxiety, worry, mortification, shock, humiliation and indignity, as well as physical pain. The word "severe," in the phrase "severe emotional distress," means substantial or enduring as distinguished from trivial or transitory. Severe emotional distress is emotional distress of such substantial quantity or enduring quality that no reasonable person in a civilized society should be expected to endure it."[3] "Severe emotional distress must be proven; but in many cases the extreme and outrageous character of the defendants' actions is in itself important evidence that the distress has existed." "Extreme and outrageous conduct is conduct, which goes beyond all possible bounds of decency so as to be regarded as atrocious and utterly intolerable in a civilized society."[4] To qualify defendants' refusal to return plaintiffs' animal, we relied on Tennessee Code Annotated (T.C.A.) 63-12-134, which addresses the conduct of licensed veterinarians towards the owners of the animals left in their custody as follows:

> Any animal placed in the custody of a licensed veterinarian for treatment, boarding or other care, shall be considered to be abandoned by its owner or its agents following ten (10) days' written notice . . . by the licensed veterinarian to the owner or his agent . . . and the failure of the owner or the agent to fulfil his contractual obligation . . . with the licensed veterinarian, and after such abandonment, may be turned over by the licensed veterinarian to the custody of the nearest humane society or dog pound in the area for disposal . . .[5]

The defendants did not give the plaintiffs the required ten days written notice   6
until after this case came to court. Therefore, the defendants had no legal right to refuse to give back the animal or to allegedly make threats to "do away with the animal." If the plaintiffs' allegations that the defendants threatened to "do away with the animal" are true, the defendants can even be said to have intended to inflict emotional distress on "peculiarly susceptible" minor plaintiffs.[6]

However, the fact that the defendants have "acted with an intent which is tor-   7
tious or even criminal, or that [they have perhaps] intended to inflict emotional distress" does not necessarily mean that they are liable to the plaintiffs.[7] Even if everything happened just as the plaintiffs alleged, the defendants were engaged in a common business transaction, debt collection. This practice, while often controversial, is hardly something "beyond all possible bounds of decency."

The defendants did not show compassion towards the plaintiffs. For example,   8
they refused to allow installment payments on the plaintiffs' debt. Perhaps they were rude and obnoxious. Certainly, their conduct could have been more considerate for the feelings of the minor plaintiffs. However, the defendants' conduct

---

[2]*Restatement (Second) of Torts* sec. 46 (1965).
[3]*Judge's Instructions to the Jury: Emotional Distress:* 120.
[4]*Judge's Instructions to the Jury: Emotional Distress:* 120.
[5]*T.C.A.* 63-12-134 (b): 126.
[6]*Restatement (Second) of Torts,* sec. 46 (1965): 134.
[7]*Restatement (Second) of Torts,* sec. 46 (1965): 132.

was not so extreme and outrageous as in itself to provide evidence of infliction of severe emotional distress.

As a result of defendants' lack of compassion the plaintiffs, especially the   9
minors were understandably upset. According to Ms. Powell's affidavit, her two minor children spent their Christmas very upset over their dog.[8] However, their distress is not of the kind, which "no reasonable person in a civilized society should be expected to endure." Rude debt collectors are part of our collective reality. Sometimes, this reality hits one over the head with an unpleasant surprise for a few weeks around Christmas. It is a testament to the durability of the human nature that even the young members of our species recover fairly quickly from this transitory distress. As jurors we took into consideration defendants' lack of compassion and tortious conduct, but concluded that the law cannot protect even the youngest members of our society from enduring certain "rough edges of our society."[9]

COMMENTARY AFTER INSTRUCTOR'S FEEDBACK

As I revised my rough draft I began to have more and more doubts about my con-   10
clusion. I realized that I had decided too early that the defendants had a stronger case than the plaintiffs. This made me realize once again, that it isn't necessary to decide which way to argue the case before plunging into it. Next time, I'll base my conclusion—the resolution of the issues—on the outcome of applying the rules to the facts of the case.

The instructor's comments made my writing more relaxed. If my rough draft was   11
overly dry and legalistic, my revision keeps in mind the expectations of the general reader. I found that I needed to do more than just quote the rules: I had to explain them. I also reduced the number of quotations, paraphrasing some of the definitions of emotional distress and that block quotation on the abandonment of animals from the Tennessee statute. I also used signal phrases to place the quotations in context and used parenthetical form instead of footnote form for citations.

I found that the best way to argue is to argue with your opponent in mind.   12
Think of what he or she is likely to say and try to incorporate these counter-arguments into your thinking. Continue with this process until finally (likely after several false alarms) you come to the crux of the matter: a fine point like whether the defendants knew that their infliction of emotional distress was directed against "peculiarly susceptible" minor plaintiffs.

Final Draft

Pay Up or We'll Kill Your Dog

Facts and Issue

Back home from my first semester in college, my jury service obligation finally   13
caught up with me, and so I had to spend my winter vacation as a juror. Fortu-

---

[8]*Lawrence v. Stanford* 665 S.W. 2d 927 (Tenn. 1983): 125.
[9]*Restatement (Second) of Torts*, sec. 35 (1965): 133.

nately, I was selected for an interesting case about infliction of severe emotional distress, *Lawrence v. Stanford*, 655 S.W.2d 927 (1983). The plaintiffs, Annette Powell, and her two minor children, Mario Edward Lawrence and Gwendlyn Daphane Lawrence, brought their injured dog to the Ashland Terrace Animal Hospital, where veterinarian J. L. Stanford treated the animal. Ms. Powell had until January 10th, 1980 to pay $155.00 for the animal's treatment. She could not afford to pay right away and so offered to pay for the services over a period of time. But the hospital and the veterinarian wanted the payment in full and in cash right away. Moreover, they refused to give the animal back until the bill was paid, and, according to the plaintiff, threatened to "do away with" the dog unless the plaintiffs were immediately paid in full. According to Ms. Powell's affidavit, the two minor plaintiffs, Mario and Gwendlyn, spent their Christmas crying and extremely upset.

To prevent the clinic and the veterinarian from disposing of the animal, and to   14
collect damages for their "outrageous and extreme conduct," the plaintiffs sued the defendants for willful infliction of emotional distress. In deciding the case, we the jury considered the issue of whether the defendants' conduct as described above was so outrageous and extreme, and their mental anguish from this conduct so intense and prolonged, as to justify the plaintiffs' claim to have suffered severe emotional distress as a result of the defendants' actions.

Rules

We were moved by emotional evidence in this case, but the judge said that it was   15
our job to assess the case by applying the law to the evidence, and not by any feelings of sympathy we might have for the plaintiffs. To explain the law, the judge defined infliction of severe emotional distress as extreme and outrageous conduct, done by the defendant intentionally and "with reckless disregard of the probability of causing plaintiff to suffer emotional distress" ("Judge's Instructions to the Jury: Emotional Distress" 119). To clarify the wording of the rule, the judge explained that "emotional distress" referred to mental distress, and other mental experiences like mental suffering or mental anguish: "It includes all highly unpleasant mental reactions, such as fright, nervousness, grief, anxiety, worry, mortification, shock, humiliation and indignity, as well as physical pain." But to fit the legal definition of "severe emotional distress," these mental reactions have to be substantial or enduring. In other words, they cannot be something that is just trivial or transitory, like the temporary stress one suffers by listening to a rude bill collector. To be considered severe, emotional distress has to be so extreme that "no reasonable person in a civilized society should be expected to endure it" ("Jury Instructions" 120).

We were still unclear, however, what kind of evidence proves that severe emo-   16
tional distress existed. According to the *Restatement of Torts*, "in many cases the extreme and outrageous character of the defendant's conduct is in itself important evidence that the distress has existed" (134). In this case, the defendants refused to give back the animal in their possession and allegedly threatened to dispose of the animal. If the law protected the defendants' conduct, it could not be considered outrageous and extreme. Therefore, we turned to the *Tennessee*

Code Annotated (T.C.A.), which addresses the conduct of licensed veterinarians towards the owners of the animals left in their custody. If the animal left in the clinic's custody was abandoned as defined by this law, then the defendants indeed had the right to turn over the animal to the nearest humane society. According to the Tennessee statute, an animal is considered abandoned when its owner or his agent refuses to fulfil his contractual obligation (for example, pay a bill) to a licensed veterinarian within ten days of a written notice (*T.C.A.* 126). However, the defendants did not give the plaintiffs the required ten days written notice until after this case came to court. Therefore, the defendants had no legal right to refuse to give back the animal or to allegedly make threats to "do away with the animal." In other words, the law did not protect the defendants' conduct.

Analysis

Having been satisfied that defendants' actions were unjustified, we turned our attention to the defendants' actions toward the plaintiffs. Apparently, the defendants were in no hurry to dispose of the dog. Instead they retained the animal in order to force payment for its treatment. Thus, their actions were both illegal and intentional. Moreover, the plaintiffs certainly suffered emotional distress in being unable to spend their Christmas in the company of their dog. However, the fact that the defendants have "acted with an intent which [was] tortious or even criminal, or that [they have perhaps] intended to inflict emotional distress" does not necessarily mean that they are liable to the plaintiffs (*Restatement* 132). This case was not about the legality of the defendants' actions in threatening to turn the dog over to the humane society, but rather about whether or not they willfully inflicted emotional injuries upon the plaintiffs. To decide whether defendants' conduct was extreme and outrageous, our first task was "to decide all questions of fact," according to the judge's instructions. One important disputed fact was whether defendants threatened to "do away with" the dog. The defendants' illegal retention of the animal, coupled with their clear intent to collect money from the plaintiffs, indicated that they likely did make this threat. Assuming that they did, the defendants' conduct was rude and inconsiderate towards the plaintiffs. [17]

However, rude debt collectors are part of our collective reality. Verdicts in previous trials have indicated that even if the manner of defendants' conduct was "rude and insolent," the defendants' conduct was not extreme and outrageous and so the defendants are not necessarily liable to the plaintiffs (*Restatement of Torts* 132). The crux of this particular case was whether the minor plaintiffs were "peculiarly susceptible to emotional distress by reason of some physical or mental condition or peculiarity," and more important, whether the defendants were aware of this "peculiar susceptibility." If a defendant proceeds in the face of such knowledge, his conduct may be considered extreme and outrageous, even if, without this knowledge, his conduct would not have been considered extreme and outrageous ("Jury Instructions" 120). According to Ms. Powell's affidavit, her two minor children spent their Christmas very upset over their dog. During the period between December of 1979 and February of 1980, two minors had to face the fact that their dog could be put to death because their family was poor and could not afford to pay for the treatment. Their impressionable young [18] age left no chance that this stress could be trivial, but rather made them particularly susceptible to emotional distress. At the same time, the fact that the fate of their dog was uncertain from December of 1979 to February of 1980 makes it impossible to believe that their emotional distress was just transient. We also think it is likely that the defendants knew about the ages of the minor plaintiffs and still retained the animal and threatened to dispose of it.

Conclusion

Based on this analysis, we found that the defendants' actions were extreme and outrageous and the distress suffered by the plaintiffs, especially the minors ones, was severe. Accordingly, we found the defendants, because of their "outrageous and extreme" conduct, liable for willful infliction of emotional distress and therefore liable to the plaintiffs for damages. 19

—Mark Tseselsky

The Law on Intentional Infliction of Mental Distress

From Restatement of the Law (Second): Torts, American Law Institute, 1965

§ [Section] 46. Outrageous Conduct Causing Severe Emotional Distress

(1) One who by extreme and outrageous conduct intentionally or recklessly causes severe emotional distress to another is subject to liability for such emotional distress, and if bodily harm to the other results from it, for such bodily harm.
(2) Where such conduct is directed at a third person, the actor is subject to liability if he intentionally or recklessly causes severe emotional distress
    (a) to a member of such person's immediate family who is present at the time, whether or not such distress results in bodily harm, or
    (b) to any other person who is present at the time, if such distress results in bodily harm.

[Comment] D. EXTREME AND OUTRAGEOUS CONDUCT. The cases thus far decided have found liability only where the defendant's conduct has been extreme and outrageous. It has not been enough that the defendant has acted with an intent 1

Restatement (Second) of Torts. As adapted and promulgated by the American Law Institute at Washington, D.C. May 25, 1963, and May 22, 1964. St. Paul, MN: West Publishing, 1965.

which is tortious or even criminal, or that he has intended to inflict emotional distress, or even that his conduct has been characterized by "malice," or a degree of aggravation which would entitle the plaintiff to punitive damages for another tort. Liability has been found only where the conduct has been so outrageous in character, and so extreme in degree, as to go beyond all possible bounds of decency, and to be regarded as atrocious, and utterly intolerable in a civilized community. Generally, the case is one in which the recitation of the facts to an average member of the community would arouse his resentment against the actor, and lead him to exclaim, "Outrageous!"

The liability clearly does not extend to mere insults, indignities, threats,   2
annoyances, petty oppressions, or other trivialities. The rough edges of our society are still in need of a good deal of filing down, and in the meantime plaintiffs must necessarily be expected and required to be hardened to a certain amount of rough language, and to occasional acts that are definitely inconsiderate and unkind. There is no occasion for the law to intervene in every case where someone's feelings are hurt. There must still be freedom to express an unflattering opinion, and some safety valve must be left through which irascible tempers may blow off relatively harmless steam.

Illustrations: 3

1. As a practical joke, A falsely tells B that her husband has been badly injured in an accident, and is in the hospital with both legs broken. B suffers severe emotional distress. A is subject to liability to B for her emotional distress. If it causes nervous shock and resulting illness, A is subject to liability to B for her illness.
2. A, the president of an association of rubbish collectors, summons B to a meeting of the association, and in the presence of an intimidating group of associates tells B that B has been collecting rubbish in territory which the association regards as exclusively allocated to one of its members. A demands that B pay over the proceeds of his rubbish collection, and tells B that if he does not do so the association will beat him up, destroy his truck, and put him out of business. B is badly frightened, and suffers severe emotional distress. A is subject to liability to B for his emotional distress, and if it results in illness, A is also subject to liability to B for his illness.
3. A is invited to a swimming party at an exclusive resort. B gives her a bathing suit which he knows will dissolve in water. It does dissolve while she is swimming, leaving her naked in the presence of men and women whom she has just met. A suffers extreme embarrassment, shame, and humiliation. B is subject to liability to A for her emotional distress. . . .
8. A, a creditor, seeking to collect a debt, calls on B and demands payment in a rude and insolent manner. When B says that he cannot pay, A calls B a deadbeat, and says that he will never trust B again. A's conduct, although insulting, is not so extreme or outrageous as to make A liable to B. . . .

[Comment] J. SEVERE EMOTIONAL DISTRESS. The rule stated in this Section applies   4
only where the emotional distress has in fact resulted, and where it is severe.

Emotional distress passes under various names, such as mental suffering, mental anguish, mental or nervous shock, or the like. It includes all highly unpleasant mental reactions, such as fright, horror, grief, shame, humiliation, embarrassment, anger, chagrin, disappointment, worry, and nausea. It is only where it is extreme that the liability arises. Complete emotional tranquility is seldom attainable in this world, and some degree of transient and trivial emotional distress is a part of the price of living among people. The law intervenes only where the distress inflicted is so severe that no reasonable man could be expected to endure it. The intensity and the duration of the distress are factors to be considered in determining its severity. Severe distress must be proved; but in many cases the extreme and outrageous character of the defendant's conduct is in itself important evidence that the distress has existed. For example, the mere recital of the facts in Illustration 1 above goes far to prove that the claim is not fictitious.

The distress must be reasonable and justified under the circumstances, and there is no liability where the plaintiff has suffered exaggerated and unreasonable emotional distress, unless it results from a peculiar susceptibility to such distress of which the actor has knowledge.   5

It is for the court to determine whether on the evidence severe emotional distress can be found; it is for the jury to determine whether, on the evidence, it has in fact existed.   6

Illustration: 7

17. The same facts as Illustration 1, except that B does not believe A's statement, and is only sufficiently disturbed to telephone to the hospital to find out whether it could possibly be true. A is not liable to B.

The Abusive Motorman

KNOXVILLE TRACTION CO. v. LANE
et ux.
(Supreme Court of Tennessee. Oct. 28, 1899.)

On July 29, 1898, the plaintiff Maggie Lane, who was a woman of good character, boarded one of the defendant's cars at or near Lake Ottosee, in the suburbs of Knoxville, for the purpose of being transported into the city, and paid the fare required by the defendant. Just before the car reached the city, the plaintiff noticed that the motorman was drinking. She was sitting near the center of the car. The motorman turned and looked towards her, and said, "You are a good-looking old girl, and I would like to meet you when you get off." She became indignant, and remarked that she would have some one attend to him when she got off. Thereafter he continued to make signs to her until the conductor interfered, and the motorman then said, "She is nothing but a whore." The plaintiff commenced to cry, and the motorman seemed to get angry, and said other abusive things to her. He stated that   1 he knew all about her, and that she "would go out to the lake and throw herself out to the men there." He did not put his hands on her, or attempt to do so. When he arrived at the station the plaintiff went to the office of the defendant company, crying, and complained of the insulting conduct of the motorman towards her. The motorman was taken off the run, and immediately discharged by the company. This motorman had theretofore shown himself to be a good and faithful employee of the company, and had never been drunk before while on duty. The defendant did not know that he drank at all. At the conclusion of the plaintiff's testimony the defendant demurred to the evidence upon the ground that the plaintiff's testimony showed that it did not know of the drunkenness of the motorman, and that it discharged him immediately upon learning of his conduct, and also upon the ground that as the injury alleged in the declaration was the willful, malicious, and unlawful employment of a drunken motorman, the plaintiff's cause of action was not made out by her own proof, as there was no evidence to support this allegation. The circuit judge overruled this demurrer to the evidence, and submitted the case to the jury to ascertain and fix the amount of damages suffered by the plaintiff. The jury rendered a verdict for $500, and, the defendant's motion for a new trial having been overruled, it appealed to this court, and has assigned errors.

The Law on Liability of Public Utility for Insults by Employees

§ 48. Special Liability of Public Utility for Insults by Servants

A common carrier or other public utility is subject to liability to patrons utilizing its facilities for gross insults which reasonably offend them, inflicted by the utility's servants while otherwise acting within the scope of their employment. . . .   1

Comment: 2

a. The rule stated in this Section is based on the public interest in freedom from insult on the part of those who undertake the obligations of a public utility. The chief value of the rule lies in the incentive which it provides for the selection of employees who will not be grossly discourteous to those who must come in contact with them, and for the making of proper rules and supervision to enforce them.

The earliest cases involved insults to passengers by the hands of employees of common carriers. The rule was then extended to innkeepers, who always have been regarded as analogous to carriers; and in the later decisions it has been further extended to other public utilities. Any such utility is subject to liability to patrons who are making use of its facilities. The earlier cases found an "implied contract" not to insult the patron; but the later decisions have based the liability on the public duty, and have found it even where there is as yet no contract. It is not necessary that the insult be offered on the utility's own premises.   3

Restatement (Second) of Torts. See p. 132.

Illustrations: 4

1. A, intending to buy a ticket on a train, enters the waiting room of the B Railroad, and sets her parcels on one of the seats. An employee of the railroad removes the parcels. When A protests, he abuses her with profane language, calls her a woman of low character, and accuses her of indecent conduct. B Company is subject to liability to A.
2. A messenger employed by the A Telegraph Company delivers a telegram to B at her home. While she is signing the receipt he makes an indecent proposal to her. A Company is subject to liability to B.

b. PATRONS. The rule stated in this Section applies only to insults to patrons who are   5
utilizing the facilities of the carrier or other public utility, for the purpose for which
they are offered to the public. If an insult is offered to any other person, it does not
fall within this Section, and he must recover, if at all, under the rule stated in § 46.
Illustration: 6

3. A enters B's hotel for the purpose of meeting her brother, who is not a guest of the hotel. While A is waiting in the lobby the hotel detective orders her to leave, and uses insulting language to her. B Company is not liable to A.

c. GROSS INSULTS. Any public utility may of course be liable for the infliction of   7
severe emotional distress by extreme and outrageous conduct, under the rule
stated in § 46 (see pp. 132–34). The rule stated in this Section goes further and
makes such a defendant liable for conduct which falls short of extreme outrage, but
is merely insulting. At the same time the rule of this Section does not extend to
mere trivialities. Even at the hands of public servants the public must be expected
and required to be hardened to a certain amount of rudeness or minor insolence,
which any reasonable man would consider offensive but harmless and unimportant. Even profanity may not be grossly insulting, where it obviously amounts to
nothing more than mere emphasis or a habit of speech, or where it is so customary
in the particular community that it may be said to be generally tolerated. An unduly
sensitive plaintiff, even though he may be badly upset and suffer illness as a result,
cannot found a cause of action upon mere hurt feelings at conduct which is essentially trivial. No passenger on a railroad can mulct the carrier in damages merely
because he is told to "Hurry up! We haven't got all night!"

The obvious condition of the plaintiff must, however, be taken into account in   8
determining whether the conduct is grossly insulting; and language addressed to
a pregnant or a sick woman may be actionable where the same words would not
be if they were addressed to a United States Marine. The defendant is never liable
for doing more than he is privileged to do, even though his manner of doing it may
be lacking in the politeness which would be desirable.
Illustrations: 9

4. A is riding on a train of the B Railroad with the wrong ticket. B's conductor tells A in a rough and rude tone of voice that she must leave the train at the next station, and requires her to do so. B Company is not liable to A.

5. A, a mature man, and B, his ten year old daughter, are in the waiting room of the station of C Railroad, waiting for their train. Employees of C in the adjoining station agent's office use vulgar and profane language, knowing that it will be overheard in the waiting room, and that the passengers are there. A is accustomed to such language and is in the habit of using it himself; B is not. C Company is subject to liability to B, but not to A.

d. SCOPE OF EMPLOYMENT. The rule stated in this Section does not make any defendant liable for insults offered by its employees while they are not acting within the scope of their employment.   10

A Department Store Billing Nightmare

Robert C. MOORHEAD and wife,
Elizabeth A. Moorhead, Appellants,
v.
J. C. PENNEY COMPANY, INC., Appellee.

Supreme Court of Tennessee.
Sept. 19, 1977.

Plaintiffs allege that they maintained a charge account with the defendant, J. C. Penney Company, and that they returned a purchased item of merchandise to the defendant's store in the West Town Shopping Mall in Knoxville with the agreement of defendant's employees there that plaintiffs would be given a credit for the returned merchandise in the sum of $16.78. Due to a mistake in the defendant's billing and accounting procedures, the plaintiffs' next monthly statement indicated a charge, rather than a credit, in the amount of $16.78. Plaintiffs promptly called this mistake to the attention of defendant's employees in Knoxville who assured them that the error would be corrected forthwith. The complaint describes the events which occurred thereafter as follows: 1

"III. Plaintiffs repeatedly called the local office of the J. C. Penney Company and it was always explained that the mistake would be corrected but the threatening letters not only continued to come from the J. C. Penney Company but service charges were added to the mistaken charge so that the bill increased in amount. Further plaintiffs began to receive correspondence requesting payment on almost a daily basis.   2

"IV. As a result of the urging of the local office of the J. C. Penney Company, it was finally attempted by the J. C. Penney Company to correct the erroneous charge but instead of correcting same and wiping the slate clean, through another grossly negligent error, the charge was actually doubled so that after all finance and service   3

Moorhead v. J. C. Penney, 555 S.W.2d 713 (1977).

charges were added it was suddenly claimed that plaintiffs owed $38.12 to the J. C. Penney Company and once again plaintiffs began to receive threatening letters from the J. C. Penney Company asking for payment of the due and total balance. . . .

"VI. In March, 1974, plaintiffs began to receive notices from the Knoxville Collection Agency which had been referred the matter (sic) by the J. C. Penney Company and following this many letters of a threatening nature came from the collection agency all at the instance of the J. C. Penney Company.

"VII. Plaintiffs went in person to the J. C. Penney Company and sat down with the manager of the store after having made copies of all the documents they received and the store manager for the West Town J. C. Penney Company local store admitted that the J. C. Penney Company had made a mistake and wrote a long correspondence to the Atlanta office beginning with the words 'We goofed.' Shortly thereafter plaintiffs received a notification which appeared to be in the nature of a lawsuit which indicated 'final notice before suit.'

"VIII. Finally in July, 1974, a letter was forwarded by the J. C. Penney Company to the Knoxville Credit Bureau indicating that in fact J. C. Penney Company had reported an error and thereupon clients (sic) received information indicating a new account had been opened for them but were shocked to find that when the new account was opened they were again charged with the erroneous purchases and once again clients (sic) began to receive threatening letters and notices with finance charges added each month indicating such information as 'our collection department now has your account!' Plaintiffs have received a notice as recently as December, 1974, and it appears that the notices will continue to be sent. Plaintiffs have now received some 42 threatening letters and bills from the J. C. Penney Company all as a result of their gross neglect and error in spite of repeated requests of plaintiffs to correct the error including long distance phone calls to the Atlanta office and many calls to the local office of the J. C. Penney Company.

"IX. Plaintiff, Robert C. Moorhead, is an accountant with the Tennessee Valley Authority and his wife, Elizabeth Moorhead, is a schoolteacher. Neither plaintiff has ever been a party to a lawsuit previously, both enjoy an excellent reputation with regard to payment of bills and both have done all within their power to try to be reasonable in straightening out this matter with the J. C. Penney Company. It is averred that this incident has caused them considerable emotional distress and has resulted in some monetary loss to them including charges for phone calls, charges for copies of documents requested by the J. C. Penney Company, car expense for two trips to the West Town J. C. Penney Company, and the necessity to miss work and use vacation time in order to try to get the matter straightened out and the incurrence of mailing expense. The home life for plaintiffs has been considerably disrupted and their integrity questioned by defendant through its gross neglect. In fact as late as October, 1974, in a phone conversation with the Atlanta office of the J. C. Penney Company, said company through its agent indicated that the logical explanation for this matter was the possibility that the plaintiffs had given a 'bad check' to the J. C. Penney Company. . . .

"XI. It is further averred that defendant's conduct in failing to correct its obviously erroneous records for its own financial benefit has been intentional and so outrageous in character and so extreme in degree as to go beyond all possible bounds of decency and same is regarded as atrocious and utterly intolerable in a civilized community. Plaintiffs rely upon the theory of outrageous conduct. . . .

"XIV. Plaintiffs aver the actions of defendant, through its agents, has been willful, wanton, gross and intentional and that said acts have been ratified by defendant. . . .

"XVI. It is further averred that in October, 1974, defendant, through its agents, called Mrs. Elizabeth Moorhead, the wife of Robert Moorhead, and falsely and maliciously indicated that Mr. Moorhead did not pay his bills, had long been in delinquent with regard to its accounts and had not heeded reasonable requests of the defendant and the conversation tendered (sic) to degrade and injury (sic) Mr. Moorhead's situation insofar as his financial reputation was concerned. In the same conversation it was demanded that the defendant be in immediate contact with Mr. Moorhead and it was explained that the only way to reach Mr. Moorhead since he was away on business was to call Mr. Moorhead's employer, explain the circumstances and ask for an emergency contact. Defendant, through its agent, demanded and requested that this be done and it is averred that both publications amount to a slander both to Mrs. Moorhead and to the employer of plaintiff, Robert Moorhead. A document was forwarded to plaintiffs indicating that the defendant would call at plaintiff's place of business unless defendant was contacted by plaintiffs.

"XVII. It is averred that the repeated correspondence and verbal communication from defendant to plaintiff contained thinly veiled threats, indicated that plaintiff would be listed 'as delinquent with your local credit bureau,' that 'immediate court action' would be taken against plaintiff for the 'principal, interest, court costs and attorneys fees' and that 'your credit privileges have been terminated.' Plaintiffs aver these threats as well as threats that plaintiff did not pay his bills on time and was the type of person who might write a bad check were calculated to (sic) by defendant and did cause severe emotional distress, exasperation, physical irritability, and nervousness, headaches, anger, and frustrations. It is averred that a good credit reputation is an important asset in today's society and that plaintiff's job as an accountant requires that he have a good credit reputation. Defendants knew and it is averred to be the fact that a mere inference of the matters being published and communicated and threatened by defendant would severely restrict plaintiff in job opportunities, in advancement opportunities, and in the ability to enjoy life in the community in which he lived. It is further averred that Mrs. Elizabeth Moorhead, being a schoolteacher, feared and justifiably feared that the mere communication of this possible bad debt would affect her ability to obtain employment. Consequently she begged her husband to pay the bill even though same was not owed and when he stood on right and principle, considerable friction and argument resulting, causing great family discord, threats regarding their marital status, and caused both parties to be greatly upset, emotionally distressed, and physically nervous and not well.

"XVIII. Plaintiffs further aver that the threats and calls to them continued for more than one year and continued long after defendant's agents had admitted that the mistake was made and after defendant had been advised fully concerning the facts of how and why the mistake was made. It is averred that the reason the harassment and threats continued from the Collection Department of the defendant is that defendant has adopted a procedure to maximize its profits whereby its Collection Department is wholly unresponsive to communication of individuals and wholly unresponsive to communication from other departments within itself. This procedure and method was calculated to result in maximum collection effort using the threat of job security and credit reputation which this defendant knew was valuable to these plaintiffs. It is averred that this method of collection is calculated to cause collection of accounts not legitimately owed by the ability to apply credit pressure from a large wealthy corporation when the defendant knew or should have known that an individual would be severely damaged even though subsequently his or her name might be cleared."

● ● ● ●

For Deliberation and Argument

1. In another financial harassment case (*Duty v. General Finance Co.*, 273 S.W.2d 64 (1954)), the court noted, "We have been furnished by a representative of the Retail Merchants' Association of Texas with an argument by *amicus curiae*[1]. . . in which the fear is expressed that a [victory for the plaintiff] would hamper the department stores, national banks and ethical professional men in the collection of obligations owing to them." To what extent is this fear legitimate? Suppose that you owned or managed a business. What would you do about customers who did not pay their bills? Where would you draw the line between ethical and unethical steps to recover payment? What steps would you consider legitimate and ethical, what steps unethical?

2. If you were a member of the *Knoxville* jury, would you find for the plaintiff, Maggie Lane, or for the defendant? Draw on the definitions and discussions in "The Law on Liability of Public Utility for Insults by Employees" in supporting and explaining your decision. During the course of your discussion,

   - compare and contrast the illustrations provided in the law to the case at hand, explaining how these illustrations help you make your decision;
   - explain whether you consider the motorman guilty of "gross insults" (for which he and his employer are legally liable) or merely "rudeness and minor insolence" (for which they are not);
   - explain the extent to which you believe the law, as stated, is a good one, or the extent to which you believe it should be modified. For example, are the practical distinctions drawn among definitions and illustrations sensible and useful ones to regulate social interaction?

3. To what degree do you believe that J. C. Penney acted maliciously toward Robert and Elizabeth Moorhead? Could the company's actions have resulted

---

[1]Latin, "friend of the court": a person or organization "that is not a party to a lawsuit but who petitions the court to file a brief in the action because [of] a strong interest in the subject matter" (*Black's Law Dictionary*).

from honest mistakes—for example, that one department did not know what the other department was doing? Why or why not? [19]

4. Summarizing the holdings of similar cases in the past, the court hearing the *Moorhead* case wrote, "The general rule is that a creditor has a right to urge payment of a just debt, and to threaten to resort to proper legal procedure to enforce this obligation. Hence, the creditor is not liable for a mental or emotional disturbance, or for a bodily injury of illness, as a result of his mere attempt, by reasonable means, to collect." To what extent, if any, does this conclusion relieve the defendants in each of these two cases (*Lawrence* and *Moorhead*) from liability for intentional infliction of emotional distress?

5. Compare and contrast *Lawrence v. Stanford* and *Moorhead v. J. C. Penney*. Once again, assume that the plaintiffs' allegations are true. From an ethical standpoint—and ignoring for the moment the legal standpoint—how do you assess the relative degrees of "outrageousness"?

6. The case summaries provided by appeals court judges provide only the essential facts of each case—those facts providing the basis of their rulings. (Fuller details, of course, are provided in the trial court testimony.) Using these essential facts, expand one of the cases treated in this group into either a newspaper or magazine article or a short story. If you prefer, select a case from one of the previous reading groups.

7. Role-play as one of the plaintiffs (or as someone related to or friendly with the plaintiffs) in one of the cases in this group. Presume that you have not yet sued the defendant. Write *either* a personal letter or a business letter (perhaps to the prospective defendant), giving your view of the matter.

8. Select one of these cases. If you were a member of the jury, would you find for the plaintiff or the defendant? Draw on the definitions and discussions in "The Law on Intentional Infliction of Mental Distress" and other relevant rules in supporting and explaining your decision.

9. Select one of these cases. Imagine yourself as attorney for the plaintiff or attorney for the defendant. Write a paper in IRAC format to make your case. Define the *issue* in question format. State or summarize the *rules* about intentional infliction of emotional distress. *Apply/Analyze* the rules, as explained in the "Judge's Instructions to the Jury"or (as the case may be) "The Law on Liability of Public Utility for Insults by Employees" to the facts of the case you have selected. Draw a *conclusion* from the application of these rules.

■ Group 3 Readings: *Distress Caused by Sexual Predators*

In matters of unwelcome sexual advances, emotional distress is almost a given. Still, in this arena, as in all others, both morality and the law must draw boundaries between the acceptable and the unacceptable. As demonstrated in Chapter 5 of this book, sexual harassment is now a major area of legal conflict. The readings in this group deal less with sexual harassment itself than with its emotional effects.

We present three cases. In the first, "Sexual Harassment," a woman claims sexual harassment by her employer. She sues, not only for assault and battery but also for intentional infliction of emotional distress. In the second, "Covert Videotaping," a woman sues a former boyfriend who secretly taped the couple's sexual activities and then showed the tape to his friends. In the third, "A Case of Stalking," a woman is terrified when a man follows her on several occasions and then intimidates her at her house.

In discussing and writing arguments about these cases, you are encouraged to apply the rules, definitions, and illustrations of emotional distress that appear earlier in the chapter. An additional standard is provided by "The Reasonable Person," a fictitious legal construct by which juries are encouraged to assess alleged acts of negligence. Jurors are often asked to consider whether a reasonable person would act as the defendant has acted, or whether a reasonable person in the plaintiff's place would have the same reaction to the situation as the plaintiff. The readings in this group conclude with an article by a trial lawyer, Larry S. Stewart, "Arguing Pain and Suffering Damages in Summation: How to Inspire Jurors"—an article that may give you some ideas for your own arguments about cases treated in this chapter.

Sexual Harassment

400 Mass. 686
Kathleen O'CONNELL
v.
Shimon CHASDI et al.

Supreme Judicial Court of Massachusetts, Norfolk.

Argued May 7, 1987.
Decided Aug. 12, 1987.

In the spring of 1980, the plaintiff, Kathleen O'Connell, was hired as assistant to   1
the director of the Institute for International Education Programs, Inc. (Institute).
The defendant, Shimon Chasdi, was the director of the Institute. Shortly thereafter, Chasdi and O'Connell departed on a business trip to South America. Beginning on the airplane flight at the start of the trip, Chasdi engaged in a series of
sexual advances and other objectionable actions of a sexual nature. On the airplane, Chasdi asked O'Connell to share a hotel room with him. When she refused
Chasdi said that it was "rigid and inflexible" on her part. He repeated this request
in the taxi from the airport. Again she refused.

During the business trip, Chasdi repeatedly made physical advances toward   2
O'Connell placing his hand on her knee, hugging her, stroking her hair and face, and
attempting to hold her hand. O'Connell resisted his advances, telling him that such

O'Connell v. Chasdi, 511 N.E.2d 349 (1987).

contact was unwelcome. Nevertheless, Chasdi persisted. He renewed his request that O'Connell share his hotel room, and when she refused, Chasdi said that she "was very unsophisticated. It was probably because of [her] Catholic background, and that kind of thing is very common when you're working internationally, and that [she] would have to learn how to deal with these things in a more sophisticated way."

As O'Connell resisted Chasdi's advances, he became increasingly critical of   3
her, and began to threaten her job. During one taxi ride from a meeting, Chasdi attempted to hold O'Connell's hand. When she withdrew her hand, Chasdi said, "I think you should go back to Boston. When I get back, we can discuss whether you should continue to work for the organization." Soon thereafter, however, Chasdi changed his mind about having O'Connell return to Boston. O'Connell felt that her job was in jeopardy if she did not continue on the trip.

Chasdi's behavior did not improve. He questioned O'Connell about her per-   4
sonal life, and criticized her for her morals, calling her "rigid and Catholic." Chasdi continually tried to touch O'Connell, and became angry and critical when she resisted. Chasdi told her, "You have no quality in your thinking. I'm elimi-nating you." Another time, Chasdi punished O'Connell for resisting his advances by not allowing her to attend meetings that day, and later told her "he didn't know if [she] was capable of the close working relationship you needed in this job." Once, when Chasdi visited O'Connell in her hotel room because she was ill, Chasdi lifted the bedcovers and stroked her thighs. Finally, when Chasdi had a maid let him into O'Connell's room while she was sleeping, O'Connell decided to return to Boston alone. She left the next day. When Chasdi returned to Boston a few days later, O'Connell confronted him. He denied that anything had happened, and said that nobody would believe her. O'Connell resigned shortly thereafter.

O'Connell brought this action against Chasdi and the Institute, asserting   5
claims against Chasdi for assault and battery and intentional infliction of emo-tional distress.

Covert Videotaping

Dan BOYLES, Jr., Petitioner,

v.

Susan Leigh KERR, Respondent.

No. D–0963.

Supreme Court of Texas.
May 5, 1993.

On August 10, 1985, Petitioner Dan Boyles, Jr., then seventeen, covertly video-   1
taped nineteen-year-old Respondent Susan Leigh Kerr engaging in sexual inter-course with him. Although not dating steadily, they had known each other a few

months and had shared several previous sexual encounters. Kerr testified that she had not had sexual intercourse prior to her relationship with Boyles.

Kerr and Boyles, who were both home in Houston for the summer, had made   2
plans to go out on the night of the incident. Before picking Kerr up, Boyles arranged with a friend, Karl Broesche, to use the Broesche house for sexual intercourse with Kerr. Broesche suggested videotaping the activity, and Boyles agreed. Broesche and two friends, Ray Widner and John Paul Tamborello, hid a camera in a bedroom before Kerr and Boyles arrived. After setting up the camera, the three videotaped themselves making crude comments and jokes about the activity that was to follow. They left with the camera running, and the ensuing activities were recorded.

Boyles took possession of the tape shortly after it was made, and subse-   3
quently showed it on three occasions, each time at a private residence. Although he showed the tape to only ten friends, gossip about the incident soon spread among many of Kerr and Boyles' friends in Houston. Soon many students at Kerr's school, Southwest Texas State University, and Boyles' school, the University of Texas at Austin, also became aware of the story. Kerr did not learn of the video until December 1985, long after she and Boyles had stopped seeing each other. After she confronted him, Boyles eventually admitted what he had done and surrendered the tape to Kerr. No copies had been made.

Kerr alleges that she suffered humiliation and severe emotional distress from   4
the videotape and the gossip surrounding it. At social gatherings, friends and even casual acquaintances would approach her and comment about the video, wanting to know "what [she] was going to do" or "why did [she] do it." The tape stigmatized Kerr with the reputation of "porno queen" among some of her friends, and she claimed that the embarrassment and notoriety affected her academic performance. Kerr also claimed that the incident made it difficult for her to relate to men, although she testified to having had subsequent sexually-active relationships. Eventually, she sought psychological counselling.

Kerr sued Boyles, Broesche, Widner and Tamborello, alleging intentional inva-   5
sion of privacy, negligent invasion of privacy, and negligent (but not intentional) infliction of emotional distress. Before the case was submitted to the jury, however, Kerr dropped all causes of action except for negligent infliction of emotional distress. The jury returned a verdict for Kerr on that claim, assessing $500,000 in actual damages. The jury also found that all defendants were grossly negligent, awarding an additional $500,000 in punitive damages, $350,000 of which was assessed against Boyles. The trial court rendered judgment in accordance with the jury's verdict.

Only Boyles appealed to the court of appeals. That court affirmed the judg-   6
ment against him, concluding that Kerr established negligent infliction of emotional distress under the facts of this case. The court of appeals also affirmed based on negligent invasion of privacy, even though Kerr abandoned this theory prior to submission of the case to the jury and did not brief or argue it as a basis for affirmance in the court of appeals.

A Case of Stalking

237 Ga. App. 10
TRONCALLI
v.
JONES.

No. A98A2143.

Court of Appeals of Georgia.
March 15, 1999.

. . . Jones and Troncalli, who previously had met briefly, were at a mutual friend's 1
house for a business-related party on April 24, 1996. Troncalli approached Jones and
talked with her. During the conversation he "brushed up" against Jones' breasts with
his arm and then looked at her to acknowledge that he had intentionally touched her.
Jones felt uncomfortable and went to a different room; Troncalli followed her. He
then gave her his business card and again intentionally touched her breasts.

Because she felt uncomfortable at the party, Jones left the party and got in her 2
car. She saw Troncalli leaving the party and quickly walking to his car. As Jones
was driving away, she noticed in her rearview mirror that Troncalli was following
her in his car. Because she was afraid, Jones ran a stop sign, and Troncalli also
ran the stop sign. Jones recalled that Troncalli followed her car very closely and
when she began speeding, he began speeding too. Jones drove through the
parking lot of a convenience store to avoid stopping at a stop sign; Troncalli followed her through the lot.

After traveling about three miles, Jones saw two police cars parked in front of 3
a gas station. She drove up to the police and told them she was being chased. Troncalli arrived in the parking lot about a half-minute after Jones arrived. The police
officers, who testified at trial, stated that Jones appeared "extremely frightened"
and upset; she told the officers about Troncalli's behavior. At this point, Troncalli
motioned at Jones as if to cut his throat. Troncalli looked angry, and Jones understood the gesture as a threat. One of the officers confirmed that the gesture
appeared threatening and recalled that after Troncalli gestured, Jones asked the
officers to tell Troncalli to go away. The officers then asked Troncalli to leave the
premises. After about five minutes, Jones left the parking area and went home.

Officer Gomez testified that he asked Jones if she wanted to file a report 4
regarding Troncalli's stalking. Jones did not want to pursue the matter. Gomez
recalled that about a week after the incident, Jones came to the police station and
asked that an incident report be made. She was also interested in getting a
warrant against Troncalli. Though no charges were filed against Troncalli, both
the incident report and the warrant were introduced as exhibits.

The evening after the business party, Jones and Troncalli were both present at a Chamber of Commerce meeting. Jones testified that before she was aware that Troncalli was present, he walked up behind her, put his mouth on her neck, and told her she had better be careful, because someone might be watching her. Jones became very frightened and tried to get away from Troncalli, but he followed her. Jones told Troncalli that he was frightening her and asked him to leave her alone, but Troncalli laughed at her request. Jones left the meeting soon thereafter. 5

On or about May 2, 1996, a little more than a week after the first business meeting, Troncalli came to Jones' house and banged loudly on the door for about five minutes. Although Jones was not at home, her teenage daughter testified that she saw Troncalli and that her mother became more frightened after this incident. 6

After these incidents Jones developed shingles, experienced nausea and vomiting, became frightened and depressed, and sought psychological counseling. 7

At trial, Paula Head and Tamara Roberts testified that Troncalli had also subjected them to unwanted attention, touched their breasts intentionally and against their will, continued to pursue them after they asked him to stop, and otherwise behaved in a sexually inappropriate manner. 8

The Reasonable Person

W. Paige Keaton

The whole theory of negligence presupposes some uniform standard of behavior. Yet the infinite variety of situations which may arise makes it impossible to fix definite rules in advance for all conceivable human conduct. The utmost that can be done is to devise something in the nature of a formula, the application of which in each particular case must be left to the jury, or to the court. The standard of conduct which the community demands must be an external and objective one, rather than the individual judgment, good or bad, of the particular actor; and it must be, so far as possible, the same for all persons, since the law can have no favorites. At the same time, it must make proper allowance for the risk apparent to the actor, for his capacity to meet it, and for the circumstances under which he must act. 1

The courts have dealt with this very difficult problem by creating a fictitious person, who never has existed on land or sea: the "reasonable man of ordinary prudence." 2

Sometimes he is described as a reasonable person,[1] or a person of ordinary prudence, or a person of reasonable prudence, or some other blend of reason and caution. It is evident that all such phrases are intended to mean very much the 3

Prosser & Keaton on the Law of Torts, 5th ed. St. Paul, MN: West Publications, 1984.
[1]"Negligence is the omission to do something which a reasonable man, guided upon those considerations which ordinarily regulate the conduct of human affairs, would do, or doing something which a prudent and reasonable man would not do." Alderson, B., in *Blyth v. Birmingham Waterworks Co.*, 1856, 11 Ex. 781, 784, 156 Eng. Rep. 1047.

same thing. The actor is required to do what such an ideal individual would be supposed to do in his place. A model of all proper qualities, with only those human shortcomings and weaknesses which the community will tolerate on the occasion, "this excellent but odious character stands like a monument in our Courts of Justice, vainly appealing to his fellow-citizens to order their lives after his own example."[2]

The courts have gone to unusual pains to emphasize the abstract and hypothetical character of this mythical person. He is not to be identified with any ordinary individual, who might occasionally do unreasonable things; he is a prudent and careful person, who is always up to standard. Nor is it proper to identify him with any member of the very jury which is to apply the standard; he is rather a personification of a community ideal of reasonable behavior, determined by the jury's social judgment.

The conduct of the reasonable person will vary with the situation with which he is confronted. The jury must therefore be instructed to take the circumstances into account; negligence is a failure to do what the reasonable person would do "under the same or similar circumstances." Under the latitude of this phrase, the courts have made allowance not only for the external facts, but sometimes for certain characteristics of the actor himself, and have applied, in some respects, a more or less subjective standard. Depending on the context, therefore, the reasonable person standard may, in fact, combine in varying measure both objective and subjective ingredients. . . .

Knowledge

One of the most difficult questions in connection with negligence is that of what the actor may be required to know. Knowledge has been defined as belief in the existence of a fact, which coincides with the truth. It rests upon perception of the actor's surroundings, memory of what has gone before, and a power to correlate the two with previous experience. So far as perception is concerned, it seems clear that, unless his attention is legitimately distracted, the actor must give to his

---

[2]A. P. Herbert, Misleading Cases in the Common Law, 1930, 12–16: "He is an ideal, a standard, the embodiment of all those qualities which we demand of the good citizen. . . . He is one who invariably looks where he is going, and is careful to examine the immediate foreground before he executes a leap or a bound; who neither star-gazes nor is lost in meditation when approaching trapdoors or the margin of a dock; . . . who never mounts a moving omnibus and does not alight from any car while the train is in motion . . . and will inform himself of the history and habits of a dog before administering a caress; . . . who never drives his ball until those in front of him have definitely vacated the putting-green which is his own objective; who never from one year's end to another makes an excessive demand upon his wife, his neighbors, his servants, his ox, or his ass; . . . who never swears, gambles or loses his temper; who uses nothing except in moderation, and even while he flogs his child is meditating only on the golden mean. . . . In all that mass of authorities which bears upon this branch of the law there is no single mention of a reasonable woman." Arguing that women are indeed rational beings, and that the standard of liability should be gender-free, see Collins, Language, History and the Legal Process: A Profile of the "Reasonable Man," 1977, 8 Rut. Cam.L.J. 311.

surroundings the attention which a standard reasonable person would consider necessary under the circumstances, and that he must use such senses as he has to discover what is readily apparent. He may be negligent in failing to look, or in failing to observe what is visible when he does look.[3] As to memory, a person is required to fix in his mind those matters which would make such an impression upon the standard person, and, unless he is startled, or his attention is distracted for some sufficient reason, to bear them in mind, at least for a reasonable length of time. The real difficulty lies with the question of experience. The late Henry T. Terry came to the conclusion that "there are no facts whatever which every person in the community is absolutely bound at his peril to know." It seems clear, however, that there are certain things which every adult with a minimum of intelligence must necessarily have learned: the law of gravity, the fact that fire burns and water will drown, that inflammable objects will catch fire, that a loose board will tip when it is trod on, the ordinary features of the weather to which he is accustomed, and similar phenomena of nature. A person must know in addition a few elementary facts about himself: the amount of space he occupies, the principles of balance and leverage as applied to his own body, the effects of his weight, and, to the extent that it is reasonable to demand it of him, the limits of his own strength, as well as some elementary rules of health.

But beyond this, it seems clear that any individual who has led a normal exis-   7
tence will have learned much more: the traits of common animals, the normal habits, capacities and reactions of other human beings, including their propensities toward negligence and crime, the danger involved in explosives, inflammable liquids, electricity, moving machinery, slippery surfaces and firearms, that worn tires will blow out, and many other risks of life. Such an individual will not be excused when the individual denies knowledge of the risk; and to this extent, at least, there is a minimum standard of knowledge, based upon what is common to the community.

The few cases which have considered the question have held that when an   8
abnormal individual who lacks the experience common to the particular community comes into it, as in the case of the old lady from the city who comes to the farm without ever having learned that a bull is a dangerous beast, the standard of ordinary knowledge will still be applied, and it is the individual who must conform to the community, rather than vice versa.

Above this minimum, once it is determined, the individual will not be held to   9
knowledge of risks which are not known or apparent to him. A person may, however, know enough to be conscious of his own ignorance, and of possible danger into which it may lead him; and if that is the case, as where a layman attempts to give medical treatment, or one enters a strange dark passage,[4] or an

---

[3]"A pedestrian is held to have seen those obstructions in his pathway which would be discovered by a reasonably prudent person exercising ordinary care under the circumstances." *Artigue v. South Central Bell Telephone Co.*, La.App.1980, 390 So.2d 211, 213, writ refused 396 So.2d 917; *Hicks v. Donoho*, 1979, 79 Ill.App.3d 541, 35 Ill.Dec. 304, 399 N.E.2d 138 (driver).

[4]"[D]arkness is, in itself, a warning to proceed either with extreme caution or not at all." *McNally v. Liebowitz*, 1980, 274 Pa.Super. 386, 418 A.2d 460, 461, reversed, 498 Pa. 163, 445 A.2d 716.

automobile driver proceeds with a mysterious wobble in his front wheels, or traverses a strange town without an attempt to discover the meaning of unfamiliar purple traffic lights which suddenly confront him, the person may be found negligent in proceeding in the face of known ignorance.

He may, furthermore, be engaged in an activity, or stand in a relation to others, which imposes upon him an obligation to investigate and find out,[5] so that the person becomes liable not so much for being ignorant as for remaining ignorant; and this obligation may require a person to know at least enough to conduct an intelligent inquiry as to what he does not know. The occupier of premises who invites business visitors to enter, the manufacturer of goods to be sold to the public, the carrier who undertakes to transport passengers, all are charged with the duty of the affirmative action which would be taken by a reasonable person in their position to discover dangers of which they may not be informed. As scientific knowledge advances, and more and more effective tests become available, what was excusable ignorance yesterday becomes negligent ignorance today.

Superior Knowledge, Skill and Intelligence; Professional Malpractice

Thus far the question has been one of a minimum standard, below which the individual will not be permitted to fall. But if a person in fact has knowledge, skill, or even intelligence superior to that of the ordinary person, the law will demand of that person conduct consistent with it. Experienced milk haulers, hockey coaches, expert skiers, construction inspectors, and doctors must all use care which is reasonable in light of their superior learning and experience, and any special skills, knowledge or training they may personally have over and above what is normally possessed by persons in the field.

Arguing Pain and Suffering Damages in Summation: How to Inspire Jurors

Larry S. Stewart

Recovery of "pain and suffering" damages is one of the most challenging tasks facing plaintiffs' attorneys today. For more than a decade the insurance industry and various other groups have been conducting an unrelenting, all-out war on the civil justice system. Many of their efforts have been deflected or defeated. But

---

[5]"Where a duty to use care is imposed and where knowledge is necessary to careful conduct, voluntary ignorance is equivalent to negligence." Gobrecht v. Beckwith, 1926, 82 N.H. 415, 420, 135 A. 20, 22.

Trial (Mar. 1992): 55–57.

they have convinced a significant part of the U.S. public that there is something inherently wrong—even evil—in a claim for pain and suffering damages.

As a result, many potential jurors enter the courthouse with a prejudice against these claims. This makes pain and suffering damages difficult to recover.   2

The prejudices prevalent today operate on two levels. First, jurors resist the very fact of pain and suffering. For some people, the term "pain and suffering" has become an emotional code for fraud or deceit. Second, jurors resist the amount of the award. Claims are presumed to be inflated or exaggerated, making the plaintiff's burden of persuasion enormous. You must counter these prejudices throughout a trial—and especially during your summation.   3

In voir dire, you should identify and exclude the more prejudiced individuals. But even the most artful jury selection cannot eliminate all vestiges of this kind of prejudice. And although the depth of the prejudice will vary from jury to jury and from jurisdiction to jurisdiction, it is a potential problem in every jury.   4

You should treat this problem as a challenge. Redouble your efforts and polish your skills. Significant general damages can still be recovered if you work diligently at every aspect of trial, select witnesses carefully, use expert testimony skillfully and exhibits and demonstrative aids imaginatively, avoid exaggeration or overstatement, and prepare plaintiffs and expert and lay witnesses meticulously. However—notwithstanding even the best preparation and presentation—if prejudice surfaces in the jury room, general damages can be denied or significantly compromised.   5

Your challenge is to defeat or avoid jurors' conditioned responses and achieve full justice for your clients. When arguing pain and suffering, adopt techniques that improve the chances of obtaining full compensation. What follows are some ideas gleaned and collected over the years—many of them from other trial lawyers.   6

Human nature makes people turn away from others' troubles. Moving jurors beyond their natural reluctance to deal with the plaintiff's problems is difficult. To do this, you must engage the jurors' emotions. Justice may be blind—but she is not heartless.   7

The emotional response you are seeking is an appreciation of the plaintiff's predicament. You can't make jurors feel the plaintiff's pain, but you can make them understand it. This requires skill and passion. You should not simply repeat the evidence in summation. You must inspire the jury to rise above just understanding the facts of the case.   8

No one is born with such advocacy skills. They can only be learned. One of the best ways is to read and practice speaking the words of great writers. Read voraciously and collect every example of moving prose you find.   9

Also, take the time to learn what your client has suffered and is experiencing in daily life. Too many attorneys think that they don't have to ask their clients what pain and suffering is because they already know. They think they can describe it to the jury solely because they are highly skilled. They are dead wrong.   10

Spend time with the client and the client's family in their normal environment. Walk in the client's shoes. Learn how the client and family have been affected by   11 the client's injury, how they hurt, and what burdens they bear every day. Discover what they have lost. Invariably the raw material for an effective argument will be there, awaiting refinement by the skillful advocate.

If the case warrants it, consider hiring one or more consultants to work with   12
you to explore damages. Sometimes another perspective can uncover key bits of evidence that would otherwise have gone unnoticed and unused.

All of your efforts will come together in the final argument. But final argument   13
is much more than merely a summary of the merits of the case. It is also the ultimate opportunity to deal with, avoid, or overcome the problems that you face. The degree to which you are successful will largely determine the amount of success your client achieves. To formulate a successful final argument, you should structure it so that you motivate the jury, dictate the jury-room dialogue, describe pain and suffering, use demonstrative aids, present dollar amounts, and prepare your rebuttal.

Motivating the Jury

Motivating and inspiring the jury will help set the stage for the recovery of intan-   14
gible damages. By raising the awareness of the jurors, you help them to rise above their prejudice and their natural reluctance to dwell on others' troubles.

You can do this at the beginning of the final argument. Here is an example: 15

> As jurors, you are part of the greatest democratic government ever devised in the history of humankind. There were democracies before the United States of America, and there was also trial by jury. But the earlier democracies and the earlier forms of trial by jury were reserved for the nobility—a privileged few. What is unique about the U.S. system of justice is that anyone—and everyone—can serve as a juror. And these people—you people—are entrusted with the sole power to right wrongs, to do justice. The law places it in your hands to decide. . . . And the law places it in your hands to award damages.

Another way to raise the jurors' awareness is to try to impress them with the   16
importance of what they are about to do, so they will render the right verdict:

> The character of our country is the sum of the characters of all the individual jurors deciding cases throughout the land. It is decided over and over, day after day, in the verdicts of juries throughout this nation. And the verdict that you render today will be part of the great sum that will decide who we are, what we value, and what we will not tolerate.

Dictating Jury-Room Dialogue

If a juror has arrived at the courthouse already prejudiced against awarding pain   17
and suffering damages, the danger is that a conditioned response may occur. You say "pain and suffering," and the juror reacts negatively. This is exactly what plaintiffs' attorneys want to avoid.

Think about how this response has been conditioned. Jurors have been brain-washed about pain and suffering, and they have never critically examined what they have been told. However, in the short time you have available for final argument, you cannot hope to convince jurors that what they believe is wrong. It is a mistake to try to persuade them that they have been sold a bogus bill of goods. But you can effectively make an end run around the prejudice by getting them to think about pain and suffering in a different way.   18

Most jurors have never considered that the right to be free from pain and suffering is a fundamental right of every person. You can go a long way toward overcoming the brainwashing by getting them to focus on this fact. It can be done by equating the fundamental human right to dignity with the freedom from pain and suffering. This puts the debate on a different plane and provides an easy transition to the damage phase of the argument. For example: 19

> The U.S. system of justice is the only one in the history of mankind that has as its foundation the value and dignity of human life. No other government has ever guaranteed to all its citizens the right to life, liberty, and the pursuit of happiness.
>
> Battlefields have run red with blood to preserve these rights for all the Bob Markhams of this country. But in the final analysis, those guarantees are a hollow promise if they cannot be enforced. You jurors must put the meaning of those rights into this case for, in the blink of an eye on June 15, 1988, Bob Markham's right to liberty and happiness was snuffed out. His pride and his dignity and his right to a life free from pain were taken from him, not just for the past _____ months but also for the next _____ years.

Another way to influence the dialogue in the jury room is to get the jurors to focus on their duty to award intangible damages. Make the jurors understand that they have certain obligations, one of which, assuming liability, is to return money damages that include pain and suffering damages. Again, a discussion of this can provide the transition from liability to damages. Here is one way to do it: 20

> Unfortunately, you do not have the power to turn back the clock and restore Mr. Markham to what he was before the accident. I wish you could. He would be eternally grateful if you could. But that cannot happen. You can only do what the law says you must do—award fair and full damages for Mr. Markham's injuries and his agony and suffering. You must do your duty as the judge will instruct you. And you must be careful to make sure that you do full justice by Mr. Markham now, because you will never again have the opportunity.

Another alternative is to appeal to the jurors' sense of justice. The message does not have to be elaborate. It could be something as simple as this.   21

> Justice resides in everyone's heart, but only the truth can let it out. By your verdict you are asked to speak the truth today and to do justice for Bob Markham.

The point is to galvanize the jury at the outset so that during deliberations the   22
jurors will not waste time arguing about whatever misinformation about the civil
justice system they have heard or read. At least you will have inspired some jurors
to object to discussions of this subject if it is raised by others.

Describing Pain and Suffering

Since one goal of advocacy is to avoid triggering preconditioned negative   23
responses, you should avoid using the term "pain and suffering" to the extent possible. View this as an opportunity rather than a limitation. The forms and shades
of human suffering are as endless as the human imagination. The dedicated advocate will discern the nuances of the case and develop ways to describe pain and
suffering that will move the jury to reach the conclusion desired.

You can describe pain and suffering without ever using those words. Vivid   24
words move jurors. You can say—

- "agony and misery" instead of "pain";
- "fear and terror" instead of "mental anguish";
- "fear and anguish are her constant companions";
- "a window to hell";
- "pain is the blood brother of death";
- "imprisoned by scars";
- "the indignity of always being a burden to others."

And to drive home the extent of the pain and suffering damages in this case,   25
consider addressing it in the following terms:

No one has ever sought pain. People have even sought death to escape pain.
Pain can break people's spirits. Pain is so horrible that it is unlawful for the
state to inflict pain in criminal cases. The state may kill you for your crimes,
but it cannot torture you.

Using Demonstrative Aids

There is no greater truism than "a picture is worth a thousand words." Yet too   26
often, plaintiffs' lawyers use demonstrative aids only when discussing liability
and ignore them when discussing general damages.

You should examine the evidence in every case to see if it can be used to   27
demonstrate pain and suffering. Invariably the raw material is there, but finding
it means an unrelenting devotion to the client's case—a willingness to find and
understand every detail of your client's tragedy.

Locate the memorabilia, pictures, videos, and other collections that show   28
what your client's life used to be like. Review personal records, school records,
and other documents that reveal the plaintiff's history. Then comb the hospital
and other medical records. These may be a catalogue of horrors. These materials
can become irrefutable proofs of the client's changed state, especially when they

are presented as blowups. If they will work as demonstrative evidence, weave them into your presentation of the case. Only by knowing what the plaintiff has lost can jurors measure the full extent of the agony suffered.

During trial, note the jewels of testimony presented by witnesses (or have an assistant do this). You can note these gems on a large flip pad in front of the jury or collect them on a large chart for final argument. The chart need not be fancy. It will serve as an effective outline for reviewing the true extent of the pain and suffering. 29

Translating Pain into Numbers

How to translate the evidence into a dollar amount runs the entire gamut of advocacy. If you have presented the evidence effectively and motivated the jury, how you arrive at the final number is the least important part of the argument—as long as you do not ask for too much. But if you have not assembled the evidence and motivated the jury, then no matter how clever your presentation, it will fall on deaf ears. 30

Some lawyers favor a per diem approach in jurisdictions where it is allowed. Some refine this approach and give a separate figure for each element (e.g., pain, injury, embarrassment). Other attorneys favor a single lump-sum approach. All good advocates will try to find the best approach for the individual case. 31

More important than how you arrive at or explain the number is your ability to present it with conviction and confidence, without hesitation or negative body language. Whatever approach you choose, you must be comfortable with it and you must present the number with credibility. 32

You should consider challenging defense counsel to give a number to the jury. Defense counsel who fail to respond may be seen by the jury as being unfair or afraid—or even as tacitly admitting the validity of the plaintiff's request. On the other hand, if defense counsel gives a ridiculously low number, this provides you the opportunity to display righteous indignation in rebuttal. 33

Preparing Rebuttal

One or two points skillfully scored with just the right amount of scorn or righteousness will echo in the jury room. Learn all you can about your opponent to anticipate what rebuttal opportunities may arise. You also need to be alert during the trial, especially during motion arguments, to see if your opponent telegraphs his punches. 34

If your opponent attacks the amount requested for pain and suffering, you should consider a response somewhat along these lines. 35

It is easy for Ms. Jones to say that these damages are too much, but consider if we were to place the following ad in the Sunday paper: "Immediate job opening paying $ _____ per day. No special job qualifications required. No age limit. No special education or experience required.

"All you have to do is to suffer pain the rest of your life, 24 hours a day, seven days a week. No time off for the Fourth of July or any other holiday. No vacations. $ _____ per day to suffer unrelenting pain the rest of your life."

Would there be any takers? Yet that is exactly what has happened to Bob Markham.

Another way to wrap up rebuttal and inspire jurors is to summon them to bring in a verdict that they can always be proud of.   36

What you do here today is extremely important. It is important to these parties, and it is important to our democratic way of life. When you leave this courtroom, your work will be done. But your verdict will live on. It will be part of the permanent records of this court. It will affect not just these parties but all those who follow.

Return a verdict that will fill you with pride, so that when you leave this courtroom it will be with your head held high, knowing in your heart that you have rendered justice—so that tomorrow, and next year, and for all the tomorrows thereafter, you can say that in [March of 1992], "I sat on a jury in [Miami, Florida], and we reached a just verdict."

Remember that summation must bear the mark of the individual lawyer.   37
There is no fixed method to follow. There is no right or wrong way to sum up a case. Your own sincere final argument is always more effective than an imitation of someone else's. Your goal must always be to motivate and inspire the members of the jury. And your only limitations are the rules of evidence and your own resourcefulness and imagination.

● ● ● ● ●

For Deliberation and Argument

1. Assess Kathleen O'Connell's claim against Shimon Chasdi. Apply the criteria for emotional distress, as indicated in the jury instructions, to the facts of this case. Was Chasdi's behavior sufficiently "outrageous" to qualify under the law as intentional infliction of emotional distress? You may want to clarify your discussion by comparing Chasdi's conduct to that of one or more other defendants in this chapter.
2. Kerr sued Boyles for *negligent*, rather than *intentional* infliction of emotional distress. Review the law and the jury instructions for each type of claim (see pp. 119–21, pp. 132–34, and pp. 163–65). Do you believe that Kerr and her attorneys made the right choice? Explain, citing relevant sections of the law, as they apply to the facts of the case.
3. Boyles's attorneys charged that the real reason Kerr sued for negligent rather than intentional infliction of emotional distress was to get at the "deep pockets" of Boyles's insurance company. They pointed out:

In Texas, a home owners policy covers only accidents or careless conduct and excluded intentional acts. Ms. Kerr's lawyers may have believed that if they obtained a judgment declaring that Boyles' conduct came within the rubric of "negligence" (inadvertence or carelessness), they could tap the homeowners policies owned by the parents of Boyles and the other defendants. Thus, this case has a lot to do with a search for a "deep pocket" who can pay. If the purpose of awarding damages is to punish the wrongdoer and deter such conduct in the future, then the individuals responsible for these reprehensible actions are the ones who should suffer, not the people of Texas in the form of higher insurance premiums for home owners.

React and respond to this argument as if you were one of Kerr's attorneys.

4. If you were on the *Troncalli v. Jones* jury, how would you vote on the question of whether Troncalli should be found liable for inflicting emotional distress on Jones? What, to you, is the most important evidence influencing your decision about whether Jones's behavior meets the criteria for intentional infliction of emotional distress outlined in both the "Judge's Instructions to the Jury" and "The Law on Intentional Infliction of Mental Distress"?

5. In addition to charging Troncalli with infliction of emotional distress, Jones also charged him with stalking, invasion of privacy, and assault and battery. Based on the following definitions, is Troncalli guilty of stalking and either or both of the other two offenses?

Stalking has been defined as follows (Delaware Stalking Statute):

(a) Any person who wilfully, maliciously and repeatedly follows or harasses another person or who repeatedly makes a credible threat with the intent to place that person in reasonable fear of death or serious physical injury is guilty of the crime of stalking.

(b) For the purposes of this section the following definitions are provided:

  (1) "Harasses" means a knowing and wilful course of conduct directed at a specific person which seriously alarms, annoys or harasses the person and which serves no legitimate purpose. The course of conduct must be such as would cause a reasonable person to suffer substantial emotional distress and must actually cause substantial emotional distress to the person.

  (2) "Course of conduct" means a pattern of conduct composed of a series of acts over a period of time, however short, evidencing a continuity of purpose. Constitutionally protected activity is not included within the meaning of "course of conduct." 11 Del. Code § 1312A; *Snowden v. State.* 677 A.2d 33 (1996).

Georgia case law defines the key element of *invasion of privacy* as "intrusion upon the plaintiff's seclusion or solitude, or into his private affairs." *Troncalli v. Jones*, 514 S.E.2d at 482.

Battery is defined as the harmful or offensive touching of another that is intentional, unconsented, and unprivileged (i.e., an action taken in self defense or in the defense or protection of another, including the plaintiff, is privileged and is not battery).

6. Role-play as one of the plaintiffs (or as someone related to or friendly with the plaintiffs) in one of the cases in this group. Presume that you have not yet sued the defendant. Write a personal letter giving your view of the matter.

7. Select one of these three cases. Imagine yourself as attorney for the plaintiff or attorney for the defendant. Write a paper in IRAC format to make your case. Define the *issue* in question format. State or summarize the *rules* about intentional infliction of emotional distress. *Apply/Analyze* the rules, as explained in the "Judge's Instructions to the Jury" and "The Reasonable Person" to the facts of the case you have selected. Draw a *conclusion* from the application of these rules.

8. After reviewing "The Reasonable Person," write a short paper detailing an experience that you or someone you know (or perhaps a fictional character) has had, measuring all of the actions detailed against the standard of "the reasonable person." To what degree did each of these actions meet the "reasonable person" standard? To what extent did they fall short? In those cases where the actions fell short, could they have been interpreted as negligence? If so, could one or more of these negligent acts have resulted in accidents that caused another or others emotional distress? If so, add to your account a formal statement by a plaintiff charging negligence that resulted in emotional disturbance.

9. Discuss your reaction to Larry Stewart's "Arguing Pain and Suffering Damages in Summation." To what extent does Stewart's advice make you think better or worse of trial lawyers and their strategies for success in the courtroom? In your discussion, keep in mind both the interests of the plaintiffs and the interests of the defendants in such cases as you have studied in this chapter.

10. Following Stewart's recommendations, draft a closing argument for one of the cases that you have studied so far in this chapter. Don't appropriate his language directly; rather, follow his general strategy, using the specific facts of whichever case you select. You may also want to incorporate (either in a preliminary paragraph, or during the course of the discussion) some "demonstrative aids" to support your argument for your client.

■ Group 4 Readings: *Witnesses to Disaster*

Most of the cases we have dealt with so far involve the intentional *infliction of emotional distress. That is, the plaintiffs have charged that the defendants, through willfulness or malice, have set out to inflict mental distress. As we have seen, the primary criterion for judging such claims is the degree to which the defendant's actions would be viewed by as "outrageous" by "the rea-*

sonable person." The conduct in question must go "beyond all possible bounds of decency so as to be regarded as atrocious and utterly intolerable in a civilized community."

Clearly, however, many people suffer emotional disturbance not because someone has purposely inflicted mental distress on them but because of the negligent acts of one or more others. One doesn't have to be a lawyer to appreciate this distinction. We generally think worse of people who intentionally set out to hurt us than we do of people whose carelessness hurts us, even though, as they protest, they "didn't mean to." Of course, to the victim or the victim's loved ones, the offender's intentions may not make any difference. The mother whose son is killed because of defective automobile brakes suffers as much emotional distress as the one whose son is murdered in an armed robbery.

Still, the law draws a distinction between emotional distress that has been intentionally inflicted and emotional distress that has been caused by negligence—or NIED, for "negligent infliction of emotional distress." Perhaps the primary way of establishing a standard of negligence is to postulate what a "reasonable person" would have done, or would not have done, under the circumstances (see "The Reasonable Person," pp. 146–49). This reasonable person is "an ideal, a standard, the embodiment of all those qualities which we demand of the good citizen." The reasonable person, according the law, would have foreseen that a given action of his or hers could have dangerous consequences, and so would not have engaged in that action. Foreseeability is an important issue when a judge or jury tries to determine negligence. For example, just as a speeding driver ought to have foreseen that his excessive speed could cause an accident, one that could injure or kill someone, he ought also to have foreseen that this accident might result in severe emotional distress to the victim's loved ones.

Until recently, however, many courts have been reluctant to allow claims for NIED alone, pointing to the subjectivity of such injuries and preferring to have plaintiffs base claims on the physical consequences of negligence. For example, a defendant may be liable for damages—including deaths, physical injuries, and property damage—caused by the negligent manufacture or installation of brakes, but not for emotional distress only (absent any damage or physical injuries) to victims or relatives of victims of accidents caused by the defective brakes. Faced with claims of emotional distress, many courts have found it difficult to assess the seriousness, or the permanence, or the genuineness of such mental injuries. When they do consider these claims, they generally take into account such factors as whether the plaintiff was present at the scene of the accident and actually witnessed it (as opposed to hearing about it from someone else) and the closeness of the family relationship between the victim and the plaintiff.

In recent years, courts have been taking a more liberal view of emotional distress claims based on negligence. In the following group of readings, we offer four cases involving NIED claims. In the first case, Dillon v. Legg, *a mother witnesses the death of her daughter in an automobile accident. In* Barnhill v. Davis, *a son witnesses an accident that only slightly injures his mother. In* Portee v. Jaffee, *a mother witnesses her seven-year-old crushed in elevator accident. In* Dunphy v. Gregor, *a woman witnesses her fiancé killed by an automobile. Following these cases, we provide "The Law on Unintentional and Negligent Infliction of Emotional Disturbance," which provides one set of standards to judge cases of emotional distress caused by negligence. Also included is a set of jury instructions on NIED. Next is "The Thing Test for NIED." This is a crucial element of a 1989 California Supreme Court decision in the case of* Thing v. La Chusa *(48 Cal.3d 644, 771 P.2d 814), which established a key set of criteria for evaluating NIED cases. This group of readings concludes with a set of standards comprising "The Psychology of Emotional Distress," through which you may be able to assess the seriousness of the emotional distress claimed by the plaintiffs.*

Accident 1

69 Cal. Rptr. 72
Margery M. DILLON et al.,
Plaintiffs and Appellants,
v.
David Luther LEGG, Defendant and Respondent.

Sac. 7816.

Supreme Court of California, In Bank.
June 21, 1968.

Plaintiff's first cause of action alleged that on or about September 27, 1964, defen-   1
dant drove his automobile in a southerly direction on Bluegrass Road near its
intersection with Clover Lane in the County of Sacramento, and at that time plaintiff's infant daughter, Erin Lee Dillon, lawfully crossed Bluegrass Road. The complaint further alleged that defendant's negligent operation of his vehicle caused it
to "collide with the deceased Erin Lee Dillon resulting in injuries to decedent
which proximately resulted in her death." Plaintiff, as the mother of the decedent,
brought an action for compensation for the loss.

Plaintiff's second cause of action alleged that she, Margery M. Dillon, "was in   2
close proximity to the . . . collision and personally witnessed said collision." She

---

further alleged that "because of the negligence of defendants . . . and as a proximate cause [*sic*] thereof plaintiff . . . sustained great emotional disturbance and shock and injury to her nervous system" which caused her great physical and mental pain and suffering.

Plaintiff's third cause of action alleged that Cheryl Dillon, another infant daughter, was "in close proximity to the . . . collision and personally witnessed said collision." Because of the negligence, Cheryl Dillon "sustained great emotional disturbance and shock and injury to her nervous system," which caused her great physical and mental pain and suffering. 3

Accident 2

Robert C. BARNHILL, Appellant,

v.

Rose Marie DAVIS and James A. Davis, Appellees.

No. 64492.

Supreme Court of Iowa.
Jan. 14, 1981.

On June 12, 1978, plaintiff Robert C. Barnhill was driving his car in West Des Moines. He was being followed by his mother, Grace Maring, who was driving her car. Barnhill stopped at an intersection and then proceeded safely through it. He pulled over to the side, about three car lengths from the intersection, to wait for his mother. When Maring tried to drive through the intersection, her car was struck on the driver's side by a car driven by defendant Rose Marie Davis and owned by defendant James A. Davis. 1

As a result of the accident, Maring was slightly bruised. She was examined by doctors shortly after the accident and also approximately six weeks later. The first examination disclosed a bruised rib cage and mild muscle strain. The second examination report stated "she did not claim or present any evidence of physical injury from the accident." Barnhill claims that he has suffered emotional distress because of his fear for his mother's safety. He contends the emotional distress has caused pain in his back and legs, dizziness, and difficulty in sleeping. 2

Barnhill v. Davis, 300 N.W.2d 104 (1981).

Accident 3

■ ━━━ ■

84 N.J. 88
Renee PORTEE, Individually and as
General Administratrix and Administratrix
ad Prosequendum of the Estate of Guy Portee,
Deceased, Plaintiff-Appellant,
v.
Edith JAFFEE, Nathan Jaffee,
Watson Elevator Company and Atlantic
Elevator Company, Defendants-Respondents.

Supreme Court of New Jersey.

Argued May 5, 1980.
Decided July 29, 1980.

Plaintiff's seven-year-old son, Guy Portee, resided with his mother in a Newark   1
apartment building. Defendants Edith Jaffee and Nathan Jaffee owned and operated the building. On the afternoon of May 22, 1976, the youngster became trapped
in the building's elevator between its outer door and the wall of the elevator shaft.
The elevator was activated and the boy was dragged up to the third floor. Another
child who was racing up a nearby stairway to beat the elevator opened it, saw the
victim wedged within it, and ran to seek help. Soon afterwards, plaintiff and officers of the Newark Police Department arrived. The officers worked for four and
one-half hours to free the child. While their efforts continued, the plaintiff watched
as her son moaned, cried out and flailed his arms. Much of the time she was
restrained from touching him, apparently to prevent interference with the
attempted rescue. The child suffered multiple bone fractures and massive internal
hemorrhaging. He died while still trapped, his mother a helpless observer.

During the unsuccessful efforts to save Guy Portee's life, the police contacted   2
the office of defendant Atlantic Elevator Company in nearby Belleville, New
Jersey. Along with defendant Watson Elevator Company, which designed and
built the elevator, Atlantic was responsible for the installation and maintenance
of the elevator. The police requested that Atlantic send a mechanic to the building
to assist in the attempt to free plaintiff's son. Apparently no one came.

After her son's death plaintiff became severely depressed and seriously self-   3
destructive. On March 24, 1979, she attempted to take her own life. She was admitted
to East Orange General Hospital with a laceration of her left wrist more than two
inches deep. She survived and the wound was repaired by surgery, but she has since
required considerable physical therapy and presently has no sensation in a portion
of her left hand. She has received extensive counseling and psychotherapy to help
overcome the mental and emotional problems caused by her son's death.

───────

Portee v. Jaffee, 417 A.2d 521 (1980).

On December 2, 1976, plaintiff brought suit against the Jaffees and the two [4] elevator companies. The complaint was premised on defendants' negligence in failing to provide a safe elevator. As both general administratrix and administratrix *ad prosequendum* of the estate of Guy Portee, plaintiff asserted survival and wrongful death claims. She also sued individually seeking damages for her mental and emotional distress caused by observing her son's anguish and death.

◼ Accident 4 ◼

136 N.J. 99
Eileen M. DUNPHY, Plaintiff–Respondent,
v.
James L. GREGOR, Defendant–Appellant.

Supreme Court of New Jersey.

Argued Oct. 13, 1993.
Decided June 2, 1994.

Eileen Dunphy and Michael T. Burwell became engaged to marry in April 1988 [1] and began cohabitating two months later. The couple set a date of February 29, 1992, for their wedding. On September 29, 1990, the couple responded to a friend's telephone call for assistance in changing a tire on Route 80 in Mount Arlington. As Michael changed the left rear tire of the friend's car on the shoulder of the roadway, he was struck by a car driven by defendant, James Gregor. After being struck by the vehicle, his body was either dragged or propelled 240 feet. Eileen, who had been standing approximately five feet from Michael, witnessed the impact, and ran to him immediately. Realizing that he was still alive, she cleared pebbles and blood from his mouth to ease his breathing. She attempted to subdue his hands and feet as they thrashed about, all the while talking to him in an effort to comfort him. The following day, after a night-long vigil at Dover General Hospital, Eileen was told that Michael Burwell had died as a result of his injuries. Since the accident, Eileen has undergone psychiatric and psychological treatment for depression and anxiety. She instituted an action seeking to recover damages for the "mental anguish, pain and suffering" experienced as a result of witnessing the events that led to the death of her fiance.

Eileen testified at her deposition that both she and Michael had taken out life- [2] insurance policies making each other beneficiaries. They had maintained a joint checking account from which they had paid their bills, and also they had jointly purchased an automobile. In addition, Michael had asked her several times to elope with him, and he had introduced her in public as his wife.

Dunphy v. Gregor, 642 A.2d 372 (1994).

The Law on Unintentional and Negligent Infliction of Emotional Distress (NIED)

§ 313. Emotional Distress Unintended

(1) If the actor unintentionally causes emotional distress to another, he is subject to liability to the other for resulting illness or bodily harm if the actor
   (a) should have realized that his conduct involved an unreasonable risk of causing the distress, otherwise than by knowledge of the harm or peril of a third person, and
   (b) from facts known to him should have realized that the distress, if it were caused, might result in illness or bodily harm.
(2) The rule stated in Subsection (1) has no application to illness or bodily harm of another which is caused by emotional distress arising solely from harm or peril to a third person, unless the negligence of the actor has otherwise created an unreasonable risk of bodily harm to the other.

Comment on Subsection (1):

a. The rule stated in this Section does not give protection to mental and emotional tranquillity in itself. In general, as stated in § 436 A [below, pp. 164–65], there is no liability where the actor's negligent conduct inflicts only emotional distress, without resulting bodily harm or any other invasion of the other's interests. Such emotional distress is important only in so far as its existence involves a risk of bodily harm, and as affecting the damages recoverable if bodily harm is sustained. [Note: In California, this rule was superseded by the *Thing* decision in 1989 (p. 166), which does not require that the plaintiff have suffered "bodily harm."]   1

b. The rule stated in this Section is unnecessary to make the actor's conduct negligent and, therefore, to subject him to liability if the actor should realize that it involves an unreasonable risk of causing bodily harm in some other manner, such as by immediate impact. . . .   2

[T]he actor who intentionally subjects another to emotional distress may under some circumstances take the risk that the other may, unknown to him, have a resistance to emotional strain which is less than that of the ordinary man although characteristic of a recognized minority of human beings. On the other hand, one who unintentionally but negligently subjects another to such an emotional distress does not take the risk of any exceptional physical sensitiveness to emotion which the other may have unless the circumstances known to the actor should apprise him of it. Thus, one who negligently drives an automobile through   3

Restatement (Second) of Torts. As adapted and promulgated by the American Law Institute at Washington, D.C. May 25, 1963, and May 22, 1964. St. Paul, MN: West Publishing, 1965.

a city street in a manner likely merely to startle a pedestrian on a sidewalk, is not required to take into account the possibility that the latter may be so constituted that the slight mental disurbance will bring about an illness.

Illustrations:

1. A is employed to drive B to a hospital. He is informed that B is desperately ill. Nonetheless, he drives at a rapid rate of speed and cuts in and out of traffic. He thereby puts B in such fear of a collision that B suffers a serious increase in her illness. A is subject to liability to B.   4

2. Under the facts assumed in Illustration 1, A would not be liable to B if he had no reason to know of B's illness.

§ 436 A. Negligence Resulting in Emotional Disturbance Alone

If the actor's conduct is negligent as creating an unreasonable risk of causing either bodily harm or emotional disturbance to another, and it results in such emotional disturbance alone, without bodily harm or other compensable damage, the actor is not liable for such emotional disturbance.   5

Comment:

a. The rule stated in this Section stands in contrast to those stated in §§ 46 [see pp. 132–34] and 48, as to the intentional infliction of emotional distress. It is also to be contrasted with the rules stated in § 436, under which an actor who has negligently created an unreasonable risk of causing either bodily harm or emotional disturbance to another becomes subject to liability for bodily harm brought about solely by the internal operation of emotional disturbance. Under the rule stated in this Section, the negligent actor is not liable when his conduct results in the emotional disturbance alone, without the bodily harm or other compensable damage. The difference is one between the negligent automobile driver who narrowly misses a woman and frightens her into a miscarriage, and the negligent driver who merely frightens, her, without more.   6

b. The reasons for the distinction, as they usually have been stated by the courts, have been three. One is that emotional disturbance which is not so severe and serious as to have physical consequences is normally in the realm of the trivial, and so falls within the maxim that the law does not concern itself with trifles. It is likely to be so temporary, so evanescent, and so relatively harmless and unimportant, that the task of compensating for it would unduly burden the courts and the defendants. The second is that in the absence of the guarantee of provided by resulting bodily harm, such emotional disturbance may be too easily feigned, depending, as it must, very largely upon the subjective testimony of the plaintiff; and that to allow recovery for it might open too wide a door for false claimants who have suffered no real harm at all. The third is that where the defendant has been merely negligent, without any element of intent to do harm, his fault is not so great that he should be required to make good a purely mental disturbance. [Note: In California, this rule was superseded by the *Thing* decision in 1989 (p. 166), which does not require that the plaintiff in an emotional distress suit have suffered "bodily harm."]   7 *c.* The rule stated in this Section applies to all forms of emotional disturbance, including temporary fright, nervous shock, nausea, grief, rage, and humiliation. The fact that these are accompanied by transitory, non-recurring physical phenomena, harmless in themselves, such as dizziness, vomiting, and the like, does not make the actor liable where such phenomena are in themselves inconsequential and do not amount to any substantial bodily harm. On the other hand, long continued nausea or headaches may amount to physical illness, which is bodily harm; and even long continued mental disturbance, as for example in the case of repeated hysterical attacks, or mental aberration, may be classified by the courts as illness, notwithstanding their mental character. This becomes a medical or psychiatric problem, rather than one of law.

Illustration:

1. A negligently manufactures and places upon the market cottage cheese containing broken glass. B purchases a package of the cheese, and upon eating it finds her mouth full of glass. She is not cut or otherwise physically injured, and she succeeds in removing the glass without bodily harm; but she is frightened at the possibility that she may have swallowed some of the glass. Her fright results in nausea and nervousness lasting for one day, and in inability to sleep that night, but in no other harm. A is not liable to B.

■ Judge's Instructions to the Jury ■

UNINTENTIONAL AND NEGLIGENT INFLICTION OF EMOTIONAL DISTRESS (NIED)

The plaintiff _____ seeks to recover damages based upon a claim of negligent infliction of emotional distress.

The elements of such a claim are:

1. The defendant engaged in negligent conduct;
2. The plaintiff suffered serious emotional distress;
3. The defendant's negligent conduct was a cause of the serious emotional distress.

Serious emotional distress is an emotional reaction which is not an abnormal response to the circumstances. It is found where a reasonable person would be unable to cope with the mental distress caused by the circumstances.

California Jury Instructions, Civil: Book of Approved Jury Instructions 8th ed. Prepared by the Committee on Standard Jury Instruction Civil, of the Superior Court of Los Angeles County, California. Hon. Stephen M. Lachs, Judge of the Superior Court, Chairman. Compiled and Edited by Paul G. Breckenridge, Jr. St. Paul, MN: West Publishing, 1994.

The "Thing Test" for NIED

We conclude, therefore, that a plaintiff may recover damages for emotional distress caused by observing the negligently inflicted injury of a third person if, but only if, said plaintiff: (1) is closely related to the injury victim; (2) is present at the scene of the injury producing event at the time it occurs and is then aware that it is causing injury to the victim; and (3) as a result suffers serious emotional distress—a reaction beyond that which would be anticipated in a disinterested witness and which is not an abnormal response to the circumstances. 1

The Psychology of Emotional Distress

Definitions of Mental Anguish

[A]¹

[A] relatively high degree of mental pain and distress. It is more than mere disappointment, anger, resentment, or embarrassment, although it may include all of these. It includes a mental sensation of pain resulting from such painful emotion as grief, severe disappointment, indignation, wounded pride, shame, despair and/or public humiliation. 1

[B]²

From a medical perspective, negligently-inflicted mental distress may be characterized as a reaction to a traumatic stimulus, which may be physical or purely psychic. Traumatic stimulus may cause two types of mental reaction, primary and secondary. The primary response, an immediate, automatic and instinctive response designed to protect an individual from harm, unpleasantness and stress aroused by witnessing the painful death of a loved one, is exemplified by emotional responses such as fear, anger, grief, and shock. This initial response, which is short in duration and subjective in nature, will vary in seriousness according to the individual and the particular traumatic stimulus. 2

Secondary responses, which may be termed traumatic neuroses, are longer-lasting reactions caused by an individual's continued inability to cope adequately with a traumatic event. Medical science has identified three frequently occurring forms of neuroses resulting from trauma. In the first, the anxiety reaction, the 3

Thing v. La Chusa, Supreme Court of California, 48 Cal. 3d 644 (1989),771 P.2d 814.
¹*Boyles v. Kerr*, 855 S.W.2d at 616.
²*Leong v. Takasaki*, 520 P.2d 758.

trauma produces severe tension, which results in nervousness, weight loss, stomach pains, emotional fatigue, weakness, headaches, backaches, a sense of impending doom, irritability, or indecision as long as the tension remains. The second, the conversion reaction is a reaction to trauma in which the individual converts consciously disowned impulses into paralysis, loss of hearing, or sight, pain, muscle spasms, or other physiological symptoms which cannot be explained by actual physical impairment. The third, the hypochondriasis reaction, is characterized by an overconcern with health, a fear of illness, or other unpleasant sensations. Thus only secondary responses result in physical injury.

The severity of mental distress may be approached in terms of the amount of 4 pain and disability caused by defendant's act. Traumatic neuroses are more susceptible to medical proof than primary reactions because they are of longer duration and usually are manifested by physical symptoms which may be objectively determined. While a psychiatrist may not be able to establish a negligent act as the sole cause of plaintiff's neurosis, he can give a fairly accurate estimate of the probable effects the act will have upon the plaintiff and whether the trauma induced was a precipitating cause of neurosis, and whether the resulting neurosis is beyond a level of pain with which a reasonable man may be expected to cope.

In a situation where only the primary response to trauma occurs, the defen- 5 dant's negligence may produce transient but very painful mental suffering and anguish. Because this reaction is subjective in nature and may not result in any apparent physical injury, precise levels of suffering and disability cannot be objectively determined. The physician or psychiatrist must rely on the plaintiff's testimony, the context in which the trauma occurred, medical testing of any physical ramifications, the psychiatrist's knowledge of pain and disability likely to result from such trauma, and even the framework of human experience and common sense to determine the amount of pain resulting naturally as a response to defendant's act, and whether it is beyond the level of stress with which a reasonable man may be expected to cope.

Thus calculation of damages becomes a simpler matter when the primary 6 response is coupled with a secondary one, because damages may be assessed by more objective standards. Nevertheless, the absence of a secondary response and its resulting physical injury should not foreclose relief. In either event plaintiff should be permitted to prove medically the damages occasioned by his mental responses to defendant's negligent act, and the trial court should instruct the jury accordingly.

[C]³

The real question . . . is whether the subsequent nervous disturbance of the plain- 7 tiff was a suffering of the body or of the mind. The interdependence of the mind and body is in many respects so close that it is impossible to distinguish their respective influence upon each other. It must be conceded that a nervous shock

---

³*Sloane v. Southern Cal Railway*, 44 P. 320.

or paroxysm, or a disturbance of the nervous system, is distinct from mental anguish, and falls within the physiological, rather than the psychological, branch of the human organism. It is a matter of general knowledge that an attack of sudden fright, or an exposure to imminent peril, has produced in individuals a complete change in their nervous system, and rendered one who was physically strong and vigorous weak and timid. Such a result must be regarded as an injury to the body rather than to the mind, even though the mind be at the same time injuriously affected. Whatever may be the influence by which the nervous system is affected, its action under that influence is entirely distinct from the mental process which is set in motion by the brain. The nerves and nerve centers of the body are a part of the physical system, and are not only susceptible of lesion from external causes, but are also liable to be weakened and destroyed from causes primarily acting upon the mind. If these nerves, or the entire nervous system, are thus affected, there is a physical injury thereby produced; and, if the primal cause of this injury is tortious, it is immaterial whether it is direct, as by a blow, or indirect, through some action upon the mind.

[D][4]

Diagnostic Criteria for 309.81, Posttraumatic Stress Disorder

   A. The person has been exposed to a traumatic event in which both of the following were present:
      (1) the person experienced, witnessed, or was confronted with an event or events that involved actual or threatened death or serious injury, or a threat to the physical integrity of self or others
      (2) the person's response involved intense fear, helplessness, or horror. **Note:** In children, this may be expressed instead by disorganized or agitated behavior
   B. The traumatic event is persistently reexperienced in one (or more) of the following ways:
      (1) recurrent and intrusive distressing recollections of the event, including images, thoughts, or perceptions. **Note:** In young children, repetitive play may occur in which themes or aspects of the trauma are expressed.
      (2) recurrent distressing dreams of the event. **Note:** In children, there may be frightening dreams without recognizable content.
      (3) acting or feeling as if the traumatic event were recurring (includes a sense of reliving the experience, illusions, hallucinations, and dissociative flashback episodes, including those that occur on awakening or when intoxicated). **Note:** In young children, trauma-specific reenactment may occur.

---

[4]*DSM-IV* 4th ed. Washington, DC: American Psychiatric Association, 1994.

    (4) intense psychological distress at exposure to internal or external cues that symbolize or resemble an aspect of the traumatic event

    (5) physiological reactivity on exposure to internal or external cues that symbolize or resemble an aspect of the traumatic event

C. Persistent avoidance of stimuli associated with the trauma and numbing of general responsiveness (not present before the trauma), as indicated by three (or more) of the following:

    (1) efforts to avoid thoughts, feelings, or conversations associated with the trauma

    (2) efforts to avoid activities, places, or people that arouse recollections of the trauma

    (3) inability to recall an important aspect of the trauma

    (4) markedly diminished interest or participation in significant activities

    (5) feeling of detachment or estrangement from others

    (6) restricted range of affect (e.g., unable to have loving feelings)

    (7) sense of a foreshortened future (e.g., does not expect to have a career, marriage, children, or a normal life span)

D. Persistent symptoms of increased arousal (not present before the trauma), as indicated by two (or more) of the following:

    (1) difficulty falling or staying asleep

    (2) irritability or outbursts of anger

    (3) difficulty concentrating

    (4) hypervigilance

    (5) exaggerated startle response

E. Duration of the disturbance (symptoms in Criteria B, C, and D) is more than 1 month.

F. The disturbance causes clinically significant distress or impairment in social, occupational, or other important areas of functioning.

Specify if:

Acute: if duration of symptoms is less than 3 months

Chronic: if duration of symptoms is 3 months or more

Specify if:

With Delayed Onset: if onset of symptoms is at least 6 months after the stressor

● ● ● ●

For Deliberation and Argument

1. Compare and contrast the four accident cases: *Dillon v. Legg, Barnhill v. Davis, Portee v. Jaffee,* and *Dunphy v. Gregor.* In all four cases, the plaintiffs sued the defendants for negligence that resulted in emotional distress. Leaving aside the law for a moment, which plaintiff or plaintiffs do you think have the strongest moral claims to restitution? Which have the weakest claims? For example, does the infant Cheryl Dillon have an equal claim to the

mother, Margery? Does Robert Barnhill have a strong moral claim, even if his mother was not seriously injured? Does Eileen Dunphy have a moral claim, even if she was not married to the victim?

2. Summarize in two paragraphs "The Law on Unintentional and Negligent Infliction of Emotional Distress." Who is entitled recover damages? Who is not entitled to recover damages? What are the reasons for distinguishing between the two types of plaintiffs? How are various types of mental disturbance distinguished?

3. Reread "The Law on Intentional Infliction of Mental Distress" (in the Group 2 Readings, pp. 132–34). In a paragraph, compare and contrast the provisions of this law to the "The Law on Unintentional and Negligent Infliction of Emotional Distress." As someone who is not an attorney, but as someone who may have suffered both intentional infliction of emotional distress and negligence leading to emotional distress, do you find the legal distinctions reasonable and fair?

4. Review the "The Psychology of Emotional Distress." To what extent do some of the symptoms in one or more of these descriptions seem to particularly apply to one or two of the accidents treated in this reading group? Explain, referring to the facts of the case(s).

5. The Iowa Supreme Court that heard the *Barnhill* case adopted the following criteria for judging bystanders' claims of emotional distress caused by witnessing accidents resulting from negligence:

   1. The bystander was located near the scene of the accident.
   2. The emotional distress resulted from a direct emotional impact from the sensory and contemporaneous observance of the accident, as contrasted with learning of the accident from others after its occurrence.
   3. The bystander and the victim were husband and wife or [were closely related].
   4. A reasonable person in the position of the bystander would believe, and the bystander did believe, that the direct victim of the accident would be seriously injured or killed.
   5. The emotional distress to the bystander must be severe.

   Strictly apply these standards to all four of the cases and render a judgment for the plaintiff or the defendant in each case. To what extent do you believe that all of these judgments are fair and reasonable?

6. Select one of these four cases. If you were a member of the jury, would you find for the plaintiff or the defendant? Draw on the definitions and discussions in "The Law on Unintentional and Negligent Infliction of Emotional Distress" or on "The 'Thing Test' for NIED" in supporting and explaining your decision. Draw also on "The Reasonable Person" and on one or more of the subsections of "The Psychology of Emotional Distress," attributing such symptoms, as appropriate, to the plaintiff.

7. Select one of these four cases. Imagine yourself as attorney for the plaintiff or attorney for the defendant. Write a paper in IRAC format to make your

case. Define the *issue* in question format. State or summarize the *rules* about intentional infliction of emotional distress. *Apply/Analyze* the rules, as explained in the "The Law on Unintentional and Negligent Infliction of Emotional Distress" or the "Judge's Instructions to the Jury: Unintentional and Negligent Infliction of Emotional Distress," or the "Thing Test" for NIED. Draw also on "The Reasonable Person" and "The Psychology of Emotional Distress." Finally, draw a *conclusion* from the application of these rules and standards.

8. Select one of the cases treated in this group. Imagine that you are representing either the plaintiff or the defendant. Compose either an opening statement or a closing argument for this case. Remember that your audience is the jury. Draw on the facts of the case in a way that is likely to have the greatest impact on the jury. Keep in mind, however, that jury members may turn against you—and your client—if they think that you are overly manipulating the facts, being deceptive, making exaggerated claims, or attempting too crudely to play on their emotions. For guidance on developing your statement, see "Models for the Opening Statement and the Closing Argument" at the end of Chapter 2. See also Larry Stewart's "Arguing Plain and Suffering Damages in Summation: How to Inspire Jurors" at the end of the Group 3 Readings in this chapter.

9. Imagine that you are either an attorney for the plaintiff or for the defendant in the *Barnhill, Portee*, or *Dunphy* case. Write a memo to the court in which you cite the precedent of the *Dillon* case, or one of the others, and explain how the similarities or differences between the two cases, as you interpret them, favor your client.

10. Role-play as one of the plaintiffs (or as someone related to or friendly with the plaintiffs) in one of the cases in this group. Presume that you have not yet sued the defendant. Write a personal letter that gives your view of the matter.

Homicide

> The very emphasis of the commandment: "Thou shalt not kill" makes it certain that we are descended from an endlessly long chain of generations of murderers, whose love of murder was in their blood, as it is perhaps also in ours.
>
> —Sigmund Freud

In most societies there is no greater crime than homicide—defined as the killing of a human being by another human being. "Thou shalt not kill" is, after all, one of the Ten Commandments. Most societies, however, recognize a difference between homicide and murder—defined as the *unlawful* killing of a human being. Thus homicide in self-defense, homicide on the battlefield, or homicide in cases of lawful execution are not *legally* considered to be murders. (The term *legalized murder* used by death penalty opponents is therefore a contradiction in terms, regardless of its rhetorical effectiveness or the merits of the arguments, one way or the other.)

Societies also generally classify unlawful homicides into various types. Most serious is murder in the first degree, generally characterized as willful, deliberate, premeditated murder with "malice aforethought." (Many of these terms will be more fully defined in the jury instructions included in this chapter.) To win a first degree murder conviction, a prosecutor does not have to prove that the premeditation took place over an extended period of time, only that there *was* time for reflection, however brief. Murder in the second degree does not involve this element of deliberation and premeditation but is characterized by malice (intent to kill) and is generally the result of a "mere unconsidered and rash impulse." The distinction between first- and second-degree murder, however, is often unclear, even to lawyers, and prosecutors will often charge defendants with second-degree murder if they believe that they do not have sufficient evidence to prove first-degree murder.

Below murder in seriousness is manslaughter, which is generally divided into two kinds: voluntary and involuntary. Voluntary manslaughter cases are often of the "heat-of-passion" type. In the classic voluntary manslaughter situation a man returns home to find his wife in bed with another man, and immediately kills the other man. He would most probably be charged with voluntary manslaughter. The judge would likely have instructed the jury that "the provocation must be of the character and degree as naturally would excite and arouse the passion, and the assailant must act under the influence of that sudden quarrel or heat of passion." Moreover, the passion must be of the type "as would naturally be aroused in the mind of an ordinarily reasonable person in the same circumstances." On the other hand, if the husband, upon finding the couple in bed, leaves the scene, goes out and buys a gun, then returns and kills the lover, he would likely be charged with murder, as his "heat of passion" would have had sufficient time to cool. In the case of involuntary manslaughter, there is neither premeditation nor intent to kill. A drunk driver who speeds through a red light and crashes into another car, killing the other driver, might, because of his "criminal negligence," be charged with involuntary manslaughter. (But if the drunk driver's conduct is sufficiently egregious, he or she may be charged with second-degree murder.)

In addition to these long-established categories of homicide, many jurisdictions have passed additional statutes on murder. For example, to deal with a horrific new social trend, California added the category of "drive-by murder" to its penal code, classifying all such killings as murder of the first degree. Another category of homicide (instituted in 1872 in California and derived from English common law) is the controversial concept of *felony murder*. Under the felony-murder doctrine, any death that results from the commission of a felony (such as robbery or arson), whether the killing be intentional or accidental, is chargeable as first-degree murder.

Types of lawful homicide include excusable homicides (accidents or unintentional killings caused through no fault or negligence of the perpetrator) and justifiable homicides (killing in defense of oneself or another).

The following chapter includes five groups of readings focusing on homicide. The first group provides an introduction to the subject; cases presented involve a barroom killing, a fatal game of Russian roulette between two children, a case of domestic violence, a gang shooting, and a "mercy" killing. It also includes a set of jury instructions on various types of homicide. The second group deals with vehicular homicide—cases in which drivers failing to exercise due caution or acting in reckless disregard of human life have killed people. The third group focuses on crimes of passion—cases in which one partner in a soured romantic relationship kills the other. The fourth group deals with "battered-woman syndrome"—cases in which a woman who has suffered repeated physical abuse at the hands of a spouse or lover finally kills the batterer. In the final group, we focus on the controversial doctrine of felony murder.

■ Group 1 Readings: *Introductory*

This introductory group offers a variety of homicide cases. They will give you an opportunity to think about and apply the legal definitions of first- and second-degree murder and voluntary and involuntary manslaughter. The first case, Commonwealth v. Carroll, *concerns a domestic dispute that turns fatal. This selection is followed by a* model student paper *by Alyssa Mellott, which analyzes the case by Alyssa's comments on her own writing process.* People v. Dewberry *concerns a barroom killing that resulted from a dispute over money.* Commonwealth v. Malone *is about a game of Russian roulette played by two youths, with tragic consequences.* Toney v. Peters *concerns a gang-type killing in a fast-food restaurant. And* State v. Forrest *deals with a "mercy killing": a son shoots his terminally ill father in a hospital.*

The group concludes with a set of jury instructions on various types of homicide.

Model Student Paper: Domestic Tragedy

412 Pa. 525
COMMONWEALTH of Pennsylvania
v.
Donald D. CARROLL, Jr., Appellant.

Supreme Court of Pennsylvania.
Nov. 12, 1963.

The defendant married the deceased in 1955, when he was serving in the Army in California. Subsequently he was stationed in Alabama, and later in Greenland. During the latter tour of duty, defendant's wife and two children lived with his parents in New Jersey. Because this arrangement proved incompatible, defendant returned to the United States on emergency leave in order to move his family to their own quarters. On his wife's insistence, defendant was forced first to secure a "compassionate transfer" back to the States, and subsequently to resign from the Army in July of 1960, by which time he had attained the rank of Chief Warrant Officer. Defendant was a hard worker, earned a substantial salary and bore a very good reputation among his neighbors.   1

In 1958, decedent-wife suffered a fractured skull while attempting to leave defendant's car in the course of an argument. Allegedly this contributed to her mental disorder which was later diagnosed as a schizoid personality type. In 1959 she underwent psychiatric treatment at the Mental Hygiene Clinic in Aberdeen, Maryland. She complained of nervousness and told the examining doctor "I feel like hurting my children." This sentiment sometimes took the form of sadistic "discipline" toward their very young children. Nevertheless, upon her discharge from the Clinic, the doctors considered her much improved. With this background we come to the immediate events of the crime.   2

In January, 1962, defendant was selected to attend an electronics school in Winston-Salem, North Carolina, for nine days. His wife greeted this news with violent argument. Immediately prior to his departure for Winston-Salem, at the   3

Commonwealth v. Carroll, 194 A.2d 911 (1963).

suggestion and request of his wife, he put a *loaded* .22 calibre pistol on the window sill at the head of their common bed, so that she would feel safe. On the evening of January 16, 1962, defendant returned home and told his wife that he had been temporarily assigned to teach at a school in Chambersburg, which would necessitate his absence from home four nights out of seven for a ten week period. A violent and protracted argument ensued at the dinner table and continued until four o'clock in the morning.

Defendant's own statement after his arrest details the final moments before   4
the crime: "We went into the bedroom a little before 3 o'clock on Wednesday morning where we continued to argue in short bursts. Generally she laid with her back to me facing the wall in bed and would just talk over her shoulder to me. I became angry and more angry especially what she was saying about my kids and myself, and sometime between 3 and 4 o'clock in the morning I remembered the gun on the window sill over my head. I think she had dozed off. *I reached up and grabbed the pistol and brought it down and shot her twice in the back of the head.*"[1]

Defendant's testimony at the trial elaborated this theme. He started to think   5
about the children, "seeing my older son's feet what happened to them. I could see the bruises on him and Michael's chin was split open, four stitches. I didn't know what to do. I wanted to help my boys. Sometime in there she said something in there, she called me some kind of name. I kept thinking of this. *During this time I either thought or felt—I thought of the gun, just thought of the gun.* I am not sure whether I felt my hand move toward the gun—I saw my hand move, the next thing—the only thing I can recollect after that is right after the shots or right during the shots I saw the gun in my hand just pointed at my wife's head. She was still lying on her back—I mean her side. I could smell the gunpowder and I could hear something—it sounded like running water. I didn't know what it was at first, didn't realize what I'd done at first. Then I smelled it. I smelled blood before. . . ."

"Q. At the time you shot her, Donald, were you fully aware and [did you] intend to do what you did?
"A. I don't know positively. All I remember hearing was two shots and feeling myself go cold all of a sudden."

Shortly thereafter defendant wrapped his wife's body in a blanket, spread and   6
sheets, tied them on with a piece of plastic clothesline and took her down to the cellar. He tried to clean up as well as he could. That night he took his wife's body, wrapped in a blanket with a rug over it to a desolate place near a trash dump. He then took the children to his parents' home in Magnolia, New Jersey. He was arrested the next Monday in Chambersburg where he had gone to his teaching assignment.

---

[1]When pressed on cross-examination defendant approximated that five minutes elapsed between his wife's last remark and the shooting.

Paper Topic: Domestic Tragedy *(Commonwealth v. Carroll)*

The trial court found Carroll guilty of first-degree murder, and he was sentenced to life imprisonment. In filing his appeal, the defendant posed the following two questions:

> (1) Does not the evidence sustain a conviction no higher than murder in the second degree?
>
> (2) Does not the evidence of defendant's good character, together with the testimony of medical experts, including the psychiatrist for the Behavior Clinic of Allegheny County [Pennsylvania], that the homicide was not premeditated or intentional, *require* the [Appellate] Court . . . to fix the degree of guilt of the defendant no higher than murder in the second degree?

Carroll also argued:

> that there was insufficient time for premeditation. This is based on an isolated and oft repeated statement that "no time is too short for a wicked man to frame in his mind the scheme of murder." Defendant argues that, conversely, a long time is necessary to find premeditation in a "good man." . . . Defendant further contends that the time and place of the crime, the enormous difficulty of removing and concealing the body, and the obvious lack of an escape plan, militate against and make a finding of premeditation legally impossible.

Discuss these questions, as if you were a making a case before the appellate court. *Take into account the facts of the case, as well as the instructions to the jury, provided at the end of this group of readings* (pp. 189–94). In an IRAC essay, explain why you believe that the original verdict should be affirmed or, on the other hand, that Carroll should either be convicted of a less serious type of homicide or acquitted.

MODEL STUDENT PAPER

COMMENTARY BY ALYSSA MELLOTT

I first read through the case and the jury instructions on homicide to get a general idea of the issues that were involved in the case. I then read through the jury instructions again and began to make connections between the facts of the case and the jury instructions. For instance, I noted that premeditation is the essential element of first-degree murder, but that the facts of the case showed no evidence that Carroll premeditated the homicide. From this first run-through I developed an issue statement that addressed the most important issues involved in the case:

> The issue in his appeal is whether the defendant, who after many hours of arguing, shot the victim in the back of the head during a break in their quarreling, committed the homicide with premeditation and malice, so that he should be found guilty of

first-or second-degree murder, or whether he acted in the sudden heat of passion, in which case he should be found guilty of voluntary manslaughter.

Based on this issue statement, the most important subjects to discuss were whether or not the defendant's actions constituted murder, and if so, was he guilty of murder in the first or second degree? The first thing I would need to decide was whether or not the defendant acted with malice aforethought. Next, I would need to discuss whether or not the defendant premeditated the murder. Finally, because the couple was engaged in an argument prior to the murder, I needed to address the rules concerning murder committed in the heat of passion. 2

I decided on the following organization plan that would flush out the issues:

A: Narrative of facts, ending with the issue statement
B: Discussion of jury instructions for murder, first-degree murder, second-degree murder, and voluntary manslaughter
C: Discussion of whether the evidence supports malice aforethought
D: Discussion of whether the evidence supports premeditation
E: Discussion of whether the evidence supports voluntary manslaughter
F: Conclusion

I then went through the facts again very carefully and included in my narrative of the facts only those that would provide adequate background preceding the argument, as well as facts related to the murder itself. For example, I included the important details explaining why the gun was placed on the window sill. I excluded such details as the fact that Mrs. Carroll had been diagnosed as a schizoid personality type. From here I sifted through the jury instructions once more to pull out the most important and concise rules to include in an introductory discussion of murder, first-degree murder, second-degree murder, and voluntary manslaughter. (In the first draft I included too many of the jury instructions in a single, difficult-to-read paragraph. I realized later that some of these could be introduced later in my discussions of the issues.) 3

- An unlawful killing is considered murder if the killing was done with malice aforethought. ("Jury Instructions on Murder and Manslaughter")
- According to the "Jury Instructions" section on deliberate and premeditated murder, "If you find that the killing was preceded and accompanied by a clear, deliberate intent on the part of the defendant to kill, which was the result of deliberation and premeditation . . . it is murder of the first degree."
- As defined by the "Jury Instructions" section on unpremeditated murder of the second degree, "Murder of the second degree is . . . the unlawful killing of a human being with malice aforethought when the perpetrator intended unlawfully to kill a human being but the evidence is insufficient to prove deliberation and premeditation."
- According to the "Jury Instructions" section on voluntary manslaughter, a homicide committed with intent to kill but without malice aforethought is considered voluntary manslaughter.

Based on the elements of these rules and the distinctions among them, I   4
then developed topic sentences to introduce each part of the paper in my outline:

- For the defendant to be found guilty of murder it must be shown that the homicide was committed with malice aforethought.
- The defendant must have performed the act with the knowledge of the danger to, and conscious disregard for, human life.
- The next issue to be determined is whether the defendant should be found guilty of first-degree murder (premeditated murder) or second-degree murder (murder without premeditation).
- Carroll's testimony and the facts of the case do not support the claim that he acted with premeditation.
- Should the defendant be convicted of voluntary manslaughter?

From here I began to apply the jury instructions to the facts of the case. For   5
instance, in my discussion of malice aforethought I included the fact that Carroll had testified that he was aware that he had reached for the gun and made the connection that if he was aware that he had reached for the gun and he then pulled the trigger, he was performing an intentional act. In my discussion of premeditation I reviewed the facts of the case, including the doctor's testimony, which suggested that Carroll had not premeditated the murder. I also made the point that the argument between Carroll and his wife precluded him from adequately reflecting on his actions.

While applying the jury instructions to the facts of the case, I included addi-   6
tional instructions that I did not mention in my initial discussion of the rules that would elaborate and strengthen the points that I wanted to make. For example, in the discussion of voluntary manslaughter I added the following rule from the "Jury Instructions" section on the cooling period of murder or manslaughter: "To reduce a killing upon a sudden quarrel or heat of passion from murder to manslaughter the killing must have occurred while the slayer was acting under the direct and immediate influence of the quarrel or heat of passion." I then argued that because the argument had gone on for hours, it was no longer sudden and that because the couple had stopped fighting in the moments when Carroll shot his wife, he was no longer under the direct and immediate influence of the quarrel or heat of passion.

As I worked through my analysis, I concluded that the homicide was com-   7
mitted with malice aforethought and was therefore murder. I further concluded that because the murder was not premeditated, the defendant should not have been found guilty of first-degree murder. I concluded my essay by briefly reiterating these points.

Once I was done with the first draft, the paper did not flow as well as it could   8
so I redeveloped the topic sentences to clarify the points that I wanted to make. In particular I cleaned up the two paragraphs in which I discussed premeditation by breaking the two paragraphs into three paragraphs, each discussing only one rule.

<u>**Final Draft**</u>

Domestic Tragedy

Facts and Issue

Donald D. Carroll was known as a hard worker. He was able to support his family [9] and was well respected among his neighbors (*Commonwealth v. Carroll*, 194 A.2d 911 (1963)). Carroll showed his dedication to his family by leaving his position in the Army to improve his family's living conditions. In January 1962 he was selected to attend a school that would require his absence from home for nine days. Mrs. Carroll reacted to the news with violent argument. She insisted that he place a loaded .22 caliber pistol on the window sill above their bed so that she would feel safe. A few weeks later, Carroll informed his wife that he had accepted a position that would require that he be gone several nights a week for several weeks. The couple argued over this matter from dinner time until approximately four in the morning. Carroll testified that slightly before 3 a.m. the couple went to the bedroom where they continued to argue sporadically. During this time, Carroll's wife lay with her back towards him. Carroll became angry at some of the things that his wife was saying about him and their children. At some point between 3 and 4 a.m., as his wife was dozing, he grabbed the gun from the window sill above the bed and shot her twice in the back of the head. He then wrapped his wife's body in a sheet and hid it in the cellar until he transferred the body to a trash dump. Carroll was arrested several days later. The trial court convicted him of first-degree murder, and he appealed his conviction. The issue in his appeal is whether the defendant, who after many hours of arguing, shot the victim in the back of the head during a break in their quarreling, committed the homicide with premeditation and malice, so that he should be found guilty of first- or second-degree murder, or whether he acted in the sudden heat of passion, in which case he should be found guilty of voluntary manslaughter.

The Law on Homicide

An unlawful killing is considered murder if the killing was done, among other things, [10] with malice aforethought ("Jury Instructions on Murder and Manslaughter" 189). The distinction between first-degree murder and second-degree murder centers on whether or not the accused committed the act with premeditation. According to the "Jury Instructions" section on deliberate and premeditated murder, "If you find that the killing was preceded and accompanied by a clear, deliberate intent on the part of the defendant to kill, which was the result of deliberation and premeditation . . . it is murder of the first degree" (190). The "Jury Instructions" section on unpremeditated murder of the second degree" defines second-degree murder as "the unlawful killing of a human being with malice aforethought when the perpetrator intended unlawfully to kill a human being but the evidence is insufficient to prove deliberation and premeditations" (190). According to the "Jury Instructions" section on voluntary manslaughter, a homicide committed with intent to kill but without malice aforethought is considered voluntary manslaughter (191).

Did the Defendant Have Malice Aforethought?

For the defendant to be found guilty of murder it must be shown that the homicide
was committed with malice aforethought. According to the "Jury Instructions"
section on malice aforethought, malice is implied when (1) "The killing resulted
from an intentional act"; (2) "The natural consequences of the act are dangerous
to human life"; and (3) "The act was deliberately performed with the knowledge of
the danger to, and conscious disregard for, human life" (189). The evidence in
Commonwealth v. Carroll supports the first element in these instructions. The
defendant testified that he was aware that the gun was in his hand at the moment
that he shot his wife in the back of the head. He further testified that he had to
reach up to grab the gun before he proceeded to pull the trigger twice. These
actions indicate that the defendant was performing an intentional act, as opposed
to firing the gun accidentally. The second element of the malice aforethought jury
instructions is also satisfied, since a reasonable person would consider that
shooting a person in the back of the head would be "dangerous to human life."
11

Finally, under the third element of the "malice aforethought" instructions, the
defendant must have performed the act "with the knowledge of the danger to,
and conscious disregard for, human life." Carroll testified that he was aware that
he was reaching for the gun. Although the defendant's testimony is not completely clear, he claimed that he was aware that the gun was in his hand and that
he was angry at the things his wife was saying, and that he was thinking of the
abuse that she had inflicted on their children. The defendant claimed that he just
"thought of the gun" (175). It is unlikely, however, that a person would think of a
gun and not immediately associate this object with its purpose: to kill. A reasonable person would argue that if one is aware that he is holding a gun, that the
gun is pointed at someone's head, and that he then pulls the trigger, he is performing a deliberate act "with knowledge of the danger to, and with conscious disregard for human life." The defendant was correctly found guilty of murder, since
the evidence shows that he acted with malice aforethought.
12

Did the Defendant Premeditate the Killing?

The next issue to be determined is whether the defendant should be found guilty of
first-degree murder (premeditated murder) or second-degree murder (murder without
premeditation). To be convicted of first-degree murder, according to the "Jury Instructions" section on deliberate and premeditated murder, the law requires that the
murder be perpetrated as a result of deliberation and premeditation where
13

> [t]he word "deliberate" means formed or arrived at or determined upon as a
> result of careful thought and weighing of considerations for and against the pro-
> posed course of action. The word "premeditated" means considered beforehand.
> (*Commonwealth v. Carroll* 190)

Prior to the night of the murder, Carroll had been, according to the testimony of
his neighbors and in terms of his dedication to his family, a very responsible
person. He had found a home for his family when living with his parents proved to
be a strain. At his wife's insistence he had also left the Army to be closer to home.
14

Furthermore, Carroll did not seek out a murder weapon prior to the instant in which the murder took place, nor did he make effective arrangements for concealing his crime. He did not take active steps indicative of someone who was deliberating murder. For example, he did not force his wife into the bedroom where the gun was. Carroll merely reached up above his head to find a gun that was placed above the bed at his wife's request. In addition, a psychiatrist from the Behavioral Clinic of Allegheny County testified that, in his opinion, the homicide was not premeditated.

The defendant argues that there was insufficient time for premeditation. 15 However, according to the "Jury Instructions" section on deliberate and premeditated murder, "[t]he true test is not the duration of time, but rather the extent of the reflection" (190). Therefore, while the defendant argues that there was insufficient time for premeditation, the amount of time allotted for reflection is incidental. Although Carroll's testimony about the amount of time the couple spent fighting once they were in the bedroom is somewhat unclear, whether it was a matter of minutes or an hour does not matter. There was "time" for the defendant to deliberate killing his wife.

However, Carroll's testimony and the facts of the case do not support the 16 claim that he acted with premeditation. For a murder to be considered premeditated, the law stipulates that the killing must have resulted from "a clear, deliberate intent on the part of the defendant to kill, which was the result of deliberation and premeditation, so that it must have been formed upon preexisting reflection and not under a sudden heat of passion or other condition precluding the idea of deliberation" ("Jury Instructions" 190). The circumstances of the murder preclude the possibility that the defendant deliberated the killing to the extent that the law requires. A reasonable person would agree that after fighting for many hours with a woman who was known to abuse one's children and had a history of violence, one may lose his ability to reflect to any significant extent on his actions. Carroll testified that it was a combination of thinking of his boys and something that his wife said about him that he could not rid from his mind. He reached for the gun in a frustrated, angry, and exhausted state, during which his actions were beyond reflection. This accounts for his testimony about his feelings that he only became aware that he had shot his wife when she began to bleed. In light of the facts presented, the circumstances of the argument prior to the murder, the temperament and reputation of the defendant, and the insufficient evidence of premeditation, Carroll should not have been found guilty of first-degree murder.

Manslaughter or Murder?

Should the defendant, then, be convicted of voluntary manslaughter? If it were 17 not for the fact that the couple had ceased their arguing long enough for the victim to turn her back toward her assailant and doze off, and if it were not for the fact that the defendant cannot narrow the time of the murder to a more accurate time frame than between 3 and 4 a.m., the evidence presented may have supported a finding of voluntary manslaughter. The "Jury Instructions" section on deliberate and premeditated murder stipulates that "there is no malice aforethought if the killing occurred [upon a sudden quarrel or heat of passion]" (191). However, the "Jury Instructions" section on the cooling period of murder or manslaughter states that "[t]o reduce a killing upon a sudden quarrel or heat of passion from murder to manslaughter the killing must have occurred while the slayer was acting under the direct and immediate influence of the quarrel or heat of passion" (192). The couple had been fighting for many hours off and on, so that the quarrel was no longer "sudden." When the homicide occurred, the couple was no longer in the middle of the argument. Rather, they had reached a break in the argument. Since the end of the last stage of the quarrel, the defendant had had up to an hour to calm down. Moreover, it is questionable that the passion aroused during the Carroll's argument which led the defendant to shoot his wife would be aroused in the mind of an ordinarily reasonable person in the same circumstances ("Jury Instructions" 191). Arguments between married couples are very common, and in most cases the parties involved either remove themselves from the situation or drop the argument and go to bed. They do not shoot their spouse twice in the back of the head. When he committed the homicide, Carroll was no longer acting under the direct and immediate influence of a sudden quarrel, and the nature of the provocation was not sufficient to elicit passion severe enough to warrant killing.

Conclusion

Since the evidence does not show that Carroll acted with premeditation, does not show that he was acting under the influence of a sudden quarrel or in the heat of passion, but does show that he killed with malice aforethought, the defendant should be found guilty of murder in the second degree.

—Alyssa Mellott

Killing in a San Francisco Bar

PEOPLE of the State of California, Respondent,

v.

John DEWBERRY, Appellant.

Cr. 6335.

Supreme Court of California,

In Bank.

Feb. 6, 1959.

The circumstances of the homicide were related at the trial by two witnesses, Jesse Mosley and defendant. Mosley testified that about 7:30 A.M. on Sunday, October 14, 1956, he went to a bar in San Francisco. He sat near the door and consumed two bourbon highballs. He had been in the bar about forty-five minutes

---

People v. Dewberry, 334 P.2d 853 (1959).

when defendant entered and sat about 10 feet from him. Mosley did not know defendant, but had seen him before and had heard his name. Defendant went to the telephone several times and complained about not being able to reach his sister.

In the course of a conversation about gambling between defendant and another customer defendant took a large roll of bills from his pocket. The two agreed to gamble and defendant stated that he did not want any foolishness about his money and that he carried his own protection. He then showed the revolver he was carrying. Defendant repocketed the pistol and the two left the bar. A short time later, defendant returned.

The deceased, Rudolf Glover, entered the bar at about 9 A.M. with a woman whom he introduced as his wife to Mosley and the others. Glover and defendant each bought a round of drinks for the six or seven other customers.

About 10:45 A.M. the television set was turned on for a Forty-Niner football game. Mosley moved to a booth in the rear to see better. About this time defendant told the bartender he wished to take care of his bill and spread his roll of money on the bar.

A few minutes later, two people sat in front of Mosley and blocked his view of the screen, so he started back to his original seat. As he was walking toward the front of the bar he heard defendant accuse Glover of taking his money and demand its return. Glover stated that he was not taking defendant's money but merely keeping it for him to protect him. Defendant told Glover that he did not need his protection, that he had his own protection. Both defendant and Glover were standing, about three bar stools or ten feet apart. Defendant again demanded that Glover return the money.

In the course of the argument, Mosley saw Glover put his hand in his pocket and pass something to Mrs. Glover. Defendant then told Mrs. Glover to put his money on the bar and repeated his demand to Glover. Thereupon defendant took out his revolver, cocked it, and fired once. Glover turned and fell. At no time did Mosley hear Glover threaten defendant or see him make a move toward defendant.

Defendant turned Glover over and went through his pockets. Mrs. Glover began to cry as she put her head on Glover's chest. She then started for the door, but defendant asked her for the rest of his money. When she failed to give it to him, he hit her in the face, knocking her down. He pointed the pistol at her and said, "If you don't give me my money I will kill you too." Mosley took the money from Mrs. Glover. Defendant had the bartender count it for him and when he was told the amount he stated that he was still about $100 short.

Meanwhile, someone had called an ambulance and the police. Officer Dobleman testified that when he arrived at the bar, defendant handed him a .38 calibre revolver with five live rounds and one discharged shell in the cylinder. Defendant told the officer, "He tried to take my money and I did it." Shortly thereafter defendant made substantially the same statement to Inspector McDonald of the homicide detail. It appeared to the officers that at the time he was questioned defendant had been drinking but was in full control of his faculties and had no trouble speaking.

Defendant testified that he was a professional gambler and a car salesman and admitted two prior felony convictions. He had spent the previous night drinking and gambling in San Mateo, had met a friend in San Francisco about 5:00 A.M., had a few more drinks, and went to the bar about 8:00 A.M. He was waiting there to get in touch with his sister to give her money for the care of his mother. While he was waiting, he talked to another customer about gambling, but he denied showing him the pistol. He went upstairs and gambled with him for about forty-five minutes and won $55.

When he returned to the bar, he had a brief conversation with the bartender about his bar bill. He paid it and then spread his money out along the bar so that the could arrange it according to denomination. He knew he had $1,252. While he was sorting and arranging the money, Mrs. Glover told him to take it off the bar. Defendant told her to mind her own business and she walked away. Glover then walked to the bar and picked up the money. Defendant stopped him and asked him to return it. Glover put some money back on the bar, but defendant could see that five $100 bills were missing. At defendant's request, the bartender counted the money and found about $700. After defendant's repeated demands for the return of his money, Glover reached in his pocket and raised his arm toward defendant. Glover had told defendant that if he did not shut up he would lose more than his money. One James McCoy had told him that the deceased had a reputation of being belligerent. Defendant said he tried to fire the pistol to the right of Glover, but with no intention to hit him. He had won the weapon in the game in San Mateo and was not sure it was loaded until he pulled the trigger. He denied threatening Mrs. Glover.

The testimony of the autopsy surgeon tended to corroborate defendant's story about Glover's raising his arm toward defendant. James McCoy, called by the People in rebuttal, denied telling defendant anything about Glover.

Teenagers and "Russian Poker"

COMMONWEALTH v. MALONE.

Supreme Court of Pennsylvania.
May 27, 1946.

This is an appeal from the judgment and sentence under a conviction of murder in the second degree. William H. Long, age 13 years, was killed by a shot from a 32-caliber revolver held against his right side by the defendant, then aged 17 years. These youths were on friendly terms at the time of the homicide. The defendant and his mother while his father and brother were in the U.S. Armed Forces, were residing in Lancaster, Pa., with the family of William H. Long, whose son was the victim of the shooting.

On the evening of February 26th, 1945, when the defendant went to a moving picture theater, he carried in the pocket of his raincoat a revolver which he had

---

Commonwealth v. Malone, 47 A.2d 445 (1946).

obtained at the home of his uncle on the preceding day. In the afternoon preceding the shooting, the decedent procured a cartridge from his father's room and he and the defendant placed it in the revolver.

After leaving the theater, the defendant went to a dairy store and there met the decedent. Both youths sat in the rear of the store ten minutes, during which period the defendant took the gun out of his pocket and loaded the chamber to the right of the firing pin and then closed the gun. A few minutes later, both youths sat on stools in front of the lunch counter and ate some food. The defendant suggested to the decedent that they play "Russian Poker."[1] Long replied: "I don't care; go ahead." The defendant then placed the revolver against the right side of Long and pulled the trigger three times. The third pull resulted in a fatal wound to Long. The latter jumped off the stool and cried: "Oh! Oh! Oh!" and Malone said: "Did I hit you, Billy? Gee, Kid, I'm sorry." Long died from the wounds two days later.

The defendant testified that the gun chamber he loaded was the first one to the right of the firing chamber and that when he pulled the trigger he did not "expect to have the gun go off." He declared he had no intention of harming Long, who was his friend and companion.

The defendant was indicted for murder, tried and found guilty of murder in the second degree and sentenced to a term in the penitentiary for a period not less than five years and not exceeding ten years.

A new trial was refused and after sentence was imposed, an appeal was taken.

Chicago Gang Shooting

Alvin TONEY, Petitioner–Appellee, Cross–Appellant,

v.

Howard A. PETERS, III, Director, Department of Corrections, State of Illinois, Respondent–Appellant, Cross–Appellee.

Nos. 92–3769, 93–1331.
United States Court of Appeals, Seventh Circuit.

Argued Nov. 8, 1994.
Decided Feb. 23, 1995.

Toney was convicted of one count of murder and two counts of attempted murder for shooting three individuals at a Chicago restaurant called Harold's Chicken Shack (Harold's) on the evening of April 29, 1985. James Love and Rodney Williams were injured; Lindsey Williams was killed.

---

[1] It has been explained that "Russian Poker" is a game in which the participants, in turn, place a single cartridge in one of the five chambers of a revolver cylinder, give the latter a quick twirl, place the muzzle of the gun against the temple and pull the trigger, leaving it to chance whether or not death results to the trigger puller.
Toney v. Peters, 48 F.3d 993 (1995).

The shootings were precipitated by an encounter between Rodney Williams and Toney's co-defendant, David Kelly.[1] Rodney Williams testified that, between 1:00 and 2:00 p.m. on April 29, he was driving to a liquor store with two friends when he saw David Kelly walking down the street. Kelly was wearing a hat tilted to the left, which Williams took as a sign that he was gang affiliated. Kelly stared into the car and Williams called out: "You [ought to] straighten your hat up where you can see." Shortly thereafter, Williams and two friends were walking to Harold's when they again encountered Kelly. Upon seeing them Kelly ran away, causing his hat to fall off.

Later that night, Williams met two other friends, James Love and Lindsey Williams, and the three entered Harold's. Williams testified that David Kelly entered the restaurant, walked straight up to him and asked if Williams remembered him now without his hat on. Williams said he did not and told him to "get out of his face." Kelly then left and, a short time later, petitioner Toney entered with a gun drawn. Williams testified that Toney pointed the gun at him and shot him. He fell against a wall and heard four more shots.

The other surviving victim, James Love, also testified for the prosecution. He stated that, on the night of the shooting, he, Rodney Williams and Lindsey Williams were sitting at the booth closest to the door at Harold's. He and Rodney Williams went to the window to place an order. David Kelly then entered, asked Rodney Williams if he remembered him, and left. Love testified that he and Rodney Williams then went to the window to pick up their orders. As they were returning to their table, Toney entered with a gun drawn. Love testified that Toney pointed the gun at Rodney Williams and shot him. Toney then shot Lindsey Williams in the head while he sat in the booth, turned the gun toward Love, and shot him in the lower right back as he was diving for cover.

Both Love and Williams denied threatening Toney or possessing weapons at the time of the shooting.

Police Officer James Haggard testified that, when he arrived at Harold's in response to a call of a shooting, he found one man dead and two others wounded. He identified a photograph of the scene of the shooting that showed a pocketknife lying on the floor.

The prosecution called several witnesses who testified that while in custody Toney made a voluntary statement confessing to the shootings. Assistant State's Attorney Romza testified that she had reduced Toney's verbal statement to writing. Toney reviewed the statement, made one minor addition, and signed it, telling Romza that it was voluntary and accurate. The statement indicated that Toney had been a member of the El Rukn gang for 16 years up to 1983 and that David Kelly was also a member of the El Rukns. On the night of the shooting, Kelly arrived at a house where Toney was present, complaining that "3 chumps were trying to move on him with guns" and that they were "up at Harold's . . . making pistol plays." According to the statement, Toney told

---

[1] Kelly was acquitted after a simultaneous bench trial.

Kelly that he would take care of the situation and left the building armed with a .32 snub-nosed revolver tucked into his pants. He entered Harold's, finding the three men inside. Kelly then entered and started arguing with them, prompting Toney to tell Kelly to leave. As Kelly headed out the door, two of the three men started to get up. Toney then drew his gun and fired six shots. According to the statement, the first two he fired at David Kelly because he "knew David started the whole thing and I told [him] not to be there." Toney then "sprayed the rest of the shots at the 3 dudes in the chicken shack," one of whom "was still in his chair when I started shooting." He did not see any of the three men holding guns.

Toney took the stand and testified that the statement was false; he had signed it as part of a deal with the interrogating officers that he would be charged with manslaughter and not murder. He said that police officers had told him that, because there was a knife found at the scene, they would charge him with manslaughter only and relocate his family if he signed the statement and cooperated with ongoing investigations into other crimes involving the El Rukn gang. He stated that officers had beaten him while he was being questioned. 8

Toney also described a different version of the shooting from that portrayed by Williams and Love and in his statement. He testified that, on the evening of April 29, David Kelly arrived at a building where Toney was present. Kelly told him that, when he went to order some chicken at Harold's, three men had threatened him with guns. The three had previously chased him and taken his hat from him. Toney accompanied Kelly back to the restaurant and both men walked inside. Toney heard Rodney Williams say to Kelly, "Yeah, Shorty, we got your cap." Toney told Williams not to harass young people like Kelly and that, if he wanted a fight, Toney would fight him. Kelly picked up his chicken order and he and Toney walked toward the exit to leave. 9

According to Toney, Rodney Williams then jumped up from the table and approached him from the side. Toney spun around and said to him, "if you are looking for some trouble, you are going to get some trouble. We did not come for [any] trouble, but if you want some trouble, you can get all the trouble that you want." Undeterred, Rodney Williams reached toward the door; Love also moved toward Toney. Love told Toney that he might as well sit down "and then [Love] reached for his pocket." Then, according to Toney's testimony, "Rodney Williams went to make a move and dropped something. I do not know what he dropped, and then that is when I started shooting." Toney first shot Rodney Williams, then Love, and then, when Lindsey Williams "went to get up, trying to come up out of the booth," Toney shot him. Toney testified that, in light of the fact that David Kelly had told him that the three had been armed, he "was not going to take [any] chances of getting shot in the back. . . . The whole thing I was thinking about is making sure they did not hurt me." Toney testified that he did not see that any of the men had guns. 10

The autopsy revealed that Lindsey Williams died from a single gunshot wound to the right side of his head, just in front of his right ear, which travelled slightly downwards. 11

A Mercy Killing?

■ ━━━ ■

321 N.C. 186
STATE of North Carolina
v.
John FORREST.

No. 705A86.

Supreme Court of North Carolina.
Dec. 2, 1987.

On 22 December 1985, defendant John Forrest admitted his critically ill father, 1
Clyde Forrest, Sr., to Moore Memorial Hospital. Defendant's father, who had previously been hospitalized, was suffering from numerous serious ailments,
including severe heart disease, hypertension, a thoracic aneurysm, numerous pulmonary emboli, and a peptic ulcer. By the morning of 23 December 1985, his
medical condition was determined to be untreatable and terminal. Accordingly,
he was classified as "No Code," meaning that no extraordinary measures would
be used to save his life, and he was moved to a more comfortable room.

On 24 December 1985, defendant went to the hospital to visit his ailing father. 2
No other family members were present in his father's room when he arrived.
While one of the nurse's assistants was tending to his father, defendant told her,
"There is no need in doing that. He's dying." She responded, "Well, I think he's
better." The nurse's assistant noticed that defendant was sniffing as though crying
and that he kept his hand in his pocket during their conversation. She subsequently went to get the nurse.

When the nurse's assistant returned with the nurse, defendant once again 3
stated his belief that his father was dying. The nurse tried to comfort defendant,
telling him, "I don't think your father is as sick as you think he is." Defendant, very
upset, responded, "Go to hell. I've been taking care of him for years. I'll take care
of him." Defendant was then left alone in the room with his father.

Alone at his father's bedside, defendant began to cry and to tell his father how 4
much he loved him. His father began to cough, emitting a gurgling and rattling
noise. Extremely upset, defendant pulled a small pistol from his pants pocket, put
it to his father's temple, and fired. He subsequently fired three more times and
walked out into the hospital corridor, dropping the gun to the floor just outside
his father's room.

Following the shooting, defendant, who was crying and upset, neither ran nor 5
threatened anyone. Moreover, he never denied shooting his father and talked
openly with law enforcement officials. Specifically, defendant made the following
oral statements: "You can't do anything to him now. He's out of his suffering." "I
killed my daddy." "He won't have to suffer anymore." "I know they can burn me

---

State v. Forrest, 362 S.E.2d 252 (1987).

for it, but my dad will not have to suffer anymore." "I know the doctors couldn't do it, but I could." "I promised my dad I wouldn't let him suffer."

Defendant's father was found in his hospital bed, with several raised spots and blood on the right side of his head. Blood and brain tissue were found on the bed, the floor, and the wall. Though defendant's father had been near death as a result of his medical condition, the exact cause of the deceased's death was determined to be the four point-blank bullet wounds to his head. Defendant's pistol was a single-action .22-calibre five-shot revolver. The weapon, which had to be cocked each time it was fired, contained four empty shells and one live round.

6

Jury Instructions on Murder and Manslaughter

8.10 MURDER—DEFINED (Pen. Code, § 187)

[Defendant is accused of having committed the crime of murder, a violation of Penal Code section 187.]

Every person who unlawfully kills a [human being] . . . [with malice afore-thought] . . . is guilty of the crime of murder in violation of section 187 of the Penal Code.

[A killing is unlawful, if it [is] [neither] [justifiable] [nor] [excusable]].

In order to prove this crime, each of the following elements must be proved:

1. A human being was killed;
2. The killing was unlawful; and
3. The killing [was done with malice aforethought]

8.11 "MALICE AFORETHOUGHT"—DEFINED

"Malice" may be either express or implied.

[Malice is express when there is manifested an intention unlawfully to kill a human being.]

[Malice is implied when:

1. The killing resulted from an intentional act,
2. The natural consequences of the act are dangerous to human life, and
3. The act was deliberately performed with knowledge of the danger to, and with conscious disregard for, human life.]

California Jury Instructions, Criminal: Book of Approved Jury Instructions. 6th ed. Prepared by the Committee on Standard Jury Instruction Criminal, of the Superior Court of Los Angeles County, California. St. Paul, MN: West Publishing, 1996.

[When it is shown that a killing resulted from the intentional doing of an act with express or implied malice, no other mental state need be shown to establish the mental state of malice aforethought.]

The mental state constituting malice aforethought does not necessarily require any ill will or hatred of the person killed.

The word "aforethought" does not imply deliberation or the lapse of considerable time. It only means that the required mental state must precede rather than follow the act.

8.20 DELIBERATE AND PREMEDITATED MURDER

All murder which is perpetrated by any kind of willful, deliberate and premeditated killing with express malice aforethought is murder of the first degree.

The word "willful," as used in this instruction, means intentional.

The word "deliberate" means formed or arrived at or determined upon as a result of careful thought and weighing of considerations for and against the proposed course of action. The word "premeditated" means considered beforehand.

If you find that the killing was preceded and accompanied by a clear, deliberate intent on the part of the defendant to kill, which was the result of deliberation and premeditation, so that it must have been formed upon pre-existing reflection and not under a sudden heat of passion or other condition precluding the idea of deliberation, it is murder of the first degree.

The law does not undertake to measure in units of time the length of the period during which the thought must be pondered before it can ripen into an intent to kill which is truly deliberate and premeditated. The time will vary with different individuals and under varying circumstances.

The true test is not the duration of time, but rather the extent of the reflection. A cold, calculated judgment and decision may be arrived at in a short period of time, but a mere unconsidered and rash impulse, even though it includes an intent to kill, is not deliberation and premeditation as will fix an unlawful killing as murder of the first degree.

To constitute a deliberate and premeditated killing, the slayer must weigh and consider the question of killing and the reasons for and against such a choice and, having in mind the consequences, [he] [she] decides to and does kill.

8.30 UNPREMEDITATED MURDER OF THE SECOND DEGREE

Murder of the second degree is . . . the unlawful killing of a human being with malice aforethought when the perpetrator intended unlawfully to kill a human being but the evidence is insufficient to prove deliberation and premeditation.

8.37 MANSLAUGHTER—DEFINED (PEN. CODE, § 192)

The crime of manslaughter is the unlawful killing of a human being without malice aforethought. It is not divided into degrees but is of two kinds, namely, voluntary manslaughter and involuntary manslaughter.

8.40 VOLUNTARY MANSLAUGHTER—DEFINED (PEN. CODE, § 192, SUBD. (A))

. . . Every person who unlawfully kills another human being without malice aforethought but with an intent to kill, is guilty of voluntary manslaughter in violation of Penal Code section 192(a).

There is no malice aforethought if the killing occurred [upon a sudden quarrel or heat of passion] [or] [in the actual but unreasonable belief in the necessity to defend oneself against imminent peril to life or great bodily injury].

In order to prove this crime, each of the following elements must be proved:

1. A human being was killed;
2. The killing was unlawful; and
3. The killing was done with the intent to kill.

[A killing is unlawful, if it was [neither] [not] [justifiable] [nor] [excusable].]

8.42 SUDDEN QUARREL OR HEAT OF PASSION AND PROVOCATION EXPLAINED (PEN. CODE, § 192, SUBD. (A))

To reduce an intentional felonious homicide from the offense of murder to manslaughter upon the ground of sudden quarrel or heat of passion, the provocation must be of the character and degree as naturally would excite and arouse the passion, and the assailant must act under the influence of that sudden quarrel or heat of passion.

The heat of passion which will reduce a homicide to manslaughter must be such a passion as naturally would be aroused in the mind of an ordinarily reasonable person in the same circumstances. A defendant is not permitted to set up [his] [her] own standard of conduct and to justify or excuse [himself] [herself] because [his] [her] passions were aroused unless the circumstances in which the defendant was placed and the facts that confronted [him] [her] were such as also would have aroused the passion of the ordinarily reasonable person faced with the same situation. [Legally adequate provocation may occur in a short, or over a considerable, period of time.]

The question to be answered is whether or not, at the time of the killing, the reason of the accused was obscured or disturbed by passion to such an extent as would cause the ordinarily reasonable person of average disposition to act rashly and without deliberation and reflection, and from passion rather than from judgment.

If there was provocation, [whether of short or long duration,] but of a nature not normally sufficient to arouse passion, or if sufficient time elapsed between the provocation and the fatal blow for passion to subside and reason to return, and if an unlawful killing of a human being followed the provocation and had all the elements of murder, as I have defined it, the mere fact of slight or remote provocation will not reduce the offense to manslaughter.

8.43 MURDER OR MANSLAUGHTER—COOLING PERIOD

To reduce a killing upon a sudden quarrel or heat of passion from murder to manslaughter the killing must have occurred while the slayer was acting under the direct and immediate influence of the quarrel or heat of passion. Where the influence of the sudden quarrel or heat of passion has ceased to obscure the mind of the accused, and sufficient time has elapsed for angry passion to end and for reason to control [his] [her] conduct, it will no longer reduce an intentional killing to manslaughter. The question, as to whether the cooling period has elapsed and reason has returned, is not measured by the standard of the accused, but the duration of the cooling period is the time it would take the average or ordinarily reasonable person to have cooled the passion, and for that person's reason to have returned.

8.45 INVOLUNTARY MANSLAUGHTER—DEFINED (PEN. CODE §192, SUBD. (B))

[Defendant is accused [in Count[s] _____] of having committed the crime of involuntary manslaughter in violation of section 192, subdivision (b) of the Penal Code.]

Every person who unlawfully kills a human being, without malice aforethought and without an intent to kill, is guilty of the crime of involuntary manslaughter in violation of Penal Code section 192, subdivision (b).

A killing is unlawful within the meaning of this instruction if it occurred:

1. During the commission of an unlawful act [not amounting to a felony] which is dangerous to human life under the circumstances of its commission; or
2. In the commission of an act, ordinarily lawful, which involves a high degree of risk of death or great bodily harm, without due caution and circumspection.

[The commission of an unlawful act, without due caution and circumspection, would necessarily be an act that was dangerous to human life in its commission.]

In order to prove this crime, each of the following elements must be proved:

1. A human being was killed; and
2. The killing was unlawful.

8.46 DUE CAUTION AND CIRCUMSPECTION—DEFINED

The term "without due caution and circumspection" refers to [a] negligent act[s] which [is] [are] aggravated, reckless and flagrant and which [is] [are] such a departure from what would be the conduct of an ordinarily prudent, careful person under the same circumstances as to be contrary to a proper regard for [human life] [danger to human life] or to constitute indifference to the consequences of such act[s]. The facts must be such that the consequences of the negligent act[s] could reasonably have been foreseen. It must also appear that the [death] [danger to human life] was not the result of inattention, mistaken judgment or misadventure, but the natural and probable result of an aggravated, reckless or grossly negligent act.

5.00 EXCUSABLE HOMICIDE—LAWFUL ACT

The unintentional killing of a human being is excusable and not unlawful when (1) committed by accident and misfortune in the performance of a lawful act by lawful means and (2) where the person causing the death acted with that care and caution which would be exercised by an ordinarily careful and prudent individual under like circumstances.

5.01 EXCUSABLE HOMICIDE—HEAT OF PASSION

The unintentional killing of a human being by accident and misfortune is excusable when committed in the heat of passion upon a sudden combat or upon a sudden and sufficient provocation.

Sufficient provocation is that which would provoke a reasonable person to fight, provided:

1. The person killing was not the original aggressor;
2. No undue or unfair advantage was taken of the other by the person killing;
3. No dangerous or deadly weapon was used by the person who killed during the fight;
4. The killing was not done in a cruel or unusual manner; and
5. The act of killing was not the result of gross negligence.

5.10 RESISTING ATTEMPT TO COMMIT FELONY

Homicide is justifiable and not unlawful when committed by any person who is resisting an attempt to commit a forcible and atrocious crime.

5.12 JUSTIFIABLE HOMICIDE IN SELF-DEFENSE

The killing of another person in self-defense is justifiable and not unlawful when the person who does the killing actually and reasonably believes:

1. That there is imminent danger that the other person will either kill [him] [her] or cause [him] [her] great bodily injury; and
2. That it is necessary under the circumstances for [him] [her] to use in self-defense force or means that might cause the death of the other person, for the purpose of avoiding death or great bodily injury to [himself] [herself].

A bare fear of death or great bodily injury is not sufficient to justify a homicide. To justify taking the life of another in self-defense, the circumstances must be such as would excite the fears of a reasonable person placed in a similar position, and the party killing must act under the influence of those fears alone. The danger must be apparent, present, immediate and instantly dealt with, or must so appear at the time to the slayer as a reasonable person, and the killing must be done under a well-founded belief that it is necessary to save one's self from death or great bodily harm.

5.13 JUSTIFIABLE HOMICIDE—LAWFUL DEFENSE OF SELF OR ANOTHER

Homicide is justifiable and not unlawful when committed by any person in the defense of [himself] [herself] [[his] [her] _____] if [he] [she] actually and reasonably believed that the individual killed intended to commit a forcible and atrocious crime and that there was imminent danger of that crime being accomplished. A person may act upon appearances whether the danger is real or merely apparent.

5.14 HOMICIDE IN DEFENSE OF ANOTHER

The reasonable ground of apprehension does not require actual danger, but it does require (1) that the person about to kill another be confronted by the appearance of a peril such as has been mentioned; (2) that the appearance of peril arouse in [his] [her] mind an actual belief and fear of the existence of that peril; (3) that a reasonable person in the same situation, seeing and knowing the same facts, would justifiably have, and be justified in having, the same fear; and (4) that the killing be done under the influence of that fear alone.

5.15 CHARGE OF MURDER—BURDEN OF PROOF
RE JUSTIFICATION OR EXCUSE

Upon a trial of a charge of murder, a killing is lawful, if it was [justifiable] [excusable]. The burden is on the prosecution to prove beyond a reasonable doubt that the homicide was unlawful, that is, not [justifiable] [excusable]. If you have a reasonable doubt that the homicide was unlawful, you must find the defendant not guilty.

5.17 ACTUAL BUT UNREASONABLE BELIEF IN NECESSITY
TO DEFEND—MANSLAUGHTER

A person, who kills another person in the actual but unreasonable belief in the necessity to defend against imminent peril to life or great bodily injury, kills unlawfully, but does not harbor malice aforethought and is not guilty of murder. This would be so even though a reasonable person in the same situation seeing and knowing the same facts would not have had the same belief. Such an actual but unreasonable belief is not a defense to the crime of [voluntary] [or] [involuntary] manslaughter.

As used in this instruction, an "imminent" [peril] [or] [danger] means one that is apparent, present, immediate and must be instantly dealt with, or must so appear at the time to the slayer.

[However, this principle is not available, and malice aforethought is not negated, if the defendant by [his] [her] [unlawful] [or] [wrongful] conduct created the circumstances which legally justified [his] [her] adversary's [use of force], [attack] [or] [pursuit].]

USE NOTE

Battered wife syndrome evidence is admissible to prove the actual and reasonable belief requirement of self-defense. When this type of evidence is received, the trial court should give CALJIC 9.35.1 [see p. 235].■

● ● ● ●

For Deliberation and Argument

1. Each of the homicides treated in this group may be viewed as symptomatic of a broader social problem or issue. For example, *Carroll* is one of many cases of homicidal domestic violence; *Toney* is a case of teenage, probably gang-related, violence; *Forrest* deals with what used to be called "mercy killing." Of the cases in this group, which, in your view, represents the most serious social problem(s)? Which generates in you the most outrage? Explain your thinking. Recommend one or more social policies that might be enacted or put into practice to help alleviate the problem(s) of which this case is symptomatic.

2. Applying the jury instructions to the facts of the *Dewberry* case, do you believe that Dewberry is guilty of first-degree murder, second-degree murder, or voluntary manslaughter, or do you believe that he is not guilty? Explain your reasoning. In particular, apply the language of the jury instructions (for example, "willful, deliberate and premeditated" or "sudden heat of passion") to the defendant's— and the deceased's—behavior, showing how such terms do or do not apply in meeting the criteria for one type of homicide or another. Specifically, did the deceased's behavior toward the defendant justify a judgment of manslaughter, as opposed to first- or second-degree murder? If the defendant could reasonably be viewed as having acted in self-defense, would a verdict of "not guilty" be justified?

3. If you were a member of the *Malone* jury, for what kind of verdict would you vote in this Russian roulette case? Focus in particular on the difference between second-degree murder and involuntary manslaughter. As you understand the jury instructions, which terms most closely describe the defendant's actions? What aggravating or mitigating circumstances do you find?

   In commenting on this case, one justice remarked that "malice [may be] implied from conduct, recklessness of consequences, or the cruelty of the crime." His implication is that a homicide may be malicious, even though it was unintentional (that is, even though it was accidental). Do you agree? Did the defendant in this case exhibit this kind of malice? If so, what are the consequences for your verdict.

4. In his appeal, Toney argued that he should have been charged, at most, with manslaughter rather than murder. In considering his argument, the court noted,

   > To be guilty of manslaughter only, Toney had to have an honestly held belief, albeit an unreasonable one, that shooting Lindsey Williams was necessary to prevent his own imminent death or great bodily harm. Toney testified that when he shot his victims, his thoughts were that he

"was not going to take [any] chances of getting shot in the back. . . . The whole thing I was thinking about is making sure they did not hurt me."

Discuss the validity of Toney's argument, and argue that he should be convicted of manslaughter, on the one hand, or murder, on the other.

5. Forrest contended that he should not have been convicted of first-degree murder because (1) he killed his dying father without the malice required for a first-degree murder conviction, and (2) there was insufficient evidence of premeditation and deliberation. In his instructions to the jury, the trial judge explained the legal definition of *malice*, and said that it was up to the jury to determine whether the defendant killed his father with malice. Based on the facts of the case, and based also on the law, do you believe that Forrest killed his father with malice and with premeditation and therefore should be convicted of first-degree murder? Or do you believe that he should be convicted of manslaughter? Explain.

6. Forrest also contended that, at most, he should have been convicted of manslaughter under the "heat of passion" doctrine. As the appeals court noted,

> According to the defendant, there is abundant evidence in the record that, upon seeing his father at the hospital, he was overwhelmed by the futile, horrible suffering before him and that, in a highly emotional state, he killed to bring relief to the man he deeply loved. The jury instruction employed by the trial court, concludes defendant, because it did not instruct on heat of passion, for all intents and purposes precluded the jury from considering these critical facts in mitigation of the offense.

To what extent do you agree with Forrest's argument? (*Note:* You may wish to combine this question with question 5 in formulating an argument on Forrest's degree of guilt.)

7. Select one of these five cases. Imagine yourself as attorney for the plaintiff or attorney for the defendant. Write a paper in IRAC format to make your case. Define the *issue* in question format. State or summarize the applicable *rules* about homicide. *Apply* the rules, as explained in "Jury Instructions on Murder and Manslaughter," as they apply to the facts of the case you have selected. Draw a *conclusion* from the application of these rules.

8. Select one of the cases treated in this group. Imagine that you are representing either the plaintiff or the defendant. Compose either an opening statement or a closing argument for this case. Remember that your audience is the jury. Draw on the facts of the case in a way that is likely to have the greatest impact on the jury. Keep in mind, however, that jury members may turn against you—and your client—if they think that you are overly manipulating the facts, being deceptive, making exaggerated claims, or attempting too crudely to play on their emotions. For guidance on developing your statement, see "Models for the Opening Statement and the Closing Argument" at the end of Chapter 2. See also Larry S. Stewart's "Arguing Pain and Suffering Damages in Summation: How to Inspire Jurors" at the end of the Group 3 Readings in Chapter 3.

■ Group 2 Readings: *Vehicular Homicide*

The next group of readings concerns vehicular homicide—that is, homicides resulting from the operation of motor vehicles. As with other types of homicides, legal culpability varies, primarily depending on the state of mind—and in particular, the intent—of the vehicle operator. In cases where the homicides are the result of an accident (for example, an unexpected blowout that causes the driver to lose control of the vehicle, which then plows into a pedestrian), a jury may arrive at a verdict of excusable homicide. On the other end of the spectrum, a driver who intentionally uses his vehicle as a deadly weapon will likely be charged with first- or second-degree murder. In some cases, a jury may arrive at a verdict of involuntary manslaughter if it concludes that the driver, while not intending to kill anyone, nonetheless acted with gross negligence.

The cases that follow illustrate a variety of types of vehicular homicide. In People v. Markham, *the defendant was charged with driving under the influence of alcohol when he struck another car, killing its two occupants.* People v. Pears *concerns another intoxicated driver, charged with second-degree murder after a fatal accident. In* People v. Madison *the passenger of a car was convicted of manslaughter for urging the driver to pursue another car, with tragic results. Finally,* People v. Spragney *concerns a driver convicted of vehicular homicide for causing a fatal accident as a result of suffering an epileptic seizure.*

Death on Highway 6

The PEOPLE of the State of California, Plaintiff and Respondent,
v.
Tyson Lee MARKHAM, Defendant and Appellant.

Cr. 5818.

District Court of Appeal, Second District. Division 1, California.

Aug. 15, 1957.

Rehearing Denied Sept. 10, 1957.
Hearing Denied Oct. 9, 1957.

The record reflects that about 7:30 or 7:45 p.m. on the evening of May 10, 1956, 1
Miss Patricia L. McKnabb saw her father William L. McKnabb and her sister Faye Jean Zander leave together in a 1954 Ford station wagon owned by the latter. Later that evening, between 9:30 and 10 p.m., Lester C. Kerwood, a truck

---

People v. Markham, 314 P.2d 217 (1957).

driver with 18 years experience, was driving a loaded truck from Mojave going towards Santa Maria. He was driving south on Highway 6 near Ward Road. The driver's seat in this truck was about 6½ feet above the roadway. While operating his truck, Mr. Kerwood witnessed an accident involving two vehicles. They were both traveling north. The first vehicle to come into his view was a Ford station wagon proceeding at 50 to 55 miles per hour. Following the Ford was an Oldsmobile traveling, in his opinion, at 80 miles per hour. The basic speed limit in this area was 55 miles per hour. This witness testified that as the Ford station wagon passed the cab of the truck, the Oldsmobile was "right on him." The truck was fifty-nine feet four inches long. Believing that the Oldsmobile had no room to "get by" the station wagon, Mr. Kerwood pulled his truck off to the side of the road. As the witness saw the Ford pass his truck, he looked back, heard the collision and saw one of the vehicles "rolling through the air." The impact occurred immediately after the Ford had passed the cab of the truck.

The truck driver did not hear the sound of brakes. The Oldsmobile, still going   2
80 miles per hour, struck the Ford station wagon in the rear, both cars went through a fence, the Ford turning over sideways. In the Ford at the time of the accident were Faye Jean Zander and William L. McKnabb, both of whom died as the result of injuries sustained in the accident.

The headlights and the tail lights of the Ford were operating until the colli-   3
sion; the road and the weather were "fair"; the visibility was "very good."

When he witnessed the accident, Mr. Kerwood was forty feet away. He   4
stopped his truck, set out flares, and "set out to get help and to see what was wrong." Fifteen or twenty minutes later, the highway patrol arrived.

Viewing the scene, Mr. Kerwood found a man thirty to forty feet from the Ford   5
who appeared unconscious. He saw a woman forty to fifty feet from the Ford who appeared to be dead. There were two occupants in the Oldsmobile; the defendant was in the driver's seat and was conscious, as was his passenger.

Charles L. Evans, a highway patrolman, arrived at the location of the accident   6
at 10:40 p.m. When he arrived, the defendant was being put into an ambulance. No sobriety test was given to him due to the nature of his injuries. He was bleeding from the mouth, his teeth were knocked out, and from his breath there emanated the odors of "strong alcohol—blood."

The defendant was taken to the hospital for treatment, and with his consent   7
blood was withdrawn from him for a blood alcohol test.

Dr. Strawn, attending physician at the Antelope Valley Hospital in Lancaster,   8
withdrew a sample of the appellant's blood for the blood alcohol test at one minute past midnight on the 11th of May, 1956.

Martin Klein, a forensic chemist, who was qualified as an expert chemist at   9
the trial, examined the appellant's blood and discovered it to contain .19 percent of alcohol by weight. He stated that the oxidation of ethyl alcohol to carbon dioxide and water produces a reduction in the amount of alcohol in the blood at the rate of .015 percent per hour or .03 for two hours, and that if no alcohol were consumed in the interim, the amount of the alcohol in the blood of a person at a

time two hours prior to the taking of the sample would be .03 higher. The accident had occurred approximately two hours prior to the taking of the sample.

In the opinion of Mr. Klein, a person having an alcohol level of .15 percent or higher would be under the influence of alcohol. That one having an alcohol level of .20 percent would be intoxicated; and that person with the alcohol level of .22 would be under the influence and intoxicated.

The Defense

Max Scollin testified that he saw defendant on the night in question at about 8 p.m. in Jerry's Cafe; that defendant consumed one bottle of beer; that they left the cafe in defendant's automobile with the latter driving and the witness occupying the front seat. That defendant was watching the road ahead and that there was nothing "unusual" about his speed; that enroute they stopped at another cafe where they each had "one beer." That they remained at the latter cafe about twenty or twenty-five minutes. That the traffic was "very light." They stopped at another place for fifteen or twenty minutes during which time defendant again consumed "one beer." They made no further stops prior to the accident. The witness testified that defendant was driving between 50 and 65 miles per hour. With reference to defendant's sobriety, this witness testified:

> "Q. Now, you have seen people under the influence of alcohol before, have you, Mr. Scollin?   A. Yes, sir.
> "Q. You work in a bar. You know what somebody looks like when they are under the influence, don't you?   A. I do.
> "Q. With regard to Mr. Markham's sobriety that evening, do you have an opinion as to his sobriety that evening that you were driving with him? A. Yes, sir, I would say he was sober."

This witness testified further that prior to the accident, he saw no vehicle ahead; nor did he see any tail lights on the road in front of the automobile in which he was riding.

As a witness in his own behalf, defendant testified that he was arrested some nine days after the accident. That on the night here in question he met the witness Max Scollin at Jerry's Cafe where they had a bottle of beer. That he and Mr. Scollin left in the former's automobile for Palmdale. That he (defendant) was driving. That they made two stops enroute and at each stop consumed a bottle of beer apiece. That he "felt no effect" from the beer, and was sober. He testified that his speed on the highway varied from 50 to 65 miles per hour "off and on, up and down." That when he went into a curve after passing a truck coming in the opposite direction, "his lights picked up a car right in his lane of traffic"; that when his lights "picked up this car right in my lane of traffic. . . . I was so close on it that I didn't have time to do anything, and I hit it. I couldn't even swerve right then. It was the car that I hit. Because, it was dark, and it just picked it up, and I was that close I hit it, and I didn't know exactly what it was there. I was knocked, not unconscious, but I don't think I was—I was beat up pretty bad." That the vehicle ahead of him, ". . . didn't have any lights on, sir, that I could see at all." The defendant testified that he allowed the doctor to make the blood test because he desired to prove that he was not under the influence of liquor while driving his automobile.

In rebuttal, Officer Anderson of the State Highway Patrol testified that when he accompanied defendant to Newhall there was considerable conversation between them and ". . . the gist of the conversation was that the impact occurred almost simultaneously with the viewing of the vehicle." In answer to a question, "Did he also tell you in that conversation that he didn't see any tail lights on that car?," the witness answered, "He said he recalled seeing nothing, just a split second before the impact." 14

■ Drunk Driving ■

Richard Paul PEARS, Appellant,
v.
STATE of Alaska, Appellee.

No. 6783.

Court of Appeals of Alaska.
Nov. 25, 1983.

The evidence produced at trial indicated that Pears voluntarily drank in a bar to the point of intoxication. After becoming intoxicated he drove recklessly, speeding, running through stop signs and stop lights and failing to slow for yield signs. His passenger at the time, Kathy Hill, told him that his driving scared her. Pears and Kathy Hill then went to another bar and had more drinks. Pears and Hill then left the bar and while they were approaching his truck on foot, Pears was stopped by two uniformed police officers in a patrol car. One of the officers told Pears not to drive because he was too intoxicated. Pears and Hill walked back toward the bar until the officers were out of sight. They then returned to his truck and drove away. Once again, with Hill protesting, Pears drove over the speed limit and ran red lights and stop signs. Pears then dropped Kathy Hill off and continued to drive around. Shortly before the fatal collision Pears was seen by Steve Call, who was turning his car onto the four-lane Steese Highway. According to Call, Pears' car ran a red light on the highway, going through the light at a high rate of speed and passing two cars which were stopped at the light. Call said he was going about forty-five miles per hour, the speed limit, but Pears was going faster. As they approached the next intersection Call could clearly see the red light against them and the cars 1

Pears v. State, 672 P.2d 903 (1983).

stopping. Pears got around the cars which were stopping by passing them in the right turn lane, going into the intersection without breaking or slowing down. Pears collided with one of the cars entering the intersection on the green light, an orange Datsun. The impact of the collision knocked the Datsun 146 feet, killing two of the three people in the car and seriously injuring the third.

The second degree murder statute under which Pears was charged, AS 11.41.110(a)(2), provides:

> A person commits the crime of murder in the second degree if . . . (2) he intentionally performs an act that results in the death of another person under circumstances manifesting an extreme indifference to the value of human life.

Pears argues that the legislature did not intend to have a motor vehicle homicide prosecuted as murder and that his offense should only have been charged as manslaughter. Manslaughter is defined in AS 11.41.120(a) and provides:

> A person commits the crime of manslaughter if he . . . (1) intentionally, knowingly, or recklessly causes the death of another person under circumstances not amounting to murder in the first or second degree.

. . . This court discussed the relationship between second-degree murder and manslaughter in *Neitzel v. State*, 655 P.2d 325, 335–38 (Alaska App. 1982). In that case we indicated that the difference between second-degree murder and manslaughter was one of degree which was a question for the jury under proper instructions:

> Under the Revised Code, negligent homicide and reckless manslaughter are satisfied by conduct creating a significant risk of death absent justification or excuse. They differ only in the actor's knowledge of the risk. In differentiating reckless murder from reckless manslaughter, the jury is asked to determine whether the recklessness manifests an extreme indifference to human life.
>
> [T]he jury must consider the nature and gravity of the risk, including the harm to be foreseen and the likelihood that it will occur. For both murder and manslaughter, the harm to be foreseen is a death. Therefore, the significant distinction is in the likelihood that a death will result from the defendant's act. Where the defendant's act has limited social utility, a very slight though significant and avoidable risk of death may make him guilty of manslaughter if his act causes death.
>
> Driving an automobile has some social utility although substantially reduced when the driver is intoxicated. The odds that a legally intoxicated person driving home after the bars close will hit and kill or seriously injure someone may be as low as one chance in a thousand and still qualify for manslaughter. Where murder is charged, however, an act must create a much greater risk that death or serious physical injury will result.

Teenage Jealousy

The PEOPLE of the State of California,
Plaintiff and Respondent,
v.
Michael MADISON, Defendant and Appellant.

Cr. 2336.

District Court of Appeal, Fourth District,
Division 2, California.
June 15, 1966.

Prior to November 27, 1964, the defendant, then age 19, had known one Cheri   1
Lilly, age sixteen, for a period of one and one-half years and had been dating her
for approximately six months. During the day of November 27, the defendant
learned that Cheri had a date that evening with Kennedy. The defendant, during
the evening of that day, was, on several occasions, heard to declare he was going
to go to Miss Lilly's home and "kick Jerry Kennedy's ass." These declarations were
made at a party at the defendant's aunt's home during the course of which alcoholic beverages were served. One witness recalled that the defendant had stated,
"I'll kill the guy," or something of similar purport. At approximately 11:00 p.m. on
that evening, the defendant asked his sixteen year old friend, Covey, if he (the
friend) would drive the defendant to Cheri's home so that the defendant could
talk to her. Covey consented and the defendant left his aunt's house at 11:30 p.m.
in Covey's car with Covey driving. At this time the defendant evidenced no sign of
anger. During all subsequent events the friend, Covey, was driving. Six other
minors ranging from age fourteen to nineteen were passengers in the car;
however, one of the passengers, a girl, was transported to her home. The car then
proceeded to Cheri's residence, arriving at approximately 12:00 o'clock midnight.
Upon arriving at Cheri's home, the car was parked, facing north, across the street
from the house. Parked one house down from Cheri's residence, facing south, was
another car containing four minors who had attended the party described above.
Of the four, one was a female and one was defendant's brother. Defendant left the
Covey car, spoke to the occupants of the other auto, and as he was returning to
the Covey car, a Volkswagen stopped in front of Cheri's home. Defendant
approached the rear of the parked Volkswagen. As defendant neared the rear of
the Volkswagen, its driver, Kennedy, became aware of defendant's presence. The
Volkswagen vehicle accelerated rapidly down the street in a southerly direction.
Someone in the Covey car shouted, "Let's follow them." Both of the waiting cars
started to pursue the Volkswagen. The Covey car had some difficulty joining the
pursuit for it had been facing the opposite direction.

People v. Madison, 51 Cal. Rptr. 2d 858 (1966).

At the end of the block the Volkswagen ran a stop-sign and turned left. The chase lasted some fifteen to twenty minutes, winding through a residential area at speeds of from thirty to forty miles per hour. All three cars disregarded stop-signs and the posted speed limits. The driver of the Volkswagen, Kennedy, drove recklessly, sometimes on the wrong side of the street, allowing the Volkswagen to "fishtail" around corners. At one or more times during this chase, defendant, who was sitting at the far right hand side of the front seat, exclaimed, "Get him, Bill," [Covey's first name] and "Don't lose him, Bill," or words of similar purport. All of the occupants of the car admittedly made similar exclamations. The Covey vehicle eventually caught up to and closely followed the Volkswagen. While passing through an intersection, the Volkswagen slowed suddenly, and the pursuing auto swung to the left to avoid striking it from the rear. The Volkswagen then swerved to the left. The two autos came into brief contact along their sides, then parted with the Covey car pulling ahead. The Volkswagen then passed the Covey car on the left and the driver "hit his brakes" several times. On the last occasion this occurred, there is evidence the Covey vehicle struck the Volkswagen from the rear. Shortly after this the Volkswagen swerved left sharply toward the curb, and struck it. While making this sudden turn, the Volkswagen left two turning skid marks approximately sixty feet long. The Volkswagen jumped the curb and over-turned in the front yard of a residence. After the Volkswagen had crashed, defendant exclaimed, "Cheri," and told Covey to stop. The occupants of the pursuing car left their car and ascertained that Kennedy was very seriously injured or dead. Admittedly, Kennedy died as a result of the accident. Defendant found Cheri and discovered she was still alive. When informed Kennedy was dead and before law enforcement officers had arrived at the scene, he exclaimed, "I have killed him, I have killed him."

The defendant and two friends were taken to the Newport Beach Police Station at approximately two o'clock on the morning of November 28, 1964. There is a conflict in the testimony as to whether at that time they were advised of their constitutional rights. After this, the defendant in a conversation with his friends admitted fault for the incident. This statement was not elicited by any questions put to defendant by the officer but was overheard by that officer. Defendant and his companions were asked to "explain the night from the beginning as to what happened." Prior to his arrest, a written statement was given by the defendant which was subsequently introduced in evidence. The interrogating officer, during the preparation of these statements, admittedly directed that the defendant delete the phrase, "Kick his ass," and change it to, "Stomp his butt." There is a conflict in evidence as to exact deletion and insertion requested by the officer. The defendant's counsel moved to strike all of the defendant's admissions of liability made at the scene of the accident, presumably on *Dorado* grounds. (*People v. Dorado*, 62 Cal.2d 338, 42 Cal.Rptr. 169, 398 P.2d 361.) However, the court held that the investigation had not then focused on the defendant and hence those statements were admissible.

The Epileptic Driver

24 Cal.App.3d 333
The PEOPLE of the State of California,
Plaintiff and Respondent,
v.
Isiah SPRAGNEY, Defendant and Appellant.

Cr. 19849.

Court of Appeal, Second District, Division 5.
March 24, 1972.

The facts concerning the accident, which resulted in the death of a ten year old 1
girl, are tragic but brief. At about 8:15 a.m. on July 7, 1970, defendant speeded
through a red light at the corner of Santa Barbara and Broadway in Los Angeles.
He collided with a Volkswagen in which the victim was a passenger. His own car
proceeded about sixty feet from the point of collision and overturned.

The balance of the relevant testimony has to do only with defendant's frame 2
of mind, using that term in the broadest sense. After the accident defendant
crawled out from his overturned car. He staggered and appeared unable to maintain his balance. He did not smell of alcohol, nor did he appear injured. He
resisted arrest but not too combatively. His coordination was wild. There was no
pattern to the way he used his hands. His movements were both rapid and slow.
His eyes were wide open, and his pupils constricted. He had a fixed stare. His
speech was slow, slurred and not understandable. He was smiling, laughing, and
muttering. His responses were rambling and unintelligent. The arresting officer,
who had somewhat limited expertise on the subject, formed the conclusion that
defendant was under the influence of drugs. He had never, however, observed the
same symptoms that appellant exhibited. He had no opinion concerning the type
of drug involved.

The car which defendant had been driving was searched. Eight pills, four of 3
which were later analyzed as barbiturates, were found. The car was not registered
in defendant's name.

At the station a Breathalyzer test revealed the absence of blood alcohol. 4
Defendant was then taken to the Central Receiving Hospital where he was seen
by a Doctor Sanderson. A blood sample was taken. It later proved negative for
alcohol or barbiturates. The blood was not tested for stimulants. At the hospital
defendant continued to be restless. Instead of walking through doors he walked
into their jambs. His balance was, however, improving, as was his orientation. He
became able to communicate.

In the opinion of Doctor Sanderson defendant was "completely out of touch 5
with reality but he was awake . . . he had what we would call an acute psychosis,

---

People v. Spragney, 100 Cal. Rptr. 902 (1972).

which is often times due to drug ingestion." He had no opinion concerning the nature of the drug. Defendant was disoriented as to time and place. "Just completely out of touch with reality." No injuries were found. Defendant's blood pressure and pulse were elevated. Whatever drugs defendant had taken they were not barbiturates. The best the doctor could say was that defendant was in an acute psychotic state, probably due to a stimulant type of drug, but he could not say with certainty.

During Doctor Sanderson's cross-examination he admitted that his impression of a drug intoxication was tentative only and that he had worked with little time to spare. Several tests which would confirm or refute his tentative diagnosis were not performed. 6

On redirect examination Doctor Sanderson expressed the opinion that defendant was not suffering from epilepsy because he observed no physical signs indicative of seizures and had no information that defendant had been in a comatose state after the accident. On recross the doctor admitted, in effect, that it was only grand mal epilepsy which, in his opinion, was not present. He admitted that petit mal epilepsy manifested itself only in brief periods of disorientation. There was also temporal lobe epilepsy, which sometimes resulted in psychomotor disorders. When under that type of seizure a person would appear to be awake, although he was out of touch with reality. In his view such a person was conscious. 7

Just before it rested, the prosecution introduced, over objection, a letter from the Department of Motor Vehicles to the effect that a thorough search of its records did not reveal that defendant had ever had a license to operate a vehicle on a California highway. 8

The first important defense witness was Doctor George N. Thompson. He had performed two electroenchephalograms on defendant about three and one-half months after the accident. One of them proved something wrong with defendant's right frontal brain lobe. The abnormality was consistent with either grand mal or psycho-motor epilepsy. The latter results in seizures in which a person acts like a robot out of touch with reality. He appears conscious but, in fact, is not. He may appear to be going through an acute psychosis. This type of seizure is not recognizable by most doctors, except neurologists. During a seizure a person is unconscious in the sense that he is unaware of his surroundings, although to the unknowing he would give the impression of being conscious. 9

Doctor Fiske, a medical psychologist, performed a battery of tests on defendant, whose IQ was found to be 76; this places him on the borderline of the mentally defective group. The tests revealed evidence of organic brain damage. If defendant had epilepsy at the time the tests were administered and had known of it, he would not have been able to conceal his knowledge. 10

Doctor DiNolfo, a psychiatrist, had examined defendant on October 2, 1970. In his opinion defendant suffered from frontal lobe epilepsy which causes seizures in which the person acts like a robot. During the seizures the patient is unconscious. During the psychiatric examination defendant told the doctor about an episode which happened three weeks before July 7, 1970. On that occasion 11 defendant had been driving and had become aware that the traffic lights at an intersection ahead were red. He had noticed a police car approaching the intersection from the opposite side. In spite of this fact he had been unable to control his reactions, had run the red light and was stopped by the police. Defendant did not know why he reacted in this fashion. Defendant told the doctor about several other episodes in his past which were "epileptic equivalent states." The doctor did not believe that defendant knew that he was an epileptic or even knew what epilepsy was. Neither did defendant know that he should not be driving a car. In the doctor's view of the events of July 7, 1970, defendant was conscious when he got into the car and lost consciousness sometime thereafter. Typically when a seizure occurs while the epileptic is driving, he starts speeding up and acts as if he were glued to the wheel; he will go right through an intersection no matter what is going on. The possibility that the seizure occurred after the accident was so minimal that it could be discarded.

● ● ● ●

For Deliberation and Argument

1. The defendant in *People v. Markham*, Tyson Lee Markham, based his appeal on three arguments. First, he claimed . . . the evidence used to convict him of manslaughter—"the conditions of the highway, the marks and debris thereon, and the speed of [his] automobile"—was based on circumstantial rather than direct (that is, eyewitness) evidence. This created a reasonable doubt as to his guilt. Second, Markham argued that the evidence was insufficient to prove that he was under the influence of intoxicating liquor at the time of the accident. Third, he claimed that because the evidence was insufficient to prove gross negligence, he should not have been convicted of manslaughter. Gross negligence has been defined in California cases as "an entire failure to exercise care, or the exercise of so light a degree of care as to justify the belief that there was an indifference to the things and welfare of others," and as "that want of care which would raise a presumption of the conscious indifference to consequences." Write an argument supporting or refuting the defendant's contentions, based on the evidence provided in the facts of the case.

2. Richard Pears, the defendant in *Pears v. State*, was convicted of second-degree murder and sentenced to twenty years imprisonment. In his appeal, Pears contended that his crime amounted to no more than manslaughter, that the murder conviction was unwarranted, and the sentence excessive. Write an argument supporting or refuting Pears's position, basing your argument on the differences between manslaughter and second-degree murder specified at the end of the facts of the case and on the following definitions and legal precedents:

   • The main legal difference between manslaughter and murder is that manslaughter is characterized by *recklessness* or *gross negligence* and murder is characterized by *malice*. *Recklessness* is defined as "conduct whereby the actor does not desire the consequence but nonetheless foresees the possibility and consciously takes the risk" (*Black's Law Dictionary*). *Gross negligence* is defined as "a conscious, voluntary act or omission in reckless disregard of a legal duty and of the consequences to another party" (*Black's Law Dictionary*). *Malice* is described as follows: "Under the law of homicide, the mental state constituting malice does not require that the perpetrator harbor any ill will or hatred toward the victim; malice is found where one acts with wanton disregard for human life by doing an act that involves a high probability that it will result in death" (*People v. Matta* (1976)).

- In *People v. Watson* (1981), the court declared,

    The definitions of implied malice and gross negligence, although bearing a general similarity, are not identical. Implied malice contemplates a subjective awareness of a higher degree of risk than does gross negligence, and involves an element of wantonness ["conduct that indicates that the actor is aware of the risks but indifferent as to the results" (*Black's Law Dictionary*)] which is absent in gross negligence. . . . [A] finding of implied malice depends upon a determination that the defendant actually appreciated the risks involved. . . . When conduct resulting in a vehicular homicide can be characterized as a wanton disregard for life, and the facts demonstrate a subjective awareness of the risks created, malice may be implied.

- In *People v. Pears*, one of the judges wrote,

    Reckless murder occupies the middle ground between (1) mere recklessness, creating a substantial risk of death, and (2) knowledge, creating a virtual certainly of death. Before Pears could be found guilty or murder, his recklessness must be found to approach knowledge that his acts were practically certain to cause death or serious physical injury.

3. Michael Madison, the defendant in *People v. Madison*, was convicted of manslaughter. The prosecution had contended during trial that Madison was an aider and abettor of the driver, Bill Covey (who was also convicted of manslaughter), and that Madison's "gross negligence" led to the death of Jerry Kennedy. Madison, on the other hand, emphasized that he was neither the owner nor the driver of the car that collided with Kennedy's Volkswagen, nor did he have control over the driver. To what extent do you believe that Madison should share (1) moral responsibility and (2) legal responsibility, specifically manslaughter, for the death of Kennedy? In formulating your response, apply the *facts* of the case to the following legal *rules* and *definitions*:

- *Manslaughter* is the unlawful killing of a human being
    (3) In the *driving* of a vehicle
        a. In the commission of an unlawful act, not amounting to a felony, with gross negligence; or in the commission of a lawful act which

might produce death, in an unlawful manner, and with gross negligence. (*California Penal Code*, sec. 102, subdivision 3a)

- *Gross negligence* is now defined to be "an entire failure to exercise care, or the exercise of so slight a degree of care as to justify the belief that there was an indifference to the things and the welfare of others." (*People v. Costa*).
- "[A passenger] who advises and encourages the commission of the crime, while present at its perpetration, surely falls within the definition of a principal" (*People v. Holford*).
- Principal: "All persons concerned in the commission of a crime . . . [who] aid and abet in its commission" (*California Penal Code*, section 31).

4. Isiah Spragney, the defendant in *People v. Spragney*, was convicted of vehicular homicide. He contended that at the time of the accident, he was unconscious and therefore could not be held legally responsible for its fatal consequences. He also maintained that the prosecution's introduction of evidence that he had never been licensed to drive in California unfairly prejudiced the jury against him since the prosecution offered no evidence that the defendant had ever been *denied* a driver's license for any reason, including epilepsy. Based on the evidence and the statute on vehicular homicide, argue in support of or against the defendant's contentions. Should the appeals court affirm or reverse his conviction? Why?

▪ Group 3 Readings: *Crimes of Passion*

Crimes of passion have always been a favorite subject of fiction and film. Typically as in Shakespeare's Othello, *a spouse discovers—or imagines—that his or her loved one has been unfaithful and then takes homicidal revenge on one or both offending parties. Courts have generally viewed such crimes of passion with more understanding and as less deserving of severe punishment than cold-blooded murders. (While convicted murderers may serve terms of twenty-five years to life, or even be executed, those convicted of voluntary manslaughter— the legal name for homicides committed in the heat of passion—generally serve five to seven years, or less, and can be paroled earlier.) In fact, it has often seemed that the court's sympathies in such cases are more with the killer than with the victim. As one court ruled in a 1944 case, "Could it be doubted . . . that this afflicted mind had lost its control, that the defendant was moved by an emotion of passion springing from continued outrage upon his marital rights, culminated on this morning by this coarse and brutal notice to him of his wife's illicit intentions?" In another case, a court declared, "In our opinion the passions of any reasonable person would have been inflamed and intensely aroused by this sort of discovery [that is, catching an unfaithful spouse in the act] . . . "*

The homicides in this group are all crimes of passion. In Davis v. State, *an elderly physician kills a man he falsely suspects of having an improper rela-*

tionship with his wife. In People v. Spurlin, *a man kills both his wife and their son after she tells him that their marriage is over. In* Whitsett v. State, *a husband kills his wife's lover after a wild car chase. Finally in* State v. Thornton, *a man kills the lover of his estranged wife after catching them in bed together.*

The Deluded Doctor

DAVIS v. STATE.
Supreme Court of Tennessee.

May 24, 1930.
On Rehearing June 28, 1930.

The plaintiff in error [archaic term for plaintiff] was indicted for killing one L. R. Noe, and convicted of murder in the second degree. 1

Noe was killed May 6, 1927, in the village of Flintville. He was a middle-aged man, a respected citizen, and a member of the county court. The plaintiff in error was sixty-seven years of age at the time of the tragedy. He was a physician, having begun the practice of medicine in 1890 in Franklin county, where he remained for about fifteen years. He then removed to the West on account of the health of one of his children, he having married and raised a family. He remained in the West for about ten years and moved back to Tennessee, taking up his abode at Lexie Cross Roads in Franklin county, Tenn., where he stayed until the latter part of the year 1925. Meanwhile his first wife had died. 2

Late in 1925 or early in 1926 he moved from Lexie Cross Roads to Flintville, at the request of citizens of the latter place, they being without a physician in their neighborhood. 3

There was a lady in Flintville named Mrs. Goodwin, who ran a drug store, she having succeeded to that business upon the death of her husband. She also owned a house, suitable for a doctor's office, and this house was rented from her by the plaintiff in error, Dr. Davis. He and Mrs. Goodwin seemed to have been attracted to each other at once, and they were married after he had been in Flintville two or three months, in February, 1926. 4

On the day of his marriage, or the day before, Dr. Davis went into Mrs. Goodwin's drug store. The deceased preceded the doctor into the store. When the doctor came in Mrs. Goodwin was apparently undertaking to hide some article which she had in her hands before either of the men entered, and Noe was talking to her. It later appeared that Mrs. Goodwin had been working on a night-gown or some article of lingerie, which she was endeavoring to conceal. 5

Upon this incident alone Dr. Davis conceived the idea that improper relations existed between Mrs. Goodwin and the deceased Noe. This idea appears not to 6

Davis v. State, 28 S.W.2d 993 (1930).

have taken possession of him until after the marriage, for the ceremony was duly consummated.

After the marriage Dr. Davis testifies that he could never enter into marital   7
relations with his wife—that the image of Noe always came between them. Later he told his wife of his belief, and she endeavored to reason with him about the matter, and he evidently endeavored to reason with himself and free his mind from the idea. He was unable, however to overcome his conviction that his wife had misbehaved herself with Noe.

Mrs. Davis testified and confirmed the statements of Dr. Davis in this partic-   8
ular. She said he was a good man, good to her and to her children, that she was fond of him, and tried to clear his mind of his derogatory belief as to her conduct, but that she was utterly unable to do so.

It should be stated in this connection that all the proof showed that Mrs. Davis   9
was a woman whose character was above reproach. There was no justification for any suspicion as to her deportment.

She stated, and Dr. Davis agreed, that it was impossible for her to live with   10
him while he entertained such ideas about her, and it was arranged between them that they should separate, and that she should file a bill for divorce. Pursuant to this arrangement Dr. Davis went to Nashville for treatment for diabetes from which he was suffering, remained some time, and his wife brought suit for divorce, which was granted to her.

Dr. Davis and this lady whom he married never lived together as husband and   11
wife. His conviction as to her relations with Noe always prevented this. It cannot be doubted on this record that Dr. Davis truly and absolutely believed that his wife had misbehaved herself. It is equally plain on the record that there was no basis whatever for this belief. It is also clear that the plaintiff in error entertained this belief as a settled conviction, that he entertained it at the time he killed Noe, and that he entertained it at the time of his trial. So much indeed is conceded by the state, and the jury so found, as will hereafter appear, and we accordingly have to deal with the criminal responsibility of a man laboring under an insane delusion.

As above stated, Dr. Davis went to Nashville for medical treatment, when it   12
was agreed between him and his wife that she should get a divorce. After leaving Nashville he moved back to Lexie Cross Roads, where he had resided before going to Flintville, and practiced medicine at the former place for some months. On May 5, 1927, he made a trip to Flintville to collect some bills owing him from persons there. He spent the night at a boarding house, putting his automobile in Copeland's garage. On the day of the 6th he was in and out of Copeland's garage several times, going about the community looking after his collections. On the afternoon of May 6, while he was seated in Copeland's garage, the deceased, Noe, accompanied by another man, stopped at the garage to get gasoline and oil for his car. It does not appear that Noe knew that Dr. Davis was at the garage, or that Dr. Davis anticipated any meeting with Noe.

While Noe's car was standing at the garage, Dr. Davis, who had been seated in   13
the house, got up, walked out to the car and began to curse Noe with the utmost violence, applying to Noe the strongest epithets possible. Noe asked or undertook

to ask what he had ever done to call forth such denunciation, and Dr. Davis then opened fire on Noe with his pistol, shooting him several times, inflicting wounds from which Noe died shortly.

The shooting was witnessed by Copeland, the owned of the garage, and Young, the man who was riding with Noe. Both of them testified that Noe was seated in the car when the shooting began, making no demonstration whatever toward Dr. Davis, and all that Noe ever did was to try and get out of the car after the shooting began. 14

In his own testimony Dr. Davis states that Noe made a move as if to draw a weapon when he (Davis) began his denunciation. This, however, is in conflict with the testimony of Copeland and Young, and counsel for the plaintiff in error appear to place no credence upon this testimony of their client. 15

Dr. Davis testified at some length and it seems rather plain from his own evidence that the sight of Noe, the man Dr. Davis believed had debauched his late wife, so aroused him that he went out and cursed him and killed him without any overt act on the part of Noe at all. 16

Plaintiff in error said that when Noe stopped at the garage and saw him (Davis) there was an indescribably mean or triumphant look in Noe's eyes; that he (Davis) thought of the wrong that Noe had done him and went out to denounce him and only intended to shoot in case Noe offered resentment, in which event Davis said he intended to shoot for his own protection. 17

Dr. Davis testified that he knew that it was wrong to assassinate a man, or to kill a man, except in self-defense. After Noe was shot Dr. Davis went back into the garage and took a seat, and said that he did this because he knew an officer would be there for him in a little while—showing in this way that he realized perfectly that he had violated the law in killing Noe. 18

There is much proof in the record as to the details of the life of Dr. Davis. It is shown that he is a gentleman and a physician of good repute, well thought of, and esteemed by all who know him. He has had much of affliction in his life, sickness and deaths in his family, and he himself having sustained many bodily afflictions. As heretofore noted, he seemed to have suffered with diabetes. He also had a paralytic stroke at one time, and was terribly burned on another occasion by the explosion of a lamp. His life was despaired of as the result of this accident, but he finally recovered. The burns caused by the explosion were so painful, and his recovery so slow, it was necessary for him to take morphine for quite a time, and he acquired the habit. At another time in his life his health was such that he resorted to the use of morphine and acquired the habit. According to his testimony, he was able on both occasions by great effort to break himself of the drug. There is no other proof in the record except his own as to this. 19

The case was tried at length and submitted to the jury. After some deliberation the jury returned to the courtroom and reported in substance that they found that the defendant below was insane on the subject of the relations between his late wife and Noe, but they further found that he knew the difference between right and wrong, and they asked the court what, under such circumstances, they should do. 20

In response, the court read to the jury a part of his charge previously given them and added some further instructions. The court rejected the contention that if, by reason of mental disease, the will power of the defendant below was so impaired, he was unable to resist the impulse to kill Noe, he would not be guilty, although he could distinguish between right and wrong as to the particular act. ₂₁

[1] The charge of the court was to the effect that, although plaintiff in error acted under an irresistible impulse produced by an insane delusion he would still be guilty if he could distinguish between right and wrong, and knew that it was wrong to kill Noe. ₂₂

Counsel contend that there may be a mental disease destroying the faculty of volition, of choosing, as well as a mental disease destroying the faculty of perception, and that either condition would relieve defendant of criminal accountability. ₂₃

The court refused to recognize as a defense destroyed volition, even as a result of mental disease, apart from destroyed perception. ₂₄

■ Sexual Escapades and Murder ■

[Crim. No. 15501. Fourth Dist.,
Div. One. May 21, 1984.]
THE PEOPLE, Plaintiff and Respondent,
v.
CLYDE RICHARD SPURLIN,
Defendant and Appellant.

Spurlin married Peggy in 1972. Scott was born in 1973 and their daughter Carrie in 1977. The first years of their marriage were uneventful. They joined a church and were viewed as a religious couple. In 1981, they embarked upon a new lifestyle, initially acting out Peggy's sexual fantasies, then moving on to involvements with others. With Spurlin's permission, Peggy dated other men and had an affair with a coworker. She reported these events to Spurlin and with his permission quit her nine-to-five job as an office worker and became a nude dancer at Dirty Dan's in San Diego. ₁

Her sexual escapades escalated to include lesbian episodes, mate-swapping and possible employment as a call girl. Spurlin contracted a venereal disease from Peggy. His reluctant acquiescence in Peggy's sexual activities began to cool and they agreed she would return to school. ₂

On the night of the murders, November 2, 1982, Spurlin picked up Peggy at Dirty Dan's, they had a couple of drinks there, returned home and had some more. ₃

People v. Spurlin, 156 Cal. App.3d 119 (1984).

The children were fed, bathed and bedded. Spurlin and Peggy felt good and sat around talking. Spurlin told Peggy about three or four call girls he had patronized in earlier years during business trips. Peggy became angry, withdrew and went upstairs to their bedroom, telling Spurlin not to bother her, and responding to his question about the marriage being over: "I don't know . . . all I feel like is I just want to die." Spurlin went to the kitchen, gulped some tequila and went upstairs to the bedroom. Peggy told him to leave her alone. He felt ill, nauseous, and went to the bathroom. Peggy looked in on him and returned to bed. Spurlin next remembered standing by her bed, hammer in hand, striking her with it, Peggy saying, "Don't hurt me, Rich," strangling her and knotting a tie around her neck. Death was caused by strangulation. The hammer was broken. Spurlin went downstairs to the garage, got another hammer, returned to the bedroom where Scott was sleeping and killed him with a hammer blow to the head. He also knotted a tie around Scott's neck. Entertaining thoughts of killing Carrie and himself, he walked around the house, crying, and concluded he could not kill Carrie. Packing up some clothes, he and Carrie drove to Los Angeles. Spurlin sold his car, used the money for tickets under an assumed name to Hawaii where they stayed two days and then returned. Spurlin wrote his employer the bodies of his wife and son were in the family home where they were found by the police on November 5, 1982. Spurlin voluntarily returned to San Diego, confessed to the crimes and related all the details to the jury.

Two Men and a Woman

John W. WHITSETT
v.
STATE of Tennessee.
Supreme Court of Tennessee.

Feb. 8, 1957.
TOMLINSON, Justice.

Plaintiff Whitsett, hereinafter called defendant, concedes his guilt of voluntary manslaughter in shooting Robert McPhearson, but insists that the evidence does not support the jury's verdict of second degree murder. The State's rather able insistence is to the contrary.   1

For about six years preceding the commencement of the events which ended in the death of McPhearson, defendant and his wife appear to have enjoyed a reasonably happy marriage. Then deceased and his wife moved into the community about two years before the homicide and became next door farm neighbors of defendant and wife. Their residences were apparently almost within calling distance.   2

Whitsett v. State, 299 S.W.2d (1951).

In about May of 1954 defendant's wife procured employment at a clothing factory of some character located in Fayetteville. The McPhearsons were employed there. The three traveled to and from their place of employment in the McPhearson automobile. McPhearson's duties took him numerous times a day to that machine to which the wife of defendant had been assigned work. There developed between them an intimacy which culminated in their first act of sexual intercourse at defendant's home sometime in July of 1954. These acts continued with frequency in defendant's home generally, and at infrequent intervals in Fayetteville. Such relations continued until shortly preceding January of 1955 when the wife surreptitiously absented her husband's home until the homicide in August, keeping her whereabouts a secret.

As is to be inferred from that which has been stated, defendant was frequently away from home for several hours, and sometimes all night when engaged in fox hunting, or the like. Generally, in making these trips he passed the home, and in view, of deceased. The probable duration of his absence was generally known by defendant's wife and deceased.

Not long after the commencement of this affair, defendant arrived home sooner one day than expected, and found deceased there. He apparently thought nothing of this, other than to advise his wife that it was imprudent from the standpoint of causing gossip. Not long thereafter, however, by reason of the deceased's presence in his home being again discovered, he became suspicious, and to the point of so informing his wife. This caused them to quarrel, and she slipped away that early November night. Defendant found her at her brother's home in Birmingham within a week, and brought her home.

The illicit intimacies were renewed. When the defendant again unexpectedly arrived home one day and saw the deceased at defendant's barn with his clothing in a rather disarranged condition he directly accused his wife, who was at the house, of having improper relations with this man. He slapped her, and said that he intended to take her to the home of deceased and there tell deceased and the latter's wife what he suspected. Mrs. Whitsett again slipped away during the night, and was gone only a few days when found and brought home by defendant.

Throughout this period, this wife seemed able, by her staunch denials of wrongdoing and her explanations of matters which had aroused her husband's suspicion, to leave her husband in doubt as to her infidelity. He did, however, tell the deceased to stay away from his home on pain of being killed. All relations between the two men were terminated from that time.

When this wife was brought home in December she likewise instructed deceased to stay away from her home; that their relations were permanently ended. Nevertheless, he went there one night in January following when he knew defendant to be away. Mrs. Whitsett refused to admit him, and warned him never to come there again. He said he would not. Nevertheless, she slipped away that night because she feared deceased would persist in returning with his presence sooner or later being discovered and followed by most dire consequences. When she learned of the homicide, in order to help her husband extricate himself, in so far as she could, from his trouble, she returned from Nashville where she had been living.

Defendant, during this interim, thought his wife to be in Detroit. He decided   9
to leave his home, go there in search of her, then procure employment at some
other distant place which he had in mind with the hope that he and his wife might
commence their married lives anew. To this end he had commenced negotiations
as to the operation of his farm with a young man named Mills, who for more than
two years had lived nearby. It was contemplated that Mills would occupy defendant's residence.

About two hours, apparently, prior to the homicide defendant had sent his   10
twelve year old nephew, who had lived with him after his wife's third departure,
to bring Mills to his home for further discussion of their contemplated trade. In
the course of such discussion, it was suggested that Mills use defendant's household furniture. Thereupon, Mills inquired as to what would happen if defendant's
wife should demand this furniture.

In the course of this conversation Mills informed defendant that with great   11
frequency when defendant left home for any appreciable period of time since July
of 1954, the deceased went to that home and remained for sometime; that this
occurred both at night and during the day. Mills caused the defendant to recollect
a night when the two had gone fox hunting, and for some reason had returned
much earlier than expected. Whereupon Mills went to defendant's barn to get his
mule, which he had ridden there. Mills then informed defendant that when the
mule shied on the way to the road from the barn Mills looked around and saw the
deceased crouched behind some bushes in defendant's garden behind the residence. He decided against telling defendant about it the next morning, though he
initially contemplated such a course of action. The truth of the incident is verified
by the wife who said that the deceased later told her that he did not believe Mills
had seen him.

According to Mills, when he related these matters to defendant that August   12
1955 morning, the latter exhibited great emotion, but regained his composure
before leaving for Fayetteville—a trip previously planned.

Defendant appears to have had a fancy for shotguns, and other firearms. He   13
hunted frequently. Apparently this had given him a reputation for familiarity with
the quality of various makes of shotguns. With that in mind, or for some other
reason, a friend by the name of Brindley requested him to buy Brindley a .16
gauge shotgun. This was done a few days before the homicide. Though defendant
had two shotguns, rifle, etc., he did not have a .16 gauge shotgun. He was curious
about what it would do as a firearm. So he borrowed it from Brindley, and procured a few shells for it.

On the evening before the homicide, Brindley phoned defendant's home and   14
requested defendant's nephew, who answered the phone, to tell his uncle to bring
the gun home the next morning; that he, Brindley, wanted to go hunting. Brindley
says that he repeated the request by phone the next morning.

As a result of Brindley's request, and because Whitsett was going to Fayet-   15
teville that morning, he placed this gun, unloaded, on, and at the back of, the
single seated pickup truck which he used for transportation. He placed the few
shells which fitted this gun in the glove compartment of the vehicle.

Shortly after defendant had commenced this previously planned journey to 16
Fayetteville accompanied by his little nephew, he overtook a neighbor, Mrs.
Porter, who was walking. She was offered, and accepted, a ride. As the three continued the journey to Fayetteville some eight miles away with defendant driving
and this nephew sitting between them, defendant and this lady engaged in casual
conversation about those every day matters, which neighbors usually talk about
in such a character of conversation.

On the highway on which defendant was driving, and at the outskirts of Fayet- 17
teville, was located a place of business known as Silers' Store. It was Mrs. Porter's
intention to stop there. She so advised defendant. At this store there is a secondary road leading from the highway on which the defendant was driving. A
short distance up this secondary road is a little settlement known as Mill Village.

When defendant's truck approached the intersection of these two roads there 18
appeared at this intersection and turning into this secondary road an automobile
being driven by the deceased with his wife seated beside him. The record is void
of any intimation that defendant anticipated a meeting with McPhearson.

But when defendant recognized deceased he turned his truck up that sec- 19
ondary road and began to pursue the McPhearson car and, in order to overtake it,
drove with an abandon indifferent of consequences and so reckless as to almost
run his truck off the road on more than one occasion, and perhaps prevented
therefrom only by the nephew's tugging at the steering wheel as the truck veered
now and then from the curvy road. And, as he so drove, the defendant in some
way got the shotgun from the seat behind him, loaded it, and began to fire wildly
at McPhearson in the car ahead, indifferent of the fact that McPhearson's wife
was in the direct line of fire. Probably three futile shots were thus fired along this
wild drive before the McPhearson car came to a halt as it was about to be over-
taken in front of the home of McPhearson's daughter.

Both men got out of their respective cars about the same time. Defendant 20
again fired at, but missed, McPhearson who approached him. But this followed by
a second shot with fatal effect. When deceased fell defendant approached and
beat him over the head with the steel barrel of his shotgun, using so much force
as to bend that barrel. Perhaps it should be noted here that defendant had never
been on that road before, and was unaware that McPhearson's daughter lived in
this settlement.

Defendant, without further delay, turned his truck around, drove to the 21
home of Brindley to whom he was returning the shotgun, told Brindley what
had occurred, and came back to Fayetteville with Brindley, to the office of a
lawyer.

The testimony of these men and other unimpeachable testimony is to the 22
effect that defendant was very highly excited and distraught. Perhaps this is
not of much importance, considering what the man had just gone through,
except in so far as it corroborates defendant's statement that he remembers
very little about the actual pursuit and killing of McPhearson. It is well to add
here that this record leaves the impression that the defendant was a man of
good repute.

The Desperate Law Student

STATE of Tennessee, Appellee,

v.

James Clark THORNTON, III, Appellant.

Supreme Court of Tennessee, at Jackson.
May 4, 1987.

As previously stated, there is almost no dispute as to the material facts in this   1
case. Appellant, James Clark Thornton, III, was thirty-one years of age at the
time of the trial of this case in June 1984. His wife, Lavinia, was twenty-seven
years of age; they had been married on May 19, 1979, and at the time of the homicide had one child, a son about three years of age. Appellant was a second-year
law student at Memphis State University, having previously received his undergraduate degree from the University of Tennessee at Chattanooga. His wife had
not completed her undergraduate work when the parties married, but at the time
of the homicide she was taking some additional class work toward her undergraduate degree. The victim, Mark McConkey, was twenty-five years of age,
single, and a third-year student at the University of Tennessee Medical School in
Memphis.

As stated, appellant had never met McConkey and did not even know his   2
name. Mrs. Thornton had met him four days before the homicide and had engaged
in sexual relations with him in the home belonging to her and appellant every
night since that time, including the night of the homicide. She testified that she
thought that when she told her husband that she might want to "date" someone
else, that this, in modern society, indicated that she intended to have sexual relations. In that manner she sought to mitigate her infidelity and misconduct toward
a husband who had never been unfaithful to her insofar as disclosed by the
record.

The marriage of the parties was in some difficulty, apparently as a result of   3
dissatisfaction of Mrs. Thornton. She had advised her husband in March 1983 that
she wanted to be separated from him for a time, and he had voluntarily taken an
apartment about two miles away from their home. He visited the home almost
daily, however, and there has been no suggestion that he was ever guilty of violence, physical misconduct or mistreatment toward his wife or son. He was particularly devoted to the child, and frequently kept the child with him at his
apartment on weekends or in the evenings.

Appellant had graduated from a public high school in Chattanooga, after   4
having taken his first three years of high school at a private institution, Baylor.
During his junior year at Baylor it was discovered that he had developed a severe

---

State v. Thornton, 730 S.W.2d 309 (1987).

case of scoliosis, or curvature of the spine, and he had undergone surgery to correct that condition. He was disabled to the point that he received a vocational rehabilitation grant which enabled him to attend undergraduate school at the University of Tennessee at Chattanooga. He was slightly built, being only five feet six inches in height and weighing about 125 to 130 pounds. McConkey was an athlete, a former basket-ball and football player in high school. He was five feet nine inches in height and weighed about 183 pounds.

Mrs. Thornton testified that she told McConkey when she first met him that   5
she was married but separated from her husband. She had consulted an attorney and had signed a divorce petition, but the same apparently had not been filed on the date of the homicide.

Appellant, according to uncontradicted testimony, was deeply disturbed over   6
the separation of the parties. He had sought assistance from a marriage counselor, and had persuaded his wife to go with him to the marriage counselor on several occasions. They had a joint meeting scheduled with the counselor on May 4, the day after the homicide. Appellant testified that the parties had agreed to a separation of six months, and both he and the marriage counselor testified that the parties had agreed that they would not have sexual relations with each other or with anyone else during that period. Mrs. Thornton denied making that agreement, but she did admit meeting with the marriage counselor on several occasions.

Mrs. Thornton was from a very wealthy family and had a generous trust fund   7
which enabled the parties to live on a much more elaborate scale than most graduate students. Appellant, however, had also inherited some property through his family. This had been sold at a profit, and all of his assets had been invested in the home which the parties had purchased in Memphis, together with substantial additions from Mrs. Thornton. It was suggested by the State throughout the trial that appellant was insincere in his concern for the marriage, and that his principal concern was for his financial security.

The record indicates that as early as May 1, two days before the homicide,   8
Mrs. Thornton had stated to her husband that she did not think that the parties would ever be reconciled. On the evening of May 3, appellant picked her and their child up at their home, and the three went to dinner. Again on that occasion Mrs. Thornton reiterated that she thought that the marriage was over, and on this occasion she told appellant that she planned to date someone else whom she had met. Appellant was concerned over the situation, but on a previous occasion his wife had told him that she had had sexual relations with another student, and this had proved to be false.

He returned his wife and child to their home at about 7:30 p.m. and then went   9
to his apartment to study for a final examination in the law school. He called two close friends of the parties, however, and discussed his marital situation with them. Both of them verified that he was very concerned about the situation, but both told him that they believed that his wife was serious about going through with a divorce. One of them advised him that his wife apparently did not believe his feelings about a reconciliation were sincere.

Acting on that suggestion, appellant returned to the home of the parties in his   10
automobile, stating that he wanted to try once more to convince his wife that he
was indeed sincere. When he arrived at the home he saw an automobile parked in
the driveway. He did not recognize the car as being one belonging to any of his
wife's friends. Accordingly he parked around the corner and walked back to the
house. Observing from the rear of the house, he saw his wife and McConkey in
the kitchen with the child. He observed as Mrs. Thornton washed some laundry
for McConkey and as they were eating dinner. Thereafter they sat and read. They
drank wine and smoked some marijuana, and appellant saw them kissing.

He decided to go home to get his camera, but before doing so he let the air out   11
of one of the tires on McConkey's car. He went to his apartment, and obtained his
camera and an old pistol which had belonged to his father. He visited a convenience store in an attempt to find film for the camera, and finally obtained some
at a drugstore. He then returned to the marital residence, arriving at about 9:30
p.m. He testified that he intended to take pictures for the purpose of showing
them to the marriage counselor on the next day and possibly also for use in evidence if divorce proceedings did ensue.

Appellant spent more than an hour in the backyard of his home observing his   12
wife and McConkey in the den and kitchen. Thereafter they left the den area, but
appellant remained behind the house, thinking that McConkey was about to
leave. When he went around the house, however, he found that McConkey's car
was still in the driveway and saw the drapes in the front guest bedroom downstairs had been closed. He listened near the window and heard unmistakable
sounds of sexual intercourse. He then burst through the front door and into the
bedroom where he found the nude couple and attempted to take some pictures.
At that point he testified that he thought McConkey was attempting to attack him.
In all events he drew his pistol and fired a single shot, striking McConkey in the
left hip. Appellant did not harm either his wife or child, although Mrs. Thornton
said that he did make some threats against her. He went upstairs and brought
down the little boy, who had been awakened and who was crying. He assisted in
giving directions to enable an ambulance to bring aid to McConkey, and he
remained at the house until the police arrived.

Appellant testified that he simply lost control and "exploded" when he found   13
his wife in bed with the victim. He testified that he had armed himself because
McConkey was much larger than he, and he felt that he needed protection if there
was trouble when he returned to the residence with the camera.

Appellant testified that he did not intend to kill McConkey, but simply to shoot   14
him in order to disable him and also because of his outrage at the situation which
he had found. The single shot was not aimed at a vital organ, but the victim ultimately died because of the spread of a massive infection from the wound.

The marriage counselor who had been seeing appellant and his wife examined   15
appellant on a number of occasions after the shooting. When McConkey died
sixteen days later, appellant attempted to take his own life. The psychologist, Dr.
Hunsacker, testified that appellant was under severe emotional pressure at the
time of shooting to the point that he believed appellant had a brief period of tem-

porary insanity and was not legally responsible for his actions. An expert on behalf of the State testified to the contrary with respect to the issue of temporary insanity, but she testified that appellant was undoubtedly under severe emotional stress on the evening in question both before and at the time of the shooting.

Appellant attempted to interpose alternative defenses of self-defense and insanity. The jury rejected both of these defenses. . . 16

• • • •

For Deliberation and Argument

1. If you were a member of the jury, would you find Dr. J. L. Davis, the defendant in *Davis v. State*, guilty of first-degree murder, second-degree murder, or voluntary manslaughter in the killing of R. L. Noe? Draw on the jury instructions for these categories of homicide, as well as on the facts of the case in arriving at and explaining your verdict. Consider also an alternate verdict of not guilty by reason of insanity. Might the defendant's mental state at the time of the killing be such as to render him incapable of distinguishing right from wrong (the legal standard for insanity)? (Such a verdict would result in his commitment to a mental institution.) Might he have been acting under the influence of an irresistible impulse produced by an insane delusion? At the trial, Davis's counsel contended that "there may be a mental disease destroying the faculty of volition, of choosing, as well as a mental disease destroying the faculty of perception, and that either condition would relieve defendant of criminal accountability." To what extent would you be inclined to agree with this reasoning?

2. In *People v. Spurlin*, consider each of the two homicides—those of the defendant's wife, Peggy, and his son, Scott—separately. As a jury member, render a verdict on each killing: first-degree murder, second-degree murder, or voluntary manslaughter. Apply the jury instructions on each of these offences to the facts of this case. Explain your reasoning. In formulating your response, consider the following additional rules:

   • The *Model Penal Code*, section 210.3, states, "Criminal homicide constitutes manslaughter when . . . a homicide which would otherwise be murder is committed under the influence of extreme mental or emotional disturbance for which there is reasonable explanation or excuse. The reasonableness of such explanation or excuse shall be determined from the viewpoint of the person in the actor's situation under the circumstances as he believes them to be." This is a statement of the *diminished capacity* defense. According to the appeals court hearing *Spurlin*, this defense may be raised "if the killing occurs while the defendant's capacity to form an intent to murder is diminished by an extreme mental or emotional *disturbance* deemed to have a reasonable explanation or excuse from the defendant's standpoint."

   • In June 1982 (almost two years before this case was heard by the appeals court), the electorate of California voted into law a ballot measure, Proposition 8, which was subsequently added to the California Penal Code. Proposition 8 provides that "the defense of diminished capacity is hereby abolished. In a criminal action, as well as any juvenile court proceeding, evidence concerning an accused person's intoxication, trauma, mental illness, disease, or defect shall not be admissible to show or negate capacity to form the particular purpose, intent, motive, malice afore- thought, knowledge, or other mental state required for the commission of the crime charged." The effect of this measure is that the defense of dimin- ished capacity "is no longer available to 'negate' malice aforethought and, thus, reduce murder to manslaughter."

3. John W. Whitsett, the defendant in *Whitsett v. State of Tennessee*, was con- victed of second-degree murder for the killing of Mr. McPhearson. In his appeal, Whitsett argued that he was guilty of nothing more than voluntary manslaughter, as he was acting under the influence of intense passion— having heard Mills confirm his wife's infidelities less than two hours before the homicide. Writing either as defense attorney or prosecuting attorney, argue for or against the appeals court changing the verdict to voluntary manslaughter. Take into account the statutory differences between murder and manslaughter, as they apply to the facts of this case. Also take into account the following points:

- The defendant testified at trial that when he unexpectedly saw Mc- Phearson just before he killed him, "all of this stuff the boy had told me that morning came back to me and him riding around with his wife and both of them looked very happy and my home tore all to pieces, I don't know what happened, I lost control of myself."
- The prosecution rebutted the defendant's contention that he had lost control by "the fact that the defendant engaged in casual conversation with Mrs. Porter on his way to Fayetteville after being given this additional information by Mills."

4. James Clark Thornton, the defendant in *State v. Thornton*, was convicted of first-degree murder for the death of Mr. McConkey In his appeal, he argued that he was guilty of manslaughter, rather than murder, as he was acting the under the influence of the *heat of passion*—rather than *malice* and *premedi- tation*—as a result of having come upon his wife and her lover having sexual relations. The appellate court judges were divided on whether Thornton should be convicted of manslaughter or second-degree murder. One judge, arguing for manslaughter, quoted another court opinion, as follows:

> It is not necessary to reduce killing to manslaughter that the passion should be so great as to render the defendant incapable of deliberation or premeditation. If the circumstances be such as are calculated to produce such excitement and passion as would obscure the reason of an ordinary man and induce him, under such excitement and passion, to

strike the blow that causes the death of the deceased, this will reduce the killing to manslaughter.

Another judge was convinced that the defendant did show the malice that characterizes murder, rather than manslaughter, and to support this view, offered his own take on the defendant's actions:

In this case, the facts demonstrate that the events on the evening of May 3, 1983, took place over about a four hour period between approximately 7:30 and 11:30 p.m. Without reciting the evidence extensively, I summarize the evidence here to emphasize the sequence and timing of the events and Defendant's state of mind during this period. After returning to the marital home following dinner with his estranged wife and son, Defendant went to his apartment several miles away, arriving there sometime close to 7:30 p.m. He was tense, distraught, and depressed and decided to make telephone calls to mutual friends of his and his wife to discuss his problems. These telephone conversations continued until about 8:30 p.m. In his desperation, Defendant returned to the marital home to talk to his wife again and upon arriving discovered an unfamiliar car parked in the driveway. Aware that his wife might be dating someone, Defendant parked some distance away and stealthily made his way to the rear of the house to see who was visiting his wife. Defendant's wife testified that the victim, Mark A. McConkey, had arrived at the house close to 8:30 p.m., her date with him having been prearranged earlier that same day. Defendant saw his son playing in the den while his wife and the victim, whom he did not recognize, were kissing and embracing. He described his emotional state as one of shock and a sickening fear. He was upset at seeing his wife being embraced by another man in front of his child. Not unreasoning, however, in view of a pending divorce, Defendant determined to return to his apartment to get his camera to take photographs of his wife's adulterous rendezvous. Before departing, Defendant deflated the left rear tire of the victim's car.

At about 9:00 p.m., according to the wife's testimony, their son was put to bed in the master bedroom on the second floor of the house. She testified that for about two hours after putting her son to bed, she and Mr. McConkey ate, read, and did laundry in the kitchen and den area on the first floor of the house. Evidently, Defendant left before his son was put to bed. At his apartment, Defendant changed clothes, obtained his camera, which had flash and telescopic lens attachments, and his loaded .45 caliber service automatic pistol. Having no film for the camera, Defendant was required to stop at two places before finding film, purchasing some at a Walgreen's Drugstore at about 9:30 p.m. He loaded the camera and drove back to his wife's neighborhood, parked around the corner from the house, and again walked to the marital home. The first photograph he took was of the license plate on the rear of the victim's car. Defendant then went behind the house to look into the windows of the kitchen and den. His wife and Mr. McConkey were in the den reading. Defendant watched this scene for some time, feeling despondent. Eventually, he saw his wife go to Mr. McConkey and lie down on top of him on the couch; they became affectionate, kissing and talking. At this point he started taking a series of twelve to fifteen photographs. Anger started welling up in him, yet he did nothing more than take photographs. They got up to complete Mr. McConkey's laundry. After folding the laundry, Defendant's wife and Mr. McConkey turned off the lights in the kitchen and den and carried the laundry to the front of the house. Believing or hoping that the victim would then be leaving, Defendant waited at the rear of the house for a short time and then walked around to the front; he saw Mr. McConkey's car still parked in the driveway. Noticing that the curtains to the guest bedroom were drawn, Defendant feared that his wife and the victim had retired to this bedroom. He drew closer to the window to listen and heard the sounds of two persons engaged in sexual relations. Defendant testified that his head started to swim and that he felt sickened.

Suddenly, at approximately 11:15 p.m., Defendant, a small man, kicked through the locked front doors of the house and went directly to the guest room. The room was dark but the door was open. His camera ready to take photographs, Defendant switched the lights on; the first thing he saw was his nude wife. Mr. McConkey, nude but covered with a sheet, was on the side of the bed nearest to the door. Defendant's first reaction was to attempt to take photographs but he could not focus the camera. He then reached down and jerked the sheet off of Mr. McConkey. Again he attempted to take a photograph but without success. While trying to work the camera, thinking that he saw the victim's hands reaching towards him in his peripheral vision, Defendant drew the loaded pistol from his coat pocket. Defendant testified that at this moment he lost control and began screaming, the pistol in his hand, saying to Mr. McConkey: "I ought to teach you screwing around with somebody else's wife. I ought to shoot you in the ass." He further testified that he intentionally pointed the muzzle of the pistol at the victim's lower body. He didn't remember cocking the single action pistol but the pistol discharged, the bullet striking Mr. McConkey in the left rear hip, passing completely through the abdomen to lodge in a wall. Defendant also testified that when he pulled the pistol, Mr. McConkey had retreated and turned away from him, exposing his left rear side to him. After being shot, the victim pulled himself off of the bed and tried to push the bed between himself and Defendant, who again was trying to take a photograph. When he realized that Mr. McConkey was injured, Defendant regained sufficient control of himself to disarm the weapon. He subsequently gave instructions on the telephone to assist an ambulance in locating the address. At about 11:41 p.m., the first police officers arrived on the scene. Asked what had happened, Defendant stated: "He was in bed with my wife and I shot him. I don't know what came over me." Defendant was then arrested.

Write an argument, from the point of view of the defense or the prosecution, supporting a verdict of either manslaughter or second-degree murder, applying the rules on these two types of homicide to the facts of the case.
5. Select one of these four cases. Imagine yourself as attorney for the plaintiff or attorney for the defendant. Write a paper in IRAC format to make your case. Define the *issue* in question format. State or summarize the applicable *rules* about homicide. *Apply/Analyze* the rules, as explained in "Jury Instructions on Murder and Manslaughter," to the facts of the case you have selected. Draw a *conclusion* from the application of these rules.

■ Group 4 Readings: *Battered-Woman Syndrome*

The next group of readings focuses on the battered-woman syndrome (also called the battered-wife syndrome). The term is used to describe the psychological state that often characterizes the relationship between a woman and her physically abusive husband or partner. It is also refers to a type of legal defense to homicide, invoked by a woman, who, fearful for her life or safety, kills her abuser.

The use of deadly force in self-defense has long been recognized as justifiable homicide. But the law, understandably enough, has laid down strict requirements for such deadly force. In the words of the "Judge's Instructions to the Jury" in this group of readings, "Homicide is justifiable and not unlawful when committed by any person in the defense of him/herself if he/she actually and reasonably believed that the individual killed intended to commit a forcible and atrocious crime and that there was imminent danger of that crime being accomplished." A key term is imminent danger. *A person may not kill another and claim self-defense if she or he merely believes that there is at some indeterminate point in the future a danger of death or serious bodily harm.*

In many battered-woman situations, however, the danger does not appear to be imminent. A woman may decide to kill the batterer before he has a chance to strike again. Faith McNulty's 1984 book The Burning Bed, *adapted into a TV movie, dramatized the true case of Francine Hughes, who killed her abusive husband by setting fire to his bed as he slept. Tried for murder, she was acquitted. In many other cases, however, women who have killed battering husbands or lovers have been convicted of manslaughter or murder. As one legal commentator has pointed out, "On the issue of imminence, it must be shown why the defendant perceived danger in a situation in which a person other than a battered woman would not have perceived danger" (Jimmie E. Tinsley, 34 POF 2d at 17). Until recent years, courts in most states have refused to recognize battered-woman syndrome as a special type of self-defense and have barred the introduction by the defense of expert testimony from psychologists and others on battered-woman syndrome. As one Ohio court ruled in 1994:*

> *the only admissible evidence pertaining to [self-defense] is evidence which establishes that defendant had a bona-fide belief that she was in imminent*

danger of death or great bodily harm, and that the only means of escape from such danger was through the use of deadly force. . . . The jury is well able to understand and determine whether self-defense has been proven in a murder case without expert testimony such as [the battered-woman syndrome] offered here.

To counter such judicial reluctance, some states have passed laws specifically recognizing battered-woman syndrome as "a matter of commonly accepted scientific knowledge" and authorizing "expert testimony that the person suffered from that syndrome as evidence to establish the requisite belief of an imminent danger of death or great bodily harm that is necessary . . . to justify the person's use of the force in question." Many of the appeals of battered women convicted of murder or manslaughter have been based on the refusal of the trial court judge to accept expert testimony on the battered-woman syndrome.

In the first case in this group, People v. Reeves, a defendant shoots her husband as he is beating her on the street. The second selection is from the article "Defending the Battered Wife," by B. Carter Thompson, a criminal defense attorney practicing in Dallas. State v. Daws, the next case, detailing a "stormy marriage," illustrates some of the elements of battered-woman syndrome discussed by Thompson. Next, a landmark case, Ibn-Tamas v. United States, deals with a woman who shoots her physician husband after enduring years of battering. In Lentz v. State, a battered woman contemplates suicide, then kills her husband instead. Finally, in State v. Smith, a woman sets out to kill her husband, with the aid of confederates. Tried for attempted murder, she invokes the battered-woman syndrome defense.

"I Didn't Think I Would Do It"

47 Ill.App.3d 406
5 Ill.Dec. 696
The PEOPLE of the State of Illinois,
Plaintiff-Appellee,
v.
Barbara J. REEVES, Defendant-Appellant.

No. 76–88.

Appellate Court of Illinois, Fifth District.
April 4, 1977.

Around 11 p.m. on August 20, 1974, defendant's sister, Patricia Reeves, and the defendant went to a tavern in Benton, Illinois known as Jolly Jack's. Charles Reeves, the deceased, came into the bar between 11:30 p.m. and 12 midnight. He

1

People v. Reeves, 362 N.E.2d 9 (1977).

argued with Barbara for several minutes and then left. No one could overhear what they were saying. After Charles left, the defendant, who was visibly upset, stated in a loud voice several times that she was going to kill that son-of-a-bitch Charlie Reeves. The bar owner testified that she also said something to the effect that you will remember me in the morning, I am the one that shot Charlie Reeves; this particular recollection was not corroborated by any other witness present in the bar that evening. The owner further testified that defendant was upset and crying during the whole time she was in the bar. Patricia called defendant's sister-in-law, Deborah Reeves, and asked her to pick them up. Deborah, accompanied by her friend, Michael Standley, drove her pickup truck from her home in Sesser, Illinois to Jolly Jack's.

After Barbara and Patricia joined Deborah and Michael, the group proceeded, at defendant's request, to defendant's rural home near Whittington, Illinois. They arrived there at approximately 1 a.m., now August 21st. Defendant entered the house while the others remained outside. Crashing noises came from the house for a period of five to ten minutes. When Deborah and Michael subsequently entered the house, they found the kitchen area in total disarray.   2

Defendant brought a shotgun from the house which she wanted to take with her to town. She may also have had a .22 caliber pistol in her hand. Deborah, after lengthy discussion, convinced defendant that taking the ammunition would be a better idea. Michael Standley was handed the shotgun by defendant or one of the other women and he unloaded it. He was forced to discharge the shotgun once since there was a shell jammed in the chamber. The shotgun was returned to its customary place in the house and a box of shells for it and a box containing as many shells for the .22 caliber pistol as could be found scattered in the house were concealed under the seat of Deborah's truck.   3

Deborah testified that the defendant wanted to take the guns or ammunition so the deceased could not use them on defendant. He had taken the guns in the past and had threatened defendant with them. Deborah had hidden the guns before during family crises when Charles was in a rage. Charles Reeves had also beaten defendant many times in the past, and on several occasions the beatings were so severe that hospitalization had been required.   4

Deborah further testified that at this time defendant was scared to death and hysterical. Defendant told Deborah that she just couldn't stand any more beatings, and Deborah tried to calm her. Michael Standley testified that, at sometime prior to his unloading the shotgun, while it was in the possession of the defendant, he heard her say she was going to wait there until he came home and kill him. No one else remembered her making this statement. Sometime later, after all of this transpired, it was decided that they would go to the Kewpee Cafe in Benton, Illinois to eat breakfast. The .22 revolver was last seen lying either on the kitchen table or the freezer in the Whittington house.   5

Defendant, Patricia, Deborah and Michael arrived at the Kewpee Cafe around 3 a.m. They all ordered breakfast, including the defendant. She did not eat all of her breakfast and appeared depressed. They started to leave the cafe around 3:40 a.m. Michael went to the register to pay for the food. The three women started   6 exiting. Patricia went first; Deborah and defendant followed her, respectively, into the entranceway. Charles Reeves came up quickly and pushed by Patricia and swung on Deborah. She managed to avoid his blow. Charles grabbed defendant around the neck and head with his left arm, in a chokehold or headlock, and drug her bodily out of the cafe and down the sidewalk in a southerly direction. He was hitting her continuously about the top of her head with his free hand as he drug her toward his car. Defendant was screaming for help but none was forthcoming.

Defendant testified that she was afraid since she knew what he was going to do and that as he drug her along he said, "Wait until I get you out in the country." She was being choked by his hold on her in addition to being struck upon the head. The distance which the deceased drug defendant was variously estimated by witnesses as being as short a distance as 20 feet to as long a distance as 75 feet. A shot was fired during the struggle as they neared the deceased's car and Charles Reeves collapsed onto the street. When patrons from the cafe reached the scene, defendant was crying and holding the .22 caliber gun seen earlier at the Whittington house. She was hysterical. The police arrived almost immediately. 7

The record shows that when the police asked for the gun the defendant took the gun from the waistband of her slacks and handed it to Officer Kellam of the Benton police. Many different exclamations were ascribed to the defendant during the period after the shot was fired but prior to the arrival of the police. Defense witness, Deborah Reeves, testified defendant said, "Oh, tell me he is not dead, I didn't mean to do it." State's witness, Michael Standley, testified she said, "Tell me he is not dead, tell me he is all right." State's witness John Miller testified as follows: "Barbara said, 'I didn't think I would do it,' she said, 'I have killed him.' First she said, 'you didn't think I would do it, did you?' or something of that nature." State's witness, Dennis Odle, testified she said, "Oh, my God, what have I done, did I really do it?" Charles Reeves died shortly thereafter as a result of a wound caused by a single .22 caliber bullet which had entered his body under his left arm and had punctured his left lung and pierced his heart. 8

Defendant, Barbara Reeves, raised the affirmative defense of self-defense or use of force in defense of person to justify the killing of Charles Reeves. The trial court, sitting as trier of fact, concluded that the evidence did not establish the justification of self-defense and found her guilty of murder. . . . 9

[According to the Illinois Criminal Code,] "A person is justified in the use of force against another when and to the extent that he reasonably believes that such conduct is necessary to defend himself or another against such other's imminent use of unlawful force. *However, he is justified in the use of force which is intended or likely to cause death or great bodily harm only if he reasonably believes that such force is necessary to prevent imminent death or great bodily harm to himself or another, or the commission of a forcible felony.*" (Emphasis added.) 10

"These elements are: (1) that force is threatened against the person; (2) that the person threatened is not the aggressor; (3) that the danger of harm is immi- 11 nent; (4) that the force threatened is unlawful; (5) that the person threatened must actually believe: (a) that the danger exists, (b) that the use of force is necessary to avert the danger, (c) that the kind and amount of force which he uses is necessary; and (6) that the above beliefs are reasonable. There is a further principle involved, when, as in the instant case, the defendant uses a deadly force. This principle limits the use of deadly force to those situations in which (a) the threatened force will cause death or great bodily harm or (b) the force threatened is a forcible felony."

The State emphasized at trial: (1) that no witness saw any bruises on defendant's face; (2) that no weapon was either seen in the deceased's hand when he drug defendant out of the cafe or anywhere near his body after he was shot; and (3) that defendant made statements prior to the shooting and immediately after it which establish an intent to murder rather than to defend herself.   12

Defending the Battered Wife: A Challenge for Defense Attorneys

B. Carter Thompson

In recent years, perhaps no new area of criminal defense has received more publicity or aroused more interest than the defense of the battered wife. With the 1984 broadcast of the NBC-TV movie *The Burning Bed,* which was adapted from the book of the same name by Faith McNulty, the public got a look at family violence in this country.   1

While the plight of the battered wife is finally getting the attention it deserves, both from the public and the social agencies equipped to deal with the problem, precious little has been said, even in legal circles, about the task of the attorney charged with defending her. In most cases, the attorney must educate himself, as well as the client, about the complexities of the case and the novel ways of mounting a defense.   2

The most common situation involves the client charged with murder in the death of her husband. While the violent relationship can take on other legal aspects, as in divorce, child custody, and even personal injury issues, it is the death of the batterer that will most often involve the criminal defense attorney.   3

I use the words "husband" and "wife" loosely, since the client and the deceased need not have been married to each other for the attorney to have a "battered wife" case on his hands. In this article, the terms will apply to unmarried live-in couples as well as married couples. . . .   4

"Defending the Battered Wife." *Trial* (Feb. 1986): 74–78.

The Battered-Wife Syndrome

Once the client has been in touch with the counselor, the attorney should become 5
familar with what is known as the battered-wife syndrome. It is this syndrome, and the way it explains the otherwise irrational behavior of the client, that distinguishes this case from any other. Unless the attorney introduces this syndrome in the case, it will turn solely on whatever self-defense or temporary insanity facts are available, and they may not be enough, especially if the evidence does not explain why a woman, repeatedly beaten by an abusive husband, would remain in such a violent relationship. Thus, the attorney must learn the psychology and legal history of the subject before sitting down with the witnesses.

While there are many works on the subject, one of the better ones is *The Bat-* 6
tered Woman by Lenore Walker. It has become something of a standard in the field, and Dr. Walker has testified in a number of murder trials.

Each abuse incident, as detailed by Dr. Walker, is divided into three phases, 7
which she terms the cycle of violence. The first, the tension-building phase, is a time of increasing tension between the woman and the batterer. The husband may make verbal assaults, attack inanimate objects, and engage in minor acts of violence against the woman. She will respond by trying to calm him down. He is angry about something, whether his job, his finances, or the children, and he takes it out on her. She will accept blame for whatever he says she has done to anger him, hoping that the matter will not escalate further. She will usually do anything, even alienate friends and family, to stay on his good side and prevent an acute battering attack.

If she succeeds, the matter will stop there. If she fails, or his anger is too great to 8
be held back, the next phase may develop, the acute battering incident. Here, both parties have lost control of the situation. The batterer lashes out with blind rage at the woman, often causing serious injury to her, in an assault that can last for hours. She, too, has lost any control she had had in being able to manipulate his anger. She can now only endure the abuse and wait for the third phase, the loving-contrite period.

Here, with his rage and energy spent, and the woman showing obvious 9
injuries, the batterer tries to make up with the woman. He swears that if she will just forgive him this time, they can solve whatever problem set him off in the first place. He sincerely wants to change things and will take positive steps to improve the situation, like quitting drinking or avoiding certain people or situations.

These steps rarely last long, and soon the cycle starts again. It is this loving phase 10
that the woman looks forward to since it may, in fact, represent the best part of the relationship. In many situations, when the woman realizes that the acute battering incident is inevitable, she may actually bring it on herself just to get to this last phase. This is the phase that has the most effect on her decision to stay with her husband.

The Decision to Stay

Indeed, why does she stay? This is the one question that the defendant will be 11
asked most often, and the one that will be thrown at the attorney repeatedly during the trial. Surely, goes the common assumption, she must either enjoy the abuse (assuming she is telling the truth), or else it cannot be as bad as she claims.

Either way, she is hardly deserving of sympathy, much less an acquittal for murdering the supposed abuser, who, after all, is not in court to tell his side of the story. So, why did she stay?

While the research goes further in explaining why the wife stays with the   12
husband, her value system can be summed up as follows:

- A strong belief in the institution of marriage,
- A desire not to harm the husband's career,
- A desire to avoid the embarrassment of admitting to physical and sexual abuse,
- A feeling of helplessness and an inability to make decisions,
- A well-justified fear of reprisal if she tries to leave, coupled with a financial inability to do so,
- The presence of children,
- A desire not to admit failure in the case of a second marriage,
- The hope that things will improve in the long run,
- A feeling that she is his property and responsible for the abuse,
- The need to believe the husband when he apologizes and swears the battering will never happen again, and
- Her contentment with the relationship between battering incidents (especially as she remembers his tenderness just following each attack).

Besides, if she were to leave him, she would be presumed to be at fault for   13
breaking up the marriage, not only from the view of her friends and her children, but often in her own mind as well. This all adds up, in her mind, to strong reasons to both stay in the relationship and keep quiet about its darker side. Even if she thinks that someday she will get out of the relationship, the see-saw emotional effects of the cycle keep her hanging on, desperately wanting to believe his assurances that the battering will never happen again.

The Batterer

What about the other side of the equation, the battering husband? An essential   14
part of the attorney's job will be to shed new light on someone who may be well-thought-of and perhaps above suspicion. (Wife abuse cuts across class, race, and income, and exists in affluent suburbs and in ghettos.) Indeed, in two cases, the battering husbands were physicians.

The research shows that the typical batterer has low-self esteem, believes in   15
the traditional stereotypes about the roles of men and women, blames others for his actions, and is jealous. He presents a dual personality, has severe stress reactions, and may use alcohol and wife abuse as a means of coping. He uses sex as a means of aggression and to enhance his self-esteem, and does not think that his violent behavior should have negative consequences.

Interestingly, these men tend to go to extremes in how they handle their emo-   16
tions. When they intend to only "teach her a lesson," they can go overboard and

severely beat the woman, long past the point of her "learning" anything. Similarly, when they become apologetic and remorseful, they might lavish her with gifts far beyond what she needs or can even appreciate. Most appear to be possessive of their wives, demanding a complete accounting of how their time is spent and often accusing them of having an affair. Indeed, so suspicious are they that they may refuse to let their wives work outside the home, maintain social contacts, or even go shopping by themselves.

Attorneys should look for the imaginary affair as a possible rationale for the assault. This may be a case of the batterer not looking for a pretext to beat his wife, but rather having a real concern about a threat to his already low self-esteem. . . . 17

Witnesses: Sources and Stories

[One] matter the attorney must deal with is if, when, and how often the client reached out for help during her ordeal. It is not uncommon, despite her loyalty to the batterer and her need to keep what has been going on secret, for her to have called the police on a few occasions. 18

The scenario normally runs as follows: Client and husband are having a "fight" (albeit one-sided); she manages to get to a phone and call the police. The police arrive at the scene and are met by a bruised, battered woman who no longer wishes to press charges, or who, upon seeing her husband being handcuffed and taken out of the house, will suddenly come to his defense and begin attacking the police. 18

Indeed, the "domestic disturbance" call is one of the most dangerous police calls. And with good reason. The woman who made the call in the first place will realize that the husband, no matter what she says, is not going to be in jail forever and that she is going to have hell to pay once he is out. She has learned that his threats are not to be taken lightly and that any cause for him to be angry must be avoided at all costs. Even if she still does want him locked up, it is in her best interest to at least *appear* to be coming to his defense for the sake of what will happen to her upon his eventual release. 20

Second, the battering itself may be over by the time the police arrive, and the husband may have entered the loving phase of the cycle. Thus, when the police arrive, she perceives them as a threat to the marriage, an outside interference into their "private" matter, and the source of an intolerable public exposé of what she has been trying to keep secret for so long. So, she honestly wants to forget she ever called. If the police press the matter and threaten to make an arrest, she will react with predictable hostility. 21

Attorneys should go through the police logs carefully. Every call she made was a plea for help, regardless of what she said when the police got there. This kind of documentation is too valuable to ignore. The prosecution will detail what she told the arriving officers; it is up to the defense to highlight the importance of the call having been made in the first place. 22

The call to the police is probably not the only way the woman reached out for help. She may have confided in a close friend or family member. In the true bat- 23 tered-wife syndrome case, this will be the exception rather than the rule, due to the client's compulsion for secrecy. Most likely, there will be witnesses to the client's injuries, the black eyes and so forth, but little firsthand knowledge as to what put them there. Nonetheless, it is vital to bring in everyone who knows the client and who may have suspected what was going on.

Attorneys should look for the batterer's drinking as a frequent scape-goat, in the minds of both witness and client. It is convenient to come up with an impersonal cause of violence, like a drinking problem, rather than to ascribe it to a personality disorder. As the counselor will point out, while abuse happens when the batterer has been drinking, the drinking itself is *not* a cause of the violence. If the client remembers back far enough, she will probably recall at least one assault that occurred when he was sober. The drinking is thought to be a catalyst for the abuse, but it is not by itself a cause.

The sooner the client and witnesses realize that, the more likely they will stop protecting and feeling sorry for the abuser. Perhaps the loss of this misplaced sympathy will allow witnesses to remember facts about the batterer and the relationship they might otherwise prefer to leave unmentioned. Attorneys should not underestimate the impact of this concern. To the impartial observer like the recently retained attorney, the abuser may be among the lowest forms of life. To the client's witnesses, however, he is still family, and may otherwise be a pretty decent sort of person.

Susan and Dwayne

104 Ohio App.3d 448
The STATE of Ohio, Appellee,
v.
DAWS, Appellant.

No. 13914.

Court of Appeals of Ohio,
Second District, Montgomery County.
Decided July 27, 1994.

Susan and Dwayne were married in 1982. Susan was already pregnant with Dwayne's child. During her pregnancy, Dwayne, in a drunken state, twisted Susan's arm and threw her into a bedroom. Susan was forced to call the paramedics to get her out.

In 1983, Dwayne joined the army, and the couple moved to Fort Campbell, Kentucky. Dwayne, apparently unhappy with military service, began to drink heavily and became more abusive towards Susan. He attempted to isolate her

---

State v. Daws, 662 N.E.2d 805 (1994).

from her family by removing the phone so that she was forced to go to a laundromat to call them. Dwayne told Susan that "things would get better" if she got pregnant again, so she did. However, during her second pregnancy, Dwayne threw Susan against a bedpost while he was drunk. As a result of this incident, Susan spotted blood for two days, but Dwayne refused to let her go to the doctor to make sure the baby was not hurt.

After Susan gave birth to this child in 1985, Dwayne decided to leave the army, and the family returned to Springboro, Ohio. Susan decided that she wanted to attend Sinclair Community College to become a respiratory therapist. Dwayne did not want her to go back to school, and the couple argued often on this topic. Ultimately both Susan and Dwayne enrolled in Sinclair's respiratory therapy program.   3

In May 1988, Susan attempted suicide.   4

One night in 1989, Susan came home to find Dwayne drunk, sitting on the stairs with a gun. He started screaming and yelling and threw Susan up against a wall. Then he shot the gun, and a bullet went between her legs. Immediately after the incident, Dwayne was apologetic and acted as if nothing had happened.   5

Thereafter, Dwayne's drinking escalated, and he became more abusive. In 1989, just prior to Thanksgiving, Susan went to a bar where Dwayne was drinking in order to transfer some items from the trunk of her car to the trunk of his car. She went into the bar to tell Dwayne what she had done, and he seemed fine. However, Dwayne followed Susan to the parking lot, struck her several times, and dragged her to his car. He then drove her to her parent's house and continued beating her in front of her mother and their children. After her mother threatened to call the police, Dwayne left. As a result of this incident, Susan's eyes were blackened, her cheekbone fractured, and her body bruised.   6

After the Christmas of 1990, Susan asked Dwayne to leave and told him that she wanted to end their marriage. Dwayne moved out of the house, and Susan contacted an attorney in order to file for a dissolution. However, Susan ultimately decided not to go through with the dissolution because Dwayne threatened to hurt himself if she did.   7

In June 1991, Dwayne moved back in with Susan, and they lived peacefully for several months. Then Dwayne began drinking again and reverted to his earlier abusive behavior. Once, while the children were watching, Dwayne dragged Susan up the stairs by her hair, threw her against the wall, and threw her against the refrigerator.   8

Later that summer, Susan and Dwayne separated again, and Dwayne moved into a condominium owned by Karen Houseman and her husband, Marshall. Dwayne and Karen began having an affair. Susan filed for a divorce in October.   9

Unhappy about the prospect of paying child support, Dwayne decided to seek custody of the children and told Susan that he would get the children because of her earlier suicide attempt. On the day of her court date, Susan, convinced that Dwayne would take her children away, again attempted suicide.   10

After Susan recovered, the divorce proceedings continued. Dwayne and Karen were not getting along, and she asked him to leave the condominium.   11

Dwayne told Susan that if she let him come back to live with her, he would not seek custody of the children. On that condition, Susan let him move back in, but she continued the divorce proceedings. In 1991, the divorce was finalized, and Susan was granted custody.

Susan allowed Dwayne to stay in her apartment after the divorce because he had stopped drinking and was attending AA meetings. She thought he deserved another chance. However, Dwayne ultimately started drinking again and quit attending the meetings. One night while he was drunk, Dwayne grabbed Susan, held a gun to her head, and screamed that he was going to kill her. 12

In July, Susan decided that they should separate again, and she told him that she wanted him to leave. Thereafter, Dwayne disappeared. Susan tried to get in touch with him and called some of his friends. She called Karen Houseman and talked to Marshall. During the conversation, Susan told Marshall that Dwayne had been having an affair with Karen for two and a half years. When Marshall became angry, Susan instantly regretted having told him and asked him not to say anything to Dwayne because Dwayne would get mad at her. 13

The next day, Dwayne called Susan from Karen's condominium. He told her that he had been in a fight with Marshall and asked that she bring him his gun. Susan talked with him for a while and determined that, although he knew she had told Marshall about the affair, he was not angry with her. He seemed to be only angry with Marshall. 14

After she hung up the phone, Susan considered what she should do. She thought that if she did not bring him the gun, Dwayne would eventually come to get it and be extremely angry that he had to do so. She was also worried that Dwayne would come to get the gun when the children were home. Finally, Susan decided to take the gun to him and "see what happened." She put the gun in her purse and drove to Karen's condominium. 15

When she arrived, Susan left her car running. As she started to get out of the car, Dwayne, his face covered with blood, opened the front door. Susan walked into the condominium and sat down on the couch. Karen started screaming at her, yelling that it was all her fault that Marshall had beaten up Dwayne and taken her children away. Then, Dwayne also started screaming. Susan reached into her purse to get a cigarette, and Dwayne lunged at her, trying to get the gun. A struggle ensued and Susan got to the gun first. She shot him in the leg and they both fell to the floor. Several shots were fired before Susan managed to disentangle herself from Dwayne. Susan ran toward the steps of the condominium, and Dwayne grabbed her and attempted to drag her back. Fearing that Dwayne would kill her, Susan pointed the gun at him and shot once or twice. At that point, Dwayne let go and stopped moving. 16

Susan went into the kitchen and called 911. 17

When the police and the paramedics arrived, they found Susan sitting in her car and Dwayne sitting on the floor of the condominium. He was still alive. Karen was not found. 18

Approximately one and a half hours later, the police transported Susan to the police station. While in the police car, Susan asked the officers if they had 19 checked the garage of the condominium for Karen's Jeep. When the officers searched the garage, they found Karen.

Both Dwayne and Karen died, Dwayne from multiple gunshot wounds to the chest and Karen from one gunshot wound to the chest.   20

On September 1, 1992, Susan was indicted for purposely causing the deaths of Karen and Dwayne in violation of R.C. 2903.02(A). Each of the two murder charges had an attached firearm specification. On September, 22, 1992, Susan pled not guilty to the charged offenses. Susan claimed that she had acted in self-defense.   21

The matter went to trial on January 12, 1993, and the jury found Susan guilty of the two lesser included offenses of voluntary manslaughter and two firearm specifications. On February 10, 1993, the trial court sentenced Susan.   22

Judge's Instruction to the Jury: Battered-Woman Syndrome

Evidence has been presented to you concerning battered women's syndrome. . . .

[Battered women's syndrome research is based upon an approach that is completely different from the approach which you must take to this case. The syndrome research begins with the assumption that physical abuse has occurred, and seeks to describe and explain common reactions of women to that experience. As distinguished from that research approach, you are to presume the defendant innocent. The People have the burden of proving guilt beyond a reasonable doubt.]

You should consider this evidence for certain limited purposes only, namely,

[that the [alleged victim's] [defendant's] reactions, as demonstrated by the evidence, are not inconsistent with [her] having been physically abused] [, or]

[the beliefs, perception or behavior of victims of domestic violence] [, or]

[proof relevant to the believability of the defendant's testimony] [, or]

[whether the defendant [actually] [and] [reasonably] believed in the necessity to use force to defend herself against imminent peril to life or great bodily injury. [In assessing reasonableness, the issue is whether a reasonable person in the defendant's circumstances would have seen a threat of imminent injury or death, and not whether killing the alleged abuser was reasonable in the sense of being an understandable response to ongoing abuse. An act that appeared to be an understandable response is not necessarily an act that was reasonable under the circumstances.]].

California Jury Instructions, Criminal: Book of Approved Jury Instructions. 6th ed. Prepared by the Committee on Standard Jury Instruction Criminal, of the Superior Court of Los Angeles County, California. St. Paul, MN: West Publishing, 1996.

The Abusive Doctor

Beverly IBN-TAMAS, Appellant,

v.

UNITED STATES, Appellee.

No. 12614.

District of Columbia Court of Appeals.

Argued June 30, 1978.
Decided Oct. 15, 1979.

A. Background Testimony

Appellant testified that when she met her husband, Dr. Ibn-Tamas, she was   1
working as a registered nurse in the prenatal care unit at Jacobi Hospital in New
York City, where he was a resident in neurosurgery. Shortly after the doctor's
divorce from his first wife in September 1972, he married appellant. They located
in Miami, Florida, where he was finishing his residency. Appellant continued to
work as a private duty nurse until the birth of their daughter the following
autumn. In 1974, the family moved to Washington, D.C., where the doctor,
assisted by his wife, established a private practice out of an office in their home.

The marriage was marred by recurring violent episodes separated by periods   2
of relative harmony. In 1974, for example, the doctor accused his wife's visiting
friend of being a lesbian and abruptly ordered her to leave their apartment. When
Mrs. Ibn-Tamas later protested his rudeness, he struck her with his fist, a shoe,
and another object, and dragged her and their six-month-old baby off a bed and
onto the floor. Several weeks later, during an argument at his mother's house, the
doctor allegedly pulled the appellant from her chair onto a cement porch and
caused her to lose consciousness by putting his knee to her neck.[1] Days later, he
threatened her with a loaded gun when she hesitated over co-signing some financial documents. Shortly thereafter, while they were driving north to Washington
to establish their new residence, the doctor and his wife argued over whether she
would have to stay at his mother's house while their new home was being prepared. He ended the argument by forcing her out of the car along an interstate
highway and driving off with their infant daughter.

Life improved for the Ibn-Tamases temporarily after their move to Wash-   3
ington; but throughout the first two months of 1976 their relationship became
increasingly marked by violence. Although Mrs. Ibn-Tamas was several months

---

Ibn-Tamas v. United States, 47 A.2d 626 (1979).

[1]At trial, appellant's description of her husband's violent behavior was contradicted only by the
testimony of Mrs. Faye Davis, the decedent's mother. She admitted seeing her son slap appellant
during the incident at her home in Washington but denied that he had rendered appellant unconscious by thrusting his knee into her neck. However, appellant's mother testified that she had
observed a bruise mark on her daughter's neck immediately after this incident.

pregnant with their second child, the doctor on two occasions in January and February punched her in the neck and hit her in the head and face with his fists,[2] leaving her in one instance with a split and bleeding lip. During this period, Dr. Ibn-Tamas also abused appellant verbally, saying that the child she was carrying was not his and threatening her with a fractured skull should she attempt to leave or seek a divorce.

In addition to this first-hand experience, Mrs. Ibn-Tamas claimed at her trial   4 to have been aware, prior to February 23, 1976, of similar violent incidents involving her husband and others.[3] The testimony of Olga Powell indicated that on April 7, 1971, Dr. Ibn-Tamas, then known as Robert Gamble,[4] ordered Ms. Powell out of the apartment that she shared with the doctor and his first wife. When she demurred, the doctor broke down her door, fired a .38 caliber revolver in her direction, and threw her belongings out the window. A criminal complaint for assault with a weapon was later reduced to an administrative fine. The decedent's first wife, Barbara Gamble Carter, testified that on March 23, 1971, she called the police after the doctor had pushed her onto the floor and hit her with a clenched fist during a fight. The doctor left for work just before the police arrived in response to her call.[5] Finally, Marshall Whitley, a relative of the decedent's sister-in-law, testified that on June 29, 1974, the doctor had come to his family home, got into an argument, and pulled a gun on Mr. Whitley and his father. As a result of the incident, Mr. Whitley filed a citizen's complaint against the doctor with the United States Attorney's Office.[6]

B. The Events on the Morning of the Shooting

Appellant testified that on February 23, 1976, she was aware of her husband's past   5 violence toward herself and others, as well as the fact that her husband kept loaded revolvers and shotguns in the house and the adjoining office.[7] That morning, a dispute erupted at the breakfast table. Despite his wife's protests that

---

[2]On cross-examination, the government challenged this testimony by implying that the alleged behavior was inconsistent with the natural inclination of a surgeon to protect his hands and with the teachings of Dr. Ibn-Tamas' Muslim faith.

[3]Appellant claimed to have been aware of these prior incidents through conversations with the decedent and through the decedent's diary and papers filed in connection with his divorce from his first wife, which the decedent had shown her.

[4]In 1971. Dr. Ibn-Tamas became an Orthodox Muslim and changed his name from Robert Gamble to A. R. Yusef Ibn-Tamas. His first wife's refusal to "embrace the Koran" was one of the factors leading to their separation.

[5]Affidavits submitted by Ms. Carter in connection with her separation and divorce from Dr. Ibn-Tamas asserted that the doctor had accused her friend, Ms. Powell, of being a lesbian in much the same way that he later accused the appellant's friend.

[6]The government suggested, in cross-examination of Mrs. Ibn-Tamas, that this incident stemmed from the decedent's desire to gain custody of the children of his first marriage.

[7]Investigation after February 23, 1976, revealed that Dr. Ibn-Tamas kept at least three guns in addition to the weapon used by Mrs. Ibn-Tamas, and hundreds of live rounds of ammunition in his house and office.

she was pregnant and that he had promised not to hit her again, Dr. Ibn-Tamas hit appellant over the head, first with a magazine and then with his fists. He then dragged her upstairs, pulled out a suitcase, and told her to pack and get out of the house by 10 a.m. Appellant further testified that when she objected, he hit her with his fists and then with a wooden hairbrush. Trying to protect her abdomen from the attack, appellant turned her body and absorbed the blows on her buttocks and thighs.[8] Dr. Ibn-Tamas then grabbed a .38 caliber revolver, pointed it at his wife's face, and said, "You are going out of here this morning one way or the other."

Thereafter, the doctor went downstairs to his office adjoining the house, and Mrs. Ibn-Tamas remained with her daughter in the bedroom. She called her husband in his office to plead with him to be reasonable, but he told her he did not want to argue anymore and that she should just pack. [6]

Shortly thereafter, the doctor came back into the main part of the house. The events which took place during the next few moments were a matter of sharp controversy at trial. There was conflicting testimony based on the recollections of appellant and of Lynette McCollom, the doctor's secretary, who had just arrived at work and overheard the shooting from the adjoining office area. [7]

Appellant testified that the doctor returned to the bedroom and resumed the attack. She was pushed toward the bureau on top of which her husband had left the gun that he had threatened her with moments earlier. Thinking that he was going to grab the gun, she picked it up, begged him to leave her alone, and fired the gun toward the bottom of the door to scare him. The doctor then left the room; and, according to appellant, she took her daughter in hand and started toward the stairway leading down to the first floor and the door. As she reached the top of the front stairway, however, her husband allegedly jumped out from behind the wall at the landing. Appellant fired twice more. Although it was not immediately apparent to appellant, one of these two shots struck the doctor in the abdomen. There was no immediate external bleeding; and the doctor remained standing as he backed down the stairs and into an examination room connected to the house by a swinging door at the bottom of the stairs. Appellant proceeded down the steps. As she reached the bottom landing, however, her daughter jumped out in front of her, looked into the examination room, and called out "Daddy." When appellant glanced through the open door, she saw her husband crouching with what she thought was a gun in his hand.[9] She fired again, striking the doctor in the head with what proved to be the fatal blow. [8]

Ms. McCollom testified that she arrived for work at approximately 9:00 a.m. The doctor let her in as he was passing through the office to return upstairs. Although Ms. McCollom did not see what occurred between appellant and her husband, she testified that she heard a shot approximately three seconds after she [9]

---

[8]A medical examination of the appellant after her arrest revealed three bruises on her arms, thighs, and buttocks.

[9]The prosecution tried to impeach this testimony by showing that appellant's statement to police following her arrest contained no reference to the fact that she thought the decedent was holding a gun at this point. Appellant replied that she did not reveal this fact to the police initially because she thought that her husband was alive and "maybe everything would be all right."

had seen Dr. Ibn-Tamas pass through the door from the examination room into the house. The shot sounded as if it had come from the landing. Ms. McCollom then heard a thumping noise, as if someone were falling down the stairs, followed by the words, "Yasmine,[10] don't shoot me anymore," and the second shot. As Ms. McCollom backed out of the office toward the door, she heard the doctor call her name. As she reached the office door leading to the street, she heard appellant say, "I am not going to leave you, I mean it"—and then she heard a third and final shot.[11]

Principally on the basis of Ms. McCollom's testimony, the prosecution suggested in its closing argument that Mrs. Ibn-Tamas, threatened with the prospect of being thrown out of her home in what she still considered a strange city, had simply decided that she had endured enough of her husband's abuse; lured him back into the house with a telephone call; ambushed him on the stairs; and followed him downstairs, shooting him in the forehead at point blank range as he lay on the examination room floor from the previous shot. Through questioning, the prosecution further suggested that appellant stood to gain financially from her husband's death, and accused her of being jealous of the other women he told her he had dated during the last few weeks before the shooting.

II. Expert Testimony about "Battered Women"

Appellant claims the trial court erred in excluding the testimony of Dr. Lenore Walker, a clinical psychologist, proffered as a defense expert on the subject of "battered women." Specifically, the defense proffered Dr. Walker for two purposes: to describe the phenomenon of "wife battering," and to give her opinion of the extent to which appellant's personality and behavior corresponded to those of 110 battered women Dr. Walker had studied. The defense claimed the testimony was relevant because it would help the jury appraise the credibility of appellant's contention that she had perceived herself in such imminent danger from her husband that she shot him in self-defense.

The trial court refused to permit this expert testimony on three grounds. First, it would "go beyond those [prior violent] acts which a jury is entitled to hear about, sift, and try to understand the circumstances under which they arose, and draw conclusions therefrom." Second, it would "invade the province of the jury, who are the sole judges of the facts and triers of the credibility of the witnesses, including the defendant." Third, Dr. Walker, "of necessity, concludes that the decedent was a batterer. And that is not being tried in this case. It is the defendant who is on trial." . . .

On direct examination, Mrs. Ibn-Tamas had testified that immediately before the shooting Dr. Ibn-Tamas had told her to pack and leave home by 10:00 a.m. When she replied that she could not, he hit her in the head, under the arms, and in the thighs, and kicked her in the stomach even though she was pregnant. She continued:

---

[10] Ms. McCollom testified that the decedent referred to his wife as "Yasmine."

[11] Police investigators found four expended shells in the weapon that Mrs. Ibn-Tamas had used. The government's theory to explain the discrepancy between this fact and Ms. McCollom's claim of hearing only three shots was that appellant had fired a test shot through her bedroom door to see if the gun was loaded sometime prior to the doctor's return to the house.

I saw he was looking over there on the bureau, so I saw the pistol, and he looked like he was going to go for the pistol. I just picked it up. I shot the bottom of the door, and I said, "Just please get out of here, and please, please leave us alone."

(The witness is crying.)

And then he was backing out of the door, and he said, "You are going now." And he just kept looking at me. And I heard him go down the steps, and so I had my little girl's hand. I knew after I shot that shot I had to get out of the house. I just knew he was going to kill me. So I had my little girl in my hand and we started to go down the steps real fast, and we got to the top and he jumps back from the landing. I thought he had gone all the way down, and so I took my leg back, pulled my little girl back, and we were next to the wall, and I just shot the gun.

He backed up against the wall, (indicating) went back to the wall, and he kept down at the steps with his eyes still on my face, and he went down the stairs, jumping two at a time, doing like that, and he kept looking back with his back to the wall, and on the way down the steps he said, "I am going to kill you, you dirty bitch."

He got at the bottom of the steps and he looked at me and he just went in the office, and I knew I had to get out of that door.

(The witness is crying.)

I knew it. And I had my little girl by the hand. She seemed like—when he got to the bottom of the steps, she thought we were supposed to follow him. She jumped like she was going in front, and she looks and she says, "Daddy." And I looked in there and he was, he was just like he was waiting for me. He was standing over just like—something like that. (Indicating.) And I just knew he had a gun. I shot in the room, and I turned to go out the front door, and after I turned my head I heard him fall. I heard him fall, and I knew I had shot him.

On cross-examination the government attempted to discredit this testimony by [14] suggesting to the jury, through its questions, that Mrs. Ibn-Tamas' account of the relationship with her husband over the years had been greatly overdrawn, and that her testimony about perceiving herself in imminent danger on February 23, was therefore implausible. For example, the government implied to the jury that the logical reaction of a woman who was truly frightened by her husband (let alone regularly brutalized by him) would have been to call the police from time to time or to leave him.[12] In an effort to rebut this line of attack by the government, the defense proffered Dr. Walker's testimony to (1) inform the jury that there is an identifiable class of persons who can be characterized as "battered women," (2) explain why the mentality and behavior of such women are at variance with the ordinary lay per-

---

[12] Q. And during the time in Miami, did you ever leave him?
  A. No, I didn't.
  Q. Did you ever call the police?
  A. No, I didn't. He told me he would kill me if I called the police.

The prosecutor stressed this theme once again during closing argument: "Maybe she put up with too much too long, although whose fault was that? She could have gotten out, you know."

ception of how someone would be likely to react to a spouse who is a batterer, and thus (3) provide a basis from which the jury could understand why Mrs. Ibn-Tamas perceived herself in imminent danger at the time of the shooting.

More specifically, Dr. Walker told the trial court, out of the presence of the   15
jury, that she had studied 110 women who had been beaten by their husbands. Her studies revealed three consecutive phases in the relationships: "tension building," when there are small incidents of battering; "acute battering incident," when beatings are severe; and "loving-contrite," when the husband becomes very sorry and caring. Dr. Walker then testified that women in this situation typically are low in self-esteem, feel powerless, and have few close friends, since their husbands commonly "accuse them of all kinds of things with friends, and they are embarrassed. They don't want to cause their friends problems, too." Because there are periods of harmony, battered women tend to believe their husbands are basically loving, caring men; the women assume that they, themselves, are somehow responsible for their husbands' violent behavior. They also believe, however, that their husbands are capable of killing them, and they feel there is no escape. Unless a shelter is available, these women stay with their husbands, not only because they typically lack a means of self-support but also because they fear that if they leave they will be found and hurt even more. Dr. Walker stressed that wife batterers come from all racial, social and economic, groups (including professionals), and that batterers commonly "escalate their abusiveness" when their wives are pregnant. She added that battered women are very reluctant to tell anyone that their husbands beat them. Of those studied, 60% had never done so before (Dr. Walker typically found them in hospitals), 40% had told a friend, and only 10% had called the police.

When asked about appellant, whom she had interviewed, Dr. Walker replied   16
that Mrs. Ibn-Tamas was a "classic case" of the battered wife. Dr. Walker added her belief that on the day of the killing, when Dr. Ibn-Tamas had been beating his wife despite protests that she was pregnant, Mrs. Ibn-Tamas' pregnancy had had a "major impact on the situation. . . . [T]hat is a particularly crucial time."

Dr. Walker's testimony, therefore, arguably would have served at least two   17
basic functions: (1) it would have enhanced Mrs. Ibn-Tamas' general credibility in responding to cross-examination designed to show that her testimony about the relationship with her husband was implausible; and (2) it would have supported her testimony that on the day of the shooting her husband's actions had provoked a state of fear which led her to believe she was in imminent danger ("I just knew he was going to kill me"), and thus responded in self-defense. Dr. Walker's contribution, accordingly, would have been akin to the psychiatric testimony admitted in the case of Patricia Hearst "to explain the effects kidnapping, prolonged incarceration, and psychological and physical abuse may have had on the defendant's mental state at the time of the robbery, insofar as such mental state is relevant to the asserted defense of coercion or duress." . . . Dr. Walker's testimony would have supplied an interpretation of the facts which differed from the ordinary lay perception ("she could have gotten out, you know") advocated by the government.

"It Was Time to Get Out, Time to Leave"

Mona Kianne LENTZ a/k/a Mona
L. Morris a/k/a Mona Kianne Morris

v.

STATE of Mississippi.

No. 07-KA-59640.

Supreme Court of Mississippi.
June 10, 1992.

Lentz met Hudspeth in June of 1986, and began living with him in August of that [1] year. Lentz testified that during this relationship, Hudspeth repeatedly battered her. She briefly separated from him in March of 1987, but resumed the relationship in April or May of 1987, until July 10th 1987, when she and her children moved to the home of her second cousin.

On September 5th 1987, Lentz decided to take her own life. She left her [2] cousin's house with her three children in the car and drove to a pawnshop where she purchased a .25 caliber automatic pistol. What prompted her decision to take her own life is not entirely clear; however, it appears she grew up in an atmosphere of domestic violence and verbal abuse; and, believing that her cousin was no longer willing to allow her to continue living in her home, was worried she could not provide food and shelter for herself and her three children.

After purchasing the pistol, Lentz drove, somewhat aimlessly, to her mother's [3] home where she intended to leave her children. Her mother was not home, so she took her children to lunch for a treat of fast-food. She then went to visit a woman to whom she planned to give what little money she had, but found the woman did not need the money as much as she had believed. Then, she returned to her mother's house and was waiting for her mother to return when she saw Hudspeth drive by the house. Upon seeing Hudspeth, Lentz decided she wanted to talk with him one last time so that she would leave good memories of herself.

She drove to Hudspeth's house, where she and Hudspeth entered into a con- [4] versation, during which Hudspeth told her that he had smoked marijuana earlier that day. Further, Hudspeth asked her to come inside the house. When she declined, he became jealous and angry and went back inside the house. Shortly thereafter, Hudspeth's cousin came out of the house and talked briefly with Lentz before going to his father's house, which was next-door to Hudspeth's. Lentz did not want Hudspeth to remember their last moment together as one of strife, so she walked to his front door, where she was met by Hudspeth, and again they talked.

Deciding she no longer wished to kill herself, Lentz asked Hudspeth for her [5] waterbed which she had left in his bedroom. They went inside the house to the

---

bedroom, whereupon Hudspeth refused to return the bed to her. Lentz told him "you know what Judge Kopf said about you using my stuff." At the mention of Judge Kopf, Hudspeth's facial expression changed, and "his eyes turned black." From previous batterings, Lentz knew it was "[t]ime to get out, time to leave. . . . Get away." She tried to "ease out" of the house, but Hudspeth saw her and said, "[i]f I have to go to jail this time, if I have to go this time, it will be for a reason." Hudspeth grabbed her, pulled her back, and she fell. Lentz testified as follows:

> [T]he next thing I remember is his back was to me. There was ringing. He was gone. And I thought, oh, my God, he's gone to get my girls. And then I thought, my girls, as I got to the door he had a pistol, himself, that he had used on me before. I did not see him with my girls. I thought he might be on the other side, maybe he got his pistol out of his car quick enough to shoot them because I had scared him. I felt I had scared him because he was not in the room.

Further, when asked on direct examination whether she remembered shooting Hudspeth, Lentz stated: 6

> I remember thinking of the pistol when he knocked me down, to scare him so I could get away and then I heard the ringing and he wasn't there, so figured I had scared him or that he was either going to lock the door to really, so no one could get in. Because that's usually what he did. He usually went and locked all the doors where the girls could not get in when I was screaming.

Although she was afraid Hudspeth would be waiting for her outside the house, she went outside where she saw him lying on the ground. She thought he was "playing," although she could hear someone breathing with difficulty, as if they had bronchitis. 7

Hudspeth's cousin testified that when Lentz arrived at Hudspeth's house, he left and walked next door to his father's house. Shortly thereafter, he heard a gunshot and ran outside where he saw Lentz running away with a gun and Hudspeth lying on the ground near the steps leading into his parents' house, which was approximately one hundred (100) feet from Hudspeth's house. The cousin's father also testified that he heard a shot and came outside where he saw Lentz running away and Hudspeth lying on the ground. The cousin's mother also testified that she saw a female running away, and Hudspeth on the ground. 8

An autopsy revealed that Hudspeth had been shot twice at close range with a .25 caliber pistol. Only one of the two wounds was fatal; the fatal bullet entered his back and passed through his heart, and another bullet entered his face, near his left cheek. According to expert medical testimony, it would not have been unusual for a person to have received a fatal wound, as was present here, and to travel a distance of one hundred (100) feet before collapsing. 9

Lentz testified that she drove from Hudspeth's house to her mother's house, where she left her children. Lentz's mother testified that Lentz told her that she had shot Hudspeth once and he had fallen down, and then she shot him again; however, Lentz stated she did not remember telling this to her mother. Lentz left her mother's house, driving somewhat aimlessly and telephoning both her mother 10 and the cousin with whom she had lived, until she came upon a Sheriff's office patrol car, driven by a Deputy Sheriff, to whom she surrendered. . . .

[We] note Hudspeth was shot twice, with the fatal bullet entering his back. [11] Further, two live rounds of ammunition and two expended shell casings were recovered at the scene of the shooting: one shell was found in Hudspeth's bedroom; a live round was found in the house in a hallway leading from the bedroom towards the front door; and both an expended shell as well as a live round were found where Hudspeth collapsed, outside the home of his relatives, which was approximately one hundred (100) feet from his home. Further, witnesses who sold the pistol to Lentz at the pawnshop testified she was unfamiliar with firearms, so they loaded the pistol for her and instructed her that in order for the pistol to fire with each pull of the trigger, it was necessary to chamber a round by pulling the top portion of the pistol back to release it. If this chambering procedure was repeated after a live round had already been chambered, a live round would be ejected from the pistol. Thus, it appears that Lentz shot Hudspeth while they were in the bedroom, and he left his house and attempted to go to his relative's house. Lentz apparently left the bedroom and went into the hallway where she chambered a live round from the pistol, and followed Hudspeth for one hundred feet to the steps of his relatives' house where she shot him again. Either before or after this second shot, she again ejected a live round from the pistol. Moreover, Lentz's mother testified her daughter told her she had shot Hudspeth once, and he fell down, after which she shot him again.

"Hit Him Again. Kill Him. Hit Him Again."

254 Kan. 144
STATE of Kansas, Appellee,
v.
Rose Marie SMITH, Appellant.

No. 68606.

Supreme Court of Kansas.
Dec. 10, 1993.

The defendant's convictions arise out of events that occurred on July 13, 1991, in [1] Halstead. The defendant had met the victim, Benedict Raya, in 1989. At the time of the offenses, they had lived together on and off for about a year and a half. The police had been called several times in response to domestic disputes during 1989 and prior to the event giving rise to the present convictions. The defendant and Raya were not living together at the time of the present offenses.

State v. Smith, 864 P.2d 709 (1993).

The defendant asked Raya to leave and took him to a motel after a dispute 2 occurred between them in March 1991. Raya could not find his glasses and other belongings after arriving at the motel. He testified that the defendant called him on July 10 and told him that he had left his glasses at her house. He stated that she told him she was no longer angry, that they could be friends, and that he could come by and pick up his glasses. Shortly after receiving that telephone call, Raya received a threatening call from Albert McClelland, warning him to stay away from the defendant because she was "his woman."

Before Raya went to work on the 3:00 to 11:00 shift on July 12, he left a note 3 on the defendant's door, telling her that he would be over that night to get his glasses. After he got off work, Raya returned to his motel room, drank, and watched television until about 1:00 a.m. He then walked over to the defendant's house, believing she would be home from her work about 1:00 a.m.

No one responded to Raya's knock at the door. When he saw a car coming, he 4 hid under a car parked in the defendant's yard because he was afraid McClelland or Pete Villarreal would be with the defendant. McClelland and the defendant got out of the car. Raya crawled out from his hiding place when McClelland saw Raya's feet sticking out from under the car. Raya told them that he had come to get his glasses. McClelland told him to leave the area, but the defendant intervened and invited Raya into her house.

The defendant brought Raya his glasses and offered him a drink. The three of 5 them sat in the living room having drinks. Raya and the defendant sat on the couch. According to McClelland, the defendant then started motioning for him to get an axe handle that was hanging on the wall behind him. McClelland initially shook his head no, but finally reached up and took it off the wall. After they each had a couple more drinks, the defendant began motioning for McClelland to "come on, come on . . . come over there." McClelland then got up and hit Raya five or six times on the head and shoulders with the axe handle. The defendant was "egging [McClelland] on" as he hit Raya, stating, "Hit him again. Kill him. Hit him again."

McClelland eventually quit hitting Raya, and the defendant helped Raya get up 6 and go into the bathroom. As McClelland was fixing another drink, he heard the defendant say, "He's getting away." The defendant told McClelland to "get him." McClelland went outside, got in his car, and went to his own house, where he fixed another drink. He testified that he was trying to "kill some time" so the defendant would believe he was out looking for Raya.

Meanwhile, the defendant had called Pete Villarreal, an old friend of hers, told 7 him Raya was "lurking around again," and asked Villarreal if he could come over. He did so, and when he arrived, he saw the defendant covered with blood and cleaning up blood from the floor. The defendant told Villarreal that McClelland had just "knocked the hell out of [Raya], and he's out looking for him." Villarreal got in his car and started looking for Raya too.

Villarreal spotted Raya walking on the street, but when Raya saw Villarreal, 8 Raya disappeared. Eventually, Raya, Villarreal, and McClelland all ended up at the defendant's house. Raya sat in the bathtub while the defendant wiped blood off of him. McClelland went into the kitchen to fix another drink and heard "whack, whack, whack," several times. He returned to the bathroom to find Villarreal reaching through the bathroom window, hitting Raya on the head with a stick.

According to McClelland, he entered the bathroom and saw the defendant, Raya, and Villarreal struggling over a knife. McClelland testified that the defendant was hitting Raya in the groin during the struggle over the knife. According to Villarreal, McClelland hit Raya on the neck with a hatchet. When Raya tried to defend himself against the hatchet, Villarreal hit him with a stick. Villarreal saw a knife lying by Raya's feet.   9

Eventually, Raya lay immobile on the floor. The defendant checked Raya's pulse and said, "He's awful tricky. You can't trust him." According to McClelland, the defendant "was standing there telling him just to lie down and die. . . . And she walked into the other room, got her pistol, came up there and put it to [Raya's] head and pulled the trigger and it didn't go off. . . . It just clicked." The defendant made some comment about "the damned thing won't work when you want it to." The defendant then put the gun down, came back, checked Raya's pulse and said, "Well, he's dead."   10

The defendant or Villarreal said something about getting garbage bags to put the body in. Villarreal suggested they dump Raya's body in Hutchinson "because that's his home." McClelland said he knew a place to "dump trash." The defendant stated that she wanted to get a sharp knife so she could cut Raya's body up into little pieces and "scatter him in the Arkansas River." According to McClelland, he and Villarreal tied Raya's hands, although it did not make much sense because they believed he was dead. McClelland also testified that they put a garbage bag over Raya's head and one over his feet "[s]o we wouldn't get blood all over the rest of the carpet and stuff." They also wrapped Raya in blankets. McClelland, Villarreal, and the defendant loaded Raya into the back seat of the car McClelland was driving.   11

They decided to take the body to a sand pit near Hutchinson. McClelland, Villarreal, and the defendant got in the front seat of McClelland's car, and McClelland drove Villarreal to get his car. McClelland and the defendant went to get gas, and Villarreal said he would meet them on the west side of town. At the gas station Raya sat up in the back seat; he had managed to free his hands and get the garbage bag off of his head. He was crying out, "Help me, they're trying to kill me." Raya kept asking the defendant, "Why?" She replied, "I want you dead. I want you out of my life."   12

Villarreal did not meet them on the west side of town, so McClelland drove without him to an area outside of Hutchinson where McClelland had dumped trash before. On the way, the defendant repeated that she needed a sharp knife so that she could cut Raya up into little pieces so no one would find his body. McClelland told the defendant that he was just going to take Raya out and dump him. Raya kept repeating that he loved the defendant and kept asking her, "Why?"   13

As McClelland and the defendant were looking for a place to dispose of Raya, he managed to jump out of the car. McClelland immediately stopped the car. The defendant told McClelland to "hit him, finish him." McClelland took his foot off of   14 the brake and accelerated a little; the defendant grabbed the wheel, and while they both held the wheel the car struck Raya and knocked him into a field. After the car struck Raya, the defendant again began talking about needing to get a knife to cut up his body so it would not be found. They left Raya in the field and headed back toward town.

On the way, the defendant told McClelland to stop on a bridge so that she 15 could dispose of the blankets, garbage bags, and rope. McClelland took the defendant home, and on the way she complained to McClelland that he could not do anything right. McClelland dropped off the defendant at her house and went home.

Raya survived the brutal attacks, gave statements to the police, and testified 16 at trial. At trial he testified that he remembered McClelland hitting him over the head until he lost consciousness at the defendant's house. When he came to, he heard someone saying "cut his throat," and Villarreal cut Raya's throat. Raya passed out again, and the next thing he remembered was someone saying to tie his hands and put a plastic bag over his head. He did not hear the defendant's voice or notice her presence at that time. He then remembered waking up in the defendant's bathtub, untied, and he may have pushed the defendant away before he got out of the house. He remembered running from house to house seeking help, but no one would answer their doors; trying to run down a road and being struck by a car; and someone say, "[S]hoot him and make sure he [is] dead," and pretending that he was dead. He did not recall the defendant's participation but recalled that he seemed to slip in and out of consciousness. When he was conscious, his vision was obstructed by blood.

● ● ● ●

For Deliberation and Argument

1. At the conclusion of the trial, the jury in *People v. Reeves* found the defendant, Barbara J. Reeves, guilty of murder. In her appeal, the defendant argued that the killing was in self-defense and therefore justifiable.

   - The Illinois Criminal Code provides that

     a person is justified in the use of force against another when and to the extent that he reasonably believes that such conduct is necessary to defend himself or another against such other's imminent use of unlawful force. *However, he is justified in the use of force which is intended or likely to cause death or great bodily harm only if he reasonably believes that such force is necessary to prevent imminent death or great bodily harm to himself or another, or the commission of a forcible felony.* [Emphasis added.]

   - In another Illinois homicide case (*People v. Williams*, 205 N.E. 2d 749), the elements of self-defense were stated as follows:

(1) that force is threatened against the person; (2) that the person threatened is not the aggressor; (3) that the danger of harm is imminent; (4) that the force threatened is unlawful; (5) that the person threatened must actually believe: (a) that the danger exists, (b) that the use of force is necessary to avert the danger, (c) that the kind and amount of force which he uses is necessary; and (6) that the above beliefs are reasonable. [In addition, the law] limits the use of deadly force to those situations in which (a) the threatened force will cause death or great bodily harm or (b) the force threatened is a forcible felony.

- The state attempted to rebut the contention that the killing was justifiable homicide by arguing

    (1) that no witness saw any bruises on defendant's face; (2) that no weapon was either seen in the deceased's hand when he drug [dragged] defendant out of the cafe or anywhere near his body after he was shot; and (3) that defendant made statements prior to the shooting and immediately after it which establish an intent to murder rather than to defend herself.

As one of the appellate judges, write an opinion arguing that the murder conviction of Barbara Reeves should be affirmed or that it should be reversed and the homicide be declared justifiable.

2. In light of the article "Defending the Battered Wife: A Challenge for Defense Attorneys," to what extent does Susan M. Daws, the defendant in *State v. Daws*, fit the pattern described by Thompson? After the jury convicted Daws of voluntary manslaughter, the defendant appealed, claiming that the homicides were justifiable. She also argued that the judge should have allowed an expert witness to testify on battered-woman syndrome regarding whether she "reasonably believed that she was in imminent danger on the night of the shootings and whether she reasonably believed it was necessary to use deadly force at the time she fired her gun." To what extent do you agree with Daws? Apply the facts of this case to the law on voluntary manslaughter and on justifiable homicide, taking account also of relevant points in Thompson's article.

3. Suppose that you are a member of the *Ibn-Tamas v. United States* jury. You have, of course, heard the conflicting testimony of the defendant, Beverly Ibn-Tamas, and Lynette McCollom as to the events in the Ibn-Tamas house on the day of the homicide. You have also heard the testimony of Dr. Lenore Walker, an expert on the battered-woman syndrome. The other jury members are divided as to verdicts of second-degree murder, voluntary manslaughter, or justifiable homicide (self-defense). Decide on a verdict and write an argument explaining it. You should not only provide reasons for your decision but also consider other verdicts and explain why you rejected them. Base your arguments on the facts of the case and on the law on each type of homicide you consider. You may wish to compare and con-

trast Ibn-Tamas's situation with those of Barbara J. Reeves and Susan M. Daws. (*Note:* In the actual trial, the jury, on the request of the defense attorney, was not permitted to consider a verdict of voluntary manslaughter. The jury was also not allowed to hear Dr. Walker's testimony, as battered-woman syndrome had not yet been sufficiently established in the law as a defense to a charge of homicide. Prosecutors argued—and the trial judge agreed—that such testimony would "invade the province" of the jury, who "are the sole judges of the facts and triers of the credibility of the witnesses, including the defendant.")

4. Mona Lentz, the defendant in *Lentz v. State*, was convicted of manslaughter. She appealed her conviction, largely because the trial judge did not allow the defense to introduce an expert to testify on battered-woman syndrome. (In certain other cases, appeals courts have reversed trial court homicide convictions when, in their opinion, the trial judge improperly disallowed such expert testimony.) The argument against allowing expert testimony in this case was that

> [battered-woman syndrome] does not supplant accountability. When a wife kills her husband under circumstances where, *objectively speaking*, it was not reasonably necessary that she do so in her own defense, she should not expect acquittal at the hands of our law, no matter how long she may have been a battered wife. . . . [W]hether a killing is justified upon grounds of self-defense is to be judged by objective standards; that is, a killing is justified if the person who kills did so under circumstances which would lead a reasonable person under similar circumstances to conclude she was in imminent danger of death or great bodily harm.

Taking the side of either a prosecuting attorney or Lentz's defense attorney, argue that the manslaughter verdict should or should not be reversed for a verdict of justifiable homicide. Consider the facts of the case—in particular the two paragraphs of direct quotation from Lentz's own testimony—and apply them to the law on (voluntary) manslaughter and justifiable homicide. Consider also the question of whether the trial court judge should have allowed expert testimony of battered-woman syndrome. To what extent would such testimony have helped the jury to arrive at an equitable verdict? (*Note:* You may wish to compare and contrast Mona Lentz's use of the battered-woman syndrome defense with its use by other defendants treated in this section—Barbara J. Reeves, Susan Daws, and Beverly Ibn-Tamas.)

5. Rose Marie Smith, the defendant in *State v. Smith*, was convicted of attempted second-degree murder. As indicated in the last few paragraphs dealing with her case, she argued that she had acted in self-defense and was entitled to have the jury consider her status as a battered woman. Assess her claims, taking into account the facts of the case, the information and the jury instructions on battered-woman syndrome, and the applicable laws on murder and justifiable homicide. Recommend a verdict. Compare and con-

trast Rose Marie Smith's use of the battered-woman syndrome with its use by other defendants treated in this section—Barbara J. Reeves, Susan Daws, Beverly Ibn-Tamas, and Mona Lentz.

6. Select one of these five cases. Imagine yourself as attorney for the plaintiff or attorney for the defendant. Write a paper in IRAC format to make your case. Define the *issue* in question format. State or summarize the applicable *rules* about homicide. *Apply* the rules, as explained in the "Jury's Instructions on Murder and Manslaughter" and apply them to the facts of the case you have selected. Draw a *conclusion* from the application of these rules.

7. Select one of the cases treated in this group. Imagine that you are representing either the plaintiff or the defendant. Compose either an opening statement or a closing argument for this case. Remember that your audience is the jury. Draw on the facts of the case in a way that is likely to have the greatest impact on the jury. Keep in mind, however, that jury members may turn against you—and your client—if they think that you are overly manipulating the facts, being deceptive, making exaggerated claims, or attempting too crudely to play on their emotions. For guidance on developing your statement, see "Models for the Opening Statement and the Closing Argument" at the end of Chapter 2. See also Larry S. Stewart's "Arguing Pain and Suffering Damages in Summation: How to Inspire Jurors" at the end of the Group 3 Readings in Chapter 3.

■ Group 5 Readings: *Felony Murder*

The doctrine of felony murder provides that any homicide perpetrated during the commission of a felony is considered first-degree murder. For example, during the course of a convenience store holdup, if the robber, in self-defense, were to kill the manager who had pulled out his own gun, then the robber's accomplice waiting in the car outside could be charged not only with being an accessory to robbery but also with first-degree murder. In such cases jurors might be instructed: "Murder which is committed in the perpetration or attempt to perpetrate robbery, is murder of the first degree, whether the murder was intentional, unintentional, or accidental."

Felony murder is a controversial doctrine because it appears to render irrelevant the issue of criminal intent, of personal responsibility for one's actions. As one judge pointed out, it "erodes the relation between criminal liability and moral culpability."[1] Moreover, it can lead to punishment that seems grossly disproportionate to the crime, and it leaves no room for the jury to consider mitigating circumstances. In effect, felony murder removes the essential elements of premeditation and malice from the definition of first-degree murder, while leaving in place the severe punishment mandated for that offense. In response to such objections, proponents of the felony murder doc-

---

[1]*People v. Washington,* 402 P.2d 130.

trine argue that persons contemplating dangerous felonies ought to foresee that their actions could have fatal, if unintended, consequences, particularly if they encounter resistance from their victims or the police. More specifically, they argue that the felony murder doctrine "presumes malice aforethought on the basis of the commission of a felony inherently dangerous to human life. . . . When a robber enters a place with a deadly weapon with the intent to commit a robbery, malice is shown by the nature of the crime."

In Tison v. Arizona, *three brothers help their father break out of jail; during the course of their escape, the senior Tison kills four members of a family whose car they have stolen. Two of the surviving brothers, who had no direct part in the killing, are charged with felony murder. In* People v. Washington, *a robber is charged with murder when his intended victim shoots and kills the robber's accomplice. In* People v. Stamp, *a robber is charged with felony murder when his victim dies of a heart attack shortly after the robbery. And in* People v. Hickman, *two robbers are charged with felony murder when one police officer accidentally shoots and kills another officer during the pursuit of the criminals.*

A Prison Breakout and the Death of a Family

■ ■

TISON v. ARIZONA
CERTIORARI TO THE SUPREME COURT
OF ARIZONA
[United States Supreme Court]

No. 84–6075.

Argued November 3, 1986—Decided April 21, 1987

Gary Tison was sentenced to life imprisonment as the result of a prison escape during the course of which he had killed a guard. After he had been in prison a number of years, Gary Tison's wife, their three sons Donald, Ricky, and Raymond, Gary's brother Joseph, and other relatives made plans to help Gary Tison escape again. . . . The Tison family assembled a large arsenal of weapons for this purpose. Plans for escape were discussed with Gary Tison, who insisted that his cellmate, Randy Greenawalt, also a convicted murderer, be included in the prison break. The following facts are largely evidenced by petitioners' detailed confessions given as part of a plea bargain according to the terms of which the State agreed not to seek the death sentence. The Arizona courts interpreted the plea agreement to require that petitioners testify to the planning stages of the breakout. When they refused to do so, the bargain was rescinded and they were tried, convicted, and sentenced to death.

1

Tison v. Arizona, 481 U.S. 137 (1987).
Footnotes 2–5 omitted, footnotes renumbered.

On July 30, 1978, the three Tison brothers entered the Arizona State Prison at 2
Florence carrying a large ice chest filled with guns. The Tisons armed
Greenawalt and their father, and the group, brandishing their weapons, locked
the prison guards and visitors present in a storage closet. The five men fled the
prison grounds in the Tisons' Ford Galaxy automobile. No shots were fired at the
prison.

After leaving the prison, the men abandoned the Ford automobile and pro- 3
ceeded on to an isolated house in a white Lincoln automobile that the brothers
had parked at a hospital near the prison. At the house, the Lincoln automobile had
a flat tire; the only spare tire was pressed into service. After two nights at the
house, the group drove toward Flagstaff. As the group traveled on back roads and
secondary highways through the desert, another tire blew out. The group decided
to flag down a passing motorist and steal a car. Raymond stood out in front of the
Lincoln; the other four armed themselves and lay in wait by the side of the road.
One car passed by without stopping, but a second car, a Mazda occupied by John
Lyons, his wife Donnelda, his 2-year-old son Christopher, and his 15-year-old
niece, Theresa Tyson, pulled over to render aid.

As Raymond showed John Lyons the flat tire on the Lincoln, the other 4
Tisons and Greenawalt emerged. The Lyons family was forced into the back-
seat of the Lincoln. Raymond and Donald drove the Lincoln down a dirt road
off the highway and then down a gas line service road farther into the desert;
Gary Tison, Ricky Tison, and Randy Greenawalt followed in the Lyons' Mazda.
The two cars were parked trunk to trunk and the Lyons family was ordered to
stand in front of the Lincoln's headlights. The Tisons transferred their belong-
ings from the Lincoln into the Mazda. They discovered guns and money in the
Mazda which they kept, and they put the rest of the Lyons' possessions in the
Lincoln.

Gary Tison then told Raymond to drive the Lincoln still farther into the desert. 5
Raymond did so, and, while the others guarded the Lyons and Theresa Tyson,
Gary fired his shotgun into the radiator, presumably to completely disable the
vehicle. The Lyons and Theresa Tyson were then escorted to the Lincoln and
again ordered to stand in its headlights. Ricky Tison reported that John Lyons
begged, in comments "more or less directed at everybody," "Jesus, don't kill me."
Gary Tison said he was "thinking about it." . . . John Lyons asked the Tisons and
Greenawalt to "[g]ive us some water . . . just leave us out here, and you all go
home." Gary Tison then told his sons to go back to the Mazda and get some water.
Raymond later explained that his father "was like in conflict with himself. . . .
What it was, I think it was the baby being there and all this, and he wasn't sure
about what to do.". . .

The petitioners' statements diverge to some extent, but it appears that both of 6
them went back towards the Mazda, along with Donald, while Randy Greenawalt
and Gary Tison stayed at the Lincoln guarding the victims. Raymond recalled
being at the Mazda filling the water jug "when we started hearing the shots." . . .
Ricky said that the brothers gave the water jug to Gary Tison who then, with
Randy Greenawalt went behind the Lincoln, where they spoke briefly, then raised

the shotguns and started firing. . . . In any event, petitioners agree they saw Greenawalt and their father brutally murder their four captives with repeated blasts from their shotguns. Neither made an effort to help the victims, though both later stated they were surprised by the shooting. The Tisons got into the Mazda and drove away, continuing their flight. Physical evidence suggested that Theresa Tyson managed to crawl away from the bloodbath, severely injured. She died in the desert after the Tisons left.

Several days later the Tisons and Greenawalt were apprehended after a   7
shootout at a police roadblock. Donald Tison was killed. Gary Tison escaped into the desert where he subsequently died of exposure. Raymond and Ricky Tison and Randy Greenawalt were captured and tried jointly for the crimes associated with the prison break itself and the shootout at the roadblock; each was convicted and sentenced.

The State then individually tried each of the petitioners for capital murder of   8
the four victims as well as for the associated crimes of armed robbery, kidnaping, and car theft. The capital murder charges were based on Arizona felony-murder law providing that a killing occurring during the perpetration of robbery or kidnaping is capital murder, and that each participant in the kidnaping or robbery is legally responsible for the acts of his accomplices. Each of the petitioners was convicted of the four murders under these accomplice liability and felony-murder statutes.[1]

. . . The judge found three statutory aggravating factors: 9

(1) the Tisons had created a grave risk of death to others (not the victims);
(2) the murders had been committed for pecuniary gain;
(3) the murders were especially heinous.

The judge found no statutory mitigating factor. Importantly, the judge specifi-   10
cally found that the crime was *not* mitigated by the fact that each of the petitioners' "participation was relatively minor." . . . The trial judge also specifically found . . . that each "could reasonably have foreseen that his conduct . . . would cause or create a grave risk of . . . death." He did find, however, three nonstatutory mitigating factors:

(1) the petitioners' youth—Ricky was 20 and Raymond was 19;
(2) neither had prior felony records;
(3) each had been convicted of the murders under the felony-murder rule.

---

[1]Arizona has recodified and broadened its felony-murder statute to include killings occurring during the course of a variety of sex and narcotics offenses and escape. See Ariz. Rev. Stat. Ann. §§13–1105(A)(2), (B) (Supp. 1986). The accomplice liability provisions of Arizona law have been modernized and recodified also. See Ariz. Rev. Stat. Ann. §§13–301, 13–303(A)(3), (B)(2) (1978 and Supp. 1986). Neither change would have diminished Ricky Tison's or Raymond Tison's legal accountability for the deaths that occurred.

Nevertheless, the judge sentenced both petitioners to death.   11

On direct appeal, the Arizona Supreme Court affirmed. The Court found: 12

"The record establishes that both Ricky and Raymond Tison were present when the homicides took place and that they occurred as part of and in the course of the escape and continuous attempt to prevent recapture. The deaths would not have occurred but for their assistance. That they did not specifically intend that the Lyonses and Theresa Tyson die, that they did not plot in advance that these homicides would take place, or that they did not actually pull the triggers on the guns which inflicted the fatal wounds is of little significance." . . .

"Intend *[sic]* to kill includes the situation in which the defendant intended, contemplated, or anticipated that lethal force would or might be used or that life would or might be taken in accomplishing the underlying felony. *Enmund, supra; State v. Emery,* [141 Ariz. 549, 554, 688 P. 2d 175, 180 (1984)] filed June 6, 1984.

"In the present case the evidence does not show that [Raymond Tison] killed or attempted to kill. The evidence does demonstrate beyond a reasonable doubt, however, that petitioner intended to kill. Petitioner played an active part in preparing the breakout, including obtaining a getaway car and various weapons. At the breakout scene itself, petitioner played a crucial role by, among other things, holding a gun on prison guards. Petitioner knew that Gary Tison's murder conviction arose out of the killing of a guard during an earlier prison escape attempt. Thus petitioner could anticipate the use of lethal force during this attempt to flee confinement; in fact, he later said that during the escape he would have been willing personally to kill in a 'very close life or death situation,' and that he recognized that after the escape there was a possibility of killings.

"The use of lethal force that petitioner contemplated indeed occurred when the gang abducted the people who stopped on the highway to render aid. Petitioner played an active part in the events that led to the murders. He assisted in the abduction by flagging down the victims as they drove by, while the other members of the gang remained hidden and armed. He assisted in escorting the victims to the murder site. At the site, petitioner, Ricky Tison and Greenawalt placed the gang's possessions in the victims' Mazda and the victims' possessions in the gang's disabled Lincoln Continental. After Gary Tison rendered the Lincoln inoperable by firing into its engine compartment, petitioner assisted in escorting the victims to the Lincoln. Petitioner then watched Gary Tison and Greenawalt fire in the direction of the victims. Petitioner did nothing to interfere. After the killings, petitioner did nothing to disassociate himself from Gary Tison and Greenawalt, but instead used the victims' car to continue on the joint venture, a venture that lasted several more days.

"From these facts we conclude that petitioner intended to kill. Petitioner's participation up to the moment of the firing of the fatal shots was substantially the same as that of Gary Tison and Greenawalt. . . . Petitioner, actively participated in the events leading to death by, *inter alia*, providing the murder weapons and helping abduct the victims. Also petitioner was present at the murder site, did nothing to interfere with the murders, and after the murders even continued on the joint venture."

Opinion of Justice A

. . . Raymond Tison brought an arsenal of lethal weapons into the Arizona State   13
Prison which he then handed over to two convicted murderers, one of whom he knew had killed a prison guard in the course of a previous escape attempt. By his own admission he was prepared to kill in furtherance of the prison break. He performed the crucial role of flagging down a passing car occupied by an innocent family whose fate was then entrusted to the known killers he had previously armed. He robbed these people at their direction and then guarded the victims at gunpoint while they considered what next to do. He stood by and watched the killing, making no effort to assist the victims before, during, or after the shooting. Instead, he chose to assist the killers in their continuing criminal endeavors, ending in a gun battle with the police in the final showdown.

Ricky Tison's behavior differs in slight details only. Like Raymond, he inten-   14
tionally brought the guns into the prison to arm the murderers. He could have foreseen that lethal force might be used, particularly since he knew that his father's previous escape attempt had resulted in murder. He, too, participated fully in the kidnaping and robbery and watched the killing after which he chose to aid those whom he had placed in the position to kill rather than their victims.

These facts not only indicate that the Tison brothers' participation in the   15
crime was anything but minor; they also would clearly support a finding that they both subjectively appreciated that their acts were likely to result in the taking of innocent life. . . .

Opinion of Justice B

[W]hile the Court has found that petitioners made no effort prior to the shooting   16
to assist the victims, the uncontradicted statements of both petitioners are that just prior to the shootings they were attempting to find a jug of water to give to the family. . . . While the Court states that petitioners were on the scene during the shooting and that they watched it occur, Raymond stated that he and Ricky were still engaged in repacking the Mazda after finding the water jug when the shootings occurred. . . . Ricky stated that they had returned with the water, but were still some distance ("farther than this room") from the Lincoln when the shootings started, . . . and that the brothers then turned away from the scene and went back to the Mazda. . . . Neither stated that they anticipated that the shootings would occur, or that they could have done anything to prevent them or to help the

victims afterward.[2] Both, however, expressed feelings of surprise, helplessness, and regret. This statement of Raymond's is illustrative:

"Well, I just think you should know when we first came into this we had an agreement with my dad that nobody would get hurt because we [the brothers] wanted no one hurt. And when this [killing of the kidnap victims] came about we were not expecting it. And it took us by surprise as much as it took the family [the victims] by surprise because we were not expecting this to happen. And I feel bad about it happening. I wish we could [have done] something to stop it, but by the time it happened it was too late to stop it. And it's just something we are going to live with the rest of our lives. It will always be there."[3]

---

[2]In addition, the Court's statement that Raymond did not act to assist the victims "after" the shooting, and its statement that Ricky "watched the killing after which he chose to aid those whom he had placed in the position to kill rather than their victims," takes license with the facts found by the Arizona Supreme Court. That court did not say whether petitioners did anything to help the victims following the shooting, nor did it make any findings that would lead one to believe that something could have been done to assist them. The lower court merely stated that petitioners did not "disassociate" themselves from their father and Greenawalt after the shooting.

[3]These expressions are consistent with other evidence about the sons' mental states that this Court, like the lower courts, has neglected. Neither son had a prior felony record. Both lived at home with their mother, and visited their father, whom they believed to be "a model prisoner," each week. They did not plan the breakout or escape; rather their father, after thinking about it himself for a year, mentioned the idea to Raymond for the first time one week before the breakout, and discussed with his sons the possibility of having them participate only the day before the breakout. The sons conditioned their participation on their father's promise that no one would get hurt; during the breakout, their father kept his word. The trial court found that the murders their father later committed were senseless and unnecessary to the felony of stealing a car in which the sons participated; and just prior to the shootings the sons were retrieving a water jug for the family. Given these circumstances, the sons' own testimony that they were surprised by the killings, and did not expect them to occur, appears more plausible than the Court's speculation that they "subjectively appreciated that their activities were likely to result in the taking of innocent life." The report of the psychologist, who examined both sons, also suggests that they may not have appreciated the consequences of their participation: "These most unfortunate youngsters were born into an extremely pathological family and were exposed to one of the premier sociopaths of recent Arizona history. In my opinion this very fact had a severe influence upon the personality structure of these youngsters. . . .

"I do believe that their father, Gary Tison, exerted a strong, consistent, destructive but subtle pressure upon these youngsters and I believe that these young men got committed to an act which was essentially 'over their heads.' Once committed, it was too late and there does not appear to be any true defense based on brainwashing, mental deficiency, mental illness or irresistable urge. There was a family obsession, the boys were 'trained' to think of their father as an innocent person being victimized in the state prison but both youngsters have made perfectly clear that they were functioning of their own volition. At a deeper psychological level it may have been less of their own volition than as a result of Mr. Tison's 'conditioning' and the rather amoral attitudes within the family home." . . .

Killing in a Gas Station

44 Cal.Rptr. 442

PEOPLE, Plaintiff and Respondent,

v.

**Edwards WASHINGTON, Defendant
and Appellant.**

Cr. 8528.

Supreme Court of California, In Bank.

May 25, 1965.

Shortly before 10 p.m., October 2, 1962, Johnnie Carpenter prepared to close his [1] gasoline station. He was in his office computing the receipts and disbursements of the day while an attendant in an adjacent storage room deposited money in a vault. Upon hearing someone yell "robbery," Carpenter opened his desk and took out a revolver. A few moments later, James Ball entered the office and pointed a revolver directly at Carpenter, who fired immediately, mortally wounding Ball. Carpenter then hurried to the door and saw an unarmed man he later identified as defendant running from the vault with a moneybag in his right hand. He shouted "Stop." When his warning was not heeded, he fired and hit defendant who fell wounded in front of the station.

The Attorney General, relying on *People v. Harrison*, 176 Cal.App.2d 330, 1 [2] Cal.Rptr. 414, contends that defendant was properly convicted of first degree murder. In that case defendants initiated a gun battle with an employee in an attempt to rob a cleaning business. In the cross fire, the employee accidentally killed the owner of the business. The court affirmed the judgment convicting defendants of first degree murder, invoking *Commonwealth v. Almeida*, 362 Pa. 596, 68 A.2d 595, 12 A.L.R.2d 183, and *People v. Podolski*, 332 Mich. 508, 52 N.W. 2d 201, which held that robbers who provoked gunfire were guilty of first degree murder even though the lethal bullet was fired by a policeman. . . .

On his appeal from the robbery conviction, defendant contends that he did [3] not participate in the robbery. He testified that on the evening of the robbery he was with Ball and a man named Johnson. He did not know that they intended to commit robbery. He was "pretty drunk" at the time and fell asleep in the automobile. When he awoke the automobile was parked near Carpenter's gasoline station, and Ball and Johnson were absent. He left the automobile to look for them. As he approached the station, Johnson ran from the vault. Carpenter shot just as Johnson ducked around a corner and dropped the moneybag. Carpenter's bullet hit defendant who fell wounded near the bag that Johnson had dropped.

. . . Defendant's testimony was corroborated by the testimony of James [4] Johnson, an inmate of the state prison for an unrelated crime at the time of defen-

---

People v. Washington, 402 P.2d 185 (1965).

dant's trial. Johnson testified that he was the man who ran from the vault with the moneybag. Carpenter controverted their testimony, however, by identifying defendant as the man who ran from the vault.

Murder by Heart Attack

[Crim. No. 12749. Second Dist.,
Div. Three. Dec. 1, 1969.]
PEOPLE, Plaintiff and Respondent,
v.
Jonathan Earl STAMP et al., Defendants and Appellants.

Defendants Koory and Stamp, armed with a gun and a blackjack, entered the rear of the building housing the offices of General Amusement Company, ordered the employees they found there to go to the front of the premises, where the two secretaries were working. Stamp, the one with the gun, then went into the office of Carl Honeyman, the owner and manager. Thereupon Honeyman, looking very frightened and pale, emerged from the office in a "kind of hurry." He was apparently propelled by Stamp who had hold of him by an elbow.

The robbery victims were required to lie down on the floor while the robbers took the money and fled out the back door. As the robbers, who had been on the premises 10 to 15 minutes, were leaving, they told the victims to remain on the floor for five minutes so that no one would "get hurt."

Honeyman, who had been lying next to the counter, had to use it to steady himself in getting up off the floor. Still pale, he was short of breath, sucking air, and pounding and rubbing his chest. As he walked down the hall, in an unsteady manner, still breathing hard and rubbing his chest, he said he was having trouble "keeping the pounding down inside" and that his heart was "pumping too fast for him." A few minutes later, although still looking very upset, shaking, wiping his forehead and rubbing his chest, he was able to walk in a steady manner into an employee's office. When the police arrived, almost immediately thereafter, he told them he was not feeling very well and that he had a pain in his chest. About two minutes later, which was 15 or 20 minutes after the robbery had occurred, he collapsed on the floor. At 11:25 he was pronounced dead on arrival at the hospital. The coroner's report listed the immediate cause of death as heart attack.

The employees noted that during the hours before the robbery Honeyman had appeared to be in normal health and good spirits. The victim was an obese, 60-year-old man, with a history of heart disease, who was under a great deal of pres-

People v. Stamp, 82 Cal Rptr 598 (1969).

sure due to the intensely competitive nature of his business. Additionally, he did not take good care of his heart.

Three doctors, including the autopsy surgeon, Honeyman's physician, and a professor of cardiology from U.C.L.A., testified that although Honeyman had an advanced case of atherosclerosis, a progressive and ultimately fatal disease, there must have been some immediate upset to his system which precipitated the attack. It was their conclusion in response to a hypothetical question that but for the robbery there would have been no fatal seizure at that time. The fright induced by the robbery was too much of a shock to Honeyman's system. There was opposing expert testimony to the effect that it could not be said with reasonable medical certainty that fright could ever be fatal.

Burglary and Death

PEOPLE of the State of Illinois,
Plaintiff-Appellant,

v.

Glenn HICKMAN and Anthony Rock,
Defendants-Appellees.

No. 72–32.

Appellate Court of Illinois,
Third District.
June 8, 1973.

The factual situation which resulted in the trial of the defendants occurred on the evening of April 2, 1970, at which time seventeen policemen from the police force of the city of Joliet were participating in a surveillance of a building known as the Illinois Wine and Liquor Warehouse. Among the officers involved in the surveillance was Sergeant James Cronk, who shortly before 10:15 P.M. noticed Robert Bruce Papes and the defendant Anthony Rock pass by the warehouse several times in a Cadillac automobile. Later several officers saw a Chevrolet automobile enter an alley south of the warehouse and stop at a side door of the building. Several people left the automobile and disappeared from sight into the doorway. The driver of this vehicle, who was Papes, walked a short distance, made a surveillance of the area, returned to the automobile and then drove out of the sight of the officers. After several minutes Papes was again seen walking in the alley and after once more looking over the area he again disappeared from the sight of the police officers when he went to the location of the side door-way of the warehouse. It was within a matter of a few seconds of Papes' disappearance that Sergeant Cronk saw three individuals exit from the side doorway of the ware-

---

People v. Hickman, 297 N.E.2d 582 (1973).

house, at which time he signaled the officers to close in from various directions towards a concrete parking lot which was to the rear and west of the warehouse.

Papes and the defendants Rock and Hickman, upon seeing the officers 2 approaching them, proceeded to run. Papes ran in a southwesterly direction and the defendants Rock and Hickman in a north-westerly direction towards some bushes located at the northwest corner of the parking lot. Papes was apprehended when a Sergeant Erwin pointed a shotgun at him. Papes submitted to an arrest and upon his person was found a loaded pistol and additional cartridges. As the defendant Rock was running he was carrying a small object in his hand. The defendant Hickman was carrying an attache case as he was fleeing.

The defendants Rock and Hickman ran through the bushes while in the mean- 3 time Sergeant Cronk ran to the rear of the warehouse where he noticed two people running in a northwesterly direction. Sergeant Cronk yelled "halt—police" several times but his commands were ignored. He lost sight of the two fleeing individuals but within seconds thereafter saw a man carrying a handgun running towards the bushes at the northwest corner of the parking lot. Sergeant Cronk, believing that this approaching individual was one of the burglars of the Illinois Wine and Liquor Warehouse, and referring to the handgun, ordered the person to "drop it." When there was no compliance to this warning Sergeant Cronk fired his shotgun at the individual, who was later discovered to be Detective William Loscheider of the Joliet police force. Loscheider was killed by this shot from his fellow officer's gun.

Approximately one-half hour later the defendants Rock and Hickman were 4 arrested as they were walking on a street approximately two and a half blocks from the warehouse. Neither of the defendants had a weapon on his person.

Subsequent to the fatal shooting of Loscheider the police officers discovered 5 that entry to the warehouse had been made by removing a panel from the side door and also by removal of the lock from the door.

During the trial of the defendants an analyst from the Illinois Bureau of Iden- 6 tification Crime Laboratory testified that the tool marks found on the side door of the warehouse were made by a screwdriver found in an attache case which was discovered on the parking lot to the rear of the warehouse.

• • • •

For Deliberation and Argument

1. The defendants in *Tison v. Arizona*, Raymond and Ricky Tison, were convicted of first-degree murder and were sentenced to death. The Arizona Supreme Court affirmed this conviction and sentence. In their appeal to the U.S. Supreme Court, the defendents ("petitioners") argued that they did not kill the victims, that they did not intend the victims' deaths, and that they played a relatively minor part in the felonies themselves (that is, the robbery of the Lyons's car and the kidnapping). Their arguments, as well as the arguments of the prosecution, are represented in the facts of the case.

Consider the arguments of both the petitioners and the prosecutors. Which do you find more persuasive? Why? Focus both on the facts of the case and on the applicable law. Focus, in particular, on how you assess the responsibility of each of the Tison brothers for the deaths of the four victims. Couch your response in the form of a petition to the Supreme Court.

2. In *People v. Washington,* the homicide was perpetrated not by one of the robbers but by the gas station owner who was being robbed. The owner first shot and killed the defendant's accomplice, James Ball, and then shot and wounded the defendant, James Washington, who was allegedly fleeing from the vault with a bag of money. Because his accomplice was killed during the course of a felony, Washington was charged with felony murder. The issue for the court was "whether a robber can be convicted of murder for the killing of any person by another who is resisting the robbery." For a person to be convicted of felony murder, should it be necessary for the felon or one of his accomplices to have committed the killing, or should it make no difference whether the killing is committed by the criminal, a victim, a police officer, or anyone else not connected with the felony?

   Write an argument, from the point of view of either Washington's defense attorney or the prosecutor of the case, on how the jury, or the appeals court, should find. Base your argument on the facts of the case as presented and on the applicable law.

3. Jonathan Stamp and his two accomplices, the defendants in *People v. Stamp,* were charged with felony murder for having caused the death of Carl Honeyman during a robbery. The defendants argued that they should not be charged with felony murder because there was insufficient evidence to prove that the robbery was the cause of Honeyman's death. They based this argument partially on the fact that the physicians testifying for the state, who said that they believed the robbery was linked to the victim's fatal heart attack, responded to a hypothetical question that was put to them, and that the doctors had answered in terms of "medical probability" rather than "beyond a reasonable doubt." Further, they argued that the victim was not killed in the perpetration of the robbery, even if his death was linked to the robbery—but was primarily caused by his heart disease and his generally poor physical condition. Finally, they argued that death of the victim from a heart attack was something that they could not reasonably have foreseen.

   How persuasive do you find the defendants' arguments? If you were a member of the *Stamp* jury, would you vote to convict or acquit on felony murder? Explain your reasoning.

4. As in the *Washington* case, the defendants Glenn Hickman and Anthony Rock (*People v. Hickman*) were convicted of felony murder even though none of the robbers actually perpetrated the homicide. Indeed, this is an unusual case of one third party killing another third party—that is, persons who were not either the defendants or the victim—while both were in the process of pursuing the felons.

   The Illinois felony murder statute provides in part that "a person who kills an individual without lawful justification commits murder if, in performing the acts which cause the death . . . he is attempting or committing a forcible felony other than voluntary manslaughter." The defendants maintained that this statute should be interpreted to mean that the person who perpetrated the killing must be the same as the one who is committing or attempting to commit a felony before the felony murder rule applies.

Further, they argued that their case should be controlled by a previous case, *People v. Morris*, in which these circumstances applied:

> In *Morris* the defendant and two cohorts entered a restaurant armed for the purpose of committing a robbery. A struggle ensued between a patron and one of the cohorts during which gunfire erupted and the cohort was killed. The defendant Morris, one of the would-be robbers, was charged with murder of his co-conspirators under the theory of the felony-murder doctrine and was convicted of the crime of murder by the trial court. The reviewing [appeals] court reversed the trial court holding that the felony-murder doctrine is not applicable against a surviving felon when a co-felon is justifiably killed during commission of a forcible felony.

On the other hand, the prosecutors argued that the *Hickman* case should be controlled by another precedent, *People v. Payne*. In this case,

> armed robbers entered the home of two brothers. One of the brothers discharged a weapon to prevent the robbery as did one of the robbers. The other brother was killed and it could not be determined whether he was killed by his brother or the robber. Our [state] Supreme Court in affirming the defendant's conviction or murder stated:

>> Where several persons conspire to do an unlawful act, and another crime is committed in the pursuit of the common object, all are alike guilty of the crime committed, if it is a natural and probable consequence of the conspiracy. . . . It reasonably might be anticipated that an attempted robbery would meet with resistance, during which the victim might be shot either by himself or someone else in attempting to prevent the robbery, and those attempting to perpetrate the robbery would be guilty of murder.

From either the prosecutor's or the defense's point of view, write an argument that the felony murder rule should or should not apply in this case. Apply the facts of this case to the law, particularly taking into account the precedents just cited. How does this case compare and contrast to *Morris*? To *Payne*?

5. Select one of these four cases. Imagine yourself as attorney for the plaintiff or attorney for the defendant. Write a paper in IRAC format to make your case. Define the *issue* in question format. State or summarize the applicable *rules* about homicide. *Apply* the rules, as explained in the "Jury Instructions on Murder and Manslaughter," and apply them to the facts of the case you have selected. Draw a *conclusion* from the application of these rules.

6. Select one of the cases treated in this group. Imagine that you are representing either the plaintiff or the defendant. Compose either an opening statement or a closing argument for this case. Remember that your audience is the jury. Draw on the facts of the case in a way that is likely to have the greatest impact on the jury. Keep in mind, however, that jury members may turn against you— and your client—if they think that you are overly manipulating the facts, being deceptive, making exaggerated claims, or attempting too crudely to play on their emotions. For guidance on developing your statement, see "Models for the Opening Statement and the Closing Argument" at the end of Chapter 2. See also Larry S. Stewart's "Arguing Pain and Suffering Damages in Summation: How to Inspire Jurors" at the end of the Group 3 Readings in Chapter 3.

Sexual Harassment

Intimate violation of women by men is sufficiently pervasive in American society as to be nearly invisible. Contained by internalized and structural forms of power, it has been nearly inaudible. Conjoined with men's control over women's material survival, as in the home or on the job, or over women's learning and educational advancement in school, it has become institutionalized.
— Catherine A. MacKinnon, *Sexual Harassment of Working Women*

In 1993 Kimberly Ellerth was hired as a merchandising assistant for Burlington Industries, a manufacturer of textiles and home furnishings. She worked well and soon was promoted to sales representative in the company's Chicago office. From the beginning of her employment, however, Ellerth had been the subject of unwelcome sexual attention from one of Burlington's vice presidents, Theodore Slowik. He made offensive jokes and comments about her body. During one business trip, Slowik, after staring at Ellerth's legs and breasts for some time, said, "You know, Kim, I could make your life very hard or very easy at Burlington." Ellerth took this to mean that she would have to have sex with Slowik if she wanted to keep her job. She sued Burlington, charging sexual harassment.

Ellerth v. Burlington eventually reached the U.S. Supreme Court, which in June 1998 issued a landmark decision setting strict new standards for sexual harassment in the workplace, increasing the liability of employers, who may now be legally responsible for the sexual harassment of their employees, even if they are not aware that such harassment is taking place.

Women in traditionally male occupations have been especially subject to sexual harassment. *Robinson v. Jacksonville Shipyards* (1991) concerns a female welder who endured verbal harassment from co-workers, obscene graffiti in her work area, and pornographic photos and drawings posted throughout the shipyard. *Llewellyn v. Celanese Corp.* (1988) involves a female truck driver who underwent similar indignities, including men who exposed themselves to her at truck stops. At one stop, someone planted a live snake in her cab. *Andrews v. City of Philadelphia* (1990) concerns a black female police officer who was severely burned when someone put lime inside the clothing in her locker. Nor are such harassments confined to blue-collar workers: *Lipsett v. University of Puerto Rico* (1988) concerns a female resident physician who was routinely harassed by the doctors who supervised (and eventually discharged) her. One told her "that women [doctors] should not go into surgery because they needed too much time to bathe, to go to the bathroom, to apply makeup, and to get dressed."

The legal basis for sexual harassment suits is Title VII of the Civil Rights Act of 1964, which prohibits discrimination on the basis of race, color, religion, national origin, or sex. The language of Title VII has been incorporated into the Equal Opportunities Employment section of the *U.S. Code* (that is, federal law), and elaborated in the *Code of Federal Regulations*. A person who believes that she or he has been sexually harassed can file a complaint with the Equal Employment Opportunity Commission (EEOC), which administers sexual harassment law, and whose guidelines are required to be posted in many workplaces. The EEOC will evaluate the case and then issue the complainant a "Right to Sue" letter, without which a Title VII case cannot be brought to court.

The explosion of sexual harassment suits in the past decade began with the Senate confirmation hearings of Clarence Thomas in 1991, when the Supreme Court candidate was accused of sexual harassment by a former employee, Anita Hill. The Paula Jones suit against President Clinton also maintained the high profile of sexual harassment suits. As an article by John Cloud points out, more than 15,000 sexual harassment suits are filed every year, and from 1991 to 1998, juries rendered more than 500 verdicts on sexual harassment.[1] A 1991 amendment to the 1964 Civil Rights Act gave sexual harassment plaintiffs the right to a jury trial (previously such cases were tried only by a judge) and significantly increased the damages that successful plaintiffs could collect. Such social change has not been without its backlash. (Camille Paglia, a maverick humanities professor, declared in "A Call to Lustiness" that "an antiseptically sex-free workplace is impossible and unnatural. . . . I want a society of lusty men and lusty women whose physical and mental energies are in exuberant free flow.")[2] And even those who fully support sexual harassment laws sometimes question their effects. According to Vicky Schultz, a professor at Yale Law School, "the problem we should be addressing isn't sex, it's the sexist failure to take women seriously as workers." She argues that

> the popular view of harassment is both too narrow and too broad. Too narrow, because the focus on rooting out unwanted sexual activity has allowed us to feel good about protecting women from sexual abuse while leading us to overlook equally pernicious forms of gender-based mistreatment. Too broad, because the emphasis on sexual conduct has encouraged some companies to ban all forms of sexual interaction, even when these do not threaten women's equality on the job.[3]

This chapter allows you to explore some of the legal, social, and moral aspects of sexual harassment in the workplace. The first group of readings pro-

---

[1] "Sex and the Law," *Time*, 23 March 1998: 53.
[2] *Time*, 23 March 1998: 54.
[3] "Sex Is the Least of It: Let's Focus Harassment Law on Work, Not Sex." *Nation*, 25 May 1998: 11, 12.

vides an introduction to the subject with three selections: "Quid Pro Quo," by Catherine MacKinnon; "What Is Sexual Harassment?" by Tracy O'Shea and Jane LaLonde; and "But Is It Sexual Harassment?," by attorney Monica E. McFadden.

The second group of readings focuses on two hypothetical sexual harassment cases—one in the form of a diary and one in the form of trial testimony. These selections are followed by model jury instructions on sexual harassment.

The third group focuses on one major type of sexual harassment, *hostile work environment*. With this type of harassment, the victim must endure sexual advances, verbal taunts, or physical assaults of the kind that create an intimidating or abusive environment and that often lead the employee to quit the job in desperation—a form of termination called "constructive discharge."

The fourth group of readings focuses on five cases of *quid pro quo* sexual harassment—the kind in which job advantages are contingent on the granting of sexual favors.

■ Group 1 Readings: *What Is Sexual Harassment?*

This first group of readings provides an introduction— from three different perspectives—to sexual harassment. The first, "Quid Pro Quo" (referring to one of the two main legal forms of sexual harassment, the other being "hostile work environment"), is excerpted from the groundbreaking book Sexual Harassment of Working Women, *by Catherine A. MacKinnon, a professor of law at the University of Michigan and at the University of Chicago. In 1977 a paper that MacKinnon wrote and gave to a federal appeals court considering a sexual harassment case became the basis for a landmark decision* (Barnes v. Costle) *that represented, as she later wrote, "the most explicit treatment of the issues to date and a holding that sexual harassment is sex discrimination in employment." This decision was the first in which a plaintiff had won a sexual harassment suit on the basis of violation of Title VII of the 1964 Civil Rights Act, which prohibits discrimination on the basis of race, color, religion, national origin, or sex. (Previously, courts had ruled that unwelcome sexual advances toward working women were "personal" and did not constitute sex discrimination.) Two years later, MacKinnon published* Sexual Harassment of Working Women, *a book that, according to Jeffrey Toobin of* The New Yorker, *"surely ranks as one of the most influential law books of the late twentieth century."*

In "What Is Sexual Harassment?," Tracy O'Shea and Jane LaLonde, pseudonyms for professionals in the publishing and banking industries, offer advice to those, like themselves, who have suffered sexual harassment. In particular, they categorize several types of sexual harassment and sexual harassers.

Finally, in "But Is It Sexual Harassment?," Monica E. McFadden, who practices law in Chicago, explains to other attorneys what constitutes sexual harassment.

Quid Pro Quo

■ _____ ■

Catherine A. MacKinnon

Women's experiences of sexual harassment can be divided into two forms which   1
merge at the edges and in the world. The first I term the *quid pro quo*, in which
sexual compliance is exchanged, or proposed to be exchanged, for an employment opportunity. The second arises when sexual harassment is a persistent *condition of work*. This distinction highlights different facets of the problem as
women live through it and suggests slightly different legal requirements. In both
types, the sexual demand is often but an extension of a gender-defined work role.
The victim is employed, hence treated, "as a woman." In the quid pro quo, the
woman must comply sexually or forfeit an employment opportunity. The quid pro
quo arises most powerfully within the context of horizontal segregation, in which
women are employed in feminized jobs, such as office work, as a part of jobs ver-
tically stratified by sex, with men holding the power to hire and fire women. In a
job which is defined according to gender, noncompliance with all of the job's
requirements, which may at the boss's whim come to include sexual tolerance or
activity, operatively "disqualifies" a woman for the job. In sexual harassment as a
condition of work, the exchange of sex for employment opportunities is less
direct. The major question is whether the *advances themselves* constitute an
injury in employment.

Quid Pro Quo

This category is defined by the more or less explicit exchange: the woman must   2
comply sexually or forfeit an employment benefit. The exchange can be anything
but subtle, although its expression can be euphemistic: "If I wasn't going to sleep
with him, I wasn't going to get my promotion";[1] "I think he meant that I had a job
if I played along";[2] "You've got to make love to get a day off or to get a good beat";[3]
"[Her] foreman told her that if she wanted the job she would have to be nice'";[4] "I
was fired because I refused to give at the office."[5]

Assuming there has been an unwanted sexual advance, a resulting quid pro   3
quo can take one of three possible shapes. In situation one, the woman declines
the advance and forfeits an employment opportunity. If the connections are
shown, this raises the clearest pattern: sexual advance, noncompliance, employ-

_____

Sexual Harassment of Working Women. New Haven: Yale UP, 1979.
Footnotes 30–54 and symbol notes used from original, renumbered here as footnotes 1–31.
[1]Working Women United Institute, "Speak-Out on Sexual Harassment," Ithaca, N. Y., May 4, 1975
(typescript), at 15.
[2]*Id.*, at 30.
[3]Peggy A. Jackson, quoted in Jane Seaberry, "They Don't Swing to Sex on the Beat," *Washington
Post*, October 13, 1975.
[4]*Monge v. Beebe Rubber*, 316 A.2d 549, 560 (N.H. 1974).
[5]*Redbook*, at 149.

ment retaliation. In situation two, the woman complies and does not receive a job benefit. This is complex: was the job benefit denied independently of the sexual involvement? Is employment-coerced sex an injury in itself or does compliance mean consent? Should the woman in effect forfeit the job opportunity as relief because she complied sexually? In situation three, the woman complies and receives a job benefit. Does she have an injury to complain of? Do her competitors? In a fourth logical possibility, which does not require further discussion, the woman refuses to comply, receives completely fair treatment on the job, and is never harassed again (and is, no doubt, immensely relieved). In this one turn of events, there truly is "no harm in asking."[6]

In situation one, the injurious nexus is between the imposition of the sexual   4 requirement and the employment retaliation following upon its rejection. To date, all of the legally successful suits for sexual harassment[7] have alleged some form of the trilogy of unwanted advances, rejection, retaliation. In Adrienne Tomkins's case[8] the advances occurred over a lunch that was to include a discussion of her upcoming promotion. She refused to comply, was threatened, demoted, and eventually terminated.[9] In the case of Paulette Barnes,[10] her supervisor repeatedly insisted that she engage in social and sexual activity with him. When she refused, he took away her duties and eventually abolished her position. A witness in Barnes's case described a classic situation of this type in her own experience with the same man:

Q. Did you ever have any problems working under Mr. Z?
The Witness: Well, the problem started when I took a trip to Puerto Rico with Mr. Z in February of 1971. When we got back he took all of my secretarial duties and gave them to E____ M____, who was white. Something happened in Puerto Rico, and he used to write me nasty little notes and things like that.
By Miss Barnes:[11]
Q. Could you tell us exactly what happened in Puerto Rico or is this confidential information?
A. Well, when we went to Puerto Rico, I was going there as his secretary to take notes on the conferences. . . . When we got there he was supposed to make hotel reservations. He took that out of my hands and when we got there he didn't do it. We waited around until 10:00 or 11:00 that night to get a hotel.

---

[6]See discussion in chap. 6 [of *Sexual Harassment of Working Women*]. The reference is to the classic formulation by Herbert Magruder of the position that a man should not be liable in tort for emotional harm resulting from his sexual advances. Magruder, "Mental and Emotional Disturbance in the Law of Torts," 49 *Harv. L. Rev.* 1033, 1055 (1936).
[7]These cases are discussed in detail in chap. 4 [of *Sexual Harassment of Working Women*].
[8]Her lawsuit is reported as *Tomkins v. Public Service Electric & Gas Co.*, 422 F. Supp. 553 (D. N. J. 1977), *reversed on appeal*, 568 F.2d 1044 (3d Cir. 1977), discussed in chap. 4, *infra*, at 69–72.
[9]*Tomkins v. Public Service Electric & Gas Co.*, 442 F. Supp. 553 (D.N.J. 1976), *rev'd*, 568 F.2d 1044 (3d Cir. 1977).
[10]Her lawsuit is reported as *Barnes v. Costle*, 561 F.2d 983 (D.C. Cir. 1977), discussed in chap. 4, *infra*, at 65–68.
[11]Ms. Barnes was not represented by counsel at this point in the proceedings.

> When we got there we went upstairs and put our bags in the room. His bags were in the room, so, he said he had to go and take someone to another hotel, and he would be back to get his things.
>
> When he came back he started undressing, and I told him that he could not stay in the same room with me. He asked me why, and I said—
>
> Mr. H____: (attorney for Mr. Z) I think we get the picture.
>
> Appeals Examiner: There was a dispute over room accommodations. Is this one of the problems?
>
> The Witness: Right.
>
> Appeals Examiner: You came back and then what happened?
>
> The Witness: He started writing me nasty little notes telling me he no longer wanted me to work for him. He started giving all of his duties to E____ instead of me, and he even asked me to quit working for him because of what happened.[12]

This structure was also presented in *Alexander v. Yale*, a case complaining of sexual harassment in education. A student who refused a professor's advances allegedly received a low grade in a course.[13] In a related situation, a woman who declined to "join [her employer] in his bed" while on a business trip was reminded at lunch the next day that she was soon to be reviewed for reappointment, that her chances depended largely upon his support and recommendation, and that she would be well served if she "linked both her professional work and her personal life more closely to his own needs." She did not do so. Subsequently she was not renewed, a decision in which his lack of support and negative recommendation were instrumental. He stated publicly that in his decision he regretfully recognized the fact that they had not been able to establish "a closer personal relationship." Women commonly report such a man's insistence that a sexual relationship is essential to their working relationship[14] and that without it the women cannot maintain their jobs.

Some employers use job sanctions to promote the sexual harassment of their female employees by male customers or clients, as well as to assure their own sexual access, and to punish the noncompliant:

> June, a waitress in Arkansas, was serving a customer when he reached up her skirt. When she asked her manager for future protection against such incidents, she was harassed by him instead. "They put me on probation," she recalled, "as if I was the guilty one. Then things went from bad to worse. I got lousy tables and bad hours."[15]

---

[12]Transcript of administrative hearing 171, 174, *quoted in* Brief for Appellant at 18–20.

[13]*Alexander v. Yale*, 459 F. Supp. 1 (D. Conn. 1977).

[14]My own research and, for example: "her new supervisor asked her to lunch to discuss a promotion. Over the meal, in a nearby hotel, he said that he wanted to go to bed with her that afternoon and that it was the only way they could have a working relationship." Ann Crittenden, "Women Tell of Sexual Harassment," *New York Times*, October 25, 1977.

[15]Leslie Phillips, "For women, sexual harassment is an occupational hazard," *Boston Globe*, September 9, 1977.

In each case, following the woman's refusal, the man retaliated through use of   7
his power over her job or career. Retaliation comes in many forms. The woman
may be threatened with demotions and salary cuts; unfavorable material may be
solicited and put in her personal file; or she may be placed on disciplinary layoff.[16]
In one case, a sexually disappointed foreman first cut back the woman's hours,
then put her on a lower-paying machine. When she requested extra work to make
up the difference, he put her to sweeping floors and cleaning bathrooms. He
degraded and ridiculed her constantly, interfered with her work so it was impossible for her to maintain production, and fired her at two o'clock one morning.[17]
In another case, failing to extract sexual favors, the supervisor belittled the
woman, stripped her of her job duties, and then abolished her job.[18] In another, a
supervisor, following rejection of his elaborate sexual advances, barraged the
woman with unwarranted reprimands about her job performance, refused routine
supervision or task direction, which made it impossible for her to do her job, and
then fired her for poor work performance.[19]

Sudden allegations of job incompetence and poor attitude commonly follow   8
rejection of sexual advances and are used to support employment consequences.
When accused of sexual harassment, men often respond that they were only
trying to initiate a close personal relationship with a woman they liked very much.
In Margaret Miller's situation,[20] her superior at the bank appeared at her door,
bottle in hand, saying, "I've never felt this way about a black chick before."[21]
"Women who refuse become just as abruptly disliked. In this case, the bank stated
that the reason for Ms. Miller's firing was her "insubordination to Mr. Taufer."[22]
Under parallel factual circumstances, one judge pointedly concluded: "Ms. Elliott
was not terminated because of . . . her insubordination except such insubordination as was embodied in her refusal to go along with Lawler's propositions."[23]

Women whose work had been praised and encouraged suddenly find them-   9
selves accused of incompetence or of sabotaging their employer's projects and
blamed for any downturn in business fortunes. The investigator in Diane
Williams's case[24] was suspicious:

---

[16]*Tomkins, supra,* note 9 illustrates these consequences.

[17]*Monge v. Beebe Rubber,* 316 A.2d 549 (N.H. 1974).

[18]*Barnes v. Train,* 13 FEP Cases 123 (D.D.C. 1974), *rev'd sub nom. Barnes v. Costle,* 561 F.2d 983
(D.C. Cir. 1977). On this motion the allegations of fact are provisionally considered as if they
were true.

[19]*Williams v. Saxbe,* 413 F. Supp. 654, 655–6 (D.D.C. 1976). Order denying motion to dismiss and
motion for summary judgment by Judge Richey.

[20]Her lawsuit is reported as *Miller v. Bank of America* 418 F. Supp. 233 (N.D. Cal. 1976), *appeal
pending,* discussed in chap. 4, *infra,* at 61–63.

[21]Clerk's Record, *quoted in* Brief for Appellant, at 39.

[22]*Id.,* at 80.

[23]Sherry Elliott's lawsuit, *Elliott v. Emery Air Frieght,* is unreported; it is discussed in chap. 4,
infra, at 72–73.

[24]Diane Williams's case is reported as *Williams v. Saxbe,* 413 F. Supp. 654 (D.D.C. 1976) and is discussed in chap. 4 [of *Sexual Harassment of Working Women*], *infra,* at 63–65.

How did an employee hired in January suddenly become so bad that during the period from July 17 through September 11, a case was built for her separation? . . . I believe a program of faultfinding, criticism and documentation of minor offenses was undertaken.[25]

Some employers do not even bother to create the appearance of actual job incompetence: 10

The man who was second in command to my boss asked me out and I fielded it. I was charming but I said no. He said that I'd be sorry. . . . Later on, my boss said he had evidence of my inefficiency on which he could fire me, and when I said it wasn't possible, he said he would make evidence. He was supported by the man who had asked me out.[26]

Situation two, the second of the three forms of the quid pro quo, requires 11 inquiry into the impact of compliance. Even less is known about women who comply than about those who refuse. But there is little to suggest that women who meet sexual conditions receive job benefits. More common is the following: "I'm told by the supervisors that the women on the oil slopes and in the camps are fired if they do and also fired if they don't."[27] This suggests that employment sanctions simultaneously prohibit and compel compliance with employment-related sexual advances. Women both must and may not comply—or face the consequences. Constantina Safilios-Rothschild suggests one possible explanation for men's failure to deliver promised job rewards:

Actually it has been quite questionable whether women did in fact obtain economic security through marriage, or desirable occupational advancement in exchange for sexual favors. In the latter case, most often adulterous men, for a variety of motivations (including guilt and fear that their infidelity will be suspected or known) have not returned favors or have done very little. Others have simply not honored the existence of any self-understood or implicit contract of exchange of favors.[28]

This implies that men believe that whenever women are advanced on the job, an exchange of sexual favors must have occurred.

---

[25]Investigative Report, No. 8, 1972, *quoted in* Brief of Appellee, at 4.

[26]Quoted in Enid Nemy, New York Times News Service, *Newark Star-News*, August 24, 1975. This is identical to the fact pattern in *Munford v. James T. Barnes & Co.*, 441 F. Supp. 459 (E. D. Mich. 1977).

[27]*Redbook*, at 217. A recent complaint filed in the Alaska federal district court alleged that the woman was rejected for the position of equal employment officer with a pipeline contractor because she refused sexual relations with the employer's senior management official. *Rinkel v. Associated Pipeline Contractors, Inc.*, 16 E.P.D. IP#8331 (D. Alaska 1977). See also Kerri Weisel, "Title VII: Legal Protection Against Sexual Harassment," 53 *Washington Law Review* 123 (1977), at 124.

[28]Constantina Safilios-Rothschild, *Women and Social Policy* (Englewood Cliffs: Prentice-Hall, 1974), at 66.

If such a compact were made and broken, a woman attempting to get the   12
benefit of her bargain would encounter little sympathy and probably less legal
support. But this misconstrues the issue. Whether or not the woman complies, the
crucial issue is whether she was sexually coerced by economic threats or
promises. Requiring her to decline would allow the employer to impose such a
deal in bad faith, secure sexual favors, and then assert she had no right to complain because she had done what he had no right to demand. Her compliance does
not mean it is not still blackmail. Nevertheless, allowing a compliant woman to
sue for sexual harassment when an exchange fails leaves open the unattractive
possibility of encouraging women to acquiesce in unwanted sex for purposes of
career advancement, knowing that they can enforce the man's promise if he does
not perform as agreed. For this reason (among others) it would seem preferable
to define the injury of sexual harassment as the injury of being *placed in the position* of having to choose between unwanted sex and employment benefits or
favorable conditions. From the standpoint of proof, situation two would then
make a woman's case weaker (although not impossible) than before she complied. It would simply undercut the plausibility of the argument that her advancement was contingent upon compliance. Such a posture would support women in
refusing unwanted sex, and discourage abuse of the cause of action through
attempts to get whatever could be gained through sexual compliance and
reserving legal resort for times when it did not work out.

"The other side" of sexual harassment is commonly thought to be raised by   13
situation three, in which women who comply with sexual conditions are advantaged in employment over men or over women who refuse. Despite the indica-
tions that few benefits redound to the woman who accedes, much folklore exists
about the woman who "slept her way to the top" or the academic professional
woman who "got her degree on her back." These aphorisms suggest that women
who are not qualified for their jobs or promotions acquire them instead by sexual
means. Do these stories raise serious difficulties for a conceptualization of sexual
harassment as integral to women's employment disadvantagement?[29]

Since so few women get to the top at all, it cannot be very common for them   14
to get there by sexual means. Yet undoubtedly some individuals, whether by calculation or in the face of discrimination and lack of recognition of their qualifications, must have followed this course. A mix of these elements is suggested in the
following (undocumented) observation: "By using sex, women were able to
diminish the social distance between important, rich or powerful men and themselves, and to obtain desirable goods such as economic security and social status
through marriage, or a desirable job or promotion through sexual relations with
an influential man."[30] Although the author of this statement qualifies it substantially in a footnote, she concludes: "There are, however, even at present a few outstanding examples of professional women, businesswomen, and artists whose

---

[29]The legal import of this and other possible complications for sexual harassment as a cause of
action is discussed in chap. 6 [of *Sexual Harassment of Working Women*].
[30]Rothschild, *supra*, note 28, at 66.

occupational success is largely due to a powerful male with whom they have a long-standing and open relationship."[31] This portrays a relationship that appears more like a consensual one than like unwanted sex acquiesced in for career advancement, although it is admittedly difficult to tell the difference.

As discussed earlier, women consistently occupy the lowest-status, lowest-paying jobs, much lower than men of the same education and experience. Given this, it is difficult to argue that women in general receive advantages even remotely comparable with the sexual harassment to which they are subjected. This, after all, is the implication of the supposed "other side": some women are hurt by the practice, it is said, but then look at all the women who benefit from it. Initially, it seems worth asking, as a hypothetical parallel, whether if some blacks are advantaged just because they are black, that is a reason why blacks who are disadvantaged because they are black should continue to be. Next, from the available data on sex discrimination, it cannot be deduced that women in general (and certainly not in individual cases) derive undeserved job opportunities from sexual compliance or by any other means. On the contrary, it would be difficult to show that cooperating women derive advantages commensurate even with the disadvantage of being female. Of course, it is impossible to estimate how much worse women's position might be without the possible contribution of unwanted sex to their side of the bargain. Overall, however, the statistics on discrimination suggest that no fulfillment of any requirement, sexual demands included, results in job status for which women are qualified, much less undeserved advancement.

Presuming for the argument that these stories have some truth, one might look at women who "succeed" this way as having extricated themselves from a situation of sexual harassment. Rather than deriving unfair advantages because of their sex, perhaps they had to meet unfair requirements because of their sex. In this perspective, the woman who "slept her way to the top" may have been the woman who would not have been hired or promoted, regardless of qualifications, without fulfilling sexual conditions, conditions equally qualified men do not have to fulfill. Moreover, for every woman who "got her degree on her back," there were men who offered rewards, supervision, and attention to her development only at a sexual price. To the extent they are true, then, these stories document a point seldom made: men with the power to affect women's careers allow sexual factors to make a difference. So the threats are serious: those who do not comply are disadvantaged in favor of those who do. (It is also seldom considered that a woman might be an attractive sexual object to her superior for the same reasons that *qualify* her for the position.)

Further, there may be compelling explanations for these stories other than their truth. How many men find it unbearable that a woman out-qualifies them in an even competition? Perhaps they assuage their egos by propagating rumors that the woman used her sexuality—something presumptively unavailable to men—to outdistance them. These stories may exemplify a well-documented inability of both sexes to see women in any but sexual terms. Willingness to believe the

---

[31]*Loc. cit.*

stories may illustrate the pervasive assumption that, since a career is so intrinsically inappropriate for a woman, her sexuality must define her role in this context, as well as in all others. This dovetails with the prior assumption that if a woman's sexuality is present at all, she must be receiving unfair consideration.

Certainly it is important to establish in individual cases whether a woman is   18
complaining about a failed attempt cynically to use sex to get ahead or a bona fide situation of sex imposed as a career requirement. But to believe that instances raised in situation three symmetrically outweigh the injury that women as a whole suffer from sexual harassment ignores the evidence and provides a convenient excuse not to take the problem seriously. Whatever they mean, people who do not take sexual harassment seriously are an arm of the people who do it.

What Is Sexual Harassment?

Tracy O'Shea and Jane LaLonde

In one of his books, Robert Fulghum wrote an essay discussing how a person's   1
identity and self-worth are tied into what can be written on a two-by-three-inch business card. He goes on to discuss how often the first question people ask when they first meet is "What do you do?" It is the answer to this question that immediately forms the basis of a person's initial impression of you. When that identity is stripped away, people's impression of you changes. In fact, your own impression of yourself changes. During my experience with sexual harassment, I often thought of this essay and the simple truth behind it. That is only one of the devastating effect of sexual harassment—it takes away your very identity.

Like a fog that rolls in slowly and unnoticed until you find yourself lost in   2
the midst of it, sexual harassment is insidious and pervasive. Besides the obvious effects—fear, discomfort in your own working environment, loss of pride in your work, to name a few—sexual harassment affects the very core of who you are as a person. Being victimized by it forces you to question yourself and to lose faith in your own judgment. This self-doubt does not confine itself to your work life; it invades your personal life as well, seeping into your relationships with friends and family. Every single comment and interaction with the harasser chips away at you slowly until suddenly one day you discover that you feel completely shattered.

Because every incident of sexual harassment is different, and because it chal-   3
lenges the fundamental dynamics of the male/female relationship, it is very difficult to create a precise, all-encompassing definition of sexual harassment. The legal definition does not touch upon what sexual harassment really means to a victim, and the impact it has on all aspects of her life—not just the professional. In an effort to clearly show how wide-ranging the effects of harassment really are,

Sexual Harassment: A Practical Guide to the Law. New York: St. Martin's, 1998.

we have expanded upon the legal definition and created what we call the "real world" definition.

Sexual Harassment: The Legal Definition

Sexual harassment is considered a type of sex discrimination and as such is covered by Title VII of the Civil Rights Act of 1964.   4

The legal precedent was established in 1986 in the case *Meritor Savings Bank*   5
v. Vinson (477 U.S. 57), in which the U.S. Supreme Court ruled that harassment is sex discrimination and is therefore illegal under Title VII of the Civil Rights Act.

In regard to sexual harassment, Title VII says the following: 6

> Sexual harassment is legally defined as any unwelcome sexual advances or requests for sexual favors. It also includes any verbal or physical conduct of a sexual nature when the following criteria are met:
>
> - Submission is made explicitly or implicitly a term or condition of an individual's employment;
> - Submission to or rejection of such conduct by an individual is used as the basis for employment decisions affecting such individual;
> - Such conduct has the purpose or effect of substantially interfering with an individual's work performance or creating an intimidating, hostile, or offensive working environment.
>
> Sexual harassment may include physical conduct, verbal conduct, or nonverbal conduct such as sexual gestures or pornographic pictures.

Under the law, there are two basic types of sexual harassment: *quid pro quo*   7
and *hostile environment*.

Quid Pro Quo

Latin for "something for something," *quid pro quo* harassment is the most blatant   8
and is what most people think of when they hear the words *sexual harassment*. Quid pro quo harassment is a request for sexual favors in exchange for a promotion, a raise, or even the right to keep a current job. More succinctly, the Equal Employment Opportunity Commission (EEOC) defines it as:

> Unwelcome sexual advances, requests for sexual favors, and other verbal or physical conduct of a sexual nature constitute "quid pro quo" sexual harassment when:
>
> Submission to such conduct is made either explicitly or implicitly a term or condition of an individual's employment or submission to or rejection of such conduct by an individual is used as the basis for employment decisions affecting such individual.

Because quid pro quo harassment is usually so blatant, one incident is usually enough to support a legal claim. The classic example of quid pro quo sexual harassment is the middle-aged manager requesting sex from his pretty young secretary as a condition to retain employment.

Hostile Work Environment

Hostile-work-environment harassment is not as clear-cut as quid pro quo. With   9
hostile-environment harassment, the victim is subjected to unwelcome sexual advances, requests for sexual favors, and other verbal or physical behavior that interferes with her work performance or creates an intimidating or offensive working environment. The main difference between hostile environment and quid pro quo is that any requests for sexual favors are not made in exchange for a raise, promotion, or as a condition for continued employment.

In an effort to clarify the definition of *hostile environment*, the EEOC created   10
the following guidelines:

> In determining whether or not an environment is hostile, it must be determined whether or not the conduct unreasonably interfered with an individual's work performance or created an intimidating hostile or offensive working environment.

The EEOC suggests that courts look at the following criteria:

- whether the conduct was verbal, physical, or both
- how frequently it was repeated
- whether the conduct was hostile or patently offensive
- whether the alleged harasser was a co-worker or a supervisor
- whether others joined in perpetrating the harassment
- whether the harassment was directed at more than one individual
- were remarks hostile and derogatory?
- did the harasser single out the charging party?
- did the charging party participate in the exchange?
- what was the relationship between the charging party and alleged harasser?

Hostile-environment claims can include many types of behavior: sexually   11
degrading or sexually explicit comments, crude jokes or stories, leering at someone's body, displaying pornographic drawings or photographs, circulating dirty cartoons, rubbing up against someone, touching a person in an inappropriate manner, sexually based teasing, sexual favoritism, forcing an employee to put up with offensive behavior, and forcing an employee into a situation that she feels uncomfortable in.

This type of sexual harassment is much more difficult to define than quid pro   12
quo because of the subjectivity involved; what one person may find offensive may not be offensive to someone else. *Therefore it is critical that the victim tell the harasser as early as possible that the behavior is unwelcome.* Silence on the part of the offended party may be construed as acceptance. Unless the actions of the harasser are particularly egregious, it takes more than one incident to constitute hostile-environment harassment.

The second sexual harassment case heard by the Supreme Court was in 1993.   13
In *Harris v. Forklift Systems, Inc.*, the Supreme Court began to define what
created a hostile workplace. In *Harris* the Court held that a victim of sexual
harassment does not have to show that she suffered "severe psychological injury"
in order to state a claim. (Until this ruling, some federal courts had been
demanding the plaintiff offer proof of psychological trauma in order to validate
her claim.) The Supreme Court established a two-pronged test:

1. The conduct complained of must "be severe or pervasive enough to create
   an objectively hostile or abusive environment that a reasonable person
   would find hostile or abusive."
2. The victim must "subjectively perceive the environment to be abusive."

If both of these criteria are met, there is sufficient proof of a hostile work environment.

In *Ellison v. Brady*, 924 F.2d (9th Cir. 1991), the "reasonable woman" standard   14
was developed. In this case it was determined that sexually harassing behavior
must be looked at from the perspective of the victim and should be based upon
the unique experience of women. The ruling states in part that "the reasonable
person standard still must consider the victim's perspective and not the stereotyped notions of acceptable behavior." Since this ruling, the EEOC and the courts
will look at whether the victim was subjected to behavior and conditions that any
reasonable woman would consider sufficiently severe or pervasive enough to
alter the conditions of employment and create an abusive working environment.

Blurred Boundaries

In an effort to develop a better understanding of sexual harassment, F. Till has   15
expanded upon quid pro quo and hostile-environment harassment to develop a
model that breaks sexual harassment into five different types. This model is helpful
because it is very easy for the victim to become confused about what is and what
isn't sexual harassment. Many comments that are borderline may or may not be considered harassment based upon the context of the behavior and the dynamics of the
victim/harasser relationship. These clearly defined categories help to organize the
victim's thoughts and solidify her perspective as to what is happening to her.

While these basic models clarify the range of sexual harassment, it is very   16
important to note that they are not mutually exclusive, nor are they all-inclusive.
It is not unusual for one case of sexual harassment to include more than one
example from the model. And, of course, there are so many types of harassment
that it is virtually impossible to develop a model for each. Of these five types,
gender harassment is the most common.

Sexual harassment can sometimes be ambiguous, and it is not uncommon for   17
a victim to wonder if she is truly being harassed. There is no one-size-fits-all definition of sexual harassment that could clearly define every scenario. The difficulty with developing a concrete definition is that person A may find person B's

actions objectionable, but person C does not. Here are some broad guidelines as to what is and what is not harassment:

Five Types of Sexual Harassment

Type 1: Gender Harassment	Generalized sexist remarks and behavior
Type 2: Seductive Behavior	Inappropriate and offensive (but essentially sanction-free) behavior with no penalty attached to noncompliance
Type 3: Sexual Bribery	Solicitation of sexual activity or other sex-linked behavior by promise of rewards
Type 4: Sexual Coercion	Coercion of sexual activity by threat of punishment
Type 5: Sexual Imposition or Assault	Gross sexual imposition such as touching, fondling, grabbing or assault

What Is Sexual Harassment	What Is NOT Considered Sexual Harassment
"You look like you need to get laid."	"You do not look very happy. Is everything okay?"
"That blouse really shows off your curves."	"You look nice in yellow."
Repeatedly asking a co-worker out once she's made it clear that she's not interested.	Asking a co-worker out on a date.
Your boss telling you your bonus is dependent on accompanying him to an out-of-town conference and that you do not need your own hotel room.	Your boss requesting your presence at a company dinner.
If the person repeatedly finds opportunities to brush up against you; if it is no longer accidental but deliberate.	Co-worker accidentally brushes up against you.
Sexually explicit jokes, e-mails, or faxes sent to your attention.	An isolated incident of an innocent "blue" joke making its way around the office, not directed at anyone specifically.

The Real-World Definition of Sexual Harassment

OK, so you know the legal definition of sexual harassment. Unlike most other civil 18
wrongs, the situation isn't over when the case is settled. The ramifications can
remain with you for the rest of your life. Sexual harassment can have many far-
reaching effects, such as a loss of self-esteem and paranoia. When we were being
victimized, we both suffered devastating bouts of self-examination. We'd constantly
ask questions such as: Am I crazy? Did I imagine this? Am I overreacting? Am I
doing something wrong? Could I be doing something differently? If this is sexual
harassment and other people witness it, why aren't they doing anything about it?

Having experienced sexual harassment firsthand, we know that it means different things to different people. While the law does a fair job of setting the 19
parameters as to what will and will not be tolerated, we found it helpful and reas-
suring to put down our thoughts as to what sexual harassment means to us.

Defining Sexual Harassment from a Victim's Perspective

To the victim, sexual harassment is a traumatic experience that undermines self- 20
esteem and builds paranoia. Other words associated with this definition are
humiliation and degradation. After experiencing sexual harassment, we developed our own definition:

To the victim, sexual harassment is very real and has many varied meanings: 21

- worrying about what other co-workers think about me and this situation
- worrying that I will be blamed
- being afraid people will think less of me for letting this happen
- second-guessing myself—what did I wear, what did I say, how did I act?
- questioning my own sensitivity to this situation
- questioning my own emotional stability
- staying awake at night wondering how to deal with the situation
- no longer deriving a sense of pleasure from my work
- having to let go of something I've worked so hard to achieve
- a terrible loss of self-esteem due to my inability to control things at work
- the real possibility of destroying either my career or my sense of self-worth
- having to confront a corporation I always thought was there to protect me
- the possibility of litigating with a corporation with resources beyond mine
- reliving every moment of interaction and wondering how I could have
  avoided it
- physical problems, such as anxiety attacks, insomnia, weight loss or gain,
  depression, dizziness, cold sweats, and stomach pain
- watching over your shoulder at all times
- being afraid and not really knowing why
- a pervasive fear of seeing this person
- being embarrassed and humiliated by the situation
- being lonely because no one really seems to understand
- not being free to do the work I was hired to do without a confrontation

- having someone making comments about my physical attributes
- being thrown off balance by having my attention taken off of a business situation and focusing it on my appearance
- feeling weak and alone
- finding out it that the situation doesn't disappear if you work harder, smarter, or faster

Sexual harassment is:

- a loss of identity and purpose
- a loss of self
- loss of your livelihood—even if you are not fired outright, you are no longer allowed to do your job without being hassled
- synonymous with shame and fear
- loss of hope for the future
- not about romance, a relationship, or physical pleasure
- about power

Sexual harassment can steal your goals and ambitions. Instead of being driven and excited about prospects for the future, just surviving through the day can be torture. Many women have left much-loved careers and decided that maybe they just were not meant to work in a particular industry or job. Many women, under the intense stress of sexual harassment, give up and come to believe that they do not have any control over their work environment and are powerless to end the abuse. We know that sexual harassment *does* have a great impact on your life. We also hope that by knowing what your options are, you will realize you are not alone, that you can safeguard yourself and your career and ultimately benefit from our experiences, and in the process manage to protect your:

- self-esteem
- career
- mental and physical health
- personal relationships
- energy
- right to do your job
- sense of security
- sense of power
- life as you know it
- hope for the future

Common Feelings and Responses

Some of the worst side effects of sexual harassment are the self-doubt and despair over the perceived lack of control over the situation. This lack of control, coupled with little factual information on how to remedy the situation, can destroy your self-esteem and often leads to depression. Some common characteristics of depression include a lack of hope and a general loss of pleasure in things that once brought you great joy.

It is typical, while undergoing sexual harassment, to cease caring about any-   23
thing. We know from personal experience that sexual harassment is such an overwhelming energy drain that just dealing with simple tasks like getting up in the morning can pose an enormously difficult challenge. Things as innocuous as crossing the street or making a phone call can become difficult. You lose confidence in your abilities and question your own judgment in even the simplest situations. As a result, you sink deeper and deeper into yourself, until you are completely isolated from your own life and numb to what is happening around you.

While these feelings and thoughts are not unusual, it is recommended that you   24
seek professional guidance. Talk to a trusted friend, family member, psychiatrist, or other health care professional. Getting professional help is nothing to be embarrassed or ashamed about; nor is it a reflection on the strength of your character. In most instances, it will not harm your legal rights. In fact, when building a case, it may be important to show that you sought professional help, especially when seeking punitive damages for intentional infliction of emotional distress. . . .

A Portrait of a Harasser: Why Do They Exhibit Such Behavior?

It is important to realize that sexual harassment is about power, not sex. In a   25
sexual harassment case, the harasser is using sex as a weapon to manipulate and to exert control over a victim. Harassers are very rarely looking for sexual gratification; their need is to feel superior and dominant to women. While the characteristics of harassers include all races, ages, professions, and even genders, a majority of harassers meet one or more of the following criteria:

- Male
- Exhibits prejudicial behavior against all groups but his own
- Views women as inferior or unequal
- Believes women should be submissive
- Believes women should be completely dependent on men for emotional and financial support
- Treats all women in a derogatory manner (not necessarily a sexually degrading manner)
- Is threatened by a change in the status quo

The easiest claims to prove are those in which the harasser is in a position of power over the victim, when he has a direct impact on the financial and professional development of the victim. However, there are extenuating circumstances in which the harasser does not have direct control over the victim.

A Co-worker as a Harasser

Because the offender is not in a position to harm the victim directly (by having   26
control over either career path or income), the courts look at the entire situation.

Victims must be able to prove that the company was aware of the situation and was given the opportunity to take action. It must also be proven that the company did not do anything to stop the harassing behavior.

A Customer or Client as a Harasser

Again, the offender is not in a position to harm the victim financially or profes- sionally. However, if the company knowingly and willingly places the victim in a situation in which she is open to harassing behavior, or if the company tries to force a person to grant sexual favors to someone the company wants to please, the company can be held liable.   27

> Tracy's situation was slightly different; it crossed the line between the harasser as a co-worker and the harasser as a client. Her harasser was a contract worker for the company and therefore could be considered a co-worker, yet because of his job responsibilities, he was perceived as being more valuable to the company, and therefore he was to be "kept happy" and treated as if he were a client.
>
> This man held no authority over her financially or professionally, yet he made her working life unbearable. Soon after the harassment began, Tracy informed her supervisor about the behavior. Nothing was done. Due to the unique nature of his job, Tracy understood that she was to "put up" with the situation. Her supervisor held the position that since Wayne would be difficult to replace, Tracy should either accept the behavior or change her lifestyle to avoid the behavior (take vacation days whenever Wayne would be in the office, or transfer some of her responsibilities to others in order to avoid working with Wayne).

Five Types of Harassers

Harassers can be broken down into five basic types; however, they are not nec- essarily exclusive: 28

Serial Offender	A person who persists in abusive behavior despite repeated warnings and even psychological treatment. Often this harasser is so weak in character and so easily threatened by change that he views harassment as the only way to preserve the status quo.
Onetime Offender	A person who, for some reason, victimizes one person and never does it again. Perhaps it is because this one victim challenged him in a way that truly frightened him, or he received treatment and learned to handle his emotions, or he was frightened into stopping the behavior by the threat of a public sexual harassment complaint.

continued

The He-Man	A person who feels the need to constantly prove his masculinity. Often this type of offender does this by degrading women. For this type of harasser, the only way to secure power and status is to steal it from those around him. Whereas most men build self-esteem and self-worth through their own achievements, the He-Man never truly rises from his own plateau, but pushes those around him down in order to make the gap appear wider.
The Laggard	A person who does not intend any offense, but still harbors the mind-set of earlier eras. The Laggard is often an older man who was raised in different times and was taught to treat women one way, but finds that the rules have changed. While he realizes that it is no longer acceptable to call woman "honey," "dear," or "sweetie," he slips into his old ways on occasion. Even though this behavior is often subconscious and unintentional, it can be detrimental to a woman because it colors how others in the working environment perceive her.
The Old Guard	Similar to the Laggard, an Old Guard harasser recognizes his behavior and defends it. Often this type of harasser is still having difficulty accepting that women are in the workforce (and that they are no longer exclusively relegated to traditional female jobs such as secretary). These men were raised to treat women as sex objects, love interests, or relatives, and now that the times have changed, they resent having to treat women as colleagues.

Why Do Men Harass Women?

Since every case is different, it is impossible to list every specific reason men harass women, but fear plays a large part. It can be fear of change in the status quo, fear of those who are different, fear of appearing to be "less of a man" because a woman can handle the same job. It can be fear of losing a promotion to a female or fear of having to report to a woman (and therefore appear subservient). 29

As discussed earlier, women in male-dominated professions are more likely to be victims of sexual harassment than women in industries with a more equitable male-to-female ratio. Men working in a previously male-only environment view female co-workers as infiltrators among their ranks. Fearful that working with a woman will change the status quo (by making them change their behavior—no more stories of sexual conquests, no more sexually explicit posters or jokes, etc.), somehow make them appear to be less masculine (the macho status of the job changes if a woman can do it), or impact their lives in some other negative way, these men use every weapon at their disposal to drive women away. This includes 30 embarrassing them, threatening them, and/or harassing them until they give up and go away (often by quitting their jobs). These men view this as a victory.

Several resources have indicated that the basic male/female gender dynamic   31
plays a part in why men harass women. Men have traditionally viewed women as sexual/feminine beings: the mother/caregiver, the wife/lover, or the sister in need of protection. It was only recently that women in large numbers took on the non-sexual role of colleagues and equals. This transition to a different mind-set has proven quite difficult for many men, and while most men are able to draw the line on what behavior is and is not appropriate in the workplace, some men are unable to do so. It is these men who cannot adjust to the new role of women who end up possibly becoming harassers.

The Male Response to Sexual Harassment

Most men recognize and abhor sexual harassment, and these men treat female   32
colleagues with the utmost respect. However, some men simply do not under-stand the concept of sexual harassment—because they believe that they would be flattered by sexual advances from a female in the workplace, they have difficulty comprehending why women get offended. Women take offense because, unlike men, they have been stereotyped by physical appearance and gender and they have had to overcome many barriers in order to be taken seriously as part of the workforce. (Remember the proverbial glass ceiling, equal pay for equal work?) After struggling for so long to be taken seriously, women get offended when all of that time and effort is minimized by a man who has never had to struggle with the same issues. In addition, women (who by far outnumber men as victims of sex crimes such as rape) live with the very real fear of physical assault and often view harassment as a prelude to physical violence.

Offenders offer several excuses for their behavior: She can't take a joke or she   33
welcomed it. Harassers interpret "stop" as playing hard to get. They view persis-tence as part of a "chase." It is also not uncommon for offenders to accuse victims of leading them on by smiling, flirting, or simply being nice. The one commonality is that they never view their behavior as wrong.

■ But Is It Harassment? ■

Monica E. McFadden

Three potential clients want to sue their employers for sexual harassment.   1

The first is a clerical worker. She is outraged that over the past several years her   2
supervisor referred to her as "a pretty girl" and made grunting noises when she passed by in a leather skirt. She estimates about six such incidents in two years. She has not complained to anyone. Friends told her she should see an attorney instead.

Trial (Dec. 1998): 48–50.

The second is a factory worker. Four months ago, her supervisor drew her into his office, rubbed his hand over her breast, and said if she would not sleep with him, he would have her changed to the night shift. She said no. He has not repeated the behavior. Last week she was changed from the day to the night shift.

The third is a male laborer in an all-male workplace. His coworkers repeatedly called him names suggesting homosexuality. One threatened to rape him. He quit.

Harassment is a hot topic in the news and in the legal community. Polls show that upwards of 25 percent of women report that they have been harassed in the workplace, with more than half of those reporting emotional harassment or inappropriate touching.[1] Men are targeted in 11 percent of the cases reported to the U.S. Equal Employment Opportunity Commission (EEOC).[2]

But not all boorish and scandalous behavior is legally considered to be sexual harassment. The first challenge for any lawyer counseling a potential victim is winnowing out the legally actionable cases. The second challenge is evaluating the feasibility of the case based on legal elements and damages.

Sexual harassment generally falls into two categories: quid pro quo harassment, or the explicit tying of job benefits to sexual acts or submission to sexual conduct, and hostile environment harassment, or the active creation of an offensive work environment.

In 1998, the U.S. Supreme Court clarified the definition of quid pro quo harassment. In *Burlington Industries v. Ellerth*[3] and *Faragher v. City of Boca Raton*,[4] the Court ruled that employers are strictly liable for a supervisor's sexual harassment when the worker's immediate (or higher) supervisor takes a tangible employment action against the worker, such as firing, failing to promote, or changing benefits. Quid pro quo harassment cases, such as the example of the factory worker above, should now be easier to identify and prosecute.

Hostile environment claims such as the examples of the clerical worker and laborer are more difficult. This article focuses on those claims.

Evaluating the Conduct

Much unpleasant behavior is not legally sexual harassment. Under the "at will" doctrine, employers have no legal obligation to create fair and pleasant workplaces. The theory is the worker who doesn't like the work environment or the attitude and behavior of his or her supervisors can leave.

But employers do have an obligation to ensure that their workplaces are free of sex discrimination. In 1986, in *Meritor Savings Bank v. Vinson*,[5] the Supreme Court ruled that sexual harassment in the workplace is sex discrimination and violates Title VII of the Civil Rights Act of 1964.[6]

---

[1]James T. Madore, *When Work Turns Ugly*, NEWSDAY, Apr. 5, 1998, at 4.
[2]*Id.*
[3]118 S. Ct. 2257 (1998).
[4]118 S. Ct. 2275 (1998).
[5]477 U.S. 57 (1986).
[6]42 U.S.C. §§2000e-2000e-17 (1998).

Since then, several cases, including three decided in 1998, have fleshed out 12 what does and what does not constitute actionable sexual harassment.[7]

Essentially, the rule is that sex-specific and derogatory language, sexual 13 advances, requests for sexual favors, and other verbal or physical conduct of a sexual nature constitute sexual harassment if the conduct is unwelcome, severe, and pervasive enough that it creates an objectively intimidating, hostile, or offensive work environment and the worker subjectively finds it abusive. These factors are "determined by only looking at all the circumstances," which may include "the frequency of the discriminatory conduct; its severity; whether it is physically threatening or humiliating, or a mere offensive utterance; and whether it unreasonably interferes with an employee's work performance."[8] Both male and female workers can be sexually harassed.

To separate boorish and scandalous behavior from sexual harassment, first 14 consider the answers to the following important questions.

1. Was the behavior directed at your client? If not, it will be difficult to make 15 out a harassment case unless the conduct is so pervasive that the entire workplace is tainted (think *EEOC v. Mitsubishi Motor Manufacturing of America*).[9] The standard legal principle applies—clients can generally only recover for harms directed at or directly harmful to them.

2. Is the conduct sexual in nature? It is vital to know the exact words or 16 conduct. If the behavior was not sexual in nature, it will not be considered sexual harassment. It might still be sex discrimination if only one gender was subjected to the language or behavior at issue.[10]

3. Was the conduct directed at your client because of his or her sex? Conduct 17 does not need to be motivated by sexual desire to be sexual harassment.[11] But the behavior does need to be discrimination on the basis of sex. The nature of the conduct will suffice to show that motivation.[12] Be aware that if both genders were treated the same way by the harasser (unlikely, but possible), this could, per *Oncale v. Sundowner Offshore Services, Inc.*, defeat a sexual harassment case. How were workers of the opposite sex treated?

4. Was the conduct unwelcome? This is a central element to any claim of 18 harassment and will be one of the first questions that will be asked during the plaintiff's deposition. If he or she welcomed the activity (e.g., a fully consensual sexual relationship) or did not find it unwelcome, there is no case. This is what distinguishes harassment from the consensual sexual affair or mutual joking relationship, even with a supervisor and even if the conduct or language was blatantly sexual. Ask carefully.

---

[7]*Faragher*, 118 S. Ct. 2275; *Ellereth*, 118 S. Ct. 2257; *Oncale v. Sundowner Offshore Servs., Inc.*, 118 S. Ct. 998 (1998); *Harris v. Forklift Sys., Inc.*, 510 U.S. 17 (1993).

[8]*Harris*, 510 U.S. 17, 23.

[9]990 F. Supp. 1059 (C.D. Ill. 1998).

[10]*See* discussion in *Doe v. City of Belleville*, 119 F.3d 563, 575–76 (7th Cir. 1997), *vacated*, 118 S. Ct. 1183 (1998).

[11]*Oncale*, 118 S. Ct. 998.

[12]*See* discussion in *Doe*, 119 F.3d 563, 575–76 (7th Cir. 1997), *vacated*, 118 S. Ct. 1183 (1998).

5. Was the conduct severe and pervasive enough to create an objectively 19
hostile environment? Many cases that pass the previous hurdles fail here. The
behavior may have been boorish and unwelcome, but unless it created an objectively hostile environment, it is not actionable.

This is an objective standard. Would a reasonable person find the behavior 20
severe and pervasive enough to create a hostile environment? Right now, a "reasonable person" is usually the one we all came to know and love in law school—
a middle-class, middle-aged heterosexual male. There is a movement to tailor the
definition of the "reasonable person" to fit the plaintiff, that is, to establish the
"reasonable woman" standard. However, that is not the general rule. Remember,
most of these cases will be resolved on summary judgment where your "reasonable person" is a federal judge. Be realistic.

Explore the factors cited in *Harris v. Forklift Systems, Inc.*:[13]   21

- How often did the conduct occur? Generally, single acts of harassment are
  not actionable. Even when harassment was repeated numerous times,
  courts have refused to find it sufficiently "severe and pervasive" when it
  was sporadic and primarily verbal in nature.[14] Also consider the time that
  elapsed between the conduct and its effect on the person. Some harassment is like water torture. At first it is mild and seems innocuous, but over
  time it becomes severely painful.

- Was the harassment verbal or physical in nature? This interacts with frequency. Generally, physical touching of private areas of the body (e.g.,
  breasts, buttocks) is considered sexual harassment, even if it occurs only
  once.[15] However, less sensitive touching (e.g., arm, hand) may require
  more frequency. Verbal comments generally require significant regularity
  to be actionable.

- Was the behavior physically threatening or humiliating? Think, for
  example, of the woman grabbed and mauled in a meeting or hallway
  where she is present as a professional (Tailhook) or the person threatened
  with rape. Remember, however, that threats and humiliation not taken
  seriously by the plaintiff are generally not actionable. Ask the plaintiff
  how he or she reacted.

- Did the conduct unreasonably interfere with the worker's performance,
  even if it was nonsexual? If, for example, a worker on the assembly line
  routinely interrupted and touched a coworker of the opposite gender
  (think *Mitsubishi*), the fact that the conduct interfered with the plaintiff's
  ability to perform might make it sexual harassment and/or discrimination.

---

[13]510 U.S. 17.

[14]*See, e.g., Brill v. Lante Corp.*, 119 F.3d 1266, 1274 (7th Cir. 1997); *c.f. Bales v. Wal-Mart Stores, Inc.*, 143 F.3d 1103 (8th Cir. 1998).

[15]*See, e.g., Fall v. Indiana Univ. Bd. of Trustees*, No. 3:96-CV-205, 1998 U.S. Dist. LEXIS 12174, at *21–22 (N.D. Ind. July 23, 1998).

Remember that "severe and pervasive" is in the eye of the beholder, the "rea-   22
sonable person." The average woman may consider the repeated use of the word
"bitch" severe and pervasive sexual harassment. The Seventh Circuit does not
agree.[16] But Justice Antonin Scalia, in *Oncale*, wrote that a smack on a male or
female secretary's buttocks could reasonably be perceived as abusive.[17] If you are
in doubt, run the facts at issue through LEXIS or WESTLAW and past nonlawyers.
You might be surprised at what the courts consider legally tolerable or intolerable
and what lawyers consider "severe and pervasive."

6. What impact has the sexual harassment had on your client? While *Harris*   23
and *Faragher* make clear there is no requirement that a victim show that his or
her work performance or psychological well-being was affected by the harassment, your client must, subjectively, find it abusive. Realistically, no judge or jury
is going to consider the harassment more severe or pervasive or having more
impact than your client does.

7. Did the employer know or should it have known of the harassment? Title   24
VII creates an employer duty not to allow a sexually hostile environment. The
courts have generally required a breach of that duty on the employer's part, that
is, it knew or should have known of the harassment and did nothing.

After the Supreme Court decisions in *Ellerth* and *Faragher*, there will appar-   25
ently be no requirement of knowledge if the harasser is a supervisor. But the
knowledge standard will probably still apply when the harasser is a coworker or
a customer.[18]

It is best if your client actually complained to the employer and can document   26
the complaints. Does your client have copies of memos to the human resources
department or the supervisor? Are there notes in the victim's or the harasser's personnel files? Are there witnesses to the harassment and your client's complaints?

Notice can be proved in all the ways available in tort, such as prior incidents   27
and complaints about the harasser or the environment and conduct so blatant and
pervasive that supervisors could not miss it. Be aware that if your client failed to
report the behavior, that fact will probably be used as a defense.

● ● ● ●

For Deliberation and Argument

1. MacKinnon draws distinctions among three types of quid pro quo sexual
   harassment but maintains that all three demonstrate the extent to which
   women have an "employment *dis*advantagement." To what extent do you
   agree with this conclusion? Base your discussion on your own observations of
   sexual harassment on the job, along with any other reading you have done on
   the subject. Consider also whether you believe that the problem of sexual
   harassment of women in the workplace may have changed since MacKinnon's
   book was first published in 1979.

---

[16]*Galloway v. General Motors Serv. Parts Operations*, 78 F.3d 1164, 1167–68 (7th Cir. 1996).
[17]118 S. Ct. 998, 1003.
[18]*See Ocheltree v. Scollon Prods., Inc.*, No. 97-2506, 1998 WL 482783, at *3 n.1 (4th Cir. 1998).

2. In "What Is Sexual Harassment?" Tracy O'Shea and Jane LaLonde focus on the legal, emotional, and psychological aspects of sexual harassment. Based on your own experience with or knowledge of the subject, how accurate, how fair do you believe their assessments of both the victims of harassment and of the harassers to be? To what extent do you find O'Shea and LaLonde's categories—"Five Types of Sexual Harassment" and "Five Types of Harassers"— useful in clarifying your ideas and in helping you to understand the social and psychological aspects of this subject? For example, do you accept the view that sexual harassment—like rape—is about power, not sex, and that it derives partly from males' insecurities about their status in a changing world and workplace?

3. Consider the three scenarios of sexual harassment with which Monica E. McFadden begins "But Is It Harassment?" in light of the seven numbered criteria she discusses. Applying these criteria, which, if any, of the scenarios would a federal judge likely consider sexual harassment? Which are not? Why?

■ Group 2 Readings: *Two Hypothetical Scenarios*

The readings in this group present two hypothetical sexual harassment scenarios. You will be asked to assess the strength of each plaintiff's case, applying the jury instructions on "Hostile Work Environment" that follow.

The first scenario is in the form of a diary kept by a plaintiff who set down in writing her experiences as a computer specialist over several weeks as she was repeatedly subjected to unwelcome sexual advances from a male co-worker and found no support from her supervisor. The second scenario is in the form of courtroom testimony, in which a former college librarian, responding to direct examination by her attorney, details the sexual harassment she endured over the course of a school term at the hands of a senior faculty member. These scenarios are followed by a set of model jury instructions for cases of hostile work environment sexual harassment.

Keeping a Sexual Harassment Journal

Monday, November 4

My first day on the job. There are ten computer technicians and fifteen computer analysts in my area. Everyone seems very nice; they even hang out together after work. After all the problems that I had at my last job, I am really happy about the

Sexual Harassment Claims: Step by Step. New York: Barron's 1998.

relaxed and friendly atmosphere here. But, I am sure that I can use the six-month probationary period to establish myself.

One of my coworkers, Ralph, came right up to me and offered to help me in 2 any way he could. The woman who sits next to me told me that Ralph is a top producer and that the boss, Bradley, relies on him very heavily.

Monday, November 11

Most of the group went out drinking after work on Friday. I did not go, but I heard 3 that Beverly, one of the techs, got drunk and danced on the table. Today, everybody is making jokes about being able to look up her skirt.

Wednesday, November 13

Ralph asked me if I want to go out drinking with the group. I said no. He then 4 asked me if my husband let me go out by myself, or whether he insisted that I be chained to him. I told Ralph to stop kidding around. Sandra, who sits near me, overheard Ralph and told him to cut it out.

Bradley, the supervisor, has an office that is just a few feet away from my 5 desk. A few times a day, he comes out of his office and stands over my shoulder and watches me work.

Friday, November 15

Ralph again invited me to go out for drinks with the group. When I said no, he 6 asked me if I intended to go right home and jump into bed with my husband: "What do you do all weekend?" he asked, "Spend all of your time under the sheets?" Embarrassed, I laughed out loud and told him that it was none of his business. Sandra overheard Ralph's comments. This time, she just smirked and looked away.

Later in the day, everyone was talking about their planned night out. This led 7 to a lot of raucous conversation about what might happen at the bar. Someone brought up a bar scene that he had seen on the Playboy channel, which started a long discussion of bar scenes in erotic and X-rated movies.

Monday, November 18

It seems that the Friday night get-together lived up to everyone's expectations. 8 Beverly again did her table dance, joined by Ralph and some of the other techs. They also did a rumba around the bar, and at some point they all crashed into each other. This gave rise to a lot of ribald discussion about body parts in the office today. Bradley was there, and it sounds like he was the life of the party. In fact, Ralph had to give him a ride home and explain his condition to his wife.

Bradley continues to watch me work. He said that I seemed to be a little slow, 9 but I told him that I was confident I would improve.

Ralph came over to ask me if I had ever danced on a table. He said, "I would sure like to look up your skirt," and he sort of grabbed at me. One of the other techs, Omar, came over and asked me if I would dance with him "cheek to cheek" next Friday. From the look on his face, I do not think he was talking about the cheeks on our faces.   10

Beverly told me that Ralph thinks he is a "ladies man." She says that, whenever he bothers her, she shrugs it off and tells him to go away.   11

One of my other coworkers, Erica, vaguely mentioned that she thought that someone had charged Ralph with sexual harassment a few years ago.   12

Tuesday, November 19

I got cornered in a conference room by Ralph, who asked me why I was not nicer to him. I felt that he was going to try to grab me, but all he did was stand very close to me and rub my arm. I told him to leave me alone, that I was not interested in him, and that I did not like him touching me. I ran out of the conference room red-faced and flustered. Erica asked me what was wrong, and I told her. She suggested that I go to Human Resources.   13

Then, as if things weren't bad enough, a few hours later Bradley came over and said that my productivity statistics were too low. I told him that I had been having trouble concentrating, and that I would try to do better in the future.   14

Human Resources sent me a copy of the personnel manual today; all new employees get it after they have been here for a short time. I skimmed through it, and it says that employees are encouraged to go to HR if they have problems and that HR will try to help them.   15

Tonight, I am going to speak to my husband about what has been going on with Ralph. Maybe he can give me some suggestions. It has finally dawned on me that Ralph's had his eyes on me since my first day at work.   16

Thursday, November 21

My husband suggested that I follow whatever the company policy is and lodge a complaint against Ralph. I had a chance to read the personnel manual. It says that any complaints must first be taken to your supervisor. I really do not want to complain to Bradley because I know that he is good friends with Ralph. I will just wait and see what happens.   17

Just a few minutes ago, Ralph called me at home. He told me that he wanted to come over, and suggested that I arrange a threesome. I told him that he was gross and that, if he bothered me again, I would have my husband take care of him.   18

Friday, November 22

Ralph gave me a nasty look when I arrived at work this morning, but he did not say anything to me.   19

Bradley came out of his office and put me on verbal warning for poor per- 20
formance. He says that I have not been able to increase my productivity very
much. I asked him what I could do to improve, and he said that we will discuss
it later.

Just before I left work, I found a card on my desk. It bore a picture of a nude 21
woman with her lips puckered up. The inside of the card said, "I'm sorry, let's
make up." It had no signature.

Saturday, November 23

Ralph called me at home to ask me if I was sorry about the way I had treated him. 22
I told him that he was never to call me again and that I was going to tell Bradley
about his antics.

Monday, November 25

I met with Bradley about my job performance. He said that I was too inexperi- 23
enced, that I made too many errors, and that I always seemed too preoccupied
and anxious to concentrate on my work. He told me that I would be put on final
warning if things did not improve. He also said that he would be reviewing my
work again at the beginning of the new year. I did not believe that my error rate
had been high, and I asked Bradley if I could have a look at my production
records.

I told Bradley that I was having a hard time doing my work because of the way 24
that Ralph had been treating me. I told him about Ralph's remarks and that Ralph
had been calling me at home. Bradley replied that this was the first time he had
heard of any problem and that Ralph could not be blamed for the errors that I
made. He said that I was in a "precarious situation" and should attend to my work
instead of complaining about my coworkers.

Later in the day, Bradley called me into his office. He told me that he had 25
spoken with Ralph, who denied bothering me in any way. Ralph claimed that the
entire staff, including the women, supported him and that I was just the "new kid
on the block." Bradley said that because Ralph was a long-term, trusted
employee and because he denied my complaint, there was nothing more that he
could do.

Thursday, December 5

The cleaning woman came upon me crying in the bathroom after I had found a 26
card on my desk, signed by "R," saying that he knew I was in trouble and that I
could come to him for help.

Beverly happened to walk past me as I was standing at my desk drying my 27
tears. I told her what I thought Ralph had done, and she told me that three or four
women had transferred from the unit because of him. She thought that one of

them might have left the company and filed a charge with an agency that handles discrimination complaints. Beverly also said that Bradley kept his "head in the sand" when it came to Ralph's behavior.

But, she also said that she had been Ralph's friend for a long time, that he did not mean any harm, and that "boys will be boys." 28

Thursday, December 19

Things have been quiet for a few weeks. Ralph went on vacation for a few days, and just before that I had no problems with him. Maybe it is because he has been put in charge of working with a group of new trainees. 29

My work seems to be okay; at least, Bradley has not made any more complaints about it. I have decided to go to the office Christmas party next week. Then, maybe I will be viewed as more of a team player. 30

Monday, December 23

Tonight was the office Christmas party. It was held at the same bar where they always hang out. No spouses were allowed to come. Entertainment was provided by two women and a man, dressed as Santa and his helpers, who slowly stripped down to nothing but red and green underwear and then walked around mingling with the guests. 31

Everyone had a lot to drink, and I even decided to have a few drinks myself. When we sat down to eat, I tried to sit far away from Ralph, just in case. But, I felt someone groping at my knees from under the table, and, sure enough, it was him. He had managed to get a seat across from me and was trying to get his hands under my dress. When the meal was over, the came up to me, said "Merry Christmas. Let me jingle your bells," and tried to put an ornament down my blouse. When I looked at it, it was a nude Santa Claus whose private parts were quite large and detailed. 32

I had had enough. I yelled at Ralph that I was sick and tired of his harassing me and that I would use any means necessary to get him to stop. I headed for the door. I looked around to see if anyone could help me, but the only person next to us was Bradley, who was in a stupor. Ralph caught up with me, spun me around, and kissed me. The restaurant manager saw him and said, "He's really got the hots for you." I kicked at Ralph's shins. He jumped back, and I ran out the front door. 33

Thursday, January 2

To celebrate the New Year, I have decided to go to Human Resources and tell them what Ralph has been doing. I hope that they can help me. I cannot spend another sleepless night worrying about what will happen in the office each day. 34

Courtroom Testimony: Hostile Work Environment at School

Q. What is your occupation?

A. I am trained as a teacher.

Q. What do you teach?

A. I hold state credentials to teach Spanish or English as a second language in high schools or junior college.

Q. Are you currently employed?

A. No.

Q. When were you last employed, and where?

A. I last worked for the defendant, _____ College, three years ago when all this happened.

Q. How old are you today?

A. Thirty-two.

Q. And where were you born?

A. I was born in Panama, near the Canal Zone.

Q. In the Canal Zone?

A. No, just west of there. I am a citizen of Panama.

Q. Where did you learn to speak English?

A. I've always loved languages and been good at them. I've always wanted to teach them, ever since I was a child. I had a good friend who was the daughter of an American serviceman.

Q. And you learned from her?

A. Yes, and then I studied a lot in school, and later made more American friends. I taught some of them a little bit of Spanish.

Q. Are you married?

A. Yes.

Q. When did you meet your husband?

A. When I was nineteen years old.

Q. How did you meet him?

A. At a dance in the Canal Zone. He was a lieutenant, I think a junior lieutenant in the American Navy. He right away helped me get a job teaching Spanish to some American sailors at the Navy base he worked at.

Q. And when did you come to the United States?

A. Eleven years ago. I was almost 21 and had been married already a year. My husband's tour of duty was over then.

Q. Is your husband still in the service?

A. No, he is something between an electronics engineer and an electronics technician, but he's unemployed now.

Q. What did you do when you came to the States?

"Hostile Environment," 50 *Proof of Facts* 2d 162 (1988).

A. We lived in _____, and I went to school to be a teacher. It took a long time because I had to keep house too, and my husband was sick for a while, and I had to take care of him. I didn't get my credential until four and one-half years ago.

Q. And what did you do then?

A. I tried to find a job, but it was hard. I was looking for almost six months. It was very disappointing, very frightening.

Q. And did you eventually find a job?

A. Yes, but not teaching.

Q. You wanted a teaching job?

A. Yes, of course.

Q. Do you have an Immigration Naturalization Service work permit?

A. Yes, and I expect to become a United States citizen next month.

Initial Hiring; First Sexual Harassment

Q. Where did you finally find a job?

A. I heard from a friend that there was an opening for an ESL— that's English as a second language—teacher at the South Campus of _____.

Q. Do you know where this friend is now?

A. No, he moved away, and I haven't heard from him in about a year. We were never very close. He was just my husband's buddy.

Q. So you applied for a job at South Campus?

A. Yes, with Mr. D.

Q. Could you describe the application process?

A. Well, my friend said to just call Mr. D's secretary and set up an appointment with him, so I did.

Q. Did you have to fill out a civil service application?

A. No, not then. Later I did, after I was hired.

Q. So you just set up an appointment with Mr. D and went and saw him, and that was it?

A. Yes. They wanted me to bring a resume and my college transcripts, and I did that.

Q. So you saw Mr. D. Do you remember what day that was?

A. Yes, it was August _____.

Q. Tell me what happened when you first got to Mr. D's office.

A. Well, the secretary asked to see my resume and transcripts.

Q. This was in Mr. D's outer office?

A. Yes. He had an outer office with a secretary, and he was in another room.

Q. Could you see Mr. D from the outer office?

A. No.

Q. The door was closed?

A. Yes, all the time, except when someone went in or out of his room.

Q. Did you give the secretary the transcripts and resume?

A. Yes.

Q. And what did she do?

A. She took them into Mr. D's room, and came back, and then she had me wait.

Q. How long?

A. Not really long, ten or fifteen minutes at most.

Q. So, you waited ten or fifteen minutes, and then what happened?

A. The secretary said that Mr. D would see me, and I went into his office.

Q. Could you describe Mr. D?

A. At that time he was in his late fifties, and I found out he was also married with grown kids. About five foot nine or 5 foot ten inches, and kind of heavy. I'd say well over 200 pounds, maybe closer to 240. Thick white hair, tanned, lots of lines on his face. . . .

Q. So what happened when you went into Mr. D's office?

A. He asked me to sit down, and he asked what job I was interested in, and I said the ESL teaching job.

Q. ESL? That means English as a second language?

A. Yes.

Q. And what did he say?

A. He said my grades weren't good enough, but that he could get me a job in the library, and if I did well there, maybe I could do substitute teaching and maybe before long be a regular teacher.

Q. What were your college grades?

A. I had a B-minus average in college, say 2.85 or so. But I think I am a good teacher, and I told him that.

Q. Was there a reason your grades were not better?

A. My grades were partly the result of personal troubles at home, my husband being sick and all. But he was better by this time.

Q. You mean at the time of your interview?

A. Yes.

Q. And did you think your grades disqualified you from teaching?

A. No. In fact, I know someone who has worse grades than I did, and she's teaching political science at that same college.

Q. So, Mr. D offered you a job in the library?

A. Yes.

Q. Did you take this job?

A. Yes, I wasn't happy, but it was better than nothing.

Q. What was the starting salary offered?

A. $_____ per month.

Q. And what did Mr. D say or do after you said you'd take the job?

A. Well, he asked if I was married, and I told him yes.

Q. And then what?

A. He said something about, "You Latina chicks are supposed to be real hot," words to that effect. And he asked if I was getting enough at home.

Q. What did you tell him in response to that?

A. I didn't—well, I didn't really say anything. I was embarrassed. And then he asked me to have a drink with him, and I said no, thank you.

Q. Were you polite?

A. Oh yes, of course. He'd just given me a job, and maybe he was going to give me a teaching job later.

Q. So then what happened?

A. He asked me if I was sure, and he said I was real sexy looking. So I said yes, I was sure, but thanks all the same, you know, and when do I start work? So he told me in September, September 10, and he gave me an application to fill out.

Q. Did you think it unusual that you filled out the application after you were hired?

A. Well, not at the time. It was my first real job in the United States. . . .

Q. How did you feel after your first interview with Mr. D?

A. I was pretty upset. I mean, I felt the man was obnoxious, and he had a lot of power, and I was afraid of him.

Q. What were you afraid of?

A. Well, he could have me fired, and I was afraid that I might have to choose between losing my job and sleeping with him, or at least enduring his coming on to me all the time.

Q. Did you tell anyone about your fears at the time?

A. No.

Q. Not even your husband?

A. No.

Q. Why not?

A. Well, in my culture there is a feeling that if a man likes a woman it's maybe because she wants it. That's what I was taught. And I don't know if maybe deep down my husband feels that same way or not, but anyway, that probably has something to do with why I didn't tell anyone then.

Q. How did these feelings affect you?

A. At first not so bad, but I did have one nightmare about Mr. D. He was chasing me down an alley in my dream, and we were naked, or I was, and he was much bigger in the dream than he is in real life, and I didn't know why he was chasing me, or what he wanted. And I was afraid to report to work the next day, but I did.

Continued Harassment; Hostile Work Environment

Q. When did you begin to work at _____ [defendant]?

A. On September 10.

Q. And when did you next see Mr. D?

A. Well, he wasn't my immediate supervisor. My immediate supervisor was the librarian, and that was who I reported to. But I often saw Mr. D in the faculty lunchroom. Sometimes I would be in there reading or eating lunch, and he would come in with his buddies. . . .

Q. Who were these buddies?

A. Senior faculty members, men, and some administrators.

Q. Can you give us names?

A. _____ [Names].

Q. To your knowledge, what positions did these people occupy at the college?

A. _____.

Q. And what would they do there?

A. Well, they told the most horrible jokes. Jokes I felt made fun of women. But especially Mr. D. He was always laughing and telling dirty jokes about Mexican women as if I weren't there, except of course he knew I was, and sometimes he would look right at me and leer as he was talking to his friends, and then they would, some of them you know, turn and stare at me too.

Q. Were there any other young Latin women working at South Campus when you were there?

A. I didn't know of any, except one girl, I didn't know her name, who worked as a night janitor. She didn't speak English very well. That's about all I knew of her.

Q. There were young Latina students?

A. Yes.

Q. What about English or Spanish teachers?

A. There was a woman from Spain in her fifties. Three or four Anglo women. The rest were men from various places.

Q. Did you get to know any of the Latina students?

A. Two or three, maybe, passingly.

Q. Did any of them know Mr. D?

A. Not that they ever told me.

Q. Did you feel isolated when you first started working at South Campus?

A. Yes, I was lonely, very alone, and kind of scared.

Q. Now, back to the lunchroom, how did those joking men make you feel?

A. Disgusted, scared.

Q. When they came into the lunchroom, what did you generally do?

A. I'd try to ignore them. When I couldn't, I'd leave.

Q. Was there any other quiet place you could go to eat lunch on campus?

A. No.

Q. You didn't have an office?

A. No.

Q. What about the library, or the cafeteria?

A. I couldn't eat in the library. And the student cafeteria was a madhouse, a zoo.

Q. Can you tell us any more about the conversations the men had in the lunchroom?

A. Well, they bragged about who they all knew that they'd all slept with, or wanted to. And they talked about racial differences in women, in bed. Things like that. They'd laugh about it.

Q. Who, in particular, said what? Can you recall specifics?

A. Well, it happened almost every day, and it varied a little from day to day. Mr. D in particular had a number of women that he liked to brag about and describe his sex life with them in graphic detail. It was very embarrassing listening to him.

Q. Did you hear him refer by name to women that you knew?

A. Yes. And also to women that I didn't know. . . .

Q. To your mind, what was his overall attitude towards the women he was discussing?

A. Contemptuous, like he hated them.

Q. How did this make you feel?

A. Personally it made me feel very small and helpless. It also made me feel sorry for the women he was making fun of.

Q. What about the other men? What did _____ say, for example?

A. I don't think he usually said much. He just joined in laughing. In fact, most of the others, besides Mr. D, just let him take the lead, and they mostly listened and laughed, as a rule.

Q. You say most of the others let Mr. D take the lead and just listened. Were there any who were more active?

A. Yes, _____ was pretty bad too. Mr. D talked about his sex life, including one incident where he forced someone at work, and _____ would egg him on and tell more dirty jokes. It almost seemed sometimes like he was competing with Mr. D in his clowning.

Q. Where did he work?

A. He was a teacher in the _____ Department.

Q. Did Mr. D ever object to anything anyone said, on the grounds that it wasn't proper conversation for work when there were other people around?

A. No.

Q. Did he ever object for any other reason to anything anyone said?

A. No, I would have remembered if he did.

Q. Why?

A. Because it would have been so out of character for him.

Q. From what you observed, was it your impression that the remarks of these men were intended especially for your ears?

A. Well, when they were sitting near me I got the feeling that they were more or less talking in my direction. Sometimes I'd look at them, although I tried to avoid them, and usually they'd be looking right at me.

Q. Did you ever object to anything that was being said?

A. Yes, just once. One time, shortly after I began work, they were being extremely obscene and quite loud, and I walked over to their table and asked them to stop it.

Q. Did they respond to your request?

A. Mr. D did. The rest of them just sat there, giggling like a bunch of embarrassed teenagers.

Q. What did Mr. D say?

A. He told me that if I didn't like it, I should leave.

Q. What did you say to that?

A. I don't recall. I could hardly speak. I think I just looked at him and returned to my table and left as soon as I could.

Q. On that particular occasion, did Mr. D's friends say anything after he made that remark to you?

A. No. They all seemed to agree with him.

Q. Were there ever other people in the room, other women?

A. Yes, sometimes.

Q. Did they talk like that around other women?

A. When I was within earshot of them, that's the way they always talked. I don't know if maybe there were some women that they showed some respect to.

Q. You said before that Mr. D said that he had forced a woman employee. Do you mean that he was implying that he had raped her?

A. Yes.

Q. Do you recall specifically what he said? . . .

A. He said it was a secretary he'd once had. That he kept pushing her into the coat closet, and she kept saying, "No, no!" And he imitated the woman with a falsetto voice like that, and they laughed. And finally she just gave up, he said, and let him do it, as he said. And another man said something like, the more they resist, the more it means they want it.

Q. And how did this make you feel?

A. Sick. Scared. Because I was afraid maybe I was next.

Unwelcome Sexual Advance; Battery

Q. Now during this period, the early months of the school year, did you ever see Mr. D, other than in the faculty lunchroom?

A. Just once.

Q. Why not more often, do you know?

A. He worked in the administration building. The library, where I worked, was in a classroom building. The one time I saw him, other than what we've already talked about, was in the library, in the stacks.

Q. About when was this?

A. Around October 10th. I think it was a Thursday, so, yes, it would have been October 10th, I looked that up. And it was about 5:45 in the early evening.

Q. What were you doing when you saw him?

A. I was on my knees, shelving and arranging books on a lower shelf. He sort of came up quietly behind me and started rubbing my neck, asked me what I was doing working so late.

Q. What were you doing, working so late?

A. I told him those were my regular hours that the librarian gave me to work. And I asked him to please stop.

Q. To stop rubbing your neck?

A. Yes.

Q. And did he stop?

A. No. He started moving his hands down the front of my shirt. And he asked me if I wanted to become a substitute teacher.

Q. And what did you say or do?

A. I didn't know what to do. I didn't say anything then. But I took his hands and moved them away.

Q. How? Gently? Roughly?

A. Gently but firmly, I'd say.

Q. And what did he do?

A. He put them back on my shoulders. And he asked me when I got off work.

Q. And did you tell him?

A. Yes.

Q. Why?

A. He was my boss, and I was scared. I needed the job since my husband still wasn't working. Then he asked me out again.

Q. And what did you say?

A. I said, no, I was busy, and to please let me work. But he said not to worry, I could take a break, that I was doing well. And then he started to talk.

Q. What about?

A. About being in the Navy, in Guantanamo, Cuba. All the Cuban girls he'd liked, he'd been with.

Q. He'd been in the Navy too?

A. Yes.

Q. Like your husband?

A. Yes.

Q. Did they know each other?

A. Oh, no, it's just coincidence they'd both been in the Navy. Mr. D was in the Navy in the late fifties, early sixties at the latest.

Q. Okay. So what did you do?

A. I listened. I didn't look at him. I kept moving the back of my neck away from his hands, flinching I guess you say. I kept shelving my books. Finally I asked him to please go away, that he was making me very nervous.

Q. And what did he do?

A. First he grabbed my neck tighter, and I turned to look at him, and I thought he was going to attack me, maybe rape me. But he didn't. He got hold of himself, like, and he walked out without saying good-bye.

Q. Did he grab you tight enough to hurt you?

A. Just a little bit. The big hurt was inside. And fear.

Q. So what did you do then?

A. I finished my work and went home.

Q. Did you tell your husband about this?

A. No, for the reasons I've already said, I didn't tell him until months later.

Q. Did you tell anyone else at the time?

A. No. I really needed that job. And at South Campus he controlled who was hired, fired, and promoted. And he had a lot more friends than I did. In fact, it seemed like everyone was his friend almost, and nobody was mine.

Increased Emotional Distress; Interference with Work Performance; Constructive Discharge

Q. Now, after this incident on October 10th, did your attitude towards your job at South Campus change?

A. Yes, in many ways.

Q. Can you describe how it changed?

A. Well, I had nightmares about Mr. D again. Murder nightmares, rape nightmares.

Q. Were you ever raped by anyone?

A. No, but almost when I was fifteen in Panama. It is often with me, asleep or awake.

Q. How did these nightmares affect your job, or your feelings towards it?

A. I was afraid to be alone in the stacks, which was a lot of my work time. And when I was alone in the stacks, I would hear footsteps, and I would turn around, terrified. And I'd be relieved it wasn't him, at least not this time. And of course I avoided the faculty lunchroom. In fact, I stopped eating lunch. I really didn't want to go to work in the morning at all.

Q. What were your work hours?

A. Usually ten to seven, with an hour for lunch.

Q. Were there restaurants in the neighborhood you could have eaten at?

A. Not in the immediate neighborhood. If I had a car I could have. But I took the bus.

Q. Did your work performance suffer from being afraid, and not being able to eat lunch?

A. Yes. I got tired easily. In November, the librarian said I was going too slow, and making mistakes in cataloguing, typing, shelving, you know, everything. I was a nervous wreck.

Q. So what did you do?

A. Well, I apologized to the librarian and said I knew I could do better, and that I'd try. And then I gathered up my courage, this was right after Thanksgiving, and went to see Mr. D to ask him about substitute teaching.

Q. And what did he say?

A. He said I couldn't teach unless things changed.

Q. Were those his exact words?

A. Yes, pretty much. That or very close to it.

Q. What did you think he meant?

A. I was afraid to ask.

Q. Did you talk about anything else with Mr. D on that occasion?

A. No, I left his office as quick as I could. He was pretty cold.

Q. What happened after that?

A. In early December I started getting terrible rashes. I went to a doctor for them, and she said that they were because of my job. . . .

Q. What did you do after you got this diagnosis from the doctor?

A. Well, since it seemed to my doctor that these rashes were work related, I felt that I had no choice but to quit my job.

Q. What were the rashes like? Itching?

A. No, burning pain.

Q. On what parts of your body?

A. Mostly my arms, legs, and chest.

Q. Did you receive medical treatment?

A. Yes, I received medication, and the rashes went away within five days after I left my job.

Q. How long did you have the rashes altogether?

A. Altogether between three weeks and a month. All through Christmas vacation, beginning maybe ten days before that. And into the first week of January, which is when I quit.

Q. What day did you leave your job?

A. I went in January third to tell them I couldn't come back.

Q. Can you tell us specifically why you left?

A. I'd given up hope of being a teacher there, unless I slept with Mr. D, which I wasn't going to do.

Q. How did you feel at the time about leaving?

A. I was glad to be gone, and at the same time I was terrified of being unemployed.

Q. Do you think you could have stayed on, given the circumstances?

A. No, how could I have?

Consequential Damages

Q. Have you worked since you left South Campus?

A. No.

Q. How much did you earn per month at the time you left?

A. $_____.

Q. How long has it been now since you worked?

A. _____ [time].

Q. Why haven't you worked in that time?

A. I've been scared, and very depressed. I've looked for a job as a teacher, off and on, with no luck. I was offered a job with an acquaintance as a word processor, but my friend said there was sexual harassment in that office too, and I just couldn't deal with that again.

Q. If a safe and appropriate job were available to you, would you be able to take it?

A. Yes.

Q. Are you presently under a doctor's care?

A. I lost my medical coverage when I left my job. I've been to someone at a community mental health center a few times, and she prescribed something, a tranquilizer, I think. I've missed a lot of appointments. I don't think the tranquilizer helps. . . .

Model Jury Instructions for Hostile Work Environment Harassment Case

■——■

B. Henry Allgood

The following jury instructions are generally applicable to an action alleging [1] hostile work environment sexual harassment and constructive discharge under federal law:

"Quid Pro Quo," 62 *American Jurisprudence Trials* 387 (1997).

Hostile Work Environment

1. The plaintiff has brought this action for alleged work place sexual harassment, and before you begin your deliberations it is obviously important for you to understand how that term is defined by the law. In your deliberations you should understand the term "sexual harassment" to refer to unwelcome sexual advances, requests for sexual favors, and other verbal or physical conduct of a sexual nature. I charge you further that in order to constitute sexual harassment, you must further find that submission to such conduct was made, either explicitly or implicitly, a term or condition of the plaintiff's employment, that submission to or rejection of such conduct by the plaintiff was used as the basis for employment decisions affecting her, or that such conduct had either the purpose or the effect of unreasonably interfering with the plaintiff's work performance or the effect of creating an intimidating, hostile, offensive working environment.

2. The definition of sexual harassment that I have just shared with you is a general definition of the term. It encompasses two forms of sexual harassment that are recognized and prohibited by federal law. The two varieties are known as quid pro quo and hostile work environment sexual harassment.

3. Members of the jury, the plaintiff in this case has asserted a cause of action for hostile work environment work place sexual harassment. In order for you to find in favor of the plaintiff on this particular claim, you must find by a preponderance of the evidence the following four elements:
   (a) that the plaintiff was subjected to unwelcome sexual harassment;
   (b) that the harassment occurred because of the plaintiff's gender;
   (c) that the harassment created an abusive work environment that affected a term, condition, or privilege of the plaintiff's employment; and
   (d) that the employer knew, or should have known, of the harassment and failed to take appropriate remedial action to rid the work environment of the harassment.

   I will charge you further with respect to each of these four elements to the hostile work environment sexual harassment cause of action.

4. As for the first element, I charge that the plaintiff must prove to you by a preponderance of the evidence that she was subjected to sexual harassment that was unwelcome by her. It is not sufficient that she prove the existence of conduct, which constitutes sexual harassment; you must also find that she did not welcome such conduct by other employees.

5. With regard to the second element of the prima facie case, you must also find by a preponderance of the evidence that the sexual harassment, if any, that occurred was due to the plaintiff's gender. By that I mean that you must find that the harassment, if any, to which the plaintiff was subjected occurred because of her gender, female.

6. Under the third element of the plaintiff's prima facie case, you must find further that the sexual harassment, if any, was sufficiently severe or pervasive that it created an abusive work environment that affected a term, con-

dition, or privilege of the plaintiff's employment. In making this determination, you are to assess the totality of the proven circumstances from the perspective of a reasonable person. It is not necessary that the Plaintiff prove that she suffered serious psychological injury. Rather, the plaintiff need only establish that the harassment was such that a reasonable person would have found the proven conduct offensive, hostile or intimidating.

7. Finally, in order to find in favor of the plaintiff on a hostile work environment theory of sexual harassment, you must also find that [defendant-employer] knew or had reason to know of the harassment's existence and yet failed to take steps reasonably calculated to rid the work environment of the harassment. With respect to this particular element of the prima facie case it is not necessary for the plaintiff to prove that the defendant had actual knowledge of the harassment. Rather, the plaintiff need only show that the employer had reason to know of the harassment, but failed to make efforts to eliminate it.

Constructive Discharge

The plaintiff has further alleged that her separation from [defendant-employer] constitutes a constructive discharge under Title VII. In order for the plaintiff to recover under a constructive discharge theory you must find by a preponderance of the evidence that the employer, by illegal discriminatory acts, made the plaintiff's working conditions so difficult that a reasonable person in the plaintiff's position would have felt compelled to resign the position. 2

● ● ● ●

For Deliberation and Argument

1. Discuss the strength of the diary writer's sexual harassment case, taking into account some of the following questions:

   - Do you think that keeping a diary was helpful to the woman in this case?
   - Are there statements in the diary that might tend to hurt her case?
   - What facts contained in the diary support a hostile work environment claim? (Refer to the "Model Jury Instructions.")
   - Does the diary help identify potential witnesses on her behalf? Who are they? Are there some people who, although witnesses to the harassment, might not want to testify in her favor?
   - Might the author's credibility be challenged? Why? Do the diary entries help or hurt her credibility?
   - Most victims do not start writing a diary until long after the harassment started. With this in mind, what facts in the diary might the writer have forgotten over time?
   - Does the diary help identify documents that would support the writer's case?

- Does the writer have potential claims against the company? Against Bradley? Against Ralph? Against any co-worker?
- What defenses might the company raise? How credible are the company's potential witnesses?
- What, if anything, could the author have done to strengthen her case?[1]

2. Suppose you were a member of the jury hearing the case of the librarian/teacher plaintiff. Basing your deliberations on the jury instructions on a hostile work environment, explain how you would vote on this case. Take into account whether the plaintiff's testimony establishes the four essential elements of sexual harassment because of a hostile work environment. Consider such key terms in the definitions of the separate elements as *severe, pervasive, reasonable person,* and *the totality of the proven circumstances.* Consider also the degree to which the school administration, as well as Mr. D., is liable for the existence of a hostile work environment, and whether or not the plaintiff's resignation of her job qualifies as a "constructive discharge" under the law. Take into account the defenses that the school district might raise and the degree to which the plaintiff's testimony can be used to rebut such defenses. Use the IRAC format as a framework for organizing your response.

3. Plaintiffs cannot recover damages for emotional distress under Title VII. However, they can file separate tort claims for emotional distress. To what extent do you think either or both of the plaintiffs in this group has a good case to recover damages for intentional infliction of emotional distress? (Refer to the jury instructions in Chapter 3 (pp. 119–21) as the standards by which to assess the plaintiff's claims.)

■ Group 3 Readings: *Hostile Work Environment*

This group presents five cases of alleged sexual harassment of the hostile work environment category. As indicated in previous selections, such as O'Shea and LaLonde, these are not cases in which the victim is threatened with loss of promotion or a job unless she or he submits to sexual demands, but rather cases in which the victim experiences the type of verbal or physical behavior that creates an offensive or intimidating work environment. The previous section presented a set of model jury instructions that specified and defined four required elements for a hostile work environment. In this group, following the cases, you will find Title VII of the Civil Rights Act of 1964, Section 703(a), the basis of contemporary sexual harassment law, along with a section of the Code of Federal Regulations (CFR) that more specifically lays out the components of sexual harassment and the obligations of employers.

In the first case, Zabkowicz v. West Bend Company, *a woman in a traditionally male occupation suffers both verbal abuse and offensive behavior*

---

[1]Questions for this piece prepared by Dale Callender, in *Sexual Harassment Claims: Step by Step.* New York: Barron's, 1998.

from her co-workers. A model student paper *by Mark Tseselsky follows this case. In* Hopkins v. Baltimore Gas and Electric, *a male photographic technician is harassed by a male co-worker.* Kopp v. Samaritan Health System *presents a case of a female cardiology technician who endures both verbal and physical abuse from a male doctor.* Ellison v. Brady *presents the case of a female IRS agent harassed by a fellow agent who writes her "weird" letters in which he claims to love her. And in* Carter v. Caring for the Homeless of Peekskill, *the working relationship between a male counselor and his female supervisor is complicated when their love affair goes sour; he contends that the hostile work environment she created eventually forced his resignation.*

Model Student Paper:
Abusive Words, Offensive Pictures

Carol ZABKOWICZ and Stanley Zabkowicz, Plaintiffs,
v.
The WEST BEND COMPANY, et al., Defendants.

No. 83–C–187.

United States District Court,
E.D. Wisconsin.

July 23, 1984.

FINDINGS OF FACT

Mrs. Zabkowicz was hired by West Bend in 1977 as a general warehouse worker   1
at the company's Oak Creek, Wisconsin, warehouse. Although the number fluctuates, about 20 workers are usually employed at the Oak Creek facility. A warehouse worker's major duty is to prepare skids for loading onto trucks. This requires the use of a forklift or handlift. At the time Mrs. Zabkowicz began to work at Oak Creek, only one other woman, Gayle Dorkey, was employed there. Robert Schommer was the plant manager. The foreman was Wesley Fredericks. After Mr. Schommer moved to a different position in October 1981, Mr. Fredericks became plant manager.

Initially, Mrs. Zabkowicz' relations with her co-workers were good. Her prob-   2
lems began when her husband's brother-in-law, Dennis Murawski, began working at Oak Creek. On more than one occasion, Mr. Murawski asked Mrs. Zabkowicz whether she was wearing a bra. When Mrs. Zabkowicz complained to Mr. Schommer, he told Mr. Murawski to "knock it off" but did not formally discipline him. The recognized forms of discipline under West Bend's policy were an oral warning, a written warning, suspension and discharge.

Zabkowicz v. West Bend Co., 589 F. Supp. 780 (1984).

From 1978 to 1980, Jon Peppey, another co-worker, exposed his buttocks to Mrs. Zabkowicz between 10 and 20 times. Ms. Dorkey, a co-worker, witnessed this conduct on more than three occasions. Mrs. Zabkowicz recalls complaining about Mr. Peppey's conduct to Mr. Schommer and Mr. Fredericks many times. On one occasion, Mr. Schommer called Mr. Peppey into his office and asked him to apologize, but Mr. Peppey refused. No disciplinary action was taken.

From about 1979 until June 1982, other co-workers joined in a campaign of abuse directed at Mrs. Zabkowicz. Defendant Larry Romans is said to have exposed his buttocks to Mrs. Zabkowicz on several occasions. In 1982, when Mrs. Zabkowicz was pregnant and under a 25-pound lifting restriction, Mr. Romans allegedly grabbed his crotch and remarked, "Carol, I bet you'd have trouble handling this 25-pounder." At other times, it is claimed that Mr. Romans grabbed his crotch and growled at Mrs. Zabkowicz.

Mrs. Zabkowicz was frequently subjected to offensive and abusive language. There was testimony that Mr. Piotrowski referred to her in her presence as a "sexy bitch" and "h & h," which meant "hot and horny." The record discloses that defendants Cyrulik, Rozina, Romans and Piotrowski, as well as Mr. Peppey, commonly addressed Mrs. Zabkowicz in such terms of abuse as "slut," "bitch," and "fucking cunt." Co-workers Paul Zierck and Carol Gabriel both testified that they heard these terms directed at Mrs. Zabkowicz.

Mr. Schommer recalled five or six occasions on which Mrs. Zabkowicz complained about abusive language. Mr. Fredericks testified that Mrs. Zabkowicz complained "more than several" times. In a file memorandum dated November 11, 1979, Mr. Schommer summarized a recent meeting with Messrs. Peppey, Rozina, and Fredericks as follows: "We discussed the verbal abusiveness going on in the warehouse, most of which is directed toward another employee." Besides this meeting, Mr. Schommer held occasional general meetings at which company rules against abusive language were recited. No other action was taken to end the abuse directed at Mrs. Zabkowicz. No one was disciplined, even informally, and no investigation was undertaken.

In the period 1979–1982, many sexually oriented drawings were posted on pillars and at other conspicuous places around the warehouse. Mrs. Zabkowicz testified that there were approximately 75 such drawings, many depicting a naked woman with exaggerated sexual characteristics, often bearing the plaintiff's initials. Mrs. Zabkowicz' co-workers also observed the drawings, which they understood as referring to Mrs. Zabkowicz. Paul Zierck recalled drawings depicting the plaintiff giving birth to a black child and having sexual relations with an animal. He testified that the drawings appeared throughout his employment with West Bend, which began in October 1979. Mr. Zierck considered the drawings "cruel."

Gayle Dorkey described numerous drawings posted at the warehouse of naked women bearing insulting messages and subscribed with the plaintiff's initials. She specifically recalled a drawing depicting the plaintiff engaged in oral sex. Kevin Kossow also referred to drawings depicting the plaintiff naked or engaged in a sex act. He characterized the drawings as "down-right demeaning."

Mrs. Zabkowicz testified that she brought offensive drawings to Mr. 9
Schommer or Mr. Fredericks about 50 times. Mr. Schommer recalled only three or
four occasions on which Mrs. Zabkowicz turned in drawings, while Mr. Fredericks did not deny that he received drawings frequently. In response to Mrs.
Zabkowicz' complaints about the drawings, Messrs. Schommer and Fredericks
occasionally called warehouse meetings at which employees were reminded of
the company's policy against posting. The situation would improve for a short
time after such meetings, but then the drawings would reappear.

The plaintiff received permission to take a medical leave of absence beginning 10
on April 26, 1982. On April 23, 1982, Mrs. Zabkowicz observed several of her co-
employees celebrating; when told that they were celebrating her imminent departure, Mrs. Zabkowicz broke into tears. Shortly thereafter, she filed a complaint
with the Equal Employment Opportunity Commission (EEOC).

An investigatory meeting of West Bend and EEOC officials was held on June 11
7, 1982. On June 8, 9, and 10, 1982, Jack DeBraal, West Bend's industrial relations
officer, conducted an investigation at the Oak Creek Warehouse. On June 14,
1982, Mr. Cyrulik was discharged, Mr. Rozina was suspended for two weeks, and
Messrs. Romans and Piotrowski were suspended for two days. In his letters to Mr.
Lyons, the union representative, Mr. DeBraal stated specifically that Mr. Cyrulik
and Mr. Rozina were guilty of verbal abuse and posting drawings. In addition, Mr.
Rozina was charged with indecent exposure. After this disciplinary action, the
posting of offensive drawings and other forms of harassment ceased.

Mrs. Zabkowicz returned to work from her medical leave of absence on May 21, 12
1982, but had to take another leave due to illness beginning on June 17, 1982. Dr.
Brian Kennedy testified that he examined Mrs. Zabkowicz in June 1982 and found
her anxious and subject to crying spells. Throughout the summer, Mrs. Zabkowicz
was seen regularly by her gynecologist, Dr. Calvin Gillespie. Dr. Gillespie testified
that Mrs. Zabkowicz was suffering from diarrhea, vomiting, severe nausea, and
cramping. He diagnosed her illness as "psychophysiological gastro-intestinal disease
due to harassment at work." Mrs. Zabkowicz returned to work on August 17, 1982.

Paper Topic: "Abusive Words, Offensive Pictures"
(Zabkowicz v. West Bend Company)

To what extent do the conditions described in *Zabkowicz v. West Bend Company*
satisfy the four elements of hostile-work-environment sexual harassment, as
specified in the jury instructions (pp. 304–05)? To what extent has the defendant
company violated Title VII of the Civil Rights Act? For example, was the harassment suffered by the plaintiff such that "a reasonable person would have found
the. . . conduct offensive, hostile, or intimidating"? Did the employer, West Bend,
fail to take effective corrective action against the harassment campaign?

During trial the defendants denied that the harassment against the plaintiff
occurred because of her sex. They contended that "a male employee with the plaintiff's same personality would have suffered equally brutal harassment, even if in a
different form." Evaluate this argument. Couch your discussion in IRAC format.

MODEL STUDENT PAPER

COMMENTARY BY MARK TSESELSKY

First I gave the "Findings of Fact" a quick read. Then I read the rules that were   1
relevant to the case. Afterwards I re-read the facts, but this time with an eye for
the facts I was going to include or accentuate in my summary of facts.

Findings of fact in this case were numerous, and the first challenge was to orga-   2
nize them. The text paralleled Mrs. Zabkowicz's complaints with how the supervisors responded to them. But I thought it would make the summary way too long to
follow that approach. My next thought was to organize the facts into separate
groups—for example, initial limited pattern of abuse and a later expanded pattern
of harassment. This way I could keep the summary of facts short and include a
paragraph on employers' actions in between the paragraphs on patterns of abuse.

But no matter how hard I tried to keep it short, my summary of facts still   3
turned out to be too long, nearly three pages at first. I formulated the issue and
quoted the rules and only then did I get a clearer picture of how to arrange the
facts. Perhaps this is the only way to approach an essay with so many facts. The
first version of the facts would be a long summary, but later with the issue and
the rules in mind, I tried to cut the facts section down.

What I realized, once I had the issue and the rules down, was that many of   4
the facts that I cited in the "facts" section were better suited for my "analysis."
Therefore, I replaced detailed facts with summaries in the "facts" section and
saved the details for making my case.

There was little I could concede to the other side in this case because the   5
facts were so blatant, so instead, I used their defense that Mrs. Zabkowicz was
abused not because of her gender, but rather because of her personality ("a male
employee with the plaintiff's same personality would have suffered equally brutal
harassment, even if in a different form"), as a way to start my essay and also to
give it a more focused theme.

I struggled about where to put the description of the management's actions   6
(or rather inactions). In the end, I realized I had to split it up a little bit to give the
beginning of my analysis a real punch.

Second Draft

Mrs. Zabkowicz was one of only two women working at West Bend warehouse   7
facility in 1977. She claims that over the course of the next five years she had
to work in a hostile environment produced by various forms of sexual harassment
from fellow co-workers and tolerated by the employers. The alleged abuse
included numerous incidents of indecent exposure, use of abusive language, and
posting of sexually suggestive drawings. Throughout her ordeal Mrs. Zabkowicz
complained to her supervisors, Messrs. Schommer and Fredericks, who discussed the situation with the offenders and recited company's harassment policy
at general meetings but did not take disciplinary actions against the offenders
(*Zabkowicz v. West Bend*, 589 F.Supp. 780 (1984)).

The harassment ceased and the disciplinary actions against the offenders were taken only after Mrs. Zabkowicz launched a complaint with the Equal Employment Opportunity Commission (EEOC). On April 23, 1983, Mrs. Zabkowicz was a few days short of her medical leave when her co-workers drove her to tears by telling her they were celebrating her imminent departure. Shortly afterwards, Mrs. Zabkowicz launched a complaint with EEOC. This forced Jack DeBraal, West Bend's industrial relations officer, to finally start an investigation, which led to the discharge of defendant Mr. Cyrulik and suspensions for defendants Rozina, Romans, and Piotrowski. Messrs. Rozina and Cyrulik were found guilty of verbal abuse and posting of drawings. In addition, Mr. Rozina was charged with indecent exposure. 8

Dr. Calvin Gillespie, Mrs. Zabkowicz's gynecologist, who treated her during the summer of 1982, testified that the plaintiff was suffering from diarrhea, vomiting, severe nausea, and cramping. These symptoms were diagnosed as "psychophysiological gastro-intestinal disease due to harassment at work." 9

The issue in this case is whether the defendant accused of violating Section 703(a) of Title VII of the 1964 Civil Rights Act failed to take appropriate and remedial action to stop unwanted "verbal and physical conduct of a sexual nature" directed toward the plaintiff because of her gender and whether this abuse was sufficiently severe or pervasive to create "an abusive work environment that affected a term, condition, or privilege of plaintiff's employment." 10

Sexual harassment—that is, "verbal or physical conduct of a sexual nature" with the purpose or effect of unreasonably interfering with an individual's work performance or "creating an intimidating, hostile, or offensive working environment"—is a violation of the sexual harassment code. Such conduct is directed toward the plaintiff because of his/her sex. It is unwanted and so severe or pervasive "that a reasonable person would have found the proven conduct offensive, hostile, or intimidating" ("Model Jury Instructions" 305). Even if such conduct is forbidden by the employer, unless an employer can show that it took immediate and appropriate corrective action, it is still responsible for its acts, those of its agents, its supervisory employees, and for conduct between fellow employees where the employer or its agents knew or should have known of the conduct. 11

Mrs. Zabkowicz suffered harassment because she was a woman, not because of her personality. Her co-workers had no trouble with Mrs. Zabkowicz's personality, person, or character until her husband's brother-in-law, Mr. Murawski, asked her whether she was wearing a bra on several occasions. Does wearing a bra have anything to do with one's personality? Clearly, such a question or comment from a man to a woman is sexual in nature and gender-based. 12

Was it Mrs. Zabkowicz's personality that suggested to Mr. Peppey to join in harassment next? From about 1978 to 1980, Jon Peppey exposed his buttocks to Mrs. Zabkowicz between 10 and 20 times. What personality flaw gave Messrs. Murawski and Peppey the idea to perform such verbal and physical conduct? Was the fact that she could not stop the harassment considered the personality flaw that opened her to brutality of her co-workers? By this line of reasoning, if she did not do enough to stop the harassment, perhaps she must have welcomed it. 13

On the contrary, Mrs. Zabkowicz did what any reasonable person would do in this situation; she unequivocally let her tormentors know that their conduct was not 14 welcome by complaining to her supervisors. According to the federal guidelines on sexual harassment, Mr. Schommer and Mr. Fredericks had the responsibility to prevent sexual harassment from taking place in the work environment by "affirmatively raising the subject, expressing strong disapproval, and developing appropriate sanctions" (29 *CFR* §1604.11). West Bend allowed the supervisors several recognized forms of "appropriate sanctions" such as an oral warning, a written warning, a suspension and a discharge. Mr. Schommer's response to Mrs. Zabkowicz's complaint was to ask Mr. Peppey to apologize and to ask Mr. Murawski to "knock it off," but no formal disciplinary action was taken in either case.

In the wake of management's indifference, from about 1979 to June of 1982 15 the harassment campaign against Mrs. Zabkowicz expanded and won new followers. In addition to exposing his buttocks, Mr. Romans used to grab his crotch and growl at Mrs. Zabkowicz. On one occasion as he allegedly grabbed his crotch, he suggested that pregnant Mrs. Zabkowicz would "have trouble handling this" because of its weight. Mr. Piotrowski referred to Mrs. Zabkowicz in her presence as "h & h" (hot and horny) and as "sexy bitch." Co-workers Paul Zierck and Carol Gabriel both testified that from roughly 1979 to 1982 Messrs. Cyrulik, Rozina, Romans, Piotrowski, and Peppey commonly addressed Mrs. Zabkowicz in such abuse terms as "slut" and "bitch." Just as questions about her bra, these terms had nothing to do with Mrs. Zabkowicz's personality, but everything to do with her gender.

Also, Mrs. Zabkowicz testified that during the same time approximately 75 16 drawings appeared, which depicted a woman with exaggerated sexual characteristics, often bearing her initials. Other co-workers understood that these drawings of a woman engaged in various sexual activities including oral and animal sex were referring to Mrs. Zabkowicz. Paul Zierck and Gayle Dorkey described these drawings as "cruel" and "down-right demeaning."

Mrs. Zabkowicz's testimony is supported not only by other co-workers, but 17 also by her supervisors. Though they disagreed about the number of complaints, both Mr. Schommer and Mr. Fredericks acknowledged the fact of Mrs. Zabkowicz's numerous complaints. Specifically, Mr. Fredericks testified that Mrs. Zabkowicz complained to him about the abusive language "more than several times" and admitted that he frequently received the paintings described as "cruel" and "down-right demeaning" to Mrs. Zabkowicz.

But just as they did not respond to the very first complaints, Messrs. 18 Schommer and Fredericks did not "take steps reasonably calculated to rid the work environment of the harassment" ("Model Jury Instructions" 305). The steps that they did take were ineffective and limited in nature. According to a file memorandum of November 11, 1979, Messrs. Schommer and Fredericks met with defendants Peppey and Rozina to discuss "verbal abusiveness" in the warehouse mostly "directed against another employee." Aside from this one time, private discussion of the management's actions were limited to recitation of company rules against verbal abuse and postings at the general meetings. Although the postings would stop for a short while after these meetings, they always promptly returned until the plaintiff was forced to leave her place of employment. Mrs.

Zabkowicz's employers clearly failed to take appropriate remedial actions against rampant sexual harassment in the workplace.

This harassment included comments about one's private parts, abusive language, and vulgar paintings. Mrs. Zabkowicz's co-workers confirmed how offensive the conduct was to her. She had to endure what no reasonable person could endure indefinitely because she was a woman working in a mostly male environment where even the supervisors tolerated treating a woman like an object. Her supervisors who had the power and the responsibility to protect Mrs. Zabkowicz from harassment knew about the abuse and yet did next to nothing to stop it. It is little wonder that after almost five years of enduring such offensive working environment Mrs. Zabkowicz suffered a severe nervous breakdown as her doctor testified. I am surprised she came back to work at all. 19

COMMENTARY BY MARK TSESELSKY

Although I was confident that I had covered all of the relevant facts and rules, I wasn't sure why this early draft of my essay seemed so meandering. My instructor then suggested that I use as an organizing principal the "four elements" of sexual harassment in the "Model Jury Instructions." I did so, and the reorganization made my essay more coherent and logical. Because I was able to take some of the detail from the preliminary narrative and use it in the later "analysis" section, the reorganization also enabled me to cut unnecessary repetition and shorten the entire essay. To further clarify my organizational plan, I added subheadings. 20

Final Draft

Abusive Words, Offensive Pictures

Facts of the Case

Mrs. Zabkowicz was one of only two women working at West Bend warehouse facility in 1977. She claims that over the course of the next five years she had to work in a hostile work environment produced by various forms of sexual harassment from co-workers, which were tolerated by the employers. The alleged abuse included numerous incidents of indecent exposure, abusive language, and posting of sexually suggestive drawings. Throughout her ordeal Mrs. Zabkowicz complained to her supervisors, Mr. Schommer and Mr. Fredericks, who discussed the situation with the offenders and recited the company's harassment policy at general meetings but did not take disciplinary actions against the offenders. These disciplinary actions were taken only after Mrs. Zabkowicz filed a complaint with the Equal Employment Opportunity Commission (EEOC). Mrs. Zabkowicz's regular physician testified that she suffered from a "psychophysiological gastrointestinal disease due to harassment at work" (*Zabkowicz v. West Bend*, 589 F.Supp. 780 (1984)). 21

Issues

This case presents two issues: (1) Did the plaintiff suffer sexual harassment that   22
was sufficiently severe or pervasive to create an abusive work environment that
affected the condition of her employment? (2) Did the defendant fail to take
appropriate and remedial action to stop unwanted verbal and physical conduct of
a sexual nature directed toward the plaintiff because of her gender?

The Law on Sexual Harassment

Sexual harassment—that is, "verbal or physical conduct of a sexual nature . . . with   23
the purpose or effect of unreasonably interfering with an individual's work performance or creating an intimidating, hostile, or offensive working environment"
(29 *CFR* §1604.11)—is a violation of Title VII of the 1964 Civil Rights Act. Such
conduct is directed toward the plaintiff because of her/his sex. It is unwanted and
so severe or pervasive "that a reasonable person would have found the proven
conduct offensive, hostile, or intimidating" ("Model Jury Instructions" 305). Even if
such conduct is forbidden by the employer, unless an employer "can show that it
took immediate and appropriate corrective action," it is still responsible for its acts,
those of its agents, its supervisory employees, and for conduct between fellow
employees where the employer or its agents knew or should have known of the
conduct (29 *CFR* §1604.11).

Was the Plaintiff Subject to Unwelcome Sexual Harassment?

From 1979 to 1982, Mrs. Zabkowicz was subjected to numerous instances of   24
abusive acts at the hands of her co-workers, including sexually insulting verbal
comments and obscene pictures posted in the workplace. Mrs. Zabkowicz
unequivocally let her tormentors and her employers know that she did not
welcome the sexual harassment that was directed against her. She testified that
she complained to her supervisors, Mr. Schommer and Mr. Fredericks, many
times about the various forms of harassment, including 50 occasions on which
she brought in obscene drawings bearing her initials, which were posted all over
the warehouse. Though they disagreed about the number of complaints, both Mr.
Schommer and Mr. Fredericks acknowledged the fact of Mrs. Zabkowicz's
numerous complaints. Specifically, Mr. Fredericks testified that Mrs. Zabkowicz
complained to him about the abusive language "more than several times" and
admitted that he frequently received the offensive drawings.

Was the Plaintiff Subjected to Harassment Because of Her Gender?

Mrs. Zabkowicz suffered harassment only because she was a woman. Although the   25
defendants contended that the abuse directed at the plaintiff was not because of
her gender ("a male employee with the plaintiff's same personality would have suffered equally brutal harassment, even if in a different form"), the facts do not
support this claim. Her co-workers had no trouble with Mrs. Zabkowicz's personality, person, or character until her husband's brother-in-law, Mr. Murawski, asked
her on several occasions whether she was wearing a bra. Was it her "personality"

or her gender that provoked such a question? Was it Mrs. Zabkowicz's personality that suggested to Mr. Peppey to join in the harassment? From about 1978 to 1980, Jon Peppey exposed his buttocks to Mrs. Zabkowicz between 10 and 20 times. What personality flaw provoked Mr. Murawski and Mr. Peppey to engage in such abusive verbal and physical conduct? Was the fact that she could not stop the harassment considered the personality flaw that opened her to the brutality of her co-workers? By this line of reasoning, if she did not do enough to stop the harassment, perhaps she must have welcomed it. The argument by the defense that any man or woman with Mrs. Zabkowicz's personality would have been subjected to brutal harassment, only in different forms, ignores the obvious sexual connotations of the defendants' conduct. Clearly, she was subjected to such abuse because she was a woman working in what had traditionally been a man's workplace.

What began as one man's sexual comments on Mrs. Zabkowicz's breasts turned into a flood of verbal abuse by other defendants, who also targeted Mrs. Zabkowicz's sexuality. Thus, co-workers Paul Zierck and Carol Gabriel both testified that from roughly 1979 to 1982, Messrs. Cyrulik, Rozina, Romans, Piotrowski, and Peppey commonly addressed Mrs. Zabkowicz as "slut," "bitch," and similarly abusive terms. Mr. Piotrowski referred to Mrs. Zabkowicz in her presence as "h & h" (hot and horny) and as a "sexy bitch." Mrs. Zabkowicz also testified that, during the same time approximately, 75 drawings appeared, which depicted a woman with exaggerated sexual characteristics, often bearing her initials. Other co-workers understood that these drawings of a woman engaged in various sexual activities including, oral and animal sex, referred to Mrs. Zabkowicz. | 26

In addition to the offensive drawings and humiliating verbal abuse, Mrs. Zabkowicz was subjected to intimidating physical conduct of a sexual nature. In addition to exposing his buttocks, Mr. Romans used to grab his sexual organ and growl at Mrs. Zabkowicz, apparently as a sign of his dominance. On one occasion as he allegedly grabbed his organ, he suggested that the pregnant Mrs. Zabkowicz would "have trouble handling" his penis because of its awesome weight. Much like other forms of abuse at West Bend, indecent exposure was not limited to a single man or to a singular event. From about 1978 to 1980, Jon Peppey exposed himself to Mrs. Zabkowicz between 10 and 20 times. On all such occasions, the sexual harassment was directed at Mrs. Zabkowicz because of her gender. | 27

Did the Harassment Suffered by the Plaintiff Create an Abusive Work Environment?

These various forms of harassment as described by Mrs. Zabkowicz and other co-workers created an abusive working environment. Gayle Dorkey, who testified to verbal abuse of Mrs. Zabkowicz, also witnessed Mr. Peppey's indecent exposure on more than three separate occasions. Ms. Dorkey and another co-worker, Paul Zierck, described the posted drawings of Mrs. Zabkowicz as "cruel" and "downright demeaning." Any reasonable person would have found the defendants' conduct offensive, hostile, and intimidating and would have felt compelled to quit his or her employment ("Model Jury Instructions" 305). | 28

Did the Employer Know of the Abuse and Fail to Take Appropriate Remedial Action to Deal with It?

According to the Federal guidelines on sexual harassment, Mrs. Zabkowicz's supervisors, Mr. Schommer and Mr. Fredericks, had the responsibility of preventing sexual harassment from taking place in the work environment by "affirmatively raising the subject, expressing strong disapproval, and developing appropriate sanctions" (29 *CFR* §1604.11). West Bend allowed the supervisors several recognized forms of "appropriate sanctions" such as an oral warning, a written warning, a suspension and a discharge. Both supervisors acknowledged Mrs. Zabkowicz's many complaints regarding various forms of sexual harassment.   29

Yet Mr. Schommer and Mr. Fredericks utterly failed to "take steps reasonably calculated to rid the work environment of the harassment" ("Model Jury Instructions" 305). They did not do anything to prevent sexual harassment or to use their disciplinary power to stop it when it first began. Thus, Mr. Schommer's response to Mrs. Zabkowicz's very first complaint was to ask Mr. Murawski to "knock it off." Mr. Peppey was asked to apologize for incident exposure, but no formal disciplinary action was taken in either case. Clearly, the two supervisors did not take the plaintiff's complaints seriously and failed to take any but the most half-hearted measures to prevent further acts of harassment.   30

Even as the harassment increased in frequency and seriousness, Mrs. Zabkowicz's employers took limited and ineffective steps to end it. According to a file memorandum of November 11, 1979, Mr. Schommer and Mr. Fredericks met with defendants Peppey and Rozina to discuss "verbal abusiveness" in the warehouse mostly "directed against another employee." Aside from this one-time private discussion, the management's actions were limited to recitation of company rules against verbal abuse and postings at the general meetings. Although the postings would stop for a short while after these meetings, they always promptly returned until the plaintiff was forced to leave her place of employment. Mrs. Zabkowicz's employers clearly failed to take appropriate remedial actions against rampant sexual harassment in the workplace. Clearly, also, the employees must have realized from their employer's inactions that management was not serious about stopping sexual harassment, and so believed that they had a free hand to continue their abusive behavior to the plaintiff.   31

Conclusion

The failure of the defendants forced Mrs. Zabkowicz to endure an offensive work environment. In the language of Title VII of the 1964 Civil Rights Act, Mrs. Zabkowicz's employers should be found liable since she suffered discrimination because of her sex, and the sexual harassment they tolerated adversely affected her conditions of employment.   32

—Mark Tseselsky

A Case of Male
Sexual Harassment

■ _____ ■

George E. HOPKINS, Jr.,
Plaintiff–Appellant,

v.

BALTIMORE GAS AND ELECTRIC
COMPANY, Defendant–Appellee.

American Civil Liberties Union Foundation;
American Civil Liberties Union of Maryland, Inc.;
Women's Legal Defense Fund; National Women's Law
Center; Equal Employment Opportunity
Commission, Amici Curiae.

No. 95–1209.

United States Court of Appeals,
Fourth Circuit.

Argued Sept. 28, 1995.
Decided March 5, 1996.

From 1985 until 1993, Hopkins worked in the Photographic Services Unit of Bal-   1
timore Gas & Electric Company (BG & E) as a color photographic technician. His
immediate supervisor was Ira Swadow. In October 1993, as part of a reduction in
force and a company-wide reorganization, BG & E eliminated the Photographic
Services Unit and its 13 positions, including those held by Hopkins and Swadow.

Hopkins contends that throughout his term of employment at BG & E,   2
Swadow subjected him to discriminatory sexual harassment, creating a hostile
work environment. Hopkins bases his claim on the following incidents:

1. Swadow frequently entered the men's bathroom when Hopkins was there
    alone. On one occasion in 1986, while Hopkins was at the urinal, Swadow
    pretended to lock the door and said, "Ah, alone at last." He walked
    towards Hopkins, making Hopkins feel "very uncomfortable."
2. In 1987, Swadow wrote "S.W.A.K., kiss, kiss," and drew small hearts on
    internal mail Hopkins received from his fiancee, a BG & E employee. On
    another occasion, Swadow added the word "Alternative" in front of the
    company name "Lifestyles" on a piece of mail addressed to Hopkins.
3. In February 1988, during a party given by Hopkins, Swadow suggested to
    a BG & E employee that Hopkins and his fiancee were getting married
    because she was pregnant. Upon Hopkins' engagement, Swadow told him
    that he would be "counting the months" to see when the baby arrives.

Hopkins v. Baltimore Gas and Electric, 77 F.3d 745 (1996).

Before Hopkins' marriage, Swadow occasionally asked him if he had gone on dates over the weekend and whether he had sex with anyone. Swadow also mentioned repeatedly that his children called him "Daddy," that it took a special person to be called "Daddy," and that he was sure Hopkins' son would never call Hopkins "Daddy."

4. At Hopkins' wedding on June 25, 1988, Swadow was the only man who attempted to greet Hopkins in the receiving line by kissing him.

5. Sometime before 1990, while Hopkins was leaning back on a table and speaking on the telephone, Swadow pivoted an illuminated magnifying lens over Hopkins' crotch, looked through it while pushing the lens down, and asked "Where is it?"

6. Sometime before 1990, Swadow asked Hopkins, "On a scale of one to ten, how much do you like me?" Hopkins felt that the question was inappropriate. He had previously told Swadow that he objected to Swadow's "sexual overtones."

7. Sometime before 1990, Swadow bumped into Hopkins and said, "You only do that so you can touch me."

8. Sometime before 1990, during a conversation with Hopkins and a vendor about a recent airplane crash, Swadow looked at Hopkins and said that in order to survive with burning fuel on the surface of the water, Swadow would "find a dead man and cut off his penis and breathe through that." Hopkins told Swadow that he was offended by such a "sick" statement.

9. In 1989 or 1990, while Hopkins was showing the color darkroom to a supervisor's female guest, Swadow came in and asked "Are you decent?"

10. In 1991, while preparing to leave on a business trip from Hopkins' home, Swadow found an unloaded gun in the house and pointed it at Hopkins.

11. On August 1, 1991, Swadow squeezed into the one-person revolving door to the darkroom with another employee. Upon exiting the door, Swadow looked at Hopkins, who was in the darkroom, and asked, "Was it as good for you as it was for me?" The other employee looked very uncomfortable. Later, Swadow attempted to force himself into the same revolving door with Hopkins. He had made physical contact with Hopkins' back before Hopkins pushed Swadow away and told him that he "objected to it" and did not want to be in the darkroom with him.

12. Throughout 1993, Swadow regularly commented on Hopkins' appearance. For example, Swadow would say, "You look nice today," "You have a really pretty shirt on," or "You look so distinguished." Once he turned over Hopkins' tie and examined it.

13. On July 2, 1993, while Swadow and Hopkins were discussing a photographic negative, Swadow, with a "very peculiar" look on his face, commented that "orientation is subjective."

Late in 1989, Hopkins complained to his supervisors about Swadow's sexual harassment, particularly his inappropriate sexual comments and jokes. He identified the events described above in paragraphs 5 and 7. In response, BG & E conducted an internal investigation, which included interviews of Hopkins, Swadow, and nine other employees in the Photographic Services Unit. A manager's report concluded that "practically all of the Section's employees engage in joking and comments of one kind or another" but that such comments were "not offensive" and were not "intended to be so." An employee case analyst, who could not conclude that Swadow's behavior was "sexually motivated," felt that Hopkins was trying to "hang" Swadow.

The matter was then referred to higher management, which assured Hopkins that Swadow was "under close scrutiny" and that "none of this would happen in the future." At the time, Hopkins appeared satisfied with BG & E's response. Without ultimately taking a position on whether Hopkins' charges were true, BG & E offered to interview him for a transfer to two different positions in other departments. Hopkins declined the offer out of a concern that his transfer would give his coworkers the impression that he was the one at fault.

Over a year later, Hopkins filed a charge of sexual discrimination with the Equal Employment Opportunity Commission (EEOC), and the EEOC issued a right to sue letter in September 1993. Hopkins filed this action in December 1993, alleging sexual harassment and retaliation in violation of Title VII of the Civil Rights Act of 1964.

The Abusive Cardiologist

Lee KOPP, Appellant,

v.

SAMARITAN HEALTH SYSTEM, INC.,
and Saadi Albaghdadi, Appellees.

No. 93–1519.

United States Court of Appeals, Eighth Circuit.

Submitted Nov. 10, 1993.
Decided Dec. 23, 1993.
Rehearing Denied Jan. 21, 1994.

Lee Kopp works for Samaritan Health System. She has worked for Samaritan (and its predecessors) for 15 years in the respiratory-cardiology department, and now is the lead cardiology technician. This position normally includes supervisory duties at two separate Samaritan sites, referred to as north and south campus. Throughout her employment, Kopp has consistently received "excellent" evaluations, and her supervisors consider her to be a dedicated employee.

Kopp v. Samaritan Health Systems, 13 F.3d 264 (1993).

Samaritan Health System is the corporate successor to Gateway Health   2
Systems, which owned Jane Lamb Hospital. In 1989, Jane Lamb and Mercy Hospital merged into the Samaritan Health System.

Dr. Saadi Albaghdadi is a cardiologist with hospital privileges at Samaritan. Prior   3
to the merger, he held privileges at both hospitals. Albaghdadi served on the executive committee of the medical staff throughout the early 1980s and has chaired several other Samaritan medical committees. He is present at Samaritan on a daily basis. In addition to his patient responsibilities, he directs hospital staff, orders them to perform tests, disciplines them when procedures fail to meet his expectations, and works in close physical contact with them. Although Albaghdadi does not have the power to hire or fire Samaritan employees, Samaritan has, at times, rearranged the location of staff members to accommodate Albaghdadi's wishes. The hospital has also changed certain staff members' schedules at his request, and has added staff in response to Albaghdadi's demands. On occasion, Albaghdadi has obtained money from the hospital for additional training for Kopp and other cardiology staff members. Moreover, the hospital has changed its supply orders to accommodate the doctor's requests. Albaghdadi generates considerable revenue for the hospital (approximately four million dollars in 1990) and is a partner in a clinic which leases an expensive piece of equipment to the hospital. From this piece of equipment alone, Albaghdadi's partnership earns $10,000 in monthly rent.

Kopp used to work with Albaghdadi on a regular basis, and has had several   4
encounters with him. On two occasions Albaghdadi shouted at Kopp. Once, he yelled and threw his stethoscope at her, because another doctor had transferred a patient before Albaghdadi could collect a fee. This behavior reduced Kopp to tears. Then, on February 1, 1991, Albaghdadi reviewed a patient's chart and noticed that an echocardiogram report was missing. He telephoned Kopp and angrily demanded to know why the report was missing. She replied that she did not know, but that she would try to find out. Before hanging up, Albaghdadi referred to Kathy McAllister, who runs Samaritan's medical records department, as "that stupid bitch."

Fifteen minutes or so later, Kopp came across McAllister and Albaghdadi in   5
the hallway. Albaghdadi attempted to secure a commitment from Kopp on a turnaround time for all echocardiogram reports to be typed and attached to patient charts. Although Kopp attempted to address Albaghdadi's concerns, she stated that she could not make a commitment about an exact turnaround time, because people over whom she had no control were involved in the process.

At this point, Albaghdadi became enraged and grabbed Lee Kopp with both   6
hands by the lapels of her scrub jacket. He also grabbed her bra straps and her skin. He pulled her close and shouted through gritted teeth, "I want to know who to come after when this happens again." He held onto her and shook her for approximately 30 seconds, then he released her and pushed her back. He also complained about the merger that created Samaritan, referred to Ron Reed, an officer of Samaritan, as a "goddamn bastard," and complained about the condition of the wallpaper.

That evening, Kopp contacted her supervisor, Bill Vogel, to tell him about the   7
incident. On February 4, she met with Samaritan administration members to discuss what had happened and, on February 6, she filed a formal complaint. Hospital officials met with Albaghdadi, and he emphatically denied ever touching Kopp.

On February 10, 1991, Dr. George York, president of Samaritan's medical staff, telephoned Kopp to schedule a meeting between Kopp and Albaghdadi. The purpose of the meeting was for Albaghdadi to apologize for his behavior. York informed Kopp that Tom Hesselman, Samaritan's CEO, had told him to arrange the meeting. When York called Kopp the next morning to set a time for the meeting, Kopp told him that she would prefer to handle the situation through administrative channels. She also indicated that she did not feel comfortable meeting with Albaghdadi. York slammed down the phone and headed for Kopp's office. When he found her he thumped her several times on the chest, saying, "Listen little lady, there are two kinds of people in this world, peace-makers and troublemakers. I know what kind you are." Kopp ran from her office into Vogel's. York followed her and continued to shout at her. Vogel stood between Kopp and York, and, eventually, York left Vogel's office. 8

Albaghdadi wrote Kopp a letter in which he apologized for upsetting her, but did not admit that he had touched her. Although the hospital could have temporarily revoked Albaghdadi's privileges and initiated proceedings to do so on a permanent basis, it did not. Instead, Vogel and Samaritan's vice-president, Wayne Sensor, told Kopp that they would require Albaghdadi to take a two-week leave of absence. Hesselman wrote Albaghdadi and told him that he either had to get some counseling or take some time off. Albaghdadi responded angrily, asserting that his apology should have been sufficient. He then attended a cardiology conference for which he had registered several weeks before the February 1, 1991, incident. No one from the hospital followed up to see whether Albaghdadi actually took the required time off or how long he was away. The hospital did not investigate the York incident, nor did Kopp receive an apology from him. 9

In 1991, before her encounters with Albaghdadi, Kopp was head of the cardiac technicians on both the north and south campuses. Samaritan performs most of its cardiac care on the north campus. After Albaghdadi's assault on Kopp, she told Vogel that she would prefer not to work with Albaghdadi on a daily basis. The hospital's response to her concerns was to locate Kopp primarily at south campus where little cardiac care occurs. As a result of this measure, Kopp no longer supervises any activity that occurs on the north campus. Kopp has had no further workplace encounters with Albaghdadi. Although Kopp continues to receive satisfactory performance evaluations and normal pay raises, she feels as if she has been demoted. She no longer supervises work on the north campus and is not involved in cardiac employee evaluations. Further, she asserts that her skills are deteriorating from lack of use. 10

In addition to the changes in her job, Kopp developed several emotional and physical problems following the Albaghdadi incident. She has suffered from insomnia, nightmares, headaches, loss of appetite, aggravation of a back problem, hypervigilance, and exaggerated startle response. These symptoms reoccur whenever she has contact with Albaghdadi. For example, she experiences some of these symptoms before and after she sees Albaghdadi at depositions. 11

Dr. Deborah Van Speybroeck, Ph.D., a clinical psychologist, diagnosed Kopp as experiencing Post Traumatic Stress Disorder as a result of the incidents at the hospital. Van Speybroeck said that Kopp had been a victim of child abuse, and 12 that the abuse made her more susceptible to long-term injury from violence. Kopp had no prior history of mental-health treatment, and denies having had any post-traumatic-stress symptoms prior to the Albaghdadi and York incidents. According to Van Speybroeck, Kopp's symptoms continue primarily because of the unpredictable chance that Kopp will have to interact, in potentially close quarters and/or alone, with Drs. Albaghdadi and York.

The record also contains considerable testimony from Samaritan employees recounting numerous instances of Albaghdadi shouting at, swearing at, throwing objects at, using vulgar names to refer to, and shoving female hospital employees. For example, in 1985, Albaghdadi pushed charged defibrillator paddles at Kelly Yaddoff Sterk, placing her and others in the room in danger. Sterk had not applied the paddles to the patient immediately upon Albaghdadi's request that she do so, because another doctor's body was in contact with the patient's bed, and Sterk did not want to harm him. At another point in time, Albaghdadi called Sterk a "stupid son of a bitch." In the mid 1980s, Albaghdadi actually shocked a female respiratory technician, Linda Carter, with defibrillator paddles, because she did not move out of the way quickly enough. In 1987, Albaghdadi threw a patient chart in anger. The chart came within inches of ward clerk Evelyn Hubbart's face. In 1987, Albaghdadi yelled at Peggy Kapp, a respiratory therapist, shouting that she was too fat and slow to do her job. He ordered her to get her "tits" out of the way when she was attending to a patient. Kapp spoke to her supervisor, hospital employee Bill Vogel, and requested an apology. Vogel responded that she should not expect one. In 1987, Albaghdadi called Nursing Director Marilyn Rhodes a "fat bitch" or "fat lady." [13]

On another occasion in 1987, Albaghdadi called nurse Jan Lauritzen a "dirty, lousy nurse," "a piece of shit," and said he wanted to "beat the shit out of [her]." In addition, he intentionally shoved her. Following Albaghdadi's encounter with Lauritzen, Mark Richardson, the hospital's former president, met with the doctor and told him that the hospital would not tolerate his abusive behavior. Albaghdadi initially denied any abuse of the staff. Richardson then questioned Pat Aldrich, a nurse manager who was present at the meeting, as to whether Albaghdadi had "intentionally intimidated, frightened or otherwise abused [the] staff." She said that the staff had felt "the effects of his personal attacks, all [were] frightened, and many would prefer not to see [his] patients." Albaghdadi then admitted that these feelings were his fault and stated that the outbursts were not beneficial to him or to Samaritan. As a result of this meeting, Richardson agreed that, even though Lauritzen had done nothing wrong, he would reorganize the schedule so that, when possible, she would not attend Albaghdadi's patients. [14]

The record also contains evidence of the hospital's knowledge of Albaghdadi's abusive behavior in the form of statements and discussions about his cultural background.[1] Throughout the time that Albaghdadi has worked at the hospital, many members of the hospital staff, including management per- [15]

---

[1]It is not proper to draw any inference about Albaghdadi's motivation from the fact that he is of Iraqi extraction. That would be an impermissible ethnic stereotype. We mention this fact only as evidence that the hospital may have recognized that Albaghdadi did not treat women and men evenhandedly.

sonnel, have discussed his behavior, speculating that perhaps it might be attributed to his culture's attitude toward women. Albaghdadi is a native of Iraq. Moreover, Albaghdadi's behavior was often a subject of discussion at hospital management meetings, and staff members suggested that nurses and technicians should not look Albaghdadi in the eye because he does not like women to do so.

The record also contains four alleged instances of Albaghdadi's abuse of male   16
staff members. First, Vogel testified that Albaghdadi might have sworn at a male respiratory technician, Ron Drish, for being slow. Second, Hesselman said that Albaghdadi initially raised his voice in their meeting about the Kopp incident. Third, Albaghdadi raised his voice and swore at Dr. James Clark, a hospital pathologist, for cancelling a test Albaghdadi had ordered. And, fourth, Albaghdadi called Ron Reed a "goddamn bastard" during the same incident in which he assaulted Lee Kopp. However, Aldrich stated that based on her observations, Albaghdadi's treatment of female employees is worse than his treatment of male employees. She also said that Albaghdadi regularly worked with Evan Davis, a male nurse, and had not had any disputes with Davis similar to those he typically had with female nurses.

The Love Letters

Kerry ELLISON, Plaintiff–Appellant,
v.
Nicholas F. BRADY, Secretary of the Treasury, Defendant–Appellant No. 89–15248.

United States Court of Appeals, Ninth Circuit.

Argued and Submitted April 19, 1990.
Decided Jan. 23, 1991.
Dissent Amended Feb. 5, 1991.

Kerry Ellison worked as a revenue agent for the Internal Revenue Service in San   1
Mateo, California. During her initial training in 1984 she met Sterling Gray, another trainee, who was also assigned to the San Mateo office. The two co-workers never became friends, and they did not work closely together.

Gray's desk was twenty feet from Ellison's desk, two rows behind and one   2
row over. Revenue agents in the San Mateo office often went to lunch in groups. In June of 1986 when no one else was in the office, Gray asked Ellison to lunch. She accepted. Gray had to pick up his son's forgotten lunch, so they stopped by Gray's house. He gave Ellison a tour of his house.

Ellison alleges that after the June lunch Gray started to pester her with unnec-   3
essary questions and hang around her desk. On October 9, 1986, Gray asked Ellison out for a drink after work. She declined, but she suggested that they have lunch the following week. She did not want to have lunch alone with him, and she

---

Ellison v. Brady, 924 F.2d 872 (1991).

tried to stay away from the office during lunch time. One day during the following week, Gray uncharacteristically dressed in a three-piece suit and asked Ellison out for lunch. Again, she did not accept.

On October 22, 1986 Gray handed Ellison a note he wrote on a telephone message slip which read: 4

> I cried over you last night and I'm totally drained today. I have never been in such constant term oil (sic). Thank you for talking with me. I could not stand to feel your hatred for another day.

When Ellison realized that Gray wrote the note, she became shocked and frightened and left the room. Gray followed her into the hallway and demanded that she talk to him, but she left the building. 5

Ellison later showed the note to Bonnie Miller, who supervised both Ellison and Gray. Miller said "this is sexual harassment." Ellison asked Miller not to do anything about it. She wanted to try to handle it herself. Ellison asked a male co-worker to talk to Gray, to tell him that she was not interested in him and to leave her alone. The next day, Thursday, Gray called in sick. 6

Ellison did not work on Friday, and on the following Monday, she started four weeks of training in St. Louis, Missouri. Gray mailed her a card and a typed, single-spaced, three-page letter. She describes this letter as "twenty times, a hundred times weirder" than the prior note. Gray wrote, in part: 7

> I know that you are worth knowing with or without sex. . . . Leaving aside the hassles and disasters of recent weeks. I have enjoyed you so much over these past few months. Watching you. Experiencing you from O so far away. Admiring your style and elan. . . . Don't you think it odd that two people who have never even talked together, alone, are striking off such intense sparks. . . . I will [write] another letter in the near future.[1]

Explaining her reaction, Ellison stated: "I just thought he was crazy. I thought he was nuts. I didn't know what he would do next. I was frightened."

She immediately telephoned Miller. Ellison told her supervisor that she was frightened and really upset. She requested that Miller transfer either her or Gray because she would not be comfortable working in the same office with him. Miller asked Ellison to send a copy of the card and letter to San Mateo. 8

Miller then telephoned her supervisor, Joe Benton, and discussed the problem. That same day she had a counseling session with Gray. She informed him that he was entitled to union representation. During this meeting, she told Gray to leave Ellison alone. 9

At Benton's request, Miller apprised the labor relations department of the situation. She also reminded Gray many times over the next few weeks that he must not contact Ellison in any way. Gray subsequently transferred to the San Fran- 10

---

[1] In the middle of the long letter Gray did say "I am obligated to you so much that if you want me to leave you alone I will. . . . If you want me to forget you entirely, I can not do that."

cisco office on November 24, 1986. Ellison returned from St. Louis in late November and did not discuss the matter further with Miller.

After three weeks in San Francisco, Gray filed union grievances requesting a return to the San Mateo office. The IRS and the union settled the grievances in Gray's favor, agreeing to allow him to transfer back to the San Mateo office provided that he spend four more months in San Francisco and promise not to bother Ellison. On January 28, 1987, Ellison first learned of Gray's request in a letter from Miller explaining that Gray would return to the San Mateo office. The letter indicated that management decided to resolve Ellison's problem with a six-month separation, and that it would take additional action if the problem recurred. 11

After receiving the letter, Ellison was "frantic." She filed a formal complaint alleging sexual harassment on January 30, 1987 with the IRS. She also obtained permission to transfer to San Francisco temporarily when Gray returned. 12

Gray sought joint counseling. He wrote Ellison another letter which still sought to maintain the idea that he and Ellison had some type of relationship.[2] 13

The IRS employee investigating the allegation agreed with Ellison's supervisor that Gray's conduct constituted sexual harassment. In its final decision, however, the Treasury Department rejected Ellison's complaint because it believed that the complaint did not describe a pattern or practice of sexual harassment covered by the EEOC regulations. After an appeal, the EEOC affirmed the Treasury Department's decision on a different ground. It concluded that the agency took adequate action to prevent the repetition of Gray's conduct. 14

Ellison filed a complaint in September of 1987 in federal district court. 15

The Aftermath of Love

■ ─── ■

Larry CARTER, Plaintiff,
v.
CARING FOR THE HOMELESS OF PEEKSKILL, INC. and Janet Foy, Defendants.

No. 91 Civ. 1913 (CLB).

United States District Court, S.D. New York.
May 20, 1993.

At the time of the incidents complained of, plaintiff was receiving a pension from the Veterans Administration based on 100% disability. He is a reformed alcoholic and former substance abuser, divorced with at least one adult child. Defendant, Dr. Janet Foy, is a psychologist practicing in the City of Peekskill, who specializes 1

---

[2] It is unclear from the record on appeal whether Ellison received the third letter.
Carter v. Caring for the Homeless of Peekskill, 821 F.Supp.225 (1993).
Footnote 1 of original omitted, remaining footnotes renumbered.

in marital counseling. She also is divorced with at least one adult child. While the ages of these parties do not appear in the record, both are mature adults.

Defendant, Caring for the Homeless of Peekskill, Inc., is a Not-for-Profit New York   2
corporation also referred to by its acronym, CHOP, Inc. It was founded by PAPA, another acronym, which stands for "Peekskill Area Pastors Association." Dr. Janet Foy was the non-salaried Chairman of the Board of Directors of CHOP, Inc. a group of approximately twenty community volunteers of various faiths, races and backgrounds brought together by PAPA and the Mayor of Peekskill, all of whom served without pay. Assisted by local service clubs, the officials of the City of Peekskill, and the public, these people were successful in establishing and opening a facility known as the Jan Peek House,[1] as a shelter for the homeless of that community.

Jan Peek House provided food and shelter as well as counseling and peace-keeping functions. It had a full time paid Executive Director, operating under a   3
budget funded primarily by contract payments (approximately $250,000.00 per year) from the Westchester County Department of Social Services, and charitable gifts.

The Facts and Contentions at Trial

In January 1988, Mr. Larry Carter was employed at Jan Peek House as a part-time Client Care worker, and became a full time Case Manager on May 9, 1988. This   4
promotion was offered by Terri Powers, the salaried Director of Jan Peek House, and was based on the understanding that he would initiate training towards becoming qualified as a "C.A.C." or "Certified Alcohol Counselor," which is a trained counselor in the field of alcohol and substance abuse. . . .

A consensual sexual relationship developed between Mr. Carter and Dr. Foy   5
in about September 1989. . . .

From the start of his employment, Mr. Carter flourished at Jan Peek House.   6
He served for a brief time as Acting Director of the Jan Peek House in the Fall of 1989, and was granted additional vacation days by the Board of Directors to reward him for this special effort. . . . Also, while a full-time paid employee of CHOP, he was allowed to take time off for his C.A.C. course of study. . . .

Throughout the course of his employment at Jan Peek House, Mr. Carter   7
received satisfactory or better performance evaluations. The corporate defendant maintained throughout this litigation that Mr. Carter was an outstanding employee, and was so regarded by his peers and by the Board, and there is no evidence to the contrary. . . . Dr. Foy wrote a glowing recommendation and personal reference to permit him to enter the C.A.C. training program, as did Terri Powers, the Director of the Jan Peek House until mid or late 1989. . . . Mr. Carter developed additional skills working at the Jan Peek House. With tuition paid by the Veterans Administration, he successfully completed his C.A.C. accreditation shortly

---

[1]Jan Peek was a Dutch navigator, who came to the locality by mistake and settled at what became known as Peek's "kill" or inlet, probably now McGregory Brook. He thought he was in Long Island Sound.

before his resignation dated October 15, 1990, which he claims and the jury found to be the result of a constructive discharge.

Following the resignation of Terri Powers and after a brief period during which 8 Mr. Carter was Acting Director, the Executive Director of the shelter became Jeannette Quinn (Lardiere). The written job description of Ms. Quinn, approved by the Board of Directors, included the power to hire and fire personnel employed at the shelter. . . . Dr. Foy, as Chairman of the Board, had neither statutory nor apparent authority to hire and fire, nor did she purport to exercise such powers, which remained with the entire Board as a matter of New York law, unless expressly delegated. . . .There is no evidence that this power was ever delegated by the Board to Dr. Foy; indeed, all evidence is to the effect that only Ms. Quinn had the delegated power, and that neither the Board nor Ms. Quinn wished to have Mr. Carter resign, or to discharge him. Section 708 of the Not-for-Profit Corporation Law of New York, with exceptions not material, clearly requires that all such actions of the Board of Directors must be taken at a meeting of the board at which a quorum is present. . . .

The path of true love seldom runs smoothly. Mr. Carter testified that he first 9 attempted to "break-off" the relationship with Dr. Foy in November of 1989, and again in December of 1989, because he felt that Dr. Foy was "very controlling and critical" of his participation in support groups and AA. . . . The couple had joint consultations, paid for by plaintiff, with Dr. James W. Walkup in November, 1989, to "identify the issues in their relationship." By plaintiff's own admission, however, Dr. Foy and he continued their tumultuous personal relationship until April or May of 1990. At this time, Mr. Carter advised Dr. Foy that he wanted to end the relationship, and that he no longer wanted her to attend his son's graduation from medical school or his own graduation from his C.A.C. certification program, to both of which he had previously invited her. Nevertheless, Mr. Carter testified that, in March of 1990, the two opened a joint savings account to save, in part, "for us to get married" and that sometime after their "final" break-up the two met on one or two occasions at her apartment for sex. . . .

As examples of the alleged sexual harassment which followed the break-up of 10 the love affair, plaintiff relies only on the following episodes to justify his resignation or constructive discharge.

According to Mr. Carter, on June 4, 1990, he appeared at Dr. Foy's own pro- 11 fessional office in Peekskill to recover a passbook for the joint savings account containing funds belonging only to him, and that the two engaged in a shouting match before Dr. Foy surrendered the passbook. This incident was off the work premises, not related to his employment at Jan Peek House and, by Mr. Carter's own admission, was instigated by him in the first place. . . .

After this incident in Dr. Foy's professional office, Mr. Carter testified that Dr. 12 Foy harassed him sexually when she attended his graduation from the C.A.C. certification program on June 4, 1990. The alleged sexual harassment by Dr. Foy during the graduation ceremony included her unwelcome attendance at the graduation (after having been invited, with the invitation subsequently withdrawn), her taking pictures and her kissing Mr. Carter when she presented him with a gift and flowers. Mr. Carter characterized this episode as "embarrassing." . . .

The next alleged incident of sexual harassment also occurred in June of 1990. Mr. 13
Carter testified, and defendant Foy concedes, that on June 5, 1990 at 10:00 AM, Dr.
Foy called Mr. Carter at work and asked him to meet over dinner that evening to
reconsider their relationship. After Mr. Carter declined the invitation, Dr. Foy then
suggested that he resign from his position at Jan Peek House "as a personal consideration" to her and asked him to take a one week vacation to consider his options.
Dr. Foy memorialized this conversation in a memorandum of the same date. . . .

Mr. Carter acknowledged during his direct and cross examination that he was 14
assured immediately and directly by Ms. Quinn, the Director of Jan Peek House,
and also by the Board of Directors of the corporate defendant, that his job was
not in jeopardy. . . . He was further advised that Jeannie Quinn would act as an
intermediary between him and Dr. Foy and that he would no longer have to report
directly to Dr. Foy, if that had ever been a requirement of his job.

Mr. Carter could cite no other examples of alleged harassment that occurred 15
during the four month period between June 5, 1990 and October 15, 1990, the date
he resigned.

Jeannie Quinn gave two week's notice of her resignation as Director of Jan 16
Peek House, on October 1, 1990, and on the following day the Board caused her
to be removed from the premises. . . .

By letter dated June 11, 1990, some three and a half months before plaintiff's 17
resignation, . . . addressed to the Executive Committee of the Board, Ms. Quinn
responds to "the many disparaging remarks about my work performance made by
the Board Chairperson [Foy] at our meeting last night" and complains:

> The issue of the personal relationship between Janet and Larry has been a dif-
> ficult one for me to manage all along as it was for my predecessor. In her zeal
> to enhance his career, Janet has made many demands of me over the months.
> At her insistence, I did the paperwork to have our site approved for CAC hours;
> budget discussions were prolonged because she argued for a higher salary for
> him; I have had to intervene when Janet bypassed me concerning shelter
> related issues and addressed her demands/requests to Larry. Limit setting was
> a tricky issue because there were very blurred, at best, lines between the per-
> sonal and professional boundaries between the two people. . . .
>
> Limits should have been set on both individuals in a firmer fashion con-
> cerning what would or would not be allowed at the shelter. I pride myself on
> being a professional and have been most uncomfortable with the lack of pro-
> fessionalism evidenced on the parts of both of them. I also strive to be a fair
> Director to all employees. I try to express respect for everyone who works here
> and focus on job performance rather than personalities. I do not like everyone
> and am not equally comfortable working with everyone, but so long as people
> perform effectively within the parameters of their particular job descriptions,
> I shall advocate on their behalf as their supervisor. I cannot become involved
> in doing personal favors at the expense of the integrity of my position.

Ms. Quinn's later resignation on October 1, 1990 . . . differs slightly from her 18
June 11th version:

. . . I am resigning as a result of harassment and attempts to undermine my position as Director dating from June 5, 1990 when Janet Foy requested me to "urge Larry Carter's resignation" and to "establish a confidential file" to help her achieve this, and I refused . . .

Mr. Carter testified that after Jeannie Quinn resigned he was required to report directly to Dr. Foy, yet he could cite no specific examples of when his job required him to do so. The uncontroverted evidence is that Mr. Carter was out sick between October 8, 1990 and the date of his resignation. . . . Accordingly, the only period of time in which any events relied on to constitute a constructive discharge could have occurred was between the second and the eighth of October, and there was no evidence of any incidents occurring between Dr. Foy and Mr. Carter during this period of time, except that on one occasion Dr. Foy yelled because she could not find the secretary and sent plaintiff to look for her. 19

Statutory Law
on Sexual Harassment

◾ ─────────────────────────────────────── ◾

Title VII, *Civil Rights Act of 1964*, section 703(a) and 42 *U.S.Code*, Ch. 21, "Equal Employment Opportunities," section 2000e-2(a)

Discrimination Because of Race, Color, Religion, Sex, or National Origin

It shall be an unlawful employment practice for an employer— 1

   (1) to fail or refuse to hire or to discharge any individual, or otherwise to discriminate against any individual with respect to his compensation, terms, conditions, or privileges of employment, because of such individual's race, color, religion, sex, or national origin; or
   (2) to limit, segregate, or classify his employees in any way which would deprive or tend to deprive any individual of employment opportunities or otherwise adversely affect his status as an employee, because of such individual's race, color, religion, sex, or national origin.

Title 29, *Code of Federal Regulations*, 14, sec. 1604.11

Sexual Harassment

(a) Harassment on the basis of sex is a violation of section 703 of title VII.[1] Unwelcome sexual advances, requests for sexual favors, and other verbal or physical 2

─────────────

Title VII, Civil Rights Act of 1964, sec. 703a; 42 *US Code*, 21, sec 2000e: 2(a).
[1]The principles involved here continue to apply to race, color, religion or national origin.

conduct of a sexual nature constitute sexual harassment when (1) submission to such conduct is made either explicitly or implicitly a term or condition of an individual's employment, (2) submission to or rejection of such conduct by an individual is used as the basis for employment decisions affecting such individual, or (3) such conduct has the purpose or effect of unreasonably interfering with an individual's work performance or creating an intimidating, hostile, or offensive working environment.

(b) In determining whether alleged conduct constitutes sexual harassment, the Commission will look at the record as a whole and at the totality of the circumstances, such as the nature of the sexual advances and the context in which the alleged incidents occurred. The determination of the legality of a particular action will be made from the facts, on a case by case basis.

(c) Applying general title VII principles, an employer, employment agency, joint apprenticeship committee or labor organization (hereinafter collectively referred to as "employer") is responsible for its acts and those of its agents and supervisory employees with respect to sexual harassment regardless of whether the specific acts complained of were authorized or even forbidden by the employer and regardless of whether the employer knew or should have known of their occurrence. The Commission will examine the circumstances of the particular employment relationship and the job junctions performed by the individual in determining whether an individual acts in either a supervisory or agency capacity.

(d) With respect to conduct between fellow employees, an employer is responsible for acts of sexual harassment in the workplace where the employer (or its agents or supervisory employees) knows or should have known of the conduct, unless it can show that it took immediate and appropriate corrective action.

(e) An employer may also be responsible for the acts of non-employees, with respect to sexual harassment of employees in the workplace, where the employer (or its agents or supervisory employees) knows or should have known of the conduct and fails to take immediate and appropriate corrective action. In reviewing these cases the Commission will consider the extent of the employer's control and any other legal responsibility which the employer may have with respect to the conduct of such non-employees.

(f) Prevention is the best tool for the elimination of sexual harassment. An employer should take all steps necessary to prevent sexual harassment from occurring, such as affirmatively raising the subject, expressing strong disapproval, developing appropriate sanctions, informing employees of their right to raise and how to raise the issue of harassment under title VII, and developing methods to sensitize all concerned.

(g) Other related practices: Where employment opportunities or benefits are granted because of an individual's submission to the employer's sexual advances or requests for sexual favors, the employer may be held liable for unlawful sex discrimination against other persons who were qualified for but denied that employment opportunity or benefit.

---

29 Code of Fed. Regulations, 14, sec 1604.11.

● ● ● ●

For Deliberation and Argument

1. Offer an interpretation of the defendants' behavior in *Zabowitz v. West Bend Company* based on the analysis of sexual harassment by Catharine MacKinnon or Monica McFadden in the first group of readings in this chapter. How would O'Shea and LaLonde classify the harassment experienced by Zabkowicz?

2. In *Hopkins v. Baltimore Gas and Electric*, assess Hopkins's charges of hostile-work-environment sexual harassment. First, do you think that the language of Title VII can be interpreted to prohibit same-sex harassment? If so, does the harassment claimed by Hopkins satisfy all of the elements specified and defined in the model jury instructions (pp. 304–05)? For example, was Hopkins harassed *because* of his gender? Were the sexual comments and innuendoes directed against him (individually or in totality) "serious or pervasive" enough to create a hostile work environment? Would a "reasonable" person have found them so? Did Baltimore Gas and Electric take effective remedial action to prevent future harassment and to punish the harassers?

3. Suppose you are an attorney for either the plaintiff or the defendant in *Kopp v. Samaritan Health System*. Argue that the plaintiff should or should not prevail on her charge of sexual harassment. Note that unlike the previous cases presented in this chapter, the offensive behavior directed at the plaintiff was not of a sexual nature. To what extent does this behavior support the finding of hostile-work-environment sexual harassment? To what extent did the plaintiff suffer harassment because of her *sex*? Apply the four elements specified in the "Model Jury Instructions" (pp. 304–05) to the behavior of Dr. Albaghdadi. Consider also the standards developed in the U.S. Code. Should the doctor—and his employer, the hospital—be liable for anything more than bad-tempered, boorish behavior? Did the hospital have sufficient knowledge of the doctor's treatment of Kopp and others? Did it take adequate steps to discipline the offender for his behavior and to prevent its recurrence?

4. In *Ellison v. Brady*, did Gray's behavior constitute sexual harassment? In developing your response, compare and contrast Gray's actions with those of other alleged harassers in this and the previous group. How are they similar? How are they different? Apply the four elements specified and defined in the model jury instructions (pp. 304–05), the Title VII elements, and those in the Code of Federal Regulations (*CFR*) to the behavior complained of by the plaintiff. Would a "reasonable person . . . have found the . . . conduct offensive, hostile, or intimidating"? Did the defendant company (and supervisor Miller) take effective action to correct the situation?

5. Apart from the legal issues, *Ellison v. Brady* raises the question of where to draw the line between acceptable and unacceptable ways of expressing both romantic as well as sexual interest in another person. We are often entertained by romantic comedies (and perhaps also by real-life stories) about one person who persists in pursuing another despite the professed disinterest of the pursued. At what point did Gray cross the line? Was it his persistence, despite Ellison's rejection of his advances, or was it his clumsiness of expression? Suppose that instead of being

co-workers Gray and Ellison lived in the same apartment building. To what extent would you consider his behavior harassment?

6. In *Carter v. Caring for the Homeless of Peekskill, Inc. and Foy*, did Foy's behavior constitute sexual harassment? Focus on the two specific incidents cited by Carter in early June of 1990. To what extent did Carter experience a hostile work environment resulting from Foy's behavior toward him? To what extent may Carter's resignation be classified as a "constructive discharge" in terms of the definition provided at the end of the "Model Jury Instructions" (pp. 304–05)? In developing your response, compare and contrast Foy's actions with those of other alleged harassers in this and the previous group. How are they similar? How are they different? Apply the four elements specified and defined in the "Model Jury Instructions" and the *Code of Federal Regulations* sec. 1604.11 to the behavior complained of by the plaintiff. Would a "reasonable person . . . have found the . . . conduct offensive, hostile, or intimidating"? Did the defendant company (and supervisor Quinn) take effective action to correct the situation?

7. Select one of the cases in this group. Imagine yourself as attorney for the plaintiff or attorney for the defendant. Write a paper in IRAC format to make your case. Define the *issue* in question format. State or summarize the *rules* about sexual harassment caused by hostile work environment. *Apply/Analyze* the rules, as explained in the "Model Jury Instructions," Title VII of the Civil Rights Act, and the *Code of Federal Regulations*. You may also wish to draw on one or more of the articles in the Group 1 Readings in this chapter. Finally, draw a *conclusion* from the application of these rules and standards.

8. Select one of the cases treated in this group. Imagine that you are representing either the plaintiff or the defendant. Compose either an opening statement or a closing argument for this case. Remember that your audience is the jury. Draw on the facts of the case in a way that is likely to have the greatest impact on the jury. Keep in mind, however, that jury members may turn against you—and your client—if they think that you are overly manipulating the facts, being deceptive, making exaggerated claims, or attempting too crudely to play upon their emotions. For guidance on developing your statement, see the "Models for the Opening Statement and the Closing Argument" at the end of Chapter 2. See also Larry S. Stewart's "Arguing Pain and Suffering Damages in Summation: How to Inspire Jurors" at the end of the Group 3 Readings in Chapter 3 and the selection by O'Shea and LaLonde in this chapter.

■ Group 4 Readings: *Quid Pro Quo*

Quid pro quo sexual harassment shares many of the features of hostile-work-environment harassment. The main difference, as one judge has bluntly put it, is that quid pro quo harassment "involves express or implied demands for sexual favors in return for job benefits: 'You have sex with me, and you will get a raise (or keep your job, or whatever)' " (Keppler v. Hinsdale). As pointed

*out in the chapter introduction, quid pro quo harassment is more difficult to
prove than hostile-work-environment harassment because the plaintiff has to
show that she was fired, demoted, not promoted, and so forth, as a result of
having refused the sexual demands of the harasser. If the employer can show
that there was a legitimate, nondiscriminatory reason for the termination or
adverse job action, then the plaintiff has no case—unless she can show that
the proffered reason for the discharge was not the true reason. For example, a
plaintiff may effectively rebut charges that she was fired for incompetence or
mediocre job performance by showing evidence of good or excellent job evaluations and challenging the employer to prove that she was warned about
unsatisfactory job performance prior to her termination.*

In Stockett v. Tolin, *a twenty-nine-year old receptionist at a film production company is harassed by the seventy-one-year old president of the firm.
In* Dockter v. Rudolf Wolff Futures, *a smooth-talking broker arranges for an
attractive woman to be hired by his firm; she is fired after she rejects his
overtures. But was she fired because she rejected them?* Equal Employment
Opportunity Commission and Papa v. Domino's Pizza *presents a case in which
a male subordinate was sexually harassed by a female boss. In* Tunis v.
Corning Glass Works, *an unpopular woman who endures catcalls, dirty pictures, and gender-biased language sues her former employer after she is fired.
And* Keppler v. Hinsdale Township High School *presents the case of a woman
fired from her job as an educational administrator after spurning the continued sexual attentions of a former lover, an influential vice principal.*

*The cases are followed by a set of model jury instructions on quid pro quo
sexual harassment.*

The Casting Couch

■ ———————————————————————————————————— ■

Michelle Ann STOCKETT, Plaintiff,
v.
Frank TOLIN, et al., Defendants.

No. 88–1550–CIV.

United States District Court, S.D. Florida.
April 24, 1992.

On February 5, 1988, Plaintiff, Michelle Ann Stockett, (herein "Stockett"), filed a   1
Charge of Discrimination with the Dade County Fair Housing and Employment
Opportunity Commission. The EEOC issued Stockett a Notice of Right to Sue,
dated May 25, 1988.

Stockett v. Tolin, 791 F. Supp. 1536 (1992).
Numbers 3–5 and 10–25 introducing paragraphs omitted from original for paragraphs 2–20 of this
reading.

Plaintiff is a 29-year-old woman, who was employed by the Defendants from December 30, 1985, through on or about April 22, 1987. On December 30, 1985, Plaintiff was accepted for an internship program sponsored by Florida State University, where students are given on-the-job training in the film industry. She worked for a short time as a receptionist before begining her internship on January 6, 1986. The internship ran through March 28, 1986. After the conclusion of the internship program, Plaintiff remained employed by Defendant corporations until she resigned late in April 1987.

Each of the corporate defendants, Limelite Studios, Limelite Video, and DPC is or was a closely-held Florida corporation with its principal place of business at 7355 N.W. 41st Street, Miami, Florida. Limelite Studios, which rents out stages, was incorporated in late 1982. Limelite Video, which is involved in the business of post-production work and off-line editing including graphic special effects such as clay animation, was incorporated on October 8, 1985. Both are active corporations. DPC, which was incorporated January 27, 1986 and produced video and film pieces, stopped doing business in the summer of 1986 and was involuntarily dissolved in October 1989.

Defendant Frank Tolin is a 71-year-old man, who at all times relevant to this lawsuit owned most of the stock in the Defendant corporations and dominated the organization and operation of the Defendant companies. At all material times, he owned approximately 95% of the 7,125 issued shares of Video stock; Ron Fenster owned the remaining 5% of Video stock. Tolin owned all of the issued shares of stock in Limelite Studios. He owned 50% of the stock of DPC. The remaining 50% of DPC's stock was owned by Ron Fenster. Tolin and Fenster were directors of Video. . . .

Stockett's involvement with Tolin and Limelite began at a Florida Film Producers Association awards affair at the Grand Bay Hotel in Coconut Grove, which she had attended with a girlfriend hoping to make some contacts that would help her either further a modelling career or break into the production industry. At the party, Plaintiff was introduced to Toby Ross, who was involved in an on-the-job internship training program sponsored by Florida State University, and to Ron Fenster and Tolin.

Stockett testified that she talked about the intern program with Fenster and Tolin. She was told that Dr. Ungarait from Florida State would be conducting interviews at Limelite in the near future; and she was invited to apply. Stockett testified that she left soon thereafter and went home alone. This Court found Plaintiff to be a credible witness and we specifically credit her account as to this first meeting. While Tolin claims to have had a physical encounter with the Plaintiff that night, we do not credit that account.

Soon thereafter, Stockett went to the Limelite complex where Fenster introduced her to Dr. Ungarait. After an interview the Plaintiff was told that she was accepted into the program, which started January 6, 1986. Before she left, Fenster offered her a job as a receptionist for a few days before the internship program formally began. Stockett accepted.

A substantial number of Limelite employees were young women seeking careers in the entertainment industry. Limelite Studios rented out sound stages for use in movies and for commercials. A modelling agency in which Tolin had an interest had offices on the premises. Casting calls were routinely held at Limelite, bringing in actresses and models.

According to the testimony of the Plaintiff Stockett, Tolin made blatantly sexual advances to her virtually from her first day at Limelite until her last. Based on our review of all the testimony adduced at the trial this Court has credited Ms. Stockett's account that the Defendant Tolin sexually harassed her repeatedly, both verbally and physically, throughout her term of employment.   9

Tolin first approached Stockett in an offensive manner late in December 1985 while she was working as a receptionist during the filming of a Pepsi commercial. The Defendant came up to her at the receptionist's desk, put his arms around her from behind, pressed his body up against her and said "I'd love to eat you all up." Stockett pushed him away and asked Tolin to stop. Stockett was confused by Tolin's conduct but not totally surprised; Amparito Vargas-Lothian, another employee, had warned Stockett when she first started working at Limelite to stay away from Tolin because "he liked young girls."   10

On two occasions in 1986 within a month of each other, in the offices of Limelite Video, Tolin confined Stockett for a few seconds in her secretarial chair, where she was sitting and typing. Coming up behind her he pressed down on her shoulders so she couldn't get up, and then reached over and squeezed her breasts.   11

In January or February 1987, Stockett was changing clothes in the ladies room after work, getting ready to go to a circus. Tolin walked into the ladies bathroom and looked around a partition, smiled and said, "Hello." She screamed for him to leave. He stood there another few seconds and left. Tolin admits encountering Stockett in the ladies room, although he claims he just stuck his head in while turning off a light, saw she was there, apologized and left.   12

On another occasion, sometime in March or April 1987, after that bathroom incident, while Stockett worked at her desk, Tolin came up behind her, stuck his tongue in her ear and told her in the crudest terms that he wanted to perform oral sex on her. Stockett testified further that in 1988, the Defendant again approached her from behind, while she was working at her desk, stuck his tongue in her ear, and said with a four letter expletive that he wanted to have sexual intercourse with Plaintiff. On still other occasions, Stockett testified that while she was working, the Defendant would corner her, run his fingers up the front of her shirt, grab her breasts and pinch her nipples. During these assaults, he laughed and said, "You like that, don't you." Tolin also grabbed Plaintiff's buttocks whenever he could get close enough, as the Plaintiff walked down the hall. Stockett testified that incidents such as these occurred weekly throughout Stockett's employment. She further testified that Tolin's behavior was deeply offensive to her, altogether unsolicited, and that she regularly told the Defendant to leave her alone.   13

A few weeks before Stockett left Limelite in April 1987, Tolin's conduct became even more blatant. One night while Stockett was working late, about 6:30 or 7:00 p.m., she encountered Tolin. She thought no one else was in the building. Tolin pushed her up against the wall and began licking her neck. According to   14

Plaintiff, Tolin said he "wanted to f— me." Tolin had his hands on Plaintiff's shoulders, his body was pressed against hers and he was "right in her face." Stockett testified that she was terrified; she couldn't think and she couldn't move. Stockett testified that a former co-worker at Video who had taken space in the complex for his own business, walked by and did nothing. Moments later, Marie Arnold, who with Tolin owned Coty International, a modelling and talent agency with offices at Limelite, walked by, noticed the look on Plaintiff's face and interrupted Defendant's embrace. Arnold's testimony, in large measure, corroborates Plaintiff's account. According to Arnold, Stockett had tears in her eyes and from the look in Stockett's eyes and on her face, it was apparent that Stockett was afraid.

Finally, on a Wednesday, Thursday or Friday of the week before Stockett left   15
Limelite in April 1987, as Stockett was leaving her office, she encountered Tolin in a hallway. Tolin told Stockett he was going away and asked how long she had been working there. When she replied that she had worked there for about one and one-half years, Tolin said to her, "you've always got an excuse, I want to f— you." He added that he was tired of waiting. Stockett told Tolin that she worked hard at her job and asked him to leave her alone. Tolin responded with a torrent of sexually explicit comments that included, "Oh, you work hard. Do you f— hard?" Tolin bragged about his sexual prowess, compared himself to a twenty year old, and, finally, demanded, "F— me or you're fired." Later that day, Stockett encountered Tolin again as he left for his trip. Tolin's parting words were, "I'll see you when I get back," a comment Plaintiff took as a direct threat. Stockett reported this incident to Marie Arnold, who, in turn, reported it to Wanda Rayle.

Stockett began thinking about leaving her job at the time of the incident Marie   16
Arnold witnessed. It was not until Tolin directly threatened her and presented her with an ultimatum, however, that she decided she could no longer work at Limelite.

The following Monday, on April 20, 1987, Stockett gave two weeks' notice to   17
Fenster and Michael Garrett that she was quitting, but stayed only a few extra days. Tolin was out of town and Stockett did not want to be there when he returned. She did not work the final two weeks in part because of Tolin's return date and in part because soon after she announced her resignation, Michael Garrett took away her desk and put her at a little schoolboy desk in the corner with no computer, no typewriter and no telephone.

The Court is satisfied from the full record that Plaintiff did not in any way   18
encourage Tolin's verbal and physical advances. Repeatedly she pushed him away and told him to stop. She avoided Tolin by going in the opposite direction when she saw him. When she went into his office, she would tell another woman not to let the door be closed. She tried never to be alone with the Defendant.

Moreover, the evidence extant strongly suggests that Stockett stayed as long   19
as she did and put up with Tolin's conduct as long as she did because she needed the work and wanted to learn the business. The Plaintiff feared that she would be fired immediately and her opportunity in the industry would be destroyed, by a man whom she perceived as being rich and very powerful.

This Court credits Stockett's testimony that she did not see an EEOC poster   20
posted anywhere on the Limelite premises.

Stockett's account of a pervasively hostile work environment marked by the 21 Defendant's repeated and explicit sexual advances is corroborated by the testimony of many other female employees at the Defendant companies.

a. Lourdes Claveria, who worked as an administrative assistant for Limelite 22 Studios between June 1986 and June 1987, testified that one time she saw the door to Stockett's office open and found Tolin sitting on Stockett's desk facing her. She could see Tolin's office door from her desk. She observed Tolin call Stockett into his office, watched Stockett hesitate by the door and ask to leave the door open. Tolin closed the door and, after having been in the office for awhile, Stockett came out visibly shaken, either crying or about to cry. Stockett did not tell Claveria what had happened.

b. Wardrobe mistress and costume designer Beverly Saffire, whose business 23 operated out of the Limelite complex, recalled Stockett, crying and upset, asking to come into Saffire's dressing room to hide from Tolin, who had been "harassing her again." This incident occurred during the filming of a movie "The Unholy" at the studios.

c. Amparito Vargas-Lothian, who at various times worked for Limelite Studios 24 and for Coty International, between 1984 and 1986, as a receptionist and an administrative secretary, overheard Stockett telling Defendant to stop and seeking to get away from him.

d. Wanda Rayle, who held a senior position in the Defendant companies for 25 many years, including the position of Executive Vice President, testified that she witnessed Defendant Tolin's sexual advances towards the Plaintiff. Specifically, Rayle observed that Plaintiff complained to her on several occasions about the Defendant's harassment. On one occasion, Rayle recalled observing the Defendant Tolin standing with his arms wrapped around the Plaintiff's breasts.

e. Chris Carrol, who worked for DPC during Stockett's internship, witnessed 26 Tolin walking arm and arm with Stockett. Gloria Reese, who worked in accounting and testified by deposition, observed Tolin talking to Stockett and walking with his arm around her.

f. Kevin Layne, a producer with offices on the Limelite premises, testified 27 that he had talked to Stockett regarding Tolin's asking her to dinner and being "flirtatious."

g. Toby Ross, a free-lance producer and director, and a member of Florida's 28 Motion Picture and Television Advisory Council, testified that Plaintiff had called him while she was still working as an intern with the Defendant companies and complained that Frank Tolin was sexually harassing her. Plaintiff told Ross that she was sure about the nature of the harassment and that it was serious. Ross added that he made a series of inquiries about the allegations, and informed Wanda Rayle about the charges. Rayle told Ross that she would make an inquiry and speak to Tolin about it. Thereafter Rayle informed Ross that she had spoken to Tolin and that if it had happened, it would never happen again. Ross further testified that he told Rayle about similar complaints from two other employees. Ross said Rayle called him back about these complaints and indicated she had spoken with Tolin and "everything is taken care of."

Harassment at a Brokerage House?

Betty DOCKTER, Plaintiff,

v.

RUDOLF WOLFF FUTURES, INC., a
New York corporation, Defendant.

No. 86 C 4236.

United States District Court,
N.D. Illinois, E.D.
April 25, 1988.

Plaintiff is an attractive female in her mid-twenties who came from Idaho to   1
Chicago, Illinois, some years ago. She has a ninth-grade education, with a con-
comitant level of diction and oral presentation, and a somewhat querulous or
testy personality. She was working as a recruiter for a local school, the National
Education Center, and as a bartender for a local pub, the Chicago Bar & Grill,
when she met James [G.] in late 1984.

Wolff is a commodity brokerage firm engaged in buying and selling com-   2
modity future contracts. Throughout the time period relevant to this case, James
was a manager at one of Wolff's two Chicago offices. He was responsible for
supervising the sales office along with his co-managers Richmond Flowers
("Flowers") and, beginning in February, 1985, Steve Bernard ("Bernard"). James
is a man of above average education, intelligence and appearance, and demonstrates that he is well aware of these assets.

James was also a frequent after-hours customer at the Chicago Bar & Grill. In   3
late 1984, he met Plaintiff while she was bartending. The two engaged in some
mutual flirting and courting whenever their paths would cross at the pub.

In early 1985, James was seeking an administrative assistant and, in an effort   4
to impress Plaintiff and secure her company in the future, he offered her the job
at a salary level far in excess of what she was then making, or was likely to make
in the foreseeable future, $25,000 per annum. Plaintiff accepted, telling James that
she was a high school graduate, that she knew how to type, and that she would
be willing to learn how to use the office's word processing machines.

Plaintiff began working for Wolff on January 27, 1985. For the first few weeks,   5
James, as he occasionally did with other female employees at the office, made
sexual overtures to—in the vernacular of the modern generation, "came on to"—
her. Although Plaintiff rejected these efforts, her initial rejections were neither
unpleasant nor unambiguous, and gave James no reason to believe that his moves
were unwelcome.

By the end of her third week with Wolff, James began to realize that his   6
preening, primping and posturing, so welcome prior to his hiring Plaintiff, were

Dockter v. Rudolf Wolff Futures, Inc., 684 F. Supp. 532 (1988).

no longer desired. After one misguided act, in which he briefly fondled Plaintiff's breast and was reprimanded by her for doing so, he accepted his defeat and terminated all such conduct.

Meanwhile, Plaintiff was suffering defeat of another sort. Incapable of performing even the simplest of tasks assigned to her by James and the other personnel in the office, she became unhappy and unpleasant. Eventually, after a number of Wolff employees had tried unsuccessfully to train her to operate the word processing equipment, only to be told that the fault lay in the machine rather than the operator, she became unwelcome as well. [7]

By April, 1985, both Flowers and Bernard had decided to terminate Plaintiff because of her incompetence and attitude. Nevertheless, until nearly the day she was fired, James continued to defend her and to request that she be given more time to adjust. Finally, on April 22, 1985, Flowers and Bernard, acting without the physical presence or other influence of James, informed Plaintiff that she was fired. Neither at this time, nor at any time during her employment with Wolff, did Plaintiff say anything about the sexual harassment she now claims to have suffered at James' hands. [8]

Plaintiff, within 180 days of the termination, filed charges with the Equal Employment Opportunity Commission ("the Commission") alleging that Wolff discriminated against her based on her sex. Within 90 days of receiving a Notice of the Right to Sue from the Commission, she filed this lawsuit. [9]

Female Manager Harasses Male Worker

■ _____ ■

EQUAL EMPLOYMENT OPPORTUNITY COMMISSION, Plaintiff,
and
David Papa, Intervenor/Plaintiff,
v.
DOMINO'S PIZZA, INC., Defendant.

No. 91–1020–CIV–T–25(A).

United States District Court,
M.D. Florida, Tampa Division.
Nov. 17, 1995.

. . . 2. David Papa ("Papa") is intervenor/plaintiff herein. Papa was the store manager of the Defendant's Port Richey store in January, 1988. [1]

3. Defendant Domino's Pizza, Inc. (Domino's) employed Papa and is an employer within the meaning of Title VII, 42 U.S.C. § 2000e(b). [2]

E.E.O.C. v. Domino's Pizza, Inc., 909 F.Supp. 1529 (1995).

4. Beth Carrier ("Carrier") was Papa's immediate supervisor and Defendant's Corporate Area Supervisor. Papa's performance under Carrier was more than satisfactory. In fact, Papa had been promoted at least twice while under her supervision. Just prior to the termination complained of herein, Carrier had nominated Papa as "Manager of the Year."

5. At various times, from January 1988 until May 1988, the following occurred between Carrier and Papa:

    a. Carrier would come into the store and place her hand on Papa and would rub his neck and back.

    b. While standing besides him, Carrier would put her hand around Papa's waist.

    c. At a business meeting at Carrier's residence, Carrier told Papa that he had a "nice ass" and that he shouldn't bend over as he did because it "turns me on."

    d. Carrier told Papa that he had a "nice ass" on one other occasion when the two of them were distributing coupons to local residences.

    e. Carrier stated, "I know you are having trouble with your wife, but you are separated now and would be interested in starting a relationship again."

    f. Carrier told Papa that she loved him and cared about him.

    g. Carrier told Papa that she would never treat him like his estranged wife did and told him "just think, Dave, you could become a supervisor and I could stay home and take care of David [Papa's young son]."

    h. On one occasion, Carrier was standing next to Papa in the store and put her arm on his back while talking to him; when he moved away, Carrier moved close, put her arm around his back again, and "reached down with her hand and she grabbed my behind and squeezed it."

    i. On one occasion, Carrier was in the store helping to make pizza when she told him that her bra had slipped off and asked if that turned him on.

    j. In April or May, Carrier came to his store and said, "You know how I feel about you. I care about you, and you and David are more than welcome to come live with me. . . . you know I love you." Papa ordered her from his office and threatened to report the conduct to her supervisor. Upon leaving the store, Carrier told Papa that she would "get him."

6. Papa claims that Carrier's sexual advances embarrassed him and made him feel uncomfortable. His testimony was corroborated by employees who observed several of the incidents described above. There is no evidence that he provoked or encouraged Carrier's sexual overtures.

7. Approximately six days after the incident described in paragraph 5(j) Carrier and Mike Haskins, Carrier's supervisor, came to the store and fired Papa.

8. The reason for termination proffered by Carrier and Haskins at the time they fired Papa, and the reason proffered by the Defendant at trial are the same. That is that Papa was fired for violating company policy. One alleged violation was the payment of an employee, Mr. Whetzel, out of the mileage account rather than the labor account. Defendants also claim that Papa hid coupons and "lates" (discounts

for late deliveries) in order to improve the appearance of the store's financial position. Defendant characterizes these activities as "manipulation of paperwork."

9. The evidence did not support Defendant's claim that Papa was responsible 8
for hiding coupons or lates, or that he directed Whetzel to seek payment from the mileage fund. Instead, the evidence showed that Carrier instructed employees to hide coupons and lates. Furthermore, months before Papa's firing, Carrier approved Whetzel's idea to rollover the labor cost into his mileage account and directed Whetzel to carry out his idea.

10. Papa did not instigate or implement the "roll over" from the labor account 9
to the travel account for Whetzel. In fact Papa did not know that it was a violation of company policy. On the contrary, Papa testified that he did not believe it a violation of company policy because Carrier approved Whetzel's idea. Furthermore, Carrier reviewed the daily paper work frequently and would have noticed the changes in Whetzel's mileage, prior to Papa being fired.

11. Defendant submitted no evidence of prior misconduct or deficient per- 10
formance on the part of Papa. Nor did Defendant show that it was notified of Papa's alleged "manipulation of paperwork" by anyone other than Carrier.

12. During the time Papa managed Domino's Port Richey store, he earned 11
$350 per week and received a bonus averaging $606 for every four-week period.

13. The Court finds that Papa did seek employment in fast-food management 12
after he was terminated from Domino's but was prevented from obtaining employment because he reported to prospective employers that he was terminated by Domino's for "manipulation of company paperwork." Papa did find work in Rhode Island and continued to work at various restaurant jobs until his back was injured in October of 1991. Thereafter, he attended Fisher College part-time and the University of Rhode Island full-time for three terms and part-time for a fourth term. In 1994, Papa discontinued his job search for work in fast food management and decided to enter college to train for another profession.

Retaliatory Discharge?

■──■

Catherine S. TUNIS, Plaintiff,
v.
CORNING GLASS WORKS, Defendant.

No. 86 Civ. 1074 (RLC).

United States District Court, S.D. New York.
Aug. 6, 1990.

Catherine Tunis was employed by Corning Glass at its Fall Brook plant beginning 1
April 1, 1976, as a process engineer in glass technology. In 1976, there were about 300 production and maintenance workers and 50 salaried employees at the plant, of which 25 were in the engineering department in which Tunis worked.

Tunis v. Corning Glass Works, 747 F. Supp. 951 (1990).

Morning production meetings were held daily. It was Tunis' job to identify 2
quality defects in the tubing where the glass was being formed and to give her
findings at the morning meetings as to the cause of the flaws she discovered. To
accomplish this assignment Tunis had to mark the defects, take samples and
examine them under a microscope in an attempt to determine the cause of the
problem. During her training period she performed these tasks under the supervision of Dennis Kauser, her immediate supervisor. After completion of her
training in May, she was expected from June onward to perform the defect analysis function on her own.

The morning meetings focused around correcting the problems which had 3
been found. From time to time, after her training period ended, Tunis was not prepared to give a full report about all the defects in the tubing. On occasion she was
unprepared to give an analysis of the defects she had found, or she had not completed the required investigation of the contents of all the operating tubing.

On or about April 15, Tunis complained to Charles Francik, plant manager, 4
about photographs of naked or nearly naked women in sexually suggestive poses
displayed on the walls along the passage-way she used in going to the glass laboratory and mix house. She told Francik that she had discussed the matter with
Equal Employment Opportunity Commission ("EEOC") officials and had been
assured that such displays were in violation of the law banning sex discrimination
in the workplace. Francik advised Tunis that public displays of the sort she
described were at odds with company policy and that he would have the photographs removed.

Francik then made an immediate tour of the area Tunis would walk through, 5
and the next morning he went through the entire plant. He found pinup photographs in the mix house, on the door of the paint shop and in the teaser
shanty—the trades area where employees involved in maintenance and construction worked. Francik ordered Carlo Merletti, department head of the trades area,
to remove the material and to make a tour of the area to look for any such material he might have missed.

On or about April 23, Tunis again complained that offensive photographs were 6
still on display. Francik sent Merletti to look for the display, but Merletti reported
he could find nothing. Francik then had Merletti accompany Tunis to locate the
material. It turned out to be a postcard on the inside cover of the tool box of one
of the maintenance employees. It was ordered removed. Thereafter, Tunis made
no further complaints to Francik about any pinup displays.

Going with Merletti to locate the postcard exposed Tunis as the individual 7
who caused the removal of the photographs. Thereafter, on trips to the glass laboratory and mix house, she was greeted with whistles, catcalls and grunts. On one
occasion two hourly employees remarked in her presence in sufficient volume for
her to hear that she was okay but they could not tell about her legs because she
always wore pants. She told them "to fuck off."

When Tunis complained to Francik about being whistled at in the trades area, he 8
personally went to the area to speak to the union representative and several other
supervisors and employees he regarded as influential. He explained to them that he

did not want such activity to continue, that it was inappropriate, that he specifically disapproved of such conduct, and he asked for their cooperation in having it stopped. He heard no further complaints from Tunis about being whistled at.

Tunis also complained to Jack Stumpf, plant manufacturing engineer and the immediate supervisor of Kauser, who was Tunis' immediate superior, about the whistling. Stumpf spoke to the union steward of the trades group and asked him to speak to the group and indicate that such conduct was inappropriate. He asked the steward to identify anyone he knew who might be doing the whistling so that Stumpf could speak to them directly.

Tunis complained subsequently that she was still being whistled at. Stumpf convened a meeting in his office with Tunis, Merletti and Art Mayo, the union committeeman. Tunis told them about the catcalls and whistles, and Stumpf indicated that such conduct was unprofessional and inappropriate in a business climate. Tunis stated that those responsible should be discharged. She could not, however, name the culprits and did not identify them by description. Her proposed solution led to protracted discussion with the union representative about what steps the union required in disciplining employees. There was an unwillingness to go to the extreme of terminating the offenders. Nothing concrete seems to have come out of this meeting, but Stumpf received no further complaints from Tunis on this subject.

Tunis was very much concerned about the use of gender based job titles, language and terminology. She would constantly interrupt people, whether she was a participant in the conversation or not, to correct their usage if gender based language or terminology was used. Steve Clair, the melting department head, and Jean Gauthier, the forming department head, complained that when they would try to explain something to Tunis she would interrupt to correct their speech. At one of the morning meetings a senior process engineer had been asked to attend to make a presentation. Tunis kept interrupting him to correct him when he would say such things as tank man or cullet man. He became so upset that he walked out of the meeting. Gauthier also testified that Tunis prolonged the morning meetings by rudely correcting people's language.

Gauthier was awakened in the early morning hours on two consecutive occasions because the log book which he used to communicate with his shift supervisors was not legible. Gender based words had been crossed out along with other words, so that what had been written made no sense. Later on he came upon Tunis in the act of crossing out words in the log book. She was told by Kauser not to do that again, and there was no repetition of log book tampering.

On March 24, 1976, before Tunis commenced her tour of duty at Fall Brook, a memorandum had been sent to company supervisory personnel changing salaried position titles to eliminate their gender based orientation. Shift foreman, for example, was changed to shift supervisor, section foreman to section supervisor, draftsman to drafting technician, etc. When Tunis complained about the continued use of sex based terminology, Francik had a new memorandum, dated May 13, 1976, sent to all personnel reiterating company policy that sex based terminology was no longer appropriate.

Tunis testified that, after she had become known as the cause of the removal   14
of the pinup displays, she was often kept locked in the outer area when she
sought entry into the plant in the morning. One had to be let into the plant by
security personnel, who would buzz you in on the showing of proper identification. After showing the proper identification, however, she would still be denied
access to the plant until other employees arrived, when she then would pass
through with them. Francik testified that the security people on duty would
become distracted by a phone call or some other matter and would at times forget
to buzz him in promptly.

The work day was 8–5. Tunis arrived at about 8:10–8:15 and worked until 6 or   15
later. In the beginning she arrived at 8, but was locked out and then she began
arriving at 8:15 or 8:20. Because of some construction which blocked access to
her office, arriving at 8 was a problem for about 6 weeks, but her late arrivals to
work continued after the construction was no longer the problem.

At the trial some emphasis was put on the tardiness issue, but it was conceded   16
that the tardiness *per se* was not management's real complaint about Tunis. Her
tardiness, however, meant that she did not arrive early enough to inspect and
analyze the defects in the tubing, and, therefore, was not properly prepared at the
morning meetings when she was supposed to give her analysis of the kind, nature
and causes of the defects she had found in her inspections and microscopic
examinations. Kauser testified that he typically arrived at work at 7:45; that he did
not go directly to his office. Instead, since Tunis was usually late getting to work
and, therefore, could not be relied on to start looking for glass defects, or be prepared to give the morning reports, he would go out in the plant to investigate the
glass formations. He would then be prepared to start the morning meetings
without her.

On one occasion Tunis found an envelope full of condoms on her desk. At the   17
trial it was testified that the envelope contained finger guards used to avoid damaging surfaces in handling the glass, not condoms. Defendant conceded, however,
that these objects had no business being placed on Tunis' desk and that investigation had failed to uncover the culprit.

Kauser was angered that Tunis had taken her complaints to Francik, rather   18
than bringing them first to him. Tunis felt that he became hostile and uncooperative thereafter. As proof of Kauser's hostility she related a story he had told her,
which one of his employers had told him, to the effect that an employer did not
have to fire an employee but could make life so unpleasant that the individual
would quit. Tunis took that as a warning that Kauser intended to make her stay at
the plant as miserable as possible.

According to Kauser, he was angry, not about the nature of her complaints,   19
but that she had gone over his head to the plant manager. While he had no direct
control over the hourly employees in whose area the offensive photographs were
displayed, he could have worked through his immediate superiors to get the
matter resolved. He said he told the story to everyone and that while it could be
interpreted to mean that an employee could be made to quit by life being made
miserable on the job, the other message was that one should never take anything

for granted. He said he understood being by-passed, but he wanted to be sure it did not happen again.

Tunis complained to Stumpf that Kauser's assignments were confusing and arbitrary and that she was not clear as to her responsibilities. Stumpf spoke to Kauser and asked him to prepare in writing an outline of Tunis' job. When Kauser gave her the outline he had prepared, she objected to the job description on the grounds that she was being required to do more than she should. 20

Stumpf met with Tunis and Kauser in his office in July to review the outline with both of them. His purpose was to make sure Tunis understood her assignments and that the designations of her responsibilities in the outline were reasonable because of her complaints about Kauser being autocratic and ambiguous. Stumpf confirmed that the job description was proper. 21

In or about July, Stumpf noticed more and more that Kauser was giving reports which Tunis should have been giving. He told Tunis at an early July meeting that her performance was not up to standard. There were complaints from the melting, quality control and forming departments that Tunis was quite rude and cold in dealing with them. She had to interact with these people every day to obtain their assistance in determining the causes for whatever glass flaws her investigations uncovered. 22

In late July Stumpf again told Tunis that her job performance was not satisfactory, that she was not interacting properly with her co-workers, and that she was not prepared at the morning meetings to give a full and complete report on many occasions. She was advised that she had to correct her interpersonal relations at the plant, get to work on time and complete her assignments satisfactorily and that if there was no improvement her job was in jeopardy. He saw no evidence of improvement. 23

Francik testified that earlier on in Tunis' training it was pointed out that she was difficult to get along with, and the two people with chief responsibility for her training did not want to train her because they found her rude and discourteous. 24

Kauser had an evaluation session with Tunis on September 17, and told her he was recommending termination. At the trial Kauser testified that the factor which triggered his recommendation that Tunis be let go was her refusal when he reviewed his evaluation with her to concede that there was anything wrong with her performance. This convinced him that she would not improve. 25

Kauser went to see Stumpf to go over the evaluation with him, and they both agreed that her performance was unsatisfactory, that she was not carrying out her responsibilities, that Kauser was required to perform her tasks, that she missed critical meetings because of tardiness, and that she was not a constructive member of the company and was disruptive in her frequent efforts to change the conduct of others. 26

While Kauser was absent from his desk, Tunis went through her personnel file which Kauser had left on his desk and found in her file a copy of *Donaldson v. Pillsbury*, a Title VII sex discrimination case, with notations which appeared to be applicable to her situation. She had the case copied. When Kauser returned, he 27 found her going through the papers. The two of them went to see Stumpf, and she was advised that she was being terminated.

Stumpf then informed Francik in the latter's office of his and Kauser's deci- 28 sion that Tunis should be let go. Francik went to the office of Dan Lammon, the affirmative action officer, to discuss the matter with a few colleagues. Stumpf attended this meeting. Kauser arrived late, reported his evaluation of Tunis as unsatisfactory and his recommendation that she be terminated.

At the trial neither Kauser nor Stumpf recalled being at this meeting. Trial 29 exhibits and Francik's testimony place both at the meeting in Lammon's office, Kauser only for a short time to report his evaluation of Tunis and his recommendation, concurred in by Stumpf that she be terminated.

The day before termination, Lammon was notified that Tunis had filed an 30 EEOC charge. . . . Francik, however, did not recall any EEOC charges being mentioned at the meeting.

Tunis was unemployed from September, 1976, until January, 1978, at which time 31 she went back to school. She received a masters degree in forestry from Duke University in December, 1980; worked for Resources for the Future from December, 1980, until May, 1983; then was unemployed until February, 1984, when she worked for the Census Bureau for a while and then for the U.S. Forestry Service, also short term employment. She was unemployed from June, 1985, until July, 1986, when she took her present job with the Environmental Protection Agency.

A Case of Soured Love

Rose KEPPLER, Plaintiff,

v.

**HINSDALE TOWNSHIP HIGH SCHOOL
DISTRICT 86, a quasi-municipal corporation of the
State of Illinois, and Roger Miller, Defendants.**

No. 88 C 8506.

United States District Court, N.D. Illinois, E.D.
June 20, 1989.

District 86 has two high schools: Hinsdale Central and Hinsdale South. The Super- 1 intendent for District 86 controls the day-to-day affairs of both schools. The Superintendent at all times relevant to this case was Dr. John Thorson. He reported directly to the District 86 Board of Education, a seven member body responsible for the termination and reduction of administrators and staff.

Keppler v. Hinsdale Township High School, 715 F. Supp. 862 (1989).

Each high school in District 86 has a principal. The principals report directly   2
to the Superintendent. Each principal has assistant principals, department
chairmen and teachers, who report directly to him.

Ms. Keppler first became employed by District 86 in 1978 as Coordinator of   3
Education Services. Because this was an administrative position, Ms. Keppler
reported directly to Superintendent Thorson. In 1982, Ms. Keppler was made
Director of Special Services, another administrative position with accountability
directly to the superintendent. Ms. Keppler's office was in Hinsdale Central, but
her authority was district wide.

In the fall of 1982, Ms. Keppler met on two occasions with Dr. Miller. Dr. Miller   4
had become employed by District 86 in 1980 as an assistant principal at Hinsdale
Central. In the fall of 1982, his marriage was in trouble and he was seeking companionship and advice. Ms. Keppler provided them.

By the end of 1982, Dr. Miller's relationship with his wife was over, and he   5
began seeing Ms. Keppler on a regular basis. They had sexual relations frequently
and, when the relationship was going well, saw each other during the week as
well as on weekends. In 1984, District 86 promoted Dr. Miller to principal of Hinsdale Central.

Dr. Miller and Ms. Keppler continued to see each other through the spring of   6
1986. Although they also saw other people, and at times contemplated terminating their relationship, they continued to have sexual intercourse on a regular
basis when they were together.

By March, 1986, however, things had taken a turn for the worse. After Dr.   7
Miller and Ms. Keppler returned from a weekend together in New Orleans in
March, during which they had sexual relations, their sexual relationship was at an
end.

From that point on, the evidence is conflicting as to who was tired of whom,   8
and just what transpired when the two were together. For the purposes of this
summary judgment motion, this court accepts as true all of the testimony of Ms.
Keppler in her deposition and in the affidavit she provided in opposing the
summary judgment motion.[1]

Ms. Keppler and Dr. Miller saw each other socially on two occasions in April,   9
1986. On a Sunday in mid-April, Mr. Miller invited Ms. Keppler to accompany him
to his parents' home. She agreed to go. Dr. Miller drove the two of them in Ms.
Keppler's car. At the end of the day, Dr. Miller drove Ms. Keppler back to his
house. He asked her to come in, but she refused. He then became angry and
insisted that their sexual relationship should continue. When she refused again,
he threw the car keys in her lap, and went inside. Ms. Keppler went home.

---

[1]The defendants have objected to Ms. Keppler's affidavit on the grounds that it contradicts the
statements she made during her deposition. This court has reviewed both, and although it does
appear that Ms. Keppler was less-than-forthcoming in her deposition testimony, nothing in it
directly conflicts with the additional statements she has made in her affidavit. Thus, while the
defendants could use the deposition testimony to impeach Ms. Keppler at trial, they cannot have
the affidavit stricken at the summary judgment stage.

Later that month, Dr. Miller asked Ms. Keppler to come to dinner with him and   10
two other couples. Again, Ms. Keppler agreed and met Dr. Miller in the parking lot
of a Marriott Hotel. After dinner, the two returned to the Marriott, and Dr. Miller
requested that Ms. Keppler come to his place for sexual relations. Ms. Keppler
refused, and left.

The next month, Judy Kozienczka (now Judy Miller) had a dinner party to   11
which she invited Ms. Keppler. Ms. Kozienczka asked Ms. Keppler to invite Dr.
Miller to the dinner. Ms. Keppler agreed to do so, and Dr. Miller agreed to go with
her. This was the last time that Ms. Keppler and Dr. Miller saw each other socially
(though not the last time that Ms. Kozienczka and Dr. Miller did so).

At some point in 1986, Ms. Keppler's administrative position was changed   12
from Director of Special Services to Director of Curriculum, Instruction, Staff
Development and Special Services ("Director of Curriculum"). As part of her new
job, Ms. Keppler continued to have considerable responsibility for special services, but also took on additional responsibilities. She still reported directly to
Superintendent Thorson.

In August, 1986, Dr. Miller told Ms. Keppler that she had lost professional   13
credibility in his eyes, and that as far as he was concerned she should leave the
district. From August, 1986 through February, 1988, Dr. Miller made a number of
negative comments to Superintendent Thorson about Ms. Keppler's performance
as Director of Curriculum. Superintendent Thorson, noting the antagonistic relationship between Dr. Miller and Ms. Keppler, decided to transfer Ms. Keppler's
office to Hinsdale South for the 1987–88 school year.

In early 1988, Superintendent Thorson met with Ms. Keppler and told her that   14
he thought that she should resign her position as Director of Curriculum. When
Ms. Keppler asked why, Thorson indicated that it was because of her poor relationship with the principals of the two district high schools. The superintendent
noted that she had tenure as a teacher and could therefore stay with the district
in that capacity, but told her that she would have to give up her administrative
role. He also indicated that he hoped she would not accept a teaching role, and
would instead leave the district. Ms. Keppler told him that she would think it over.

On February 15, at a Board meeting, Superintendent Thorson recommended   15
that the Board terminate Ms. Keppler's position as Director of Curriculum. An
extensive discussion ensued, but the members agreed not to take any action until
Ms. Keppler decided whether or not to resign.

On February 28, Ms. Keppler met with Dr. Richard Spiegel, president of the   16
Board. Dr. Spiegel informed Ms. Keppler that he thought she should resign. At
that point, Ms. Keppler informed Dr. Spiegel of her previous relationship with Dr.
Miller, and of her belief that the principal's attitude toward her was engendered in
part by the fact that she had terminated the relationship. She also stated that she
would consider legal action if the Board decided to terminate her administrative
position.

At a Board meeting on March 28, 1988, the Board agreed that Ms. Keppler's   17
position would probably be terminated for the following year, but also decided
that Ms. Keppler should be given the opportunity to meet with Superintendent

Thorson one last time before the Board took final action. Dr. Thorson sent Ms. Keppler a letter that day suggesting a meeting, but Ms. Keppler never responded.

On April 4, 1988, the Board voted unanimously to terminate Ms. Keppler's position as Director of Curriculum, and to do away with that position, at least in the near future, for financial reasons. Ms. Keppler was then transferred to a position as special education teacher for the 1988–89 school year, and to a salary level commensurate with that position. 18

Ms. Keppler thereafter filed this action against Dr. Miller and District 86. Count I seeks relief under 42 U.S.C. § 1983 and alleges that Dr. Miller violated her equal protection rights by discriminating against her on the basis of her sex. Count II also seeks relief under § 1983, but against District 86 for violating her rights to due process by depriving her of her position as Director of Curriculum without a hearing. Count III arises under Title VII, and alleges that District 86, as Ms. Keppler's employer, discriminated against her on the basis of sex by relying on Dr. Miller's recommendation that her administrative position be terminated. 19

Model Jury Instructions for Quid Pro Quo Harassment Case

B. Henry Allgood

The following are appropriate jury instructions for a plaintiff's claim of quid pro quo sexual harassment under federal law: 1

1. The plaintiff has asserted a cause of action for quid pro quo sexual harassment. In order to find for the plaintiff on this particular count of the complaint you must find by a preponderance of the evidence that the following four elements have been established:
   (a) that the plaintiff belongs to a group protected by law;
   (b) that the plaintiff was subject to unwelcome sexual harassment;
   (c) that the harassment complained of was based on the plaintiff's gender; and
   (d) that the plaintiff's reaction to the harassment complained of affected tangible aspects of her compensation, or terms, conditions, or privileges of her employment. Proof of these four elements constitutes proof of a prima facie case.
2. With respect to the first element, I charge you that both men and women are protected from work place sexual harassment under federal law.
3. I charge you further that, in order to recover, the plaintiff must prove to you by a preponderance of the evidence that any harassment proven was unwelcome by the plaintiff. If you find that harassment occurred, but that

it was welcomed by the plaintiff, then in that case you must find for the defendant.

4. The third element that the plaintiff must prove by a preponderance of the evidence as part of the prima facie case is that the harassment was based on the plaintiff's gender. That is, you must find that the harassment occurred because the plaintiff is a woman.

5. The fourth and final element of the prima facie case requires proof by a preponderance of the evidence that the plaintiff's response to the harassment actually affected tangible aspects of her compensation, or of some other term, condition, or privilege of her employment. In this regard I charge that you must find that a term or condition of the plaintiff's employment was actually affected by the plaintiff's response. It is not enough for the plaintiff to establish that a threat of adverse consequences was made; you must find that an adverse consequence in fact resulted from the plaintiff's reaction.

6. If you find that these four elements that I have just explained and defined have been proven by the plaintiff by a preponderance of the evidence, then in that case you should find in favor of the plaintiff.■

● ● ● ●

For Deliberation and Argument

1. Based on the account of the facts in *Stockett v. Tolin,* how strong of a case do you believe that the plaintiff has against the defendants in charging quid pro quo sexual harassment? Apply the four elements of quid pro quo harassment, as specified and defined in the jury instructions. Consider also whether the plaintiff has a case for "constructive discharge," as defined in the jury instructions for hostile-work-environment sexual harassment (pp. 304–05). Finally, you may wish to speculate on other offences with which Stockett could charge Tolin (for instance, intentional infliction of emotional distress, pp. 119–20, 132–34). Couch your response in IRAC format.

2. Courtroom testimony in *Stockett v. Tolin* provided many instances of Tolin's harassing other young women, besides Stockett, at his studio. While admitting these incidents, he explained them by maintaining that they were "jokes" or that he was "in love" or that "something came over me at that particular moment." Attempt to account for Tolin's behavior in the light of O'Shea and LaLonde's discussion of sexual harassers in the latter part of their selection (pp. 281–84). To what extent does Tolin represent a common type of harasser? How might he be categorized, according to O'Shea and LaLonde?

3. Taking the role of either the plaintiff's or the defendant's attorney in *Dockter v. Rudolf Wolff Futures,* write an argument, in IRAC format, arguing that your client should prevail in this quid pro quo sexual harassment suit. (Note that the defendant in this case is the Wolff brokerage firm, not James G.) Apply the four elements of quid pro quo harassment described in the jury instructions. Determine whether Dockter was fired in retaliation for not acceding to James G.'s

sexual demands. Cite other relevant cases in this and the previous groups, comparing and contrasting them as necessary, as precedents for this case. To what extent can the plaintiff also make a plausible argument for hostile-work-environment harassment?

Note that the plaintiff in this case may also file a lawsuit against James G. as an individual (as opposed to the firm that employed him) for *battery*, defined as an "intentional and offensive touching of another." (See rules on p. 92.) To what extent does Dockter have a good case for battery against James G.?

4. If you were a member of the jury in *EEOC and Papa v. Domino's Pizza*, would you find for the plaintiff or for the defendant? Was the termination of David Papa a case of quid pro quo sexual harassment? In developing your answer, apply the relevant jury instructions and compare this case to *Stockett v. Tolin* and *Dockter v. Rudolf Wolff Futures*. To what extent can Papa demonstrate the existence of a hostile work environment? Were the offensive actions of Carrier sufficiently severe or pervasive? Did they "alter the conditions of [the victim's] employment and create an abusive working environment"?

To what extent should Domino's Pizza—as opposed to Carrier—be held liable? Note that, according to the law, "where the harasser is the employer or an agent of the employer the employer is directly liable [even if] Domino's had neither actual or constructive knowledge of the hostile atmosphere created by Carrier." To what extent was Carrier acting as an agent of Domino's?

5. Discuss the following questions in *Tunis v. Corning Glass Works*: (1) Did the plaintiff establish the existence of a hostile work environment? (Compare this case to *Zabkowicz v. West Bend*, pp. 307–09.) (2) Did the plaintiff establish her claim of quid pro quo sexual harassment? (3) Was the plaintiff a victim of a retaliatory discharge?

Apply the jury instructions for both hostile-work-environment and quid pro quo sexual harassment to the facts of the case. In addressing the hostile-work-environment question, consider the sexually provocative photos, the catcalls of Corning employees, co-workers blocking Tunis's entrance to the plant, and the prevalent use of gender-biased language by co-workers. Consider also the responses of Corning management to these matters.

In addressing the question of quid pro quo sexual harassment and retaliatory discharge, note that the plaintiff conceded that she was never sexually propositioned. Consider, however, whether the plaintiff can establish that she was fired "because she refused to be passive and accepting about the hostile environment issues or because she filed a [sexual harassment] charge with the E.[qual] O.[pportunity] E.[mployment] C.[ommission]." Or has the defendant established that there was "a legitimate, non-discriminatory reason for the adverse employment decision"? Has the plaintiff established that "the proffered reason [for her termination] was not the true reason for the discharge"?

Finally, consider the extent to which conflicts of personality, such as existed between Tunis, and her co-workers, can or should be a legitimate consideration in determining suitability for promotion or continued employment.

6. In *Keppler v. Hinsdale Township High School District,* assess the plaintiff's charge that she was the victim of quid pro quo sexual harassment. Apply the relevant jury instructions to the facts of this case. Consider in particular (1) the extent to which Keppler's and Miller's prior sexual relationship affects the legitimacy of her charges; (2) whether Keppler's termination was a result of sex [gender]-based discrimination; (3) whether or Keppler was terminated because she refused to continue the sexual relationship with Miller; (4) whether the plaintiff has a good case for hostile-work-environment sexual harassment; (5) whether, apart from any of the preceding factors, Kepper was treated fairly by Miller. In discussing this case, you may want to clarify your arguments by comparing and contrasting its circumstances with those of one or more other sexual harassment cases in this chapter.

7. Select one of the cases in this group. Imagine yourself as attorney for the plaintiff or attorney for the defendant. Write a paper in IRAC format to make your case. Define the *issue* in question format. State or summarize the *rules* about quid pro quo sexual harassment. *Apply/Analyze* the rules, as explained in the model jury instructions and Title VII of the Civil Rights Act ("Statutory Law") and the *Code of Federal Regulations,* sec. 1604.11. You may also wish to draw on one or more of the articles in the Group 1 Readings. Finally, draw a *conclusion* from the application of these rules and standards.

8. Select one of the cases in this group. Imagine that you are representing either the plaintiff or the defendant. Compose either an opening statement or a closing argument for this case. Remember that your audience is the jury. Draw on the facts of the case in a way that is likely to have the greatest impact on the jury. Keep in mind, however, that jury members may turn against you—and your client—if they think that you are overly manipulating the facts, being deceptive, making exaggerated claims, or attempting too crudely to play on their emotions. For guidance on developing your statement, see "Models for the Opening Statement and the Closing Argument" at the end of Chapter 2. See also Larry S. Stewart's "Arguing Pain and Suffering Damages in Summation: How to Inspire Jurors" at the end of the Group 3 Readings in Chapter 3 and the selection by O'Shea and LaLonde in this chapter.

Freedom of Speech

Congress shall make no law respecting an establishment of religion, or prohibiting the free exercise thereof; or abridging the freedom of speech, or of the press; or of the people peaceably to assemble, and to petition the government for a redress of grievances.

—First Amendment to the U.S. Constitution

In 1992, a high school student in Norfolk, Virginia, suspended for wearing a T-shirt proclaiming "Drugs Suck!", sued the school district for violating her First Amendment rights. (She lost.) A trivial incident, to be sure, light-years removed from the noble language—and intent—of the First Amendment, but it does indicate the pervasive degree to which freedom of speech is taken for granted in American society. Such freedom was not specifically articulated in the original Constitution. But in response to popular demand, a Congress mindful of the abusive restrictions on freedom of speech both in England and in the American colonies insisted on enshrining this democratic right in the Bill of Rights, adopted in 1791. One of the most eloquent defenses of the often controversial First Amendment was articulated by Judge Learned Hand: "[The First Amendment] presupposes that right conclusions are more likely to be gathered out of a multitude of tongues than through any kind of authoritative selection. To many this is, and always will be, folly, but we have staked upon it our all."[1]

The right to freedom of speech was tested almost immediately in the new American republic with the passage of the Alien and Sedition Acts of 1798. The Sedition Act was used by John Adams' Federalist administration to retaliate against criticism by members of Jefferson's Democratic-Republican party, and the tables were turned with the accession of Jefferson. Although the Alien and Sedition Acts were never tested in court, they were soon thrown out as unconstitutional by Congress, which repaid all fines levied. Since that time, the limits of First Amendment freedoms have been tested many times, particularly during wartime and other periods of heightened national tensions. In the twentieth century, perceived threats of Communist subversion during the cold war, and antiwar protests, such as occurred during the Vietnam War, have repeatedly raised questions of just how much freedom of speech can be tolerated in a democratic society.

---

[1]*United States v. Associated Press*, 52 F.Supp. at 372 (1943).

Of course, freedom of speech has never been absolute. The most well-known example of its limits is Supreme Court Justice Oliver Wendell Holmes's remark that freedom of speech does not give one the freedom to falsely shout "fire!" in a crowded theater.[2] Similarly, a person who used a bullhorn to make a political statement in a residential street at 2 A.M. would most likely be charged with disturbing the peace—and would be unsuccessful in claiming First Amendment protection. The First Amendment has always been subject to a balancing of interests: is the harm done by the speech act greater than the harm that would be done by restricting it? Speech that breaches the peace is often not protected because whatever social value it may have "is clearly outweighed by the social interest in order and morality."[3]

The First Amendment does not give one the right to slander or libel others by knowingly making false statements about them that would harm their reputation. Nor does it give one the right to solicit others to commit crimes or to blackmail them, to disclose state secrets, or to incite people to riot. And a continuing source of controversy is whether the First Amendment allows someone to publish or circulate obscene materials—a particularly difficult question because the definition of obscenity is so subjective and changeable over time.

In the past century, some of the most vigorous First Amendment battles have been fought over the "clear and present danger" test, "fighting words," and "symbolic speech." The "clear and present danger" test originated in the wake of World War I as a means of prohibiting oral or printed speech that appeared to threaten national security (in this case, leaflets intended to encourage active resistance to the war effort, though the test was used later during the cold war). Primarily a means of preventing acts that incite violence, the "clear and present danger" test has been invoked by liberals as well as conservatives: for example, not only against antiwar protestors but also against the Ku Klux Klan.

The First Amendment does not provide protection for "fighting words"— words that are highly likely to provoke a violent reaction from the person or persons to whom they are directed. However, words that merely annoy or even deeply wound others are protected, as long as they are not likely to result in physical violence. In recent years, many have debated whether "hate speech" should enjoy First Amendment protection—whether, for example, it is constitutional for college administrators to prohibit people from making statements that attack others on the basis of their race, ethnicity, or sexual orientation.

"Symbolic speech" deals with nonverbal acts of communication, such as burning a crucifix, burning an American flag (or, in the 1960s, one's draft card), wearing an armband to protest a war, or wearing a T-shirt saying "Drugs Suck!" to promote an antidrug message.

The readings in this chapter allow you to explore some of these issues. The first group deals with the symbolic speech involving the flag. Is burning the

---

[2]*Schenck v. United States*, 249 U.S. at 52 (1919).
[3]*Chaplinsky v. New Hampshire*, 315 U.S., 568 (1942).

American flag an act protected by freedom of speech? And does the state of Georgia have the right to adopt an emblem of the Confederacy, a symbol to many citizens of slavery and white supremacy? The second and third groups of readings deal with the First Amendment in American high schools. In the second group, a student gives a sexually suggestive speech; two pages of a student newspaper are pulled by the school principal on the grounds that they contain objectionable stories; and a teacher is fired when her students dramatize plays they have written containing an abundance of "street" language. The third group of readings deals with the constitutionality of student dress and grooming codes. To what extent do objectionable T-shirts and long hair qualify for First Amendment protection?

■ Group 1 Readings: *The Flag as Symbolic Speech*

On September 12, 1989, Representative Thomas Petri (R-Wisc.) told his House colleagues, who were then debating . . . [a law against] flag burning as a form of political protest, that recently a constituent had telephoned his office "and moved my staff to tears telling how her husband had fought and died for our country and its flag, and that flag had draped his coffin and she could not imagine how we could allow anyone to desecrate the symbol for which so many had given up their lives." He added, however, that another constituent had personally visited his Capitol office and told him that "she had supported me for years, but her husband had fought and died to protect the freedom of all Americans to burn our flag if they so wished, and she could not imagine why I would undermine the freedom of speech for which the flag stands."

The foregoing account, from Robert Justin Goldstein's 1996 book Burning the Flag: The Great 1989–1990 American Flag Desecration Controversy, *crystallizes the debate among those who feel that it is wrong to desecrate or otherwise maltreat the American flag and those who feel that it is wrong to make such desecration a criminal act. At the heart of the conflict is the question of just how far the First Amendment applies to a kind of "symbolic speech" or "expressive conduct" that is profoundly offensive to numerous people. Surely, the First Amendment is meaningless if it protects only speech that most people agree with. But surely, also, the protections of the First Amendment are not absolute.*

Two cases in this section illustrate many of the sensitive issues about free speech and the flag. In Texas v. Johnson, *a political protestor appeals his conviction for burning the American flag. Many readers of this case, described here by Randall P. Bezanson, are likely to feel that the First Amendment should extend to acts such as flag burning, even if they do not themselves agree with such an act of protest. But how far should symbolic acts concerning the flag extend? Should the state of Georgia be allowed to adopt as its official state flag a design based on the old Confederate battle flag? After all, such a design is offensive to thousands of citizens, both black and white, for whom this flag represents a celebration of slavery and white supremacy. Is it consistent to oppose anti-flag burning laws on the basis of freedom of speech, while at the same time opposing the display of flags symbolizing a tradition of racial oppression?* Coleman v. Miller, Gov. of Georgia *provides an opportunity to consider this troubling question. Two editorials and a newspaper article provide additional material for consideration of these issues.*

"He Soaked It, Ignited It, and the Flag Burned."

(Texas v. Johnson)
Randall P. Bezanson

The year 1984 was the year of the Reagan landslide. President Ronald Reagan was completing his first term; inflation was down and the economy was expanding; and America was in the midst of a remarkable military buildup that would, in the view of many, soon result in the breakup of the Soviet Union, Reagan's "evil empire."

The Republican Party held its 1984 National Convention in Dallas, Texas. Dallas was, generally, friendly country for the Republicans. Texas was the home state of Vice President George Bush. But even in Dallas there were demonstrations against the military policies of the Reagan administration and against the corporate interests that benefited from them.

A series of such demonstrations was planned for the streets of Dallas on August 22, 1984, during the course of the convention. Dubbed the "Republican War Chest Tour," the demonstrations consisted of protests, "die-ins," and related events at a series of corporate and government offices in downtown Dallas, with the participants marching from site to site, ending in a demonstration and speeches in front of City Hall.

The demonstration, as it turned out, was not large, consisting of only a hundred or so people. One of the protesters was Gregory Lee Johnson. Johnson and his fellow demonstrators marched through the streets, stopped to stage "die-ins" at some corporate offices, spray-painted slogans on the side of a few buildings, and proceeded ultimately to City Hall.

The demonstrators were accompanied by Dallas police officers. One of the officers testified at trial that when the demonstrators arrived at the Mercantile Bank Building, "several of the protesters bent a flagpole" in front of the building and "removed an American flag." The flag was then handed to Johnson, who "wadded it up and stuck it under his T-shirt."

The demonstrators then moved on to other downtown sites. "When they got to City Hall," the officer "saw Mr. Johnson remove the flag from under his shirt.

Speech Stories: How Free Can Speech Be? New York and London: New York UP, 1998.

He tried to light it with a cigarette lighter. It would not light. Someone from the crowd then handed him the can of lighter fluid. He soaked it, ignited it, and the flag burned." As the flag burned, the group chanted "America, the red, white, and blue, we spit on you."

The flag burning was the demonstration's catharsis. Shortly after it occurred, the demonstration ended and the protesters, including Johnson, left the area in front of City Hall.   7

As the demonstrators disbursed, a man who had witnessed the flag burning quietly walked to the place where Johnson had ignited the flag. He proceeded carefully, even reverentially, to collect the ashes and remains from the ground, took them home, and buried them in his yard.   8

Within a half hour or so of the flag burning Johnson was arrested, along with a number of other protesters. Johnson, alone, was charged with a crime. The charge was desecration of a venerated object, in this case the American flag, a Class A misdemeanor. Johnson was tried, convicted, and sentenced to a year in jail and a $2,000 fine.   9

After one unsuccessful appeal to the Texas District Court of Appeals, Johnson succeeded in having his conviction overturned in the Texas Court of Criminal Appeals. The State of Texas then brought an appeal to the United States Supreme Court, arguing that the First Amendment to the United States Constitution did not give Johnson the right to desecrate the American flag by publicly burning it as part of a protest against the government of the United States.   10

At one level the Johnson case presented a pretty simple and straightforward question for the justices of the Supreme Court to decide. Johnson was clearly expressing his political views at the time he burned the flag, and the flag-burning was indisputably part of his expression. Speech protected by the First Amendment, in other words, was clearly taking place.   11

But at another level the case posed a difficult problem. The State of Texas agreed that Johnson was exercising his freedom to speak, but claimed that he was not arrested for speaking but, instead, for burning the flag. The question thus posed was what relation the act of setting the flag afire had to Johnson's speech. This question, it turns out, was *not* a simple and straightforward one. Was the flag, itself, speech because of its symbolic meaning? Or was the flag the medium through which Johnson's protest message against nuclear war was expressed? If it was the medium, what contribution did it make to the speech, and what amount of protection, if any, should it have *as a medium* under the First Amendment?   12

In its argument before the United States Supreme Court, the State of Texas took the position that burning the flag, even as part of Johnson's effort to communicate his sentiments about the Reagan military buildup and the threat of nuclear war, was not protected by the First Amendment. The state's position was presented—*very* ably, it should be said—by Kathi Alyce Drew, an assistant district attorney for Dallas County, in the oral argument that was held before the Supreme Court at 2:00 P.M. on Tuesday, March 21, 1989.   13

Ms. Drew: The issue before this Court is whether the public burning of an American flag which occurred as part of a demonstration with political overtones is entitled to First Amendment protection. We believe that preservation of the flag as a symbol of nationhood and national unity is a compelling and valid state interest. We feel certain that Congress has the power to both adopt a national symbol and to . . . prevent the destruction of that symbol.

Question from the Court: Now, why does—why did [Johnson's] actions destroy the symbol? His actions would have been useless unless the flag was a very good symbol for what he intended to show contempt for. His action does not make it any less a symbol.

Ms. Drew: Your Honor, we believe that if a symbol over a period of time is ignored or abused, it can, in fact, lose its symbolic effect.

Question: I think not at all. I think . . . when somebody does that to the flag, the flag becomes even more a symbol of the country. It seems to me you're running quite a different argument: not that [Johnson] was destroying its symbolic character, but that he was showing *disrespect* for it; that you want not just a symbol, but you want a venerated symbol. But I don't see how you can argue that he's making it any less of a symbol than it was.

Ms. Drew: Your Honor, I'm forced to disagree with you.

Texas is not suggesting that we can insist on respect. We are suggesting that we have the right to preserve the physical integrity of the flag so that it may serve as a symbol [and that] its symbolic effect is diluted by certain flagrant public acts of flag desecration.

All Texas is suggesting . . . is that we have got to preserve the symbol by preserving the flag itself because there really is no other way to do it.

Oh, Say Can You See
. . . the Point?

John Leo

It's certainly true, as Rep. Henry Hyde says, that the proposed constitutional   1
amendment against desecration of the American flag "is an effort by mainstream Americans to reassert community standards."

But it has less to do with real-life behavior (i.e., flag burning, which hardly   2
occurs anymore) than with returning fire, very late, in a long war over symbols.

The truth is that the cultural left has shown an uncanny ability to conduct   3
symbolic warfare. One example is the long campaign by some gay groups against the Roman Catholic Church, on display recently with simulated acts of anal sex outside St. Patrick's Cathedral during a gay pride march in Manhattan.

US News & World Report, 10 July 1995: 17.

That campaign has mostly skipped the normal methods of democratic protest and concentrated on an attempt to enrage Catholics and degrade the whole symbolic structure of the Catholic religion—male protesters dressed as nuns, loony-looking bishops' miters, cartooned Communion rites, swishy Jesuses in parades.

This cultural style—find out what the mainstream holds dear, then go out of your way to degrade and mock it—erupted in the '60s and made the flag its primary target. Oddly, the flag burnings to protest the Vietnam War, which caused most of the commotion, at least showed an inverted form of respect for the symbolic power of the flag. However provocative, these acts were conducted with full seriousness.   4

But the wider campaign to undermine the flag as potent symbol of national unity, taking place against a backdrop of grave government deception and fraud in conduct of the war, took on a different, jokey character. It went well beyond an attack on militarism and superpatriotism. Like the New York gays' attack on Catholicism, the antiflag campaign aimed to trivialize and enrage. Protesters sprouted shirts and hats made of flags—a taboo in those days—and if that didn't push all the buttons of ordinary citizens, you could always whip out a flag handkerchief and blow your nose on it.   5

Isolated images. Mostly, the energies of that campaign have been spent. They still drift down to us through isolated images—Roseanne Barr's crotch-grabbing rendition of the national anthem, for example, or the Chicago art exhibit that invited museumgoers to walk across the flag.   6

The fallout from the campaign—the trivialization of the flag by printing its image on napkins, sweaters, bikinis and underpants—vastly irritates older Americans who remember the web of understandings and etiquette built around respect for the flag. The chattering classes nowadays show an apparently irrepressible tendency to mock those understandings as a primitive form of idolatry or fetishism. The *Washington Post* Style section recently said, "No, son, you won't go to jail for letting the flag touch the ground." But care in handling the flag is nothing to smirk about. Mankind lives by symbols, and the flag is worth respecting. It represents our shared experience, our connection to America's past and future and our responsibility for one another, regardless of class, age or race.   7

But that meaning has to grow out of the lives of the citizens. Respect for the flag as a symbol can't be compelled through a constitutional amendment. First of all, there is no crisis here that demands the dramatic and very serious business of amending the Constitution. The number of people eager to burn a flag to call attention to a cause or to themselves is very small. By one count, only three flag burnings are known to have occurred since 1993.   8

The only absolutely certain way to revive the flag-burning instinct among American misfits is to pass an amendment forbidding it. "The cultural left is enormously exhibitionistic and enormously juvenile," says Fred Siegel, a historian at Cooper Union in New York City. "An amendment would let them become martyrs. They would be able to cloak their hostilities in constitutional issues." It's politi-   9 cally much smarter to ignore the occasional flag burner. Without an arrest and big emotional reaction, the burning comes to nothing.

Then there are the practical difficulties in policing symbolic protest. All the 10
near-theological issues—What is a flag, and what is merely a image of a flag? What actions constitute disrespect or desecration? Which are truly worth the time of prosecutors and judges?—will come into play, perhaps with yet another 1,200-page government manual to explain the rules. Surely a new crop of dedicated burners will evolve many methods of skirting the flag-burning regulations, while still vastly irritating the general population.

But the biggest reason not to pursue an amendment is that it would bring one 11
more huge effort dedicated to the politics of gesture. Purely emotional satisfactions and theatrical gestures that don't bring much social change have exerted much too strong a pull on conservatives. The reason why so many people want this amendment is that their sensibilities were outraged years ago by a few street-corner provocateurs and they want to strike back now. Or they want to lash out symbolically at some other bothersome group of protesters and imagine that a flag-protection amendment would do the trick.

It's not worth it. Political seriousness means not wasting time and money, and 12
tinkering with the Constitution, to chase a few cranks with flags and matches.

Here's a Thought: Flag Amendment Is a Bad Idea

Benjamin Zycher

The House of Representatives has passed a proposed amendment to the Consti- 1
tution that would allow Congress to impose criminal penalties upon those who physically desecrate the American flag. The standard arguments against such an amendment are driven by the traditional American protection of political speech under the 1st, 9th and 14th amendments and, more broadly, under the natural law doctrines of the Declaration of Independence. Opposition recognizes as well the dangers inherent in the introduction of politically inspired exceptions to the general protection of individual liberties.

That standard argument is correct as far as it goes, but it does not go far 2
enough. It is a matter of long-standing tradition for torn or soiled American flags to be burned, an act reflecting solemn respect. That respect is fundamentally a political statement. The only difference between that act and the burning of a flag by a protester is the nature of the political statement, or, more precisely, the thought that goes through the individual's mind when he strikes the match. In short: A law imposing criminal penalties for the desecration of the flag seeks literally to outlaw a particular thought.

Los Angeles Times (editorial), 2 July 1999: B13.

Many liberals opposing the proposed amendment—always so smug in their 3
purported concern for individual liberty—make precisely the same error in their
support for laws imposing relatively heavy penalties for "hate" crimes. Consider
two individuals assaulted while walking along a road. The first is attacked because
the assailant is in a bad mood; the second is attacked because of the color of his
skin. The respective criminal acts are identical. The respective injuries to the
victims are identical. The only difference in the two cases—literally—is what the
assailants were thinking. "Hate" legislation—as well as the larger dogmas of political correctitude—seeks to penalize a particular set of thoughts.

Clearly, it matters more to individuals if a vandal spray-paints upon a syna- 4
gogue a swastika, as opposed to "Joe was here." The burning of a flag as a symbol
of the community matters differently than the burning of a pile of leaves. But law
can make such distinctions only crudely if at all; would it be "hate," say, to attack
someone because of the color of his hair? Such laws inexorably must make distinctions based on the nature of particular thoughts, and the criminalization of
such thoughts, however worthy they are of contempt, represents a very real step
toward a world of totalitarianism.

Georgia Governor Wants to Lower Confederate Flag

Eric Harrison and Edith Stanley

More than a century after the end of the Civil War, the governor of Georgia thinks 1
it is time to lower the Confederate battle flag for good.

Bowing to pressure from civil rights groups and others who called the emblem 2
offensive and an embarrassment to the state, Gov. Zell Miller said Thursday he
will introduce a measure when the Legislature convenes in January to change the
Georgia flag, which currently incorporates the striking red and blue design of the
Confederacy.

"It's just time to make a change," Miller said. "I think it is the final step that 3
Georgia must take to really become a member of the New South."

Besides Georgia, three other states fly Confederate flags over their capitols in 4
some form—Alabama, Mississippi and South Carolina.[1] The NAACP [National
Association for the Advancement of Colored People] and other civil rights organizations have fought unsuccessfully since 1987 to have them removed. Their
efforts have been staunchly opposed by many whites who see the flag as a symbol
of ethnic and regional pride.

Los Angeles Times, 29 May 1992: A1+.
[1]By July, 2000, after the South Carolina legislature yielded to the economic pressure of an NAACP
boycott—and after it had become an issue in the Republican primary earlier that year—there
were no more Confederate battle flags flying over state capitols.

But Miller said Thursday that the current Georgia state flag, which was 5
adopted in 1956 to protest integration, stood only for a shameful, divisive past.

"The Georgia flag is a last remaining vestige of days that are not only gone but 6
also days that we have no right to be proud of," he said. "We need to lay the days
of segregation to rest, to let bygones be bygones and rest our souls. We need to
do what is right."

The battle over the flag is part of an agonizing larger process of change that 7
has been going on throughout the South as the region struggles in the post-civil
rights era to redefine itself, to recast its symbols and mythology to encompass the
history of both whites and blacks.

While whites might see the Confederate flag as representative of Southern 8
honor and a proud heritage, blacks see something else altogether. Miller alluded
to that Thursday when he said, "What we fly today is not an enduring symbol of
our heritage, but the fighting flag of those who wanted to preserve a segregated
South in the face of the civil rights movement."

The first-term Democrat previously had steadfastly refused to take a stand on 9
the issue. He made it clear that a primary reason for his change of heart is the
state's reputation. Atlanta will be the site of both the 1994 Super Bowl and the
1996 Olympics.

"I want the world to see Georgia as a vibrant growing state, a state that is 10
moving ahead," he said, "and not as a state that is entrenched and holding fast to
the symbols of a time when we resisted efforts to right the wrongs of our past."

Organizations that had been fighting to change the flag hailed Miller's change 11
of heart, even though the new design he endorsed—the state's pre-1956 flag—also
incoroporates Confederate elements.

"The flag is a compromise," said Douglas Alexander, chairman of Georgians 12
for the Flag—an organization pushing for return to the pre-1956 flag. "It has some
Confederacy in it. . . . It has the Confederacy without such a divisive Confederate
emblem."

The National Assn. for the Advancement of Colored People had been in favor 13
of readopting the state's original flag—the Georgia seal on a blue field. Miller
endorsed a later design in which the seal and blue field cover the left third of the
flag and the remainder is occupied by two horizontal red bands enclosing a band
of white. [See diagrams on pp. 365, 366, 368.]

That flag was a variation of the little-known official Confederate flag adopted 14
in 1861. The more familiar Confederate emblem bearing the large blue star-
studded "X" on a red field was used in battle to better distinguish the Confederate
flag from the Union banner.

"You cannot take the Confederacy away from Georgia," said Frank L. Redding 15
Jr., a Democratic representative who has introduced legislation during the past
six sessions to change the flag. "History is important. We should learn from our
history.

"I think the Confederate battle cross has a place, but that place is in the 16
museum so children can learn about the history of the state."

He praised the governor's proposal and predicted it will pass. 17

Miller indicated that he is flexible on which old design is chosen. "I don't have any great deal of problem about what we go back to," he said. "I just think we should not have this flag." 18

The governor's position is sure to be unpopular with many for whom the symbols of the Confederacy remain sacred icons. Throughout the Deep South, these symbols are as common as the kudzu vines that cover the hillsides. The flags adorn caps and clothing and are waved in great number at Ol' Miss football games. The song "Dixie" is still a favorite of high school marching bands and "Rebels" remains a popular athletic team name. 19

The Sons of the Confederate Veterans, a 15,000-member organization made up of descendants of Rebel soldiers, is among those opposed to changing the flag. 20

"Georgia is not a part of the United States today from its own free will," said Charles Lunsford, a spokesman for the group. "We were defeated and destroyed and made to pay penance for 100 years. It's certainly appropriate for us, as a sub-jugated region, to fly the flag of our once independent nation." 21

Claiming that most black people don't care what the flag looks like, he accused the NAACP of initiating the campaign against the flag to increase its membership. "For 100 years nobody attacked our symbols or our songs," Lunsford said. 22

But blacks who have fought against government endorsement of Confederate symbols since the 1960s said that to them, the flag symbolized slavery, racism and oppression. 23

"We are offended by the flag and we abhor having to be forced to pay any kind of salutation to it," said Earl Shinhoster, southeast regional director of the NAACP. 24

In Atlanta, the self-proclaimed capital of the progressive New South and a largely black city, the Confederate battle emblem today flies over the state capitol. It hangs—on almost every block, it seems—in front of downtown hotels and from government and school buildings. For blacks from out of state unac-customed to the flag, it is a startling sight. 25

"Black people never *not* see it and people never become comfortable with it," Shinhoster said. "It's an ongoing symbol of the Confederacy, which is a symbol of oppression. It is a divisive symbol and it is a symbol that is not representative of all the people of the state." 26

For Melissa Metcalfe, state director of Common Cause, one of 90 organiza-tions that form the Civil Rights Network, the symbol has new meaning in light of the rioting that erupted in Atlanta and other cities after the verdicts in the Rodney G. King beating case. 27

Violence related to the verdicts "stresses the fact that people feel disenfran-chised," she said. "Here we have these students in Atlanta saying the justice system doesn't work for them. And when they go to court [to face charges from the disturbance], in front of that court-room is going to be the Georgia flag with the Confederate battle flag on it. That is a strong statement that justice has nothing to do with them in Georgia courts." 28

But while black people may strongly oppose the flag, whites feel at least as strongly in favor of it. An informal telephone survey published by the *Atlanta* 29

Journal and Constitution in April received more than 43,000 calls. About 75% of the respondents wanted the flag left alone. A scientific poll conducted by the same paper in December found that 75% of white Southerners saw the flag as a symbol of Southern pride while more than 50% of black Southerners viewed it as a racist symbol.

Many whites oppose eliminating Confederate symbols, said University of North Carolina sociologist John Shelton Reed, because "they feel they're being asked to spit on the graves of their ancestors, and that's something you shouldn't ask anybody to do."   30

He said the issue is not whether the symbols should be outlawed, but whether they should be displayed by government bodies.   31

Charles Reagan Wilson of the University of Mississippi's Center for the Study of Southern Culture agreed: "[The flag] has historical significance, but turning it into a public symbol suggests something more. Symbols have to be things that unite the community. . . .   32

"In the last 30 years, we've been involved in the process of redefining what the Southern community is," said Wilson. "In the old days blacks were not consulted on symbols as well as on anything else. Whites made the decisions."   33

In the post-civil rights era, "the region is having to deal with the fact that the Southern culture now includes blacks and whites. We're trying to redefine symbols and come up with new ones. The flag issue is very central, I think."   34

The flag debate is such an emotional issue in Georgia that politicians have been reluctant to take a stand. Even Maynard Jackson, Atlanta's black mayor, has skirted the issue.   35

"Most elected officials, even black ones, will tell you that they have other fish to fry," said Shinhoster, who attributed the reluctance to get involved to fear of the political consequences.   36

In what was seen as a courageous move, state Atty. Gen. Michael J. Bowers, in a letter published in the Constitution on May 15, came out in favor of changing the flag. First confirming his Confederate ancestry, Bowers took note of the Rodney King case and consequent rioting and called on his fellow whites to "reach out and show our love for our black neighbors. . . ."   37

"The need is obvious and has nothing to do with image concerns associated with the upcoming Olympics," he said. "It's just a question of right and wrong."   38

As recently as two weeks ago, Miller had dismissed their efforts, saying: "There are more important issues than how our flag looks." But in his press conference Thursday, he said that while issues such as teen-age pregnancy, infant mortality rates and school dropouts are more important, he wanted to put an end to the divisive flag issue "and get it behind us."   39

While many who argue in favor of keeping the flag as it is do so on historical grounds, the fact is that the flag was not adopted until 1956, in the wake of the historic *Brown vs. the Topeka Board of Education* school desegregation case.   40

Reed, the University of North Carolina sociologist, called it an "in-your-face" gesture of defiance by a state government opposed to integration.   41

A Symbol of White Supremacy on the Georgia Flag?

James Andrew COLEMAN, Plaintiff-Appellant,

v.

Zell MILLER, Governor, State of Georgia,
Defendants-Appellees,
Georgia Division, Sons of Confederate
Veterans, et al., Proposed Intervenors.

No. 96-8149.

United States Court of Appeals,
Eleventh Circuit.
July 21, 1997.

In 1879, Senator Herman Perry introduced a bill in the Georgia General   1
Assembly proposing . . . that they adopt his proffered design as the first official
state flag. . . . That flag, a variation on the Stars and Bars [see Figure 1], which
was intended to honor the Confederacy, was modified slightly in 1902 to add

Figure 1

Coleman v. Miller, 912 F.Supp. 522 (1997).
Only footnote 3 (renumbered as footnote 1) remains from original; all others are omitted.

the State coat of arms. . . . The 1902 flag remained the official flag of the State of Georgia until 1956. It looked like this [see Figure 2].[1]

The publication of Margaret Mitchell's book *Gone With The Wind* in 1936 and its release as a movie in 1939 generated a wave of interest in southern history and culture throughout the United States. Although this revived interest was particularly evident in the South, there were few concrete manifestations of it until the mid-1950's, at which time interest in Confederate history coalesced with public outcry to desegregation mandates by the United States Supreme Court.   2   7

In 1952, the Georgia General Assembly passed a resolution providing that the Confederate memorial on Stone Mountain near Atlanta, Georgia should be completed. . . .   3

In 1954, the United States Supreme Court decided *Brown v. Board of Education*, holding that racial segregation in public schools violated the Equal Protection Clause. Later that year, Georgia voters ratified a constitutional amendment allowing parents to withdraw their children from public schools and diverting public money to nonsectarian, segregated private schools.   4

In January 1955, the Georgia General Assembly passed a resolution urging completion of the Confederate memorial on Stone Mountain, finding that inadequate progress had . . . been made since the 1952 resolution. . . .   5

In April 1955, John Sammons Bell, counsel to the County Commissioners Association of Georgia and Chairman of the State Democratic Party, presented his idea of redesigning the state flag to the annual conference of County Commissioners. The County Commissioners approved of the design and voted to   6

Figure 2

---

[1]This example contains a variation on the State coat of arms which first appeared in the mid-1920's.

support his efforts. As is stated in Bell's affidavit, he had been a lifelong student of Confederate military history and a collector of Confederate memorabilia. As such, he stated that he had thoughts of redesigning the flag to incorporate the Confederate battle flag long before the 1950's.

In May 1955, the Supreme Court decided *Brown v. Board of Education*, . . .   7 which required the desegregation of public schools to proceed "with all deliberate speed." The Court's decision fomented great controversy and deep emotion in Georgia. Politicians, including Governor Marvin Griffin, advanced a policy of massive resistance to desegregation in response.

In June 1955, Thurgood Marshall came to Atlanta to help organize citizens to   8 attack segregation. Two months later, the Georgia School Board ordered all teachers belonging to the National Association for the Advancement of Colored People to resign from the organization or have their teaching licenses revoked. At approximately the same time, the State Attorney General prepared for distribution to public schools and universities a background paper advocating the doctrine of interposition, which essentially maintains that states may interpose themselves to block the enforcement of unconstitutional federal mandates such as *Brown*. During this time, the Ku Klux Klan displayed the Confederate battle flag.

In September 1955, the United States Postal Service issued a stamp com-   9 memorating Robert E. Lee.

In November 1955, the Supreme Court decided *Holmes v. City of Atlanta*, . . .   10 which required the desegregation of Atlanta's public golf courses and, by exten- sion, all public facilities, including buses, parks, beaches, and swimming pools.

In December 1955, Rosa Parks refused to give up her seat on a Montgomery,   11 Alabama bus and Rev. Martin Luther King, Jr. instituted a bus boycott there which lasted for over a year. In Georgia, the Board of Regents voted to permit the Georgia Tech football team to play an away game against a team with one black player; however, they also passed a resolution to play no intrastate games against teams with black players.

At the beginning of the 1956 legislative session, Governor Griffin stated in an   12 address to the States' Rights Counsel of Georgia that "the rest of the nation is looking to Georgia for the lead in segregation." In his 1956 state of the State address, Governor Griffin declared that

> there will be no mixing of the races in public schools, in college classrooms in Georgia as long as I am the governor. I campaigned with segregation as the number one plank in my platform. We must not desert future generations of Georgians. We must never surrender. All attempts to mix the races, whether they be in the classrooms, on the playgrounds, in public conveyances, or in any other close personal contact on terms of equality harrow the mores of the South.

The General Assembly had no African-American members at that time.

In early February 1956, Senator Willis Hardin sponsored a bill to adopt John   13 Sammons Bell's new design for the state flag. The bill passed in the Senate within three days. The only discussion on its adoption involved the Civil War centennial and the fact that few surviving Confederate veterans remained to participate. In the House, members debated the cost of changing the flag and whether Bell owned a copyright on . . . his design such that he would profit from the change. The United Daughters of the Confederacy opposed changing the flag, arguing that the Confederate battle flag belonged to all Southerners and no single state had the right to appropriate it.

The bill passed 107 to 32 with 61 abstentions. Because of the unusually high number of abstentions, the bill passed by only a fourteen-vote margin. The flag adopted in 1956, which today remains the official flag of Georgia, looks like this [see Figure 3]. 14

Nothing in the record of the flag bill's debate reveals discussions of segregation or white supremacy. This is pointed out in a number of affidavits of former legislators. (See, e.g., affidavits of S. Ernest Vandiver, Jr., Carl E. Sanders, Harold L. Murphy, Denmark Groover, Jr., and Robert G. Stephens, Jr.). One former member, James Mackay, however, testified that the flag was adopted as a symbol of resistance to *Brown*. 15

The remainder of the 1956 session of the General Assembly reflected its members' interests in segregation and southern history. Of the 150 acts passed in the session, ten bills and two resolutions dealt with massive resistance to desegregation. One such law passed after the flag bill, the Interposition Resolution, declared the *Brown* cases and all similar decisions to be null and void. Finding that the Supreme Court had usurped powers reserved to the states in *Brown*, it repudiated the Court's right to declare state laws unconstitutional. It also asserted that Georgia had the right to decide for itself how to educate its children in keeping with the State's segregated social structure. The resolution passed with twenty-five abstentions and only one dissent. 16

Many observers felt that by 1956, the Confederate battle flag had degenerated into a Dixiecratic symbol of white supremacy and defiant resistance to federal efforts at integration. (See, e.g., affidavits of Dan Carter, Joseph H. Beasley, 17

Figure 3

Joseph E. Lowery, and Teresa Nelson.) To some, the battle flag represented the Ku Klux Klan. In fact, the Klan's stationery in 1995 depicts this flag.

Plaintiff makes the following legal arguments: (1) the flag violates his equal protection rights because a discriminatory purpose motivated the General Assembly to adopt the flag, which has a discriminatory effect; (2) the flag violates Plaintiff's First Amendment rights because it forces him to adopt a symbolic message which discriminates against African-American citizens; (3) the flag violates the Due Process Clause by depriving him of his fundamental privacy interest in associating with white people free from unwarranted governmental intrusion; (4) the flag's intimidating presence infringes on his right to the full and equal enjoyment of public facilities in violation of 42 U.S.C. § 2000(a); and (5) the flag intimidates African-Americans into refraining from exercising their right to vote. 18

. . . [1] Defendants make the following arguments in reply: (1) Plaintiff lacks standing to sue because his subjective assertions of injury are too speculative and the claimed connection between Plaintiff's injury and the flag is too remote; (2) the complaint fails to state a legal issue, raising instead a political question; (3) Plaintiff's § 1983 claims are barred by laches or Georgia's two-year statute of limitations for personal injury claims; and (4) Plaintiff has failed to demonstrate the prerequisites for issuance of a preliminary injunction, most importantly, that there is a substantial likelihood that he will prevail on the merits. 19

● ● ● ●

For Deliberation and Argument

1. *Texas v. Johnson* came before the Supreme Court in 1989. As Randall P. Bezanson explains, Gregory Lee Johnson, the protester who burned the flag, was initially convicted of desecrating a venerated object. When his conviction was overturned by the Texas Court of Criminal Appeals, the state of Texas appealed to the Supreme Court. As an attorney representing the state of Texas or an attorney representing Gregory Lee Johnson, write a memorandum to your superior assessing the merits of your case. In the first section, lay out the arguments on both sides. First, what do you see as the main issue—the question of law on which *Texas v. Johnson* turns? Next, what are the arguments for upholding Johnson's initial conviction? For sustaining the overturning of his conviction? In the second section, explain why you believe that your position is the stronger one and should prevail.

   Take into account the difference between *speech* and *conduct*. Government is much freer to regulate conduct than it is to regulate speech. Speech can be prohibited or restricted only if it is libelous or treasonous, if it solicits criminal acts, if it consists of "fighting words" likely to provoke violence, or if it otherwise is likely to incite breaches of the peace. Conduct can be regulated freely, as long as the conduct is *not* seen as primarily communicative in purpose. Conduct that is intended to communicate an idea is termed *symbolic speech* or *expressive conduct*. Note also that the Supreme Court has said that "the First Amendment literally forbids the abridgment only of 'speech,' but we have long recognized that its protection does not end at the spoken or written word." Did

Johnson's act in burning the flag constitute "expressive conduct," and as such is it protected by the First Amendment? How do you assess Texas attorney Kathi Drew's argument that Johnson should not be allowed to destroy a symbol of the country—that the "symbolic effect [of the flag] is diluted by certain flagrant acts of flag desecration"?

2. Recent years have seen many attempts both by state legislatures and by members of the U.S. Congress to pass laws against flag desecration. For example, one man who wore a small cloth patch of the U.S. flag sewn into the seat of his pants was prosecuted under a Massachusetts statute that read, in part, "Whoever publicly mutilates, tramples upon, defaces or treats contemptuously the flag of the United States . . . whether such flag is public or private property . . . shall be punished by a fine . . . or by imprisonment" (*Smith v. Goguen*, 415 U.S. 566). And in 1989 Congress passed the Flag Protection Act, which provided that "whoever knowingly mutilates, defaces, physically defiles, burns, maintains on the floor or ground, or tramples upon any flag of the United States shall be fined under this title or imprisoned for not more than one year, or both." In 1995, some legislators proposed a constitutional amendment that read, "The Congress and the States shall have power to prohibit the physical desecration of the flag of the United States." This attempt was defeated, but the House of Representatives passed a similar bill in 1999. (Note that it has always been permissible to dispose of worn or soiled flags by burning them; such treatment is legally considered respectful rather than "contemptuous.")

Discuss your own ideas about a constitutional amendment to prohibit treating the flag disrespectfully. Can such a law be reconciled with First Amendment protection of freedom of speech? Or should mistreatment of the flag be put in the same category as other long-established exceptions to unrestricted freedom of speech, such as slander or yelling "fire" in a crowded theater? In composing your response, you may want to consider John Leo's editorial, "Oh, Say Can You See . . . the Point?" Leo supports the conservative attitude on revering the flag yet opposes a constitutional amendment to prohibit flag burning. Why? To what extent do you share his viewpoint about "the cultural left" and about the problems of a flag amendment?

3. Why does economist Benjamin Zycher believe that many liberals are inconsistent in opposing a constitutional amendment to prohibit burning the flag while at the same time supporting heavy penalties for "hate" crimes? Do you agree with him? To what extent can his ideas be extended to the kind of speech codes that have been instituted on many college campuses—codes that prohibit or sanction the expression of racially or ethnically offensive speech? To what extent can support for such codes be reconciled with belief in the First Amendment?

4. The selections on the Georgia state flag controversy show two ways of dealing with what many people saw as a highly controversial issue. In 1992, Governor Zell Miller introduced a measure that would have changed the state flag, dropping the Confederate battle flag design adopted in 1956 and reverting to one of the more neutral designs in effect earlier. As the article by Harrison and Stanley indicates, the measure was extremely controversial among both legislators and the Georgia electorate, and it became unlikely that either a majority of the legislature or the

voters would support it. Miller eventually gave up the fight, saying that the issue had become too divisive. The following year, however (three weeks after the Atlanta-based Super Bowl), the Atlanta-Fulton Country Recreation Authority voted to remove the state flag from the County Stadium, home of the Atlanta Braves. And a number of local school boards and many county agencies and business also stopped flying the official state flag. During the 1996 Olympics in Atlanta, some activists picketed events where the state flag was flying.

Coleman v. Miller illustrates another approach to the issue. James Coleman, an African American, brought suit against the state of Georgia and its governor (who had already expressed support for doing away with the confederate emblem), claiming that its flag was unconstitutional—that it violated both his equal protection rights and his First Amendment rights. In the context of the controversy over the Georgia state flag, how do you assess Coleman's claims? Consider especially the merits of his argument that the flag violated his First Amendment rights. Consider, also, the opposite argument: that the court could not compel the state of Georgia to change its flag because such compulsion would violate the state's (and its citizens') First Amendment rights.

Consider, finally, both the moral *and* the constitutional issues. *Should* the state of Georgia, through its elected officials and its electorate, be entitled to adopt whatever state flag it wants? Does the court have the right, on constitutional (First Amendment) grounds, to require the state to drop the Confederate design on its flag?

■ Group 2 Readings: *Student Speech*

The three cases treated in this section have to do with freedom of speech in public schools. Do the First Amendment rights enjoyed by adults also apply to minors? Does society—as represented in school boards and school administrators—have a right (indeed, an obligation) to impose restrictions on what students may say and write? Should administrators be able to prohibit speech or writing that, in their view, disrupts the educational process, violates privacy, or offends certain individuals? Before rushing to a conclusion, consider whether a student should have the right to hurl racial epithets at another student. Even on college campuses, the decision to forbid or allow "hate speech" has been a controversial one.

The cases here will allow you to explore some of these questions. In Bethel School District v. Fraser, *an honors student is suspended after making a nominating speech filled with sexual innuendo. The* model student paper *in this chapter, by Mark Tseselsky, derives from the next case,* Hazelwood School District v. Kuhlmeier, *in which student reporters file suit against a school after the principal pulls two stories he deemed objectionable from the student newspaper. The third case,* Lacks v. Ferguson Reorganized School District, *involves a teacher who lost her job after her students wrote poems and plays containing "street" language.*

The Obscene Election Speech

BETHEL SCHOOL DISTRICT NO. 403 et al.

v.

FRASER, A Minor, et al.

No. 84-1667

Supreme Court of the United States
478 U.S. 675; 106 S. Ct. 3159; 1986
U.S. LEXIS 139; 92 L.
Ed. 2d 549; 54 U.S.L.W. 5054

July 7, 1986, Decided

A

On April 26, 1983, respondent Matthew N. Fraser, a student at Bethel High School   1
in Pierce County, Washington, delivered a speech nominating a fellow student for
student elective office. Approximately 600 high school students, many of whom
were 14-year-olds, attended the assembly. Students were required to attend the
assembly or to report to the study hall. The assembly was part of a school-sponsored educational program in self-government. Students who elected not to
attend the assembly were required to report to study hall. During the entire
speech, Fraser referred . . . to his candidate in terms of an elaborate, . . . graphic,
and explicit sexual metaphor. [See text of speech, p. 375.]

Two of Fraser's teachers, with whom he discussed the contents of his speech   2
in advance, informed him that the speech was "inappropriate and that he probably should not deliver it," . . . and that his delivery of the speech might have
"severe consequences." . . .

During Fraser's delivery of the speech, a school counselor observed the reac-   3
tion of students to the speech. Some students . . . hooted and yelled; some by gestures graphically simulated the sexual activities pointedly alluded to in
respondent's speech. Other students appeared to be bewildered and embarrassed
by the speech. One teacher reported that on the day following the speech, she
found it necessary to forgo a portion of the scheduled class lesson in order to
discuss the speech with the class. . . .

A Bethel High School disciplinary rule prohibiting the use of obscene lan-   4
guage in the school provides:

"Conduct which materially and substantially interferes with the educational   5
process is prohibited, including the use of obscene, profane language or gestures."

The morning after the assembly, the Assistant Principal called Fraser into her   6
office . . . and notified him that the school considered his speech to have been a
violation of this rule. Fraser was presented with copies of five letters submitted
by teachers, describing his conduct at the assembly; he was given a chance to

---

Bethel School District v. Fraser, 478 US 675 (1984).

explain his conduct, and he admitted to having given the speech described and that he deliberately used sexual innuendo in the speech. Fraser was then informed that he would be suspended for three days, and that his name would be removed from the list of candidates for graduation speaker at the school's commencement exercises.

Fraser sought review of this disciplinary action through the School District's   7
grievance procedures. The hearing officer determined that the speech given by respondent was "indecent, lewd, and offensive to the modesty and decency . . . of many of the students and faculty in attendance at the assembly." The examiner determined that the speech fell within the ordinary meaning of "obscene," as used in the disruptive-conduct rule, and affirmed the discipline in its entirety. Fraser served two days of his suspension, and was allowed to return to school on the third day.

B

Respondent, by his father as guardian ad litem, then brought . . . this action in the   8
United States District Court for the Western District of Washington. Respondent alleged a violation of his First Amendment right to freedom of speech and sought both injunctive relief and monetary damages under 42 U. S. C. § 1983. The District Court held that the school's sanctions violated respondent's right to freedom of speech under the First Amendment to the United States Constitution, that the school's disruptive-conduct rule is unconstitutionally vague and overbroad, and that the removal of respondent's name from the graduation speaker's list violated the Due Process Clause of the Fourteenth Amendment because the disciplinary rule makes no mention of such removal as a possible sanction. The District Court awarded respondent $278 in damages, $12,750 in litigation costs and attorney's fees, and enjoined the School District from preventing respondent from speaking at the commencement ceremonies. Respondent, who had been elected graduation speaker by a write-in vote of his classmates, delivered a speech at the commencement ceremonies on June 8, 1983.

The Court of Appeals for the Ninth Circuit affirmed the judgment of the District Court . . . holding that respondent's speech was indistinguishable from the   9
protest armband in *Tinker v. Des Moines Independent Community School Dist.*, 393 U.S. 503 (1969). [See pp. 403–04.] The court explicitly rejected the School District's argument that the speech, unlike the passive conduct of wearing a black armband, had a disruptive effect on the educational process. The Court of . . . Appeals also rejected the School District's argument that it had an interest in protecting an essentially captive audience of minors from lewd and indecent language in a setting sponsored by the school, reasoning that the School District's "unbridled discretion" to determine what discourse is "decent" would "increase the risk of cementing white, middle-class standards for determining what is acceptable and proper speech and behavior in our public schools." . . . Finally, the Court of . . . Appeals rejected the School District's argument that, incident to its responsibility for the school curriculum, it had the power to control the language used to express ideas during a school-sponsored activity.

High Court to Test Student Free-Speech Rights

■ ─── ■

Philip Hager

There was no mistaking the ominous tone of the announcement over the public   1
address system at Bethel High School [in Tacoma, Washington] in the spring of
1983: "Matt Fraser, please come to the principal's office—immediately."

Fraser, a senior honor student and the state's top-ranked debater, soon was   2
headed down the hall for a confrontation with administrators over a speech laden
with sexual innuendo he had made before 600 classmates at a student election
assembly. He was promptly suspended for making an "indecent" speech that violated a school rule against disruptive conduct.

But Fraser, an aspiring law student, decided to make a federal case out of it—   3
and won an appellate court ruling that will be reviewed Monday before the
Supreme Court in a pivotal test of student free-speech rights against the authority
of school officials to maintain order. The justices' ruling, expected by this
summer, could have a broad impact on the students, teachers and administrators
in the nation's 22,000 public secondary schools.

Broad Power Cited

States generally give school authorities broad power to establish rules and stan-   4
dards for student conduct, and some specifically allow disciplinary action for
vulgar or profane language. In California, habitual use of such language is grounds
for punishment.

In the past, the justices, noting that high school students do not shed free-   5
speech rights "at the schoolhouse gate," have upheld the students' right to wear
black armbands in an anti-war protest. But the court also has recognized that
authorities must be permitted to promote moral values in the schools and that, in
some instances, they can curtail conduct by students that would be fully permissible for adults.

The Reagan Administration and a wide-ranging coalition of school adminis-   6
trators have joined Bethel officials in asking the high court to overturn the appellate ruling and grant school authorities the same "reasonable" power to restrict
indecent speech that the justices granted them last year to search students for
weapons and other contraband.

But Fraser, backed by the American Civil Liberties Union and some teacher   7
and student press groups, says that his speech was neither obscene, disrespectful
nor disruptive and thus is protected by the First Amendment. A ruling for the
school district, he says, could lead to curtailed student speech and press, teaching
an "ugly lesson" of suppression instead of constitutional rights.

───────────

Los Angeles Times, 2 Mar. 1986.

Text of Speech Made by Student for Nomination

This is the speech Matthew Fraser made in 1983 nominating a fellow student to a class office.

"I know a man who is firm—he's firm in his pants, he's firm in his shirt, his character is firm—but most of all, his belief in you, the students of Bethel, is firm.

"Jeff Kuhlman is a man who takes his point and pounds it in. If necessary, he'll take an issue and nail it to the wall. He doesn't attack things in spurts, he drives hard, pushing and pushing, until finally—he succeeds.

"Jeff is a man who will go to the very end—even to the climax—for each and every one of you.

"So vote for Jeff for ASB vice president—he'll never come between you and the best our high school can be."

"I think it's really important that the First Amendment actually be in existence in high school," Fraser, now a student at UC Berkeley, said in an interview there. "You can't expect students to learn about it if they're not able to exercise it. 8

"I think it's good for students to challenge authority to find out what the legal boundaries are. But in this case I was nowhere near passing the boundaries." 9

An attorney for the school district, Clifford D. Foster Jr., says the school has a duty to regulate student speech to preserve a stable and civil environment for learning. 10

"We're not a bunch of right-wing Neanderthals," Foster said. "We're not saying he can't express an idea. The issue here is the way he expressed it. That's the only power we're asserting. He could have gone to a park and given the same speech and there'd be no problem. But a school assembly—that's different." 11

For Fraser, the controversy was born almost by accident. On short notice, he was asked to speak in behalf of Jeff Kuhlman, a nominee for student body vice president. He composed a speech filled with sexual metaphors and showed it to three teachers—two of whom recommended against giving it. Both sides agree that he was not specifically warned he would be suspended if he gave it. 12

Fraser went ahead with the speech, drawing hoots, hollers and applause. Some students were seen mimicking sexual gestures during the speech, and the next day one teacher reported that pupils seemed more interested in discussing the speech than in doing class work. Kuhlman, the candidate Fraser nominated, was elected to office. 13

School officials charged Fraser with violating the school's rule against conduct that "materially and substantially interferes with the educational process." He was suspended for three days and told he would not be eligible to be on a forthcoming ballot for graduation speaker. 14

Elected Class Speaker

Fraser made a quick telephone call to the ACLU and later, with his parents' permission, filed a federal civil rights suit against the school district. Meanwhile, he 15 received enough write-in votes to be elected graduation speaker but still was denied the right to speak by school officials.

At trial in June, 1983, U.S. District Judge Jack E. Tanner ruled that Fraser's 16 rights had been violated and awarded him the $278 he sought as damages—the equivalent of a teacher's pay for the time he was suspended—and attorneys' fees of $12,750. The judge also issued an injunction allowing him to speak at graduation.

Last year a federal appellate panel in San Francisco upheld the decision by a 17 vote of 2 to 1, rejecting the district's claim that it could restrict student speech it considered indecent.

"We fear that if school officials had the unbridled discretion to apply a standard 18 as subjective and elusive as 'indecency' . . . it would increase the risk of cementing white, middle-class standards for determining what is acceptable and proper speech and behavior in our public schools," Judge William A. Norris wrote for the court.

The appeals court acknowledged that officials could exercise substantial 19 control over the classroom but found that a "voluntary activity" like the election assembly amounted to an "open forum," where the First Amendment protected Fraser from punishment.

In their appeal to the Supreme Court (*Bethel vs. Fraser*, 84-1667), the school 20 district's attorneys contend that the assembly was not an open forum but an edu- 18 cational activity, where authorities had a duty to promote community standards of decency and civility. They also denied that the rule they enforced was vague and overly broad or that they should be required to provide students with specific written warnings of potential punishment.

The Justice Department, in a "friend of the court" brief supporting the district, 21 contends that the appellate ruling erroneously bars school officials from punishing students for speech that is anything less than legally obscene or physically disruptive. The public schools, in their role of inculcating basic values, should be empowered to prohibit indecent speech just as they bar racial or religious slurs, the department says.

The district also is backed in a brief filed by the Pacific Legal Foundation and 22 the National School Safety Center on behalf of several school administration groups and officials. They point to the justices' decision last year holding that students' right to privacy must give way to school officials' power to make reasonable searches to maintain order. In this case, they say, students' right of free speech must give way to reasonable limits to guard against disruption.

Speech Defended

Fraser's attorney, Jeffrey T. Haley of Seattle, argues that the speech is not even 23 indecent—let alone obscene—and that Fraser's use of sexual metaphor in a student political assembly should not have been punished by school officials.

"Restrictions within the classroom are fine," Haley said. "There's nothing 24 wrong with enforcing good grammar or requiring certain forms of address to teachers. But a voluntary student assembly is different. If students are to be punished for the kind of speech Matt made, they will get a very distorted view of free-speech rights. In our system, we can generally say what we want."

The Student Press Law Center, citing the right of students to speak out against 25
school administrators, backs Fraser in the case. So does the National Education
Assn., which concludes that the speech presented no threat to teachers or administrators but was merely a non-disruptive expression of opinion on a subject he
was fully entitled to discuss.

For his part, Fraser retains the suspicion that he was "singled out" for pun- 26
ishment by school authorities because he had criticized administrators in editorials in the student newspaper and in confrontations in student gatherings.

"They thought I was a troublemaker," he said. "I think they were happy to 27
finally have an opportunity to suspend me."

There was divided feeling at the high school over the incident. Following 28
Fraser's suspension some students put up posters and placards in his support—
some of them containing sexual references. But later, when as the result of a
court order he gave the graduation address, some in the audience left in protest.

The theme of his graduation talk was the importance of standing up for one's 29
rights. But in Fraser's view, his suspension had a "chilling effect," as he puts it, on
the willingness of students to speak out against authority.

"It's too bad," he said. But, he added with a smile. "They don't recognize how 30
much fun it can be."

Model Student Paper:
The Censored High School Newspaper

U.S. Supreme Court
HAZELWOOD SCHOOL DISTRICT v. KUHLMEIER,
484 U.S. 260 (1988)
484 U.S. 260

Hazelwood School District et al. v. Kuhlmeier et al.
on Writ of Certiorari to the United States Court
of Appeals for the Eighth Circuit
No. 86–836.

Argued October 13, 1987
Decided January 13, 1988

Spectrum was written and edited by the Journalism II class at Hazelwood 1
East. The newspaper was published every three weeks or so during the
1982–1983 school year. More than 4,500 copies of the newspaper were dis-

---

Hazelwood School District v. Kuhlmeier, 484 US 260 (1988).
Footnote 1 omitted.

tributed during that year to students, school personnel, and members of the community.

The Board of Education allocated funds from its annual budget for the printing of *Spectrum*. These funds were supplemented by proceeds from sales of the newspaper. The printing expenses during the 1982–1983 school year totaled $4,668.50; revenue from sales was $1,166.84. The other costs associated with the newspaper—such as supplies, textbooks, and a portion of the journalism teacher's salary—were borne entirely by the Board.

The Journalism II course was taught by Robert Stergos for most of the 1982–1983 academic year. Stergos left Hazelwood East to take a job in private industry on April 29, 1983, when the May 13 edition of *Spectrum* was nearing completion, and petitioner Emerson took his place as newspaper adviser for the remaining weeks of the term.

The practice at Hazelwood East during the spring 1983 semester was for the journalism teacher to submit page proofs of each *Spectrum* issue to Principal Reynolds for his review prior to publication. On May 10, Emerson delivered the proofs of the May 13 edition to Reynolds, who objected to two of the articles scheduled to appear in that edition. One of the stories described three Hazelwood East students' experiences with pregnancy; the other discussed the impact of divorce on students at the school.

Reynolds was concerned that, although the pregnancy story used false names "to keep the identity of these girls a secret," the pregnant students still might be identifiable from the text. He also believed that the article's references to sexual activity and birth control were inappropriate for some of the younger students at the school. In addition, Reynolds was concerned that a student identified by name in the divorce story had complained that her father "wasn't spending enough time with my mom, my sister and I" prior to the divorce, "was always out of town on business or out late playing cards with the guys," and "always argued about everything" with her mother. . . . Reynolds believed that the student's parents should have been given an opportunity to respond to these remarks or to consent to their publication. He was unaware that Emerson had deleted the student's name from the final version of the article.

Reynolds believed that there was no time to make the necessary changes in the stories before the scheduled press run and that the newspaper would not appear before the end of the school year if printing were delayed to any significant extent. He concluded that his only options under the circumstances were to publish a four-page newspaper instead of the planned six-page newspaper, eliminating the two pages on which the offending stories appeared, or to publish no newspaper at all. Accordingly, he directed Emerson to withhold from publication the two pages containing the stories on pregnancy and divorce. He informed his superiors of the decision, and they concurred.

Respondents subsequently commenced this action in the United States District Court for the Eastern District of Missouri seeking a declaration that their First Amendment rights had been violated, injunctive relief, and monetary damages.

Opinion of Justice A

The initial paragraph of the pregnancy article declared that "[a]ll names have been changed to keep the identity of these girls a secret." The principal concluded that the students' anonymity was not adequately protected, however, given the other identifying information in the article and the small number of pregnant students at the school. Indeed, a teacher at the school credibly testified that she could positively identify at least one of the girls and possibly all three. It is likely that many students at Hazelwood East would have been at least as successful in identifying the girls. Reynolds therefore could reasonably have feared that the article violated whatever pledge of anonymity had been given to the pregnant students. In addition, he could reasonably have been concerned that the article was not sufficiently sensitive to the privacy interests of the students' boyfriends and parents, who were discussed in the article but who were given no opportunity to consent to its publication or to offer a response. The article did not contain graphic accounts of sexual activity. The girls did comment in the article, however, concerning their sexual histories and their use or nonuse of birth control. It was not unreasonable for the principal to have concluded that such frank talk was inappropriate in a school-sponsored publication distributed to 14-year-old freshmen and presumably taken home to be read by students' even younger brothers and sisters.

8

The student who was quoted by name in the version of the divorce article seen by Principal Reynolds made comments sharply critical of her father. The principal could reasonably have concluded that an individual publicly identified as an inattentive parent—indeed, as one who chose "playing cards with the guys" over home and family—was entitled to an opportunity to defend himself as a matter of journalistic fairness. These concerns were shared by both of Spectrum's faculty advisers for the 1982-1983 school years, who testified that they would not have allowed the article to be printed without deletion of the student's name.

9

Opinion of Justice B

[My fellow justice] relies on bits of testimony to portray the principal's conduct as a pedagogical lesson to Journalism II students who "had not sufficiently mastered those portions of the . . . curriculum that pertained to the treatment of controversial issues and personal attacks, the need to protect the privacy of individuals" . . . and "the legal, moral, and ethical restrictions imposed upon journalists. . . ." In that regard, [he] attempts to justify censorship of the article on teenage pregnancy on the basis of the principal's judgment that (1) "the [pregnant] students' anonymity was not adequately protected," despite the article's use of aliases; and (2) the judgment that "the article was not sufficiently sensitive to the privacy interests of the students' boyfriends and parents. . . ." Similarly, [he] finds in the principal's decision to censor the divorce article a journalistic lesson that the author should have given the father of one student an "opportunity to defend himself" against her charge that (in the Court's words) he "chose 'playing cards with the guys' over home and family. . . ."

10

But the principal never consulted the students before censoring their work.   11
"[T]hey learned of the deletions when the paper was released. . . ." Further, he
explained the deletions only in the broadest of generalities. In one meeting called
at the behest of seven protesting *Spectrum* staff members (presumably a fraction
of the full class), he characterized the articles as " 'too sensitive' for 'our immature audience of readers,' " and in a later meeting he deemed them simply "inappropriate, personal, sensitive and unsuitable for the newspaper." [My fellow
justice's] supposition that the principal intended (or the protestors understood)
those generalities as a lesson on the nuances of journalistic responsibility is
utterly incredible. If he did, a fact that neither the District Court nor the Court of
Appeals found, the lesson was lost on all but the psychic *Spectrum* staffer.

Paper Topic: "The Censored High School Newspaper" (*Hazelwood School District v. Kuhlmeier*)

To what extent do you believe that the principal of the Hazewood School District
(*Hazelwood v. Kuhlmeier*) was justified in deleting from the school newspaper
the pages that contained the two articles to which he objected? To what extent do
you believe that the principal violated the First Amendment rights of the student
journalists?

In developing your argument, take into account not only the First Amendment
itself but also the circumstances of this case and the excerpts from the two opinions
(by justices of the Supreme Court) following the facts of the case. Draw compar-
isons and contrasts between this case and *Bethel School District v. Fraser*, in which
a student was disciplined for making an obscene speech in a school assembly.

You may also want to include, as part of your argument, the kinds of things
that the parties concerned—that is, the student journalists, their journalism
teacher, and the principal—might have done to avoid having this matter become
a full-fledged First Amendment issue that went all the way to the Supreme Court.
For example, was it possible for the students to fulfill their journalistic responsibilities while protecting the privacy of the individuals about whom they reported?
Was it possible for the principal to have acted in such a way as to deal with both
the privacy issue and the freedom of speech issue?

MODEL STUDENT PAPER

COMMENTARY BY MARK TSESELSKY

At first, I felt that my task in this assignment was fairly straightforward. I knew   1
immediately which way to argue. More important, because of previous experience, I had IRAC to follow. The tricky part was that the judges had already written
out most of the arguments for me. All that was missing was the verdict. However,
I had an impressive number of facts to mull over, and it was hard to decide which

facts to include. As I was working on the rough version I caught myself not including enough facts. Throughout this assignment I had the feeling I forgot to include something. It seemed to be an easy assignment, but completing it was difficult.

Since I have read the *Hazelwood* and *Bethel* cases several times, it was hard for me to pick up on the fact that my own writing lacked important explanations about the content. It helped to put away the writing even for a short time and then to look at it with a fresh eye to discover that many important facts were still missing. 2

Once I was satisfied with presenting the relevant facts, I had trouble deciding which rules to include. It was easy enough to cite the First Amendment, but how was I to connect this abstract notion to the specific case of freedom of speech in high schools? 3

At this moment I felt that the assignment was too broad. It had at least three components: the issue of constitutionality of the principal's actions, the extent to which his actions were justified, and alternatives to his conduct and to the style of the articles. Which was I to tackle first? How could I incorporate all of the components into a single whole so that my argument flowed instead of being choppy? 4

First, I approached it from the justification point of view. Basic plan: list what the principal was concerned about and then say whether or not his concerns were justified. But I was not happy with that approach because it left out other important aspects, like constitutionality and alternatives. How to include them? 5

In the end, I decided to use a reliable tactic. Acknowledge the validity of the opposite point of view to the greatest extent possible. This meant starting out by saying that the principal had some real causes for concern. The two arguments that the justice arguing for the school district used were privacy concerns and journalistic fairness. I showed how these concerns could have been handled. And the principal's real concern over the appropriateness of the material for the high school students was beyond his powers, according to the law. 6

My essay was still missing a few components, such as discussion of the harm involved in what the articles said and the harm involved in prohibiting the discussion of these subjects. Also, I needed to say more about what the students themselves could have done to avoid a lawsuit. 7

Rough Draft

Three former students of Hazelwood East High School in St. Louis, Missouri, alleged violation of their constitutional freedom of speech over the decision by the principal of the high school to delete articles dealing with divorce and teen pregnancy from *Spectrum*, the school newspaper that the three students edited. *Spectrum* was intended for high school students but also widely read by teachers and members of the local community. The newspaper was mostly supported by contributions from the local Board of Education, which explains why it was customary for teacher-supervisors of *Spectrum* like Howard Emerson to submit for review the proofs of the newspaper to Robert Eugene Reynolds, the principal of Hazelwood East High School. According to this practice, on May 10, 1983, 8

Emerson delivered proofs of the newspaper to Principal Reynolds. There were three days left before the newspaper had to go to print.

Reynolds thought that two particular articles in this edition were controversial. One of these articles discussed the experiences of three Hazelwood students with pregnancy. Their names were changed to protect their identity. However, a teacher testified that "she could positively identify at least one of the girls, and possibly all three" (*Hazelwood* 379). In another controversial article a student accused her father of not spending enough time with his family prior to the divorce. In the version that Reynolds saw she was quoted as saying that her father would rather spend time with his card-playing buddies than with his own family. Neither the father nor the boyfriends of the pregnant girls gave their consent to the articles, nor were they in a position to offer a response.

Principal Reynolds was concerned about the lack of journalistic fairness toward boyfriends and parents mentioned in the articles. He also felt that the protection of privacy interests of all the parties discussed in the articles was inadequate. In particular, he felt concerned about the lack of protection for the pregnant students whose names were already falsified in the article. Moreover, he did not think that it was appropriate for a high school newspaper to mention the sexual history of the pregnant girls and their use or nonuse of contraceptives. He judged that three days was not enough time to correct the problems and believed his only viable option was to delete the offending articles or to issue no newspaper at all. The legal question to answer in this matter is whether deleting the offending articles was a justified act of a concerned educator or a violation of students' freedom of speech rights. But it is also important to discuss what the principal and the students could have done to avoid turning a journalistic matter into a complex legal question worthy of a Supreme Court ruling.

Freedom of speech is protected by the First Amendment of the U.S. Constitution, which states that "Congress shall make no law . . . abridging the freedom of speech." The amendment is straightforward, but its interpretation is complex. So in practice the Supreme Court and other federal court rulings determine how the amendment is applied to real-life situations such as freedom of speech in schools. In large measure the judicial interpretation of the First Amendment depends on whether "the harm done by the speech act [is] greater than the harm that would be done by restricting it" (Introduction to "Freedom of Speech" 354). In weighing the balance of these opposite interests, the U.S. courts have determined that school districts cannot "control the language used to express ideas . . . [in] a school-sponsored activity" (*Bethel School District v. Fraser*, 478 U.S. 675 (1986)).

The articles as they were presented to the principal certainly contained some cause for concern over privacy and perhaps even journalistic fairness. For example, to include the name of the student who sharply criticized her father made her vulnerable and her father unfairly prevented from responding to some serious accusations. Moreover, despite the fact that the names of the pregnant girls were changed, other students could have still identified the girls because of their condition.

But both problems were fixable and did not justify the principal's decision to delete the articles. For example, the name of the student sharply critical of her father was dropped from the final version just as both teachers involved with

Spectrum recommended. This eliminated the need to protect the privacy interests of an already torn family, as well as the need to provide the father's consent and response to accusations of indifference. To further protect the identities of the pregnant girls, the principal could have suggested that the subject of the article be changed from teenage pregnancy in Hazelwood East High to teen pregnancy in general to avoid implicating pregnant girls of Hazelwood in particular. If Principal Reynolds' only concerns were over-protection of privacy and journalistic fairness, he could have used these articles as an important opportunity to teach the students about the journalistic craft without necessarily abridging their right to freely express themselves. But Reynolds chose instead to simply delete the offending articles in their entirety without consulting the students, which suggests that he was simply determined to prevent publication of articles he considered to be "too sensitive . . . for our immature audience of readers."

However, based on the existing legal precedent, an educator cannot control   14
the language, much less the free flow of ideas, in a school-sponsored organization. According to the Supreme Court's ruling in *Bethel v. Fraser*, high school students have a constitutional right to freely express themselves. Moreover, such expression does not have to be approved by their teachers. Matthew N. Fraser delivered a speech to a group of Bethel High School students who were required to either attend the meeting or report to study hall. To this essentially "captive audience" of teenagers, Fraser delivered an election speech, which contained implicit sexual innuendoes. He was suspended and removed from the list of candidates for graduation speakers because the school officials judged his actions obscene and disruptive of the educational process.

However, the appellate court judges' ruling in *Bethel* held that the school   15
board could not dictate what was the proper discourse to its students because it would impose white, middle-class values on everyone (376). Similarly, Principal Reynolds imposed his views that teenage pregnancy and inattentive parenting are inappropriate subjects for high school students. Thereby, he violated students' freedom of speech rights.

Second Draft (Final Six Paragraphs)

But both problems were fixable and did not justify principal's decision to delete the   16
articles. For example, the name of the student sharply critical of her father was dropped from the final version just as both teachers involved with *Spectrum* recommended. This eliminated the need to protect the privacy interests of an already torn family, as well as the need to provide the father's consent and response to accusations of indifference. To further protect the identities of the pregnant girls, the principal could have suggested that the subject of the article be changed from teenage pregnancy in Hazelwood East High to teen pregnancy in general to avoid implicating pregnant girls of Hazelwood in particular. Thus, with a little innovative thinking, the possible harm done by the speech act would have been greatly diminished.

On the other hand, to restrict the controversial articles harmed the interests   17
of the young journalists as well as the young readers of the newspaper. The very essence of the First Amendment is to provide everyone, but especially a jour-

nalist living in a democratic republic, with the freedom and the opportunity to delve into important and controversial subjects, of which the authorities may not approve. The principal could have taught Journalism II students how to exercise this sacred journalistic right responsibly. But instead, what kind of lesson in democracy did the principal provide to his students by simply deleting the controversial articles?

If Principal Reynolds' only concerns were protection of privacy and journalistic 18
fairness, he could have used these articles as an important opportunity to teach the students about the journalistic craft without necessarily abridging their right to freely express themselves. But Reynolds chose instead to simply delete the offending articles in their entirety without consulting the students, which suggests he was simply determined to prevent publication of articles he considered to be "too sensitive . . . for our immature audience of readers." But with a little fix these articles could have helped a young reader to cope with an ongoing divorce and perhaps some young girls would have thought twice about premature sexual relations if they knew more about teen pregnancy. Were the interests of "our immature audience" really served well by complete lack of information on these teen issues?

Concern for sensitive material reaching young children was also a part of the 19
issue in *Bethel v. Fraser.* Matthew N. Fraser delivered an election speech, which contained implicit sexual innuendoes to a "captive audience" of Bethel High School students who were required to either attend the meeting or report to study hall. He was suspended and removed from the list of candidates for graduation speakers because the school officials judged his actions obscene and disruptive to the educational process.

In both cases, freedom of expression had to be balanced with protecting the 20
needs of a vulnerable young audience. In *Bethel v. Fraser,* the harm done by Fraser's speech, which bordered on the obscene, was greater than the harm done by restricting it. Fraser's electoral speech was supposed to be a lesson in democracy, but both the content and the manner of the speech made a mockery of our political process because sexual prowess should have nothing to do with politics. Fraser's sexual innuendoes took the minds of the young students far away from politics and contained no ideas worthy of the First Amendment protection.

On the other hand, the imperfect but important attempt to deal with signifi- 21
cant teen issues by the young Hazelwood journalists deserved First Amendment protection. Unlike the Fraser speech, the controversial articles contained nothing remotely similar to obscenity. The pregnancy article's frank discussion of girls' sexual history did not contain any graphic depiction of the sexual acts and only served to make a valid point about an important teen issue. Both privacy and journalistic fairness concerns were fixable, so there was nothing about either the content or the style of the articles that had the potential to harm the students. On the contrary, to restrict their access to important knowledge and to quash the journalistic aspirations of Journalism II students produced greater harm than the articles. The fact that these articles were written for a school-sponsored news-

paper did not give Principal Reynolds the right to violate the students' right to free expression of important ideas, which these articles contained. Clearly, the principal did not work hard enough to balance his responsibilities as protector of the innocent with his job as an educator of future citizens and journalists of a democratic republic.

Commentary by Mark Tseselsky

As I was trying to finish this piece, I was challenged by the unique position of   22
freedom of speech in high school in the context of the greater First Amendment issue. To prevent influencing the way in which students argued in this essay, it was necessary for the instructor to exclude important information about the actual outcome of this case. If the professor had provided me in advance with the decisions of the courts in *Bethel* and *Hazelwood*, the essays would have been one-sided. On the other hand, without knowing the reasoning behind these important decisions it was difficult to comprehend the special restrictions on freedom of speech in high schools, as opposed to in society at large.

After reading the professor's comments, I realized that I had gotten carried   23
away with my comparison of *Bethel* and *Hazelwood* at the expense of some crucial aspects of First Amendment law. In calling Fraser's speech unworthy of First Amendment protection, I missed the very point of the amendment, which is that *all* speech—except for very narrowly defined exceptions, such as libel, obscenity, "fighting words," incitement to riot, etc.—is protected.

In terms of organization and structure, the challenge in the final stages of the   24
essay was incorporating the *Bethel* case. Since the focus was on *Hazelwood,* my argument about this particular case had to come first, but it was also important to compare it with the *Bethel* case. At the same time I wanted to avoid repeating in the comparison the arguments I had made earlier.

Final Draft

The Censored High School Newspaper

Facts and Issue

Three former students of Hazelwood East High School in St. Louis, Missouri,   25
alleged violation of their constitutional freedom of speech over the decision by the high school principal to delete articles dealing with divorce and teen pregnancy from *Spectrum*, the school newspaper that the three students edited (*Hazelwood School District v. Kuhlmeier* (1988)). *Spectrum* was intended for high school students but was also widely read by teachers and members of the local community. The newspaper was mostly supported by contributions from local Board of Education, which explains why it was customary for teacher-supervisors of *Spectrum* like Howard Emerson to submit the proofs of the newspaper for review to Robert Eugene Reynolds, the principal of Hazelwood East High School. Following this practice, on May 10, 1983, Emerson delivered proofs of the newspaper to Principal Reynolds with only three days left before the newspaper had to go to print.

Reynolds thought that two particular articles in this edition were controversial. One of these pieces discussed the experiences of three Hazelwood students with pregnancy. Their names were changed to protect their identity. However, a teacher testified that "she could positively identify at least one of the girls, possibly all three" (*Hazelwood* 379). In another controversial article, a student accused her father of not spending enough time with his family prior to his divorce from her mother. In the version that Reynolds saw, the student was quoted as saying that her father would rather spend time with his card-playing buddies than with his own family. Neither the father nor the boyfriends of the pregnant girls gave their consent to the articles, nor were they in a position to offer a response.   26

Principal Reynolds was concerned about the lack of journalistic fairness toward boyfriends and parents mentioned in the articles. He also felt that the protection of privacy interests of all the parties discussed in the articles was inadequate. In particular, he felt concerned about the lack of protection for the pregnant students whose names were already falsified in the article. Moreover, he thought that it was inappropriate for a high school newspaper to mention the sexual history of the pregnant girls and their use or nonuse of contraceptives. He believed that three days was not enough time to correct the problems and that his only viable options were either to delete the offending articles or to issue no newspaper at all. The issue in this case is whether deleting the offending articles was the justified act of a responsible educator concerned with journalistic fairness and protecting the privacy of individuals discussed in the article or whether it was instead a violation of students' freedom of speech rights.   27

The First Amendment and the Balancing of Interests

Freedom of speech is protected by the First Amendment of the U.S. Constitution, which states that "Congress shall make no law . . . abridging the freedom of speech." The amendment is straightforward, but its interpretation is complex. So in practice the Supreme Court and other federal court rulings determine how the amendment is applied to specific concepts such as the freedom of speech in public high schools. In large measure, the judicial interpretation of the First Amendment depends on whether "the harm done by the speech act is greater than the harm that would be done by restricting it" (Introduction to "Freedom of Speech" 354). In weighing the balance of these opposite interests, the federal courts have determined that school districts cannot "control the language used to express ideas . . . [in] a school-sponsored activity" (*Bethel v. Fraser*, 478 U.S. 675 (1986)).   28

Freedom of Speech vs. Privacy and Sensitive Subject Matter

As they were presented to the principal, the articles certainly gave some cause for concern over privacy and perhaps even journalistic fairness. For example, to include the name of the student who sharply criticized her father made her vulnerable and unfairly prevented her father from responding to some serious accusations. Moreover, despite the fact that the names of the pregnant girls were   29 changed, other students could have still identified the girls because of their pregnancies.

But both problems were fixable and did not justify the principal's decision to delete the articles. For example, the name of the student sharply critical of her father was dropped from the final version, just as both teachers involved with *Spectrum* recommended. This eliminated the need to protect the privacy interests of an already torn family, as well as the need to provide the father's consent and response to accusations of indifference. To further protect the identities of the pregnant girls and to avoid implicating pregnant girls at Hazelwood, in particular, the principal could have suggested that the subject of the article be changed from teenage pregnancy in Hazelwood East High to teen pregnancy in general. Thus, with a little innovative thinking, the possible harm done by the speech act would have been greatly diminished.

On the other hand, to restrict the controversial articles harmed the interests of the young journalists as well as the young readers of the newspaper. The very essence of the First Amendment is to provide everyone, but especially a journalist living in a democratic republic, with the freedom and the opportunity to delve into important and controversial subjects, of which the authorities may not approve. The principal could have taught Journalism II students how to exercise this vital journalistic right responsibly. But instead, what kind of lesson in democracy did he provide to his students by simply deleting the controversial articles?

If Principal Reynolds' only concerns were protection of privacy and journalistic fairness, he could have used these articles as an important opportunity to teach the students about the journalistic craft without abridging their right to freely express themselves. Reynolds chose instead to simply delete the offending articles in their entirety without consulting the students, which suggests he was simply determined to prevent publication of articles he considered to be "too sensitive . . . for our immature audience of readers." But with a little fix these articles could have really helped its readers. Perhaps some young women would have thought twice about premature sexual relations if they knew more about teen pregnancy and some young readers would have been better able to cope with an ongoing divorce. Were the students' interests really served well by blocking information from other teenagers' point of view on these important teen issues?

Concern for sensitive material reaching young children was also a part of the issue in *Bethel v. Fraser.* Matthew N. Fraser delivered an election speech, which contained implicit sexual innuendoes to a "captive audience" of Bethel High School students who were required to either attend the meeting or report to study hall. He was suspended and removed from the list of candidates for graduation speakers because the school officials judged his actions obscene and disruptive of the educational process.

In both legal cases, freedom of expression had to be balanced with protecting the needs of a vulnerable young audience. To meet a vital societal interest in the proper education of the young, the school districts in both cases felt responsible for what reached the ears and eyes of the young students. In

Bethel v. Fraser, the harm done by Fraser's speech, which bordered on the obscene, was greater than the harm done by restricting it. Fraser's electoral speech was supposed to be a lesson in democracy, but it actually disrupted the educational process because Fraser's sexual innuendoes took the minds of the young students (some as young as 14 years of age) far away from politics. According to a school counselor, some of the students imitated sexual activities alluded to in the speech, others "appeared bewildered and embarrassed by the speech" (*Bethel* 372). Perhaps Fraser's punishment was overly harsh, but the school district had a vital interest to protect its vulnerable audience from disruptions to the educational process.

On the other hand, an imperfect but important attempt to deal with significant teen issues by the young Hazelwood journalists was not a disruption of the educational process. Moreover, with a little help from the principal these articles could have become an important part of this process. Unlike the Fraser speech, the controversial articles contained nothing remotely similar to obscenity. The pregnancy article's frank discussion of girls' sexual history did not contain any graphic depiction of the sexual acts and served only to make a valid point about an important teen issue. Both the privacy and journalistic fairness problems were fixable, so that there was nothing about the articles that had the potential to harm the students or disrupt the educational process. On the contrary, restricting their access to important knowledge and quashing the journalistic aspirations of Journalism II students produced greater harm than the articles themselves would have.

Conclusion

The fact that these articles were written for a school-sponsored newspaper did not give Principal Reynolds the right to violate the students' right to free expression of important ideas. These ideas could have enriched the students' education with a teen perspective on the important issues. Clearly, the principal did not work hard enough to balance his responsibilities as protector of the innocent with his job as an educator of future citizens and journalists of a democracy.

—Mark Tseselsky

Cissy Lacks: A Teacher Who Didn't Play Safe

James Nicholson

For 25 years, Cissy Lacks has been receiving awards for her work in the classroom, including citations as one of the 15 best teachers in America. But suddenly, in January of 1995, the St. Louis, Mo. educator was fired because, as Lacks puts

American Theatre 14.3 (Mar. 1997): 34–35.

it, "I decided drama was important in language classes." The fallout made her a "Person of the Week" on ABC's *World News Tonight,* the subject of a segment on *Dateline NBC,* an interviewee on *CBS This Morning* and the most carefully observed educator in the country.

Characters in Conversation

Lacks's students at the predominantly African-American Berkeley High School 2 tackled a drama assignment in the fall of 1994. "I asked them to develop a dialogue about things that are important to them," Lacks says, "showing how natural conversation is created from characters." The teacher and her students were anticipating the opportunity, thanks to a grant Lacks had secured from the School Partnership Program, to work with actors from neighboring St. Louis Black Repertory Company. Their scenes [dealt with] such issues as teen pregnancy, gang violence and drugs, and were replete with the kind of language those subjects elicit. Following a classroom documentation policy suggested by the district, Lacks videotaped the students performing the scenes for in-class critique.

The scenes might have been alien to the majority of St. Louis's Ferguson- 3 Florissant School District, but were all too real for the students at Berkeley. "I've been teaching for 25 years, and in all those years, I have not censored creative writing in the early stages," Lacks notes. "My students have been productive, they have understood voice and how to use it, and they were taking responsibility for writing."

Three months after the taping, without explanation or warning, Berkeley's 4 principal Vernon Mitchell removed the videotapes from Lacks's locked classroom cabinet and proceeded to remove the teacher from the classroom. The tapes were distributed to local and national media without the students' permission and without explaining the assignment. News reports focused sensationally on the street language the characters were using in the scenes.

The district fired Lacks for violating a profanity code that applies to student 5 classroom behavior, but not to the district's own creative writing policy, which states, "Don't tell writers what should be in their writing . . . build on what writers know and have done." At Lacks's hearing, assistant superintendent of curriculum Barbara Davis stated that any teacher allowing a student to read aloud any play, poem or novel that contained profanity could be subject to termination. The district then went on to censor a high school production of *Oklahoma!,* ordering that all "hells" and "damns" be removed.

Dubbed the "Profanity Queen" by St. Louis talk shows, Lacks set out to fight 6 for her academic freedom and reputation, quickly gaining an impressive array of supporters: the National Education Association and the National Council of Teachers of English rapidly weighed in with their backing, and New York's Young Playwrights, whose work with school-age children served as a model for Lacks, also voiced its support. Last April, she received the PEN/Newman's own First

Amendment Award for "her courage in defending her young writers' right to self-expression at great risk to herself."

In November, Lacks sued the district in Federal Court, claiming that it had   7
violated her First Amendment rights and that race was a motivating factor in her firing. Young Playwrights artistic director Sheri Goldhirsch—after an initial challenge that her presence in the courtroom was irrelevant, as she was "from New York"—testified that Lacks's teaching technique parallels a curriculum created by the company which has been in use throughout the country for the past 15 years. "Young playwrights need to be able to be free to say and write about what interests them if they are to continue to write," reasoned Goldhirsch.

Drama Is the Perfect Tool

The widely-seen tapes, Goldhirsch explained, were not examples of the students   8
cursing, but "acting out a role." For his part, however, principal Mitchell testified that he only saw "white folks video-taping black students acting the fool." School board president Leslie Hogshead concurred, contending that she saw nothing "racial" in distributing a press release that called the tapes "a violation of our black community."

Lacks's students felt differently. One of them, Reginald McNeary, who won a   9
district-wide contest for a poem written in Lacks's class, said, "Ms. Lacks explained to us that writing was just what is inside you—what you feel and what's on your mind." However, a different view was voiced by psychologist Judith Tindale, a special witness for the district, who questioned a technique that allows students to explore their "dark side" and stated that such exploration should not be allowed. When asked specifically about McNeary's award-winning poem, Tindale indicated that it should never have been written.

The jury disagreed. On Nov. 18 it ruled that the school district had violated   10
Lacks's First Amendment fights because she was not given fair warning and that the district has no right to prohibit classroom methods that have a legitimate academic purpose. The jury awarded the educator $500,000 for her claim of improper firing and $250,000 for her claim that she was discriminated against because of her race. A week after these decisions, Judge Catherine Perry ruled that Lacks should also receive back pay and benefits. (The Fergusson-Florissant Board of Education voted to appeal both rulings; at press time, Lacks's job status, awards and pension were still pending.)

Lacks was particularly pleased because "a jury of ordinary citizens under-   11
stood how important it is for a teacher and students to have mutual trust and how the creative process differs from other learning processes.

"Theatre is one of the most under-used mediums in teaching," Lacks con-   12
tinues. "This is unfortunate, as it is the perfect tool for teaching language. Drama is important to education and it is sad that, precisely because of its effectiveness, teachers tend to pull back and play it safe."

"The Profanity Queen"

Cecilia LACKS, Plaintiff,

v.

FERGUSON REORGANIZED SCHOOL
DISTRICT, R–2, Defendant.
No. 4:95CV1024 CDP.

United States District Court, E.D.
Missouri, Eastern Division.
Aug. 15, 1996.

[Lacks] admitted that she does not censor profanity in her students' creative   1
works. The issue, therefore, is whether plaintiff had an "intent to violate or
disobey a particular regulation," *i.e.*, board policy 3043. The board made no specific finding as to plaintiff's intent to violate policy 3043, but presumed such intent
because plaintiff was aware that policy 3043 incorporated the student discipline
code that prohibited student profanity. Plaintiff argues, however, that she did not
know that policy 3043 applied to profanity in class-related creative assignments.
[School District] argues that there is no exception for class-related profanity on
the face of policy 3043. Defendant also argues that plaintiff had been put on
notice that the policy applied to creative works by Principal Mitchell's warnings
to plaintiff regarding profanity in the student newspaper. Plaintiff denies having
received any warnings about profanity in the newspaper.

The record as a whole clearly indicates that there was in practice an unwritten   2
exception in the district for profanity in class-related activities. The evidence presented to the board was overwhelming that many administrators and teachers in
the district allowed class-related profanity depending on the context and degree
of profanity. The relevant evidence can be summarized as follows:

- In the 1993/94 school year, plaintiff showed Mitchell a student journal
  entry containing the words "honkey" and "chink," and the statement if "I
  ever see a white are [sic] a Jew touch me I'm going two kill them . . ." and
  Mitchell did not discuss the language with plaintiff or the student, nor did
  he discipline either plaintiff or the student.
- A play written and performed by Berkeley students for the entire
  student body and attended by Mitchell contained profanity, including at
  least the word "damn," as well as other conduct classified as Type II violations of policy 3043. Neither the teacher supervising that play nor the
  students performing it were disciplined in any way.

Lacks v. Ferguson Reorganized School District, 936 F.Supp. 157 (1996).
Footnote 2 omitted, following footnote renumbered.

- Dr. John Wright, assistant superintendent, testified regarding the plays produced in plaintiff's class that "if [the students] were not doing this in a play, they would have been suspended, it would have been Type I or Type II behavior in the classroom."
- Wright testified that he did not know whether a student who reads profanity aloud from another author's work could be punished
- Karen Price, Chair of the English Department at Berkeley, testified that she was not aware of a rule that required teachers to censor profanity in creative works. Price also testified that she was not aware that a student reading profanity from literature could be charged with violating the student discipline code.
- Dr. Larilyn Lawrence, the district's Curriculum Coordinator for Language Arts, testified that she did not know of a policy prohibiting students from reading profanity in literature aloud.
- Delores Graham, principal at a middle school in the district, was not aware that a student reading profanity from a creative work of literature or that student's teacher would be violating the student discipline code.
- James Nicholson, a playwright who visited plaintiff's classes [see pp. 388–90], testified that he was present when district administrators heard students read profanity from their own creative works, but no administrator ever told him or plaintiff to disallow profanity in the students' creative expression. Nicholson testified that no policy was "verbalized to me or given to me in print."
- C.S., a former student of plaintiff, testified as follows: "I didn't realize that expressing yourself in a play when, you know, I didn't realize if you express yourself, you could get in trouble for that. But I realize that if you are using profanity and doing other things in the hallway or any place else in the school, that you could get in trouble."
- P.S., a former student of plaintiff, testified that she performed creative writing assignments containing profanity in the presence of a district administrator and the administrator "didn't give a reaction, so we just basically, we went with the flow."

Defendant submitted no evidence indicating that the district in fact enforced policy 3043 to prohibit students from reading aloud or otherwise using profanity in creative works.[1]

---

[1]Defendant [school district] attempts to characterize Mitchell's alleged warnings to plaintiff about profanity in the student newspaper as evidence that plaintiff knew profanity was not allowed in any student creative works. Defendant's attempt is unconvincing because there is a separate board policy (number 2053) entitled "student publications" that requires teachers and students to judge the "appropriateness" of materials and to edit "obscene" and other material from the student newspaper and yearbook. Mitchell's enforcement of this specific policy does not translate to an interpretation that profanity is not allowed in student poems and plays under policy 3043, which governs student behavior. In fact, policy 2053 begins with the following statement: "The Board recognizes creative student expression as an educational benefit of the school experience. One medium of expression is student journalism." The policy proceeds to expressly limit the content of student journalism, but does not address limitations on any other form of creative student expression.

Excerpt from Judge A, Appeals Court Opinion (1998)

[T]his case . . . involves issues of exceptional importance. The panel [of judges] high- 4
lights the fact that offensive and profane words were used more than 150 times in
approximately forty minutes of the student-written plays. The panel also points to
the fact that "as part of a poetry-writing exercise, Lacks had permitted a student to
read aloud in a classroom two of his poems which contained profanity and graphic
descriptions of oral sex." Of course, when these facts are viewed in isolation, one
might wonder how suppressing or censoring such profanity could raise any First
Amendment or educational issues of exceptional importance. Again, these facts,
standing alone, present only a one-sided, fractional portion of the evidence. The jury
was presented with a much bigger picture. For example, Lacks testified at length
about the two poems mentioned above and the context in which they were read to
the class. Her testimony revealed that those two poems—vulgar and shocking as
they were—were the first utterances in the class by a boy named Reginald, who previously had refused to participate in class and had repeatedly been sent to the principal's office because he did nothing but put his head on his desk during class. While
Lacks does not deny that she allowed Reginald to read those two poems aloud in
class, she also testified that no one was aware of their content before he read
them. . . . More importantly, however, she explained that, after he wrote and read
aloud those two poems, Reginald went on to write several more for her class, the last
of which, entitled "Alone," won academic awards. These facts were entirely ignored
in the panel opinion (as they apparently were ignored by the school board).

Lacks's trial testimony regarding Reginald's story is set forth below. I urge that 5
this part of the record be fully and thoughtfully considered.

Q. I would like to show you, Cissy, what's been marked as Exhibit 18, and ask if
you can identify this document?
A. Yes.
Q. What is it?
A. This document is a series of poems that I showed to the administrators in my
District that was done by one of my students, Reginald McNeary, when he was
in ninth grade.
Q. And when was that?
A. That was in 1992.[2]
Q. At the Berkeley High School?
A. Yes.
Q. And these poems were done in which class?
A. These poems were done in the ninth grade English class.
Q. What do they illustrate, Cissy?

. . . .

Lacks v. Ferguson Reorganized School District, 154 F.3d 904 (1998). The two excerpts beginning
on this page and on page 400 are from the appellate court decision on the school district's appeal,
following the district's loss in trial court.

[2]It is worth nothing that the events involving Reginald occurred three years before the events
concerning the student plays, which led to the school board's termination of Lacks.

A. They illustrate how a student can grow in a very short period of time using the student-centered teaching method. They illustrate that a student can learn a lot of techniques in a very short time if he or she cares about what he is doing, and they show that what a student says in the beginning is not at all the way a student might want to express him or herself, but it's what they start with because they may not have had the experience to do or say anything else.

Q. And you said you showed these poems to your administrators?

A. Yes.

Q. When did you do that?

A. I did that in a meeting that I had with them on January 25th.

Q. 1995?

A. 1995.

Q. And that was after you were suspended?

A. Correct.

Q. All right, can you start with the first poem on the top there and explain to us the significance of this poem in that learning process that you just described?

A. This poem that I'm going to read is the last poem that Reginald wrote.

Q. The last poem he wrote in what period of time?

A. In three weeks.

Q. This was a three-week poetry unit?

A. Yes.

Q. In ninth grade English?

A. Yes.

Q. First of all, tell us the story of Reginald. When he came into your class, what did you observe about him?

A. Reginald came into my class and he wanted to do absolutely nothing but put his head on his desk in the back of the room. He did not talk to anyone. He did not talk to me. He wouldn't do assignments. I would send him to the guidance office, he would throw away the sheets of paper. I would send him to the principal, I would get a note back saying that I should send him during my class but he wouldn't go. I continued to send—nothing worked for Reginald. He was totally silent, totally disengaged, totally disconnected from me, from school, and he also, I learned later, because I asked about him, had had a very difficult—

MR. SUSMAN: Objection, hearsay.

THE COURT: That will be sustained.

Q. Did Reginald have any observable problems in learning, to your knowledge?

A. Yes.

Q. What were they?

A. He seemed to have a very difficult time talking to people or looking at them. I saw him write something once and he seemed to have an eye hand coordination problem in terms of writing.

Q. All right, did he later stop putting his head down in the class?

A. Yes.

Q. About when did that occur?

A. When we started doing the poetry writing.

Q. How did you organize physically the classroom when you began the poetry writing?

A. The class was in a circle so we could talk to each other and share work.

Q. And did Reginald sit in the circle?

A. No.

Q. Where did he sit?

A. He sat in the back of the room with his head on his desk.

Q. What did the other students do?

A. They told me that if they had to sit in the circle, Reginald would have to sit in the circle, I should force Reginald into the circle.

Q. What did you tell them?

A. I told them there was no way I could force Reginald in the circle short of picking up the desk, but that they could get him in the circle by doing things so interesting to him that he would be jealous and come into the circle.

Q. Did that happen?

A. It did.

Q. How soon after did it happen?

A. Two days after we started doing things in poetry, he started moving into the circle.

Q. Okay, and this first poem that is listed on Exhibit 18 was written you say about three weeks after he moved into the circle?

A. Yes.

Q. Okay, would you read it for us, please?

A. Sure. It's called "Alone."

> I'm all alone in this world today.
> No one to laugh with, no one to play.
> It's been like that since the age of three.
> No one to love care or hold me.
> I guess that's why I'm the way I am.
> No one loved me so I don't give a damn.
> No one to pick me up when I fall.
> No one to measure growth or how tall.
> Alone, how it hurts inside.
> If I were to die, no one would cry.
> I never gave a damn about any other.
> I love my shoes more than I love my mother.
> You might think I'm the devil or call me Satan.
> I have no love, I'm so full of hating.
> I guess that's why I have low self-esteem.
> The only time I show love is in my dreams. . . .

Q. Let me ask you Cissy, did this poem win any awards?

A. This poem, a somewhat corrected one won awards. This poem won the first place in the poetry contest at Berkeley High School, and then I believe it also won the district-wide poetry contest in a corrected version.

Q. Corrected in what way?

A. Corrected in the grammar, and corrected a bit in the way the stanzas are organized.

Q. Did Reginald agree to enter the poem in the contest?

A. Yes.

Q. Did he read this poem in class?

A. Yes.

Q. And you said you videotaped it?

A. Yes.

Q. Why did you do that?

A. At the end of the poetry unit when people have decided what they wanted to share with people, in this particular instance for poetry, we agree to tape them and then use them again in other classes, so each year they can see what students did the year before.

Q. Okay, and then can you explain to us the process that you went through with Reginald to get him to this award-winning poem?

A. Well, Reginald heard the things that we were talking about in terms of writing, and the first exercise I believe that he saw, a tape by Quincey Troupe talking about poetry writing, and Reginald wrote a poetry exercise for us when we were reading out loud in the class, and he asked if he could read it out loud. It was the first time Reginald said anything in the class to any of us.

Q. Okay, would you like to show us what he did at that point?

A. Uh-huh.

Q. At the beginning?

A. I'm sorry, what do you mean, show it? Are you going to put it up?

Q. First of all, Exhibit 18, could you turn to the first poems that you just mentioned?

A. Okay. There is a poem called "Hard Core Gangsta Pimp."

Q. And the second poem?

A. It's called "Click."

Q. Let's see if I can get that. This "Hard Core Gangsta Pimp" poem?

A. Uh-huh.

Q. Is that the first poem he wrote in poetry class?

A. Yes.

Q. And would you agree there is a great deal of street language in there?

A. Yes.

Q. Profanity?

A. Yes.

Q. The second poem as well, the second poem called "Click," the name of this poem is "Click"?

A. Uh-huh.

Q. Same thing?

A. Yeah.

Q. How did this poem come to be read to the class?

A. When we were doing the poetry exercises, we're just experimenting and nobody knows what anybody else has written, but when asked if they would like to share it, Reginald said that he would like to share what he had written.

Q. So he stood up and read it?

A. Yes.

Q. What did you say to him after he read these poems to the class?

A. Well, I was a little taken aback because it was also read with a lot of anger, and I told him in the class that I thought that his writing had a lot of anger in it, and that sometimes you can use anger to write extremely effective poems, and that he should listen to what we were doing in the rest of the classes when we talk about technique and process, and see if he could use some of that technique to express his anger in other ways.

Q. You did not criticize him for the street language in here?

A. No.

Q. Why not?

A. I would have—I was so pleased that Reginald did something, that he made an effort to talk, it was the first time he shared anything with anybody and did anything at all in the class, I was not going to shut him down, I was going to take that and work with it. It was something, finally I had something that he had done that I could work with, and the class could see him somewhat as part of the class and begin to respond to him. I thought it was a good moment in teaching.

Q. Did he write any poems immediately after those two?

A. Yes.

Q. Can you tell us what the next poem was in the series?

A. The next poem was called "Hate."

Q. When did he write "Hate" in relation to those first poems?

A. I think probably about a week and a half later.

Q. Okay?

A. Week later.

Q. Could you read "Hate" for us?

A. There is so much hate in the world today.
   We are so busy hating we don't even pray.
   Some whites hate blacks and some Germans hate Jews.
   But they are wrong because no one can choose.
   How dark or bright or fat or light people are to be.
   If it was up to me I would love all my brothers, white, Jews or any other.
   For Christmas instead of begging for jewelry, instead I'm going to pray for peace.

Q. Did you see any progress then between those first poems and this one?

A. Yeah, Reginald was beginning to use all techniques and styles we had talked about. He had opened up. He was beginning to talk about the feelings that he had, but in a way, I think, that he thought other people would listen to him and that was what he now thought was effective poetry.

Q. Did he write any other poem in that three week period of time?

A. Yes.

Q. What was the next poem he wrote?

A. He wrote a poem called "Why."

Q. And is there a date on this poem?

A. December 8th, 1992.

Q. Could you read "Why" for us?

A.   Why.

Why do they stare at me when I'm [maxin']?
Is it 'cus I'm not the color that they are [axin'].
They whisper in silence.
I guess they think I'll cuss.
Violence, why, why couldn't God make us one color
Instead of black and white, and many others.
Why, why when you look at me you look in fear
When I have never beat you up or made you shed a tear.
Why can't we all just get along living in harmony.
Is that too wrong?
My sisters are labeled hooker and whore bangin',
And they have got my brothers dope and gangbangin'.
Why are my people living in poverty and the rich don't care how they be?
Now I know this is the worst poetry you [ever heard] but it comes from the heart.
I wrote every word.

Q. Did you see any progress here?

A. I saw incredible progress. He is starting to use a certain style now and a rhythm to his writing, and it's real clear that he also has a position and he wants other people to know what it is and when he read it he told us what this poem came from.

Q. And then the last poem in the series was the "Alone" poem you read to us.

A. The last poem was the "Alone" poem.

Q. And how would you evaluate "Alone" as a piece of poetry?

A. I think that the person who wrote this poem is not a student poet but a poet. I think he is like Langston Hughes.* He has an incredible way with words, and it makes people cry, in class, or just be so moved by what he is saying the doing, it's, you know, it's really amazing as a poem.

Q. Who chose his poem to win the district-wide poetry contest?

A. I'm not sure. I didn't. There were judges in the District who did.

Q. And by the way, the poem "Alone" which won the district-wide poetry contest, does that have any street language in it?

A. Yes, it does.

Q. "I never gave a damn about any other"?

A. Uh-huh, twice.

---

*Langston Hughes (1902–67) African American poet and writer, one of the twentieth century's most notable interpreters of the black experience.

Q. Considerably less than that what Reginald included in his first two poems, would you agree?

A. Yes.

Q. And how do you explain that progress?

A. Well, to me I see it all the time, that once a student opens up and starts expressing himself or herself and then learns the process or the techniques and they hear people listening to them, they just want to begin to change what they are doing, so it's quite, it just seems to me it is a quite natural learning process. It's part of the student-centered method.

Q. You also talked to us about peer critique, and I'm interested to know how did the class respond to Reginald's first two poems? . . .

Q. Did the class respond to Reginald's first two poems?

A. The class as I recall was taken aback. They just listened, but at the same time said, "Reginald, good, you talked," that's what I remember. "Reginald, you said something."

Q. Okay, and how did they react to the poem "Alone"?

A. They actually cheered and clapped for him when he read it. . . .

Q. Okay. You told us earlier that you took these poems to the administrators to explain to them your teaching process in January of '95 after you had been suspended. Did you take all the poems to them?

A. Yes.

Q. Did you explain to them as you explained to us today the teaching process?

A. Yes.

Q. Who did you explain this to?

A. I explained it to John Wright, Vernon Mitchell and Barbara Davis.

Q. Now, you went to the Board termination hearing regarding your termination, is that correct?

A. Yes.

Q. And the District included a couple of Reginald's poems in its evidence against you, didn't it?

A. Yes.

Q. How did they come to have these poems?

A. I brought them all five of these poems, that's how they came to have them.

Q. Did the administrators show the Board Reginald's award-winning poem?

A. No.

Q. What did you think about that?

A. I was so discouraged, I didn't even know what teaching was about any more. They showed the first two poems that Reginald wrote and didn't show anything else, somehow seemed to have lost or forgotten all the other poems. Very discouraging for a teacher and also for the student who had written the poems.

. . . I am not condoning the use of profanity in our schools or every aspect of Lacks's teaching methodology. But the jury found in this case, based upon *all* the evidence and their assessments of credibility, that Lacks was not given reasonable notice that profanity was prohibited in her creative writing assignments. If she had been given such notice, this whole matter could have been avoided. In this day and age, while our children are being exposed to the worst aspects of society through the media, entertainment, and sometimes even in their own homes, we expect public school teachers to erase the effects of that environment and make even the most uninspired children learn and achieve. Meanwhile, we require our teachers to pick their way through a mine field of competing and conflicting expectations, and changing and elusive legal standards. This case stands for the proposition that, for all her hard work and devotion to *all* her students, this teacher was in the end fired for stepping on a political land mine—one which she never even knew was there.

Excerpt from Judge B, Appeals Court Opinion (1998)

In order to prevail the school board must prove that Lacks violated the board policy prohibiting profanity, and that she knew that the board policy applied to the profanity used by her students. After a careful review of the evidence, [I believe] that the record contains sufficient evidence for the school board to have concluded that Lacks willfully violated board policy.   7

Lacks admitted that she allowed students to use profanity in the classroom in the context of performing the plays they had written and reading aloud the poems they had composed. . . . At the hearing, and in her brief, Lacks defended this practice by arguing that she thought that the board's policy on profanity applied only to "student behavior" and not to students' creative assignments. . . . She also argued that her teaching method, which she describes as the "student-centered method" and which she explained at length at the hearing, required her to allow her students creative freedom, which included the use of profanity. . . . Lacks could not say with certainty that she would be able to teach at Berkeley High School if her students were not given the freedom to use profanity in their creative activities. . . . As evidence that Lacks believed that the anti-profanity policy did not apply to students' creative assignments, the District Court noted that testimony at the hearing indicated some confusion within the school district as to whether reading aloud literature which contained profanity might violate the school board's prohibition on profanity. . . . For example, Larilyn Lawrence, a curriculum coordinator for language arts at the school district, believed that a videotaped production of a play with students using profanity could fall within acceptable course parameters. . . . On the other hand, Barbara Davis, the assistant superintendent for curriculum instruction, testified that teachers in the school district should not allow students to read aloud profanity contained in literary works. . . .   8

The school board also heard testimony from Lacks's principal, Vernon Mitchell, that he told Lacks that profanity was not permitted in the school newspaper. Mitchell testified that he specifically spoke to Lacks in 1993 about profanity in the school newspaper, and told her that use of profanity in the newspaper was not allowed. . . . Mitchell said that he had reviewed a draft of the newspaper and was concerned that the students were including profanity in the paper by writing "S   9

Lacks v. Ferguson Reorganized School District, 154 F.3d 904 (1998).

blank blank T" and "F blank blank K" rather than writing every letter of the profane words. . . . Mitchell testified that he discussed the use of profanity in the newspaper with Lacks "[t]wo or three times." . . . Mitchell also noted that signs posted in Lacks's classroom read "No Profanity." . . . When the board issued its opinion terminating Lacks's contract, it based its decision in part on its finding that Lacks had been warned about the use of profanity by Mitchell.

Lacks claimed that Mitchell never warned her about the use of profanity in the　10 newspaper. . . . However, under Missouri law, assessing the credibility of witnesses is the function of the school board, not the reviewing court. . . . Because the school board heard testimony that Lacks was directly warned by the principal in her school that including "S blank blank T" and "F blank blank K" in the student newspaper violated the school board's profanity policy, the board could have reasonably found that Lacks knew that profanity was not allowed in students' creative activities. While Lacks did produce some evidence that confusion existed in the school district as to the profanity policy, and while she denied that she had been warned about it, we must read the record in the light most favorable to the school board's decision, together with all reasonable inferences.

The policy prohibiting profanity was explicit and contained no exceptions. It　11 was not ambiguous. The board was free to find that Mitchell gave Lacks an express and particularized direction about the student newspaper. [I] think it was not unreasonable for the board to treat student writing for the newspaper and student writing for the class as alike. Isolated instances of profanity had been overlooked or tolerated in the past, but what went on in Lacks's classroom went far beyond the reading aloud of a novel containing the occasional "damn." The board might have chosen a lesser form of discipline, especially in view of Lacks's long and devoted service. It was not required to do so by law. [I believe] that the board's decision was reasonable and supported by substantial evidence on the record as a whole.

●　●　●　●

For Deliberation and Argument

1. Compare and contrast the treatment of the *Bethel* case in Philip Hager's *Los Angeles Times* article, "High Court to Test Student Free-Speech Rights," and in the U.S. Supreme Court's description of the same case. Comment on the differences in style, organization, and emphasis. What elements does Hager include in his article that are absent from the court's description of the same events? What do you think is the reason for these differences?

2. To what extent do you think the school district was justified in taking disciplinary action against Matthew Fraser—that is, suspending him for three days and not allowing him to give the commencement address? To what extent do you think that Fraser's First Amendment rights were violated? In developing your answer, consider the following points:

   - Should public school administrators and teachers have the right to prohibit "vulgar and obscene language" in classrooms and assemblies?
   - Did Fraser's speech violate the school's rule prohibiting obscene language?

- Was his language disruptive to the educational process?
- To what extent do you believe that Fraser was aware of the rule he had violated and of the penalties for violating it?
- What is the significance, for you, of Fraser having showed his speech to three teachers before delivering it?

3. Study the four sources on the Cissy Lacks case (*Lacks v. Ferguson Reorganized School District*). The first is an article by playwright James Nicholson (who visited Lacks's classes and testified on her behalf at the trial), the second is an excerpt from the trial court opinion, and the third and fourth are opposing opinions by appeals court judges. (The third excerpt includes an extended piece of testimony from Lacks herself at the trial.) Based on these sources and on your responses to them, do you believe that the appeals court should affirm or reverse the decision of the trial court? Take into account not only the broader questions relating to freedom of speech but also the narrower question of whether Lacks violated the school board policy on profanity ("policy 1043"). As one judge notes, "In order to prevail the school board must prove that Lacks violated the board policy prohibiting profanity, and that she knew that the board policy applied to the profanity used by her students."

   Based on the sources you have read, has the board proved these two contentions? What evidence supports your conclusion? In developing your response, you may want to compare and contrast the *Lacks* case to *Bethel*, which also involved a school district's enforcing a policy against objectionable language. What are the similarities and differences between the issues in these two cases? How do you view the conflicting claims of social policy and individual rights to freedom of speech? Take into account Matthew Fraser's purpose in giving his nominating speech and Cissy Lacks's purpose and strategy as a classroom teacher. Is the issue in these two cases essentially the same? If so, what is it? If not, how should the differences affect the outcome (if at all)?

4. Select one of the cases treated in this group. Imagine that you are representing either the plaintiff or the defendant. Compose either an opening statement or a closing argument for this case. Remember that your audience is the jury. Draw on the facts of the case in a way that is likely to have the greatest impact on the jury. Keep in mind, however, that jury members may turn against you—and your client—if they think that you are overly manipulating the facts, being deceptive, making exaggerated claims, or attempting too crudely to play on their emotions. For guidance on developing your statement, see "Models for the Opening Statement and the Closing Argument" at the end of Chapter 2.

■ Group 3 Readings: *Student Dress and Hair Codes*

Like those in the previous group, the next few cases deal with the First Amendment rights of high school students. Here is another instance of the First Amendment involving a balancing of interests: on the one hand, students are no less citizens than adults and should—theoretically—be entitled to the same First Amendment protections. On the other hand, courts have historically granted wide latitude to school districts in setting standards of both speech and conduct inside the school, and specifically in allowing school administrators to prohibit speech and conduct they deem "disruptive" to the educational process. Perhaps the most delicate aspect of weighing the balance is in devising "content-free" rules—that is, in making sure that whatever restrictions are placed on student speech are based on the form *and the manner,* rather than on the *content of the speech or the symbolic speech. (A school cannot prohibit one student from making an antiwar statement if it permits another to make a pro-war statement.) But this is not always easy to do.*

In Tinker v. Des Moines Independent Community School District, *a school is faced with students who wear black armbands to protest America's participation in the Vietnam War. Another T-shirt case is illustrated by* Pyle v. South Hadley School Committee, *when a student whose father is a professor of constitutional law sets out to test the limits of his First Amendment protections.* Brownlee v. Bradley County Board of Education *and* Church v. Board of Education of Saline Area School District *both involve male students with hair that is too long for the taste (and the dress codes) of the school districts concerned; but the issues in the two cases are significantly different.*

Illegal Arm Bands

TINKER et al. v. DES MOINES INDEPENDENT COMMUNITY SCHOOL DISTRICT et al.
U.S. Supreme Court

Certiorari to the United States Court
of Appeals for the Eighth Circuit.

Petitioner John F. Tinker, 15 years old, and petitioner Christopher Eckhardt, 16 years old, attended high schools in Des Moines, Iowa. Petitioner Mary Beth Tinker, John's sister, was a 13-year-old student in junior high school.   1

In December 1965, a group of adults and students in Des Moines held a meeting at the Eckhardt home. The group determined to publicize their objections to the hostilities in Vietnam and their support for a truce by wearing black armbands during the holiday season and by fasting on December 16 and New Year's Eve. Petitioners and their parents had previously engaged in similar activities, and they decided to participate in the program.   2

The principals of the Des Moines schools became aware of the plan to wear armbands. On December 14, 1965, they met and adopted a policy that any student wearing an armband to school would be asked to remove it, and if he refused he would be suspended until he returned without the armband. Petitioners were aware of the regulation that the school authorities adopted.   3

Tinker v. Des Moines Independent Community School District, 393 US 503 (1969).

On December 16, Mary Beth and Christopher wore black armbands to their   4
schools. John Tinker wore his armband the next day. They were all sent home and
suspended from school until they would come back without their armbands. They
did not return to school until after the planned period for wearing armbands had
expired—that is, until after New Year's Day.

Coed Naked Band: Do
It to the Rhythm T-Shirts

Jeffrey J. PYLE and Jonathan H. Pyle, By
and Through his father and next friend,
Christopher H. PYLE, Plaintiffs,

v.

The SOUTH HADLEY SCHOOL COMMITTEE,
Charles F. Kimball, Individually and in his capacity
as Interim Superintendent of South Hadley
High School, Paul Raymond, Individually
and in his capacity as Interim Principal of
South Hadley High School, and Donna Theroux-Cole,
Steven M. Marantz, Chairman, Robert L. Gouin,
Mary Jo Moore, Kevin Taugher, Individually,
and in their capacity as Members of the
South Hadley School Committee, Defendants.

Civ. A. No. 93-30102-MAP.

United States District Court, D. Massachusetts.
Aug. 26, 1994.

I. Introduction

This case is a reminder that it is easy to assume a tempest in a teapot is trivial,   1
unless you happen to be in the teapot.

II. Facts

A. The Parties

Plaintiff Jeffrey Pyle ("Jeffrey"), is now an eighteen-year-old freshman at Trinity   2
College in Hartford, Connecticut. In 1993, he was a student at South Hadley High
School and participated in the band and the drama club. Jeffrey's father, Christopher Pyle, a professor of constitutional law at Mount Holyoke College, is also a
plaintiff, bringing this action on behalf of his minor son Jonathan, a sixteen-year-

---

Pyle v. South Hadley School Committee, 861 F. Supp. 157 (1994).
Footnote 1 is text from page 170 of the original source.

old sophomore still attending the high school. It is undisputed that both Jeffrey and Jonathan have achieved an excellent record, both academically and with respect to their extracurricular activities. They have been good students and good citizens of their school.

Defendants are: the South Hadley School Committee and its individual members;   3
Charles Kimball, individually and in his capacity as Interim Superintendent of the South Hadley High School; and Paul Raymond, interim principal of the high school.

South Hadley is a town of approximately 16,000 inhabitants, located at the   4
foot of the Holyoke Mountain range in Western Massachusetts. The area is rich in both history and culture. South Hadley has a strong commitment to the education of the town's students and is influenced, in part, by the presence of Mount Holyoke College as well as many of the excellent academic institutions nearby. The first public school in South Hadley was built in 1754. In 1870 the high school held a graduation for its first class—of two students. By 1900 the population of South Hadley had increased to approximately 4,500 and in 1904 the first woman school committee member, Mary Brainard, a retired high school teacher, was elected. In 1907, the high school graduated a "large" class of 16 students. Over the years, South Hadley has continued to grow, and the location of the high school has changed several times due to the demand for more space. Presently, approximately 785 students attend South Hadley High, in the eighth through twelfth grades, ranging in age from twelve to eighteen years old.

B. Findings of Fact

The following facts emerged from the bench trial, which took place from March   5
28, 1994 to April 1, 1994.

The controversy over T-shirts in South Hadley can be traced back to some   6
time during the 1991 school year. Prior to this time, an informal system was in place at the school. If a student wore an objectionable T-shirt to class, a teacher would ask the student to remove it or turn it inside out. The number of times this occurred in the past was minimal.

Then came the "Button Your Fly" controversy. Charles Kimball, principal of   7
the high school in 1991, sent home a student wearing a T-shirt with this popular Levi-Strauss logo. At that time, the dress guidelines at South Hadley High School were set out in the folder given to each student at the beginning of the school year. A section entitled "Personal Appearance" stated:

> Personal appearance should not disrupt the educational process, call individual attention to the individual, violate federal, state, or local health and obscenity laws, or affect the welfare and safety of the students, teachers, or classmates. Students will be asked to change inappropriate attire.

Under this provision, Kimball sent the student home to change his T-shirt. Unfortunately, on his way from school the student fell off his moped and broke his arm.

The next day, approximately 20 to 30 students wore "Button Your Fly" T-shirts   8
to school and staged a peaceful sit-in to protest the banning and the injury to their classmate. Jeffrey, then a sophomore at the high school, participated in this

demonstration. Jonathan, a student in the middle school at the time, also wore the "Button Your Fly" T-shirt to his school.

In response to the protest, Principal Kimball eventually decided to allow the   9
students to wear the T-shirts pending a school committee meeting on the subject. As now, the school committee consisted of five members.

At a meeting on May 24, 1991, the school committee decided, by a 3-2 vote, to   10
allow the students to wear the "Button Your Fly" T-shirt. To no one's surprise, the logo's popularity plummeted following this decision, and until the Spring of 1993 the dress code issue lay dormant.

Troubles began to brew again on March 24, 1993, when Jeffrey wore a T-shirt   11
to his gym class bearing the slogan "Coed Naked Band; Do It To The Rhythm" ("Coed Naked Band"). This shirt was a Christmas gift given to Jeffrey by his mother celebrating Jeffrey's involvement in the school band. After viewing the T-shirt, Jeffrey's gym teacher told him that it was unacceptable. Although she allowed Jeffrey to wear the shirt for the rest of her gym class, she warned him not to return to her class wearing the Coed Naked Band T-shirt.

In response, Jeffrey wrote a letter to Acting Principal Paul Raymond. In his   12
letter, Jeffrey explained that, because he felt his constitutional right to freedom of expression was being violated, he intended to wear the T-shirt again. He noted that he had worn the Coed Naked Band T-shirt on several previous occasions and had not received any complaints. In addition, he had seen both boys and girls wearing "Coed Naked" T-shirts with various tag-lines at South Hadley High and never saw them cause a disruption. He concluded, "I am respectfully informing you that I plan to wear this shirt, and similar shirts, in the future. Of course, if any of my shirts were to cause a genuine disruption, I would change it immediately." Acting Principal Raymond did not respond to Jeffrey's letter.

When the next gym class met, Jeffrey wore his Coed Naked Band T-shirt to class   13
again. This time the teacher asked Jeffrey to change his shirt. When Jeffrey refused, he was given three detentions for insubordination and sent to the office. Acting Principal Raymond met with Jeffrey, and they both looked at a publication sponsored by the Massachusetts Department of Education, entitled "Check it Out," for guidance on the issue of dress codes. Raymond, unsure whether Jeffrey's T-shirt was permissible under the dress code then in effect, decided to seek guidance from the members of the school committee and put Jeffrey's detentions on hold until the April 6, 1993 meeting.[1]

---

[1]After some struggle, the defendants determined that not all Coed Naked T-shirts should be prohibited. For example, Jonathan's contrived "Coed Naked Gerbils" and "Coed Naked Censorship" T-shirts were permitted. Only Coed Naked T-shirts that displayed an overt sexual tag line were deemed off limits. Other T-shirts in the "Coed Naked" line arguably go further. For example:

1. "Coed Naked Law Enforcement: Up Against the Wall and Spread 'Em."
2. "Coed Naked Gambling: Lay Them on the Table."
3. "Coed Naked Auto-Racing: Lapping the Competition."
4. "Coed Naked Firefighters: Find 'Em Hot, Leave 'Em Wet."
5. "Coed Naked Lacrosse: Ruff and Tuff and in the Buff."
6. "Coed Naked Billiards: Get Felt on the Table."

The defendants here decided to draw the line somewhere between "Button Your Fly" and "Do It to the Rhythm." Other lines are easy to conceive, perhaps between "Do It to the Rhythm" and "Up Against the Wall and Spread 'Em" or perhaps somewhere else.

In the days prior to April 6, Jeffrey deliberately continued to test the rules by   14
wearing two new T-shirts to gym class. One T-shirt depicted two men in naval
uniform kissing each other with a tag line "Read My Lips." The second T-shirt
depicted a marijuana leaf and stated "Legalize It." Neither prompted an objection.

At the April 6, 1993 school committee meeting Jeffrey orally presented his   15
views regarding censorship and the boundaries of a student's First Amendment
rights. Also speaking at that meeting was Jeffrey's gym teacher, who explained
her ground rules of acceptable behavior. Students were not allowed to wear T-
shirts that targeted or harassed a person because of race, sex, religion, or sexual
orientation. During the past few years, this teacher had used the "Coed Naked"
series of shirts as an example of what she considered unacceptable dress in her
gym class. . . .

During the meeting, Jeffrey requested that the school committee formally   16
draft a dress code because, in his opinion, the current guidelines were too vague.
The school committee believed that the school's informal policy of requesting a
student to change an objectionable T-shirt had proved successful. They were at
first reluctant to attempt a more formal dress code.

By the end of the April 6th meeting, however, the school committee agreed   17
not to enforce the three detentions given to Jeffrey and to consider the dress code
issue further. On April 7, 1993, Jeffrey sent a letter to the members of the School
Committee outlining once more his request that the school committee adopt a
new, formal dress code.

On April 20, 1993, the school committee held a second meeting at which it   18
considered proposals to amend the existing guidelines. . . .

On April 22, 1993, Christopher Pyle, Jeffrey and Jonathan's father, sent School   19
Committee Chairperson Steven Marantz a ten page single-spaced letter, setting
forth specific objections to the newly adopted dress code and offering several
suggestions to cure what he viewed as its constitutional infirmities. The School
Committee did not respond to Professor Pyle's letter.

On April 29, 1993, the students, faculty, staff, and parents of students at South   20
Hadley High School were sent the following notice.

TO: Students, Faculty, Staff and Parents
FROM: Paul R. Raymond, Interim Principal
Subject: Dress Code at South Hadley High School

On Tuesday, April 20, 1993 and again on Tuesday, April 27, 1993 the South
Hadley School Committee voted to amend the current dress code to read as
follows:
CURRENTLY IN THE DRESS CODE:
Personal appearance should not disrupt the educational process, call singular attention to the individual, violate federal, state, or local health and
obscenity laws, or affect the welfare and safety of the students, teachers, or
classmates.
ADDITIONS TO THE DRESS CODE:
Students, therefore, are not to wear clothing that:
1. Has comments or designs that are obscene, lewd or vulgar.

2. Is directed toward or intended to harass, threaten, intimidate, or demean an individual or group of individuals, because of sex, color, race, religion, handicap, national origin, or sexual orientation.

3. Advertises alcoholic beverages, tobacco products, or illegal drugs.

If such clothing is worn to school, students will be required to change or will be sent home to do so.

Clothing expressing political views is allowed as long as the views are not expressed in a lewd, obscene or vulgar manner.

This policy will become effective per the direction of the South Hadley School Committee on Monday, May 3, 1993.

On May 3, 1993, the day the code was to take effect, Jeffrey wore a T-shirt to school with the slogan "Coed Naked Civil Liberties: Do It To The Amendments" ("Coed Naked Civil Liberties" T-shirt) to signify his opposition to the new dress code.[2] The same day, Jonathan, a sophomore, wore a T-shirt bearing the slogan: "See Dick Drink. See Dick Drive. See Dick Die. Don't Be A Dick" ("See Dick" T-shirt). Jonathan and Jeffrey wore these T-shirts for about four periods with no incident. Later in the day, Jeffrey and Jonathan were sent down to the administration office where Acting Principal Raymond and Acting Vice-Principal Zajac told them that their T-shirts were unacceptable. They were given the usual three options: First, turn the T-shirt inside out; second, change into another T-shirt, or third, go home and change. Jeffrey and Jonathan decided to go home and did not return to school until the next day.   21

Following a letter from plaintiffs' counsel, the school committee took no action regarding the dress code from May 4 to May 11, so that they could meet and discuss counsel's concerns regarding the constitutionality of the amended dress code. On May 5, 1993, on the advice of counsel, the school committee agreed to retract the prohibition on the "Coed Naked Civil Liberties" and "See Dick" T-shirts pending a May 11, 1993 school committee meeting. Jeffrey and Jonathan were notified of this new position and wore these two T-shirts on May 7, 1993, without incident.   22

On May 11, 1993, the school committee reconvened and discussed the dress code with plaintiffs' counsel. This meeting had several results. First, the school committee reaffirmed the guidelines set forth in the April 29 memorandum. Second, the committee defeated a motion to continue to permit the "See Dick" and "Civil Liberties" T-shirts. These shirts were therefore again off limits. Third, the committee granted the school administration (Kimball, Raymond and Zajac) the authority to interpret and enforce the code.   23

That same day, May 11th, Jonathan protested the dress code by wearing a homemade T-shirt bearing a picture of a gerbil and the tagline "Coed Naked Gerbils" on the front and "Some People Will Censor Anything" on the back. Jonathan was sent to the office where his T-shirt was reviewed by Kimball, Raymond, and Zajac. Kimball said that while he personally found the shirt to be   24

---

[2]This T-shirt was a gift to Jeffrey's father Christopher Pyle from his Mount Holyoke students.

inappropriate, it did not violate the dress code. Jonathan was then given a pass to return to class.

On May 14, 1993, Jonathan wore a T-shirt that read "Coed Naked Censorship—They Do It In South Hadley." One of his teachers sent Jonathan down to the office to get an evaluation of the T-shirt. Kimball looked at the T-shirt and found that it did not violate the dress code. Once more, Jonathan was given a pass to return to his class. Jonathan wore this T-shirt to school on another day and did not experience any problems. He also wore a T-shirt celebrating the Smith College centennial, and reading "A Century of Women on Top," without incident.

Jonathan and Jeffrey both admit that they selected these T-shirts to protest censorship and to test the capacity of the administration to distinguish prohibited from permitted messages. At least three of the shirts (Coed Naked Censorship, Coed Naked Civil Liberties and Coed Naked Gerbils) were custom-created to test, and lampoon, the borders of the permitted range.

On May 17, 1993, Jeffrey wore the Coed Naked Civil Liberties T-shirt again to school. Jeffrey was sent to the office, where Principal Kimball reviewed the shirt and, this time, found that it did not violate the dress code. Jeffrey returned to class and wore the T-shirt for the rest of the school day. That same day, Jonathan wore the "See Dick" T-shirt again. Vice-principal Zajac told Jonathan that the T-shirt was unacceptable. Unwilling to change, Jonathan left school.

On May 18, 1993, Jeffrey tested the waters again with his "Coed Naked Band" T-shirt. By first period, he was sent down to Kimball's office, where he was told the shirt was not acceptable. Concerned with missing more classes, Jeffrey decided to change into a non-objectionable T-shirt. A short time later, Jeffrey graduated from South Hadley High School.

On May 18, 1993, Kimball sent a memorandum to the faculty at South Hadley High school regarding the dress code. In it, Kimball advised that

> [t]he faculty should understand that every shirt or hat or whatever that you personally feel is off color or in bad taste will not automatically be found in violation of our present dress code. The code is designed to prevent lewd, obscene and vulgar statements on clothing and to prevent people from intimidating, demeaning or harassing students and staff on the basis of sex, creed, national origin, etc.

Kimball concluded that if a teacher had any questions regarding the appropriateness of a student's clothing, the student should be sent down to the office for a decision.

In the 1993–94 school year, South Hadley's Dress Code read, in pertinent part:

> e. Students are not to wear clothing (including hats) which cause a disruption to the educational process or the orderly operation of the school. This includes clothing that:
>
> 1. Has comments, pictures, slogans, or designs that are obscene, profane, lewd or vulgar.
>
> 2. Harasses, threatens, intimidates or demeans an individual or group of individuals because of sex, color, race, religion, handicap, national origin or sexual orientation.

3. Advertises alcoholic beverages, tobacco products, or illegal drugs.

If such clothing is worn to school, students will be required to change or cover said clothing or will be sent home to do so. Refusal to change or cover said clothing will result in the students not being allowed to attend class until they have complied with the code. The students should understand that failure to attend class may subject them to a penalty under the existing class attendance and truancy regulations at South Hadley High School and the South Hadley School Department.

On this rendition of the code, defendants inadvertently omitted the provision concerning protection for expression of political views. On February 15, 1994, the defendants amended the September 1, 1993 dress code and added one final sentence.   31

Clothing expressing political views clearly is allowed as long as the views are not expressed in a lewd, obscene, profane or vulgar manner. . . .

This dress code now remains in effect at South Hadley High School and is, in part, the subject of this lawsuit.   32

The Hostility of Long Hair

**David BROWNLEE, a minor, b/n/f
Donald S. Brownlee and Mary S. Brownlee
v.
BRADLEY COUNTY, TENNESSEE
BOARD OF EDUCATION; William R. Walker,
Superintendent; and Bill Schultz,
Principal of Bradley Central High School.**

Civ. A. No. 5827.

United States District Court,
E. D. Tennessee, S. D.
April 10, 1970.

This lawsuit involves the subject of human hair and its grooming on the male of the species, a subject not often thought of as grist for the federal judicial mills. For reasons which find their justification more often in the emotions than in logic, lengthening hair and changing hair style in males has become a strangely sensitive subject both among those who practice the change and among those who resist the change. Some might write the subject off as but an illustration of the wisdom of Ecclesiastes when some three thousand years ago he proclaimed all human foibles to be but "vanity of vanities, all is vanity." (Ecc. 1:2 and 12:8) Others might feel that   1

Brownlee v. Bradley County Board of Education, 311 F. Supp. 1360 (1970).

Alexander Pope, the English poet, said all that need be said to bring the errant to their senses in his famous poem, "The Rape of the Lock." Pope introduces his poetic treatment of the subject with the well known line, "What mighty contests rise from trivial things!" This lawsuit however does not deal with the trivial, as will become apparent to those who pursue the legal ramifications involved. Where male hair length and style is made a condition of admission to a public school, the subject is of more importance than might first appear, for it raises federal constitutional issues and constitutional issues are never of little importance.

This is an action to test the constitutionality of a public school regulation   2 regarding the permissible length of hair upon male students. The plaintiff, David Brownlee, a student at Bradley Central High School, Bradley County, Tennessee, elected not to comply with the regulation and upon his expulsion brought this lawsuit seeking to have the regulation declared void as being in violation of his constitutional rights under the First, Third, Fourth, Fifth, Ninth and Fourteenth Amendments to the United States Constitution. . . .

The plaintiff, David Brownlee, is a resident of Bradley County, Tennessee. He   3 first entered Bradley Central High School in the Fall of 1968 as a member of the freshman class and attended throughout that school year. He again re-entered in the Fall of 1969. At that time his hair was not of the conventional length for students in the school, but in order to be eligible to play football he submitted to having his hair trimmed. By the winter semester, however, his hair was again of a length sufficient to cover his ears and extend below his collar. Meanwhile, during January of 1970 the student counsel formulated a "dress code" for students at the school. The plaintiff was advised of the fact that such a code was under consideration by the student council and afforded an opportunity to make any representations to that body that he might desire, but he did not avail himself of this opportunity. Upon recommendation of the student council, the principal of the school adopted the "dress code" as a part of the school program. With regard to hair length to be worn by male students, the code provided as follows: "Boys' hair should be out of the eyes, not over the collar, not covering the ears. No moustaches nor beards to be grown by students."

An announcement with regard to the dress code was made over the public   4 address system at the school in the early part of February, 1970, prior to the events leading to the plaintiff's expulsion from school, but there had been no written publication of the code at that time. Even prior to the adoption of the code the principal had asked the plaintiff upon two or three occasions to have his hair trimmed, but the plaintiff had declined to do so and no further action was taken. Following adoption of the dress code, the plaintiff was sent to the principal's office by a faculty member on February 5, 1970, for failure to comply with the provisions of the code regarding hair length. At that time the principal advised him that he must have his hair trimmed in a manner that would comply with the code. At that time the plaintiff was not formally suspended from school, but he did depart for the day. The next day he went to the Superintendent of Schools office for a conference on the subject of his hair length, and he was again advised that he must have his hair trimmed to comply with the dress code before he would be permitted to return to his classes. On Monday, February 9, 1970, the plaintiff attempted to return to school without having trimmed his hair and, on instructions of the Superintendent of Schools, he was denied admission to classes and was advised that he was formally expelled from school until such time as he should have his hair trimmed in compliance with the dress code. Thereafter on February 11, 1970, the plaintiff's mother held a further conference of some two hours' duration with the Superintendent of Schools regarding the plaintiff's expulsion from school, but without any change in the position previously taken upon each side of the issue. No further requests were made by the plaintiff or his parents for conferences with school authorities in regard to the resolution of the matter. Although it was contended by the plaintiff that some discrimination was practiced in the application of the dress code, the evidence does not support this contention. On the contrary, the evidence reflects no discrimination in the application of the dress code, but rather reflects that other offending students elected to comply when requested to do so by school authorities. The plaintiff, electing not to comply with the dress code, filed this lawsuit as a means of obtaining readmission to the school.

No attempt was made on the part of the plaintiff to give reasons in support of   5
his preference for maintaining his long hair. He does not contend that it represents an expression of any particular attitude or idea upon his part. Rather, it is apparently merely a matter of personal preference with him.

Among the reasons advanced by or on behalf of the school authorities as jus-   6
tification for adoption of the dress code, and particularly that portion of the code dealing with the length of hair of male students, were the following: (1) behavioral problems predominated among male students adopting the long hair style; (2) academic performance declined among male students adopting the long hair style; (3) male students adopting the long hair style sometimes did so as a symbol of hostility toward school attendance or toward school authority, either of which attitudes was undesirable and deserving of discouragement; (4) male students adopting the long hair style caused classroom disruptions and distractions by centering student attention on their unconventional appearance with the result that classroom decorum was disturbed and an adverse teaching situation was created; (5) the reputation of the school suffered in the eyes of visitors by allowing male students to grow unconventionally long hair; and (6) the dress code as developed and recommended by the student council and as approved by the school principal and the school superintendent, was an expression of a sense of school pride and a reasonable expression of the prevailing sense of propriety within the student body and within the community.

The precise question to be considered by the Court is whether public school   7
authorities may limit the hair length of male students as a condition for admission to a public school without violating some constitutional right of the student. . . .

As noted above, the plaintiff contends that the hair code here adopted by   8
school authorities violates various provisions of the Bill of Rights. These contentions can appropriately be dealt with rather briefly. It is first contended that male hair length is a mode of symbolic expression and as such may not be limited by public school authorities without violation of the Freedom of Speech Clause of the First Amendment. . . .

[T]here is no evidence in the record in this case to support the plaintiff's First   9
Amendment contention. The record is devoid of any evidence that the plaintiff
chose to wear long hair as a means of conveying any thought or belief on his part
or as a means of symbolic expression of speech. It is not suggested that the plaintiff's long hair was either aimed or aimless "protest." Rather, it appears from the
evidence merely to have been a matter of personal choice with him. No First
Amendment problem could arise on this state of the record.

Having commenced with the poet, Alexander Pope, it would not appear inap-   10
propriate to allow him the final words, too:

> "O hadst thou, cruel! been content to seize Hairs less in sight, or any hairs but
> these!"

Hair and the War

Don Leslie CHURCH, Jr., a minor, by his Father and Next Friend, et al., Plaintiffs,

v.

The BOARD OF EDUCATION OF SALINE AREA SCHOOL DISTRICT OF WASHTENAW COUNTY, MICHIGAN, et al., Defendants.

Civ. A. No. 35399.

United States District Court,
E. D. Michigan, S. D.
March 9, 1972.

On September 10, 1970, Plaintiff Don Leslie Church, Jr., was informed by Defen-   1
dant, Clement Corona, Assistant Principal of the Saline High School, that Plaintiff's hair style did not conform to the school dress and grooming code adopted in
May, 1970, by the Defendant Board of Education. That Code, which is still in
effect, provides as follows:

> Long hair cuts are not desirable. The hair must be cut or groomed so that the
> area above the eyebrows is visible, the ears must not be covered, and in the
> back the area of the neck immediately above the normal collar position
> should be visible.

It is stipulated that Plaintiff's hair style violated this rule, and at the present time,
continues to violate this rule.

Church v. Board of Education of Saline Area School District, 339 F. Supp. 538 (1972).
Introductory paragraph numbers 1–14 omitted.

On September 11, 1970, Plaintiff accompanied by his parents conferred with   2
Defendant Corona and informed him that Plaintiff did not intend to cut his hair in
order to comply with this rule. Thereupon Plaintiff was informed by Defendant
Corona that he was suspended from school until he cut his hair in compliance
with the rule.

On September 16, 1970, Plaintiff accompanied by his parents appeared before   3
the Defendant Board of Education to urge that the Board rescind its hair style rule
and permit him to reenter school. The Defendant Board refused Plaintiff's
request. . . .

On September 21, 1970, Plaintiff filed suit in the United States District Court   4
for the Eastern District of Michigan, alleging that the hair style rule violated the
United States Constitution. Following a show cause hearing, the Court, Honor-
able Damon J. Keith, on September 30, 1970, issued a preliminary injunction
requiring that Plaintiff be permitted to attend school without cutting his hair, until
final disposition of this suit. Since that order, Plaintiff has attended the Saline
High School. There has been no disruption of classes or other disturbance in the
school as a consequence of Plaintiff's long hair. Plaintiff's scholastic grades have
improved from a B+ to an A– average during the past academic year and he has
been an active participant in school affairs.

Plaintiff is a student in good standing at the Saline High School. In September,   5
1971, he will enter the twelfth grade at this school, and upon graduation he
intends to pursue a college education. Plaintiff currently maintains an A- average.
For his six academic courses during the past year, Plaintiff received four A's, one
A-, and one B+ grades. In addition, Saline High School gives six Citizenship marks
in each academic course. During the past year, of the 36 grades, Plaintiff received
32 "excellents" (the highest mark) and four "goods" (the second highest mark of
five possible marks). Plaintiff is a member of the National Honor Society. On May
14, 1971, Plaintiff was elected by the Student Body at large to the Saline High
School Student Council. He was appointed by the Student Council on May 29,
1971, to the Adult-Student Communications Liaison Committee on General
Issues.

On November 11, 1969, Plaintiff accompanied by his parents attended a large   6
public meeting in Ann Arbor, Michigan, organized to protest United States presence in Vietnam. Prior to that meeting, Plaintiff had been deeply troubled about
the morality of this country's actions in Vietnam. At that meeting, the arguments
made by many of the speakers brought together many of the Plaintiff's misgivings,
and firmly persuaded him that United States presence in Vietnam was wrong and
must be opposed by all lawful means. Plaintiff then spoke out, in his high school
history class (which devoted one day each week to current affairs discussions)
and informally to other students. His position was vehemently opposed by most
students. Plaintiff was particularly disturbed that few of his peers were willing to
dispute his arguments on their merits, but instead argued that his views were
wrong because those views were also held by "bad people." To this effect, one
student called him a "Communist" for believing that the United States must leave
Vietnam. Others stated in effect that "long-haired, violent, drug-taking radicals"

also held that viewpoint, and since Plaintiff agreed with them, he must be one of them. These kinds of exchanges between Plaintiff and his peers continued throughout the 1969–70 school year.

As a direct consequence of the events described in Paragraph [6], Plaintiff decided, by the end of the 1969–70 school year, that he should permit his hair to grow long. His immediate purpose was to present to his peers, and those in the adult community in Saline whom he knew to hold identical beliefs, with a tangible, continuously visible symbol of his personal viewpoint on the Vietnam War. Plaintiff knew that his long hair would be identified by those in the Saline community with opposition to the War. [7]

A second, equally important purpose motivated Plaintiff to grow long hair. The vehement opposition to his expressed viewpoints regarding the Vietnam War crystallized for Plaintiff his misgivings about intolerance for dissent generally in the Saline community. Saline was originally exclusively a farming community and is, with the gradual advent of small manufacturing enterprises, only slowly losing the characteristics of a semi-rural, totally homogeneous community. In Plaintiff's view, dissent has never been easily tolerated in Saline. As the dominant majority of the community sees the advent of some changes in Saline's social and economic composition, in Plaintiff's view, the "old guard" of the community appears even less tolerant of differences of viewpoint. In addition, Saline is located only about ten miles from Ann Arbor, and the desire of many Saline residents to keep away any change from their community often is expressed as a desire to differentiate Saline from Ann Arbor. That University community has often been described to Plaintiff by Saline residents as a "haven of long-haired drug-addict hippies." The school hair code was thus seen by Plaintiff and by many Saline residents as an attempt to accentuate the community's difference from Ann Arbor, and to reinforce its self-image as a totally homogeneous community in which all "good citizens" not only looked alike, but thought alike. Outward appearance was, for Plaintiff and for many Saline residents, the visible sign of inward conformity of thought. This oppressive intolerance for any dissent, which was made vehemently evident when Plaintiff expressed his dissent regarding the Vietnam War, was paradigmatically expressed by the Saline community in its school hair code. Therefore, in order to symbolize the importance of dissent in general as well as his dissent on the specific issue of the War, Plaintiff believed that he must grow his hair long. [8]

Plaintiff's decision to grow his hair long in order to express his convictions regarding intolerance for dissent in Saline, and particularly intolerance for dissent regarding the Vietnam War, was directly paralleled by a similar decision of Plaintiff's father, Don Leslie Church, Sr. Mr. Church, Sr., is a tool and die maker and has resided in Saline since 1959. Until September, 1970, he was an officer and active member in the Saline Masonic Lodge. Mr. and Mrs. Church attended the Ann Arbor anti-war rally with the Plaintiff (mentioned above in Paragraph [6]). Following that rally Mrs. Church decided that she would wear an anti-war button. At a subsequent social gathering in the Church home, several guests—one an elected official of Washtenaw County, and others who were long- [9]

standing residents of the community—were outspokenly critical of Mrs. Church's viewpoint. Mr. Church indicated that he shared her view that the war should be ended. One guest then stated that if they held such views, the Churches were "son of a bitch Communists."

This episode crystallized for Mr. and Mrs. Church their previous dissatisfac-   10
tions at, in their view, the intolerant narrow-mindedness and overweening pressures for ideological conformity that was the dominant tone of the Saline community. As a consequence of this re-examination, Mr. Church resigned from the Saline Masonic Lodge (though it was likely that he would have been designated the next Grand Master of the Lodge). At the same time, Mr. Church decided that he would let his hair grow long, to symbolize his attitudes toward the intolerance and intellectual conformity of the Saline community regarding opposition to the War and any dissident opinion. At the present time, Mr. Church's hair falls well below his collar, and in order to keep his hair from his eyes when he works, Mr. Church often wears a headband.

Though Plaintiff and his father let their hair grow long at the same time, and   11
for directly parallel reasons, the parallelism in their thinking was not fully perceived by either until after this suit had been filed. At a pre-hearing conference of the Church family and their attorneys in this litigation, both father and son informed one another for the first time that each had been called a "Communist" for the views that each had expressed regarding the Vietnam War and each acknowledged to the other the role these experiences had played in determining that each would grow his hair long.

That in addition to the open defiance, as viewed by Defendant School District,   12
that has been displayed by the Plaintiff Don Leslie Church, Jr., one of the teachers of the Saline Area School District resigned because of other students' defiance of discipline and changing attitudes of the children.

Plaintiff's . . . argument is that the regulation in question infringes his right to   13
freedom of speech under the First Amendment to the U.S. Constitution.

● ● ● ●

For Deliberation and Argument

1. How do you think the court should decide in the *Tinker* case? What do you see as the central issue involving the school board, on the one hand, and the students, on the other? In your argument take into account the following opinions by the Supreme Court in the two cases covered in this chapter:

   • "In our system, state-operated schools may not be enclaves of totalitarianism. School officials do not possess absolute authority over their students. Students in schools as well as out of school are 'persons' under our Constitution. They are possessed of fundamental rights which the State must respect, just as they themselves must respect their obligations to the State. In our system, students may not be regarded as closed-circuit recipients of only that which the State chooses to communicate. They may not be confined to the expression of those sentiments that are officially approved. In the absence of a specific showing of constitutionally valid reasons to regulate their speech, students are entitled to freedom of expression of their views."

- "The process of educating our youth for citizenship in public schools is not confined to books, the curriculum, and the civics class; schools must teach by example the shared values of a civilized social order. Consciously or otherwise, teachers—and indeed the older students—demonstrate the appropriate form of civil discourse and political expression by their conduct and deportment in and out of class. Inescapably, like parents, they are role models. The schools, as instruments of this state, may determine that the essential lessons of civil, mature conduct cannot be conveyed in a school that tolerates lewd, indecent, or offensive speech or conduct."

Finally, note that over the years both the Supreme Court and other federal courts have allowed school districts to restrict both student speech and student conduct that in their judgment disrupts the educational process.

2. In *Pyle v. South Hadley School Committee*, one of the chief questions faced by the court is whether the South Hadley dress code that students were charged with violating (by wearing various T-shirts) is constitutional. The first two provisions of the code prohibit clothing that

- "has comments, pictures, slogans, or designs that are obscene, profane, lewd or vulgar."
- "harasses, threatens, intimidates or demeans an individual or group of individuals because of sex, color, race, religion, handicap, national origin or sexual orientation."

Consider each of these provisions separately. Does the wearing of the T-shirts violate either or both provisions of the code? And do you believe that either (or both) of these provisions violate the First Amendment? More specifically, can a school district restrict the *content* of nonvulgar, nondisruptive "speech" if that content appears to harass or demean one or more individuals or groups? Based on your response to these questions, how do you think the court should rule in the *Pyle* case? Explain.

3. Compare *Pyle* to *Bethel*, which involves a student, Matthew Fraser, who gave a sexually suggestive nominating speech at a school assembly. To what extent are the plaintiffs' actions in these two cases comparable? To what extent do they differ? How do both cases compare to the *Tinker* case at the beginning of this group?

4. If you were the judge on the *Brownlee* case, how would you rule on the question of whether, by sanctioning David Brownlee for wearing long hair, the Bradley County Board of Education violated the student's First Amendment rights? Develop your argument by comparing and contrasting *Brownlee* with one or more of the other cases in this group. See also the Supreme Court opinions quoted in question 1 (pp. 416–17).

5. Compare and contrast the *Church* case with the *Brownlee* case. Both, of course, involve students sanctioned for wearing long hair. How do you think the judge should rule in *Church*? Provide depth to your argument by discussing other relevant cases in this group: *Tinker* and *Pyle*.
6. Consider the two Supreme Court statements quoted in question 1 (pp. 416–17). In one sense they appear contradictory: The first appears to give children and adolescents the same freedom of speech rights as adults; the second appears to restrict the rights of younger citizens, for the sake of a "civilized social order." To what extent do you think it is possible to reconcile these statements? To what extent are they incompatible? Does the interest of society in educating and socializing young people take precedence, under certain circumstances, over unrestricted freedom of speech? If so, why? If not, why not?
7. Select one of the cases treated in this group. Imagine that you are representing either the plaintiff or the defendant. Compose either an opening statement or a closing argument for this case. Remember that your audience is the jury. Draw on the facts of the case in a way that is likely to have the greatest impact on the jury. Keep in mind, however, that jury members may turn against you—and your client—if they think that you are overly manipulating the facts, being deceptive, making exaggerated claims, or attempting too crudely to play on their emotions. For guidance on developing your statement, see "Models for the Opening Statement and the Closing Argument" at the end of Chapter 2.

Search and Seizure

The right of the people to be secure in their persons, houses, papers, and effects, against unreasonable searches and seizures, shall not be violated, and no warrants shall issue, but upon probable cause, supported by oath or affirmation, and particularly describing the place to be searched, and the persons or things to be seized.

—Fourth Amendment to the U.S. Constitution

The Fourth Amendment to the Constitution was designed by the founding fathers to prevent the kind of searches and seizures routinely practiced against the American colonists by officers of the English crown. It required that all such searches and seizures (including arrests and detentions) be based on probable cause—that is, reasonable grounds to believe that a person had committed a particular crime or that a place contained certain specified items connected with a crime. Without probable cause, no warrants or court orders would be issued, and without a warrant, police officers could not lawfully enter premises without the consent of the owner. Nor could search warrants be general: They had to specify the persons or articles to be searched for.

Such rights had long been enjoyed by the English. As early as 1604, a British court had observed that "the house of every one is to him as his castle,"[1] and in 1765, the English jurist William Blackstone had observed "the law of England has so particular and tender a regard to the immunity of a man's house, that it stiles his castle, and will never suffer it to be violated with impunity, agreeing herein with the sentiments of ancient Rome."[2] In 1948, Supreme Court Justice Felix Frankfurter wrote, "The knock at the door, whether by day or by night as a prelude to a search, without authority of law but solely on authority of the police, did not need the commentary of recent history to be condemned as inconsistent with the conception of human rights enshrined in the history and the basic constitutional documents of English-speaking peoples."[3]

Of course, just as with the First Amendment, the Fourth Amendment is not absolute. Note that the language of the amendment does not prohibit all searches and seizures, but only "unreasonable" ones. What counts as "unreasonable" has

---

[1] *Barnard v. Bartlett,* 10 Cush. (Mass.) 501, 502-503; cf. *State v. Smith,* 1 N.H. 346.
[2] 4 *Commentaries on the Laws of England* 223 (1765-69).
[3] *Wolf v. Colorado,* 338 U.S. 25 (1949).

occupied courts at all levels since the founding of the republic. Over the years, however, the outlines of the law have become clearer. For example, no warrant is required when police are in "hot pursuit" of a suspect and when taking the time to obtain a warrant would allow the suspect to escape. Police may arrest someone in a public place if they have probable cause to suspect that person of a crime; if the person retreats to a house, they must obtain a warrant before making an arrest. Even if provided with a warrant, police must knock and announce their presence. Only if permission to enter is refused may they then break open the door. The knock and announce rule need not be observed, however, if (1) such action will increase the likelihood of injury to themselves or to others, (2) the premises are clearly unoccupied, or (3) the evidence is likely to be destroyed—a particular problem in drug searches where evidence can so easily be "flushed."

To enforce the Fourth Amendment, courts early in the twentieth century introduced the *exclusionary rule*. Also termed *the "fruit of the poisonous tree" doctrine*, the exclusionary rule prohibits the use of evidence obtained through unlawful searches. Such searches may be unlawful because the warrants or the arrests are later determined by the trial or appellate court judge to be based on insufficient probable cause or because the seizures are determined to be unlawful. For example, unless an item is specified in a warrant, it must be in "plain view" before it can legally be seized. Police may not search through drawers, for example, looking for something—anything—to connect the suspect to a crime. As a result of this rule, suspects caught with incriminating evidence must often be released because prosecutors are prohibited from using it in court. The exclusionary rule has been the subject of a great deal of controversy. As one justice wrote, "The criminal is to go free because the constable has blundered." In recent years, the exclusionary rule has been modified somewhat; in *United States v. Leon* (1984), the Supreme Court ruled that when police rely in good faith on a warrant that is later ruled deficient, the evidence they seize may still be used in court (unless the evidence on which the warrant is based has been fabricated by police or prosecutors).

The following chapter focuses on two areas related to the Fourth Amendment: police brutality and the exclusionary rule as it applies to searches of students at school. Police brutality cases—which revolve around the use of excessive or unreasonable force during an arrest or while a suspect is in police custody—are generally treated as violations of both the Fourth Amendment and of the Fourteenth Amendment. The latter provides that all citizens are entitled to due process and equal protection of the law. Persons who believe their Fourth and Fourteenth Amendment rights have been violated are entitled to sue the offender(s) under the authority of Title 42, Section 1983 of the U.S. Code (see p. 430).

The first group of readings provides a hypothetical case, in the form of a section of courtroom testimony, dealing with the arrest of a person suspected of violating a municipal law. You are invited to apply the statements of law following the testimony to the facts of this case in order to develop an argument about whether the officer was acting lawfully in attempting to detain and arrest the suspect. The second group of readings focuses on a set of cases involving possible police brutality. The third group focuses on searches of students for contraband—drugs or weapons—carried to school buildings or grounds. It invites you to determine whether the searches or arrests were legal and whether the evidence seized should be excluded from legal proceedings against the student.

■ Group 1 Readings: *A Hypothetical Scenario of Arrest and Excessive Force*

The following is a hypothetical section of testimony, in which the defense attorney of a client who has been arrested for a misdemeanor (firing a rifle within city limits) and a felony (auto theft) interrogates his client on the witness stand. This interrogation has two main purposes: (1) to present the essential facts of the case and (2) to establish the basis for a civil claim against the arresting officer for using excessive force. The testimony originally appeared in Proof of Facts, *a set of volumes that helps attorneys to prepare particular types of cases, especially the evidence they need to provide to fully support their claims. The scenario represented here is drawn from a number of actual cases, although the facts may have been somewhat modified. In parenthetical remarks, the editor explains the reasons that the defense attorney adopts these particular lines of questioning.*

The transcript is followed by extracts from the law that provide the legal underpinning of the cases in the rest of the chapter: the Fourth and Fourteenth Amendments to the Constitution; Section 1983 of Title 42 of the U.S. Code (a compilation of federal laws), which covers civil actions for deprivation of rights guaranteed under the Fourth and Fourteenth Amendments; and sections from case law that has developed from previous search and seizure cases, and that focuses particularly on the degree of force that police may use in arresting suspects and preventing their escape from custody.

Courtroom Testimony

■ ─── ■

Testimony of Arrestee

. . . *[After introduction and identification of witness.]*

Q. How old are you?
A. Seventeen.

───────────

9 *Proof of Facts* (POF) 2d 392 (1976) (edited and modified) (Bancoft Whitney/West Pub.).

Q. Are you employed?
A. No, I am a student at _____ *[high school]*.
Q. Did you have any contact with _____ *[defendant police officer]* on _____, 19___?
A. Yes.
Q. In what connection?
A. I was shooting at some bottles with my rifle when he tried to stop me.
Q. Where were you doing this shooting?
A. In a vacant lot at the corner of _____ Street and _____ Street *[within city limits]*.

[Request Court to take judicial notice that the offense is a misdemeanor under state law. See 29 AM JUR 2d, Evidence § 27.]

§ 14. Use of Deadly Force against Misdemeanant Resisting Arrest but Not Endangering Officer's Life

Q. How did you happen to have contact with _____ *[defendant]*?
A. Well, I was lying down firing at the bottles when I heard a voice behind me say to put the gun down and to get over there.
Q. What did you do?
A. I looked over my shoulder and saw _____ *[defendant]* standing near the sidewalk, so I got up and went over to him.
Q. Did you take your rifle with you?
A. No, I left it on the ground.
Q. What did _____ *[defendant]* do when you got over to him?
A. He grabbed my arm and dragged me over to his squad car and threw me against it. Then he told me I was under arrest and to get into the car.
Q. What did you do then?
A. I refused to get in.
Q. Why?
A. I told him I hadn't done anything wrong and that I wasn't going with him.
Q. Did you know that firing a rifle in the city was against the law?
A. No.

☐ **Practice Observation:** Evidence concerning the crime the arrestee allegedly committed would normally be introduced by the arresting officer in order to justify his actions. In some instances, however, counsel for the arrestee may find it advantageous to present evidence on this matter, such as to establish that the crime was a misdemeanor or, if a felony, that it was one that did not involve a danger to life. The arrestee may, of course, recover damages for the arresting officer's excessive use of force regardless of his guilt or innocence of the crime involved, although the advisability of admitting guilt may depend upon the status of any criminal charges against the arrestee. In any event, if guilt is admitted, counsel for the arrestee should introduce any mitigating factors surrounding the commission of the crime since such factors may be relevant in explaining the arrestee's reaction to being arrested and any action he subsequently took.

Q. What did _____ *[defendant]* do when you refused to get into his car?

A. He grabbed me by the arm and neck and tried to force me into the car.

Q. What did you do?

A. I pushed his hands away.

Q. What did he do then?

A. He grabbed me again, only harder this time.

Q. Did you continue to resist?

A. Well, I kept trying to push his hands away from me so he couldn't get me into the car.

Q. How long did this struggle go on?

A. Oh, about 10 to 15 seconds, I guess.

Q. Did either of you fall to the ground during this time?

A. No.

Q. Did you hit _____ *[defendant]* during the struggle?

A. No, I was only trying to keep from getting put into his car.

Q. Did you have any weapon of any type in your possession during the struggle?

A. No. I had left my rifle on the ground when _____ *[defendant]* first yelled at me.

Q. How far away was the rifle while you and _____ *[defendant]* were struggling?

A. About 20 yards.

Q. What are your height and weight?

A. Five feet, eleven inches and about 170 pounds.

Q. How would you say that that compared with _____ *[defendant]*'s height and weight?

A. We seemed to be about the same size. He might be a few pounds heavier.

Q. What happened after you and _____ *[defendant]* struggled?

A. Well, I remember that after struggling for a while _____ *[defendant]* backed off a few feet, and I noticed him going for his gun.

Q. What did you do when you noticed _____ *[defendant]* reaching for his gun?

A. We were standing next to his car, so I began to edge around the car.

Q. Then what happened?

A. I saw him point his gun toward me and I ducked down behind the front of his car. Just as I was doing this, I heard his gun go off.

Q. Were you hit?

A. No.

☐ **Practice Reminder:** An action for assault can be brought against the arresting officer even though he never actually touched the arrestee. See *Hutchinson v. Lott,*—**Fla** —, 110 S2d 442.

Q. Did you hear the bullet strike anything?

A. Yes, I heard it hit the right front bumper near where I was.

Q. Did _____ [defendant] say anything to you before he fired?

A. As he was pulling his gun out, he said he was going to take me in one way or the other.

☐ **Practice Reminder:** Statements introduced as circumstantial evidence of the speaker's state of mind, rather than as evidence of the facts asserted therein, are not hearsay and may be received as evidence. 29 *Am Jur 2d*, Evidence § 650.

§ 15. Use of Force against Nonresisting Misdemeanant

Q. After the shot was fired, what did you do?

A. I wanted to run, but I was afraid he would shoot me, so I tried to keep the car between him and me.

Q. What did _____ [defendant] do?

A. He started edging around the car towards me real slow like. When he would move some, so would I, so that the car stayed between us. A couple of times he would change his direction and start to move the other way around the car. When he did this, so did I.

Q. While this was going on, where was _____ [defendant]'s gun?

A. In his right hand.

Q. Did he fire it during this time?

A. No.

Q. Did he say anything to you?

A. No.

Q. Did you ever break away from the car?

A. Yes, we finally moved completely around the car so that I was on the side facing the field where I had been firing my rifle.

Q. What happened then?

A. There were some trees over to the left along the street on that side of the field, so I decided to run for them for cover.

Q. Did you make the trees?

A. No, right after I left the car, I had to go down a small hill leading on to the field where I had been firing, and I fell down as I was going down this hill.

Q. Were you able to get up and keep running?

A. No, before I had gotten completely up I felt something hit me on the back of the head which stunned me and I fell back down on my stomach.

Q. Were you hit any more?

A. I was then kicked four or five times in the side and once on the side of the head.

Q. What were you doing while this was going on?

A. I was just lying there. I was still groggy from the first blow on the head.

Q. How long were you lying there?

A. I'm not sure, but it seemed like a long time.

Q. Were you hit any more?

A. Yes, after awhile I rolled over and sat up. Then I saw _____ [defendant] putting away his gun. He then took his nightstick and hit me in the face with it.

Q. What exactly were you doing when you were hit with the nightstick?

A. I was sitting on the ground holding my side where I had been kicked.

☐ **Case Illustration: Excessive use of force against a nonresisting misdemeanant.** A recovery of damages for personal injuries was sustained upon evidence that the suspect, after assaulting a state policeman, had withdrawn and had started to walk away when the policeman, either to satisfy his blind rage or to arrest the suspect for a misdemeanor, shot him after pointing his weapon directly at his body. The court stated that the shooting, for either reason, was not justified. *Padilla v. Chavez*, 62 NM 170, 306 P2d 1094.

Q. Did _____ *[defendant]* say anything at the time he struck you with his nightstick?

A. Yeah, he said that this is the only thing you _____s *[racial slur]* understand.

§ 16. Rebuttal of Possible Claim of Self-Defense by Arresting Officer

Q. What happened next?

A. I was dragged over to the squad car and thrown against it.

Q. Did you get in?

A. No, _____ *[defendant]* opened the front door and reached inside for something. When he did this I took off.

Q. Why did you take off?

A. I was afraid that _____ *[defendant]* would start hitting me again.

Q. Which direction did you run?

A. I started back across the field.

Q. Where you had been firing?

A. Yes.

Q. What, if anything, happened to your rifle?

A. I ran by it and picked it up and kept moving.

Q. Why did you pick it up?

A. I didn't want to lose it.

Q. Then what happened?

A. I was hit in the right arm by a bullet.

Q. Where was your rifle when you were hit?

A. I was holding it in my right hand.

Q. I show you plaintiff's Exhibit _____ for identification and ask if you recognize it.

A. Yes. That's my rifle.

Q. The one you were firing on the day in question?

A. Yes.

Q. How do you recognize it?

A. It has my initials carved on the stock, right there. _____ *[Witness points to the initials]*.

[Rifle may be introduced as evidence.]

☐ **Practice Observation:** If required by the court, each person who had possession of the rifle from the time it left the arrestee's possession until introduced in evidence may be called to establish the chain of possession. See 29 AM JUR 2d, Evidence § 774. However, if the article can be identified sufficiently to satisfy the court, it is not always necessary to place each custodian on the witness stand. See *Witt Ice & Gas Co. v. Bedway*, 72 Ariz 152, 231 P2d 952.

Q. What exactly were you doing when you were hit in the right arm?
A. Well, I was running and had turned slightly to look back when I was hit.
Q. Which way did you turn to look back?
A. Over my right shoulder.
Q. How were you holding your rifle at that time?
A. It was in my right hand and I was holding it on the upper part of the stock just below the trigger guard.

☐ **Practice Reminder:** At this point, and whenever else necessary, counsel should consider having the witness demonstrate exactly what he did. See 29 AM JUR 2d, Evidence § 769. Also, counsel may wish at appropriate times to introduce diagrams showing the location of the participants.

Q. Do you remember the direction the barrel of the rifle was pointing when you were hit?
A. No.
Q. Did you fire the rifle at this time?
A. No.
Q. Did you knowingly point the rifle at _____ *[defendant]* at this time?
A. No.
Q. Did you have any intention of firing the rifle at _____ *[defendant]?*
A. No. I just wanted to get out of there.

☐ **Case Illustration: Reasonableness of officer's belief that his life was endangered.** As the arresting officer was pursuing a boy who was suspected of having fired a rifle in the city, it appeared, according to the officer's testimony, that the boy turned around so that the officer felt threatened by the gun which the boy was carrying. The officer responded by firing at and wounding the boy, and, as a defense, claimed that he acted in self-defense. In rejecting this claim, the court noted that the officer was approximately 40 yards behind the suspect, that both parties were running, and that the suspect was holding a BB gun in front of his body. On the basis of this evidence, the court concluded that the officer could only have imagined that his life was going to be endangered, since there were no facts to indicate that from his viewpoint his life was in apparent danger. A bare fear, the court explained, is not sufficient to justify a shooting. *Palmer v. Hall* (DC Ga) 380 F Supp 120.

Q. When you looked back over your right shoulder, did you see _____ *[defendant]?*
A. Yes.
Q. What was he doing?

A. He was running towards me and pointing his pistol in my direction.

Q. Did he say anything to you?

A. No.

Q. How far away from you was he when you looked back?

A. About 15 yards.

Q. What time of day did this take place?

A. About two o'clock in the afternoon.

Q. What was the weather like then?

A. It was a bright, sunny day.

Q. What happened to your rifle when you were hit?

A. I dropped it on the ground and kept running.

§ 17. Commission of Felony

Q. Where were you running to?

A. No place in particular. I was just trying to get away.

Q. Where did you end up?

A. Well, I went to the trees alongside _____ Street that I mentioned earlier and began running along the road.

Q. Was _____ [defendant] following you?

A. Yes, but he was further behind me now.

Q. How far behind?

A. About 30 or 35 yards.

Q. What happened next?

A. I saw a lady on the other side of the street opening the door to a car that was parked there. I ran across the street and grabbed her keys and jumped in the car and drove it away.

§ 18. Rebuttal of Possible Claim That Arrestee's Injuries Were Received in Car Crash

Q. When you drove away, what direction were you heading in relation to _____ [defendant]?

A. I was heading back toward him, but before I got to him I began making a right turn onto _____ Street.

Q. What happened then?

A. Just as I was making the turn, I heard shots and then I lost control of the car. The street I was turning into was a narrow street and when I lost control of the car it veered over to the left-hand side of the road, and before I could gain control of the car I hit a car that was parked over there.

Q. How fast were you going when the crash occured?

A. I don't know, but it wasn't very fast. As soon as I lost control of the car, I hit the brakes, and I was fairly well stopped by the time I crashed.

Q. Did your head collide with anything during the crash?

A. No.

Q. Were you hurt in any way during the crash?
A. No.

§ 19. *Availability of Means, Other Than Deadly Force, to Arrest Felon*

Q. What did you do after you crashed?
A. I got out of the car and started running again.
Q. Was _____ *[defendant]* following you?
A. Yes. By the time I got out of the car and started running down the street where the crash occurred, he was about 25 yards behind me.
Q. Did he do anything to try and get you to stop?
A. I heard one shot, but I wasn't hit.
Q. Did you hear where the shot hit?
A. Yes, it hit the sidewalk near my feet.
Q. What did you do when you heard the shot?
A. Soon after that, I came to a corner and turned left and then turned left again down an alley.
Q. Did you keep going down the alley?
A. No. I went a short way down it and saw that it was a dead end.
Q. What did you do then?
A. I went back up the alley to the street, but just as I got there I saw _____ *[defendant]* coming around the corner, so I went back into the alley.
Q. Why did you do that?
A. It was the only thing I could think of at the time. I was afraid that if I went back out onto the street _____ *[defendant]* would shoot me. He wasn't very far away by that time.
Q. What happened after you went back into the alley?
A. I looked for some way out but couldn't find any. There was about a 10-foot stone wall at the end of the alley, and I tried to get over that.
Q. Did you make it?
A. No, it was too high. It was also slick and there weren't any places to get a hand or foothold. I tried once but I slipped back to the ground.
Q. Did you make any other attempt to get over the wall?
A. Yes. I moved over to the right side of the wall where it joined the building on that side of the alley and tried to use the building to work my way up.
Q. Did you succeed?
A. No.
Q. How close did you come to getting over the wall?
A. I never managed to get a hand up on top of the wall. I didn't get close at all to getting over it.
Q. After your second attempt, what happened?
A. I looked back over my shoulder and saw _____ *[defendant]*.
Q. How far from you was he?
A. About 20 feet.

Q. Was he moving?

A. No, he was just standing there.

Q. What happened then?

A. I remember looking back at the wall and then I heard a gun go off and was hit in the back.

Q. Did _____ [defendant] say anything before you were hit?

A. No.

Q. When you looked back at the wall just before you were hit, what were you thinking?

A. I had decided to give up. There was no place to run, and by that time I was feeling pretty weak from the beating and the gun wound I had already received.

☐ **Case Illustration: Type of circumstances required to show that officer had reasonable belief that use of deadly force was necessary.** The officer testified that as he was pursuing the suspect, the suspect disappeared into the darkness and that when, by using a flashlight, he finally located the suspect, he was in the process of attempting to get over a fence that was more than three feet high. The officer stated that by the time he could have reached the fence, the suspect would have been over it and into the next yard. Thus, after giving a command to halt, which went unheeded, the officer fired at and wounded the suspect. On the basis of this evidence, the court concluded that even though the officer was only 15 feet from the suspect when he fired the shot, and although two other officers were in the general neighborhood, the jury was fully justified in finding that the officer reasonably believed that the shooting was necessary to prevent the suspect's escape into the darkness of the night. *Martyn v. Donlin*—**Conn** —, 198 A2d 700.

Statutory Law

U.S. Constitution
Amendment IV

The right of the people to be secure in their persons, houses, papers, and effects, against unreasonable searches and seizures, shall not be violated, and no warrants shall issue, but upon probable cause, supported by oath or affirmation, and particularly describing the place to be searched, and the persons or things to be seized.

Amendment XIV

(The proposed amendment was sent to the states June 16, 1866, by the Thirty-ninth Congress. It was ratified July 9, 1868.)

Section 1

All persons born or naturalized in the United States, and subject to the jurisdic-   3
tion thereof, are citizens of the United States and of the State wherein they reside.
No State shall make or enforce any law which shall abridge the privileges or
immunities of citizens of the United States; nor shall any State deprive any person
of life, liberty, or property, without due process of law; nor deny to any person
within its jurisdiction the equal protection of the laws.

U.S. Code, Title 42
§ 1983. Civil Action for Deprivation of Rights

Every person who, under color of any statute, ordinance, regulation, custom,   4
or usage, of any State or Territory or the District of Columbia, subjects, or
causes to be subjected, any citizen of the United States or other person within
the jurisdiction thereof to the deprivation of any rights, privileges, or immunities secured by the Constitution and laws, shall be liable to the party injured in
an action at law, suit in equity, or other proper proceeding for redress. For the
purposes of this section, any Act of Congress applicable exclusively to the District of Columbia shall be considered to be a statute of the District of
Columbia.

Jury Instructions

ARREST BY PEACE OFFICER WITHOUT WARRANT

A peace officer may, without a warrant, lawfully arrest a person:

Whenever the officer has reasonable cause to believe that the person to
be arrested has committed a public offense in the officer's presence.

When a person arrested has committed a felony, although not in the
officer's presence.

Whenever the officer has reasonable cause to believe that the person to
be arrested has committed a felony, whether or not a felony has in fact been
committed. . . .

USE OF FORCE BY POLICE IN LAWFUL ARREST OR DETENTION—EXCESSIVE
FORCE AS BATTERY

A peace officer who is making a lawful [arrest] [or] [detention] may use reasonable force to make such [arrest,] [or] [detention,] to prevent escape, or to
overcome resistance.

California Jury Instructions, Civil: Book of Approved Jury Instructions. 8th ed. Prepared by
the Committee on Standard Jury Instruction Civil, of the Superior Court of Los Angeles County,
California. Hon. Stephen M. Lachs, Judge of the Superior Court, Chairman. Compiled and edited
by Paul G. Breckenridge, Jr. St. Paul, MN: West Publishing, 1994.

The officer need not retreat or desist from [his] [her] efforts by reason of the resistance or threatened resistance of the person being [arrested] [or] [detained].

Where a peace officer is making an [arrest] [or] [detention], and [the] [a] person being [arrested] [or] [detained] has knowledge, or by the exercise of reasonable care should have knowledge, that [he] [she] is being [arrested] [or] [detained] by a peace officer, it is the duty of the person to refrain from using force [or any weapon] to resist such [arrest] [or] [detention] [unless unreasonable or excessive force is being used to make the [arrest] [or] [detention]].

A peace officer who uses unreasonable or excessive force in making a lawful [arrest] [or] [detention] commits a battery upon the person being [arrested] [or] [detained] as to such excessive force[.] [and the person being [arrested] [or] [detained] may use reasonable force in self defense against such excessive force.]

Case Law

An arrest without probable cause violates a person's right under the Fourth Amendment to be free from unreasonable searches and seizures. (*Swanson v. Fields*, 814 F.Supp. at 1013 (1993))   1

The Fourth Amendment is not violated when a person is arrested with probable cause. (*Swanson v. Fields*, 814 F.Supp at 1013 (1993))   2

Probable cause to arrest exists when the officer has knowledge or reasonably trustworthy information sufficient to warrant a person of reasonable caution in the belief that an offense has been or is being committed. (*Swanson v. Fields*, 814 F.Supp at 1013 (1993))   3

Personal encounters between law enforcement officers and citizens are "seizures" on occasions when officer, by means of physical force or show of authority, has in some way restrained liberty of citizen. (*Courson v. McMillian*, 939 F.2d 1479 (1991))   4

Apprehension by force is "seizure" subject to Fourth Amendment's reasonableness requirement. (*Meyers v. Becker County*, 833 F.Supp. 1424 (1993))   5

Under due process clause of Constitution, person has federally protected right to be free of unreasonable and unnecessary force at hands of police officers making otherwise lawful arrests of them. (*Conklin v. Barfield*, 334 F.Supp. 475 (1971))   6

In analyzing claim of use of excessive force in making arrest under reasonableness standard, court must balance nature and quality of intrusion on individual's Fourth Amendment interests against importance of governmental interests alleged to justify intrusion, paying careful attention to facts and circumstances of each case, including severity of crime at issue, whether suspect poses immediate threat to safety   7 of officers or others, and whether suspect is actively resisting arrest or attempting to evade arrest by flight. (*Meyers v. Becker County*, 833 F.Supp 1424 (1993))

Reasonableness of particular use of force to make arrest must be tested from perspective of reasonable officer on scene and critical inquiry is whether officers' actions are objectively reasonable in light of facts and circumstances confronting them, without regard to their underlying intent or motivation. (*Meyers v. Becker County*, 833 F.Supp. 1424 (1993))   8

Traffic violations may constitute probable cause for arrest. (*Courson v. McMillian*, 939 F.2d 1479 (1991))   9

To prevail on excessive force claim under § 1983, arrestee must show significant injury, which resulted directly and only from use of force that was clearly excessive to need and was objectively unreasonable. (*Reese v. Anderson*, 926 F.2d 494 (1991))   10

When physical contact is caused by arrestee's resistance, leaves no significant abrasions, bruises or other injuries on arrestee's body, and is weaponless attempt to contain and control rather than to abuse or dominate, no excessive force exists. (*Franklin v. City of Boise*, 806 F.Supp. 879 (1992))   11

The "reasonableness" of a particular use of force must be judged from the perspective of a reasonable officer on the scene, rather than with the 20/20 vision of hindsight. . . . "Not every push or shove, even if it may later seem unnecessary in the peace of a judge's chambers," violates the Fourth Amendment. The calculus of reasonableness must embody allowance for the fact that police officers are often forced to make split-second judgments—in circumstances that are tense, uncertain, and rapidly evolving—about the amount of force that is necessary in a particular situation. . . . [T]he "reasonableness" inquiry in an excessive force case is an objective one: the question is whether the officers' actions are "objectively reasonable" in light of the facts and circumstances confronting them, without regard to their underlying intent or motivation. (*Graham v. Connor*, 490 U.S. 386 (1989))   12

Peace officer may arrest one without warrant for a public offense committed in his presence and he need not inform such person for what he was being arrested when such person is engaged in commission of the offense and when peace officer notifies individual who is committing public offense of intention to arrest him and he resists, officer may use all necessary means to effect his arrest. (*Schell v. Collis*, 83 N.W.2d 422 (1957))   13

The law protects an officer who is trying to do his duty as long as he does not use more force than is necessary, and in making arrest he is under no obligation to retreat but has both the legal right and official duty to press forward and accomplish his object by overcoming any resistance offered, and if after notice of intention to arrest, defendant either flees or forcibly resists, officer may use all necessary means to effect his arrest. (*Schell v. Collis*, 83 N.W.2d 422 (1957))   14

Police officer in defending himself against attack during arrest of plaintiff was entitled to act on reasonable appearance of danger from plaintiff and was not   15 required to nicely measure or narrowly gauge force to amount required from a deliberate retrospective view. (*Conklin v. Barfield*, 334 F Supp.475 (1971))

In making an arrest, an officer may use whatever force is reasonably neces- 16 sary. Reasonable force is generally considered to be that which an ordinarily prudent and intelligent person, with the knowledge and in the situation of the arresting officer, would have deemed necessary under the circumstances. (*Breese v. Newman*, 140 N.W.2d 805 (1966))

Generally, an officer has no right to shoot or kill a person who is committing a 17 misdemeanor except in self-defense. (*Breese v. Newman*, 140 N.W.2d 805 (1966))

An officer must not intentionally inflict unnecessary bodily harm or death on 18 a fleeing misdemeanant. (*Haviev v. Partin*, 492.P.2d 481 (1972))

Police officer has no right to attempt to shoot or kill a person being arrested for 19 a misdemeanor if the person sought to be arrested is making no effort to resist arrest but is only attempting to avoid it by flight. (*Palmer v. Hall*, 380 F.Supp. 120 (1974))

Police officer, like any other person, may shoot another in defense of his own 20 life provided that the danger apprehended by the officer is urgent and pressing or apparently so; a bare fear is not sufficient to justify the shooting. (*Palmer v. Hall*, 380 F.Supp 120 (1974))

Police are authorized to use deadly force to apprehend felon if they have prob- 21 able cause to believe that felon poses risk of serious harm to officers or others. (*Carter v. Buscher*, 763 F.Supp. 392 (1991))

Police officer in effecting arrest has right to use such force as he feels rea- 22 sonably necessary, but he is responsible for use of any excessive force, or for wanton abuse of discretion in determining amount of force reasonably required to effect arrest. (*Wimberly v. City of Paterson*, 183 A.2d 691 (1962))

If resistance to lawful arrest is encountered, officer may repel force with force 23 even to extent of killing offender if that extremity becomes necessary to effect arrest or to protect himself from serious bodily injury. (*Wimberly v. City of Paterson*, 183 A.2d 691 (1962))

Although peace officer has privilege of self-defense, as does any other citizen. 24 he is in that respect governed by the ordinary rules of law; but where the peace officer is in the exercise of the privilege of protecting the public peace and order, he is entitled to the even greater use of force than might be in the same circumstances required for self-defense. (*Wirsing v. Krzeminski*, 213 N.W.2d 37 (1974))

If, under the circumstances, no force at all would be required by a reasonable 25 and prudent police officer to effect an arrest, then any force would be excessive and constitute assault. (*Wirsing v. Krzeminski*, 213 N.W.2d 37 (1974))

Under Fourth Amendment, police officer's use of force must be objectively rea- 26 sonable in light of facts and circumstances surrounding arrestee's actions; thus, even unreasonable force applied without malice violates Fourth Amendment and may be challenged under § 1983. (*Smith v. Delamaid*, 842 F. Supp. 453 (1994))

In actions to obtain damages for civil rights violations, police officers are enti-   27
tled to a qualified immunity from liability based on good-faith belief in the propriety of their actions and reasonable grounds for that belief. (*Landrum v. Moats*,
576 F.2d 1320 (1978))

In evaluating police conduct relating to an arrest for purpose of determining   28
whether the conduct violated the arrestee's civil rights, the court's guideline is
good faith and probable cause. (*Landrum v. Moats*, 576 F.2d 1320 (1978))

In assessing the propriety of force used by the police to effect an arrest, for   29
purpose of determining any liability for civil rights violations, police officers are
entitled to the defense of good faith, even if their use of force turns out to have
been illegal or excessive, if the officers believed that a certain amount of force
was necessary to make an arrest and that use of that amount of force was lawful
under the circumstances and if the officers had reasonable grounds for each of
those beliefs. (*Landrum v. Moats*, 576 F.2d 1320 (1978))

● ● ● ●

For Deliberation and Argument

1. Consider the first selection. You are the arrestee's defense attorney preparing a
   brief—a formal argument—on behalf on your client. He has charged the defendant police officer with violating his Fourth and Fourteenth Amendment rights
   and is claiming relief under Title 42, section 1983 of the U.S. Code. Assume that
   the essential facts provided by your client in his testimony are not contradicted
   by the defendant. Study the testimony and the law as explained in the relevant
   amendments, in section 1983 of Title 42 of the U.S. Code, and in the case law
   excerpts provided. In assessing the charges you intend to make against the
   defendant, consider at what point(s) he was acting *within* the law and at what
   point(s) he was acting *outside* the law, explaining your conclusions.
   In your brief, address the following questions:

   - Did the officer have *probable cause* to arrest your client?
   - In first arresting your client, did the officer use *excessive force*?
   - In first trying to get your client into the police car, did the officer use exces-
     sive force?
   - Comment on the legality of the officer using (a) his gun and (b) his night-
     stick to subdue your client.
   - After your client picked up his rifle, to what extent might the officer have
     had a reasonable, good-faith belief that in shooting at your client, he was
     acting in self-defense?
   - Robbery—the taking of property from another person by violence or intim-
     idation—is a felony. To what extent was the officer justified in firing at the
     car that your client had just stolen in order to prevent his escape?

- After the car crash, to what extent was the officer justified in shooting your client to prevent his escape over the wall of the dead-end alley?

2. Continuing your role as defense attorney, compose a transcript of your interrogation of the police officer whom you are charging with violating your client's constitutional rights.

■ Group 2 Readings: *Police Brutality*

The police, of course, have the power to arrest suspected lawbreakers. While most do so with considerable professionalism, enough police officers abuse their authority to make "police brutality" a major source of social injustice in this country. During the 1930s, police were often used by corporate owners and managers as strikebreakers, injuring and killing workers exercising their right to strike. During the 1960s, police frequently used violence to quell civil rights workers and antiwar demonstrators. In more recent times, police brutality— often brutality of white officers against African-American or Latino suspects— has remained in the forefront of the news. In 1992, Americans were shocked by a videotape of four white police officers savagely beating an African American, Rodney King, whom they had arrested for speeding. In 1997, several New York City officers were placed on trial for a brutal attack against Abner Louima, sodomized with a broom handle in a police station rest room. The main perpetrator of the attack, Justin Volpe, later pled guilty. An article in Newsweek *magazine showed that this was not an isolated instance of police brutality:*

> *Within hours of Volpe's guilty plea, an unarmed 16-year-old Bronx youth, Dante Johnson, was shot and seriously wounded by a member of the NYPD's Street Crimes Unit. The Street Crimes Unit was also involved in the February death of Amadou Diallo, a 22-year-old African immigrant who was shot 19 times despite the fact that he was unarmed and had no criminal record. In Riverside, Calif., the FBI is investigating the death of 19-year-old Tyisha Miller, who was shot 12 times by four white officers while passed out in her car, with a gun in her lap, last Dec. 28. In Los Angeles, a 54-year-old black woman, Margaret Mitchell, was shot to death on May 21 by an LAPD officer. Mitchell, who was mentally ill, apparently lunged at the cop with a screwdriver—but she was only 5 feet 1, and the officer had his partner as a backup.*

When are police officers justified in making an arrest? And how much force are they legally entitled to use in doing so and preventing an arrestee from escaping? In general, police are entitled to make an arrest if (a) they have a warrant signed by a judge authorizing them to arrest one or more particular individuals, who are reasonably suspected of having committed a crime, or if (b) they have probable cause *to do so—that is, if they have a reasonable ground to suspect a person of committing a particular crime. They are authorized to use only as much force as is reasonably necessary under the particular circumstances. If the arrestee offers no resistance, then the officer should use no force at all. If the arrestee does resist, then the police may use only such force as is reasonably necessary to acomplish the arrest or to prevent an escape. Deadly force may be used only (a) in self-defense or (b) against an arrestee attempting to flee, if he or she is suspected of having committed a violent felony and if allowing the arrestee to escape would threaten the safety of others.*

In Palmer v. Hall, *a southern sheriff enraged by civil rights and antiwar demonstrators, issues a "shoot to kill" order to police. At least one officer takes him literally and shoots a twelve-year-old boy in the back. In* Franklin v. City of Boise, *a young man trying to escape arrest is tackled by a police officer and the two fall into a deep pond. The young man drowns; the officer is charged with violating the man's constitutional rights. In* Lewis v. Downs, *an officer arrests two members of a family, severely hurting them in the process. Did he use excessive force? In* Wyche v. City of Franklinton, *an officer shoots and kills a mentally deranged man. And in* Courson v. McMillian *a woman who was forced to lie face down on the ground for thirty minutes charges the arresting officer with false arrest and using excessive force.*

Shoot to Kill!

Quinton David PALMER, By next friend, Marie Palmer, Plaintiff,

v.

Roger HALL et al., Defendants.
Civ. A. No. 2912.

United States District Court,
M. D. Georgia, Macon Division.
July 29, 1974.

Quinton David Palmer, a thirteen year old Macon child, brought this lawsuit against Macon Police Officers Roger Hall and Larry Foster, Macon Mayor Ronnie Thompson and the individual aldermen of the City of Macon for his being unconstitutionally and unlawfully shot by Police Officer Hall on February 18, 1973.   1

1. Mayor Thompson

Defendant Ronnie Thompson, Mayor of the City of Macon since November 8, 1967, a former Alderman, and the acknowledged "acting head" of the police department of the City of Macon, on June 19, 1970, issued the following written order: 2

Palmer v. Hall, 380 F. Supp. 120 (1974).
Footnotes 1–5 are omitted, original footnote 6 is renumbered as footnote 1. All reference numbers have been omitted as well.

CITY OF MACON

GEORGIA 31201

June 19, 1970

EXECUTIVE ORDER

FROM: MAYOR RONNIE THOMPSON

TO: CHIEF J. F. FLYNT

As you know we are receiving more and more threats from a few dissenting people who are interested only in violence.

Anyone trying to cause violence in the City of Macon must be dealt with accordingly.

People engaged in burning, looting, killing and the destruction of property, etc. must answer to the strongest reply available.

Lawlessness designed to produce anarchy and the destruction of the City of Macon will not be tolerated.

No policeman, no volunteer policeman will be asked to face the enemy unarmed. See that we have sufficient arms, ammunition and equipment.

Those people engaged in lawlessness and anarchy must be stopped. SHOOT TO KILL!

[Exhibit P-10]

_____

/s/ Ronnie Thompson, Mayor

This order was widely published in and about the City of Macon and as a matter of common knowledge, rapidly became and continued to be, a topic of public debate. Among the public statements made by Mayor Thompson was the following given in response to a question propounded during a television interview over station WSAV (Savannah) on June 20, 1970, asking whether or not death isn't too extreme:

I think it's positive, and I think it's permanent, and I think during this period of history it's necessary. If it takes using firearms, if it takes shooting people and killing people in order to enforce the law in the City of Macon, that's exactly what I am going to do, and I'm not going to put up with burners and looters and killers and thugs.

Around September 3, 1970, during an Atlanta television interview conducted by four or five Atlanta newsmen, Mayor Thompson was asked whether or not this order meant that the police were to shoot someone who had stolen a $1.95 shirt. He in effect said, "We would want him shot." Mayor Thompson also said, "If he was engaged in any anarchy or civil disobedience, the police are to shoot whoever is involved." 3

Mayor Thompson "made a lot of statements" about his "shoot to kill" order and as a matter of common knowledge has continued to do so. 4

Not only has the Mayor been the acting head of the police department, but he has also assumed active command of the department on various occasions such as in July 1970 when according to the Mayor he was shot at by a sniper and he fired back with a carbine. 5

Aware that many people listened to the police radio, Mayor Thompson had the simulated sound of a machine gun broadcast over the police radio and as a matter of common knowledge regularly talked at night over the police radio on this subject. 6

In July 1971, according to the Mayor "There were a band of people out violating the law. The City was under an emergency curfew, and they refused to get off the streets. And they were listening to everything on police radio. The police reported to me that many of them had their radios in their hands listening, and the report came back that they refused to obey the policemen and get off the street—40 or 50 of them. And for their consumption I said, 'Well, get them off the street if you have to take them to the hospital or to the mortuary.' Yes, I made that statement on the radio for their consumption. And they did get off the street." 7

The newspaper report of that incident stated "When police were alerted that 25 armed people were gathering in one area Thompson issued an order to take them to the hospital or to the mortuary." 8

Around February 5, 1972 Mayor Thompson "instructed Macon policemen to 'shoot first and ask questions later' while investigating armed robberies and burglaries if there is the 'slightest indication' that they might be harmed." 9

Around February 17, 1972, defendant Thompson issued an order to shoot on sight any person engaged in armed robbery and that same month issued instructions to the Macon police to shoot first and ask questions later. 10

In the spring of 1972 Mayor Thompson unveiled his peace symbol which is described in the April 4, 1972, *Macon Telegraph* as follows: 11

Mayor's Peace Symbol Goes 'Pow'

A "peace" symbol designed by *Mayor Ronnie Thompson* is being used to counter the "peace" symbol adopted by thousands of anti-war protesters.

Yesterday, the Thompson unveiled a "peace" symbol which he designed and which he will use in promotion work, much as the "Thompson" machine gun lapel pin was used in last fall's mayoral compaign.

The insignia shows a red, white, and blue colored hand which forms a pistol outline with the thumb and index finger extended. The word "peace" is printed below the finger (which apparently corresponds to the gun-barrel of a pistol). Rising from the finger tip is a small puff of smoke, symbolizing that the "peace" symbol has been fired.

A small "Thompson" machine gun links the white cuff of the otherwise unseen shirt.

The stripes on the hand are colored red, the finger is a solid blue, and the other outlined images are also blue.

Mayor Thompson said yesterday he is using the smaller rectangular sticker to seal outgoing mail. He also has a larger decal type insignia of his "peace" symbol which is suitable to affix to glass. The Mayor said the stickers were not paid for with city funds.

Thompson noted the significance of the "peace" symbol yesterday: "When a person's coming after you this way," he said waving his arms, "do you stop him by doing this?" he asked forming his fingers into the traditional "V" peace symbol.

"I stop 'em this way," he said, holding his hand in the shape of a pistol and saying "pow."

The mayor has repeatedly emphasized his "shoot to kill" ideas in law enforcement, the latest coming almost two weeks ago over the police radio following a late night robbery.

[Plaintiff's Exh. 19].

As a matter of common knowledge defendant Thompson continued to espouse his "shoot to kill" order as he went about his duties as Mayor of Macon and as he campaigned for election to the Congress of the United States during the November 1972 general election. Preceding the incident in question such orders were never rescinded. Indeed, they continued in full force and effect through and including February 18, 1973, and in spite of the pendency of this complaint, continue today. 12

2. Defendant Aldermen

The defendant Aldermen have taken no action in the Police Committee or in any meeting of mayor and council to countermand Mayor Thompson's "shoot to kill" orders. 13

3. February 18, 1973

Police Officer Roger Hall, with the Macon Police Department since 1969, and   14
Police Officer Larry Foster were patrolling together on Sunday afternoon,
February 18, 1973. Defendant Hall was driving. Around 5:00 p.m. they stopped to
eat and about 5:36 p.m. they overheard radio instructions to another car to go to
Appleton and Progress Streets on a code signal 10 which was shooting, colored
males with rifles. Since they were close by, Officers Hall and Foster volunteered to
take the call and after doing so proceeded about one-half block to Progress Street.

Officer Hall was still driving. He turned the police car to the right onto   15
Progress at a speed of about 25–30 m.p.h. As he turned the corner he saw three
males standing about one hundred fifty yards away at the corner of Progress and
Appleton with rifles pointed upwards. Defendant Hall accelerated the car, and the
three males broke and ran up on the railroad tracks. The officers drove down
Progress to Appleton and as soon as they turned right, parked on Appleton near
the railroad tracks, jumped out of the police car and gave chase, Officer Hall
going after the plaintiff who had run up on the tracks and in a westerly direction
and Officer Foster going after the plaintiff's two companions who had run up on
the railroad tracks and in an easterly direction. As he chased, Officer Foster withdrew his .357 Magnum pistol from his holster and the circumstances indicate
Officer Hall did the same. . . .

The police officers saw the three males run up onto the tracks. It was late in   16
the day, dusk was approaching, and visibility was poor. Plaintiff, a tall twelve year
old Negro boy was wearing a heavy coat and was running down the railroad
tracks. He did not have a hat on and with both hands he held a Daisy air rifle in
front of him as he ran. The Daisy air rifle in question is what is commonly known
as a "BB gun"; it has a brown plastic stock, a brown plastic grip, a black frame and
barrel and a total overall length of thirty-two inches. The "BB gun" in question has
a carbine type hand operated lever that is used to pump the gun preparatory to
shooting one "BB."

When Officer Hall reached the top of the path and the tracks and first saw the   17
plaintiff running down the tracks, the plaintiff according to Officer Hall was then
some 60 to 100 yards away. According to Officer Foster who could hear but not
see what went on, Officer Hall twice yelled "stop, drop the rifle." The plaintiff did
not stop. When Officer Hall was within some 40 yards of the plaintiff and he and
the plaintiff were both running in a westerly direction, according to Officer Hall
the plaintiff "looked back" at him in such a manner as to cause the barrel of the
"BB gun" to turn towards him. When he saw the barrel of the gun come around,
he fired his .357 Magnum revolver. The bullet entered the rear of plaintiff's left leg
about half-way between the back of the knee and the lower portion of his buttocks at a point somewhat towards the inside portion of his left leg. It exited
about four inches above the top of the knee cap and several inches toward the
inside of the front of the left leg.

Officer Hall had presumed that what he saw in the plaintiff's hand was a rifle.   18
As far as he then knew the plaintiff had been doing nothing more than shooting a

rifle in the city which he also knew was a misdemeanor.[1] While he had heard of Mayor Thompson's "shoot to kill" and "shoot first and ask questions later" orders, he says he shot only because he was in fear of his life.

The plaintiff agrees with the officer's description of his running down the 19 tracks but says that he did not hear the officer order him to stop and did not even look back at the officer. He denies in any way pointing his "BB gun" towards Officer Hall. He says that he first knew that the officer was behind him when he heard the explosion of the gun and felt the bullet enter his leg.

According to *The Gunner's Bible* by Bill Riviere, 1973 Revised Edition, the 20 .357 Magnum handgun that Officer Hall fired is second in the handgun power field and has a muzzle velocity of more than 1410 feet per second.

The path of the bullet—entered the rear and towards the inside of plaintiff's left 21 leg and exited the front and towards the inside of plaintiff's left leg—shows that at the time the bullet entered plaintiff's body, plaintiff's body was positioned so that the toes of both feet were away from Officer Hall and the heel of each foot was towards Officer Hall; plaintiff's direction of body travel was straight ahead and away from Officer Hall; the entire rear of plaintiff's body was towards Officer Hall. Since Officer Hall was some 40 yards or 120 feet away from plaintiff when he fired his .357 pistol and since the bullet traveled at a speed of at least 1410 feet per second, plaintiff could not have moved or changed his body position to any extent in the less than one-tenth of a second that it took the bullet to travel to him. The court therefore finds that at the time Officer Hall fired his .357 pistol at the plaintiff, the rear of plaintiff's body was towards him—Officer Hall was looking at plaintiff's back.

After he was shot the plaintiff felt pain, saw blood running down his leg and 22 fell on to the tracks near the westerly end of the bridge. Officer Hall came up, saw the plaintiff and his condition and immediately used his belt to stop the bleeding. Officer Hall saw that plaintiff's gun was a "BB gun"; Officer Foster ran up, observed that the plaintiff had been shot, grabbed the "BB gun" and went to the patrol car to call an ambulance. Officer Hall picked up David Palmer and ran with him to the patrol car. The plaintiff was then carried by ambulance to the emergency room of the Macon Hospital which is about one-half mile away. After going to the emergency room, Officers Hall and Foster charged plaintiff David Palmer as a juvenile with shooting in the city and aggravated assault. According to Officer Hall the charges were from evidence at the scene—the "BB gun" and a paper bag containing robins, the latter having been found after the plaintiff was shot. Officer Hall knew that aggravated assault was a felony.

Dr. Triana examined plaintiff in the emergency room, found that there was a 23 trauma to his left body which entered posteriorly and exited anteriorly, found an absence of pulse below the wound and determined there was an injury of the main artery—the femoral artery—going down to plaintiff's leg. Plaintiff was taken

---

[1]An ordinance of the City of Macon then provided:

"Sec. 14-24. *Firearms—Shooting Inside City Prohibited.*

"It shall be unlawful for any person to discharge a firearm and airgun within the City. (Code 1947, Section 72–101)."

to the operating room. During the operation Dr. Triana found that the bullet had pierced the main vein and artery—the femoral vessels—that supply the leg. Using a piece of vein obtained from the right thigh, the artery was reconstructed. After doing so an absence of pulse in the foot was noted. The cause could not then be determined, so at the end of about a three hour procedure the wound was closed, having in mind that if a pulse was not regained in about eight hours another operation would have to be performed.

The following morning Dr. Smith examined the plaintiff and finding no pulse,   24 performed an arteriogram which showed a blood clot in the area of the injury. Another operation was performed and the artery was again reconstructed with another piece of vein from the same leg. The plaintiff remained in the hospital until February 27, suffered after leaving the hospital but with the passage of time has virtually fully recovered. The doctors who treated plaintiff are of the opinion that he will not have any permanent difficulties. The plaintiff, however, says that he cannot now run and play to the same extent that he could before being shot. If he runs or exercises or anything, he has to stop and rest; and if he exercises too much, his leg will swell.

The plaintiff has not gone to juvenile court in connection with the juvenile   25 charges placed by Officers Hall and Foster.

Death in the Dredge Pond

**Delores FRANKLIN, Individually and as
Natural Mother of Ronald Earl Walker, Deceased,
and on and for the Behalf
of Ronald Earl Walker. Deceased, Plaintiff,**
v.
**The CITY OF BOISE, Michael Paul Konst,
Ted Littlefield, Angela Louise Bevier
and John Does I Through VIII, Defendants.**

Civ. No. 91-0218.

United States District Court, D. Idaho.
Nov. 6, 1992.

This litigation began when Ronald Walker drowned in a dredge pond after a   1 struggle with Boise City police officers. Walker's mother, Delores Franklin, has brought this action for damages against the three individual police officers involved in the altercation, and the City of Boise. Her main claims are that the police used excessive force, botched rescue attempts, and discriminated against

---

Franklin v. City of Boise, 806 F. Supp. 879 (1992).
Cross references omitted from original.

Walker because he was an African-American. A thorough understanding of the facts is necessary to resolve these claims.

In the early morning hours of August 15, 1990, an apartment tenant called the Boise City Police to complain of loud music coming from the dredge pond a short distance away. The police dispatcher directed Officer Angela Bevier to respond at 1:26 a.m. Officers Bevier and Littlefield obtained a signed complaint from the tenant, and proceeded to the dredge pond. At this time Acting Field Commander Michael Konst was waiting near an entry road to the dredge pond. When Officer Konst saw a pickup truck leave from the dredge pond area, he was concerned that the noise perpetrators might flee. He decided not to wait any longer for officers Littlefield and Bevier, but to go to the pond immediately. He did so, and upon arriving found five vehicles and about ten to twelve individuals. Officer Konst testified that upon his arrival, "somebody had a stereo turned up pretty loud."

> Plaintiff has argued in her brief that all three officers went to the Park Center dredge pond. Upon their arrival, there was no loud music or excessive noise. . . . Officer Konst observed a pickup truck leaving the Park Center dredge pond prior to all three officers arriving. Given the fact that the excessive noise had ceased by the time the officers arrived, it is only logical to conclude that the vehicle that left the pond was the major source of the complained noise.

This argument completely ignores the undisputed testimony that Officer Konst arrived first at the dredge pond and heard loud music. While it is true that by the time Officers Bevier and Littlefield arrived at the dredge pond the music had ceased, this does nothing to advance plaintiff's argument in light of Officer Konst's testimony that there was loud music when he arrived there. Even if the pickup truck that left earlier was a source of the loud music, it was obviously not the only source.

Officer Konst waited in his car for the other officers. When they arrived, all the officers exited their cars to investigate the loud noise complaint. Officer Konst first approached two individuals—Mike Randall and Kevin Anderson—who were drinking beer and sitting on the tailgate of a white pickup truck. These two individuals were both Caucasians. Because these two men appeared to be of age and not the source of the loud music, Officer Konst proceeded to the next car.

There, he found Dagmar Danney, a white female who owned the car, seated in the driver's seat, with Ronald Walker seated in the passenger seat. Officer Konst asked for identification, and Danney produced her driver's license. Although Walker had no license, he gave Officer Konst his name, birthdate, and Social Security number. Officer Konst told Danney and Walker to stay put while he investigated the information they had given him. Dagmar Danney testified that as Officer Konst was taking this identification information back to his patrol car to run a warrant check, she heard him say, "These f—— kids and their f—— music." Officer Konst denies this use of profanity. Officer Konst then called the dispatch center and requested a check on whether there were any outstanding warrants on Danney and Walker. At 1:50 a.m. Officer Konst was informed that Danney's record was clear but that there was a possible arrest warrant on Walker. Officer Konst requested confirmation and then proceeded to investigate a suspicious-acting individual near a copper-colored pickup truck. Officer Konst determined that this individual was a Michael Hendrikse, obtained information from him, and ran a check on him through police dispatch.

Meanwhile, Officers Bevier and Littlefield were questioning the main group of young people to investigate the source of the loud noise and to determine if any underage drinking was going on. Officer Littlefield wrote an under-age drinking citation to Michelean Wilson and was in the process of writing one to Cecelia DeCosta when he ran out of citation forms. Officer Littlefield then approached Officer Konst to obtain more forms, whereupon Officer Konst informed Officer Littlefield about the possibility that an arrest warrant was outstanding on Walker. Officer Konst—as Field Commander—instructed Littlefield to finish writing citations and then to begin instructing the youth to leave so that there would be less obstruction from bystanders if Walker had to be arrested. Officer Littlefield agreed and went off to finish writing a citation to Cecelia DeCosta. 6

At about this time, Officer Konst noticed that Randall and Anderson, who had been drinking beer on the tailgate of the white pickup truck, were missing. Looking around, he saw that the two men were in the pond swimming away from the scene. He yelled at them to return; Mike Randall complied but Kevin Anderson did not. Anderson continued to swim away and eventually escaped. 7

Officer Konst then instructed Mike Randall to stay put until he could return to him. About this time, 1:53 a.m., police dispatch called Officer Konst with the results of its record check on Hendrikse and also confirmed the outstanding arrest warrant on Walker. Dispatch told Officer Konst that Hendrikse was clear, but confirmed that there was a day-night misdemeanor warrant on Walker for a failure to appear with bond set at $250.00. Then, at 1:56 a.m., Officer Konst called dispatch to run a records check on Mike Randall, which turned up nothing. 8

At this time, Officer Bevier was telling the congregated youth to leave. Dagmar Danney testified that she heard Officer Konst shout, "Get those f—— cars out of here." Officer Konst denies this use of profanity. 9

Officer Bevier, not knowing about the outstanding warrant on Walker, then instructed Walker that he should leave with a friend. Walker complied by exiting the Danney vehicle. When Officer Konst saw Walker leaving, he told Walker to get back in the Danney car, and Walker complied. Officer Konst denies using any profanity here, but Danney testified that he directed Walker to "Get back in the f—— car, you son-of-a-bitch." 10

Officer Konst then informed Officer Bevier about the warrant on Walker. About this time, Walker re-emerged from the car and walked toward Officer Konst. There is no indication in the testimony that Walker was fleeing at this time; instead, it appears that he was approaching Officer Konst to find out why he (Walker) could not leave with all the others.[1] 11

---

[1]At least two other witnesses, Mori Bagby and Michael Randall, testified that Walker did not leave his car, and that Officer Konst came up to the vehicle, told Walker to exit, and then told Walker he was under arrest. This difference in the testimony is insignificant for purposes of this summary judgment.

At this time, Officer Konst told Walker that there was a warrant outstanding   12
for Walker's arrest, and that Walker should turn around and put his hands behind
his back. Dagmar Danney testified that Officer Konst yelled at Walker in an angry
tone of voice. When Officer Konst reached out to grab Walker in an attempt to
handcuff him, Walker fled, running toward the dredge pond. Officer Konst
caught Walker from behind and pulled him to the ground. Officer Bevier
attempted to secure Walker's hands so that the handcuffs could be applied. But
Walker broke free and again ran off with Officers Konst and Bevier in pursuit.
For a second time, Officer Konst pulled Walker to the ground although Walker
again escaped. Dagmar Danney testified that during this struggle she saw Officer
Konst strike Walker on a single occasion in the face with his fist. Officer Konst
denies this.

These struggles had brought the parties to the ledge of an embankment that   13
led down about six feet to the edge of the dredge pond. Officers Konst and Bevier
and Walker lost their footing at the top of this embankment and tumbled down to
the water's edge. Walker once again broke free from the grasp of Officer Konst,
but Officer Bevier was still holding on. Walker dragged her for a ways as he ran
along the water's edge. Officer Bevier then let go just as Officer Konst grabbed
Walker around the waist. As the men struggled, they entered the dredge pond up
to their knees. Officer Konst had not been in the pond prior to this night and did
not know the depth of the water. The floor of the dredge pond drops off sharply,
and although these two men began their struggle in knee-deep water, they were
moving toward the drop-off that would leave them both unable to touch the
bottom.

As they struggled, Officer Konst put a bear-hug around Walker by wrapping   14
his arms around Walker in an attempt to pin Walker's arms to his sides. But about
this point, the men lost their balance, toppling over and out into the deep part of
the pond. Officer Konst quickly discovered that he could not touch the bottom,
and he thought to himself:

> This isn't worth it, in my mind, only thought process anyway, this isn't worth it,
> I'm awfully tired you know, I'm not going to drown out here over a misdemeanor
> warrant. And I pushed myself away from Mr. Walker to make it clear to him that
> he was free to go and I didn't want anything to do with him at that point.

Officer Konst surfaced, and he saw Walker surface. Officer Konst then swam   15
for shore. When he reached a point where he could stand, he looked back and saw
Walker sinking below the surface. One witness says she saw Officer Konst at this
point with his nightstick in his hand, although she never saw him use it. Officer
Konst then proceeded to shore where he removed his duty belt and shoes. He
instructed Officer Bevier to move the patrol cars to the embankment where the
headlights could illuminate the site, and he and Officer Littlefield started diving
to find Walker. Officer Bevier called in a "Code 3" to the dispatcher, meaning that
all available units should respond as quickly as possible. She also called the
paramedics. Although unknown by the officers at this time, it appears that Walker
could not swim.

As Officers Konst and Littlefield were diving, they were joined by Michael   16
Randall. Randall wanted to assist the officers in rescuing Walker, and stated that
he knew cardiac pulmonary resuscitation. Although Randall said that he had only
had one and one-half beers that evening, the officers felt that he was highly intoxicated because they had seen him earlier sitting on a tailgate of a pickup truck
drinking beer with numerous empty beer cans at his feet. At one point, the officers observed that Randall was having difficulty in the water and so Officer Konst
ordered Randall to the shore and prohibited him from any further rescue
attempts.

At 2:02 a.m. the Boise Fire Department dive team was requested, and they   17
arrived at 2:09 a.m. The dive team dove for an hour but could not locate Walker.
When efforts were continued the next day, the dive team did locate Walker's body
at about 11:30 a.m.

An autopsy was conducted, and the Ada County Coroner, Erwin L. Sonnen-   18
berg, concluded that Walker died "by fresh water drowning and that no physical
violence was a direct cause of Mr. Walker's death." The coroner further concluded
as follows:

7. Based upon my review of the Tucker Coroner's Report and Dr. Keen's
   report and upon my own observations, knowledge and experience, I conclude the following:
   (a) That the multiple small abrasions appearing around Mr. Walker's right
       eye along with the multiple small scratches and abrasions on Mr.
       Walker's face appear to be post-mortem and most likely caused by fish;
   (b) That the multiple small abrasions around Mr. Walker's right shoulder
       appear to be post-mortem;
   (c) In addition, Mr. Walker appears to have a number of other small abra-
       sions and/or pock marks under the corner of his right eye, his lower
       left lip, lower left neck at the shoulder, lower left arm, upper right arm,
       above and below the left knee, and below the right knee.
8. All of the abrasions were superficial in nature.

The coroner further testified that the autopsy revealed that Mr. Walker had a   19
blood alcohol level of .185. In addition, a blood analysis revealed traces of
cocaine.

Walker's mother has filed this action under 42 U.S.C. §§ 1983 and 1985 seeking   20
damages for her son's death. Her complaint can be divided roughly into claims for
excessive force and claims for inadequate rescue. She summarizes her constitutional claims as follows:

The plaintiff alleges violations of Ronald Walker's rights under the Fourth,
Fifth and Fourteenth Amendments to the United States Constitution.

One, the arrest constituted an unreasonable seizure and violation of
Ronald Walker's Fourth Amendment rights, as incorporated by the Fourteenth Amendment, which unreasonable seizure resulted in Ronald Walker's
death.

Two, the actions of the defendants in carrying Ronald Walker to a place of danger and leaving him there to drown, refusing and failing to rescue him, and preventing others from attempting to rescue him, deprived Ronald Walker of his life in violation of his rights to due process under the Fifth and Fourteenth Amendments.

Three, the actions of the defendants in singling Ronald Walker out for arrest and abusive treatment denied him the equal protection of the law, in violation of the Fourteenth Amendment.

Furthermore, the plaintiff alleges these acts were carried out in furtherance of the defendant City's policies, and/or custom, and were the direct and proximate result of the City's failure to properly train its police officers.

■ "An Inflammable Situation" ■

Thomas LEWIS, et al.,
Plaintiffs-Appellees, Cross-Appellants,
v.
J. D. DOWNS and V. W. Geil,
Defendants-Appellants,
Cross-Appellees.

Nos. 84–5738, 84–5739.

United States Court of Appeals,
Sixth Circuit.

Argued Aug. 1, 1985.
Decided Oct. 9, 1985.

This case grows out of an unfortunate racial incident. Ethel and Thomas Lewis, both of whom are Caucasian, reside in a neighborhood in which the minority of the residents are white with their two children Tony and Lois. During the afternoon of the day in question, an argument began between Lois and a black neighbor, concerning the place where Mr. Lewis had parked his truck. Although innocuous in its beginnings, this argument continued to escalate to the point where later that afternoon Lois, allegedly because she could not sleep due to the noise, called the Memphis Police Department.

Downs, a reserve police officer, and Geil, a regular police officer, both of whom are white, responded to the call. Upon arriving at the scene, the officers found both the Lewises and numerous neighbors yelling and cursing at each other. Mrs. Ethel Lewis, who by this time was quite agitated, was repeatedly yelling, "Get your guns now. We have got something for you." The officers imme-

1

2

---

diately attempted to discern what had happened and repeatedly asked Mrs. Lewis to stop screaming and cursing. Due to Mrs. Lewis' failure to comply with the officers' requests to quiet down and because Mrs. Lewis' conduct was creating an "inflammable situation," Officer Downs informed Mrs. Lewis that she was under arrest.

In order to effect the arrest, Officer Downs reached over the four foot chain [3] link fence which surrounded the Lewises' home to grab Mrs. Lewis. At this time, the Lewises' dog jumped up and grabbed Officer Downs' arm (Officer Downs' shirt was not ripped nor was his skin broken from this encounter). In response, both officers drew their revolvers and Officer Downs told Mrs. Lewis that if she did not restrain the dog he would kill it, which caused Mrs. Lewis to go into hysterics. Despite Mrs. Lewis' mental condition, she complied with Officer Downs' request and placed the dog inside the Lewises' house. Officer Geil then proceeded into the Lewises' front yard to arrest Mrs. Lewis. Officer Geil gained physical control over Mrs. Lewis near the front porch and by severely twisting her arm, was able to place his handcuffs on her wrists. After Mrs. Lewis was handcuffed, she either slipped due to muddy conditions or was thrown by Officer Geil to the ground.[1] While Mrs. Lewis lay handcuffed and face down on the ground, Officer Geil kicked her in the back and buttocks area.

Tony, in a "foolish" attempt to prevent the apprehension of his mother, started [4] to move towards Officer Downs with an iron rake. Officer Downs responded by drawing his revolver and asking Tony to put down the rake; after three such requests, Tony dropped the rake. Officer Geil then grabbed Tony to effect an arrest of him. In the process of subduing and handcuffing Tony, Officer Geil resorted to pulling Tony's hair, twisting his arm, and placing him in a choke hold. At this time, Mr. Lewis, "in a very foolish manner, commensurate with his physical . . . inadequacy," sought to intervene on his son's behalf by grabbing Tony's waist in order to prevent Officer Geil from taking him away. Mr. Thomas Lewis' brother, Eugene Lewis, however, intervened and grabbed Mr. Lewis around his waist and restrained him. While being held by his brother, Mr. Lewis was kicked by Officer Geil in the groin and, simultaneously, struck on the top of his head by Officer Downs with his nightstick. Mr. Lewis immediately went to the ground. Bleeding profusely and on his knees, Mr. Lewis was forced to crawl unaided to the gate. Due to Mr. Lewis' condition, the officers had him taken by ambulance to a hospital where he was diagnosed as suffering a cut to his head with an underlying hematoma.

Following his father's aborted attempt to intervene, Tony Lewis was hand- [5] cuffed and taken to the police car. While being led away, Officer Geil without justification struck Tony in the mouth with his nightstick. Tony later received several stitches due to the injury to his mouth.

Mr. and Mrs. Lewis were, subsequently, charged with several crimes, including [6] disorderly conduct, assault, and battery. The Lewises were acquitted on all counts.

---

[1] The district court never explicitly explained how Mrs. Lewis ended up handcuffed and on the ground. Mrs. Lewis alleged that Officer Geil threw her to the ground. In contrast, Officer Geil testified that they both slipped and fell due to the muddy conditions.

"You're Going to Have to Kill Me"

Doris WYCHE, individually and as
Administratix of the Estate
of Darryl Sherman Wyche, Plaintiff,

v.

The CITY OF FRANKLINTON, a body of
Politic; Ray Gilliam, individually and in
his official capacity as Chief of Police of
the City of Franklinton; and Antonio
Eugene Caldwell, personally and in his
official capacity as a Police Officer for
the City of Franklinton, Defendants.

No. 93–141–CIV–5–H.

United States District Court,
E.D. North Carolina, Raleigh Division.

Nov. 5, 1993.

Defendant Caldwell, a police officer employed by the Town of Franklinton, worked   1
the third shift from 8:00 p.m. until 8:00 a.m. He was the only officer on duty in
Franklinton during the third shift. At midnight, the Franklinton Police Department
building was locked and dispatching duties were handled by Franklin County.

At approximately 1:00 a.m. on February 12, 1991, Caldwell received a call   2
from the Franklin County dispatcher concerning a mentally disturbed person on
Mason Street in Franklinton. When Caldwell arrived on Mason Street, he was
stopped by John Bullock who told the officer that his friend Darryl Wyche
("Wyche") had "gone crazy." From his encounter with Bullock, Caldwell learned
that Wyche had ripped two doors off of their hinges, that he was saying "God had
called him home," and that Wyche's family was supposed to be taking him to a
mental hospital the next day. Caldwell then placed a call for backup assistance.

Caldwell next encountered Ms. Katie Crudup. Crudup was upset and con-   3
firmed that Wyche was acting "crazy." She stated that Wyche was headed towards
the Snack Shack convenience store. After making a second call for backup, Caldwell received a call concerning an emergency at the Snack Shack. Caldwell drove
the short distance to the Snack Shack and pulled in the parking lot with his
vehicle's blue lights activated. From the parking lot, he observed Wyche walking
up and down the aisles of the Snack Shack with blood on his arms. He could not
see the two employees on duty at the Snack Shack. Caldwell exited his vehicle
carrying a PR-24 baton. Although Caldwell had never received training in the use
of a PR-24 baton, Caldwell carried it in the hope that the sight of it would keep
Wyche from giving him any trouble.

Wyche v. City of Franklinton, 837 F.Supp. 137 (1993).

When Wyche saw Caldwell in the parking lot, he kicked open the doors of the   4
Snack Shack and yelled to Caldwell that he was going to kill him. Caldwell
attempted to calm Wyche, but Wyche responded "you're going to have to kill me."
Caldwell again placed a call for backup, indicating that urgent help was needed
and noting that he was dealing with a person exhibiting abnormal mental behavior.
Wyche began chasing Caldwell around the parking lot and adjacent street,
screaming as he ran that he was going to kill Caldwell. Caldwell, knowing that
backup was on its way, turned and ran from Wyche in an effort to buy time. As
Wyche was chasing Caldwell, he continued to yell threats and tried to grab him.

While running from Wyche, Caldwell again attempted to call for backup from   5
his walkie-talkie. The chase continued for several minutes, during which time
Caldwell became very tired. Finally, Caldwell stopped running, turned to face
Wyche, and demanded that he stop, saying "Stop, or I'm going to have to shoot
you." Wyche was approximately three to five feet away and continued to advance
toward Caldwell. Although Caldwell had not previously seen a weapon in Wyche's
possession, he saw Wyche reach behind him as he lunged forward. Caldwell then
fired a shot in a downward direction, hitting Wyche in the left leg. Wyche's body
jerked, but he continued to advance toward Caldwell. Caldwell then fired a
second shot, hitting Wyche in the abdomen. Wyche fell to the ground, and Caldwell immediately called for rescue. Wyche died later that night. Sometime after
the shooting, backup arrived.

■ Detained and Abandoned ■

Sharon COURSON, Plaintiff–Appellee,
v.
Quinn A. McMILLIAN, individually and
as Sheriff of Walton County, a political
subdivision of the State of Florida, Defendant,
Jim Roy, Defendant–Appellant.

No. 90–3400.

United States Court of Appeals,
Eleventh Circuit.

Aug. 30, 1991.

On the night of May 12, 1985, plaintiff-appellee Sharon Courson and two male   1
companions were "four wheeling" in an all-terrain vehicle on a Walton County,
Florida beach.[1] When they were ready to leave the beach, Courson, who did not

---

Courson v. McMillian, 939 F.2d 1479 (1991).
Cross references to depositions and affadavits omitted.
[1]Courson was twenty-three years of age when the incident in question occurred, and her male
companions were in their mid to late thirties.

drink any alcoholic beverage, was concerned that her two male companions had consumed a sufficient amount of beer to inhibit their driving ability. Nevertheless, one of the males drove west from the beach on U.S. Highway 98 at approximately 10:00 P.M.; Courson rode as a passenger.

Their vehicle passed defendant-appellant Lieutenant Jim Roy, a deputy sheriff for Walton County, in a no passing area at a speed between 60 and 80 miles per hour in a 45 or 55 miles per hour zone. Roy, who had been conducting surveillance of marijuana fields, had noticed that evening a dark, four-wheel drive vehicle, similar to the one that passed him and contained Courson and her companions, in the vicinity of the cultivated marijuana fields. He activated his siren and flashing blue light, and pursued the vehicle. Courson, seated in the front seat between the two males, became aware of Roy's presence as soon as he activated his flashing blue light.

Subsequently, the vehicle stopped on the side of the paved surface of the highway at a condominium construction site, located between two developments. One of the developments was townhouse rental property. The other, which had a guard house at the entrance to the property, was a resort with units available for rent and sale.

Roy stopped his patrol car behind the vehicle and, in a loud voice, requested the occupants to exit. When none of the occupants exited the vehicle, Roy reiterated his instruction. Thereafter, the male driver only left the vehicle. After Roy again repeated his order that all occupants exit, Courson and the other male exited.[2]

Roy observed that each of the three individuals had difficulty getting out of the vehicle. As Courson and her male companions approached, Roy, who was alone, withdrew a shotgun from his patrol car. One of the males became and continued to be verbally abusive and belligerent;[3] he also challenged Roy's authority to conduct the stop and investigation. Roy immediately requested the assistance of backup units. Because he was outnumbered and uncertain whether the three apprehended individuals were involved in criminal activity, Roy instructed them to lie face down on the ground.[4] He continued to hold his shotgun toward the three detainees while he awaited backup assistance.[5]

---

[2]Courson contends that the vehicle occupants did not hear Roy's instruction to exit the vehicle. Her deposition testimony, however, contradicts the fact that the occupants did not hear Roy's request. Evidenced by his exit, the male driver heard the instruction.

[3]The parties dispute whether the abusive language occurred upon the male's exit from the vehicle or after the three were directed to lie on the ground.

[4]Courson testified that she was reluctant to obey Roy and questioned him as to whether he meant for her also to lie on the ground. In response, she stated that Roy chambered his shotgun and repeated his instruction that all three individuals lie on the ground, whereupon she complied.

[5]Roy explained his actions subsequent to the stop of the vehicle and the exit of the occupants:

> In light of the circumstances I encountered, I withdrew from my vehicle a shot gun, directed it in the general direction of the occupants of the vehicle and instructed them to stop and lay upon the ground. One of the male occupants of the vehicle who had exited from the passenger side was cussing, yelling and challenging my authority to conduct this stop and investigation. I also immediately requested the assistance of back up units.
>
> While awaiting the arrival of back up units, I remained at the front of my vehicle, continuing to exhibit the shot gun and requiring the occupants of the vehicle to remain prone on the ground. This was done as a result of their initial failure to stop, their initial failure to exit the

Subsequently, a Florida highway patrolman arrived. Roy gave his shotgun to   6
the patrolman to guard Courson and her male companions while he searched
their vehicle by shining a flashlight into the interior. Thereafter, four Walton
County deputy sheriffs arrived at the scene. In addition to Roy's patrol car,
Courson's best recollection was that there were two or three patrol cars trans-
porting the backup officers.

Both of the males were arrested, handcuffed, and taken to the Walton County   7
sheriff's department for booking in separate patrol cars. The male driver was
charged with driving under the influence of alcohol, speeding, and with fleeing
and attempting to elude a law enforcement officer. The other male, who physically resisted arrest and injured one of the officers, was charged with resisting
arrest with violence, disorderly intoxication, obstruction of justice, assault on law
enforcement officers, and battery on a police officer. The lawfulness of these
arrests has not been challenged by Courson or her arrested companions.

During the investigation and arrest of male companions, Courson was kept on   8
the ground until both males were taken into custody. Including the wait for
backup assistance with her companions, the total time that Courson remained on
the ground was approximately thirty minutes; little traffic passed on the highway
during that period. She was not directly interrogated, searched, touched, harmed
in any way, or charged with any crime.[6]

---

vehicle as instructed and the belligerent attitude of at least one of the occupants. *Additionally,
I was outnumbered and uncertain of whether the individuals apprehended were involved in
any other manner of criminal activity, such as the marijuana cultivation I had been investigating earlier in the evening.* (emphasis added)

[6]Roy explained his reasoning in keeping Courson on the ground until her male companions were
taken into custody:

The female passenger in the vehicle was also instructed to lay on the ground. Although she was
not uncooperative, the number of individuals involved and the circumstances led me to believe
that the most prudent course of action for me was to require all of the individuals to lay upon
the ground until I was able to obtain assistance. The female was kept on the ground until both
of the other male individuals had been taken into custody. She was then allowed to stand.

The female was not searched, touched, struck or harmed in any way. She was not directly
interrogated and did not say much to me or any of the other officers on the scene. She identified herself as Sharon Courson. . . .

*Ms. Courson was not arrested or otherwise charged with any criminal offense, nor was
she detained beyond the time necessary to determine her involvement in the events that had
transpired that evening.* (emphasis added)

Courson testified that she was not harmed physically by Roy or any other officer during her
detention:

Q. You were not I gather physically struck or otherwise harmed on the night in question?
A. [Courson] No, sir, I was not.
Q. *What you described does not sound as though Lieutenant Roy or any other law enforce-
ment officer ever made physical contact with you?*
A. *No, sir.*
Q. *You were not grabbed, or held, or anything of that nature?*
A. *No.*
[Deposition of Sharon Courson (emphasis added).]

After Courson's male companions had been taken to the station for booking, Courson was told that she was free to go. Roy put his shotgun away. The officers assisted Courson in searching for her car keys, which she said were left in the vehicle in which the three individuals had been riding. The keys were not found, and the vehicle was towed away. Courson did not ask Roy or another officer to take her anywhere.[7] She walked a short distance to the guard house at the adjacent resort and called a friend, who came to take her home, at which she arrived at approximately midnight.[8]

Courson lost no time from work as a result of this incident.[9] She testified that she was not physically injured during her detention by Roy, that she suffered no

---

[7]Roy's affidavit states that he asked Courson's two male companions if they would allow her to drive the vehicle home. Upon their refusal, he states that Courson informed him that she would walk to the guard house at the adjoining resort where she would call someone to transport her home. Courson did not request Roy to transport her anywhere.

> I asked both of the male occupants of the vehicle if they would allow Ms. Courson to drive the vehicle home. They refused to agree to allow Ms. Courson to drive the vehicle and therefore it was towed.
>
> After the arrest of the male occupants of the vehicle, Ms. Courson was advised that she was free to go. She did not request that I transport her home, or to any other location and, to the best of my recollection, stated that she could contact someone who would transport her home. She indicated that she would walk to a phone, which she apparently did, by walking to the guard shack at the Sea Scape. I presumed she made a telephone call and arranged for transportation on her own. [Affidavit of Jim Roy.]
>
> Courson testified that one of the other officers asked Roy if she could take the vehicle home, and Roy refused because the vehicle did not belong to her. According to Courson, Roy showed no interest in her transportation home, but she concedes that she did not ask him or any other officer to transport her anywhere.
>
> Q. Okay, so after Roy says you can't take the truck, what happens then?
> A. [Courson] That officer that asked him [Roy] that turned around and he didn't say another word. Uh, I said to Lieutenant Roy, "Well how am I going to get home[?]" And as I said "home" he just dropped the pad down and he said, he said, "I hope that you can find a way home." And I just stood there and he turned around, walked and got in his car and drove away. And the other officer was gone also.
> Q. *Did you ask him [Roy] to take you anywhere?*
> A. *No, sir.*
> Q. Did he offer to take you anywhere?
> A. No, sir.
> Q. *How about the other deputy, did you ask him to take you anywhere?*
> A. *No, sir.*
> Q. Did he offer to take you anywhere?
> A. No, sir.
> (emphasis added)

[8]Courson testified that her walk from the scene of her detention to the guard house, where she called her friend to transport her, was "[a]bout a mile," but also admitted that the length of a football field was a suitable frame of reference. [Deposition of Sharon Courson.] The photographs, attached to Roy's affidavit, show the scene of Courson's detention by the condominium construction site and the adjoining resort and guard house. The pictures evidence that the distance of Courson's walk was consistent with her football field analogy.

[9]Although Courson subsequently did leave the employer for whom she was working at the time of the incident in question, she testified that her work, and not this experience, was the reason for her departure. [Deposition of Sharon Courson.]

physical consequences, and that she had no medical treatment and received no medication for any condition resulting from this incident.[10] Courson's only residual effect from the experience is her claimed mistrust of police officers.[11]

Courson initiated this action in the Walton County, Florida circuit court. Her four-count complaint alleged violation of her Fourth, Fifth and Fourteenth Amendment rights resulting from her detention, including excessive force, and abandonment as well as related state tort claims.

● ● ● ●

For Deliberation and Argument

1. Imagine that you are David Palmer's attorney (*Palmer v. Hall*). Write a brief for the appellate court in which you argue that your client is entitled to damages for violation of his civil rights under section 1983 of Title 42 of the U.S. Code. In your argument address the *separate* and *comparative* responsibilities of (a) Mayor Thompson, (b) the town aldermen, (c) Officer Hall, and (d) Officer Foster (Hall's partner). In assessing damages (if any), you may want to consider the amounts of *actual* damages and *punitive* damages. Actual damages are assessed to compensate the plaintiff for pain, suffering, and mental anguish, past and future, resulting from the unlawful actions of the defendant(s). Punitive damages are designed to penalize the defendant(s) for willful or malicious violations of the plaintiff's rights. Apply the applicable law in the Group 1 Readings (pp. 429–34) to the facts of this particular case, including the actions of each defendant or set of defendants. In assessing the responsibility of the alderman, note that the Macon city charter provides that "the mayor *and* the council constitute the legislative department [of the city government]. They stand on an equal footing. Neither has the duty to supervise and/or take the other to task for what either does or fails to do as elected city officials."

---

[10]Deposition of Sharon Courson.

[11]Courson described her residual, nonphysical effects of the incident:

> Q. Describe for me if you will how you were, or have been injured as a result of this incident?
> A. [Courson] There's, uh, I feel like there's a permanent and definite mistrust and fear of police officers. I'm afraid to be stopped by a police officer. . . .
> Q. You alleged in your complaint that you have and will suffer mental and physical pain. Can you tell me a little bit about the mental aspects, fear, nervousness, and so forth? Is there any physical pain or physical consequences that you can identify or describe for me that has [sic] resulted from this incident?
> A. Nothing other than the stress, and, uh, the headaches from the stress that have happened. But nothing physical or anything. You know I told you that I was not harmed that night as far as a physically hurt or anything like that.

[Deposition of Sharon Courson.] Although Courson does not appear to consider her headaches a physical ailment, we note that our review of the record indicates that the headache condition apparently occurred as a direct result of her detention and is not alleged to be a persisting or permanent condition resulting from this incident.

2. Based on your reading of the *Franklin* case and of the applicable law in the Group 1 Readings, assess the likelihood of the plaintiff, Delores Franklin, mother of Ronald Walker, prevailing against the defendants. In particular, consider the following key questions, and support your responses with evidence based on the facts of the case:

   - Did the police have probable cause to arrest Ronald Walker? Was the seizure unreasonable, and did it violate Walker's Fourth Amendment rights?
   - Was the arrest of Walker discriminatory? That is, does the evidence support the plaintiff's claim that the officers singled out Walker, an African-American, for special treatment?
   - To what extent, if any, did the officers use excessive force in arresting Walker and attempting to prevent his escape?
   - To what extent can the officers be held liable for failing to rescue Walker, and in particular, for refusing to allow Michael Randall to assist in the rescue efforts?

3. Consider the facts of *Lewis v. Downs*. Then, assuming the role of either prosecuting or defense attorney, write a brief in which you comment on (a) whether Officers Downs and Geil were justified in arresting Ethel Lewis and her son Tony Lewis and (b) whether the officers used excessive force against the two arrestees. Refer to the applicable law in the Group 1 Readings, pages 429–34. Note that in considering this case, the appellate court declared that

   > in determining if a police officer's conduct rises to the level of a constitutional deprivation, factors such as the need for the force, the relationship between the need and the amount applied, the extent of the injury inflicted, and the motivation of the police officer in applying the force must be considered. Finally, the circumstances surrounding the use of force must be carefully considered. . . . [quoting an opinion from another case:] "A court . . . should take care to consider whether the police are acting in a swiftly developing situation, and in such cases the court should not engage in unrealistic second-guessing."

   An additional relevant fact: Tony Lewis weighed 120 pounds; he was being restrained by his brother Eugene, who weighed 175 pounds.

4. Based on your reading of *Wyche v. City of Franklinton* and your understanding of the law, was Officer Caldwell justified in using deadly force against Darryl Wyche? In its opinion, the court noted that defendant Caldwell contended that "his actions were objectively reasonable in light of the facts and circumstances." The plaintiff, on the other hand, contended that

   > Wyche posed no serious threat to the safety of Caldwell or other because he was not armed . . . and that the amount and degree of force used against Wyche was unnecessary under the circumstances and, therefore,

unreasonable. This contention is based upon the fact that Caldwell did not attempt to employ a lesser degree of force before resorting to deadly force. The plaintiff argues that Caldwell should have first resorted to hand-to-hand combat or, at the very least, the use of his baton, which he carried throughout the encounter.

In formulating your conclusions, apply the relevant statements on the law in the Group 1 Readings to the particular facts of this case.

5. The plaintiff in *Courson v. McMillian*, Sharon Courson, brought three main charges against officer Jim Roy: first, that he violated her constitutional rights by detaining her for thirty minutes; second, that he violated her rights by using excessive force against her in forcing her to lie face down on the ground and pointing a shotgun at her and her companions; and third, that he violated her rights under section 1983 by abandoning her—leaving her alone on a highway at night without transportation home. Based on the evidence in the facts of the case, the sections of testimony by the plaintiff and the defendant, and the relevant law in the Group 1 Readings, explain whether you believe that the plaintiff is likely to prevail on the constitutional questions of unlawful arrest and excessive force. To answer the first question, you will need to consider whether Roy had probable cause to stop the vehicle and detain its occupants— that is, to "conduct an investigatory stop." To answer the second, you will need to consider whether Roy's actions were "objectively reasonable" in light of the particular "facts and circumstances" of this case. On the question of abandonment, consider whether Roy violated Courson's constitutional rights by not taking her home. And if you have read the chapter on emotional distress, you may also want to consider whether Courson would likely prevail if she were to bring an additional (nonconstitutional) charge of intentional or negligent infliction of emotional distress for the defendant's act of abandonment.

6. Select one of the cases treated in this group. Imagine that you are representing either the plaintiff or the defendant. Compose either an opening statement or a closing argument for this case. Remember that your audience is the jury. Draw on the facts of the case in a way that is likely to have the greatest impact on the jury. Keep in mind, however, that jury members may turn against you— and your client—if they think that you are overly manipulating the facts, being deceptive, making exaggerated claims, or attempting too crudely to play on their emotions. For guidance on developing your statement, see "Models for the Opening Statement and the Closing Argument" at the end of Chapter 2. See also Larry S. Stewart's "Arguing Pain and Suffering Damages in Summation: How to Inspire Jurors" at the end of the Group 3 Readings in Chapter 3.

■ Group 3 Readings: *Searches of Students*

Do high school students have the same constitutional rights—more specifically, the freedom from unlawful search and seizure—as adults? In the Tinker *case (see Chapter 6) the Supreme Court declared that "It can hardly be argued that either students or teachers shed their constitutional rights at the school-house gate." Further, "state-operated schools may not be enclaves of totalitari-anism. School officials do not possess absolute authority over their students. Students in school as well as out of school are 'persons' under our Constitu-tion." At the same time, the Supreme Court and lower courts, have circum-scribed the rights of students to a greater degree than the rights of adults because, as they have argued, courts must balance the interests of society in providing a proper educational environment for students against the rights of the individual student to be free from intrusive searches. We have seen how freedom of the student press is not quite the same as freedom of the press in society at large.*

What is true of students' First Amendment rights is to some extent true of students' Fourth Amendment rights. While courts have ruled that students may not be searched or seized without good reason, the standard is not the relatively high one of "probable cause" (which requires solid evidence from reliable sources) but rather "reasonable suspicion" that illegal or illicit activity has occurred. The justification for this lower threshold was stated by the court in of Brousseau v. Town of Westerly: *"Fourth Amendment inquiry into reasonableness of search in public school setting cannot disregard schools' custodial and tutelary responsibility for children, and must take into account the fact that, in some respects, students within school environ-ment have lesser expectations of privacy than members of the population generally."[1]*

The following group of cases focuses on searches of students suspected of possessing contraband items—either drugs or weapons. In all of these cases, the student plaintiffs have claimed that their Fourth Amendment rights were violated, and they were therefore seeking to have the incriminating evidence suppressed under the exclusionary rule. As discussed in the introduction to this chapter, under the exclusionary rule, items obtained during the course of an illegal search cannot be used as evidence against the accused. The rule is intended to act as a deterrent both to police and to magistrate judges (who sign search warrants) for overstepping constitutional boundaries by denying them the fruits of illegal searches.

A model student paper, *by Alyssa Mellott, accompanies the first case in this group,* State v. Engerud. *In the landmark* New Jersey v. T.L.O. *case, a school official who searched a fourteen year old female student on suspicion of smoking tobacco found evidence that she was dealing, as well as smoking marijuana. In* Coronado v. State, *a young man who left school to attend his "grandfather's funeral" was recalled to the office; though drugs were not found on his person, they were later discovered in the trunk of his car. In another landmark case,* Acton v. Vernonia School District, *parents of a fourteen-year-old student refused to sign the consent form that requires student athletes to submit to random drug testing; as a result, he was barred from athletic*

---

[1] F.Supp.2d 177 (1998).

activity. Williams v. Ellington *concerns a female student who was strip-searched on suspicion of carrying drugs.* People v. Dilworth *concerns a student who had hidden cocaine inside a flashlight. Finally,* People v. Pruitt, Cheatham, and Brooks *focuses on three students who carried concealed guns to school. Preceding the cases are extracts from case law that has developed from searches and seizures of students.*

Case Law

High school students are protected from unreasonable searches and seizures, even in the school, by state employees, whether police officers or school teachers. (*People v. Scott D.*, 34 N.Y.2d 483 (1974))   1

Public school authorities have special responsibilities, and therefore correspondingly broad powers, to control school precincts in order to protect students in their charge. (*People v. Scott D.*, 34 N.Y.2d 483 (1974))   2

Obligation of public school authorities to maintain discipline and provide security is derived from state law and is delegated by local boards of education and, in exercising their authority in performing their duties, public school teachers act not as private individuals, but as agents of the state. (*People v. Scott D.*, 34 N.Y. 2d 483 (1974))   3

That primary purpose of school searches may be to protect school environment and not to secure a criminal conviction changes basis for probable cause and also standards of reasonableness of searches and seizures under constitutional limitations, but does not permit random causeless searches. (*People v. Scott D.*, 34 N.Y.2d 483 (1974))   4

Fourth Amendment inquiry into reasonableness of search undertaken in public school setting cannot disregard schools' custodial and tutelary responsibility for children, and must take into account fact that, in some respects, students within school environment have lesser expectation of privacy than members of population generally. (*Broussou v. Town of Westerly*, 11 F.Supp. 2d 177 (1998))   5

Search of a student in a public school does not require showing of probable cause; rather, legality of search depends simply on its reasonableness, under normal circumstances. (*Widener v. Faye*, 809 F.Supp. 35 (1992))   6

To be reasonable, search of a public school student must be justified at its inception, and it must be reasonably related in scope to circumstances at hand. [T.L.O. test] (*Widener v. Faye*, 809 F.Supp. 35 (1992))   7

State cannot compel attendance at public schools and then subject students to unreasonable searches of legitimate, noncontraband items that students carry onto school grounds. (*People v. Pruitt*, 662 N.E.2d 540 (1996))   8

For purposes of determining legality of search, search of student by teacher 9 or other school official will be justified at its inception when there are reasonable grounds for suspecting that search will turn up evidence that student has violated or is violating law or rules of school; such search will be permissible in its scope when measures adopted are reasonably related to objectives of search and not excessively intrusive in light of age and sex of student and nature of infraction. (*People v. Pruitt*, 662 N.E.2d 540 (1996))

Students possess legitimate, yet limited, expectation of privacy within school 10 environment. (*Commonwealth of Pennsylvania v. Cass*, 709 A.2d 350 (1998))

Although primary and secondary public school students possess legitimate 11 expectation of privacy in their assigned lockers at school, that privacy expectation is minimal within meaning of constitutional search and seizure provision; lockers are school property and although students can provide their own locks, combination to locks must be provided to school. (*Commonwealth Pennsylvania v. Cass*, 709 A.2d 350 (1998))

General searches by school officials are compatible with limited protection 12 provided to school students under constitutional search and seizure provision, so long as they are carried out based upon neutral, clearly articulated guidelines. (*Commonwealth of Pennsylvania v. Cass*, 709 A.2d 350 (1998))

Student's expectation of privacy in school locker is not absolute but must be 13 balanced against school's need to maintain order and discipline. (*Dumas v. Pennsylvania*, 515 A.2d 984 (1986))

Requirement that search of student be "justified at its inception" does not 14 mean that school administrator has right to search student who merely acts in way that creates reasonable suspicion that student has violated some regulation or law but, rather, search is warranted only if student's conduct creates reasonable suspicion that particular regulation or law has been violated, with search serving to produce evidence of that violation. (*Cornfield v. Consolidated H.S. District 230*, 991 F.2d 1316 (1993))

Determining reasonableness of any search involves a twofold inquiry as to 15 whether the action was justified at its inception and whether search as actually conducted was reasonably related in scope to circumstances which justified interference in the first place. (*New Jersey v. T.L.O.*, 105 S.Ct. 733 (1985))

Search of student by teacher or other school official would be permissible in 16 its scope when measures adopted are reasonably related to objectives of search and not excessively intrusive in light of sex of student and nature of infraction. (*New Jersey v. T.L.O.*, 105 S.Ct. 733 (1985))

State-compelled collection and testing of urine constitutes "search" under 17 Fourth Amendment. (*Vernonia School District v. Acton*, 115 S.Ct. 2386 (1995))

Where, at time of Fourth Amendment's enactment, there was no clear prac- 18 tice, either approving or disapproving type of search at issue, "reasonableness" of search is judged by balancing intrusion on individual's Fourth Amendment interest against promotion of legitimate governmental interest. (*Vernonia School District v. Acton*, 115 S.Ct. 2386 (1995))

While public school children have lesser privacy expectations with regard to   19
medical examinations and procedures than general population, student athletes have even less legitimate privacy expectation, for purpose of determining reasonableness on drug urinalysis "search." (*Vernonia School District v. Acton*, 115 S.Ct. 2386 (1995))

Doctrine of "in loco parentis," which literally means in the place of a   20
parent, is common law doctrine which means that parent may delegate part of his parental authority, during his life, to tutor or schoolmaster of his child, who is then in loco parentis, and has such portion of power of parent committed to his charge for purposes of restraint and correction as may be necessary to answer purposes for which he is employed. (*People v. Dilworth*, 661 N.E.2d 310 (1996))

Miranda rights did not attach, and warnings were not required, where   21
middle school student was detained and questioned by school authorities after he had admitted to smoking in school lavatory. (*In Re S.K.*, 647 A.2d 952 (1994))

Student does not lose his Fourth Amendment expectation of privacy in coat   22
or book bag merely because he places those objects in his locker. (*In Re Adam*, 697 N.E. 2d 1100 (1997))

The resolution of whether school officials act as agents of the police when   23
they conduct a search, so as to subject them to same Fourth Amendment standards, is determined by an examination of the totality of the circumstances, including consideration of: (1) the purpose of the search; (2) the party who initiated the search; and (3) whether the police acquiesced in the search or ratified it. (*In Re D.E.M.*, 727 A.2d 570 (1999))

For purposes of determining whether school officials acted as agents of the   24
police when they conducted search, so as to subject them to same Fourth Amendment standards, the mere fact that school officials cooperated with the police does not establish that the police acquiesced in or ratified the search. (*In Re D.E.M.*, 727 A.2d 570 (1999))

Random metal detector weapon searches of high school students did not   25
violate Fourth Amendment ban on unreasonable searches and seizures; need of school to keep weapons off campus was substantial, no system of more suspicion-intense searches was workable, and searches were minimally intrusive in that only random sample of students was tested and students were not touched during search and were required to open pockets or jackets only if they triggered metal detector. (*In Re Latasha W.*, 70 Cal. Rptr. 886 (1998))

Model Student Paper:
Search the Locker

■ _____ ■

STATE of New Jersey,
Plaintiff-Respondent,

v.

Jeffrey ENGERUD, Defendant-Appellant.

Supreme Court of New Jersey.

Argued May 10, 1983.
Decided Aug. 8, 1983.

On January 29, 1980, a vice-principal at Somerville High School met with a   1
Somerville police detective in the high school office. The detective had just
received a telephone call from a person claiming to be the father of a student. The
caller said that the defendant, an eighteen year old student at the school, was
selling drugs in the school and if the police did not stop it, he would take matters
into his own hands. Their conversation lasted five minutes and the detective left
the building.

The vice-principal then relayed this information to the assistant principal and   2
the principal. The principal had heard a "rumor" a year earlier that the defendant
was selling drugs at the school. He and the assistant principal opened the defendant's locker through the use of a pass-key that could open any locker in the
building even though the lockers are equipped with combination locks. The two
men made a complete search of the locker and its contents. In the defendant's
coat pocket they found two plastic bags containing packets of a white substance
that turned out to be methamphetamine (speed). Each packet was marked with
its weight in fractions of a gram. They also discovered a package of marijuana
rolling paper.

The vice-principal called the police and defendant's parents and took the   3
defendant out of class. The principal asked the defendant to empty his pockets.
This disclosed a small quantity of marijuana and $45 in cash.

Engerud was charged with unlawful possession of a controlled dangerous   4
substance and unlawful possession of a controlled dangerous substance with
intent to distribute. . . . On June 18, 1981, the Law Division judge denied a motion
to suppress the evidence obtained from the locker and pocket searches. In his
view the search was "responsible and diligent under all of the circumstances."

On July 9, 1981, defendant pleaded guilty to the second count of the indict-   5
ment and was sentenced to an indeterminate term at Yardville, not to exceed five
years. His sentence was stayed pending appeal.

_____

State v. Engerud, 463 A.2d 934 (1985).

Paper Topic: "Search the Locker" (State v. Engerud)

In *State v. Engerud*, apply the legal standards articulated in the case law (pp. 458–60) to determine whether (a) the search of Engerud's locker was legal and (b) the evidence found during the search should be suppressed, under the exclusionary rule, in prosecuting the charge of delinquency.

In particular, note the test established by the Supreme Court in the *T.L.O.* case: "Search of student by teacher or other school official would be permissible in its scope when measures adopted are reasonably related to objectives of search and not excessively intrusive in light of sex of student and nature of infraction" (*New Jersey v. T.L.O., 105 S.Ct. 733* (1985)).

COMMENTARY BY ALYSSA MELLOTT

After reading through the case and the case law on searches of students I decided that the boy should have been searched. The majority of the decisions indicated that while students are protected from unreasonable searches, their expectation of privacy is limited because of the necessity of schools to protect their students. I then chose the cases I would use to discuss the rules regarding searches of students. Next, I picked cases from the case law that would support my position. I also made note of the case law that could be used to argue against the legality of the searches. It always makes for a stronger argument when you address the other side's viewpoint. [1]

Next I developed my *issue statement*: [2]

Was the initial search of the defendant's locker, which was prompted by a call to the police from a man claiming to be a student's father and a "rumor" heard a year prior to the search, legal, and should the evidence uncovered during the search be suppressed, under the exclusionary rule, in prosecuting the defendant?

I then decided on the following organization: [3]

A. Narrative of facts—issue statement
B. General rules from case law regarding searches of students
C. The *T.L.O.* test
D. Further discussion of *T.L.O.* test using *People v. Pruitt*
E. Potential conflict between competing case law: *In Re Adam* and *Commonwealth of Pennsylvania v. Cass.* (how much Fourth Amendment protection do students have?)
F. Second search (pockets) was legal because first search (locker) was legal
G. Conclusion

I then began to develop my topic sentences and made note of which cases I wanted to discuss in each section of my essay: [4]

Schools are generally considered to have broad powers to conduct searches   5
of students because of their duty to protect the students on the school premises.
(*People v. Scott D.,* 483 (1974)).

- *Commonwealth of Pennsylvania v. Cass*
- *Widener v. Frye*
- *New Jersey v. T.L.O.*

In determining whether the searches were legal, it is necessary to ignore what   6
the search actually found and instead to investigate what prompted the search.

- *New Jersey v. T.L.O.*

Further support of the conclusion that the search was not intrusive in light of   7
the nature of the infraction is provided by the ruling in *People v. Pruitt,* 662 N.E.2d
540 (1996), in which the court specified that when determining the legality of a
search the "search of student by teacher or other school official will be justified at
its inception when there are reasonable grounds for suspecting that search will turn
up evidence that student has violated or is violating law or rules of the school."

The defendant could argue that the fact that the drugs were found in his coat   8
pocket rather than in plain view in his locker renders the evidence impermissible
under the exclusionary rule.

- *In Re Adam*
- *Commonwealth of Pennsylvania v. Cass*
- *Brousseau v. Town of Westerly*

However, because the search of the defendant's locker was legal in its   9
inception and scope, the related search of the defendant's pockets was legal
as well.

- *People v. Dilworth*
- *Dumas v. Pennsylvania*

In conclusion, both the search of the defendant's locker and the search of the   10
defendant's pockets were legal as the measures adopted were reasonably
related to the objects of search and were not intrusive in light of the nature of
the infraction (*New Jersey v. T.L.O.*). Because the searches were legal, the evidence uncovered should not be suppressed, under the exclusionary rule, in prosecuting the defendant.

In the final draft, in addition to clarifying my meaning and polishing the sen-   11
tences, I added a discussion of how the defendant's status as a student affected
the legality of the search. To be justified in searching students, school officials
need only a "reasonable suspicion" that their search will produce evidence of

illegal activity. Searches of people who are not students must be based on the higher standard of "probable cause." This new discussion is included in paragraph 7 of my final draft—between "D" and "E" of the outline.

Final Draft

Search the Locker

Facts and Issue

On January 29, 1980, a Somerville police detective received a call from a person who claimed to be the father of a student at Somerville High School. (*State v. Engerud*, 3 A.2d 934 N.J. (1983)) The caller claimed that Jeffrey Engerud, an eighteen-year-old student at the school, was selling drugs at the school and declared that if the police did not do something about it, he would. The detective informed the vice principal of the call, who told the assistant principal and the principal. A year earlier, the principal had heard a "rumor" that Engerud was selling drugs at the school. The two school officials went to Engerud's locker, opened it with a pass-key and searched the locker and its contents, including Engerud's coat. In Engerud's coat pocket, they found methamphetamine, a controlled substance. **12**

The vice principal then called the police and Engerud's parents and summoned Engerud from class. The student was asked to empty his pockets. This search produced more incriminating evidence: marijuana and $45 in cash. The student "was charged with unlawful possession of a controlled dangerous substance and unlawful possession of a controlled dangerous substance with intent to distribute." A motion to suppress the evidence from the searches of the locker and the pocket was denied. The defendant pleaded guilty to the second count of the indictment and was sentenced to a prison term of up to five years. He appealed. The issues in this appeal are (1) whether the initial search of the defendant's locker, prompted by a call to the police from a man claiming to be a student's father and a "rumor" heard a year prior to the search, was legal, and (2) whether the evidence found during the search should be suppressed, under the exclusionary rule. **13**

The Law on Search and Seizure

Schools are generally considered to have broad powers to conduct searches of students because of their duty to protect the students on their premises (*People v. Scott D.*, 34 N.Y. 483 (1974)). Consequently, students have limited protections against search and seizure as compared with the general adult population under the Fourth Amendment (*Brousseau v. Town of Westerly*, 11 F. Supp. 2d 177 (1998)). As stated in *Commonwealth of Pennsylvania v. Cass* (709 A.2d 350 (1998)), however, "Students possess legitimate, yet limited, expectation of privacy within the school environment." The courts have limited students' expectations of privacy by requiring that searches be based on "reasonable suspicion" rather than on the higher standard of "probable cause" (*Widener v. Frye*, 809 F. **14**

Supp. 35 (1992)). In *New Jersey v. T.L.O.* (105 S. Ct. 733 (1985)), the court developed a test to determine the reasonableness of searches such that an inquiry be done into "whether the action was justified at its inception and whether search as actually conducted was reasonably related in scope to circumstances which justified interference in the first place."

The T.L.O. Test

In determining whether the searches in this case were legal, we must ignore what the search actually produced and instead investigate what prompted the search. Two causes prompted school officials to search the defendant's locker. The first was a call to the police from someone who claimed to be the parent of a student who stated that the defendant was selling drugs. The second was a "rumor" that had circulated a year before the search that the defendant was selling drugs at the school.   15

In *New Jersey v. T.L.O.*, the court ruled that "search of student by teacher or other school official would be permissible in its scope when measures adopted are reasonably related to objectives of search and not excessively intrusive in light of sex of student and nature of infraction." The nature of the infraction called for action by the school officials to investigate whether the allegation made by the parent was true and to subsequently remove any illegal substances from the school grounds. Schools are expected to protect students under their care as well as to provide for a learning environment free of distraction and potential harm. The possibility that the defendant was dealing drugs posed a potential risk to the students. The school was therefore obligated to conduct a thorough search of the defendant's locker to determine whether it indeed contained drugs. Therefore, the measures adopted were reasonably related to the objectives of the search. Furthermore, given the risk posed to the students, the search was not excessively intrusive. (Engerud was not strip-searched.) Because it passed the *T.L.O.* test, the search conducted by the school officials at Somerville High School was reasonable and legal.   16

Further support of the conclusion that the search was not intrusive in light of the nature of the infraction is provided by the ruling in *People v. Pruitt* (662 N.E.2d 540 (1996)), in which the court specified that when determining the legality of a search the "search of student by teacher or other school official will be justified at its inception when there are reasonable grounds for suspecting that search will turn up evidence that student has violated or is violating law or rules of the school." A reasonable person would conclude that a parent would call a detective to report that another student at the school was dealing drugs only if he or she had sufficient cause to do so. Even if the parent were reporting false information, the potential danger to the other students required the school to investigate the situation. Moreover, the fact that the parent called the police first and threatened to take care of the problem himself shows the caller's perception of the urgency of the situation. Had the call been the only evidence offered that the defendant was dealing drugs, perhaps the search would have been questionable because it was not the defendant's parent who contacted the police. In   17 addition to the call, the principal had also heard a "rumor" that the defendant was dealing drugs. Although it is doubtful that either the call or the rumor alone would have been sufficient to justify a search of the locker or the student, the combination of the call and the rumor provided the school officials with reasonable grounds to suspect that the search would turn up evidence that the defendant was violating the law.

Limitations on Student Expectations of Privacy

Because the defendant was eighteen years of age at the time of the search, it could be argued that he should have been accorded the full Fourth Amendment protections against search and seizure, which require "probable cause" as the basis for search. The purpose of the Fourth Amendment is to protect citizens from the power of the state to prosecute and to take away freedom. The government is limited, however, in its powers to prosecute minors. Minors are not subject to the same criminal justice system as adults and conversely are not accorded the same freedoms and rights as adults. The defendant in this case was legally an adult. However, because he was also a student, the lower standard of "reasonable suspicion," rather than the higher standard of "probable cause," was the basis for the search. Had the defendant been subject to the higher standard, the search of his locker would not have been warranted based on an uncorroborated phone call and a potentially unreliable rumor. [18]

The argument that the defendant should have been subject to "probable cause" needs to be considered in view of the fact that the school officials conducted the search not as agents of the police but as school officials. The court in *In Re D.E.M.* (727 A.2d 570 (1999)), ruled that, in deciding whether school officials acted as agents of the state such that they should be subject to the same Fourth Amendment standards, it is necessary to consider (1) "the purpose of the search," (2) "the party who initiated the search," and (3) "whether the police acquiesced in the search or ratified it." The purpose of the search was to protect the school environment, not to make a criminal conviction. This purpose changes the "probable cause" basis for search (*People v. Scott D.*). The party that actually initiated the search was the school officials acting on a tip from the police, not the police themselves. Finally, the police did not acquiesce to the search or ratify it. The police detective met with the vice principal for five minutes and then left the school, allowing school officials to handle the matter independently of the police. These facts show that the school officials were not acting as agents of the police and thus subject to Fourth Amendment standards; therefore the search was legal as conducted, under the "reasonableness" standard. [19]

Was the Search of the Defendant's Pockets Legal?

The defendant might argue that because the drugs were found concealed in his coat pocket rather than in plain view in his locker, the evidence should be inadmissible, under the exclusionary rule. The court in *In Re Adam* (697 N.E.2d 1100 [20]

(1997)) found that "student does not lose his Fourth Amendment expectation of privacy in coat or bookbag merely because he places those objects in his locker." However, in *Commonwealth of Pennsylvania v. Cass*, the court ruled that the student's expectation of privacy is "minimal within the meaning of constitutional search and seizure provision; lockers are school property and although students can provide their own locks, combination to locks must be provided to the school."

At first glance, these rules may seem contradictory. Together, however, they 21 imply that, whereas individual students are protected against arbitrary searches of their lockers and their contents, the school has broad powers to protect the larger student population from harm. This responsibility affords schools broader search powers in regard to students who, in some instances, "have lesser expectation of privacy than members of population generally" (*Brousseau v. Town of Westerly*, 11 F. Supp. 2d 177 (1998)). The use of a pass key that could open any locker in the building, even though the lockers had combination locks, is legal under *Commonwealth of Pennsylvania v. Cass*.

It follows that because the search of the defendant's locker was legal in its 22 inception and scope, the related search of the defendant's pockets was legal as well. The law requires under the *T.L.O.* test that a search be justified in its inception. The two plastic bags containing packets of a white substance that turned out to be methamphetamine in the legal search of the locker provided the officials at Somerville High School with the reasonable suspicion of violation of the law by the defendant to justify the search of the defendant's pockets. Further, the search was legal under the "two-fold" inquiry required by the *T.L.O.* test that the search be reasonably related in scope to the circumstances that justified interference in the first place. We have already determined that the locker search was legal. Because that legal search turned up evidence that the defendant was dealing drugs at the school, a search of the defendant's pockets was reasonably related in scope to the first search.

Moreover, at this point the defendant's parents had been notified of the situation. As explained in *People v. Dilworth* (661 N.E. 2d 310 (1996)), the doctrine of *in loco parentis* allows parents to delegate part of their parental authority to the teacher of their children who then "has such portion of power of parent committed to his charge for purposes of restraint and correction as may be necessary to answer purposes for which he is employed." Therefore, the vice principal and the principal were entitled to call the defendant out of class and request that he empty his pockets in order for them to find any remaining drugs and evidence of wrongdoing in order to meet the school's need to maintain order and discipline, which trumps students' expectation of privacy (*Dumas v. Pennsylvania*, 575 A.2d 986 (1986)).

Conclusion

Both the search of the defendant's locker and the search of the defendant's 24 pockets were legal because they were "reasonably related to the objectives of search" and were not "excessively intrusive" in light of the nature of the infraction (*New Jersey v. T.L.O.*). Because the searches were legal, the evidence uncovered should not be suppressed, under the exclusionary rule, in prosecuting the defendant.

—Alyssa Mellott

"You Lied to Me."

469 U.S. 325, 83 L.Ed.2d 720
NEW JERSEY
v.
T.L.O.

No. 83–712.

Argued March 28, 1984.
Reargued Oct. 2, 1984.
Decided Jan. 15, 1985.

On March 7, 1980, a teacher at Piscataway High School reported that fourteen year old T.L.O. and another student were smoking in the girls' restroom. School regulations forbade smoking in that area and the teacher took the students to the assistant principal's office. He asked the students whether they had been smoking. T.L.O.'s companion admitted smoking and the assistant principal assigned her to a three-day smoking clinic. [1]

T.L.O. denied smoking in the lavatory or indeed smoking at all. The assistant principal asked T.L.O. to go with him into a private office. He closed the door and asked her to turn over her purse. At this time they were both seated at a desk, he behind and she in front. When he opened the purse on the desk, he saw a pack of Marlboros. He picked up the cigarettes and said "You lied to me." As he reached into the purse for the cigarettes, he saw rolling papers in plain view. That fact, his experience told him, meant that marijuana was probably involved. He therefore looked further into the purse and found a metal pipe of the kind used for smoking marijuana, empty plastic bags and one plastic bag containing a tobacco-like substance. His search also revealed an index card reading "People who owe me money," followed by a list of names and amounts of $1.50 and $1.00, and two letters, one from T.L.O. to another student and a return letter, both containing language clearly indicating drug dealing by T.L.O. The purse also contained $40, most of it in one-dollar bills. [2]

The assistant principal called T.L.O.'s mother and the police. A police officer asked the mother to bring T.L.O. to police headquarters for questioning. There, T.L.O. admitted selling marijuana to other students. She was charged with delinquency based on possession of marijuana with the intent to distribute. [3]

New Jersey v. T.L.O., 463 A.2d 934 (1985), 105 S. Ct. 733 (1985).
Footnote 1 and N.J.S.A. references omitted from original.

T.L.O. moved to suppress the evidence seized from her purse and her confession, claiming that the search tainted the confession. She also argued that she had not knowingly waived her right to remain silent. 4

"Truancy. That's What I Was Trying to Establish."

■ ■

Jose Eduardo CORONADO, Appellant,

v.

The STATE of Texas, Appellee.

No. 529–91.

Court of Criminal Appeals of Texas,
En Banc.
June 24, 1992.

The relevant facts developed at the hearing on appellant's motion to suppress evidence are as follows. On April 27, 1989, Kim Benning, an assistant principal, received information that appellant attempted to sell drugs to another student. Benning questioned and patted down appellant, then had appellant turn his pant pockets inside-out, remove his shoes, and pull down his pants. The search, which Benning testified was "standard," produced no contraband or weapon. However, Benning did find $300.00 in cash in appellant's billfold. At the search, Benning asked appellant, "Do you sell drugs?" and appellant replied, "Not on campus." 1

On May 5, 1989, the school secretary informed Benning that appellant was leaving school at 9:30 to attend his grandfather's funeral. Benning informed both Ernest Randall, a sheriff's officer assigned to the school, and the regular school security guard that appellant "was attempting to leave the campus and that [Benning] suspected his motives for leaving campus." Benning saw appellant at an outside pay phone and asked appellant "to come inside." Benning asked appellant where appellant's vehicle was parked and appellant responded that he did not drive. Benning contacted appellant's relatives who stated that appellant's grandfather had not died. In response to another question, appellant's relatives told Benning that appellant drove a Buick to school that morning. Appellant, however, identified his vehicle as a red Camaro, which was not parked on campus. Benning had a teacher question a student who rode to school with appellant and determined that appellant's vehicle was in the student parking lot. Benning then sent the school security officer to locate the vehicle. 2

Coronado v. State, 835 S.W.2d 636 (1992).
Original footnotes 2–4 now 1–3.

Benning called Randall to Benning's office after verifying that appellant's   3
reasons for leaving school were false. Although Randall testified he acted as an
"advisor," the record reflects Randall was employed with the Galveston County
Sheriff's Department Organized Crime Division on special assignment to the
Clear Creek High School. Randall had an office on the school premises and his
duties were to investigate alcohol and drug activities and "anything else that violates the penal code." Randall testified he did not have probable cause to search
appellant nor did he observe appellant commit any illegal acts.

Benning testified that he detained appellant to ascertain a "reasonable suspi-   4
cion" for appellant's actions. While in Benning's office, Randall testified that appellant was evasive in his answers and told several different versions of how
appellant travelled to and from school. Benning claimed he had cause to search
appellant due to the April 27 tip that appellant had attempted to sell drugs.
However, Benning conceded that he did not observe appellant commit any illegal
act and was only trying to determine whether appellant was "skipping school."
Benning stated that truancy applied only to students under seventeen years of age.
Appellant was nineteen at the time of the search. If appellant had "skipped school,"
Benning could have assigned appellant to detention or an "alternate learning
center."

At the hearing on appellant's motion to suppress evidence, the following   5
exchange occurred between Benning and appellant's trial counsel:

Q. [Did you observe anything] illegal according to the laws of the State of Texas
   or the laws of the United States?
A. Possible truancy. *That's what I was trying to establish.*[1]
Q. So aside from possible truancy, had he committed any illegal law violations
   regarding any laws of the State of Texas or laws of the United States? Yes, or
   no?
A. No.
Q. And you proceeded to search him even though you had not seen him commit
   any illegalities in your presence?
A. Do you want me to comment on that?
Q. I want you to answer it, yes, or no?
A. He would not tell me where his car was parked.
Q. Again, during this time, he had not committed any illegal acts or had violated
   any law of the State of Texas or violated any law of the United States?
A. To that point, I could not establish any illegal acts.

Benning "patted down" appellant, out of a concern for safety, but found only   6
keys and a wallet with $197.00 in currency. Benning, with Randall observing, then
asked appellant to remove his shoes and socks. After finding no contraband,
Benning then had appellant pull down his pants.[2] Randall acknowledged that

---

[1] Unless otherwise indicated, all emphasis herein is supplied by the author [judicial officer].
[2] Benning testified that appellant only "loosened" his pants to "see if anything would fall out."

Benning was irate and shaking in anger during the searches and testified that the proceedings in Benning's office lasted approximately forty-five minutes. After finding no contraband on appellant, Benning and Randall searched appellant's locker, but found no contraband. Benning, Randall and appellant returned to Benning's office. While in the office, appellant was not permitted to leave except to go to the restroom.

Later, Benning, Randall, and the school security guard accompanied appellant   7
to his vehicle where Benning demanded appellant open the vehicle. The Court of Appeals stated: "Coronado then volunteered to take the two men to the car and told Benning that it would be all right for him to search the car." However, that statement is not supported by the record. Benning testified as follows:

Q. When you went to [appellant's] car with all three of you with him, Mr. Randall demanded that [appellant] open the car door?
A. [I] demanded that [appellant] open the car. I was conducting the search.
Q. And Mr. Randall had the keys to the car?
A. I don't recall.
Q. Did you have the keys?
A. I don't recall. It was demanded that he open the car upon my request.
Q. Upon your request with two other men next to him, one being an officer, police officer, and the other being a security guard and he acquiesced to your request?
A. Yes.

When appellant opened the trunk, Benning saw appellant attempt to hide a   8
paper bag. Subsequently, Randall discovered bags of white powder, a triple beam balance, and what appeared to be marijuana. After searching the vehicle, including the trunk and engine compartment, Randall arrested appellant.

After the arrest, Randall handcuffed appellant to a chair in Randall's office for   9
two to three hours. Appellant eventually gave a statement revealing prior and pending drug deals. Appellant claims he gave the statement because he thought he would get the vehicle back.

Appellant testified that Benning and Randall forced him to go to the principal's   10
office for the initial search. Appellant balked at pulling down his pants, but Randall told appellant to do what the principal said. According to appellant, Randall held appellant's wallet and keys until the group arrived at appellant's vehicle.[3] Randall gave appellant the keys and appellant was forced to open the vehicle. According to appellant, Randall and the security guard searched the vehicle along with Benning. Appellant never attempted to escape. Neither Benning nor Randall ever told appellant of the right to refuse a search of the locker or vehicle.

---

[3]Benning testified that he returned appellant's keys "at some point" after the search in the office so that appellant could open the vehicle.

Athletes and Drug Testing

Wayne and Judy ACTON, guardians ad litem for James Acton, Plaintiffs,

v.

VERNONIA SCHOOL DISTRICT 47J, Defendant.

Civ. No. 91–1154–MA.

United States District Court,
D. Oregon.
May 7, 1992.

I. Background

Vernonia, Oregon, is a small logging community of approximately 3000 persons   1
including all those living within or near the city limits. Plaintiffs Wayne and Judy
Acton reside in Vernonia and their son James, age 12, is enrolled in the seventh
grade of Washington Grade School. Due to its small size and somewhat remote
location, Vernonia is typified by its central interest in school district activities in
general and athletics in particular. Witnesses explained that the entertainment
opportunities in Vernonia are fairly limited so that interscholastic athletics play a
dominant role in the community and student athletes are well known and
admired. Approximately 60–65% of the high school students and 75% of the elementary school students participate in district sponsored athletics.

The school district employs a small but stable and closely knit teaching staff   2
with deep ties to the community. For instance, two of the teachers who testified at
trial grew up and attended school in Vernonia. Randall Aultman, the current principal of Washington Grade School, has a long tenure with the district and has held
the positions of Assistant Superintendent and principal of the high school. Other
teachers who testified had years of experience in the district, and I was impressed
by their knowledge and concern for the community, its students and school system.

Aultman and the teachers testified that, up until the early 1980s, discipline at   3
the Vernonia schools was not a problem. The teachers were well acquainted with
the students and their families and students were generally cooperative and
respectful both in the classrooms and during after-school activities. Drug and
alcohol use, although present, was limited to certain small "fringe" elements of
the student population. Then, in the mid-to-late 1980s, the staff began noticing a
startling and progressive increase in students' use of drugs and alcohol. As the
administration became more aware of the problem, it began investigating its possible source. Aultman met with the teaching staff and asked them to look for any
signs of drug or alcohol use to gauge the magnitude of the problem and to try to
determine what responsive steps should be taken.

Acton v. Vernonia School District, 796 F. Supp. 1354 (1992).

In the meantime the glamorization and use of drugs and alcohol became more blatant. All of the teachers who testified at trial expressed how appalled and helpless they felt as students increasingly expressed their attraction to, and vocal defense of, the use of drugs. Students boasted about drug use and regaled one another with stories of the latest "high" or "party." Class decorum suffered. One teacher, who had never experienced classroom discipline problems in the past, was ready to give up 15 years of service because of her frustration and apparent inability to deal with this new situation. Outbursts of profane language during class, rude and obscene statements directed at other students, and a general flagrant attitude that there was nothing the school could do about their conduct or their use of drugs or alcohol typified a usual day. Organizations formed within the student drug culture taking such names as the "Big Elks" or the "Drug Cartel." Loud "bugling" or "head butting" were the calling cards of these groups. Drug paraphernalia was confiscated on schools grounds, and open use of drugs was observed at a local cafe across the street from the high school.

Drug and alcohol use also invaded the sports program. Students consumed alcohol on a bus after a game. Others stole alcohol from a store after a track meet. Ron Svenson, a teacher and wrestling coach, testified that suspected drug use contributed to the injury of a wrestler who failed to execute a basic maneuver. When visiting the hotel room of the student the next day the smell of marijuana permeated the area. Svenson also gave convincing testimony that drug use affected certain football players in that they ignored or forgot well-drilled safety routines. He also expressed a concern that the use of intoxicants would slow down their reaction time and hence, make them more susceptible to injury. Svenson's concerns were corroborated by the testimony of Dr. DuPont, who explained the deleterious effects of drugs and alcohol on a person's motivation, memory, judgment, reaction, coordination and performance.

Svenson also explained that a student injured in a regular physical education class is much more apt to disclose an injury than one engaged in interscholastic activity, given the highly competitive atmosphere of the latter. This sense of pride and desire to stay in the game, when coupled with the numbing influence of drugs, became a significant concern to all involved in the athletic program.

School officials had a clear perception that the discipline problems they were experiencing were the result of substance abuse. Informal interviews with responsible students and parents confirmed that fact. Based upon the administration's investigation, it also became clear that the leaders of this activity were also the leading student athletes. Thus, the very center of activity of the school and the community was endangered. Further, the administration was concerned that the corruption of the school's leading athletes might have a significant poisoning impact upon the broader student population, including the younger and more impressionable elementary school students who would eventually seek to emulate their elders. No evidence was presented that refuted any of the facts set forth nor the conclusions reached by the school officials.

Following its initial investigation, the school administration attempted to address this problem and deter drug and alcohol use through education. Special classes were held on the effect and addictive nature of drugs. Special speakers were invited who the school hoped would have a particular charm with the students. Seminars within classes, polls, and theatrical presentations were all tested and failed to achieve any significant impact on the disruptive atmosphere. The day after the presentation of a play directed at the evils of drug use, several sophomore athletes were caught cutting classes to hold a party where arrests took place for the use of intoxicants. The administration even brought in a specially trained dog to sniff for drugs in locker area, but none of these efforts deterred the students. As Dr. DuPont confirmed, youth who use drugs are typically in denial and think they can control their drug use. Thus, simply telling them that drug use is bad for their health and that they should stop using is invariably ineffective. DuPont testified that what youth really need is a compelling reason or incentive to stop using drugs.

The evidence amply demonstrated that the administration was at its wits end   9
and that a large segment of the student body, particularly those involved in interscholastic athletics, was in a state of rebellion. Disciplinary actions had reached "epidemic proportions." The coincidence of an almost three-fold increase in classroom disruptions and disciplinary reports along with the staff's direct observations of students using drugs or glamorizing drug and alcohol use led the administration to the inescapable conclusion that the rebellion was being fueled by alcohol and drug abuse as well as the student's misperceptions about the drug culture. It also became readily apparent to staff that, unless it took immediate action, the problem was going to get far worse and widespread before it got better. At one point, the administration felt that the only practical solution was mass expulsion. Fortunately for the city of Vernonia, school officials remained vigilant in their efforts and continued to pursue less drastic alternatives.

Spurred on by an article in the local *Oregonian*, the idea of a drug testing   10
program was considered. While the idea had been discussed before, concerns over its legality had deferred its consideration in favor of exhausting other alternatives. But sometime in 1988, borne out of necessity, the idea was investigated. A study was made of such programs across the country. Legal opinions were studied, legal counsel obtained, and parent meetings were held. Finally, with the blessing of the administration, a unanimous vote of parents at the meeting, and approval of the superintendent a plan was submitted to the School Board and approved for implementation beginning in the fall of 1989.

II. Defendant's Drug Testing Policy

All students who desire to participate in interscholastic athletics are required to   11
sign a form authorizing the District to conduct a test on a urine specimen provided by the student as a prerequisite to participation in the athletic program. The test requirement is applied to all students and is limited to determining whether the student has been using illegal drugs and/or alcohol.

All students in the athletic program are tested at the beginning of each athletic   12
season in which they participate. During the season, student athletes are tested at

random on a weekly basis. The names of all students participating in sports during that season are placed in a "pool" and approximately ten percent of the names are drawn from the "pool" each week. A student draws numbers representing names from the "pool," but is not aware of the names he or she draws. Students whose numbers are drawn are tested one at a time throughout that day.

The procedure for the test varies slightly for boys and girls. Boys begin the 13 process by filling out a portion of a specimen control form which assigns the student a number. The student is then given a testing packet which contains a cup and a vial. The student enters an empty locker room with a male school official acting as a monitor. The monitor opens the packet and provides the student with the cup. The student then proceeds to a urinal to produce the sample. While producing the sample, the student remains fully clothed and has his back to the monitor. The monitor is present to assure that there is no tampering and remains 12 to 15 feet behind the student.

After producing the sample, the student returns the cup to the monitor. The 14 monitor checks the sample for temperature and signs of tampering. The monitor then transfers the sample into a vial, and the student places a lid on the vial. The vial is sealed with security tape which the student signs and dates. The vial is assigned a number which coincides with the student's number on the specimen control form and then is placed in a plastic bag which is also sealed and signed and dated by the student. Finally, the student completes the specimen control form by verifying that the specimen is his and that the specimen and package were securely sealed in his presence.

The procedure for girls differs only in that a female school official acts as a 15 monitor and the sample is produced in an enclosed stall with a toilet. The monitor remains outside the stall and listens for signs of tampering.

The samples are sent for testing to Metrolab under security procedures 16 designed to protect the chain of possession. Metrolab technicians do not know the identity of the person being tested and rely solely upon the assigned numbers for identification. The test screens for amphetamines, cocaine, marijuana, and alcohol and has an accuracy of approximately 99.94%. Test results are reported by telephone to authorized Vernonia School District personnel. Positive results are also mailed to the district superintendent.

If a student's test is positive, a second test will be administered as soon as pos- 17 sible to confirm the results. Parents will be notified after the second positive test. If the second test is negative, no further action will be taken. If the second test is positive, the school notifies the parents or guardians and conducts a hearing with the student and his or her parents. At this hearing, the student will be given the option of either participating in an assistance program and taking a weekly drug test for six weeks or suspension from the athletic program for the remainder of the current season and the next athletic season. The student will be retested before beginning the next season for which he or she is eligible.

At trial, Aultman testified that, though not spelled out in the written policy, a 18 student athlete who commits a second offense may also continue participating in the athletic program if he or she submits to counseling and weekly urinalysis.

III. Basis of the Plaintiffs' Claim

In the Fall of 1991, James Acton, a seventh grade student attending Washington   19
Grade School in the Vernonia School District, signed up to participate in district-
sponsored football. To participate in football, James had to take a physical examination.[1] James attended the first football practice and received the District's consent
form for drug and alcohol testing. After discussing the form with his parents, they
decided not to sign it. James and his parents scheduled a meeting with Aultman.

At the meeting, the Actons explained to Aultman that they objected to the   20
drug testing policy because it required James to submit to a urinalysis in the
absence of any evidence that he had used drugs or alcohol. Aultman informed the
Actons that James could not participate in district-sponsored athletics without a
signed consent form. The Actons notified the district superintendent, Ellis Mason,
of their decision. Mason confirmed that James could not participate in district-
sponsored sports without a signed consent form. There is no dispute that the
policy was applied to James in the same manner as it was applied to all other students who sought to participate in interscholastic athletics and was not based
upon any individualized suspicion that James had used drugs or alcohol.

■ Illegal Strip Search? ■

**Angela Lee WILLIAMS, a minor, by her
father and next friend, William Hardy
WILLIAMS, Plaintiff–Appellant,**

v.

**Jerald M. ELLINGTON, et al.,
Defendants–Appellees.**

No. 90-5993.

United States Court of Appeals,
Sixth Circuit.

Argued March 21, 1991.
Decided June 24, 1991.

I.

The record before us reveals that on Tuesday, January 19, 1988, Graves County   1
High School Principal Jerald Ellington received a telephone call from a student's
mother who expressed concern over a situation in which her daughter, Ginger,
was confronted with drugs. Although no names were disclosed, the mother
reported that a student had offered drugs to her daughter. Later that day,

---

[1]The physical examination included giving a urine sample.
Williams v. Ellington, 936 F.2d 881 (1991).

Ellington called Ginger into his office to learn more about the incident. Ginger reported that during typing class on the day before, she had seen [Angela] Williams and another girl, Michelle, with a clear glass vial containing a white powder. Ginger also stated that the two girls placed the powder on the tips of their fingers and sniffed it. One of the girls then offered the powder to Ginger, but she refused it. Ellington asked Ginger if she had any problems with the girls, and was satisfied there was no animosity between them to provide Ginger with an ulterior motive for reporting the incident.

Ellington then spoke with Williams' typing instructor, Brenda Cobb, in whose   2
class the alleged drug use occurred. When asked if she had noticed anything peculiar during class on the day of the purported drug use, Cobb indicated that Michelle's behavior was strange. Cobb approached Michelle, who told the teacher she had the "flu." Ellington then relayed Ginger's report to Cobb, prompting her to remember an incident involving Williams the previous semester. During the first semester, Cobb found a typed note under Williams' desk in which she had referred to parties involving her friends and the use of the "rich man's drug." When Cobb questioned Williams about the letter, the student passed it off as a joke, and a few months later when Cobb seemed satisfied that there was not a problem, she threw the letter in the trash.

During the next few days, Ellington also spoke with Mary Jean Young,   3
Williams' aunt and school guidance counselor, and Michelle's father, so that both families would be apprised of the situation. Michelle's father expressed concern that Michelle might be using drugs and disclosed that Michelle had recently stolen $200.00 from his bureau drawer.

Also during this same week, Michelle came to Ellington and reported that   4
another student, Kim, and Kim's boyfriend, Steve, were inhaling a substance called "rush." "Rush" is a volatile substance that can be purchased over the counter, and while possession of "rush" is legal, inhalation of it is illegal under Kentucky law.[1] Coincidentally, Kim and Steve also came to Ellington and insisted that it was not them, but other students, who were using the substance. Following these reports, Ellington questioned the motives of these students in coming forward and the validity of the information.

On Friday of this same week, January 22, Ginger stopped in to see Ellington   5
during her fifth period geometry class to report "those girls are at it again," or words to that effect, and indicated she had observed the two girls with the white powdery substance again. Ellington sent Ginger back to class and

---

[1]Section 217.900 reads, in pertinent part:

(1) As used in this section:

"Volatile substance" means any glue, cement, or paint or other substance containing a solvent or chemical having the property of releasing toxic vapors or fumes which when inhaled may cause a condition of intoxication, inebriation, stupefaction, dulling of the brain or nervous system, or distortion or disturbance of the auditory, visual or mental processes.

(2) It shall be unlawful for any person to intentionally smell or inhale the fumes of any volatile substance, or to induce any other person to do so for the purpose of inducing a condition described in subsection (1) of this section. . . . Ky.Rev.Stat. 217.900.

decided to act on the information before the end of fifth period. Ellington contacted Assistant Principal Maxine Easley and apprised her of the week's events. Ellington and Easley then went to the geometry class and called Williams and Michelle out into the hall. Although Ellington observed that neither student appeared disoriented or intoxicated, the two girls were taken to the administrative offices. After escorting the girls into his office and confronting them with his suspicions, Michelle produced a small brown vial from her purse that contained "rush." Michelle claimed the vial belonged to Kim, and although both girls denied possession of any drugs, Ellington wanted to search the girls' lockers because the brown vial did not match the description given by Ginger.

At that time, Assistant Principal Donald Jones, who was also aware of the week's events, went to search Williams' assigned locker. No drugs were found in this locker, nor in the locker Williams had been using to store her personal items. Likewise a search of Williams' books and purse conducted by Assistant Principal Easley produced no evidence of drugs. Finally, Ellington asked Easley to take Williams into her office and search her person, in the presence of a female secretary.[2] Inside Easley's office, Williams was asked to empty her pockets which she promptly did. Easley's then asked the girl to remove her T-shirt. Although she hesitated and appeared nervous, Williams complied after Easley repeated the request. Williams was then required to lower her blue jeans to her knees. In her deposition, Williams testified that Easley pulled on the elastic of her undergarments to see if anything would fall out, but Easley disputes this contention. The district court concluded this factual discrepancy was not material for summary judgment purposes, and as troubling as that conclusion may be, the veritable inconsistency need not be addressed in light of the rationale set forth below. Finally, Williams was told to remove her shoes and socks. Easley found no evidence of drugs as a result of this search.

William Hardy Williams, Appellant's father, lodged a complaint regarding the incident with the Graves County School Board of Education. The Board, in ratifying the conduct in question, believed there existed reasonable suspicion under the search and seizure policy to justify the actions of Defendants Ellington, Jones and Easley. Angela Williams, by her father and next friend William Hardy Williams, then instituted the present suit, pursuant to 42 U.S.C. § 1983, seeking damages and injunctive and declaratory relief.

---

[2]The "search and seizure policy," in effect at the time petitioner was searched, was instituted by the Board in 1985 and states the following:

1. A pupil's person will not be searched unless there is a reasonable suspicion that the pupil is concealing evidence of an illegal act. . . .When a pupil's person is searched, the person conducting the search shall be the same sex as the pupil; and a witness of the same sex shall be present during the search.

Graves County High School Student Handbook, 1987–88, p. 34.

Cocaine in the Flashlight

169 Ill.2d 195
214 Ill.Dec. 456
The PEOPLE of the State of Illinois, Appellant,

v.

Kenneth DILWORTH, Appellee.

No. 78274.

Supreme Court of Illinois.
Jan. 18, 1996.

Certiorari Denied May 13, 1996.
See 116 S.Ct. 1692.

Defendant was a 15-year-old student at the Joliet Township High Schools Alternate School. The Alternate School is unlike a regular public school in that only students with behavioral disorders attend it. A little more than 100 students attended the school at the relevant times. [1]

According to the Alternate School handbook, which was admitted into evidence, the goal of the school's program is to create an environment that will allow students to modify their behavior in a positive direction. Students who improve their behavior are allowed to return to regular school. The school staff was listed as consisting of 11 teachers, four paraprofessionals, one social worker, one psychologist, one counselor, and, significantly, one liaison officer. [2]

The liaison officer was Detective Francis Ruettiger. Ruettiger was a police officer employed by the Joliet police department and was assigned full-time to the Alternate School as a member of its staff. His primary purpose at the school was to prevent criminal activity. If he discovered criminal activity, he had the authority to arrest the offender and transport the offender to the police station. Ruettiger also handled some disciplinary problems. Like the teachers, Ruettiger was authorized to give a detention, but not a suspension. Only the school principal and the director could suspend a student. [3]

On November 18, 1992, two teachers asked Ruettiger to search a student, Deshawn Weeks, for possession of drugs. The teachers informed Ruettiger that they had overheard Weeks telling other students that he had sold some drugs and would bring more drugs with him to school the following day. The next day, Ruettiger searched Weeks' person in his office and found nothing. He then escorted Weeks back to his locker. [4]

Defendant and Weeks met at their neighboring lockers. According to Ruettiger, the two adolescents began talking and giggling "like they put one over on [him]." Ruettiger further testified that they turned toward him and they were "looking, laughing at [him] like [he] was played for a fool." Ruettiger noticed a [5]

---

flashlight in defendant's hand and immediately thought that it might contain drugs. He grabbed the flashlight from defendant, unscrewed the top, and observed a bag containing a white chunky substance underneath the flashlight batteries. The substance later tested positive for the presence of cocaine. Defendant ran from the scene, but was captured by Ruettiger and transported to the police station. While there, defendant gave a statement admitting that he intended to sell the cocaine because he was tired of being poor.

Ruettiger explained that he had two reasons for seizing and searching the flashlight. He was suspicious that the flashlight contained drugs. Secondly, Ruettiger believed it was a violation of school rules to possess a flashlight on school grounds because a flashlight is a "blunt instrument." The school's disciplinary guidelines, of which all students must be informed when they enroll, prohibited the possession of "any object that can be construed to be a weapon." Ruettiger had never seen a student with a flashlight at the school before. He admitted, however, that students were never specifically informed that flashlights were prohibited. Also, he did not consider a flashlight to be "contraband *per se.*"

Ruettiger further related that he had daily contact with each student at the Alternate School. Although he did not talk with each student individually every day, he did go into each classroom. Prior to arresting defendant, Ruettiger saw defendant during school several times a day and had always gotten along with him pretty well. On one occasion, two weeks before the arrest, a teacher had suspected defendant of selling drugs in class and asked Ruettiger to search him. Ruettiger did so and found nothing. At that time, defendant told Ruettiger that he did not have any drugs, but named another student who did. A search of the other student revealed marijuana and resulted in the student's arrest.

Defendant's teacher, Danica Grabavoy, testified that sometime soon after defendant was enrolled in the Alternate School, she reviewed the entire school handbook with him and his guardian. Among other things, the handbook explains the school's policies and disciplinary guidelines. On a page entitled "Alternate School Search Procedures," the handbook states:

> **To protect the security, safety, and rights of other students and the staff at the Alternate School, we will search students.** This search may include the student's person, his/her belongings, and school locker. Search procedures may result from suspicions generated from direct observation or from information received from a third party.
>
> Search is done to protect the safety of students. However, if in the process any illegal items or controlled substances are found in a search, these items and the student will be turned over to the police. (Emphasis in original.)

Prior to trial, defendant moved to suppress the evidence found in his flashlight. He argued that Ruettiger's seizure and search of the flashlight violated the fourth and fourteenth amendments to the United States Constitution.

Of Guns and Metal Detectors

278 Ill.App.3d 194
214 Ill.Dec. 974
The PEOPLE of the State of Illinois,
Plaintiff–Appellant,
v.
Serrick PRUITT, Anthony Brooks,
and Johnnie Cheatham, Defendants–Appellees.

Nos. 1–94-2387, 1–94–2388 and 1–94–2538.

Appellate Court of Illinois,
First District, First Division.

Feb. 26, 1996.

Serrick Pruitt

Pruitt testified he was searched before he reached the two lines of metal detec- 1
tors, one for boys and one for girls, that had been set up inside the Fenger High
School on November 24, 1993. He admitted a loaded .38 caliber handgun was
found in his pants pocket.

The trial judge rejected Pruitt's testimony and accepted the police officer's 2
testimony.

The State called Officer Edward Sonne. He testified that on November 24, 3
1993, he was assigned to assist in a random metal detector search at Fenger. The
school did not use metal detectors every day. When the school decided to conduct
a metal detector search, the Chicago police department, by request of the school,
would assist.

On November 24, 1993, about 40 Chicago police officers were assigned to the 4
Fenger School to assist in the metal detector operation. Seven or eight officers
were stationed in the area of the metal detectors. Officer Sonne, dressed in
uniform, was stationed at the metal detector used to screen the boys.

Pruitt passed through the metal detector at about 7:50 that morning. The 5
machine registered a positive reading, indicating that he was carrying something
metal on his person. Because of the positive reaction of the magnetometer, a protective pat-down search was made. In the pat-down, Officer Sonne felt a large
metal object that felt like a gun. The object, located in Pruitt's pants pocket, was
removed. It proved to be a .38 caliber revolver with a 2-½–3 inch barrel.

After the gun was discovered, Officer Sonne escorted Pruitt to a conference 6
room where paper work regarding Pruitt's arrest was completed. . . .

People v. Pruitt, Cheatham, Books, 662 N.E.2d 540 (1996).

As part of its offer of proof, the State presented the testimony of Linda C. ⁷ Layne, principal at Fenger. She explained that the school's rules and regulations are set forth in a handbook, which all students are given and required to keep with them. In the "Safe School Zone" section on page 10, the handbook notified students that "possession of guns, knives, or other weapons is forbidden and will result in arrest and expulsion from Fenger . . ."

Principal Layne also testified that she wrote a letter to the director of safety ⁸ and security for the Chicago public schools on November 2, 1993, requesting a metal detector search. The request was supported by the school's council. The letter was prompted by a shooting incident which occurred near the school on October 15, 1993, and involved Fenger students on their way to school in a bus. Shots were fired from outside the bus. There was no evidence of the identity of the shooters.

The Bureau of Safety and Security for the school system provided Fenger with ⁹ two metal detectors. They were set up for the operation on November 24, 1993. On that day about 40 police officers, who are normally assigned to various schools as part of the school patrol unit of the Chicago police department, came to Fenger school to assist. The police were under the direction of Principal Layne and the Safety and Security Bureau officer. Approximately 900 students passed through the metal detectors that day. It took five or six seconds for each student to walk through.

Principal Layne saw Pruitt in line. She did not see him pulled out of line before ¹⁰ going through the metal detector. . . .

Johnnie Cheatham

On April 13, 1993, Johnnie Cheatham was a 15-year-old student at Chicago Voca- ¹¹ tional High School. He was arrested that day after he was discovered carrying a loaded .22 caliber automatic pistol.

The arresting officer, Kimberly Taylor, was a Chicago police officer assigned ¹² as a school patrol officer to Chicago Vocational. She and her partner, Officer Grissett, were permanently assigned to the school as liaison officers. Under an agreement between the Board of Education and the Chicago police department two officers are assigned to each Chicago public school to work with the school administration. Their purpose is to maintain security in the school.

Officer Taylor was the only witness to testify at the hearing on defendant's ¹³ motion to suppress the gun.

On April 13, 1993, she received a message from a school security agent, Jesse ¹⁴ Richardson, regarding a student having a weapon. Immediately, Officer Taylor contacted Richardson. He told her that a student informed him that Cheatham had a gun in school that day.

Officer Taylor, accompanied by her partner, Officer Grissett, obtained ¹⁵ Cheatham's class schedule and then went to his classroom. Officer Taylor waited by the door of the classroom. Officer Grissett spoke to the teacher, who pointed Cheatham out. Officer Grissett approached Cheatham and asked if they "could have a word with him." Cheatham nodded and then left the classroom with the officers. They went to Room 127, a disciplinary office shared by the school patrol officers and the dean of boys. The room was located four doors down from the classroom Cheatham had been in.

Inside the office, Cheatham was asked "if he had anything in his possession   16 that could get him in trouble." Cheatham pointed to his left coat pocket. He then was asked what it was. He told them it was a gun. Officer Grissett then removed the gun from Cheatham's pocket.

Anthony Brooks

Two witnesses testified at the hearing—Isaiah Kurry, Dean of Students at Simeon   17 Vocational High School, and Chicago police officer David Rozell.

Kurry testified that on December 3, 1993, he received a communication from   18 another teacher, Mrs. Vaughn, regarding a stranger in the school. Kurry immediately went to Room 317, where he spoke with Mrs. Vaughn.

She told him the stranger (later identified as Brooks) was seen coming up the   19 rear staircase. Students are restricted from using that staircase. In addition, he was wearing a jacket. Students are not allowed to wear jackets in the school. She told Kurry the boy's behavior had been suspicious, "unnatural, he seemed to be nervous about something." Mrs. Vaughn told Kurry she saw the boy do something with his hand: ". . . it was a movement and a reaching inside of the jacket that he had on, something of that nature."

Kurry then confronted Brooks, whom he did not recognize as a student at   20 Simeon. Brooks told Kurry his name and said that he was a student. Kurry asked Brooks to come to the office with him so he could verify his identify.

Kurry described Brooks as "cooperative and relaxed" as they walked to the   21 office. When Kurry asked why he was not in class and had no hall pass, Brooks said he had just been reinstated at the school.

Kurry took Brooks to an administrative room that is also used by two Chicago   22 police officers assigned to the school on a full-time basis. They went to this room because the other disciplinary room was in use. While in the office, a school administrator, Mr. Evans, came in and identified Brooks as a Simeon student.

Kurry had notified Officer Rozell, one of the two officers assigned to the   23 school. Kurry told Officer Rozell about Mrs. Vaughn's report and her concerns about the suspicious stranger. Kurry asked Rozell "to be present in the room with me" during the interview with Brooks. Officer Rozell, in uniform, came into the office to observe the interview with Brooks.

After 45 minutes to an hour in the room, Kurry told Brooks to empty his   24 pockets: "I asked him to empty out his pockets to, you know, further see just who he was and what, because the actual suspicion was that he had something on him that was suspicious—by his movements."

Before that moment, Brooks had been "totally cooperative," and had caused   25 no difficulties. He had been identified as a Simeon student and he provided proof that he had been reinstated. The Court asked:

"You personally did not entertain any fear from the defendant, fear of harm by the defendant, did you?"

Kurry: "No. Not at that time nor any time really."

When told to empty his pockets, Brooks began to comply. At that point, Officer Rozell conducted a pat-down of Brooks. He did that, he testified, because of what Kurry had told him about Brooks and because he noticed "a bulge" in Brooks' inside jacket pocket. During the pat-down Rozell felt a metal object in Brooks' inside jacket pocket. He immediately arrested Brooks, handcuffed him, and advised him of his rights. Then he reached into Brooks' pocket and retrieved the handgun. 26

● ● ● ●

For Deliberation and Argument

1. In *New Jersey v. T.L.O.*, apply the legal standards articulated by the Supreme Court in its ruling on the case to determine whether (a) the "seizure" of T.L.O. by the assistant principal was legal, (b) the search of her purse was legal, and (c) the evidence found during the search should be suppressed, under the exclusionary rule, in prosecuting the charge of delinquency. Consider such questions as whether the principal had cause to detain T.L.O. and whether he was justified in continuing to search T.L.O's purse *after* he had discovered the pack of cigarettes. Note that he had detained her in the first place on the suspicion that she was smoking cigarettes rather than the suspicion she was using or selling marijuana.

2. Compare and contrast the circumstances of the *Engerud* case with those of *T.L.O.* To what extent are the essential elements similar? To what extent are they different? Do the same legal standards that apply to the search of a purse in the student's presence also apply to the entry into and search of a student's locker when the student is not present? Should the evidence from the locker be suppressed, under the exclusionary rule?

3. Write about *Coronado v. State*, arguing that the search of the defendant's car for drugs was or was not legal. Apply the case law in this section in formulating your conclusion. (Cite case law, either in the text itself, ("According to *Chimel v. California*") or in parenthetical citations "(*Chimel v. California*)".) Consider especially the *T.L.O.* test for whether or not searches are justified. Also consider related questions, such as whether the initial pat down and strip search of Coronado by Assistant Principal Kim Bennning was legally justified and whether the defendant's subsequent truancy gave the sheriff's deputy, Ernest Randall, the right to search the car. Why do you think the court quoted Benning's testimony verbatim in its description of the facts of the case? Compare and contrast this case to *T.L.O.*, in terms of the elements of "reasonable suspicion" and of whether the search itself met the standard of "reasonableness."

4. In *Acton v. Vernonia School District*, the parents of James Acton contended that the school's drug testing policy, and school officials' decision that James could

not participate in district-sponsored sports unless they signed the consent form, violated their son's Fourth Amendment rights. When asked why he refused to submit to drug testing, Acton replied, "Because I feel they have no reason to think I was taking drugs." Taking the role either of the parents' attorney or the school district's attorney, write a brief in which you argue that James Acton's Fourth Amendment rights *are* or *are not* being violated by the drug testing policy. Apply the standards discussed in the *T.L.O.* case, as well as the other case law in this section, in pursuing your argument. Cite case law as indicated in question 3. In developing your argument, consider some of the following elements:

- the nature, extent, and dangers of the drug problem in the Vernonia School District; in particular, the degree to which the interest of the district and its population as a whole should be weighed and balanced against the invasions of individual privacy
- whether drug tests should be administered only in cases of *probable cause* or *reasonable suspicion*—as opposed to "blanket searches" or random testing of the entire student athlete population
- the availability of alternatives to random drug testing
- the school's consultation with parents and others in attempting to deal with the problem
- the nature, fairness, and accuracy of the drug tests
- the punitive and administrative measures taken when testing yielded positive results

5. After considering the facts of *Williams v. Ellington,* write a brief in which you argue that the search of Williams violated or did not violate her Fourth Amendment rights. Apply and cite the relevant case law, including the *T.L.O.* "twofold inquiry": (1) Was the search justified at its inception? (2) Was the ensuing search reasonable in its scope, and were the measures taken reasonably related to the objectives of the search and not excessively intrusive? Consider also the quantity and quality of the information supplied to principal Ellington and whether this information was sufficient and reliable enough to give the principal a reasonable suspicion that the student in question was concealing illegal drugs. Compare the circumstances of this case to those of the other drug search cases in this section—*T.L.O., Engerud,* and *Coronado*—pointing out the significance of the similarities and differences.

6. In *People v. Dilworth,* the defendant argued that Detective Ruettiger's seizure of the flashlight violated his Fourth and Fourteenth Amendment rights. To what extent do you agree with Dilworth? Apply the standards discussed in the *T.L.O.* case, as well as the other case law in this section, in pursuing your argument. In particular, consider whether the officer had a basis for a reasonable suspicion that the flashlight contained contraband items.

7. In *People v. Pruitt, Cheatham, and Brooks,* the court combines three cases involving high school students who, after searches of their persons, were found to be carrying concealed guns. Compare and contrast these cases,

applying the *T.L.O.* standards and the case law in this section. Determine for each case whether the search was "reasonable" under the law and whether the weapon found should be suppressed as evidence under the exclusionary rule. In your discussion you may want to focus on some of the following elements:

- the competing interests of public safety and individual expectations of privacy
- the constitutionality of magnetometers (metal detectors) in school buildings—and the difference, if any, between magnetometers in schools and in airports and other public buildings
- the availability of measures other than magnetometers to deal with the problem of guns in public schools
- whether police officers had a "reasonable suspicion" (based on the tip from another student) that Cheatham had a gun when they detained him
- whether the search of Cheatham was unnecessarily intrusive
- whether Dean Kurry was justified in ordering Brooks to empty his pockets; whether the subsequent pat-down was justified

8. Select one of the cases treated in this group. Imagine that you are representing either the plaintiff or the defendant. Compose either an opening statement or a closing argument for this case. Remember that your audience is the jury. Draw on the facts of the case in a way that is likely to have the greatest impact on the jury. For guidance on developing your statement, see "Models for the Opening Statement and the Closing Argument" at the end of Chapter 2.

8

A Legal Grab Bag

> The Law is the true embodiment
> Of everything that's excellent.
> It has no kind of fault or flaw,
> And I, my Lords, embody the Law.
>
> —The Lord Chancellor, in *Iolanthe*
> by William S. Gilbert and Arthur Sullivan

■ Broken Engagements

The course of true love never did run smooth, quoth the Bard, but it's a genuine bummer when the bride calls off the wedding and the groom demands the return of his engagement ring. What to do? In the following three cases, you can try your hand at devising an equitable decision to resolve the conflict between two parties who are hopelessly at odds. Each of the three short narratives is excerpted from an appellate court decision dealing with a broken engagement and focusing on the ultimate disposition of the ring: White v. Finch, Coconis v. Christakis, and Lyle v. Durham. There are few legal guidelines (i.e., rules) in this area, so you are on your own in arriving at your decisions!

White v. Finch
■ ———————————————————————————————— ■

3 Conn. Cir. 138

Paul A. WHITE

v.

Susan FINCH.

No. CV 9–645–1800.

Circuit Court of Connecticut,
Ninth Circuit.

Dec. 17, 1964.

In October, 1962, the plaintiff, then a teacher in the public school and a church   1
organist in the town of Clinton, met the defendant. Going out together, they devel-

---

White v. Finch, 209 A.2d 199 (1964).

oped a mutual fondness, one for the other, and, before Christmas, 1962, the plaintiff proposed marriage to the defendant. More unready than unwilling, the defendant demurred, claiming that she wanted time "to think it over." On February 13, 1963, appropriately the day preceding Valentine's Day, the proposal was renewed and accepted. One week thereafter the engagement ring, subject of this action, was given to the defendant by the plaintiff. The engagement was not announced publicly immediately. This is important only in that the defendant's failure to take immediate action to relay the joyous information to the world became a bone of contention between the parties.

There were other problems. The previous constant companionship became   2
infrequent meetings. The plaintiff, a ski enthusiast, sought out the snowcapped hills, leaving the defendant, uninvited, alone in Clinton. The plaintiff, a forceful man, announced to his immediate friends that the wedding was to be in August, although his bride-to-be had not as yet set the date. This no more pleased her than did his gift of a book of etiquette, "so that she might plan the wedding correctly," but their status as an engaged couple remained the same.

The climax came in the summer of 1963, coincidentally with the tercentenary   3
celebration of the founding of the town of Clinton. Among the planned festivities, there was to be a beauty contest which the defendant had been asked to enter, representing her mother's garden club. To this the plaintiff had multiple objections, the most cogent of which was that he was, as he stated, to be a judge in the contest. The ethical argument won out, and the defendant withdrew, attending the contest as an observer. The plaintiff, far from being a judge, was not even there. He had gone to the defendant's home and, not finding her there, suspected the worst.

However unfounded were these suspicions, they remained with the plaintiff   4
until the next day, when the defendant came to the plaintiff's lodging to seek the return of a punchbowl given them as an engagement present. The purpose of the quest was innocuous. She wanted to use it. The plaintiff at first refused to return it, saying that it had been given to them for their home and there was to be no home. Then followed his statement, "As far as I am concerned, this engagement is through." The following day the defendant returned to the plaintiff all gifts given her by him. She did not return the engagement ring. Subsequently, an announcement was made in the newspaper, at the defendant's bidding, that the engagement had been terminated "by mutual consent."

The question whether the engagement was broken by one of the parties or ter-   5
minated by mutual consent cannot be determined by a newspaper article, calculated to preserve the dignity of both parties as far as the rest of the world was concerned. The defendant could have done little else.

Whether the defendant would have retreated from the engagement before the   6
plaintiff said the fateful words is not in issue. Whatever words were spoken and whatever action was taken to terminate the engagement were spoken and taken by the plaintiff.

Coconis v. Christakis

■ ━━ ■

70 Ohio Misc. 29
COCONIS
v.
CHRISTAKIS.

No. 81CV–F–192.

Belmont County Court of Ohio,
Western Division.

Nov. 24, 1981.

In August 1980, plaintiff and defendant formalized previous discussions on the   1
subject of their marriage through the delivery by plaintiff to defendant of a
diamond ring. No announcement of the engagement was made through the local
print media, as is local custom, and no wedding date was set.

As was understood between the parties, both returned to their respective col-   2
leges in September, contemplating their joint return for the Thanksgiving holidays
and an engagement party for formal announcement at that time.

Because of their geographic separation (she in Athens, Ohio, and he in Regina,   3
Saskatchewan, Canada), the parties primarily communicated while in college
through pre-arranged telephone calls. Defendant testified that in several of these
calls prior to October 6, 1980, plaintiff exhibited an attitude toward her call which
she perceived to be frivolous or disinterested.

On October 6, plaintiff placed a non-prearranged late night call to defendant.   4
The parties dispute the substance of that conversation. Plaintiff claims defendant
stated that she had "second thoughts" with respect to the marriage; defendant
claims that she was too tired to carry on the conversation and requested plaintiff
to call back the next evening at an earlier hour.

It is undisputed that no such call was placed by plaintiff, and no further com-   5
munication occurred between the parties until May 1981, when plaintiff returned
from school and demanded return of the ring. Defendant, however, subsequent to
the October 6 conversation placed five additional calls to plaintiff's number. On
each occasion she was advised by one of plaintiff's four roommates that plaintiff
was unavailable. Defendant requested that plaintiff be given a message to return
the call. Plaintiff claims that he never received any of said messages.

Neither the engagement party nor the wedding occurred. Defendant has con-   6
tinued to retain possession of the diamond ring.

─────────

Coconis v. Christakis, 435 N.E.2d 100 (1981).

Lyle v. Durham

16 Ohio App.3d 1
LYLE, Appellee,
v.
DURHAM, n.k.a. Mink, Appellant.

Court of Appeals of Ohio,
Hamilton County.

Feb. 15, 1984.

In August 1980, plaintiff and defendant mutually agreed to become engaged to be married and purchased a matching engagement ring and wedding band. Plaintiff paid $1,700 for the rings and defendant paid the $50 balance when she picked them up. Plaintiff kept the wedding band, and defendant publicly wore the engagement ring.   1

In January 1981, plaintiff broke off the engagement for reasons that are in dispute. The parties continued to see each other until August 1981, trying without success to resolve their differences, and during this period defendant kept the engagement ring. Sometime during February or March 1981, defendant stole the wedding band from plaintiff in anger. After plaintiff discovered the wedding band was missing, in November 1981, he demanded in writing the return of both rings. Defendant refused, and plaintiff filed this action against defendant in March 1982. In July 1982, defendant offered plaintiff a check for the amount of the wedding band, which he refused.   2

In November 1981, defendant became engaged to another man. They went to a jeweler and used the two rings plaintiff had purchased in trade for the engagement ring and wedding band that defendant now wears. Defendant states in her deposition that after plaintiff broke up with her, he told her several times that she could keep the rings.   3

● ● ● ●

For Deliberation and Argument

1. Select one of these unhappy cases and explain whether the plaintiff is entitled to the return of his ring. Indicate both what you think *should* happen as a matter of justice and also what you think the law provides about such cases. (These may or may not be the same.) What are the most important factors in determining the most equitable outcome, both for justice and for law?

Lyle v. Durham, 473 N.E.2d 1216 (1984).

2. Write a short story based on one of these three cases.
3. Write a narrative describing some dispute you have experienced over owner-ship of a piece of property. How was this dispute resolved? Of course, it prob-ably wasn't resolved in a court of law, but in remembering the experience, you may be able to explain what principles of equity or fairness were used—or not used—in determining the outcome.

■ Hot Coffee Spills

Probably the most popular legal horror story of the decade is the notorious McDonald's coffee case—you know, the one about the woman who ordered hot coffee at a McDonald's drive-through, spilled it on herself while driving out, sued McDonald's, collected a cool $2.7 million from the deep pockets of the fast food corporate empire, and laughed all the way to the bank. Of course, this description is mostly fantasy. In actual fact, the seventy-nine-year-old woman was not driving when the spill occurred, sustained third-degree burns over 6 percent of her body, required eight days of hospitalization and painful skin grafts, and eventually saw her judgment reduced to $480,000. McDonald's, which had been warned for years by previous plaintiffs and their lawyers about the abnormally high temperature of its coffee (180–90 degrees Fahrenheit), had initially refused to settle for $20,000.

The McDonald's case is an example of a product liability *lawsuit—one in which the plaintiff sues because of injuries suffered owing to a defective or dangerous product. Other high-profile product liability cases in recent years involve cigarettes, asbestos, automobiles, and silicon breast implants. There were coffee cases before the McDonald's case, and there have been coffee cases afterward. In a 1941 Louisiana case, Miller v. Holsum Cafeteria, a woman sued a restaurant after the waiter accidentally spilled coffee down her neck and back, splashing her eye in the process. She itemized her damages as humiliation ($150), first-degree burns ($350), nervous collapse and confine-ment to her bed and residence ($1,000), and injuries to her eyes, pain and suffering and for the infection of her tonsils ($6,000). She collected, but the judge reduced her damage award to $1,450. Three years after the McDonald's case, another woman, who spilled coffee on herself while driving over a dip at a Hardee's restaurant in Virginia (she claimed that the lid was improperly attached), didn't collect anything, having failed to prove that the product she had purchased was defective.*

The following segment gives you an opportunity to decide damages in some other hot coffee cases: Harris v. Black, Pasela v. Brown Derby, Inc., Rudees v. Delta Airlines, *and* Nadel v. Burger King. *Also provided is the Ohio Product Liability Law (which is fairly typical of its type) and a set of jury instructions for determining comparative fault (relative degrees of fault of the defendant and the plaintiff) in product liability cases.*

Harris v. Black

130 Ga.App. 807
HARRIS, INC.
v.
Randy G. BLACK.

No. 48842.

Court of Appeals of Georgia,
Division No. 2.

Feb. 12, 1974.

The evidence as to how the plaintiff's injuries occurred is in conflict. The defendant's sole witness, the employee allegedly causing the injuries, testified that the plaintiff and his friends had come into the restaurant at approximately 2:30 a.m. from a party at which alcoholic beverages were consumed, and that the plaintiff, upon being refused service because of unruly behavior and profane language, twisted the witness' arm, causing her to spill the coffee on him. The plaintiff's witnesses, all participants in the party with him, testified that their group was not noisy or rowdy, but that they were unable to obtain service; that the plaintiff used profanity to describe what the restaurant was not worth, whereupon the employee picked up a pot of coffee and threw it on the plaintiff. The jury had the opportunity to give more credibility to the defendant's sole witness than to those of the plaintiff, but declined to do so, even though the plaintiff's witnesses who were all teenagers, according to his own testimony, held their party in a motel rather than in a private home because they could not be trusted not to steal things. 1

Pasela v. Brown Derby, Inc.

71 Ohio App.3d 636

PASELA et al., Appellants,

v.

BROWN DERBY, INC. et al., Appellees.[1]

No. 58247.

Court of Appeals of Ohio,
Cuyahoga County.

Decided April 1, 1991.

In the early afternoon of July 27, 1983, appellant Christine Pasela, then just under   1
one year old, was taken to a Brown Derby Restaurant for lunch by her mother,
Karen Pasela, and grandmother, Margaret Sinko. An older sister, Nicole, was also
present. The party was seated at a table by the restaurant's hostess and cashier,
Joann Sclimenti. Defendant-appellee Sclimenti brought a high chair for Christine
to sit in and appellant Karen Pasela then placed her daughter in the chair. Karen
Pasela notified Sclimenti that the high chair did not fasten properly and that there
were no straps on the seat to secure Christine. Sclimenti never replaced the chair.
Karen Pasela moved the high chair so that Christine was seated to her immediate
left. Both Karen Pasela and Margaret Sinko were given large menus and were then
asked by defendant-appellee, waitress Nancy Filler, if they would like coffee.
They responded affirmatively. While Karen and Margaret were reviewing the
menus, appellee, waitress Susan Heffner, brought two pots of coffee to the table
where the party was seated without alerting the women that she had done so. One
pot was placed on Karen Pasela's left side, near the high chair where Christine
was seated. Filler, who was in charge of training Heffner, saw the placement of
the coffee pots on the table.

Karen Pasela indicated that while waiting for the coffee, she was reviewing   2
the menu, trying to appease Nicole, who was hungry and cranky, and reaching
into a diaper bag on the floor to retrieve some baby food. Karen testified that
while she was reaching into the diaper bag, she heard Christine cry and turned
towards her to find that a pot of coffee had spilled on Christine's high chair and
on the front of Christine's clothing, causing severe burns to Christine's arms,
chest, abdomen and right leg. Karen stated that she had only looked away from
Christine for fifteen to twenty seconds. Margaret Sinko claimed that she glanced
at Christine every ten seconds but had not witnessed the accident. Karen and

Pasela v. Brown Derby, Inc., 594 N.E.2d 1112 (1991).

Footnote 1 text reference changed from original.

[1]The plaintiffs-appellants in the instant action are Christine Pasela, a minor, by and through her
parents and next friends, Karen Pasela (mother) and Edward Pasela (father), and Edward Pasela
and Karen Pasela. The defendants-appellees in the action are Brown Derby, Inc., Susan Heffner,
Joann Sclimenti and Nancy Filler.

Margaret both testified that they never saw a waitress bring two pots of coffee to their table, nor did they have any idea how the coffee pots had gotten on the table or how the accident had happened.

Christine was taken by ambulance to Cleveland Metro General Hospital, where she was treated for her burns by Dr. Robert Gerding. Christine's burns began to heal after several months, but the record reflects that she has suffered permanent scarring.   3

Rudees v. Delta Airlines

Marvin RUDEES, Appellant,

v.

DELTA AIRLINES, INC., Appellee.

**Court of Appeals of Tennessee,
Western Section.**

April 26, 1977.

Certiorari Denied by Supreme Court
July 5, 1977.

The plaintiff boarded the defendant's DC-9 airplane at Memphis for a flight to   1
Atlanta, Georgia. The passengers were asked to keep their seat belts fastened due to the possibility that the plane might encounter air turbulence. At a point approximately 100 miles from Atlanta, a stewardess came down the aisle of the airplane carrying at waist level an open tray which contained several cups of scalding coffee. The plaintiff was seated on an aisle seat with his seat belt fastened; he had not ordered coffee. The airplane apparently hit some clear air turbulence which made the stewardess sway in the aisle and spill the contents of the cups on the plaintiff's lap. This resulted in rather severe burns to the plaintiff's thighs and groin area.

The defendant, on motion for directed verdict, argued that the plaintiff had   2
not proved any negligence on its part. Counsel for the defendant argued, and the trial judge apparently agreed, that the plaintiff could not recover because he failed to prove that the pilot was negligent or that the defendant knew or should have known about the air turbulence.

The foregoing argument overlooks the basis of the lawsuit. The plaintiff   3
alleged that the stewardess was negligent: (1) in spilling the coffee; (2) in her manner of carrying scalding coffee down the aisle of the plane; (3) in carrying the coffee in uncovered containers; and (4) in attempting to serve scalding coffee during flight. The issue is the negligence of the stewardess; therein lies the lawsuit.

Rudees v. Delta Airlines, 553 S.W.2d 85 (1977).

Nadel v. Burger King

■ ── ■

119 Ohio App.3d 578

NADEL et al., Appellants,

v.

BURGER KING CORPORATION

et al., Appellees.

No. C–960489.

Court of Appeals of Ohio,
First District, Hamilton County.

Decided May 21, 1997.

On a morning in early December 1993, plaintiff-appellant Paul Nadel was driving   1
his son, plaintiff-appellant Christopher, and two younger daughters, Ashley and
Brittany, to school. Paul's mother, plaintiff-appellant Evelyn Nadel, was seated
next to the passenger window. Christopher was seated in the front seat between
Evelyn and Paul, with one foot on the transmission hump and one foot on the passenger side of the hump. Brittany and Ashley were in the back seat. On the way,
they ordered breakfast from the drive-through window of a Burger King restaurant owned and operated by defendant-appellee Emil, Inc. ("Emil") under a franchise agreement with defendant-appellee Burger King Corporation ("BK"). Paul's
order included several breakfast sandwiches and drinks and two cups of coffee.
The cups of coffee were fitted with lids and served in a cardboard container
designed to hold four cups, with the two cups placed on opposite diagonal
corners. Emil's employee served the coffee through the car window to Paul, who
passed it to Christopher, who handed it to Evelyn.

Evelyn testified that she tasted the coffee in the cup on the right side of the   2
container, by raising the flap on its lid, and found it too hot to drink. She also testified that the lid of the coffee "jiggled off" and burned her on her right leg after
she lifted the flap. After bending the flap of the lid so that it was closed, Evelyn
returned the cup, covered by the lid, to the container. She then either started to
place the container of coffees on the floor next to Christopher's foot or placed the
container on the dashboard, or she had already placed the container on the floor
next to Christopher's foot, when Paul drove away from the restaurant, making a
left turn onto a street. At that point Christopher began screaming that his foot was
burned. Christopher, Paul, and Evelyn discovered that one or both of the cups had
tipped, and that hot coffee had spilled on Christopher's right foot. Neither the
cups, the lids, nor the container are in the record. Christopher was treated for
second-degree burns on his right foot.

────────

Nadel v. Burger King, 695 N.E.2d 1185 (1997).
Footnotes deleted from original.

In their complaint, the Nadels (Brenda Nadel is the mother of Christopher   3
Nadel) raised several claims, including (1) breach of a warranty of merchantability
and breach of a warranty of fitness for a particular purpose, both based on the allegation that the coffee was too hot to consume, (2) products liability for a defective
product and a failure to warn of the dangers of handling liquid served as hot as
appellees' coffee, and (3) negligence both for failing to instruct employees how to
properly serve hot coffee and for failing to warn business invitees of the danger of
handling coffee at the temperature Emil's coffee was served.

. . . In support of its claim for summary judgment, Emil cited the deposition of   4
Paul, in which he testified that he knew that coffee is served hot, that he expected
coffee to be served hot, that he knew Emil's coffee was served hot, that coffee
would burn someone if it was spilled on him or her, and that whoever was handling hot coffee needed to be careful not to spill it. Evelyn testified that she knew
the coffee that was spilled was hot, and that it had burned her. Emil's owner's affidavit averred that BK's operating manual required coffee to be served at approximately one hundred seventy-five degrees, that the coffee machine thermostats
were set at that temperature, and that Emil was unaware of any problems
resulting from coffee being served at that temperature.

BK also moved for summary judgment and pointed to evidence in the deposi-   5
tions that appellants knew that the coffee was hot and that coffee was purchased
and served as a hot beverage. It also contended that under the circumstances,
Evelyn's and Paul's actions were intervening, superseding causes precluding any
actionable negligence on its part.

In opposition to the motions for summary judgment, the Nadels argued that   6
Emil and BK knew or should have known that second-degree burns could occur
as a result of coffee served at one hundred seventy-five degrees, because "the
whole industry has long been aware of the danger of liquid this hot," and they
cited several journal articles in their supporting memorandum. The Nadels also
attached the affidavit of their attorney with Christopher's medical records
affixed, which averred that the medical records were true copies of what was
received through discovery.

■ Statutory Law ■

"A manufacturer is subject to liability for compensatory damages based on a   1
product liability claim *only* if the claimant establishes, by a preponderance of the
evidence, *all* of the following:

> "(1) [T]he product was defective in manufacture or construction, . . . was
> defective in design or formulation, . . . was defective due to inadequate
> warning or instruction, . . . or was defective because it did not conform
> to a representation made by the manufacturer. . . .

The Ohio Products Liability Law, R.C. 2307.73(A).

"*[AND]*
"(2) [A] defective aspect of the product . . . was a proximate cause of harm for which the claimant seeks to recover compensatory damages.
"*[AND]*
"(3) The manufacturer designed, formulated, produced, created, made, constructed, assembled, or rebuilt the product."

[This statute] defines a product liability claim as a claim "asserted in a civil action and that seeks to recover compensatory damages from a manufacturer or supplier for death, physical injury to person, emotional distress, or physical damage to property other than the product involved, that allegedly arise from any of the following:

"(1) The design, formulation, production, construction, creation, assembly, rebuilding, testing, or marketing of that product;
"(2) Any warning or instruction, or lack of warning or instruction, associated with that product;
"(3) Any failure of that product to conform to any relevant representation or warranty."

Jury Instructions on Negligence

The plaintiff _____ seeks to recover damages based upon a claim of negligence.
   The essential elements of such a claim are:

1. The defendant was negligent;
2. Defendant's negligence was a cause of injury, damage, loss or harm to plaintiff.

Negligence is the doing of something which a reasonably prudent person would not do, or the failure to do something which a reasonably prudent person would do, under circumstances similar to those shown by the evidence.
   It is the failure to use ordinary or reasonable care.
   Ordinary or reasonable care is that care which persons of ordinary prudence would use in order to avoid injury to themselves or others under circumstances similar to those shown by the evidence.

California Jury Instructions, Civil: Book of Approved Jury Instructions. 8th ed. Prepared by the Committee on Standard Jury Instruction Civil, of the Superior Court of Los Angeles County, California. Hon. Stephen M. Lachs, Judge of the Superior Court, Chairman. Compiled and edited by Paul G. Breckenridge, Jr. St. Paul, MN: West Publishing, 1994.

You will note that the person whose conduct we set up as a standard is not the extraordinarily cautious individual, nor the exceptionally skillful one, but a person of reasonable and ordinary prudence.

One test that is helpful in determining whether or not a person was negligent is to ask and answer the question whether or not, if a person of ordinary prudence had been in the same situation and possessed of the same knowledge, [he][or][she] would have foreseen or anticipated that someone might have been injured by or as a result of [his][or][her] action or inaction. If the answer to that question is "yes," and if the action or inaction reasonably could have been avoided, then not to avoid it would be negligence.

Contributory negligence is negligence on the part of a plaintiff which, combining with the negligence of a defendant, contributes as a cause in bringing about the injury.

Contributory negligence, if any, on the part of the plaintiff does not bar a recovery by the plaintiff against the defendant but the total amount of damages to which the plaintiff would otherwise be entitled shall be reduced in proportion to the amount of negligence attributable to the plaintiff.

Comparative fault is negligence on the part of a plaintiff which combining [with the negligence of a defendant][or][with a defect in a product][or][with negligent or wrongful conduct of others] contributes as a cause in bringing about the injury.

Comparative fault, if any, on the part of plaintiff does not bar recovery by the plaintiff against the defendant but the total amount of damages to which plaintiff would otherwise be entitled shall be reduced by the percentage that plaintiff's comparative fault contributed as a cause to plaintiff's injury.

If you find that a cause of plaintiff's injury was [a defendant's negligence][or][a defect in the product] and that the comparative fault of the plaintiff was also a cause of said injury, you will determine the amount of damages to be awarded by you as follows:

First: You will determine the total amount of damages to which the plaintiff would be entitled under the court's instructions if plaintiff had not been comparatively at fault.

Second: You will determine what percentage of the combined causes of plaintiff's injury is attributable to plaintiff's comparative fault and what percentage of such combined causes is attributable to the [defective product][and][or][a defendant's negligence].

Third: You will then reduce the total amount of plaintiff's damages by the percentage that plaintiff's comparative fault contributed as a cause to plaintiff's injury.

Fourth: The resulting amount, after making such reduction, will be the amount of your verdict.■

● ● ● ●

For Deliberation and Argument

1. Assume that you are either an attorney for the plaintiff *or* an attorney for the defendant. Which of these coffee cases do you think would be easiest to win for your client? Which would be most difficult? Consider the rules relating to product liability and negligence following the cases and apply them to the facts of the case you have selected as the most difficult.
2. For any one of these cases, what additional information would you need as a jury member to cast your vote for the plaintiff or the defendant? Explain.
3. Select one of these cases and write an essay in which you argue your conclusion in IRAC format.

■ Parental Responsibility for Destructive Acts by Children

In April 1999, two youths in Littleton, Colorado, went on a shooting rampage in their high school. Thirteen students and a teacher died, and many more were wounded before the shooters turned their weapons on themselves. When police searched the youths' homes, they found in plain view (among quantities of hate literature) a sawed-off shotgun and pipe bomb ingredients. In the wake of the tragedy, many people wondered about the responsibility of the parents of the two young killers: Didn't they see the danger signs? Didn't they realize that their sons were walking time bombs? To what extent might they share responsibility for the terrible acts of their children?

The question has no easy answer, either in a particular case like this or in a more general social context. Most societies, however, recognize the crucial role of parents in shaping the moral, as well as the emotional and intellectual, development of their children, and our society imposes liability, in some cases, on parents who are negligent in this area.

Negligence in law is the failure to exercise the standard of care that a reasonably prudent person would have exercised in a given situation. One can be negligent by doing something that a reasonable person would not do, or by not doing something that a reasonable person would do. While parents cannot be found criminally liable for the acts committed by their children, they can be found civilly liable if their own negligence has made it possible or easier for their children to harm others. A father who keeps a loaded gun in an unlocked drawer may be found liable for negligence if his child takes the gun and uses it, even unintentionally, to shoot someone.

A parent may also be liable for negligence if he or she knows, based on past experience, that a child's conduct may pose a danger to others and fails to exercise sufficient control over the child to prevent harm from occurring or fails to warn the victim of the potential danger. Of course, the plaintiff in a lawsuit must show that the parent has control—both legal control, in terms of custody, and the ability to deter harmful conduct of the child. Generally, courts do recognize that it is more difficult to control a troubled seventeen-year-old than a five-year-old.

The cases that follow deal with the liability of parents for acts committed by their children. In these cases the victims or families of the victims have brought lawsuits for negligence against the parents, and they seek damages in the form of financial recompense. (Note that in these cases the children are sometimes referred to as "infants," even though they may be teenagers; this is simply legal terminology for minors.) This brief chapter begins with an article on parental liability, "When the Sins of the Child Point to Parents, Law's Grip Is Tenuous," by Kim Murphy and Melissa Healy. Four cases follow: Costa v. Hicks, Moore v. Crumpton, Reida v. Lund, *and* Roberton v. Wentz. *The chapter also includes statements on the law that concern parental liability for the acts of children.*

When the Sins of the Child Point to Parents, Law's Grip Is Tenuous

Kim Murphy and Melissa Healy

Should Steven Pfiel's parents have seen the signs of their son's murderous outburst? 1

At 7, he allegedly set fire to a motor home. As a grammar school student in 2 suburban Chicago, he was accused of singing death chants to a classmate. After the student complained, Pfiel admitted to police that he had vandalized the student's home with a knife and had spray-painted satanic symbols on its side. According to friends, Pfiel dropped rocks on cars from over-passes.

When he was old enough to drive, he would swerve his car in hopes of picking 3 off small animals.

Still, when he turned 17, his birthday gift from his parents was a hunting knife 4 with a serrated, 5-inch blade. And three weeks later, on July 12, 1993, Pfiel used the knife to murder 13-year-old Hillary Norskog, and 17 months later, while awaiting trial, Pfiel beat his brother with a bat, slit his throat and then fled with three of his father's guns.

He is now serving a life prison sentence in Illinois, having pleaded guilty to 5 both murders. And Pfiel's parents, a business executive and a stay-at-home mother who volunteered at his school, are facing a lawsuit from Norskog's mother.

"There are a whole lot of parents out there who act as if being a parent is just 6 their right and it doesn't come with responsibilities," says Donald Pasulka, the Chicago attorney who brought the suit on behalf of Norskog's family.

Los Angeles Times, 30 Apr. 1999, pp. A1+.

"We sometimes view the parents as victims," Pasulka said. "When they see the 7
school shootings in Arkansas and Littleton [Colo.] and Kentucky, people are
starting to wake up and say, 'Wait a minute: If you're not going to control your
children, we're going to start controlling them—and you.' "

Across the country, 25 states have extended some form of legal sanctions 8
against parents whose children commit crimes, although rarely have they been
invoked for major crimes.

Los Angeles County has prosecuted 40 parents for not sending their children 9
to school under California's 11-year-old parental responsibility law, one of the
toughest in the nation. An Oregon woman got a hefty fine under a local ordinance
when her son was repeatedly arrested for tobacco, marijuana and curfew violations. In Michigan, a pizza baker was ordered to pay a $300 fine for overlooking
the fact that his son had in his bedroom property from a string of burglaries.

Increasing Cases in Civil Courts

Increasingly, parents are also being held accountable in civil courts for the wrong- 10
doing of their offspring. The National Center for Victims of Crime has tracked as
many as 100 cases in the past decade in which parents like the Pfiels have been
sued for negligent care. And the volume is rising sharply, said staff attorney Lisa
Ferguson.

Parents of school shooters in Jonesboro, Ark., West Paducah, Ky., and Moses 11
Lake, Wash., all face substantial lawsuits from families of the victims—alleging
they should have done more to control their children.

And President Clinton, as part of a package of proposals unveiled last week, 12
called for making it a felony for parents to knowingly or recklessly allow children to use guns to commit crimes. Illinois last week became the 17th state to
pass similar legislation.

Yet drawing a firm connection between what children do and what their 13
parents could have done to stop it remains difficult and constitutionally problematic, say lawyers and almost any parent who has tried to tell a teenager:
"Don't."

In the case of the recent high school shootings in Littleton that left 13 inno- 14
cent victims dead, authorities have said they are looking at a diary, bomb-making
equipment and part of a shotgun found in the home of one of the two teenage
assailants, 18-year-old Eric Harris, to help determine whether the parents should
face criminal charges.

"Parents of children in most states are subject to civil liability when they fail 15
to exercise appropriate control over their children and their children cause
harm. But in terms of criminal law, current legal principles provide significant
obstacles to any significant prosecution of the parents, and I think for good
reason," said Peter Arenella, professor of criminal law at UCLA.

"In this country, we believe that people should only be held accountable for 16
their own criminal acts or the criminal acts of others they've encouraged.
Clearly, you have here at best parents who were aware of the fact that their chil-

dren had access to weapons. That doesn't mean they were aware of the possibility that their children would engage in such horrendous acts, much less that they encouraged them," Arenella said.

Tom Higgins, head of the Los Angeles County district attorney's juvenile division, suggests that in balancing a child's right to some measure of privacy and a parent's oversight responsibilities, the principle of probable cause ought to play a role.   17

"I don't go searching through my kids' bedroom," Higgins said. "They have drawers, they have boxes. I occasionally go in there to tell them to pick their stuff up off the floor, or wake them up when the alarm goes off. But I don't search my kids' room. So, 'should have known' needs to be prefaced with, is there something in their behavior that should have prompted them to search their kid's room?   18

"And let's just suppose they knew. And let's suppose they said, 'I'm taking that stuff out of your room, and I'm destroying it or I'm calling the cops, make your choice.' If they made the effort, and the kid [responded with] some expletive, what does a parent do? If there were reasonable efforts made and they failed, then I don't think they would fall under a parental accountability law."   19

Liability Laws Have Proliferated

Most states have had statutes on contributing to the delinquency of a minor since the 1950s and 1960s. Occasionally, they are brushed off to prosecute a pimp or an adult who serves alcohol to a minor.   20

But, experts say, specific parental liability laws have proliferated amid a surge in youth crime that has scared Americans and prompted a search for what—or who—is to blame. In pressing their cases, lawmakers and attorneys frequently draw on the argument that, along with their rights to raise children free of government meddling, parents bear the responsibility to provide adequate oversight.   21

In 1988, California amended its statute to target parents who do not "exercise reasonable care, supervision, protection and control" over their children. Penalties can include a year in jail and a $2,500 fine.   22

Although similar laws have been attacked as unconstitutionally vague, the California Supreme Court upheld the law in 1993, overruling lawyers for the American Civil Liberties Union who said it was "unfair to blame poor parents for something that is a failure of our society as a whole."   23

Since then, the revised California law has been used sporadically: against parents who served alcohol to a juvenile who then went out and injured someone in an automobile accident, for example, or parents who left a gun in the house unlocked. Its primary target in Los Angeles has been parents of elementary school children who are chronically absent from school.   24

In recent years, parents of 40,000 truant children have been threatened with prosecution under the law. Only about 40 have had criminal charges filed—the longest jail term was nine months—because most parents opt to send their children to school instead, Higgins said, adding that "in fact, our goal is not court but to turn the behavior around."   25

Oregon, Louisiana, Alabama, Wyoming and Hawaii all adopted laws in recent 26
years threatening parents with fines or prison for negligent parenting, although
some have been struck down in the courts. An Oklahoma law requires parents to
complete community service or pay a fine of up to $2,000 if their child possesses
a firearm at school. Florida requires parents to pay the cost of their child's criminal prosecution, and in Tennessee, parents must pay the cost of medical exams,
treatment and pretrial placement of their children.

Citations Drop after Supervision Ordinance

Silverton, Ore., whose 1995 parental supervision ordinance became a model for 27
the state law, has seen its citations under the law go down from 14 the first year
to two last year. There has been a 35% reduction in overall juvenile crime during
the same period, said Police Chief Rick Lewis. "So the word has gotten out. The
parents understand what their role is in their kids' lives."

Most of the crimes prosecuted in Silverton involve relatively minor infractions, 28
like marijuana possession and alcohol offenses. Criminal charges against parents in
a case like Littleton have been rare or nonexistent, most legal experts said, because
of the difficulty in proving criminal recklessness: that a parent knew there was a
substantial risk the child was going to commit a crime but did nothing to prevent it.

"A criminal charge is kind of like a cake recipe. We have to have a number of 29
elements that go into it, and if we don't have them all, we don't have a crime," said
John Knodell, prosecuting attorney in Grant County, Wash. "We've got to show
that the parents were more than oblivious, that they actually knew that what they
were doing was causing the problem."

Knodell is familiar with what it takes to charge a parent with such a crime 30
because he strongly considered charging the parents of Barry Loukaitis, a 14-year-
old who, wearing a black trench coat to hide two handguns and a deer rifle, fatally
shot two students and a teacher at a Moses Lake junior high school in 1996.

His mother, JoAnn Phillips, admitted in testimony at his criminal trial that a 31
month before the killings she told her son that she was going to tie up her ex-
husband and his girlfriend and shoot herself as they watched.

Barry, she said, a former straight-A student, had been listening to her talk 32
about her marital problems for years but became worried and depressed after she
told him of her plan to kill herself.

"Testified That They Were Lousy Parents"

Phillips also admitted that she had helped her son buy the trench coat and that 33
she had taken him target shooting not long before the high school attack, Knodell
said. Indeed, at least one of the guns used in the shooting had been left in the back
of the father's car, he said.

"They both testified that they were lousy parents, their lousy parenting was 34
what led Barry to snap and become delusional or aggressive. Dad was absent

most of the time," Knodell said. But neither parent had the requisite mental state to support criminal charges, he said.

"It had to be more than simple negligence, it had to be criminal recklessness," ₃₅ he said. "There's a difference between moral culpability and legal culpability."

Lawyers in civil cases need only prove negligence and by a lesser standard ₃₆ than the proof "beyond a reasonable doubt" required in criminal cases.

A Chicago-area family won a $300,000 settlement from the well-to-do parents ₃₇ of 16-year-old David Biro, who broke into a townhome in an affluent suburb and murdered a man and his pregnant wife in 1990. Attorney John Corbett introduced evidence that Biro had previously shot his BB gun out of his bedroom window at passers-by, injuring at least two, and had tried to poison his family by pouring wood alcohol into their milk.

A search of the boy's room, according to evidence introduced at trial, turned up ₃₈ two guns, a set of handcuffs, a bag of burglary tools and a bounty of satanic writings.

"I don't think they ever went into his room," Corbett said of the parents. "They ₃₉ were pretty much oblivious."

A judge in Kentucky last week refused to dismiss a case filed against the ₄₀ parents of Michael Carneal, who pleaded guilty in the shooting deaths of three fellow middle school students in West Paducah in 1997.

"People are appreciating the fact that if they're going to stop the violence in ₄₁ the schools, it's going to have to start someplace, and the home is the best place to do that," said Michael Breen, the attorney representing parents of the victims. "What better way to get Mom and Dad to start taking care of what's going on at home than to start putting them in jail?"

"The analogy is of a vicious dog," added Bobby McDaniel, who is suing the ₄₂ parents of 12-year-old Andrew Golden and 14-year-old Mitchell Johnson on behalf of three of the five students killed at a Jonesboro, Ark., middle school last year. "An owner of a dog is liable for harm inflicted by the dog if the owner knew, or should have known, the dog would do it.

"I believe the law takes the position that a parent cannot say, 'I didn't see this ₄₃ problem, I had no idea, I didn't realize, I looked but I didn't see, I listened but I didn't hear.' The parent must have the responsibility to know, appreciate and understand what their child is doing."

But Michael Borders, the Chicago lawyer defending the Pfiels in a case set to ₄₄ go to trial in October, said it is too easy to "flyspeck" a family's history and come out with a pronouncement that "you should have known."

"Everybody is all too quick to judge parents after something like this," said ₄₅ Borders, who dismisses virtually all of the charges alleged in the Norskog lawsuit as "rumor and innuendo without a shred of evidence."

"Children Have Their Own Minds"

Parents who have never experienced this with their own children "can't appre- ₄₆ ciate that children have their own minds, make their own decisions, not only on the basis of what they learn at home but from society, that teenagers are notorious for not sharing with their parents what they want to hide," Borders added.

"It's a tragedy, but it's not going to be cured by dragging a bunch of parents into court."

Indeed, some people caution, holding parents liable for their children's crimes could have the result of further fracturing troubled families. . . .   47

"If parents feel they're going to get prosecuted because their children are planning something or hiding something, and that leads to parents being more intrusive in terms of checking out the children's bureau drawers and their computer and stuff like that, what's that going to do to parent-child trust issues?" asked Howard Davidson, director of the American Bar Assn.'s Center on Children and the Law. "Do we want to promote parents being snoops and informers against their kids?"   48

The Law on the Duty of Parent to Control Conduct of Child

§ 316. Duty of Parent to Control Conduct of Child

A parent is under a duty to exercise reasonable care so to control his minor child as to prevent it from intentionally harming others or from so conducting itself as to create an unreasonable risk of bodily harm to them, if the parent   1

    (a) knows or has reason to know that he has the ability to control his child, and

    (b) knows or should know of the necessity and opportunity for exercising such control.

Comment:

a. While the father as head of the family group is no longer responsible for the actions of all the members of his household or even for those of his minor child, he is responsible for their conduct in so far as he has the ability to control it. This duty is not peculiar to a father. It extends to the mother also in so far as her position as mother gives her an ability to control her child.   2

b. The duty of a parent is only to exercise such ability to control his child as he in fact has at the time when he has the opportunity to exercise it and knows the necessity of so doing. The parent is not under a duty so to discipline his child as to make it amenable to parental control when its exercise becomes necessary to the safety of others.   3

c. In order that the parent may be liable under the rule stated in this Section, it is not necessary that the actions of the child which he fails to prevent or control   4

Restatement of the Law, Second: Torts, 2nd. As Adapted and promulgated by the American Law Institute, Washington, D.C. May 25, 1963, and May 22, 1964. St. Paul, MN: West Publishing, 1965. Text references omitted from original.

are such as to make the child himself subject to liability. The child may be so young as to be incapable of negligence, but this does not absolve the parent from the performance of his duty to exercise reasonable care to control the child's conduct. Indeed, the very youth of the child is likely to give the parent more effective ability to control its actions and to make it more often necessary to exercise it.

Illustration:

1. A is informed that his six-year-old child is shooting at a target in the street with a .22 rifle, in a manner which endangers the safety of those using the street. A fails to take the rifle away from the child, or to take any other action. The child unintentionally shoots B, a pedestrian, in the leg. A is subject to liability to B.

Case Law: Seifert v. Owen[1]

[Parental liability for acts of children applies:][1]

(1) where the parent permits the child to have access to an instrument which, because of its nature, use and purposes is so dangerous as to constitute, in the hands of a child, an unreasonable risk to others (Firearms, dynamite, etc.)

(2) where the parent permits the child to have access to an instrumentality which, though not "inherently dangerous," is likely to be put to a dangerous use by a *known* propensity of the child (Matches, baseball bat, bicycle ridden on a busy sidewalk, etc.) and

(3) where the parent fails to restrain the child from vicious conduct imperiling others and the parent *knows* of the child's propensity toward such conduct (Beating up little children, etc.)

Costa v. Hicks

98 A.D.2d 137
Peter COSTA, et al., Appellants,
v.
Walter HICKS, et al., Respondents.

Supreme Court, Appellate Division,
Second Department.

Dec. 27, 1983.

The defendant father [Walter Hicks] purchased, by personal check, a 1976, 250CC Bultaco "trials" motorcycle for his 14-year-old son Walter, Jr., approximately one   1

---

[1]*Seifert v. Owen*, 460 P.2d 19 (1969).
Costa v. Hicks, 470 N.Y.S.2d 627 (1983).

month prior to the collision. The bill of sale was made out to "Walter Hicks," without the suffix "Jr." According to defendants, Walter Jr. repaid his father from money he had saved and the proceeds from the sale of the fifth motorcycle the boy had owned over a five-year period—a 125CC Power Dyne. Neither defendant could recall if the repayment equalled the cost of the motorcycle. Since the 250CC Bultaco motorcycle was a trials competition bike, it was not equipped with a rear view mirror, horn, or headlight. The motorcycle was neither inspected nor registered and Walter Jr. did not have a motorcycle license. Walter Jr. had participated in trials competition with smaller motorcycles, but the 193-pound, 250CC Bultaco was the largest machine the 14-year-old boy had ever used. The maximum speed the five-gear motorcycle could attain was 35 miles per hour.

Walter Hicks placed restrictions on his son's use of the motorcycle because he   2 knew that absent such limitations, the vehicle's use was dangerous to his son and others. Therefore, Walter Jr. was directed not to operate the motorcycle off his father's property unless accompanied by either his father or his older brothers, all of whom owned motorcycles. Walter Jr. admitted that he had violated said restriction on prior occasions and the father admitted that he possessed knowledge of the violations. Furthermore, the father acknowledged that the motorcycle was capable of being locked, chained or otherwise secured at the house, which would have prevented its use off his premises when neither he nor an older son was present. Such measures were not taken and Walter Jr. continued to have unimpeded access to the motorcycle. On the day of the collision Walter Jr. was violating his father's restrictions by operating the motorcycle off his father's premises, without his permission and unaccompanied by an older member of the family.

The scene of the accident is a residential neighborhood where many small   3 children are accustomed to playing on the dirt and gravel streets and in the nearby woods. Old Haverstraw Road is the only paved street in the neighborhood, running in a north-south direction. The defendants' residence is located on Chester Avenue, a dirt and gravel road, running east and west. Parallel with and to the south of Chester Avenue is Central Avenue. Central Avenue's road surface is similarly composed of dirt and gravel. Both Chester Avenue and Central Avenue are dead-end streets which intersect with Old Haverstraw Road to the east. A path through the woods, about 200 feet long, connects Chester Avenue with Central Avenue. The wooded path stops at the northern edge of Central Avenue, approximately 250 feet west of the intersection of Central Avenue and Old Haverstraw Road. On the south side of Central Avenue, across from the wooded path, is the Vassallo residence. On the day of the accident a six-inch high sand pile was located a short distance west of the wooded path, in the middle of Central Avenue. A milk truck was parked on the north side of Central Avenue, approximately 20 feet west of the sand pile. West of the parked milk truck was another path through the woods, leading to the residence of Walter Jr's. friend, Doug Bull.

Aside from the infant plaintiff (Michael) and defendant Walter Jr., the only   4 eyewitnesses to the accident were Joseph Griffin, then age eight, and Michael's younger brother, Jeffrey Costa, then age five; both testified on behalf of the plaintiffs.

According to plaintiffs' eyewitnesses, the infant plaintiff, his brother Jeffrey   5
and Joe Griffin, were standing on the front lawn of the residence of the Plesach
family, which is located at the end of Chester Avenue. They observed Walter Jr.
riding his motorcycle, "fairly fast," back and forth on Chester Avenue. During
these runs, Walter Jr. performed more than one "wheelie," meaning he raised the
front wheel off the ground and rode on the rear wheel only. Walter Jr.'s father
acknowledged that a "wheelie" was a dangerous maneuver, especially in the
vicinity of children. Two other children, under the age of five, were also present
on the Plesach's front lawn. The memory of the witnesses as to the number of
wheelies performed and whether Walter Jr. performed them at the children's
request differed.

Subsequently, Walter Jr. proceeded to drive the motorcycle south along the   6
wooded path connecting Chester Avenue with Central Avenue. The children followed. Some discrepancies in the plaintiffs' witnesses' testimony exist as to the
events which occurred after the children arrived at the edge of the wooded path,
where it exits onto Central Avenue.

Joseph Griffin, age 12 at the time of the trial, testified that upon arriving at the   7
edge of the wooded path, where it exits onto Central Avenue, he observed Walter
Jr. turning his motorcycle around at the intersection of Central Avenue and Old
Haverstraw Road. Walter Jr. then drove west on Central Avenue, passing the
witness. After Walter Jr. passed the parked milk truck, he turned his motorcycle
around and proceeded east on Central Avenue. Jeffrey Costa was standing in the
path of the motorcycle, i.e., the area between the sand pile and the Vassallo's front
lawn. The motorcycle was "[c]lose" to and "about to run Jeffrey down," when the
infant plaintiff Michael ran off the sand pile and pushed his younger brother out
of the way. Michael pushed Jeffrey in the direction of the Vassallo's house. The
motorcycle then hit the infant plaintiff.

Jeffrey Costa, age nine at the time of the trial, testified that while standing   8
at the edge of the wooded path, he saw Walter Jr. drive past him, going east on
Central Avenue, toward Old Haverstraw Road. During this run, Walter Jr. did
one "wheelie." When Walter Jr. reached Old Haverstraw Road, he turned around
and proceeded to drive to the west end of Central Avenue, passing the children.
Walter Jr. stopped at the parked milk truck, turned around and drove east, back
toward Old Haverstraw Road. All the boys, including the witness, were standing
near the edge of the wooded path, but Jeffrey could not remember his brother
Michael's nor Joe Griffin's exact location. The witness recalled that his brother
began to run across Central Avenue toward the Vassallo's house when Walter
Jr.'s motorcycle was "stopped" near the milk truck. Jeffrey next saw the motorcycle collide with Michael at the edge of the Vassallo's yard during Walter Jr.'s
operation of the motorcycle in an easterly direction, toward Old Haverstraw
Road.

Michael Costa, the infant plaintiff, age 11 at the time of the trial, testified that   9
while standing on the sand pile on Central Avenue he saw Walter Jr. ride past him
on the motorcycle and do wheelies. He did not recall how many times Walter Jr.
drove past him, but it was more than once. The last thing he remembered was

seeing Walter Jr. drive around the parked milk truck, going west on Central Avenue. He did not see the motorcycle after it went around the milk truck, but he thought "it was on the other side." The next thing he recalled was waking up in a car on the way to the hospital.

Walter Hicks Jr., age 18 at the time of trial, a high school graduate and an auto mechanic, presented a different version of the events leading up to the collision. Although he admitted that he twice raised the front wheel of the motorcycle off the ground and dropped it while riding up and down Chester Avenue, he explained that he was not doing wheelies, but was checking the front wheel suspension after having changed the fork oil. He observed a number of children on the Plesach's lawn, but he did not have a conversation with them. He then drove through the wooded path to Central Avenue. He did not see any children following him; the motorcycle was not equipped with a rear view mirror. At the end of the wooded path, he drove west on Central Avenue, past the parked milk truck, to another wooded path which leads to the house of his friend, Doug Bull. He never turned east on Central Avenue to go toward Old Haverstraw Road, nor did he do wheelies on Central Avenue. Upon arriving at Bull's residence, he observed that his friend's van was not in the driveway so he proceeded to drive home, retracing his prior route. When he reached the parked milk truck on Central Avenue, he saw six or seven children playing in the sand pile. He did not slow down, but continued to proceed east along the path which ran between the sand pile and the Vassallo's front lawn, at a speed of approximately 10 to 15 miles per hour. When he was 10 feet from the sand pile, all the children started running in different directions. The infant plaintiff and his brother ran south, toward Vassallo's residence. While applying his back brakes, Walter Jr. turned south, off the path and onto the Vassallo's lawn. On the lawn, at the point approximately 10 feet from the edge of Central Avenue, the left handlebar of the motorcycle collided with the infant plaintiff's forehead. The motorcycle fell to the ground about three feet past the point of impact.

Whether defendant Walter Hicks, Jr. exercised reasonable care in operating the motorcycle under the circumstances of this case was dependent upon several factors, not the least important of which was speed.

Walter Jr. maintained that he was proceeding at 10 to 15 miles per hour. The credibility of this statement is suspect when evaluated in light of the testimony of plaintiffs' expert that the subject motorcycle was equipped with five gears, which enables it to accelerate to its maximum speed of 35 miles per hour over a shorter period of time and distance than the average motorcycle, and the statement of defendant Walter Jr., in his deposition, that the motorcycle was in fourth gear when the accident happened.

. . . The motorcycle was equipped with front and rear brakes, yet Walter Jr. applied only the rear brakes. Although a degree of skill is required to safely apply the front brakes of a motorcycle, he conceded that he had applied the front brakes on occasions prior to the accident. Expert testimony was elicited that the stopping distance could be reduced by half if both brakes were applied. The motorcycle came to rest three feet from the point of impact.

Moore v. Crumpton

Alice MOORE

v.

**John C. CRUMPTON, Carol Crumpton,
and John C. Crumpton, Jr.**

No. 76PA82.

Supreme Court of North Carolina.

Oct. 5, 1982.

The plaintiff brought this personal injury action against the defendant, John C. Crumpton, Jr. and his parents, the defendants John C. Crumpton and Carol Crumpton, alleging that John, Jr. had raped her during the early morning hours of 28 June 1978. On that date John, Jr. was 17 years old having been born on 19 October 1960. The plaintiff further alleged that the defendants John and Carol Crumpton knew or had reason to know that John, Jr. used drugs and was of a dangerous mental state and disposition which made it foreseeable that he would intentionally injure others unless reasonable steps were taken to supervise and control him. The plaintiff asserted that the defendants John C. Crumpton and Carol Crumpton had a legal duty to exercise reasonable care to control and supervise John, Jr. so as to prevent him from intentionally injuring others. She alleged that they failed to perform this duty, in that they failed to prevent John, Jr. from having access to and using illegal drugs and deadly weapons and failed to prevent him from going abroad alone at night after having used such drugs and after having gained possession of such deadly weapons. She further alleged that, as a proximate result of the negligence of the defendants John and Carol Crumpton, the defendant John C. Crumpton, Jr. broke into her home while under the influence of illegal drugs and repeatedly raped her by force and against her will after using a deadly weapon, a knife, to overcome her resistance. . . .

The . . . evidence of the parties established that John Crumpton, Jr. was one of five children of John and Carol Crumpton. John, Jr. was born with a club foot and was found during early childhood to have hypoglycemia, diabetes and ulcerative colitis. During his childhood and early adolescence, his family life was comfortable and secure. He went with his parents and grandparents on regular hunting, fishing and golfing activities as well as on frequent trips to the beach.

He began using marijuana and other controlled substances at an early age, however, and was a regular user of various controlled substances by the time he was thirteen years old. His parents were aware of his use of controlled substances and attempted by various methods to discourage his use of these illegal substances. John, Jr. continued the use of controlled substances, purchasing them at times with the allowance money his parents still gave him on an irregular basis and at times with money he earned from part-time jobs. During this period of his life, John, Jr. frequently argued with his parents and skipped school. He was once arrested for carrying a concealed knife. He also impregnated a young girl and apparently was hospitalized on one occasion for a drug overdose. Prior to the rape of the plaintiff, John, Jr. owned or was in possession of various hunting knives and guns given to him by his parents. Although his parents kept alcoholic beverages in the home, the pint of bourbon which John, Jr. drank on the night of the rape was apparently obtained at a friend's home.

During May of 1978, Carol Crumpton and John Crumpton separated and she   4 moved to a new address. By agreement of the couple, Carol Crumpton took their three youngest children to live with her, and John Crumpton had custody of John, Jr. and one other child of the marriage. On 28 June 1978, Carol Crumpton was on vacation at the beach. Sometime prior to that date, John Crumpton completed plans for a vacation for himself and the other child in Hawaii. Before leaving home, he made arrangements for John, Jr. to visit with grandparents in Roxboro. Apparently, after his father left Chapel Hill on vacation, John, Jr. drank a large amount of whiskey, took some type of controlled substances, got "high" and broke into the plaintiff's home on 28 June 1978 and raped her.

The forecasts of evidence of the parties also tended to indicate that the   5 defendants John and Carol Crumpton consulted a psychologist when John, Jr. was nine years old due to problems associated with his physical infirmities. They sought the help of school guidance counselors and various mental health professionals when John, Jr. was in junior high school and had developed academic and drug related problems. The parents made frequent attempts to discipline John, Jr. and to reason with him. They sent him to a private high school during the tenth grade in order to provide a change of environment, and he performed well there. They returned him to the private high school for the eleventh grade, but John, Jr. refused to stay and returned home early during that school year. John, Jr. and his parents went to numerous mental health professionals for counseling. In addition to this counseling, John, Jr. was treated by John A. Gorman, Ph.D., a clinical psychologist, and Landrum S. Tucker, M.D., a psychiatrist. Each of these men saw, diagnosed and treated John, Jr. on several occasions. Dr. Tucker saw John, Jr. on five occasions in January and February of 1978 and among other things reviewed his psychological testing. Both Dr. Gorman and Dr. Tucker indicated to the defendants John and Carol Crumpton that John, Jr. was not disposed toward violent or dangerous behavior and that he was not a person who should or could be involuntarily committed. Although both doctors indicated that John, Jr. would require continued treatment, he broke off his counseling with both of them. His parents could not or did not require him to return.

Reida v. Lund

■ ── ■

18 Cal.App.3d 698
William Eugene REIDA et al., Plaintiffs
and Appellants,

v.

Robert H. LUND et al., Defendants
and Respondents.
Civ. 36520.

Court of Appeal, Second District,
Division 2.

July 13, 1971.
Hearing Denied Sept. 8, 1971.

Michael Clark, aged 16, left his home in Long Beach shortly after 8 o'clock on the   1
evening of 24 April 1965, taking without permission a family automobile, credit
cards, and his father's 6.5 x 55 millimeter Swedish Mauser military rifle equipped
with telescopic sight. About 6 o'clock the following morning he stationed himself
near Santa Maria on a hill overlooking Highway 101 and began firing at passing
automobiles, as a consequence of which three persons were killed and others
seriously wounded. When the police moved in on his position, Michael put the
rifle to his head and killed himself.

William, Lucille, and Kim Reida, victims of Michael's shooting, brought this   2
action for personal injuries and wrongful death against Michael's estate and
against Forest Clark and Joyce Clark, Michael's parents. The complaint charged
the parents with negligence in the training, supervision, and control of Michael,
and negligence in marking firearms available to him. A summary judgment was
entered in favor of the Clarks, and the Reidas have appealed.

. . . Forest Clark was a Long Beach businessman, a veteran of two wars, an   3
active member of his church, and the father of three children, Michael, 16,
another son 15, and a daughter, 10. Michael, a student of average scholastic ability
in the eleventh grade at Woodrow Wilson High School, was friendly, quiet, neat, a
member of the Boy Scouts, and a member of the Sea Scouts. He liked music,
dances, and sports, and he played saxophone in the high school band. He got
along well with others, including his brother and sister. He regularly attended
church with his family, he did not use alcohol or drugs, he never displayed emotional instability, nor had he ever been in trouble with the school authorities, the
police, or the juvenile authorities. According to the father's declaration Michael
had never intentionally harmed anyone prior to the shootings. In 1961 Forest
Clark purchased a Mauser rifle and converted it into a hunting rifle with telescopic sight. On two occasions, the first on a rifle range and the second on a
hunting trip, he showed Michael how to operate the rifle. Together with a sack of

──────────

Reida v. Lund, 96 Cal. Rptr. 102 (1971).

steel-jacketed military ammunition, the rifle was stored in the garage in a locked cabinet to which there were two keys, one which was regularly kept in the father's dresser drawer in a location known to Michael, and the other which had disappeared earlier but whose whereabouts were known to the younger son. On the night of Michael's disappearance the father did not know the rifle had been taken, and he did not discover it until the morning of the shootings.

Joyce Clark, a housewife and school teacher, declared that to her knowledge her son Michael had been congenial, nonaggressive, and without emotional problems. He never intentionally injured any living thing and she could not explain why he had acted the way he had. She had not known the rifle was missing until after the shootings took place.   4

In opposition to the motion plaintiffs filed the declaration of a psychologist, who said he had read the Clark's declarations, the transcript of the coroner's inquest, and newspaper articles about the shootings. On the basis of his reading he concluded: that Michael suffered from schizophrenia, paranoid type; that the symptoms of this disease must have been apparent to the Clarks; that the Clarks knew or should have known that Michael was capable of violent, irrational acts and might use any weapon available to him; that their denials of such knowledge were inconsistent with Michael's behavior at Santa Maria and therefore incredible.   5

Plaintiffs' complaint in effect charged two kinds of negligence: (1) failure of the Clarks to train, control, and supervise Michael, and (2) failure of Forest Clark to keep the rifle out of Michael's hands.   6

■ California Civil Code ■

[California] *Civil Code* section 1714.1 subdivision (a) was amended in 1983 (Stats.1983, ch. 981. § 1), and now reads in full: "(a) Any act of willful misconduct of a minor which results in injury or death to another person or in any injury to the property of another shall be imputed to the parent or guardian having custody and control of the minor for all purposes of civil damages, and the parent or guardian having custody and control shall be jointly and severally liable with the minor for any damages resulting from the willful misconduct. [¶] The joint and several liability of the parent or guardian having custody and control of a minor under this subdivision shall not exceed ten thousand dollars ($10,000) for each tort of the minor, and in the case of injury to a person, imputed liability shall be further limited to medical, dental and hospital expenses incurred by the injured person, not to exceed ten thousand dollars ($10,000). The liability imposed by this section is in addition to any liability now imposed by law."   1

California Civil Code, 1714.1, 1714.3.

[California] *Civil Code* section 1714.3: . . . "Civil liability for any injury to the [2] person or property of another proximately caused by the discharge of a fire-arm by a minor under the age of 18 years shall be imputed to a parent or guardian having custody or control of the minor for all purposes of civil damages, and such parent or guardian shall be jointly and severally liable with such minor for any damages resulting from such act, if such parent or guardian either permitted the minor to have the firearm or left the firearm in a place accessible to the minor. [¶] The liability imposed by this section is in addition to any liability now imposed by law. However, no person, or group of persons collectively, shall incur liability under this section in any amount exceeding fifteen thousand dollars ($15,000) for injury to or death of one person as a result of any one occurrence or, subject to the limit as to one person, exceeding thirty thousand dollars ($30,000) for injury to or death of all persons as a result of any one such occurrence."

Robertson v. Wentz

187 Cal.App.3d 1281
Horace B. ROBERTSON, Plaintiff
and Appellant,
v.
Marilyn WENTZ, Defendant
and Respondent.
A029699.

Court of Appeal, First District,
Division 1.

Dec. 16, 1986.

On January 20, 1982, Roy Wentz, Jr. (hereafter Roy), then a minor, robbed a book- [1] store in San Lorenzo, and in the process shot and killed Renee Robertson. Roy was apparently under the influence of drugs at the time of the crimes. Appellant, who is Renee Robertson's surviving spouse, filed an action against respondent for wrongful death, based both upon her alleged negligence in controlling and supervising her minor son, and statutory violations. The dispute before us concerns the lower court's entry of summary judgment in favor of respondent on all causes of action.

Roy is the son of respondent [defendant] and Roy Wentz (hereinafter Roy, Sr. [2] or the father.) respondent and Roy, Sr. were married in 1957, and filed for divorce in May of 1976, The decree becoming final in March of 1978. The custody provision awarding respondent sole legal custody of Roy was never modified, and was in effect at the time of the shooting. Respondent was also awarded child support. Respondent remarried and moved to Middletown, California, in Napa Valley.

Roy lived with respondent after the divorce until 1979, when he moved in with his father in San Lorenzo. Between July and September of 1981, Roy resided with his employer, Gordon Sales. Then in September of 1981, Roy returned briefly to respondent's house in Middletown. Respondent received no child support payments during the time Roy lived with his father, or during the three months in 1981 when he again resided with her. In mid-January of 1982, Roy left respondent's house and recommenced living with his father. 3

Roy was introduced to guns early in life, receiving a .22 caliber weapon for his fifth birthday. However, as the record shows, his parents allowed him to actually hold the gun only after he had taken a safety course at about age 10. Respondent was aware that, by the time Roy moved back with her, he owned two rifles, a shotgun, and two pellet pistols. To respondent's knowledge, Roy had never misused the guns or demonstrated a propensity to do so. She believed him well-disciplined in the use of firearms. 4

Roy began drinking on a social basis and smoking marijuana at age 13. Respondent testified that she did not become aware of her son's drinking until 1981, when he was about 16 years old. She discovered his use of cocaine and marijuana in the summer of 1981, when it seemed that "every cent" he earned went for drugs supplied by his employer. In the summer of 1981, Roy asked respondent if he could move back in with her to "get away from the drugs, the booze, the whole thing." Respondent testified that neither she nor her present husband ever took any disciplinary action other than spending many hours counseling Roy about his problems and imposing strict rules upon him. 5

Respondent knew of only one disciplinary problem her son had at school: after discovering that he had not passed the GED exam (a high school equivalency test), Roy went to school "irate" and threw a cigarette on the school grounds; thereafter when Roy denied the vice principal's accusations, respondent was called in to discuss the boy's behavior. She was also aware of a single criminal incident, a misdemeanor arrest for possession of marijuana. Respondent spoke with her son about these incidents, but did not otherwise discipline him. 6

Respondent characterized Roy as an average student, very athletic, who played football and wrestled. She testified, however, that as her son approached 18 years, he became scared; "he was not prepared to go out and face the world." According to Respondent, Roy had no self-confidence. She perceived her son as "a 12 year-old boy in this great big grown-up body." 7

The shooting took place five days before Roy turned 18. The morning of the incident, respondent's daughter, Kelly, called her to say that Roy was coming back to Middletown to get his own apartment and go to school. Kelly was very upset and told respondent that Roy sounded "really weird;" she felt that "something was really wrong." Roy was highly intoxicated on hallucinogenic mushrooms and alcohol, and had taken his father's loaded .38 caliber special that morning from an unlocked bedside table drawer. Although respondent testified that she had reason to believe Roy's father kept guns in his house, she was not sure that he did so. She had never been to the home of Roy's father in San Lorenzo, and had not discussed his guns with her former husband prior to the shooting. 8

Roy's living arrangements at the time of the shooting are not entirely clear.   9
Roy felt that he was then residing with his mother, and merely visiting his father.
Respondent testified, however, that she and Roy, Sr. had agreed that their son was
to stay with his father, get counseling and possibly visit military recruitment
centers. She felt that Roy needed guidance and counseling. On January 15, 1982,
respondent had discovered Roy in bed with his 13 year-old girlfriend, and had
ejected him from the house. After Roy left, respondent called Roy, Sr. to tell him
their son was coming. Respondent knew of no immediate or long range plans for
her son to move back in with her.

• • • •

For Deliberation and Argument

1. In *Costa v. Hicks*, should the plaintiffs, Peter and Michael Costa, be able to
   recover damages from Walter Hicks, father of Walter Hicks, Jr., who unintentionally ran down young Michael with his motorcycle? (The boy suffered a
   fractured skull in the accident.) Keep in mind that the defendant in this case
   is not the driver of the motorcycle but rather his parent, who is being sued for
   negligence. Based on the law on parental liability, as outlined in the *Restatement of Torts*, Sec. 316, and on the case law in *Seifert v. Owen* (pp. 505–06),
   to what extent was the father negligent in failing "to exercise reasonable care
   so to control his minor child"? Did the father have reason to believe, based on
   his past experience, that his son might operate the motorcycle off his property, and should he have foreseen that his son might operate it in a way that
   might be dangerous to others? Cite evidence to support your views. You might
   also add what the elder Hicks could have done to reduce the possibility of
   such an accident.
2. You are on the jury of *Moore v. Crumpton*. How would you vote on the civil liability of John C. Crumpton and Carol Crumpton for negligence in controlling
   her son, who committed a rape? Consider each parent's liability separately.
   Apply the standards of the *Restatement of Torts*, Sec. 316 (pp. 505–06). How
   much did each parent know of John, Jr.'s violent propensities? What steps did
   each take to control him? To what extent should they have foreseen the crimes
   that their son committed? You may want to respond to a larger, not necessarily
   legal question: What could they have done, if anything, to prevent what had
   happened?
3. Based on the facts provided in *Reida v. Lund*, discuss the liability of each
   parent, Forest Clark and Joyce Clark, for "negligence in the training, supervision, and control of Michael, and negligence in making firearms available to
   him"? Apply the standards of the *Restatement of Torts*, Sec. 316 and in *Seifert
   v. Owen* (pp. 505–06). Also take into account sections 1714.1 and 1714.3 of the
   California Civil Code (following the facts of the case). To what extent did the
   Clarks have foreknowledge of their son's violent propensities? Did Forest
   Clark take adequate steps to secure his rifle and keep it out of the hands of his
   son? How do you assess the evidence provided by Michael's psychologist?

4. In *Robertson v. Wentz*, you are either an attorney for the plaintiff (Roy Robertson, husband of the deceased) or of the defendant (Marilyn Wentz, mother of Roy Wentz, the killer of Renee Robertson). As an attorney for the plaintiff, argue that the defendant is liable for negligence; or as an attorney for the defendant, argue that she is not liable. Use the *Restatement of Torts*, Sec. 316, and the California Civil Code, Secs. 1714.1 and 1714.3, as the applicable legal standards. Did the defendant have foreknowledge of her son's violent or destructive tendencies? Should she have foreseen that her son posed a risk to others? Was she in a position to exercise control? Did she have custody of her son? To what extent was the death of Renee Robertson a consequence, even if indirectly, of something that the defendant either did or failed to do? You may want to sharpen your discussion of this case by comparing it to *Reida v. Lund*—in particular, the extent to which the defendant had foreknowledge of her son's violent tendencies.

5. Based on your reading and discussion of the cases in this chapter, what do you think parents can do to prevent the kinds of damages and crimes illustrated here? To what extent should the law be a factor in enforcing parents' responsibility to control and supervise their children's activities? To what extent is it a good idea to allow victims and families of victims to sue the parents of minors who injure or kill others? In formulating your response, draw also on the opening article, "When the Sins of the Child Point to Parents, Law's Grip Is Tenuous."

6. Select one of the cases treated in this group. Imagine that you are representing either the plaintiff or the defendant. Compose either an opening statement or a closing argument for this case. Remember that your audience is the jury. Draw on the facts of the case in a way that is likely to have the greatest impact on the jury. Keep in mind, however, that jury members may turn against you—and your client—if they think that you are overly manipulating the facts, being deceptive, making exaggerated claims, or attempting too crudely to play on their emotions. For guidance on developing your statement, see "Models for the Opening Statement and the Closing Argument" at the end of Chapter 2. See also Larry S. Stewart's article, "Arguing Pain and Suffering Damages in Summation: How to Inspire Jurors" at the end of the Group 3 Readings in Chapter 3.

■ Aborted Crimes

Three people plan to rob a convenience store. They case the store a day in advance; they develop their plan for the robbery, the getaway, and the division of the proceeds. The morning of the planned robbery, however, one of the would-be robbers gets cold feet and decides to abandon the enterprise. Furious with him, the others nevertheless determine to proceed. The crime goes off as planned, but a day later the two robbers are caught. After the police interrogate them, the third man, the one who withdrew and took no part in the actual crime, is arrested and charged as an accomplice. Is he likely to be convicted?

Whether the third man has a strong "abandonment" or "withdrawal" defense depends on a number of factors. First, did he withdraw voluntarily

*from the planned enterprise and cease offering aid and advice? Involuntary
withdrawal, occasioned by the fear of being caught or the discovery by out-
siders of some elements of the planned crime, will generally vitiate a withdrawal defense. Second, did he* communicate *his plan to withdraw to his
confederates? Third, did he withdraw* in sufficient time *before the planned
crime to allow his confederates to also abandon the plan? In addition, many
courts will require the defendant who claims he withdrew to show that he did
everything possible to prevent the carrying out of the planned crime,
including, in some cases, notifying the police. Unlike the normal criminal
case, in which the burden is on the prosecution to show that the defendant
committed a crime, when a defense of abandonment is claimed, the burden is
on the defendant to show that he or she actually did withdraw from the crime.*

*The following cases allow you to consider whether defendants charged
either as principals or accomplices actually did withdraw from the crimes
they were contemplating.* Commonwealth v. Perry *and* Commonwealth v.
Mangula *deal with armed robbery.* May v. State *is about a drug deal.* People v.
Staples *is about the attempted burglary of a bank. The first case is followed by
some relevant case law and definitions.*

Commonwealth v. Perry

COMMONWEALTH
v.
Charles E. PERRY.

Supreme Judicial Court of Massachusetts,
Suffolk.

Argued March 2, 1970.
Decided April 2, 1970.

At 9:30 P.M. on November 6, 1968, Kempner and Salibe were working as clerks at   1
the Murray Kempner Company liquor store in the Dorchester district of Boston.
Three men entered the store. One of the men had a gun, and they robbed Kempner
of his wallet and some money and assaulted Salibe with the intent to rob him.
Both clerks testified that the defendant was not one of the three robbers who
entered the store, and that they had never seen him before.

The defendant did not testify. The only evidence relating to him was testimony   2
from a police sergeant who said that he arrested him on March 26, 1969, that he
"gave the defendant the warnings required by the Miranda Case," that "he advised
him of no other rights," and that the defendant then made a statement to him as
follows: On November 6, 1968, he was at the apartment of one Carlson on Beacon

---

Commonwealth v. Perry, 256 N.E.2d 745 (1970).
Cross references from original omitted.

Street in Boston, and that one Wiggins and Gary Murphy were also there. Wiggins and Murphy talked about holding up a liquor store later that night. Murphy had formerly been a truck driver in the area of the Kempner liquor store and he suggested that they hold up that store. They all agreed and they went to that area by public transit. The defendant had formerly lived with a sister in that area and on occasions he had made purchases at the Kempner store. In view of this he feared that he would be recognized. He therefore arranged with the other three that after the holdup they would pick him up at the Y.M.C.A. which was a block away from the store. He waited at the Y.M.C.A. for them, but they did not come. He then went to his home in Boston by the public transit system. Wiggins came to his home about 11 P.M. that evening. They discussed the holdup and Wiggins said they got no money from the store. Wiggins told him that Murphy stayed near the door with a gun and Carlson went to the register looking for money. Two or three days later the defendant met Carlson who also told him they got no money.

The police sergeant testified that the Y.M.C.A. was about 400 feet from the 3 entrance to the Kempner store. This was not a statement made by the defendant. There was no evidence whether the Y.M.C.A. was on the same street as the liquor store, or whether it was possible to see from one place to the other.

The motions for directed verdicts of not guilty raise the question whether 4 there was sufficient evidence of the defendant's guilt to warrant submission of the cases to the jury. Although each indictment charges the defendant as a principal, he could be convicted on proof that he was an accessory before the fact to the crimes charged.[1]

There was evidence that the defendant knew the three persons who 5 entered the liquor store and committed the robbery and assault, that he associated with them, and that he was in their company both before and after the robbery. . . .

There was also evidence that the defendant knew before the robbery and 6 assault that Carlson, Wiggins and Murphy were going to the liquor store to commit those crimes, and that he knew later that they had committed them. . . .

The Commonwealth's evidence . . . does not show that the defendant coun- 7 seled, hired or otherwise procured the three other persons to commit the robbery or the assault with intent to rob, or that he did any other act which would make him an accessory before the fact to such crimes. It appears that it was Murphy who counseled and procured the others to rob the liquor store. Moreover, the Commonwealth made no showing that there was an agreement for the defendant to stand by, at or near the scene of the crimes to render aid, assistance or encouragement to the perpetrators if it became necessary, or to assist them in making their escape from the scene. Finally, there was no showing that he was in any location or position where he could aid in any way in the commission of the

---

[1]General Laws c. 274, § 2, as amended by St. 1968, c. 206, § 1, approved April 30, 1968, reads: "Whoever aids in the commission of a felony, or is an accessory thereto before the fact by counselling, hiring or otherwise procuring such felony to be committed, shall be indicted, tried and punished as a principal."

crimes. He did not act as a lookout or decoy for the perpetrators of the crimes. He had no car or other means by which he could assist them to escape.

Case Law

With reference to the defense of withdrawal from the alleged conspiracy, the burden of establishing withdrawal is on the Defendant. In order for such defense to prevail, a Defendant must demonstrate some type of affirmative action which disavows or defeats the purpose of the conspiracy either by making a clean breast to the authorities or communication of the abandonment in a manner reasonably calculated to reach co-conspirators. A withdrawal defense requires that the abandonment be complete and in good faith. A withdrawal that is caused by a Defendant's fear of immediate apprehension is not a bona fide defense to the charge of conspiracy. (*United States v. Diaz*, 662 F.2d 713 (1981)) 1

The communication of intent to withdraw and not the naked fact of withdrawal determines whether one who advised, encouraged or incited another to commit a crime is to be released from liability as an accessory before the fact, and withdrawal must be such as to give his coconspirators a reasonable opportunity to follow his example and refrain from further action before act is committed, and it must be possible for trier of fact to say that accused had wholly and effectively detached himself from criminal enterprise before act with which he is charged is in process of consummation or has become so inevitable that it cannot reasonably be stayed. (*People v. Brown*, 186 N.E.2d 231 (1962)) 2

Our courts have come up with a variety of "tests" which try to distinguish acts of preparation from completed attempts. "The preparation consists in devising or arranging the means or measures necessary for the commission of the offense; the attempt is the direct movement toward the commission after the preparations are made." (*People v. Murray*, 14 Cal. 159 (1859)) 3

However, it would seem that the character of the abandonment in situations of this type, whether it be voluntary (prompted by pangs of conscience or a change of heart) or nonvoluntary (established by inference in the instant case), is not controlling. The relevant factor is the determination of whether the acts of the perpetrator have reached such a stage of advancement that they can be classified as an attempt. Once that attempt is found there can be no exculpatory abandonment. (*People v. Claborn*, 224 Cal.App.2d 38, 41 (1964)) 4

One of the purposes of the criminal law is to protect society from those who intend to injure it. When it is established that the defendant intended to commit a specific crime and that in carrying out this intention he committed an act that caused harm or sufficient danger of harm, it is immaterial that for some collateral reason he could not complete the intended crime. (*People v. Camodeca*, 338 P.2d 903, 906 (1959)) 5

Mere knowledge that a crime is to be committed, even when coupled with subsequent concealment of the completed crime, does not make one guilty as an 6 accessory before the fact or as a principal to the crime about which he has knowledge.(*Commonwealth v. Perry*, 256 N.W.2d 745 (1970))

A defendant who agrees with other persons to commit a crime and does [7] nothing more is guilty of criminal conspiracy, but that alone does not make him an accessory before the fact or a principal to the substantive crime which was objective of the conspiracy. (*Commonwealth v. Perry*, 256 N.E.2d 745 (1970))

In order to convict as a principal in the second degree, it must be proved, that [8] accused was in a situation in which he might render assistance by agreement with perpetrator of crime or with his previous knowledge, consenting to crime, and for purpose of rendering aid and encouragement in commission of it. (*Commonwealth v. Mangula*, 322 N.E.2d 177 (1975))

Guilt of accessory accused of crime other than felony murder is established [9] when it is shown that he intentionally assisted principal in commission of crime and that he did this, sharing with the principal the mental state required for crime; however, it is sufficient if accomplice possesses conditional or contingent intent, i. e. a willingness to see some action occur should it become necessary to effectuate plan. (*Commonwealth v. Mangula*, 322 N.E.2d 177 (1975))

Aiding and abetting requires that person undertake conduct, either verbal or [10] overt action, which as a matter of objective fact aids another person in execution of a crime, and that he consciously desires or intends that his conduct will yield such assistance. (*May v. State*, 293 N.W.2d 478 (1980))

If a person is not a party to a crime as a conspirator, either because he never [11] conspired or because prior to its commission he withdrew from the conspiracy, he is still a party to the crime if he either directly commits it or if he intentionally aids and abets in its commission. (*May v. State*, 293 N.W.2d 478 (1980))

Commonwealth v. Mangula

COMMONWEALTH
v.
Antonio MANGULA.

Appeals Court of Massachusetts, Middlesex.

Argued May 20, 1974.
Decided Jan. 17, 1975.

One of two principal witnesses for the Commonwealth was Judy Varoski, who [1] described the circumstances of the robbery in which the defendant was allegedly involved. Varoski testified that, on April 21, 1971, while visiting Peter Kyriazopoulos (the eventual victim) at his apartment in Lowell, she was shown five $1,000 bills belonging to Kyriazopoulos.

The next morning, Varoski received a telephone call from one Luis Alvarez,   2
who told her that he needed money for a friend named Luis Perez. As a result of this conversation, Alvarez, accompanied by Perez and his friend "Tony" Mangula, the defendant on this appeal, joined together with Varoski and proceeded to downtown Lowell in Perez's car in order to find Kyriazopoulos at the place where he worked.

During the ride to Lowell, Perez asked Varoski if she was sure there was   3
money at Kyriazopoulos' apartment. Unable to find Kyriazopoulos, they drove to his apartment. Varoski took Alvarez into the apartment building to show him in which apartment Kyriazopoulos lived.

When they returned, Varoski noticed the defendant and Perez standing   4
together beside the car. She observed that Perez had a rifle in his possession. Perez said he wanted to shoot the locks off the window of Kyriazopoulos' apartment. The defendant then offered to break the window in order to gain access to the apartment and to secure the money. This plan was opposed by Varoski and Alvarez, and no further action was taken at that time. The four of them got back into the car and continued their search for Kyriazopoulos.

In the car, another conversation ensued in which Varoski said she would get   5
Kyriazopoulos out of his apartment by 5:00 P.M. that afternoon and told the others that she had given Perez Kyriazopoulos' telephone number to call to make sure he was not at home. They were then to break into the apartment.

During the course of that afternoon and evening, Varoski made continuous   6
telephone calls to Kyriazopoulos' apartment but was unable to reach him. She did not however, call Perez to tell him she was unable to contact Kyriazopoulos.

Alvarez also testified concerning the events leading up to the crime and the   7
crime itself. After talking with Varoski on the morning of April 22, Alvarez went to see Perez and the defendant. In the presence of the defendant, Alvarez told Perez about the money at Kyriazopoulos' apartment and that Varoski knew where it was.

At the trial Alvarez essentially corroborated Varoski's testimony concerning   8
the conversations in Perez's car and outside the car at Kyriazopoulos' apartment.

In the afternoon, Alvarez and the defendant entered a car which Perez was   9
driving. Alvarez sat in the front seat and the defendant in the back seat. Alvarez noticed a rifle behind the defendant's head in the back seat.

At about 4:30 P.M. they parked at Kyriazopoulos' apartment building. Alvarez   10
and Perez then got out of the car and proceeded to the apartment building, but the defendant remained in the car. Perez went straight to the building door and opened it. Alvarez went past him into the building. Alvarez testified he did not see Perez with the rifle at that point. When Perez later rushed by Alvarez into the apartment "he had a gun with him." Alvarez recounted the circumstances of the robbery and the shooting of Kyriazopoulos by Perez.

Alvarez testified that when he ran from the apartment building the defendant   11
was sitting in the back seat of the car on the driver's side with the door open.

Upon reaching the car, Alvarez threw a bank book containing $1,000 bills at the defendant and told him that the money was "fake" and that Perez had shot Kyriazopoulos. Perez returned four or five minutes later and gave the rifle to the defendant, who replaced it on the back window shelf. The defendant also received items taken from the apartment by Perez.

Lillian Oates, a girlfriend of the defendant, testified that "some time later" the defendant told her that he was inside the car and not in Kyriazopoulos' apartment at the time of the robbery. Oates also testified that on the day after the crime she and the defendant accompanied Luis Perez to New Hampshire and then to New York. 12

The defendant, although charged as a principal, was in theory being charged as an accomplice or principal in the second degree.[1] The Commonwealth has proceeded on the theory that the defendant was engaged in a joint enterprise and is therefore criminally liable for the armed robbery which occurred. The defendant concedes that there may have been a joint enterprise but argues that the very essence of the common design was to avoid confronting the eventual victim. He therefore argues that while the joint enterprise might have included a plan to break into the apartment and commit larceny, it did not extend to the commission of armed robbery. 13

May v. State

■ ─── ■

97 Wis.2d 175
Charles MAY, Plaintiff in
error-Petitioner,
v.
STATE of Wisconsin, Defendant
in error.

No. 77-853-CR.

Supreme Court of Wisconsin.

Argued June 4, 1980.
Decided June 27, 1980.

At the time of the incident which is the basis of the instant prosecution, Charles May, the petitioner (hereinafter defendant), and Cheryl Olson were living together in an apartment in Madison, Wisconsin. Both had prior criminal records, each was receiving some public assistance, and May was on parole. 1

---

[1] In order to convict as a principal in the second degree "[i]t must be proved, that he was in . . . a situation [in which he might render assistance] by agreement with the perpetrator of the crime, or with his previous knowledge, consenting to the crime, and for the purpose of rendering aid and encouragement in the commission of it." *Commonwealth v. Knapp*, 9 Pick. 495, 517 (1830). To be in a position where one might have given aid is sufficient.
May v. State, 293 N.W.2d 478 (1978).

Leon Dandurand, a Madison police officer who worked as an undercover narcotics agent, testified that on May 4, 1977, he went to the apartment occupied by the defendant and Olson to purchase "speed," an amphetamine. He was accompanied by an informant who was an acquaintance of the defendant and who introduced him to the defendant. Dandurand told the defendant he wanted to look at whatever he had. The defendant went to the kitchen cupboard, took out a plastic container and showed Dandurand a quantity of capsules which he said were "speed." The defendant said they were $2 apiece and asked Dandurand how many he wanted. Dandurand said five and gave the defendant $10 for them. He asked whether the capsules were of good quality, and the defendant said that they were "okay," but that in a couple of days he would have a quantity of "black cadillacs," which are a stronger form of "speed." Dandurand asked if he could stop by in a couple of days. The defendant indicated that he could and that if he had the "black cadillacs," they could make a deal. Olson was in the living room watching TV while this transaction occurred.   2

Two days later, on May 6th, Dandurand went to the apartment at about 7 p.m. He was admitted to the apartment by Olson and he asked her if the "black cadillacs" which he had discussed with the defendant had arrived. She indicated that she knew nothing about them and that he should contact the defendant who would probably be back within an hour.   3

Dandurand left and returned to his office. At approximately 8:10 p.m. he telephoned the apartment. Olson answered the phone and Dandurand asked if the defendant was there. When the defendant came to the phone, Dandurand asked him if he had the "black cadillacs," and the defendant said he did, but that he only had ten of them. The defendant said that the price was $3.50 apiece and that Dandurand could come over and get them.   4

Dandurand arrived at the apartment at 8:24 p.m. Olson let him in and he said he was the person interested in the "black cadillacs." She went to the kitchen cupboard and got a plastic container in which there were capsules of various colors. The defendant at this time was in the living room talking to a man. Olson showed the capsules to Dandurand and he said he was only interested in the "black cadillacs" and wanted ten of them. She took the black capsules from the container, wrapped them in plastic wrap and gave them to Dandurand, who gave her $35. They discussed the possibility of future drug deals and Dandurand left.   5

The black capsules were subsequently examined by a chemist and were found to contain amphetamine.   6

As a result of the transaction on May 6, 1977, both the defendant and Olson were charged with being parties to the crime of delivering a controlled substance. Olson pleaded guilty to the charge. She testified that she and the defendant had a close relationship and lived together intermittently for about one and a half years. She sold "speed" and other controlled substances and the defendant assisted her in so doing by directing people to her. On May 4, 1977, just prior to the first transaction with Dandurand, Olson told the defendant that he should attempt to sell what she believed to be cold capsules as "something else" because she needed the money. She was present in the apartment during the transaction with Dandurand   7 and the proceeds of the sale were given to her by the defendant. The defendant told her that Dandurand was interested in different types of "speed" and wanted "cadillacs." She told the defendant that she would try to obtain some in the next couple of days and did so on May 5th. After the defendant completed his telephone conversation with Dandurand on May 6, 1977, for the second transaction, the defendant told her that he suspected a police "set-up" and wanted nothing to do with Dandurand when he came over and advised her to do the same. Her financial needs were such, however, that she was not concerned about the possibility of her criminal involvement.

The defendant testified that he would from time to time facilitate transactions   8
between Olson and persons who were interested in buying "speed." He was a seller of marijuana and his customers would ask him if he knew where they could get "speed"; he would tell Olson he had a customer for her and would sell her "speed" to his customers on her behalf. Immediately after the May 6th telephone conversation with Dandurand, the defendant changed his mind about delivering the amphetamine to Dandurand. He told Olson that she should abandon the sale because he believed the caller was a police officer. The defendant said he was not going to have anything to do with the delivery. He was present when Dandurand arrived, but did not attempt to involve himself in the delivery and received nothing from the transaction. Olson also so testified.

People v. Staples

6 Cal.App.3d 61
The PEOPLE of the State of California,
Plaintiff and Respondent,
v.
Edmund Beauelore STAPLES, Defendant
and Appellant.

Cr. 15693.

Court of Appeal, Second District,
Division 5.

March 27, 1970.
Hearing Denied May 21, 1970.

I. The Facts

In October 1967, while his wife was away on a trip, defendant, a mathematician,   1
under an assumed name, rented an office on the second floor of a building in Hollywood which was over the mezzanine of a bank. Directly below the mezzanine

---

People v. Staples, 85 Cal. Rptr. 599 (1970).

was the vault of the bank. Defendant was aware of the layout of the building, specificially of the relation of the office he rented to the bank vault. Defendant paid rent for the period from October 23 to November 23. The landlord had 10 days before commencement of the rental period within which to finish some interior repairs and painting. During this prerental period defendant brought into the office certain equipment. This included drilling tools, two acetylene gas tanks, a blow torch, a blanket, and a linoleum rug. The landlord observed these items when he came in from time to time to see how the repair work was progressing. Defendant learned from a custodian that no one was in the building on Saturdays. On Saturday, October 14, defendant drilled two groups of holes into the floor of the office above the mezzanine room. He stopped drilling before the holes went through the floor. He came back to the office several times thinking he might slowly drill down, covering the holes with the lineoleum rug.[1] At some point in time he installed a hasp lock on a closet, and planned to, or did, place his tools in it. However, he left the closet keys on the premises. Around the end of November, apparently after November 23, the landlord notified the police and turned the tools and equipment over to them. Defendant did not pay any more rent. It is not clear when he last entered the office, but it could have been after November 23, and even after the landlord had removed the equipment. On February 22, 1968, the police arrested defendant. After receiving advice as to his constitutional rights, defendant voluntarily made an oral statement which he reduced to writing.

Among other things which defendant wrote down were these:

> Saturday, the 14th . . . I drilled some small holes in the floor of the room. Because of tiredness, fear, and the implications of what I was doing, I stopped and went to sleep.
>
> At this point I think my motives began to change. The actutal [sic] commencement of my plan made me begin to realize that even if I were to succeed a fugitive life of living off of stolen money would not give the enjoyment of the life of a mathematician however humble a job I might have.
>
> I still had not given up my plan however. I felt I had made a certain investment of time, money, effort and a certain psychological commitment to the concept.
>
> I came back several times thinking I might store the tools in the closet and slowly drill down (covering the hole with a rug of linoleum square). As time went on (after two weeks or so). My wife came back and my life as bank robber seemed more and more absurd.

II. Discussion of Defendent's Contentions

Defendant's position in this appeal is that, as a matter of law, there was insufficient evidence upon which to convict him of a criminal attempt under Penal Code section 664 [see p. 527]. Defendant claims that his actions were all preparatory in

---

[1] This is defendant's characterization of what occurred after his initial drilling session.

nature and never reached a stage of advancement in relation to the substantive crime which he concededly intended to commit (burglary of the bank vault) so that criminal responsibility might attach.

In order for the prosecution to prove that defendant committed an attempt to burglarize as proscribed by Penal Code section 664, it was required to establish that he had the specific intent to commit a burglary of the bank and that his acts toward that goal went beyond mere preparation.   4

Defendant relies heavily on the following language: "Preparation alone is not enough [to convict for an attempt], there must be some appreciable fragment of the crime committed, *it must be in such progress that it will be consummated unless interrupted by circumstances independent of the will of the attempter*, and the act must not be equivocal in nature." (Italics added.) (*People v. Buffum*, *supra*, 40 Cal.2d 709, 718, 256 P.2d 317, 321.) Defendant argues that while the facts show that he did do a series of acts directed at the commission of a burglary—renting the office, bringing in elaborate equipment and actually starting drilling—the facts do not show that he was interrupted by any outside circumstances. Without such interruption and a voluntary desistence on his part, defendant concludes that under the above stated test, he has not legally committed an attempt. The attorney general has replied that even if the above test is appropriate, the trial judge, obviously drawing reasonable inferences, found that defendant was interrupted by outside circumstances—the landlord's acts of discovering the burglary equipment, resuming control over the premises, and calling the police.   5

California Penal Code

Section 459. Every person who enters any house, room, apartment, tenement, shop, warehouse, store, mill, barn, stable, outhouse or other building, tent, vessel, . . . floating home, . . . railroad car, locked or sealed cargo container, whether or not mounted on a vehicle, trailer coach, . . . any house car . . . inhabited camper, . . . vehicle . . . when the doors are locked, aircraft . . . or mine or any underground portion thereof, with intent to commit grand or petit larceny or any felony is guilty of burglary . . .   1

Section 664. Every person who attempts to commit any crime, but fails, or is prevented or intercepted in the perpetration thereof, is punishable.   2

● ● ● ●

For Deliberation and Argument

1. Should Charles Perry, the defendant in *Commonwealth v. Perry*, be found guilty of being an accomplice to robbery? Or does the fact that he was a block away from the crime free him from legal responsibility? Did he, in fact, abandon or withdraw from the criminal enterprise carried out by

Wiggins, Murphy, and Carlson? Apply the case law, as well as the information in the chapter headnote (pp. 517–18), to the facts of this case. Use IRAC format.

2. Imagine that you are a prosecutor trying "Tony" Mangula, the defendant in *Commonwealth v. Mangula*. Argue in IRAC format why he should be convicted of being an accomplice to robbery. Compare and contrast the defendant in this case with the defendant in *Commonwealth v. Perry*. Pay particular attention to the narrative's final paragraph, where both the prosecution's (the Commonwealth's) and the defense's theory of Mangula's liability or lack of liability for this crime are explained. To what extent does the evidence show that Mangula intended only to participate in a burglary (a break-in of a building), rather than an armed robbery? To what extent does it show that he was an accomplice to armed robbery?

3. In *May v. State*, does the evidence show that Charles May had abandoned his participation in the drug purchase before the crime actually occurred? Keep in mind that his admission to selling marijuana has nothing to do, legally, with this particular crime, which involves amphetamine. May argues that he took no part in the transaction, having withdrawn in advance from this particular criminal enterprise. The prosecution contends that he acted as an accomplice to Olson. Whose case is more persuasive, and why?

4. If you were on the jury in *People v. Staples*, would you vote to convict the defendant of attempted burglary? Study the narrative's final paragraph, which highlights the differences between the crux of the defense's case and that of the prosecution. How do you interpret the quoted *People v. Buffum* opinion as it relates to *Staples*? Of course, the crucial question is this: Should Staples's actions be legally considered an "attempt"? If you do not believe that his actions constituted a legal attempt, then how much further would he have had to proceed in his plans before you would vote to convict? Develop your response in IRAC format.

5. Leaving aside the matter of the legal culpability of the defendants in this chapter, how do you assess their *moral* responsibility for the actions they took? Focus on one or (for contrast) two individuals and weigh their activities and decisions against an ethical standard of your own devising.

6. Select one of the cases treated in this group. Imagine that you are representing either the plaintiff or the defendant. Compose either an opening statement or a closing argument for this case. Remember that your audience is the jury. Draw on the facts of the case in a way that is likely to have the greatest impact on the jury. Keep in mind, however, that jury members may turn against you—and your client—if they think that you are overly manipulating the facts, being deceptive, making exaggerated claims, or attempting too crudely to play on their emotions. For guidance on developing your statement, see "Models for the Opening Statement and the Closing Argument" at the end of Chapter 2.

■ High School Sports Injuries

In 1953 a high school football player from Nyssa, Oregon, was paralyzed after being tackled by two players on the opposing team. His parents sued the school district. They won, but the judgment was reversed on appeal.[1] The case, of course, is tragic. But it raises a familiar question: Should the law have been involved at all in a situation that was clearly an accident?

Two sometimes conflicting principles are at work here. On the one hand, there's the principle of assumption of risk. *People who freely choose to engage in a potentially dangerous activity like high school football—or, for that matter, skiing, scuba diving, or skydiving—should be aware of the dangers inherent in the sport. In engaging in the activity regardless of the known hazards, they take on themselves a degree of risk. There are inherent risks in all athletic activities—anyone playing football has to expect a few scrapes and bruises—and no degree of vigilant care on the part of those responsible for supervising the activity can eliminate such inherent risks.*

On the other hand, there's the principle of negligence—*embodied in many lawsuits. Negligence has been defined as "doing something which an ordinary, prudent person would not have done under similar circumstances or in failing to do something which an ordinary, prudent person would have done under similar circumstances."[2] Participants in an athletic activity are only required to assume the risks of known dangers: They are not expected to assume the risk of negligence on the part of those responsible for supervising the activity. Negligence might be manifested in unsafe facilities or equipment or in inadequate coaching or supervision. Also, whether or not the degree of supervision was negligent depends on the age and experience of the participants: Ten-year-old Little Leaguers will need more supervision than college football players. In attempting to rebut charges of negligence, defendants will often claim* contributory negligence *on the part of student athletes—negligence by the plaintiff that is partially responsible for the injury.*

This section allows you to consider questions on negligence as they relate to four cases: Whipple v. Salvation Army *(football)*, Grant v. Lake Oswego School District *(springboard)*, Clary v. Alexander Country Board of Education *(windsprints in basketball practice)*, and Lynch v. Board of Education of Collinsville Community Unit School District *(women's "powerpuff" football). The chapter also includes statements on the law as it relates to negligence and assumption of risk.*

---

[1] *Vendrell v. Malheur County School District*, 376 P.2d 406 (1962).
[2] *Brahatcek v. Millar School District*, 273 N.W.2d at 681 (1979).

Whipple v. Salvation Army

Robert P. WHIPPLE, Jr., by and through his guardian ad litem, Robert P. Whipple, Appellant,
v.
The SALVATION ARMY, a California corporation, Respondant.

Supreme Court of Oregon, In Banc.

Argued and Submitted Nov. 2, 1971.
Decided April 4, 1972.

Plaintiff was a 15-year-old boy participating in the Salvation Army Boys Club   1
youth program conducted by defendant in the city of Medford. The defendant
employed a Mr. Gene Reagan as supervisor of the group's activities. Reagan took
a group of club members, including plaintiff, to a park and there initiated a game
of tackle football between the boys who had divided themselves into two teams.
Reagan acted as quarterback for both teams. During the course of the game he
sent plaintiff downfield and threw him a pass. Plaintiff jumped, caught the ball,
and he was almost immediately tackled, receiving a wrenched or torn knee carti-
lage from which he suffered residual difficulty.

Plaintiff claims . . . there was evidence that Reagan did not use a whistle to   2
stop the play, and that the resulting "piling on" contributed to plaintiff's injury.
Plaintiff's testimony concerning the manner of his injury was as follows:

"Q. Can you describe for the jury what happened when you were injured, Bob?
"A. Well, I went out for a pass. Gene [Reagan] told me to go out. Stand by the
goal. Gene threw the ball. I was fairly clear. It was kind of high so I jumped
up for it. When I got the ball I think I got hit and fell to the ground. Somebody
hit me from behind.
"Q. Now—
"A. Then I fell to the ground and *then somebody hit me from [the] front before I
hit the ground. A bunch.* When it was all over there was a bunch of kids on
top of me.
"Q. Now, when you were first hit where were you hit?
"A. From behind.
"Q. And then what happened?
"A. Well, then somebody hit me from the front and I hit the ground.
"Q. How did you fall when you fell down?
"A. Well, the back of me.

Whipple v. Salvation Army, 495 P.2d 739 (1972).

"Q. You fell on your back?

"A. Well, not first. I hit my backside. You know my—

"Q. Where were your legs?

"A. Oh, about the side of me. You know. I was kind of cockeyed.

"Q. Did anybody else fall on your legs?

"A. Yes.

"Q. Do you know when in this procedure you were hurt?

"A. Well, the first time I knew I was hurt was when I was hit from behind.

"Q. And did it hurt later as other people were piling on you?

"A. Yes, sir." . . .

"Q. And in fact, this particular tackle on this October 23rd, except for your being injured, wasn't really anything unusual except you got hurt?

"A. Except for the people piling on top of me.

"Q. Okay. But as I understand your testimony, you got hurt when you were hit, while you were still in the air?

"A. Yes.

"Q. When the first guy hit you, is that true?

"A. Yes, that is true.

"Q. And that's when you received the injury is when the first guy hit you?

"A. Yes.

"Q. So, the piling on and that, you'd already been injured by then?

"A. Yes, The piling on hurt it even more." (Emphasis ours.)

Despite this testimony, when the piling on occurred remains unclear. Was plaintiff piled upon *after* he had been brought to the ground, or *as he fell* to the ground because several of the boys tackled him almost simultaneously? The following testimony of one of the boys who tackled the plaintiff suggests the latter:

"Q. Okay. Were you one of the boys that tackled Bob?

"A. Yes.

"Q. Do you recall where you tackled him; in other words, what part of your body did you come in contact

"A. About the thighs.

"Q. Pardon me?

"A. About the thighs.

"Q. In what position from him; front, back or what?

"A. In the side.

"Q. Okay. Had he caught the ball?

"A. Yes.

"Q. And did anybody else tackle him?

"A. Yes.

"Q. Do you recall who else tackled him?

"A. Billy Meadows, Roger Ricker and Frank Arnold." . . .

"Q. Did he [Reagan] ever blow a whistle at any time to stop people from piling on?

"A. Not that I know.

"Q. Did he blow any whistle to stop people from piling on Bob after Bob was knocked down?

"A. No. He just ran over there and got us, took, told us to get off.

"Q. There were a bunch of you laying on him, is that right?

"A. About four.

"Q. Could there have been more than four?

"A. The rest of them were all out in the field. Just four of us on top of him.

"Q. The rest of them were gathered around him?

"A. No. The rest of them were scattered out in the field, blocking each other." . . .

"Q. Who were the ones that piled on after he was down?

"A. *Well, nobody actually went on top of him. We were all angling onto him from all sides.*

"Q. Well, did two of you tackle him and then the other two come as he was down. Is that what happened?

"A. Well, like one hits him and the other two or three, whatever it was, come in right after Frank Arnold hit him in front." (Emphasis ours.)

The only other boy who participated in the particular incident and who gave 4 evidence in the case also testified that four boys had tackled plaintiff.

Plaintiff's younger brother, who saw the incident in question, testified as 5 follows:

"A. Well, my brother went out for a pass and, and the boy threw it and then these two boys from each side hit him.

"Q. Then did anybody else then fall on him after that?

"A. Yes.

"Q. How many other people, do you know?

"A. About 10 or 15.

"Q. Several of the other people fell on him?

"A. Yes.

"Q. Do you know how many, really?

"A. No.

"Q. Did you hear any whistle of any kind? Answer out loud.

"A. No."

As is evident, this witness finally decided he did not know how many boys were on plaintiff, nor did he ever say that anyone piled on his brother *after he was down.* He testified only that others "fell" on plaintiff after he was hit on each side. The ages of all of the boys involved in the game were not given; however, it is known that plaintiff was fifteen, whereas the two witnesses who had helped make the tackle were only ten and twelve years of age. It is not surprising that it would take more than one of these boys to bring plaintiff down.

Plaintiff alleged negligence against defendant in the following particulars: 6

> "1. It allowed plaintiff and other boys playing in said football game to play tackle football without adequate calisthenics, physical exercise and preparation for said playing of tackle football.
>
> "2. It allowed plaintiff and other boys playing in said football game to play such football without adequate uniforms or equipment.
>
> "3. It allowed the playing of tackle football without adequate refereeing or supervision.
>
> "4. It encouraged and allowed untrained boys at an excessively early age, without adequate preparation and training for such a sport, to play tackle football. That these young and inexperienced boys included plaintiff herein."

Defendant's duty can be treated in the context of assumption of risk in its 7 primary sense. Plaintiff correctly contends that because there is an inherent danger of injury in football, defendant did owe him a duty not to allow or encourage him to play unless plaintiff realized the danger involved.

Plaintiff testified as follows: 8

"Q. And, in other words, you'd be involved in tackling and being tackled all this particular year and the year before?

"A. Yes, sir.

"Q. And it was the same type of tackling that had been going on?

"A. Yes.

"Q. Now, were you aware that you might get hurt in tackling or getting tackled?

"A. I didn't think I'd get hurt very bad.

"Q. But you knew you could get hurt?

"A. Probably get a scraped elbow or maybe get kicked in the nose. Something like that.

"Q. Or the knees or bumps and bruises?

"A. I never thought I'd get my knee twisted out of place, no, sir.

"Q. But you at least knew that you could get hurt in playing tackle football?

"A. You could get hurt, yes.

"Q. And even though you knew this you enjoyed playing and continued to play?

"A. Yes. Because I didn't think I'd get hurt that bad.

"Q. It was just a question of how bad you could get hurt that you hadn't considered?

"A. Yes.

"Q. But you knew you could get hurt?

"A. I could get a little scrape and get hurt falling down on the ground."

Statements of Law on Assumption of Risk, Negligence

Assumption of Risk

[T]he common law, . . . proceeding from the people and asserting their liberties, naturally regards the freedom of individual action as the keystone of the whole structure. Each individual is left free to work out his own destinies; he must not be interfered with from without, but in the absence of such interference he is held competent to protect himself. While therefore protecting him from external violence, from imposition and from coercion, the common law does not assume to protect him from the effects of his own personality and from the consequences of his voluntary actions or of his careless misconduct. (Bohlen, "Voluntary Assumption of Risk," 20 *Harv.L.Rev.* 14 (1906))   1

Voluntary participants in lawful games, sports, and even roughhouse, assume the risk of injury at the hands of their fellow participants (and of course of 'hurting themselves'), so long as the game is played in good faith and without negligence. . . . (Harper and James, *The Law of Torts*, § 21.5, page 1181)   2

. . . Those who participate or sit as spectators at sports and amusements assume all the obvious risks of being hurt by roller coasters, flying balls, fireworks, explosions, or the struggles of the contestants. The timorous may stay at home. . . . (*Prosser on Torts*, page 307)   3

Assumption of Risk from *Restatement of the Law, Second: Torts, 2nd*

§ 496 A, comment c, 1–4:

1. In its simplest form, assumption of risk means that the plaintiff has given his express consent to relieve the defendant of an obligation to exercise care for his protection, and agrees to take his chances as to injury from a known or possible risk. The result is that the defendant, who would otherwise be under a duty to exercise such care, is relieved of that responsibility, and is no longer under any duty to protect the plaintiff.   4

2. A second, and closely related, meaning is that the plaintiff has entered voluntarily into some relation with the defendant which he knows to involve the risk, and so is regarded as tacitly or impliedly agreeing to relieve the defendant of responsibility, and to take his own chances. Thus a spectator entering a baseball park may be regarded as consenting that the players may proceed with the game   5

Restatement of the Law, Second: Torts, 2nd. As Adapted and promulgated by the American Law Institute, Washington, D.C. May 25, 1963, and May 22, 1964. St. Paul, MN: West Publishing, 1965.

without taking precautions to protect him from being hit by the ball. Again the legal result is that the defendant is relieved of his duty to the plaintiff.

3. In a third type of situation the plaintiff, aware of a risk created by the negligence of the defendant, proceeds or continues voluntarily to encounter it. For example, an independent contractor who finds that he has been furnished by his employer with a machine which is in dangerous condition, and that the employer, after notice, has failed to repair it or to substitute another, may continue to work with the machine. He may not be negligent in doing so, since his decision may be an entirely reasonable one, because the risk is relatively slight in comparison with the utility of his own conduct; and he may even act with unusual caution because he is aware of the danger. The same policy of the common law which denies recovery to one who expressly consents to accept a risk will, however, prevent his recovery in such a case.

4. To be distinguished from these three situations is the fourth, in which the plaintiff's conduct in voluntarily encountering a known risk is itself unreasonable, and amounts to contributory negligence. There is thus negligence on the part of both plaintiff and defendant; and the plaintiff is barred from recovery, not only by his implied consent to accept the risk, but also by the policy of the law which refuses to allow him to impose upon the defendant a loss for which his own negligence was in part responsible.

§ 496 D. *Knowledge and Appreciation of Risk.* Except where he expressly so agrees, a plaintiff does not assume a risk of harm arising from the defendant's conduct unless he then knows of the existence of the risk and appreciates its unreasonable character.

Comment:

. . . b. The basis of assumption of risk is the plaintiff's consent to accept the risk and look out for himself. Therefore he will not be found, in the absence of an express agreement which is clearly so to be construed, to assume any risk unless he has knowledge of its existence. This means that he must not only be aware of the facts which create the danger, *but must also appreciate the danger itself and the nature, character, and extent which make it unreasonable.* Thus the condition of premises upon which he enters may be quite apparent to him, but the danger arising from the condition may be neither known nor apparent, or, if known or apparent at all, it may appear to him to be so slight as to be negligible. In such a case the plaintiff does not assume the risk. His failure to exercise due care either to discover or to understand the danger is not properly a matter of assumption of risk, but of the defense of contributory negligence.

c. *The standard to be applied is a subjective one*, of what the particular plaintiff in fact sees, knows, understands and appreciates. In this it differs from the objective standard which is applied to contributory negligence. . . . *If by reason of age, or lack of information, experience, intelligence, or judgment, the plaintiff does not understand the risk involved in a known situation; he will not be taken to assume the risk*, although it may still be found that his conduct is contributory negligence because it does not conform to the community standard of the reasonable man. . . .

e. Whether the plaintiff knows of the existence of the risk, or whether he understands and appreciates its magnitude and its unreasonable character, is a question of fact, usually to be determined by the jury under proper instructions from the court. The court may itself determine the issue only where reasonable men could not differ as to the conclusion.

(Emphasis supplied.)

§ 496 E

(1) A plaintiff does not assume a risk of harm unless he voluntarily accepts the risk.
(2) The plaintiff's acceptance of a risk is not voluntary if the defendant's tortious [wrongful] conduct has left him no reasonable alternative course of conduct in order to . . . exercise or protect a right or privilege of which the defendant has no right to deprive him.

Jury Instructions

NEGLIGENCE—ESSENTIAL ELEMENTS

The plaintiff _____ seeks to recover damages based upon a claim of negligence.

The essential elements of such a claim are:

1. The defendant was negligent;
2. Defendant's negligence was a cause of injury, damage, loss or harm to plaintiff.

Negligence is the doing of something which a reasonably prudent person would not do, or the failure to do something which a reasonably prudent person would do, under circumstances similar to those shown by the evidence.

It is the failure to use ordinary or reasonable care.

Ordinary or reasonable care is that care which persons of ordinary prudence would use in order to avoid injury to themselves or others under circumstances similar to those shown by the evidence.

You will note that the person whose conduct we set up as a standard is not the extraordinarily cautious individual, nor the exceptionally skillful one, but a person of reasonable and ordinary prudence.

California Jury Instructions, Civil: Book of Approved Jury Instructions. 8th ed. Prepared by the Committee on Standard Jury Instruction Civil, of the Superior Court of Los Angeles County, California. Hon. Stephen M. Lachs, Judge of the Superior Court, Chairman. Compiled and edited by Paul G. Breckenridge, Jr. St. Paul, MN: West Publishing, 1994.

One test that is helpful in determining whether or not a person was negligent is to ask and answer the question whether or not, if a person of ordinary prudence had been in the same situation and possessed of the same knowledge, [he][or][she] would have foreseen or anticipated that someone might have been injured by or as a result of [his][or][her] action or inaction. If the answer to that question is "yes," and if the action or inaction reasonably could have been avoided, then not to avoid it would be negligence.

Contributory negligence is negligence on the part of a plaintiff which, combining with the negligence of a defendant, contributes as a cause in bringing about the injury.

Contributory negligence, if any, on the part of the plaintiff does not bar a recovery by the plaintiff against the defendant but the total amount of damages to which the plaintiff would otherwise be entitled shall be reduced in proportion to the amount of negligence attributable to the plaintiff.

[See also the extended definition of "The Reasonable Person" in Chapter 3, (pp. 146–49).]

Case Law on Negligence

1. Negligence is defined as doing something which an ordinary, prudent person [13] would not have done under similar circumstances or failing to do something which an ordinary, prudent person would have done under similar circumstances.

2. In an action for negligence, the burden is on the plaintiff to show that there [14] was a negligent act or omission by the defendant and that it was a proximate cause of the plaintiff's injury or a cause which proximately contributed to it.

3. Negligence must be measured against the particular set of facts and cir- [15] cumstances which are present in each case.

4. Where lack of supervision by an instructor is relied on to impose liability, [16] such lack must appear as the proximate cause of the injury.

5. "Proximate cause" as used in the law of negligence is that cause which in [17] the natural and continuous sequence, unbroken by an efficient intervening cause, produces the injury and without which the injury would not have occurred.

6. Inattention to the duty to exercise care in a situation which reasonably may [18] be regarded as hazardous is evidence of negligence, notwithstanding the act or omission involved would not in all cases, or even ordinarily, be productive of injurious consequences.

7. The law does not recognize precision in foreseeing the exact hazard or con- [19] sequence which happens. It is sufficient if what occurs is one of the kind of consequences which might reasonably be foreseen.

Brahatcek v. Millard School District, 273 N.W.2d 680 (1979).

Grant v. Lake Oswego
School District

Carol GRANT, by her Guardian ad litem,
Marian Grant, Appellant,

v.

LAKE OSWEGO SCHOOL DISTRICT NO. 7,
CLACKAMAS COUNTY, Oregon, and
Toni Berke, Respondents.

Court of Appeals of Oregon.

Argued and Submitted Oct. 2, 1973.
Decided Nov. 13, 1973.
Rehearing Denied Dec. 6, 1973.
Review Denied Jan. 5, 1974.

Plaintiff Carol Grant, a child, by . . . Marian Grant, her mother, brought this action   1
against defendants for personal injuries sustained in an accident that occurred
during a physical education class on January 4, 1971. Plaintiff was a 12-year-old
seventh grade student at the time of the accident. Defendants are the School District and Toni Berke, the physical education teacher in charge of the class. The
injury occurred when plaintiff jumped off a springboard and struck her head on
the low doorway beam.

Evidence showed that on January 4, 1971 a class of 17 seventh grade girls was   2
having its first instruction in gymnastics in a school "exercise room" with a high
ceiling. When class began, a springboard was in place on a mat in the center of the
room. Defendant Toni Berke was in charge of the class, aided by two eighth grade
student assistants. During the class period some of the students took turns jumping
off the springboard, others practiced the use of a balance beam or practiced tum-
bling. Plaintiff testified that she used the springboard up to 20 times during the class
and that all the girls did was to jump off the springboard and land on their feet. One
girl testified that she had merely followed the example set by the other girls in using
the springboard. Plaintiff testified that one of the student assistants had demonstrated at the beginning of the class the exercise to be performed. Near the end of
the class plaintiff and three other girls, on instruction of defendant Toni Berke,
dragged the springboard from the middle of the exercise room to an entrance alcove
where the springboard was normally stored. The alcove had a low ceiling and was
separated from the exercise room by a doorway that had a seven-foot clearance.

Plaintiff and two of the other girls testified that the teacher had told them to   3
drag the springboard "over here." Plaintiff admitted she understood that she was
putting the springboard away. Defendant Toni Berke testified that she had told
the girls to put the springboard away and tip it up on its side against the wall in
the alcove where it was stored.

After instructing the girls to move the springboard, defendant Toni Berke   4
turned her attention elsewhere in the exercise room. She was standing in a position where she had no view into the entrance alcove. Plaintiff and the others testified that they dragged the springboard into the alcove and left it there upright. The springboard was pointed toward the exercise room with the end just behind the doorway. Plaintiff then jumped off the springboard. She felt that she would propel herself into the exercise room. The lighting was good and she was aware of the low clearance of the doorway. She struck her head on the beam above the door and fell, injured. Another girl was standing behind her intending to jump into the exercise room after plaintiff.

Plaintiff alleged that defendants were negligent: 5

"1. In placing a springboard under a low ceiling and doorway.
"2. In failing to turn the springboard on its side or otherwise making it harmless.
"3. In failing to warn the students of the danger of hitting the low ceiling and/or doorway.
"4. In failing to supervise the students in the use of dangerous exercise equipment."

Defendants School District and Berke alleged that the plaintiff was contribu-   6
torily negligent in jumping on the board without permission at a time and place when and where it was not supposed to be used, in using the springboard with too much force, and in failing to maintain a proper lookout.

Clary v. Alexander County Board of Education

285 N.C. 188
Roger Dale CLARY and Phyllis Clary,
Administratrix of the Estate of
Fred H. Clary
v.
ALEXANDER COUNTY BOARD OF
EDUCATION.

No. 12.

Supreme Court of North Carolina.

April 10, 1974.

On 8 October 1968, Roger Dale Clary, a seventeen year old senior student in the   1
Stony Point High School, was in the school gymnasium as a candidate for the school basketball team. He and other candidates for the team, by direction of and

---

Clary v. Alexander County Board of Education, 203 S.E.2d 820 (1974).

under the supervision of the coach, engaged in conditioning exercises, including windsprints.

The gymnasium was slightly longer and somewhat wider than a basketball court. At each end of the court, there was a space of approximately three feet between the end line of the court and the end wall of the room. The wall at the back end of the room was solid brick. Immediately behind the basketball goal at this end of the room, there was suspended and hanging against the wall a gymnasium mat, to protect the players against injury from running against the wall. At the opposite or front end of the room there were no mats. At that end, immediately behind the basketball goal, were two double swinging doors, providing ingress and egress to the building, each door having a center glass panel. Adjoining these doors on each side was a large, glass window, beginning about three feet from the floor and extending to the top of the doorway. Glass panels, or transoms, were also over each window and each door. All of the glass was what is known as wire glass, having small "chicken" wire enclosed within the glass itself.

On the occasion of the injury, the members of the basketball squad were arranged in four lines, beginning at or just outside of the end line of the basketball court and extending back to the doors or windows and then alongside such doors or windows as required by the length of the line of boys. Roger Dale Clary was in the line in front of one of the windows. The windsprints ordered by the coach required the front boy in each line to run, at full speed, to the opposite end of the court and then back, at full speed, to touch the hand of the next boy in the line, who would then take off on a similar sprint, the boy who had concluded his sprint then taking his place at the back end of the line to await another turn.

On his first such sprint that afternoon, Roger Dale Clary, running at full speed, touched the hand of the next boy in line and endeavored to stop but was unable to do so until he crashed into the glass window and shattered it, sustaining severe cuts on his arm and body.

On other occasions both Roger Dale Clary and other players, as well as the coach, himself, had, while engaging in windsprints and when driving toward the basket for "layups," run into these doors and windows, but no one had ever before shattered the glass. Roger Dale Clary had been on the school basketball team for three years prior to this occurrence, playing in the same gymnasium. He had seen other boys run into the window, not being able to stop before striking it.

On previous occasions, the school janitor had replaced sections of glass which had been cracked. These were in the transoms above the doors or windows and the glass had been broken on those occasions by thrown basketballs. On each former occasion when cracked panels of glass were replaced, the janitor replaced them with the same type of glass; that is, wire glass. At the time of this accident, other types of glass, less likely to shatter into jagged pieces, were available. Wire glass is not "safety glass." Its principal function is to make it more difficult for an intruder to enter a building by breaking a pane of glass, since such intruder would also have to cut through the wire. On the occasion in question, Roger Dale Clary's arm, head and upper body went through the glass and wire, leaving jagged fragments of the glass panel which apparently were the cause of the severe injuries.

On this occasion, the coach in charge of the exercises ordered the boys to   7
engage in windsprints. He testified that the boys were supposed to run on the gym floor at full speed from one end line of the court to the other and back. He had observed other players collide with the glass on other occasions and had done so himself. He never warned any of the players about the glass at the front end of the gymnasium.

The defendant is alleged to have been negligent in that: (a) It permitted the   8
installation of such glass partition when it knew or should have known that it constituted a severe hazard to basketball players, (b) through its coaching staff, it directed players on the basketball team to run sprints toward a point immediately in front of the partition, and (c) it maintained the gymnasium in a hazardous condition with respect to such partition.

Lynch v. Board of Education of Collinsville Community Unit School District

72 Ill.App.3d 317
28 Ill.Dec. 359
**Cynthia L. LYNCH, A Minor by her father
and next friend, Raymond L. Lynch, and
Raymond L. Lynch, Individually,
Plaintiffs-Appellees,**
v.
**BOARD OF EDUCATION OF COLLINSVILLE
COMMUNITY UNIT SCHOOL
DISTRICT NO. 10, County of Madison,
State of Illinois, a body politic and corporate,
Defendant-Appellant.**

No. 78–393.

Appellate Court of Illinois,
Fifth District.

May 16, 1979.

Plaintiff Cynthia Lynch testified that the "tackle" powderpuff football game had   1
been a tradition at Collinsville High School for at least three or four years. Previously it had been held at halftime of the boys' Homecoming games, but principal

Rodney Woods later testified that when he became principal, he had ordered those games to be halted. Plaintiff Lynch testified that she had heard of the game via the school public address system announcements, posters at school, and statements made by a teacher who coached the senior girls in the game. Miss Lynch then joined the junior girls team which was coached by two teachers at the high school. The teachers conducted five or six practices for the junior girls and instructed them to purchase and wear mouthguards. Miss Lynch attended some of the practices, which were held on school property, and she changed clothes in the school locker room. There was minimal instruction on football rules given to the girls prior to the game.

On October 27, 1974, the game was played at the school football bowl. The field was surrounded by a fence and could have been barred to the players by closing the gates. One team consisted of senior girls, and junior girls made up the other. During the second half of the game, which the seniors eventually won 52-0, Miss Lynch played quarterback and was hit in the face by a girl on the opposing team. She had just passed the ball when she was hit. She fell or was knocked over backwards, hitting her head on the ground. Her face was bloodied and her nose broken, and she had to be assisted from the field. She was treated at a hospital and released that evening and missed two days of school as a result of her injury. Miss Lynch testified that her behavior changed eight or nine months later, after which she couldn't get along with people. She ran away in her father's car with several other people and was apprehended by the police in both Colorado and Utah. She was taken into custody in Wyoming after the car was wrecked. She had six jobs between the time of the accident and the time of the trial, and she was fired from five of them.

Raymond Lynch testified that one of the reasons he permitted his daughter to play in the game was that he felt the game would be kept under control by the teachers present. He said that a few weeks after the game, his daughter started being harder to get along with. After the incident in Wyoming, his daughter was admitted to a hospital in Belleville for two weeks. She was forcibly restrained while in the hospital with leather straps on her legs and arms, and she was medicated. She was treated by Dr. Busch and Dr. Jerome.

Several friends of the plaintiff and her family testified that her behavior had changed after the accident. They generally agreed that before 1974 she was friendly, outgoing, got along well with others, was not disruptive and did not have a lot of disciplinary problems; however, they observed that after the accident, she was hard to get along with, got mad easily, was a totally different person, and would be different from one second to the next.

Several school friends of the plaintiff who had participated in the powderpuff game testified that the girls were really not advised of the rules of tackle football, such as the rule against rushing the passer. Also, there was testimony that the game had been announced over the school address system, and pictures of the game appeared in the paper and the school yearbook.

Dr. Anthony K. Busch, a psychiatrist, testified that he began treating Miss Lynch on June 25, 1975, when he saw her in the hospital emergency room. At that time, she was uncooperative and had to be placed in leather restraints. He pre-scribed Dilantin, a medication commonly used for epileptics, and ordered that an electroencephalogram (E.E.G.) be made. The E.E.G. disclosed that plaintiff had an abnormal brainwave pattern which Dr. Busch diagnosed as permanent or of lifelong duration. He testified that the abnormal brainwave can occur as a result of a injury and that one could fairly definitely say that she had had an injury. He felt that in all probability an injury was the cause for her difficulties. In response to a hypothetical question, Dr. Busch stated that quite probably Miss Lynch's abnormal brainwave pattern and behavioral difficulties were caused by the head injury which she received in the powderpuff football game.

Donald Eugene Arnold, an instructor in football at the University of Illinois, testified that the purpose of the rules in football is to promote the safety of the participants. He testified that he was not aware of any other tackle football game ever being played without any equipment whatsoever and that the football helmet is mandatory at practices at all times because of the possibility of severe head injuries. He also testified that specific rules prohibit a player from roughing the passer because of the vulnerable position of the passer after he releases the ball.   7

Rodney Woods, the principal of Collinsville High School, Greenwood Campus, testified that the powderpuff game in which plaintiff was injured took place at the football bowl of the school's Vandalia campus. Before Woods became principal, the powderpuff games were sponsored by the school and took place at halftime of the boys' Homecoming games, but he ordered that these games cease when he became principal. In his opinion, the game in which plaintiff was injured was not sponsored by the school. In fact, prior to the game, several students had requested that the school sponsor the game, but that request was denied. Several students were also denied permission to announce the game over the school public address system, but he did hear that an unauthorized announcement had been made, at which time he ordered an announcement countermanding it and to advise the students "that the football game that was announced on the intercom before was not correct." He also said that student groups were allowed to adver-tise on school bulletin boards only after first securing the permission of an assis-tant principal, but that often unauthorized notices are posted on the boards until discovered and removed by the assistant principal. Woods related that teachers do supervise authorized athletic events and there were teachers present at the powderpuff game. He admitted that the athletic field where the game was played was fenced and could have been closed to unauthorized use. He also testified that he never told the teachers that they could not supervise or coach the powderpuff game.   8

Charles Suarez, a teacher of defendant school district and coach of the junior team in the October, 1974, powderpuff game, testified that the principal never told him he could not coach the girls in the powderpuff game. He stated that he was a Spanish teacher, not employed by the school as a coach, and that he received no compensation for coaching the game.   9

Reese Hoskins, an assistant principal at Collinsville High School, testified that he was aware that the powderpuff game was going to take place. He did not know   10 how the girls were able to use the high school field, how they were afforded practices or why they had several teachers with them during the practices and game since the game was not authorized or permitted. He also testified that he knew that it would be a tackle game and played without equipment.

In Count I, Cynthia Lynch alleged ordinary negligence on the part of defendant   11
in failing to provide adequate and appropriate equipment. In Count II, she alleged wilful and wanton misconduct on the part of defendant in failing to adequately supervise the powderpuff football game.

Statutory Law

Section 24-24 of the Illinois School Code (Ill.Rev.Stat.1973, ch. 122, par. 24-24)   12
provides:

> Teachers and other certificated educational employees shall maintain discipline in the schools. In all matters relating to the discipline in and conduct of the schools and the school children, they stand in the relation of parents and guardians to the pupils. This relationship shall extend to all activities connected with the school program and may be exercised at any time for the safety and supervision of the pupils in the absence of their parents or guardians.

● ● ● ●

For Deliberation and Argument

1. After reading *Whipple v. Salvation Army,* consider the four counts of negligence with which the plaintiff, Robert P. Whipple, Jr., charges the defendant, the Salvation Army. As a member of the jury, would you vote to find the defendant liable for any or all of these counts? Consider the statements on negligence and assumption of risk following the case. Did the plaintiff voluntarily accept the risk of injury in playing football at the defendant's facility, and if so, should his assumption of risk relieve the defendant from liability for the knee injury suffered by the plaintiff? Note that the assumption of risk principle relieves the defendant of liability only if the plaintiff knows of the existence of the risk. If the defendant, through its negligence, creates a risk of which the plaintiff is unaware, then the latter may be able to recover damages for any injuries suffered as a result of this unknown risk.

2. In *Grant v. Lake Oswego School District,* the plaintiff, Carol Grant, charged four counts of negligence by the school district that resulted in her injuries from jumping on a springboard. The defendant responded that Grant's injuries were at least partially caused by her contributory negligence. Note that in the jury instructions on negligence, contributory negligence is defined as "negligence on the part of a plaintiff which, combining with the negligence of a defendant, contributes as a cause in bringing about the injury." Damage awards are reduced if a jury determines that there was contributory negligence on the

part of the plaintiff. However, as the court noted in this case, negligence on the part of the plaintiff depends partially "upon what a hypothetical child of like age, intelligence, and experience should have known given similar circumstances." This raises the question of how fully the plaintiff was aware of the risk she took in jumping on the springboard once it had been moved to its new location. As a member of the jury, how would you vote on each of the counts of negligence charged by Grant? Explain your reasoning, referring to the applicable statements on the law dealing with negligence.

3. You are an attorney for the plaintiff or for the defendant in *Clary v. Alexander Country Board of Education*. Applying the rules on negligence to the facts of this case, argue either that the defendant is liable or is not liable for the injuries sustained by Dale Clary. Consider each of the three counts of negligence charged by the plaintiff. Couch your discussion in IRAC format.

4. The court's discussion of *Lynch v. Board of Education* turned primarily on whether the "powderpuff" football game was authorized (or sponsored) by the school and whether the defendant had a duty to supervise the game. In reviewing the facts, one judge noted,

> The game was a tradition at the school; it was announced on the school public address system and school bulletin boards; the girls were coached by teachers; practices and games were on school property; the principal and assistant principal knew that the game was tackle football without equipment and that teachers were coaching the girls; the playing field was fenced and could have been locked to keep the girls out; and the principal did not tell the teachers they could not coach the girls. . . . [T]eachers and other certified educational employees are charged with the duty of maintaining discipline in the schools in all events; and . . . in the absence of the students' parents or guardians, they may exercise the status . . . for the safety and supervision of the pupils. It is impossible to conclude that defendant was relieved of the duty to provide safe equipment for the participants in a tackle football game on the grounds that the plaintiff's parents were physically present.

Disagreeing, another judge wrote,

> A school board has no legal duty to supervise the type of activity as shown by the facts of [this] case. Although physical education and varsity athletics are integral parts of most all school programs, there is no evidence . . . that the powder-puff football game had any connection with such programs or with any other school program. The game did not take place at the halftime of a varsity football game. Neither the school board, the principal of the school, nor anyone in authority authorized the game. Unpaid teachers were present at the game, but there is no record of anything that they did while there being authorized, directed or controlled by the school authorities. . . . Failing to instruct a teacher not to participate in after-school or weekend activities of pupils by the prin-

cipal or other school authorities does not in my opinion constitute consent to, approval of, or result in responsibility for such activities. The plaintiffs totally failed to prove any conduct of the school board or its authorized agents that was the proximate cause of plaintiff's injuries.

Based on these arguments, on the facts of the case, on the rules of negligence, and on Section 24-24 of the Illinois School Code (following the case), write an argument on whether the school district should be found liable for Cynthia Lynch's injuries.

5. Select one of the cases treated in this group. Imagine that you are an attorney representing either the plaintiff or the defendant. Compose either an opening statement or a closing argument for this case. Remember that your audience is the jury. Draw on the facts of the case in a way that is likely to have the greatest impact on the jury. Keep in mind, however, that jury members may turn against you—and your client—if they think that you are overly manipulating the facts, being deceptive, making exaggerated claims, or attempting too crudely to play on their emotions. For guidance on developing your statement, see "Models for the Opening Statement and the Closing Argument" at the end of Chapter 2. See also Larry S. Stewart's article, "Arguing Pain and Suffering Damages in Summation: How to Inspire Jurors" at the end of the Group 3 Readings in Chapter 3.

Glossary of Legal Terms

Like every other profession (and perhaps more than most), the law has its own special language—a language often so complicated and obscure that even lawyers have difficulty understanding it. Here is a glossary of legal terms that you will encounter while reading this book. The definitions, for the most part, are from The Plain Language Law Dictionary, *edited by Robert E. Rothenberg. In some cases (indicated by "[Black's]" after the definition), they are taken from* Black's Law Dictionary: New Pocket Edition, *edited by Bryan A. Garner. In a very few other cases (indicated in brackets) we have provided definitions that do not appear in the dictionaries. Not included here are terms that are defined in the text itself—for example, when a statute or judicial instruction defines what is meant by "defective condition" or explains the meaning of "involuntary manslaughter."*

abettor One who promotes or instigates the performance of a criminal act.

accessory A person who aids or contributes in the commission of a crime; an accessory is usually liable only if the crime is a felony.

accessory before the fact An accessory who assists or encourages another to commit a crime but who is not present when the offense is actually committed. [The term is now generally obsolete, as most courts treat such an offender as an *accomplice* or as a *principal*.]

accomplice A person who knowingly, voluntarily, and intentionally unites with the principal offender in committing a crime and thereby becomes punishable for it.

ad litem For the purpose of the lawsuit (Latin).

affidavit A written statement of facts, sworn to and signed by a deponent before a notary public or some other authority having the power to witness an oath.

a fortiori More effective; with greater reason. (Latin)

aid and abet To assist or facilitate the commission of a crime, or to promote its accomplishment; aiding and abetting is a crime in most jurisdictions.

allegata [Statements that have been declared to be true in a legal proceeding, without yet having been proven.]

alleged Claimed; charged.

amend To correct; to change; to alter, so as to correct defects in a document.

appeal The request for a review by a higher court of a verdict or decision made by a lower court.

1

appellant The party who appeals a case from a lower to a higher court.

appellate court A court with the authority to review the handling and decision of a case tried in a lower court.

appellee The respondent; the party against whom an appeal is taken.

breach A violation.

brief A written statement setting out the legal contentions of a party in litigation, especially on appeal. [*Black's*]

burglary Breaking and entering any building with the intent to commit a felony [not necessarily theft].

case A contested issue in a court of law; a controversy presented according to the rules of judicial proceedings.

civil Of or relating to private rights and remedies that are sought by action or suit, as distinct from criminal proceedings. [*Black's*]

civil law Law dealing with civil [private], rather than criminal matters.

codify A code is a collection of laws; the published statutes governing a certain area, arranged in a systematic manner [thus, to "codify" is to render into law].

common law 1. Law declared by judges in area not controlled by government regulation, ordinances, or statutes. 2. Law originating from usage and custom, rather than from written statutes.

comparative negligence A term that is used in a suit to recover damages, in which the negligence of the defendant is compared to that of the plaintiff. In other words, if the plaintiff was slightly negligent but the defendant was grossly negligent, the plaintiff may be awarded damages. Or, if the plaintiff was grossly negligent and the defendant only slightly negligent, no award may be granted.

compensatory damages The precise loss suffered by a plaintiff, as distinguished from punitive damages, which are over and above the actual losses sustained.

conspiracy An agreement by two or more persons to commit an unlawful act; in criminal law, conspiracy is a separate offense from the crime that is the object of the conspiracy.

constructive discharge Resignation by an employee caused by the employer's, supervisor's, or co-worker's having made working conditions intolerably difficult; the term is used in sexual harassment cases.

continue To postpone or adjourn a case pending in court to some future date.

contributory negligence Negligence in which there has been a failure on the part of the plaintiff to exercise ordinary, proper care, thus contributing toward an accident. Such contributory negligence on the part of the plaintiff in a damage suit often constitutes a defense for the defendant.

counsel A lawyer, an attorney, a counsellor. To counsel means to advise.

court A place where justice is administered.

criminal law That branch of the law that deals with crimes and their punishment. In other words, this type of law concerns itself with public wrongs, such as robbery, burglary, forgery, homicide, etc.

culpable At fault; indifferent to others' rights; blamable; worthy of censure.

decedent A person who has died.

decision A judgment or decree issued by a judge or jury; the deciding of a lawsuit; findings of a court.

declaration [A statement, usually written.]

defendant A person sued in a civil proceeding or accused in a criminal proceeding. [*Black's*]

demurrer A pleading stating that although the facts alleged in a complaint may be true, they are insufficient for the plaintiff to state a claim for relief and for the defendant to frame an answer; in most jurisdictions, such a pleading is now termed a *motion to dismiss*. [*Black's*]

deposition The written testimony of a witness, given under oath. Such a statement may be presented in a trial, before a trial, at a hearing, or in response to written questions put to a witness. A deposition is also called an affidavit or a statement under oath. *Deponent*: One who gives a deposition.

directed verdict A situation in which a judge tells the jury what its verdict must be [because the evidence is so compelling that only one decision can reasonably follow—*Black's*].

discovery Compulsory disclosure by a party to an action, at another party's request, of facts or documents relevant to the action; the primary discovery devices are interrogatories, depositions, requests for admissions, and requests for production [*Black's*].

diversity jurisdiction The exercise of federal court authority over cases involving parties from different states and amounts in controversy greater than $50,000. [*Black's*]

duty A legal obligation.

element [A constituent part of a rule of law which must be proved by the plaintiff or the People. Thus to prove a change of battery, the plaintiff must establish each of the following elements: (1) there was a touching; (2) the touching was harmful or offensive; (3) it was intentional; (4) it was unconsented; (5) it was unprivileged (e.g., it cannot be justified as self-defense).]

enjoin To forbid; to issue an injunction, thus restraining someone from carrying out a specific act; a court order demanding that someone not do, or do, something.

evidence Anything that is brought into court in a trial in an attempt to prove or disprove alleged facts. Evidence includes the introduction of exhibits, records, documents, objects, etc., plus the testimony of witnesses, for the purpose of proving one's case. The jury or judge considers the evidence and decides in favor of one party or the other.

ex parte For the benefit of one party. (Latin) An *ex parte* procedure is one carried out in court for the benefit of one party only, without a challenge from an opposing party.

fact Something that took place; an act; something actual and real; an incident that occurred; an event.

felony A major crime, as distinguished from a minor one, or misdemeanor. Felonies include robberies, burglaries, felonious assault, murder, etc.

finding of fact A conclusion reached by a court after due consideration; a determination of the truth after consideration of statements made by the opposing parties in a suit.

findings The result of the deliberations of a court or jury; the decisions expressed by a judicial authority after consideration of all the facts.

forms of action Various kinds of suits brought in the common law.

grand jury A group of citizens whose duties include inquiring into crimes in their area for the purpose of determining the probability of guilt of a party or parties. Should a grand jury conclude that there is a good probability of guilt, it will recommend an indictment of the suspects.

highest court A court of last resort; a court whose decision is final and cannot be appealed because there is no higher court to consider the matter.

id Used in a legal citation to refer to the cited authority immediately preceding. [*Black's*]

impanel To make a list of those selected for jury duty.

indictment An accusation by a grand jury, made after thorough investigation, that someone should be tried for a crime. When an indictment is handed down, the accused must stand trial for the alleged offense, but the indictment in itself does not necessarily mean that the accused will be found guilty.

infra Used as a citational signal to refer to a subsequently cited authority. [*Black's*]

injunction A restraining order issued by a judge that a person or persons can or cannot do a particular thing.... Injunctions may be temporary or permanent.

inter alia Among other things. (Latin)

interlocutory Temporary; not final or conclusive, as an interlocutory decree of divorce or an interlocutory judgment.

interrogatories A set of written questions presented to a witness in order to obtain his [or her] written testimony (deposition) while he [or she] is under oath to tell the truth. Interrogatories are part of the right of discovery that a party in a suit has of obtaining facts from his [or her] adversary. They often take place prior to the commencement of the trial.

judge A public official, appointed or elected, authorized to hear and often to decide cases brought before a court of law.

judicial Anything related to the administration of justice; anything that has to do with a court of justice.

jurisdiction The power and right to administer justice; the geographic area in which a judge or a court has the right to try and decide a case.

jury A specified number of men and/or women who are chosen and sworn to look into matters of fact and, therefore, to determine and render a decision upon the evidence presented to them.

justice The attempt by judicial means to be fair and to give each party his [or her] due, under the law.

law The rules, regulations, ordinances, and statutes, created by the legislative bodies of government, under which people are expected to live. The law is interpreted by the nature, and our experiences in living.

lawsuit A dispute between two or more parties brought into court for a solution; a suit; a cause; an action.

liability Legal responsibility; the obligation to do or not do something; an obligation to pay a debt; the responsibility to behave in a certain manner.

litigation A lawsuit; a legal action; a suit.

lower court A trial court, or one from which an appeal may be taken, as distinguished from a court from which no appeal can be taken.

malice Hatred; ill will; the intentional carrying out of a hurtful act without cause; hostility of one individual toward another.

matter The subject of a legal dispute or lawsuit; the substance of the issues being litigated; the facts that go into the prosecution or defense of a claim.

Miranda rule The requirement that, before any custodial interrogation, a person must be informed of the right to remain silent so as to avoid self-incrimination and the right to have a private or court-appointed attorney present; if the giving of these warnings (commonly called *Miranda warnings*) or a waiver of the named rights is not demonstrated at trial, any evidence obtained in the interrogation cannot be used against the defendant.

negligence Failure to do what a reasonable, careful, conscientious person is expected to do; doing something that a reasonable, careful, conscientious person would not do. *Contributory negligence*: Negligence in which there has been a failure on the part of the plaintiff to exercise ordinary, proper care, thus contributing toward an accident. *Criminal negligence*: Negligence of such a nature that it is punishable as a crime. *Gross negligence*: Conscious disregard of one's duties, resulting in injury or damage to another. Gross negligence exists when an individual, by exercising ordinary good conduct, could have prevented injury or damage. *Ordinary negligence*: Negligence that could have been avoided if only one had exercised ordinary, reasonable, proper care. Ordinary negligence is not wishful or purposeful, but rather "unthinking." *Willful negligence:* Conscious, knowing neglect of duty, with knowledge that such conduct will result in injury or damage to another.

oath A pledge to tell the truth; a sworn promise to perform a duty; a calling on God to witness a statement.

obligation Something a person is bound to do or bound not to do; a moral or legal duty. Penalties may be imposed upon people who fail in their obligations.

ordinance A local law; a law passed by a legislative body of a city or township or other local government; a statute; a rule.

party 1. A person engaged in a lawsuit, either a plaintiff or a defendant. 2. A person who has taken part in a transaction, such as a party to an agreement or contract.

plaintiff The party who is bringing a lawsuit against a defendant; the person or persons who are suing.

plaintiff in error Archaic term for *plaintiff*.

pleading The written statements of each side of a lawsuit as to their claims and defenses. These pleadings will form the basis of the trial to decide the case.

prejudice, with Indicates [that] a matter has been settled without possibility of appeal.

prima facie True or valid on first impression; evident without proof. [*Black's*]

privilege A special legal right, exemption, or immunity granted to a person or class of persons; *or* an affirmative defense by which a defendant acknowledges at least part of the conduct complained of but asserts that the defendant's conduct was authorized or sanctioned by law [e.g., self-defense privilege]. [*Black's*]

probable cause A reasonable ground to suspect that a person has committed a particular crime or that a place contains specific items connected with a crime; under the Fourth Amendment, probable cause—which amounts to more than a bare suspicion but less than legal evidence—must be shown before an arrest warrant may be issued.

probata (probatum) Something proved or conclusively established; proof (Latin). [*Black's*]

proximate cause The immediate cause of an injury or accident; the legal cause; the real cause; a direct cause. [A cause that directly produces an event and without which the event would not have occurred—*Black's*.]

punitive damages An award to a plaintiff beyond actual possible loss. Such damages are by way of punishing the defendant for his [or her] act.

question of fact The question of the truth, such question to be decided after hearing evidence from both sides in a case. It is the judge's or jury's function to decide questions of fact.

question of law A matter for the courts to decide, based on interpretation of existing laws pertaining to the matter at hand.

reasonable man Someone who acts with common sense and has the mental capacity of the average, normal sensible human being, as distinguished from an emotionally unstable, erratic, compulsive individual. In determining whether negligence exists, the court will attempt to decide whether the defendant was a reasonable person.

reasonable suspicion A particularized and objective basis, supported by specific and articulable facts, for suspecting a person of criminal activity; a police officer must have a reasonable suspicion to stop a person in a public place.

rebuttal The presentation of facts to a court demonstrating that testimony given by witnesses is not true.

reckless Careless; indifferent to the outcome of one's actions; heedless; negligent; acting without due caution.

recovery The award of money given by a court to the person or persons who win the lawsuit.

redress The receiving of satisfaction for an injury one has sustained.

requisite [Required; necessary.]

respondent A person against whom an appeal is brought. [opposite of *appellant*]

Restatement of Torts [A codification of the common law relating to torts (private wrongs) compiled by legal practitioners and scholars; most jurisdictions accept the Restatements as the equivalent of law, even though states have often passed their own laws on matters covered by the Restatements. The first series of Restatements (Restatement First) was begun in 1923; the second (Restatement Second) was begun in 1953. Restatements have been written in many other areas of civil law, such as contracts, property, and trusts.]

restraining order An order issued by the court without notice to the opposing party, usually granted temporarily to restrain him [or her] until the court decides whether an injunction should be ordered. In actuality, a restraining order is a form of an injunction.

reversal The annulment or voiding or a court's judgment or decision. Such reversal usually results from a higher court overruling a lower court's action or decision.

review 1. To re-examine, consider. 2. The consideration by a higher (appellate) court of a decision made by a lower (inferior) court.

ruling The outcome of a court's decision either on some point of law or on the case as a whole. [*Black's*]

statute A law passed by the legislative branch of a government.

stipulation An agreement between the opposing parties in a lawsuit in respect to some matter or matters that are connected to the suit. Such stipulations are made in order to avoid delays in the conducting of the trial. Many stipulations consist of the admission of facts to which both parties agree.

strict liability Liability that does not depend on actual negligence or intent to harm, but is based on the breach of an absolute duty to make something safe.

summary judgment A means of obtaining the court's decision without resorting to a formal trial by jury. Such judgments are sought when the opposing parties are in agreement on the facts in the dispute but wish to obtain a ruling as to the question of law that is involved.

supra Earlier in this text: used as a citational signal to refer to a previously cited authority. [*Black's*]

testimony Evidence given under oath by a witness, as distinguished from evidence derived from written documents.

tort A wrong committed by one person against another; a civil, not a criminal wrong; a wrong not arising out of a contract; a violation of a legal duty that one person has toward another. Every tort is composed of a legal obligation, a breach of that obligation, and damage as a result of the breach of the obligation. *Tort-feasor:* A wrong-doer.

tortious Hurtful; harmful; wrongful; injurious; in the nature of a tort.

trier of fact [A jury or judge authorized to hear testimony and consider evidence and come to a determination about whether or not certain events took place. Also called *finder of fact*.]

vacate To cancel; to annul; to set aside.

verdict The finding or decision of a jury, duly sworn and impaneled, after careful consideration, reported to and accepted by the court.

warrant A writ directing or authorizing someone to do an act, especially one directing a law enforcer to make an arrest, a search, or a seizure.

witness 1. An individual who testifies under oath at a trial, a hearing, or before a legislative body. 2. To see or hear something take place. 3. To be present, and often to sign, a legal document, such as a will or deed.

writ A formal order of a court, ordering someone who is out of court to do something.

Credits

Chapter 1

p. 1 Use of segment from Robert Bolt's *A Man for All Seasons* reprinted with permission of Heinemann Educational Publishers. A division of Reed Educational & Professional Publishing Ltd./Robert Bolt, *A Man for All Seasons*, © Random House, Inc.

p. 2 "The American Legal System." *Law School Basics: A Preview of Law School and Legal Reasoning.* Copyright © 1996, 1997 by David Hricik. Published by Nova Press.

p. 12 "A Crumbling Hive of Humanity Fit for Dickens." Copyright 1999, Los Angeles Times. Reprinted by permission.

p. 22 "About Real Lawyers." Courtesy of Judge Vic Fleming, Little Rock, Ark. © 1993.

p. 26 "September and October: Learning to Love the Law" from *One L* by Scott Turow. Copyright © 1997 by Scott Turow. Reprinted by permission of Farrar, Strauss and Giroux, LLC.

p. 32 "The Memo," pp. 94–101 from *Double Billing* by Cameron Stracher. Copyright © 1998 by Cameron Stracher. Reprinted by permission of HarperCollins Publishers, Inc.

p. 41 "The Imperfection of Law and the Death of Lilly," Ji-Zhou Zhou from *My First Year as a Lawyer,* ed. Mark Simenhoff. Reprinted with permission of Walker & Co.

p. 46 "To Work for Social Change," Robert C. Johnson, Jr., and Richard W. Moll. From *The Lure of the Law* by Richard Moll, Copyright © 1990 by Richard Moll. Used by permission of Viking Penguin, a division of Penguin Putnam Inc.

p. 51 Mr. Havlena's Verdict," Karel Capek. © 1994 Catbird Press by permission of the publisher. Translated by Norma Comrada.

Chapter 2

p. 57 Excerpt from *Law and Men: Papers and Addresses of Felix Frankfurter,* 1939–1956, copyright © 1956 by Felix Frankfurter and renewed by Estelle Frankfurter and Philip Elman, reprinted by permission of Harcourt, Inc.

p. 59 "IRAC: How to Argue Your Case Systematically and Logically," Veda Charnow et al ., *Clear and Effective Legal Writing,* 2nd ed. Chapter 9: pp. 130, 136–42, 187–89, 192–96. © Aspen Law & Business /Panel Publishers.

p. 72 "Use Plain English." Excerpt from *Plain English for Lawyers,* 4th ed., by Richard Wydick, © 1994. Published by Carolina Academic Press.

p. 76 "10 Ways to Know If Your Story Is Ready To Tell in Court," © Joel ben Izzy.

p. 81 Copyright © 2/94 by Bedford/St. Martin's Press, Inc. From *Legal Writing: The Strategy of Persuasion* by Brand & White. Reprinted with permission of Bedford/St. Martin's Press, Inc.

p. 91 Used with permission of Leonard Tourney.

p. 98 Reprinted with permission of *Trial* (6/99) Copyright the Association of Trial Lawyers of America.

Chapter 3

p. 107 Excerpt from Calvert Magruder, "Mental and Emotional Disturbance in the Law of Torts," 49 *Harvard Law Review* 1033 (1936).

p. 110 Howie Carr, "Take $2000 and Call Me In the Morning," *Boston Herald,* 3/9/95.

p. 112 Copyright © 1990 by the New York Times Co. Reprinted by permission.

p. 115 "Photojournalism, Ethics, and the Law," Mike Sherer. Reprinted with permission: The National Press Photographers Association © 1997.

p. 119 From *California Jury Instructions, Civil: Book of Approved Jury Instructions,* 8th ed. Reprinted with permission of the West Group.

p. 132 From *Restatement (Second) of Torts.* © by the American Law Institute. Reprinted with permission. Reprinted with permission of the West Group.

p. 146   From *Prosser & Keaton on the Law of Torts*, 5th ed. Reprinted with permission of the West Group.

p. 166   Reprinted with permission from the *Diagnostic and Statistical Manual of Mental Disorders*, fourth ed. Copyright 1994 American Psychiatric Association.

Chapter 4

p. 189   From *California Jury Instructions, Criminal: Book of Approved Jury Instructions*, 6th ed. Reprinted with permission of the West Group.

p. 228   "Defending the Battered Wife." Reprinted with permission of *Trial* (February 1986). Copyright the Association of Trial Lawyers of America.

p. 235   From *California Jury Instructions, Criminal: Book of Approved Jury Instructions*, 6th ed. Reprinted with permission of the West Group.

Chapter 5

pp. 264, 267   Catherine MacKinnon, *Sexual Harassment of Working Women*, Chapter 3: pp. 32–40, footnotes pp. 251–52. Published by Yale University Press. © 1979 Yale University Press.

p. 274   Copyright © 1998 by Tracy O'Shea and Jane LaLonde. From *Sexual Harassment, A Practical Guide to the Law, Your Rights, and Your Options for Taking Action* by Tracy O'Shea and Jane LaLonde. Reprinted by permission of St. Martin's Press, LLC.

p. 284   "But Is It Harassment?" by Monica E. McFadden. Reprinted with permission of *Trial* (December 1998). Copyright the Association of Trial Lawyers of America.

p. 289   *Sexual Harassment Claims* by Dale Cullenden, © 1998 Barrons Educational Series Inc.

p. 294   "Courtroom Testimony: Hostile Work Environment at School." Reprinted with permission of the West Group.

p. 303   "Model Jury Instructions for Hostile Work Environment Harassment Case," B. Henry Allgood. Reprinted with permission of the West Group.

p. 349   "Model Jury Instructions for Quid Pro Quo Harassment Case," B. Henry Allgood. Reprinted with permission of the West Group.

Chapter 6

p. 356   Reprinted by permission of NYU Press from Randall P. Bezanson, *Speech Stories: How Free Can Speech Be?* © 1998, pp. 190–92.

p. 358   "Oh, Say Can You See the Point?" John Lee. Copyright July 10, 1995, *U.S. News and World Report*. Visit us at our Web site at www.usnews.com for additional information.

p. 360   "Here's a Thought: Flag Amendment Is a Bad Idea," Benjamin Zycher. Copyright 1999, Los Angeles Times. Reprinted by permission.

p. 361   "Georgia Governor Wants to Lower Confederate Flag," Eric Harrison and Edith Stanley. Copyright 1992, Los Angeles Times. Reprinted by permission.

p. 374   "High Court to Test Student Free-Speech Rights," Philip Hager. Copyright 1986, Los Angeles Times. Reprinted by permission.

p. 388   "Cissy Lacks: A Teacher Who Didn't Play Safe," James Nicholson. Reprinted by permission from the March '97 issue of *American Theatre* Magazine, published by Theatre Communications Group.

Chapter 7

p. 421   "Courtroom Testimony." Reprinted with the permission of the West Group.

p. 430   *California Jury Instructions, Civil: Book of Approved Jury Instructions*, 8th ed. Reprinted with the permission of the West Group.

Chapter 8

p. 497   Restatement of Torts, 2d Section 316. © 1965 by the American Law Institute. Reprinted with permission from the West Group.

p. 500   "When the Sins of the Child Point to Parents, Law's Grip is Tenuous," Kim Murphy and Melissa Healy. Copyright 1999, Los Angeles Times. Reprinted by permission.

p. 505   "The Law on the Duty of Parent to Control Conduct of Child." © by the American Law Institute. Reprinted with permission. Reprinted with permission of the West Group.

Glossary

p. 547   From *The Plain Language Law Dictionary* by Robert E. Rothenberg, copyright © 1981 by Medbook Publications, Inc. Used by permission of Penguin, a division of Penguin Putnam, Inc.; *Black's Law Dictionary*, pocket edition. Reprinted with permission of the West Group.

Index